June 15–17, 2011
Hamburg, Germany

 **Association for
Computing Machinery**

Advancing Computing as a Science & Profession

WiSec'11

Proceedings of the Fourth ACM Conference on
Wireless Network Security

Sponsored by:
ACM SIGSAC

In cooperation with:
ACM SIGMOBILE

Supported by:
**Nokia, DFN-Cert, Hamburg University of Technology,
Hamburg University of Applied Sciences (HAW),
Belgian Fundamental Research on Cryptology & Information Security**

Association for Computing Machinery

Advancing Computing as a Science & Profession

The Association for Computing Machinery
2 Penn Plaza, Suite 701
New York, New York 10121-0701

ISBN: 978-1-4503-0692-8

Additional copies may be ordered prepaid from:

ACM Order Department
PO Box 30777
New York, NY 10087-0777, USA

Phone: 1-800-342-6626 (USA and Canada)
+1-212-626-0500 (Global)
Fax: +1-212-944-1318
E-mail: acmhelp@acm.org
Hours of Operation: 8:30 am – 4:30 pm ET

ACM Order Number: 537116

Printed in the USA

WiSec'11 Chairs' Welcome

It is our great pleasure to welcome you to the *2011 ACM Conference on Wireless Network Security – WiSec'11*. This year's conference continues the tradition of being the premier forum for presenting research results and experience reports on cutting edge topics in wireless network security, where results on the attacks and threats facing wireless communication as well as techniques to address them are presented, and new directions for future research and development can be identified. Settings of interest include cellular, metropolitan, mesh, local area, personal-area, home, vehicular, sensor, ad hoc, satellite, and underwater networks as well as cognitive radio and RFID. ACM WiSec gives researchers and practitioners a unique opportunity to share their perspectives with others interested in the various aspects of wireless network security.

The call for papers attracted 87 submissions from Asia, Canada, Europe, and the United States. The program committee accepted ten full papers and nine short papers that cover a variety of topics including address space randomization for mobile devices, interactive decryption of DECT phone calls, jamming attacks on wireless broadcast communications, lightweight remote attestation, or inferring users' online activities through traffic analysis to name a few. In addition, the program includes a panel organized by Srdjan Capcun on the subject 'What constitutes good research in wireless security?' and two keynote speeches from academia and industry: Ingrid Verbauwhede (K.U. Leuven) is giving a talk on 'Low budget cryptography to enable wireless network security' and Jan Müller (Airbus) provides insights into 'Wireless Sensor Applications in Aviation - Applications and Design Drivers'. We hope that these proceedings will serve as a valuable reference for security researchers and developers.

We would like to thank the colleagues at the Universities who "volunteered" to help with the organization namely Silke Kracht, Maryna Krotofil, Osman Ugus, Harald Sauff, and Heiner Perrey. Special thanks go to Adrienne Griscti from the ACM. Adrienne handles the paperwork at ACM to initiate the ACM-Sheridan Proceedings Service. Assisted by Lisa Tolles, she has taken care of processing the papers in a timely manner.

Putting together *ACM WiSec'11* was a team effort. We first thank the authors for providing the content of the program. We are grateful to the program committee that worked very hard in reviewing papers and providing feedback for authors. Moreover, special thanks go to Alban Hessler (Web Chair), Frank Kargl (Poster/Demo Chair), John Solis (Publication Chair), Ivan Martinovic (Publicity Chair) and, last but not least, the Program Co-chairs Gene Tsudik and N. Asokan. Finally, we thank the hosting University for Applied Sciences (HAW) Hamburg and TUHH, ACM SIGSAC, and our generous corporate supporters, NOKIA, and the DFN-CERT.

We hope that you will find this program interesting and thought-provoking and that the WiSec'11 conference will provide you with a valuable opportunity to share ideas with other researchers and practitioners from institutions around the world.

We hope you enjoy the conference and the beautiful Hamburg.

Dieter Gollmann
WiSec'11 General Chair
TUHH, Germany

Dirk Westhoff
WiSec'11 General Chair
HAW Hamburg, Germany

Program Co-Chairs' Foreword

It is our distinct pleasure to present the Proceedings of the Fourth ACM Conference on Wireless Network Security **(WiSec'11)**. The call for papers attracted 92 submissions from all regions of the globe, including: Asia, Africa, Europe, Australia and North America. Two submissions were withdrawn by the authors and three were rejected for not conforming to submission instructions. The program committee reviewed the remaining 87 submissions and – following an intensive discussion period – accepted 10 full and 9 short papers that cover a variety of topics in wireless security. In addition, the program features two excellent keynote speakers who bring fresh perspectives to the WiSec audience.

Putting together WiSec'11 program was very much a team effort. We first thank the authors of all papers for their support of this important venue and for providing the content for the conference program. We are very grateful to all program committee members for their selfless dedication, objectivity and overall community service. They worked very hard (under tight deadlines) reviewing/discussing submissions and, in some cases, shepherding conditionally accepted papers. We also thank all external reviewers.

We are significantly indebted to John Solis, our proceedings chair, who did lots of hard work putting together these proceedings and helping before, during and after the reviewing process. We gratefully acknowledge the contributions of General Co-Chairs: Dirk Westhoff and Dieter Gollmann, with whom we fruitfully collaborated on many organizational issues.

In addition, Ivan Martinovic (Publicity Chair), Frank Kargl (Poster/Demo Chair) and Alban Hessler (Web Chair) have each done a great deal to make WiSec'11 a success. We are very grateful to them!

Our thanks also go to Adrienne Griscti from ACM for organizing the necessary paperwork for the ACM-Sheridan Proceedings Service, and to Lisa Tolles, who has taken care of processing accepted papers in a timely manner.

Last, but certainly not least, we appreciate the trust and the guidance of the WiSec Steering Committee.

In summary, we hope that this year's WiSec program is interesting as well as thought-provoking, and provides many opportunities for researchers and practitioners to share cutting-edge research ideas and results.

N. Asokan
Nokia Research Center

Gene Tsudik
University of California, Irvine

Table of Contents

Session 5: Mobile Platforms and Systems

Session 6: Cryptographic Authentication

Session 7: VANETS

Author Index

WiSec 2011 Conference Organization

General Chairs: Dieter Gollmann (*TU Hamburg, Germany*)
Dirk Westhoff (*HAW Hamburg, Germany*)

Program Co-Chairs: Gene Tsudik (*University of California, Irvine, USA*)
N. Asokan (*Nokia Research Center, Helsinki, Finland*)

Panels Chair: Srdjan Capkun (*ETH, Zurich, Switzerland*)

Proceedings Chair: John Solis (*Sandia National Labs, CA, USA*)

Web Chair: Alban Hessler (*NEC Laboratories Europe, Heidelberg, Germany*)

Publicity Chair: Ivan Martinovic (*University of Kaiserslautern, Germany*)

Poster & Demo Chair: Frank Kargl (*University of Twente, the Netherlands*)

Steering Committee Chair: Jean-Pierre Hubaux (*EPFL, Switzerland*)

Steering Committee: Levente Buttyan (*BME, Hungary*)
Claude Castelluccia (*INRIA, France*)
Virgil Gligor (*Carnegie Mellon University, USA*)
Douglas Maughan (*DHS/HSARPA, USA*)
Peng Ning (*North Carolina State University, USA*)
Adrian Perrig (*Carnegie Mellon University, USA*)
Radha Poovendran (*University of Washington, USA*)
Nitin Vaidya (*University of Illinois, USA*)
Cliff Wang (*Army Research Office, USA*)
Dirk Westhoff (*NEC Europe Network Lab, Germany*)

Program Committee: Imad Aad (*Nokia Research Center, Switzerland*)
Giuseppe Ateniese (*Johns Hopkins University, USA*)
Gildas Avoine (*UC Louvain, Belgium*)
Sonja Buchegger (*Royal Institute of Technology, Stockholm, Sweden*)
Mike Burmester (*Florida State University, USA*)
Levente Buttyan (*BME, Hungary*)
Srdjan Capkun (*ETH, Zurich, Switzerland*)
Claude Castelluccia (*INRIA, France*)
Hao Chen (*University of California, USA*)
Yingying Chen (*Stevens Institute of Technology, USA*)
Robert Deng (*Singapore Management University, Singapore*)
Roberto Di Pietro (*Università di Roma Tre, Italy*)

Program Committee
(continued): Xuhua Ding (*Singapore Management University, Singapore*)
Karim El Defrawy (*Hughes Research Laboratory, USA*)
Pasi Eronen (*Poplatek, Finland*)
Stephen Farrell (*Trinity College Dublin, Ireland*)
Mark Felegyhazi (*ICSI Berkeley, USA*)
Aurélien Francillon (*ETH, Zurich, Switzerland*)
Christian Gehrmann (*Swedish Institute of Computer Science, Sweden*)
Philip Ginzboorg (*Nokia Research Center, Finland*)
Ian Goldberg (*University of Waterloo, Canada*)
Urs Hengartner (*University of Waterloo, Canada*)
Frank Kargl (*University of Twente, The Netherlands*)
Jihye Kim (*Seoul National University, South Korea*)
Loukas Lazos (*University of Arizona, USA*)
Janne Lindqvist (*Carnegie Mellon University, USA*)
Di Ma (*University of Michigan, USA*)
Mark Manulis (*TU Darmstadt, Germany*)
Ivan Martinovic (*TU Kaiserslautern, Germany*)
Rene Mayrhofer (*Upper Austria University of Applied Sciences, Austria*)
Chris Mitchell (*Royal Holloway, UK*)
Refik Molva (*Institut Eurecom, France*)
Yi Mu (*University of Wollongong, Australia*)
Peng Ning (*North Carolina State University, USA*)
Cristina Nita-Rotaru (*Purdue University, USA*)
Kaisa Nyberg (*Aalto University, Finland*)
Gabriele Oligieri (*CNR Pisa, Italy*)
Jörg Ott (*Aalto University, Finland*)
Kasper Rasmussen (*ETH Zurich, Switzerland*)
Nitesh Saxena (*Polytechnic Institute of New York University, USA*)
Jens Schmitt (*TU Kaiserslautern, Germany*)
Claudio Soriente (*Universidad Politécnica de Madrid, Spain*)
Frank Stajano (*University of Cambridge, UK*)
Michael Steiner (*IBM Research, USA*)
Wade Trappe (*Rutgers, USA*)
Jonathan Trostle (*Johns Hopkins University, USA*)
Ersin Uzun (*Palo Alto Research Center, USA*)
Susanne Wetzel (*Stevens Institute of Technology, USA*)
Shouhuai Xu (*University of Texas at San Antonio, USA*)
Jeong Yi (*Soongsil University, South Korea*)
Xinwen Zhang (*Samsung, USA*)
Yanchao Zhang (*Arizona State University, USA*)
Sencun Zhu (*Pennsylvania State University, USA*)

Additional reviewers:

Gergely Acs
Werner Backes
Oleksandr Bodriagov
Stanislav Bulygin
Mario Cagalj
Shaoying Cai
Xavier Carpent
Rex Chen
Mauro Conti
Emiliano De Cristofaro
Boris Danev
Stefan Dietzel
László Dóra
Amit Dvir
Kaoutar Elkhiyaoui
Tzipora Halevi
Tamas Holczer
Xinyi Huang
Ghassan Karame
Bastian Könings
Han Jin
Junzuo Lai
Yao Liu
Yunzhong Liu
Feng Mao

Claudio Marforio
Tania Martin
Gerald Ostermayer
Sai Teja Peddinti
Gábor Pék
Daniele Perito
Christina Poepper
Joel Reardon
Jae Hong Seo
Elaine Shi
Boyeon Song
Vinh Thong Ta
Bjorn Terelius
Nils Tippenhauer
Jonathan Voris
Matthias Wilhelm
Qianhong Wu
Wei Wu
Li Xu
Qiang Yan
Po-Wah Yau
Davide Zanetti
Rui Zhang
Qingji Zheng

ACM WiSec 2011 Sponsor & Supporters

Sponsor:

In cooperation with:

Supporters:

The Communication and Computation Cost of Wireless Security – Extended Abstract

Dave Singelée[†], Stefaan Seys[†], Lejla Batina[‡], Ingrid Verbauwhede[†]

[†] ESAT–COSIC
Katholieke Universiteit Leuven – IBBT
3001 Heverlee-Leuven, Belgium
{f rst.last}@esat.kuleuven.be

[‡] CS Department/Digital Security group
Radboud University
Nijmegen, The Netherlands
lejla@cs.ru.nl

Categories and Subject Descriptors

C.2.0 [**Computer-Communication Networks**]: General—
Security and protection

General Terms

Algorithms, Security

Keywords

Keywords: Wireless security, RFID, Authentication, Cryptography, Energy Consumption

1. INTRODUCTION

Ambient intelligence, the future internet, smart dust, all lead to the immersion of electronics in the human environment. E-health applications are one example: patients will carry intelligent sensors and actuators which are wireless connected to monitoring devices and health professionals. All these applications carry heavy security and privacy risks. Strong authentication is needed such that the correct medical doses can be administered or that brain stimulants cannot be hacked. On top, these devices have typically an extremely limited power, energy and area budget.

Adding security and privacy to these and similar wireless applications has a cost. Security and privacy relies mostly on cryptographic algorithms and associated protocols. To run these protocols on wireless embedded devices requires energy from the battery, which is limited. Therefore it is important to get insight into the global energy cost of secure wireless communications. The two most important factors contributing to the energy cost are the 'computation' cost and the 'communication' cost.

Some protocols rely on light-weight computations on the device of Alice, but require a lot of communication with the device of Bob, which could be another device, a reader, a server or another terminal. Other protocols require maybe

heavy public-key operations but only need a small amount of communication.

The goal of this paper is to get some insight into this com-putation-communication trade-off. It will be illustrated with several well-known authentication schemes for RFID and similar small devices.

The rest of this extended abstract is divided into the following sections. Section 2 defines what we mean with cost and with benefits. In section 3 we illustrate the communication cost of different wireless standards. In section 4 we deal with the platforms and costs of different cryptographic algorithms. The next section describes the four protocols we have chosen for our evaluation. These protocols are secret key, public key, hash and stream-cipher based. Finally, we conclude in section 6.

2. COSTS AND BENEFITS

Cost as well as benefits are difficult to measure concepts. There are many aspects to cost. One can measure area, e.g. the number of gates or the number of transistors which is typically done for hardware designs. Software designs will measure the memory footprint. Another measure of cost is the execution time needed for calculating cryptographic primitives. Yet another measure is design time and design effort.

In this presentation we will focus on the energy cost. Energy for wireless security has two main components: communication cost and computation cost. The communication cost is associated with the wireless transmission and reception. It includes all the radio parts, the digital and analog circuits to process, transmit and receive the information bits. Computation cost is associated with the execution of the cryptographic algorithms on the embedded platform.

For communication as well as communication we will need energy from the battery. Our unit of measurement is the amount of energy need to transmit and/or receive one bit of information, expressed typically in nJ/bit.

For each of the wireless standards and for each of the cryptographic algorithms there are many implementation options. E.g. the energy difference between a hardware and a software implementation of the same cryptographic

	Range	Throughput	Freq.	Power		Energy/bit	
				TX	RX	TX	RX
	(m)	(kbps)	(GHz)	(mW)	(mW)	(nJ/bit)	(nJ/bit)
802.11G	30–100	54,000	2.4	2,300	1,900	42.59	35.19
Zigbee	75	250	2.4	46.44	33.30	185.76	133.20
NFC/RFID	0.2	424	13.56E-3	60.00	60.00	141.51	141.51
Bluetooth classic	30	2,100	2.4	99.90	67.50	47.57	32.14
Bluetooth low energy	5	1,000	2.4	48.00	39.20	48.00	39.20
Nordic RF	5	1,000	2.4	21.47	25.65	10.74	12.83
BAN	5	1,000	2.4	2.60	0.73	2.60	0.73

Figure 1: Comparing wireless standards.

algorithm can vary over a few orders of magnitude. So, the numbers given in this presentation are used to give an indication of the cost and to provide insight into the alternatives.

3. COMMUNICATION COST OF DIFFERENT WIRELESS STANDARDS

As a first exercise we have compared different wireless standards. We choose wireless standards which are currently in use and which are aimed mostly at "low power" applications. The different wireless standards are GSM, Wifi, 802.11, Bluetooth, Zigbee, RFID and a state-of-the-art Body Area Network (BAN). Table 1 shows that the numbers vary substantially for different standards. This fact implies that the background of the schemes i.e. various cryptographic primitives have to be carefully scanned in terms of costs.

4. COST OF CRYPTOGRAPHY ON EMBEDDED PLATFORMS

As mentioned above obtaining security and privacy for pervasive applications is a challenging problem, mainly due to the low power/energy budgets. A basic security protocol for almost all RFID security protocols is authentication. Although it can be obtained by means of symmetric-key cryptography, using public-key algorithms for this purpose is also possible. In this way, we obtain not just a tag (or a reader) authentication, but we can also meet some privacy requirements. This issue is especially important for RFID applications as a user often does not want to be known or even linked on the basis of several authentications. Hence, we observe that in literature, a wide variety of authentication and security protocols is described using symmetric key and public key primitives.

A typical platform for a wireless node is an embedded microcontroller. Examples include an 8051, an AVR or an ARM platform. Wireless sensor nodes are typically battery operated devices. Hence the total amount of energy taken from the battery is important. On the other hand, a passive RFID tag consists of a small chip that is powered during the communication with a reader. These two cases are intrinsically different in terms of implementation strategies as well as for the cost issues. Namely, the peak power consumed by a tag is the main concern in the RFID scenario, while it influences the total energy only partially in the wireless node case. Hence, a systematic evaluation of computation and communication costs needs to consider examples of both cases and for both platforms, micro-controller and ASIC based. To complete the cost evaluation an example

primitive is selected from each group mentioned above. As a block-cipher algorithm we choose AES that is the main standard for encryption and has been already evaluated in several previous studies [6, 11]. As a public-key primitive Elliptic Curve Cryptography (ECC) has proven to be the best choice for constrained environments ever since it invention in the mid 80's. As a consequence, a majority of research on compact low-power public-key hardware architectures for RFID is dedicated to ECC [10, 5]. To complete the study we also choose one hash function and one stream cipher. For the hash function we look at the SHA3 competition and choose one of the finalists [8]. Unfortunately, as a result of the heavey security requirements from NIST, each of these finalists is quite large and power hungry. As stream cipher we select Trivium, a light weight version of the eStream portfolio, [12].

5. SELECTION OF PROTOCOLS

We based our selection of the protocols solely on the cryptographic building blocks that are used. The idea is to compare RFID authentication protocols that are exclusively based on a cryptographic hash function, a symmetric block cipher, a symmetric stream cipher, or an asymmetric cryptographic primitive. It is very important to note that each of these protocols have different security and privacy properties. Some are designed to merely offer tag-to-server authentication, while others also offer mutual authentication, or provide various means of privacy protection. The protocols also differ in terms of scalability and key management complexity.

- *Basic zero-knowledge device authentication protocol of Engbert et al.*: Engberg, Harning and Jensen were one of the first to propose an RFID authentication protocol [3]. They present a modular zero-knowledge protocol which relies exclusively on the use of a cryptographic keyed hash function. The authors also discuss how their protocol can be extended to offer advanced security and privacy protection.

- *ISO 9798-2 mutual entity authentication protocol based on AES*: Most RFID authentication protocols are challenge-response protocols which use symmetric and/or asymmetric cryptographic primitives. Protocols for symmetric challenge-response techniques based on encryption are defined in the ISO/IEC 9798-2 standard [7]. Feldhofer et al. [4] proposed to employ these symmetric challenge-response protocols in the context of RFID networks, using the symmetric block cipher AES.

2

- *PEPS protocol of Billet et al.*: Billet, Etrog and Gilbert recently proposed the PEPS protocol [1]. This privacy-preserving RFID authentication protocol relies exclusively on the use of a stream cipher. Since the protocol makes use of a symmetric primitive, the reader and RFID tag share a secret key K.

- *ECC-based Randomized Schnorr protocol*: Recently, various RFID authentication protocols (such as [9]) have been proposed that rely exclusively on the use of Elliptic Curve Cryptography (ECC), since these offer some interesting security and privacy properties. One of these protocols is the Randomized Schnorr protocol [2], proposed by Bringer, Chabanne and Icart.

The communication- computation cost of these selected protocols will be discussed during the presentation. For communication cost, we look at the number of transfers between Alice and Bob, together with the size of the messages. For computation cost, we look at the cryptographic calculations taking place. As can be seen from Table 1, the distance between Alice and Bob plays an important role in the communication cost. Hence, for very short to short distances, it makes sense to move some of the computation burden to the side with a high energy supply.

6. CONCLUSIONS

Future internet means that humans find electronics everywhere in their environment. Body Area networks, sensor nets, RFID, NFC and many more wireless applications will offer novel experiences to the human. All of these applications carry security and privacy risks. Many novel protocols with varying security properties have been proposed. In this presentation, we aim at connecting these security properties with the physical constraints, more specifically with the limited power and energy budgets of many applications. By taking both, communication and computation cost into account, we aim at providing a more holistic insight into the actual cost of security protocols. During our presentation, we will illustrate this with specific examples.

7. ACKNOWLEDGEMENTS

This work was supported in part by the IAP Programme P6/26 BCRYPT of the Belgian State, by the European Commission under contract number ICT-2007-216676 E-CRYPT NoE phase II, by EU Project UNIQUE (FP7) and by the K.U. Leuven-GOA TENSE (GOA/11/007).

8. REFERENCES

[1] O. Billet, J. Etrog and H. Gilbert. Lightweight Privacy Preserving Authentication for RFID Using a Stream Cipher. In *17th International Workshop on Fast Software Encryption (FSE '10), LNCS*, volume 6147, pages 55–74. Springer-Verlag, 2010.

[2] J. Bringer, H. Chabanne, and T. Icart. Cryptanalysis of EC-RAC, a RFID Identification Protocol. In *International Conference on Cryptology and Network Security (CANS'08), LNCS*, volume 5339, pages 149–161. Springer-Verlag, 2008.

[3] S.J. Engberg, M.B. Harning and C.D. Jensen. Zero-knowledge Device Authentication: Privacy & Security Enhanced RFID preserving Business Value and Consumer Convenience. In *Second Annual Conference on Privacy, Security and Trust (PST '04)*, pages 89–101. 2004.

[4] M. Feldhofer, S. Dominikus, and J. Wolkerstorfer. Strong Authentication for RFID Systems using the AES Algorithm. In M. Joye and J. J. Quisquater, editors, *Cryptographic Hardware and Embedded Systems (CHES'04), LNCS*, volume 3156, pages 357–370. Springer-Verlag, 2004.

[5] D. Hein, J. Wolkerstorfer, and N. Felber. ECC is Ready for RFID - A Proof in Silicon. In: R. Avanzi, L. Keliher, F. Sica (eds.) *Selected Areas in Cryptography, Lecture Notes in Computer Science*, volume 5381, pages 401–413. Springer-Verlag, 2009.

[6] A. Hodjat, and I. Verbauwhede. The Energy Cost of Embedded Security for Wireless Sensor Networks. In *Sensor Network Operations*, G. Griffin, T. La Porta, and S. Phoha (eds.), John Wiley & Sons, pp. 510-522, 2006.

[7] ISO/IEC 9798-2. Information Technology – Security Techniques – Entity Authentication – Part 2: Mechanisms Using Symmetric Encipherment Algorithms, 1999.

[8] M. Knezevic, K. Kobayashi, J. Ikegami, S. Matsuo, A. Satoh, U. Kocabas, J. Fan, T. Katashita, T. Sugawara, K. Sakiyama, I. Verbauwhede, K. Ohta, N. Homma, T. Aoki, "Fair and Consistent Hardware Evaluation of Fourteen Round Two SHA-3 Candidates," to appear in IEEE Transactions on VLSI, 13 pages, 2011.

[9] Y. K. Lee, L. Batina, D. Singelée, and I. Verbauwhede. Low-Cost Untraceable Authentication Protocols for RFID (extended version). In S. Wetzel, C. N. Rotaru, and F. Stajano, editors, *Proceedings of the 3rd ACM Conference on Wireless Network Security (WiSec '10)*, pages 55–64. ACM, 2010.

[10] Y. K. Lee, K. Sakiyama, L. Batina, and I. Verbauwhede. Elliptic Curve Based Security Processor for RFID. *IEEE Transactions on Computer*, volume 57(11), pages 1514–1527, November 2008.

[11] G. de Meulenaer, F. Gosset, F.-X. Standaert, and O. Pereira. On the Energy Cost of Communications and Cryptography in Wireless Sensor Networks, (extended version). *IEEE Int. Workshop on Security and Privacy in Wireless and Mobile Computing, Networking and Communications (SecPriWiMob'2008)*, pages 580 - 585, October 2008.

[12] The eSTREAM project, end of phase 3, http://www.ecrypt.eu.org/stream/endofphase3.html, 2008.

Short Paper: The NetSANI Framework for Analysis and Fine-tuning of Network Trace Sanitization

Phil Fazio, Keren Tan, Jihwang Yeo and David Kotz
ISTS, Dartmouth College, Hanover NH, USA
fazio, keren, jyeo, kotz @cs.dartmouth.edu

ABSTRACT

Anonymization is critical prior to sharing wireless-network traces within the research community, to protect both personal and organizational sensitive information from disclosure. One difficulty in anonymization, or more generally, sanitization, is that users lack information about the quality of a sanitization result, such as how much privacy risk a sanitized trace may expose, and how much research utility the sanitized trace may retain. We propose a framework, NetSANI, that allows users to analyze and control the privacy/utility tradeoff in network sanitization. NetSANI can accommodate most of the currently available privacy and utility metrics for network trace sanitization. This framework provides a set of APIs for analyzing the privacy/utility tradeoff by comparing the changes in privacy and utility levels of a trace for a sanitization operation. We demonstrate the framework with an quantitative evaluation on wireless-network traces.

Categories and Subject Descriptors: C.2.3 [Network Operations]: network monitoring, H.4 [Information Systems Applications]:decision support

General Terms: Design, Measurement, Security

Keywords: sanitization, network traces, APIs, privacy, utility, tradeoff

1. INTRODUCTION

Computer-network research advances more quickly when researchers are able to analyze traffic from live networks. Collecting trace data from production networks is often difficult, however, because it is difficult to obtain permission to install infrastructure and collect trace data. Thus, it is critical for the research community to share traces, leveraging this effort to benefit multiple research projects. Fortunately, a culture of sharing network traces exists [4, 9, 16], including CRAWDAD [8] for wireless networks.

Since traces collected from production networks capture the everyday business of network users, the privacy of these users is an increasing concern when sharing trace data. Researchers who wish to share traces must therefore properly "anonymize" the trace to remove personally identifiable information [12]. The researcher may also wish to "sanitize" the trace to conceal other sensitive information (e.g., network structure, critical server identities). We use the term *sanitization* to incorporate both of these goals. It takes great effort and care to correctly sanitize traces; from our own experience, and from other examples in the literature, researchers can make mistakes when sanitizing traces: they may not understand a tool's capabilities, be forced to write their own tools, or miss subtle ways in which information can leak from a trace. Many recent papers [18, 2, 6, 11] demonstrate methods to extract private information from traces thought to be suitably sanitized. Ma et al. [14] show, through analysis of wireless-network traces, that even a small amount of external information is enough for an adversary to infer a victim's true identity in a set of anonymized mobility traces from CRAWDAD. In a recent user survey [21], only 34% of survey participants with experience sanitizing traces used a third-party tool; the rest either used home-grown software or manually edited the traces. These solutions are inevitably likely to include errors affecting the privacy and/or utility of the resulting trace. Moreover, 84% of those with experience sanitizing traces stated that they did not use any quantitative metrics to measure sanitization strength. For a comprehensive survey of state-of-art network trace sanitization and de-sanitization research, we refer interested readers to our previous work [19].

Trace sanitization represents a tradeoff between removing information to protect privacy interests, and retaining information to allow meaningful analysis of the sanitized trace. Most users lack the means either to determine the privacy risks or the research utility of a sanitized trace. This information would allow the user to understand the quality of the sanitization result, controlling the tradeoff between privacy and utility to meet their desired privacy and utility goals.

In this paper, we address the following problems:

1. How can users evaluate sanitized traces in terms of privacy and utility, especially given the presence of a variety of existing metrics?

2. How can we provide users an easy framework to control and fine-tune the tradeoff between privacy and utility?

We thus propose a framework called NetSANI (Network Trace Sanitization and ANonymization Infrastructure), with which we can analyze and control this tradeoff between privacy and utility. To solve the first problem, we take a "framework" approach such that our evaluation tools can accommodate most currently available privacy metrics [10, for example]. We demonstrate that this framework can measure the degree of utility for some typical uses of network traces (e.g., mobility analysis, network intrusion detection), and analyze the privacy and utility tradeoff by comparing changes in privacy and utility levels of a trace for a sanitization operation. To address the second problem, NetSANI provides tradeoff analysis results from different analyses of the same trace to allow the user to control and fine-tune this tradeoff. This allows the user to easily repeat the process with different sanitization parameters. Where possible, we seek to provide analysis results at several granularity levels, from encompassing the entire trace to analyzing individual fields or objects. To the best of our knowledge, NetSANI is the first framework to systematically support a broad range of tradeoff analyses for both wired and wireless network traces.

2. PRELIMINARY

In this section, we introduce the trace model and briefly describe the two broad types of metric in network trace analysis: *privacy metrics* measure how well a sanitization method fulfills predefined privacy or secrecy requirements, and *utility metrics* measure how much a sanitized trace remains useful to a researcher performing trace analysis.

Network trace model. We assume that a network trace has a table structure analogous to a relational database (i.e., trace $\mathcal{T}$ consists of N rows of M fields each). For example, in a packet trace, a packet may be represented by a row whose fields represent fields located within that packet's header. A *network object* is an entity whose identity the trace publisher seeks to protect and/or seeks to gain utility (e.g., host, subnet, user handle). Network objects may be defined by more than one packet in the trace; likewise, a packet (or collection of packets) may belong to one or more network object. For example, suppose that a TCP/IP packet trace includes source and destination IP addresses among its fields, then each host (as a network object) is defined by one or more packets (as rows) that include the IP address of the host in either source or destination IP-address field.

Threat models and privacy. There are two well-known models for privacy in data sets: *network-based* and *microdata* models, and our framework is designed to accommodate either in analyzing the privacy of trace data. In both models, the adversary's goal is to identify sanitized objects using available knowledge about unsanitized objects. However, the difference between the two lies in the forms of the available knowledge and how the adversary uses the available knowledge.

In this paper, due to space limitations, we focus on the network-based model. In a future expanded version of this paper, we will address the micro-data model.

In the network-based threat model, one assumes that given sanitized trace $\mathcal{T}'$ (corresponding to $\mathcal{T}$), the adversary has some external knowledge about some unsanitized objects of trace $\mathcal{T}$. Although secondary traces containing unsanitized objects are rarely available, knowledge may come in other forms, including statistical information (e.g., port-usage distribution) about unsanitized objects or other more generic information (e.g., network topology).

Several information-theoretic measures of privacy have been proposed for this threat model [5, 6, 17]. Kelly et al. describe most of the currently available privacy metrics [10].

One basic indicator of anonymity, agnostic to data type, uses Shannon's entropy $H(s)$:

$$H(s) = -\sum_{j=1}^{L} P(s = o_j') \log P(s = o_j'), \qquad (1)$$

where $P(s = o_j')$ is the probability that sanitized object s can be obtained by applying a sanitization operation to raw object o_j. Lower entropy values correspond to stronger similarity between s and o_j.

Utility metrics. When anonymizing a network trace, a researcher must balance the need to protect privacy with the desire to retain as much useful data in the anonymized trace as possible. Since anonymization techniques may potentially disturb the analysis of a trace [15], we seek a metric that quantifies how the research utility of a trace changes because of the anonymization. Developing universal utility measures to apply to network traces is difficult due to the inherent complexity and interdependent nature of a network trace [7]. Application-dependent utility metrics (that measure values useful in common cases) may be more applicable to many network traces [3, 13, 15], such as comparing the number of alarms generated by an intrusion-detection system (e.g., Snort) pre/post anonymization [15]. Compared to anonymization algorithms, there has been far less research on utility metrics. A framework like NetSANI allows researchers to try a variety of metrics, or to define their own.

3. METHODS

In this section, we describe the requirements for a network trace-sanitization framework, and introduce the ideas behind the NetSANI framework.

3.1 Challenges

Properly evaluating the privacy of an anonymized trace requires the framework to address several specific challenges.

First, the framework should provide a flexible interface with which to transform trace data $\mathcal{T}$ from one of several formats (e.g., pcap, NetFlow, WLAN user association log) into a consistent relational table structure.

Second, the framework should allow its users (data publishers) to define their assumptions about adversary resources or deanonymization techniques (e.g., access to a portion of the unsanitized trace, or the distribution of features in the unsanitized trace). The framework should allow the publisher a choice of several threat models (e.g., network-based or microdata-based models) and sanitization configurations (e.g., different sanitization operations with differing degree of privacy and utility).

Finally, the toolset must provide a "pluggable" interface such that publishers may easily define and apply different metrics to a sanitized trace, and to implement custom metrics as a plug-in to the framework without modifying the core evaluation tool.

NetSANI first requires that its user, the data publisher, describe the subset of fields to be processed and analyzed by the system. This includes basic information such as data type (e.g., IP and MAC addresses, GPS coordinates) and how to access the field when transforming the raw trace file into relational database form.

Since a network object may be defined by several fields, we must provide an abstraction allowing the publisher to define an object as a function of the fields F. Examples of network objects include network users, mobile hosts, wireless access points, or network servers.

Finally, the publisher specifies the format of the trace input, and provides a method for converting raw trace data into table form compatible with the NetSANI database. A trace parser module should be easily implementable, able to use external parsing modules (e.g., libpcap), and still be flexible enough to allow the publisher to create a parser for custom complex formats. We also store additional information about the trace, such as its name, field descriptions, and network objects.

When choosing the network-based threat model, the publisher provides assumptions regarding the adversary's knowledge about unsanitized objects, with two levels of granularity: a unit of knowledge about network objects (e.g., the distribution of field values across a single object) and about the trace (e.g., the full collection of distributions across all objects). Since the adversary's type of knowledge may vary greatly in different uses of the framework, the definition of these types of knowledge is deliberately vague, allowing the user flexibility.

Given the adversary's knowledge, the framework calculates an "uncertainty degree" for the adversary to map between each sanitized object and its best-matched unsanitized object. It is assumed that the more uncertain the adversary is of the mapping, the stronger the privacy of the sanitized objects is maintained. In other words, the uncertainty degree obtained from a sanitization operation indicates the degree of privacy the sanitization operation can provide.

To calculate the uncertainty degree, we first calculate a "knowledge distance", which indicates a quantitative difference between the adversary's knowledge about each unsanitized object and the characteristic of the corresponding sanitized objects. We then determine the uncertainty degree of the mapping.

3.2 Utility evaluation

Universal utility measures are difficult to interpret due to their inherently complex and interdependent nature [20]. Supporting all application-specific utility measures is impossible, because the variety of uses for trace data lead to a broad range of different utility metrics. As a compromise, our framework allows users to apply their own utility measure to network traces, as well as the ability to use some common utility measures. Users explicitly provide the framework with a function to compute per-object utility values in both the original and sanitized traces, as well a function to compute distance between the utility values to calculate a utility measure of each sanitized object.

To put it formally, the users provide a set of values V, and a classifier function $f_v : O \cup O' \to V$, where O and O' are sets of objects in $\mathcal{T}$ and $\mathcal{T}'$, respectively. The users also define a utility distance function $Dist_u : U, U \to \mathcal{R}$. The utility difference between raw object o_i and sanitized object o'_i is thus defined as $\Delta U(o_i) = Dist_u(f_v(o_i), f_v(o'_i))$, where $Dist_u$ is a user-provided function and D_{max} is the (user-provided) maximum value of $Dist_u$. The *object utility* of sanitized object o'_i is defined in range [0..1] as:

$$Util(o'_i) = 1 - \frac{Dist(o_i, o'_i)}{D_{max}} \qquad (2)$$

Given the object utilities, one can compute the average, standard deviation, median and other summary utility metrics over all the objects of a sanitized trace.

3.3 Tradeoff analysis

In this section, we describe how to use our framework to analyze the tradeoff between privacy and utility in a sanitized trace. The tradeoff is presented through comparisons of measured values of privacy and utility. Our framework can support the tradeoff analysis at three different levels: *objects*, *fields*, and *trace*.

In the object-level tradeoff analysis, we compare the privacy and utility values measured on each sanitized object s using the object privacy metric and the object utility metric, i.e., $Util(s)$. The purpose of the object-level tradeoff analysis is to identify the sanitized network objects that are most vulnerable to privacy risk, or those that become much less usable than other sanitized objects.

The data publisher should not only be able to understand the vulnerability or utility of a network object, but should also be able to use the analysis results to apply different sanitization techniques to better satisfy the privacy and utility requirements of the sanitized trace. Thus, we need to provide guidance about which fields contribute more to the adversary's privacy attack or to the loss of utility than other fields. NetSANI provides a field-level tradeoff, though only for fields used by the utility metric function.

Trace-level analysis allows the data publisher to receive a broad overview of the security and usefulness of a sanitized network trace. When calculating an overall "score" for privacy and utility of an entire trace, the metric implemented within the framework may take into consideration prior calculations (e.g., a trace is as secure as its least secure object) and/or perform additional analysis of the trace structure at a level above individual fields or network objects. This type of analysis can help the user to easily identify and summarize the tradeoff between privacy and utility for a given sanitization configuration.

3.4 Tradeoff evaluation algorithm

Algorithm 1 shows our tradeoff evaluation algorithm, the NetSANI *Evaluation* module. It takes as inputs a raw trace, a sanitized trace, the adversary's knowledge file (which contains external knowledge about the raw trace), and a file for describing the mapping of objects between the raw trace and the sanitized trace. The evaluation algorithm compares the adversary's knowledge and each sanitized object so as to calculate object privacy for the object-level analysis.

The algorithm also calculates a degree of uncertainty for mapping a given sanitized object to an unsanitized object, and the per-object utility $Utils(i)$ according to Equation 2. Note that to calculate the object utility the *actual* mapping between sanitized objects and corresponding raw objects must be known to the tool.

3.5 Tradeoff control flow

Users can control the tradeoff between privacy and utility by selecting different sanitization configurations (e.g., changing a sanitization method on a trace field) within the framework until they are satisfied with the privacy and utility values ($Privs, Utils$) measured by the evaluation algorithm. In Figure 1, in which we show the overall flow during trace sanitization and analysis, the outer loop represents this manual iteration. In the inner loop of Figure 1, the tool adopts an

Algorithm 1: The NetSANI Evaluation algorithm

Input: A raw trace $RawTr$, the corresponding sanitized trace $SaniTr$, a file $MFile$ for mapping objects between $RawTr$ and $SaniTr$, and the adversary's knowledge file $KFile$.

Output: Per-object privacy values $Privs$, per-object utility values $Utils$

1 Parse $RawTr$, $SaniTr$ and $KFile$;
2 Extract from $RawTr$ network objects $RObjs$; $N_r = 0$;
3 **foreach** *Network object $RObj$ in $RObjs$* **do**
4   Calculate a utility value $RawUtils[N_r]$ according to Equation (2);
5   Extract a knowledge unit $KUnit[N_r]$ from $KFile$;
6     $N_r = N_r+1$;
7 Extract from $SaniTr$ network objects $SObjs$;
8 Extract from $MFile$ the mapping between $SObjs$ and $RObjs$ as $Mappings$;
9 $i = 0$;
10 **foreach** *Network object $SObj$ in $SObjs$* **do**
11     $MinObjIdx = -1$;
12     $MinDist = \infty$;
13   **for** $j = 0$ to N_r-1 **do**
14   Calculate a knowledge distance between $SObj$ and $KUnit[j]$, into $KGap[j]$;
15   **if** $KGap[j] < MinDist$ **then**
16             $MinDist = KGap[j]$;
17             $MinObjIdx = j$;
18   Calculate a degree of uncertainty for mapping between $SObj$ and $RObjs[MinObjIdx]$, into $Privs[i]$;
19   Calculate the object utility of $SObj$ into $SaniUtil$;
20   Calculate utility difference between $SaniUtil$ and $RawUtils[Mappings[i]]$ into $Utils[i]$;
21     $i = i+1$;

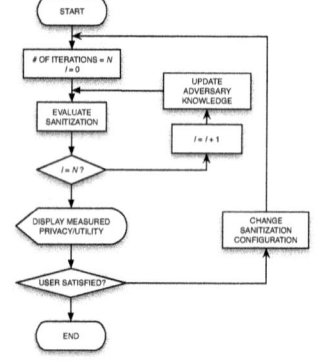

Figure 1: Tradeoff Control Flow

iterative approach to evaluating privacy (much as in Coull's work [6]). After assembling an initial adversary knowledge base, the framework evaluates that knowledge base against the chosen privacy metric, updating the knowledge base to reflect any new information derived when computing the metric. There may be a predetermined number of iterations ($N >= 1$ in Figure 1), or the engine may run until a certain goal is achieved (e.g., all sanitized objects are successfully mapped to an unsanitized equivalent). Utility is calculated on the first iteration only.

This approach not only simulates a common de-sanitization method by the adversary, but (if one were to log the progress of the algorithm) also shows the changes of privacy risks during repeated de-sanitization attempts.

Table 1: NetSANI API – Evaluation Functions

Function	Description
$MyUtility$	define a utility value
$MyUtilityComp$	compare two utility values
$MyObjectUtility$	define an object utility value ($Util$)
$MyKDist$	define a distance between a network object and knowledge units ($Dist_F$)
$MyUncertainty$	define a degree of uncertainty to map a sanitized object to a raw object
$MyMDMetric$	calculate an overall microdata metric

Table 2: NetSANI API – Classes

Class	Description
$NetSANIFramework$	master class abstracting away internal data storage and configuration
$Field$*	define a basic data type
$DataDescriptor$	describe a set of columns or fields
$NetworkObject$*	abstract a network object as defined in Section 2
$SensitiveField$	designate an field as "sensitive" as described in Section 3.1
$Trace$	abstract a trace
$TraceParser$*	transform raw trace data into relational table model
$TraceRow$	abstract a row in a trace file
$KnowledgeUnit$*	abstract an additional unit of information not found in trace itself
$AdversaryKnowledge$*	abstract the adversary's knowledge

4. THE NETSANI API

In this section, we briefly describe the NetSANI API, primarily by example. When designing the API, we placed particular emphasis on maintaining balance of the *generality*, *elegance*, and *efficiency*.

We allow users to provide their own code as *user-defined functions* (shown in Table 1) or as *user-defined subclasses* of the classes shown in Table 2. Each of the starred classes in Table 2 is the Python equivalent of an abstract base class. We encourage the publisher (or programmer) to extend, augment, and reuse as much functionality as possible.

We have space here for only one example, as follows.

4.1 SNMP traces and mobility research

In this example, we used a log of wireless network association data collected in Winter 2010 and containing the MAC address of the user, the identification of the access point (AP), and timestamps indicating the start and end of that users' session at that AP. The access-point identification is stored in "building.floor.ID" format. We wish to evaluate sanitization techniques in terms of the tradeoff between privacy and utility for specific research goals outlined below, focusing on a network-based privacy metric.

To sanitize the traces, we used a custom anonymization script that supports the following operations: prefix-preserving transform (p), zero-truncation (z), and one-to-one mapping (m). We sanitized four fields: MAC address "user", access point name "ap", and timestamps "start" and "end".

We evaluated the results for three configurations:

- *pm-pm-z*: a sanitized trace with the vendor prefix of the MAC address preserved and three least significant bytes of randomly mapped (pm), the building and floor prefix of AP identifier preserved and ID values randomly mapped (pm), and the timestamp truncated (zero) to the minute (z).

- *pz-pz-z*: a sanitized trace with the vendor prefix of the MAC address preserved and three least significant bytes of zeroed (pz), the building prefix of AP identifier preserved and floor and ID values are zeroed (pz), and the timestamp truncated (zero) to the hour (z).

- *pm-pz-z*: a sanitized trace with the vendor prefix of the MAC address preserved and three least significant bytes of randomly mapped (pm), the building and floor prefix of AP identifier preserved and ID values zeroed (pz), and the timestamp truncated (zero) to the minute (z).

4.1.1 User-defined functions and classes

We implemented the *DataDescriptor* as a set of four subclasses of *Field*: one of type *MACAddr*, one of type *AP-Name*, and two of type *Integer*. These correspond to the fields "user", "ap", "start", and "end" respectively. In this trace, "ap" consists of a three-tuple of 8-bit integers corresponding to building, floor, and ID, respectively; thus, for convenience, *APName* is a simple subclass of *IPv4Address*.

We needed two *NetworkObject* classes for this example: *DeviceAddress* and *AccessPoint*. A *DeviceAddress* object is defined as a unique MAC address represented in the trace, and an *AccessPoint* is a unique access point identifier represented in the trace.

To parse the raw and sanitized traces (which are in comma-separated text files) into *Trace* objects, we used an existing module built into the NetSANI framework: *TraceCSV*, which subclasses *TraceParser* to serve as a wrapper around the Python standard library CSV parsing module, csv.

The "adversary's knowledge" represents what the adversary knows prior to attempting deanonymization. Many existing network-based metrics are incompatible with this trace, despite its simplicity. Because this trace does not consist of sender-receiver pairs, metrics such as *combinatorial anonymity degree* (CAD) are unavailable [10]. We therefore used a non-iterative L1-similarity metric ($N = 1$) as described in Kelly et. al [10]. The whole of the adversary's knowledge is represented in the *KellyL1* subclass of *AdversaryKnowledge*, described by Equation 3, where X is an anonymized object, Y is an unanonymized object, and $z \in X \cup Y$.

$$sim(X, Y) = 2 - \sum_z |P(X = z) - P(Y = z)| \quad (3)$$

Rather than iterate over the sanitized trace several times, we instead chose to use a threshold value of sim_{min} to represent the minimum acceptable value of the metric before an adversary may be able to gain unintended information. With 2 as the maximum value that $sim(X, Y)$ may take, we let $sim_{min} = 1.8$, similar to prior work by Coull [6].

We implemented *MyUtilityComp* to reflect the use of trace data by a researcher involved in analysis of wireless-network mobility behavior. We used an existing paper from Balazinska [1] to simulate various uses of SNMP trace data for use in wireless network mobility and usage research, and assigned utility scores for the ability of an object to contribute to a given experiment present in the paper. Utility scores increase with granularity (e.g., knowledge of user distribution across all access points is weighted more heavily than user distribution across buildings). For a listing of utility value assignments for this experiment, see Table 3, and for details of each experiment, see Balazinska [1].

Table 3: Value Assignment to Utility Classes

Class	Value
users present per day per building	0.1
users present per hour per building	0.2
number of access points per floor	0.1
number of access points per building	0.2
users associated with building at given time	0.1
users associated with floor at given time	0.2
users associated with AP at given time	0.3
idle time per building	0.1
idle time per AP	0.2
buildings visited per user	0.1
access points visited per user	0.2
building prevalence per user	0.1
access point prevalence per user	0.2
building persistence per user	0.1
access point persistence per user	0.2
v_{max}	2.4

Table 4: Object Privacy and Utility (Normalized)

	Privacy		Utility
Config	*DeviceAddress*	*AccessPoint*	*v*
pz-pz-z	0.993	0.995	0.000
pm-pz-z	1.0	1.0	0.458
pm-pm-z	0.986	0.984	1.000

4.1.2 Tradeoff analysis/control result

Table 4 displays the analysis of the NetSANI framework and compares the sanitization configurations in terms of overall privacy and utility. The overall utility and privacy results are normalized: the fraction of objects that meet the minimum privacy threshold sim_{min}, and the utility defined by methods outlined in Section 3.2.

We see a considerable difference in utility based on the configuration of trace sanitization. We can infer that the zero utility values of the *pz-pz-z* configuration is caused at least in part by stripping away unique user identity in the "user" field, since each of the factors in the utility metric (Table 3) depend on the ability to uniquely identify users.

Configuration *pm-pz-z* instead applies a one-to-one mapping to the least significant bytes of the user's MAC address. We see a slight gain in the anonymity of both network objects; all objects' privacy values exceeded our minimum similarity threshold. From the utility results, we can confirm that the ability to maintain the identities in the "user" field is the reason for the considerable increase in utility.

Finally, in configuration *pm-pm-z*, rather than zeroing the ID number within the access point name, we applied a one-to-one mapping to that portion of the field. We may infer from the framework results that allowing the researcher access data accurate down to the access point level, we obtain our optimum utility values, albeit with a sacrifice in privacy. It is to be expected, since this configuration reveals the most information of any, that it also has the lowest privacy for both network objects analyzed.

5. DISCUSSION

The NetSANI framework can accommodate most of the currently available privacy metrics; Table 5 shows how to implement other currently available metrics in Kelly et al. [10] using the NetSANI APIs. Our framework can use network-based metrics by implementing the user-defined functions *MyKUnit*, *MyKDist* and *MyUncertainty*. Most of the network-based metrics can define *either* the representation and distance of the adversary's knowledge (e.g., Anonymity Set Size or Individual Anonymity Degree) *or* the uncertainty of an

Table 5: Implementation of metrics using NetSANI

Metrics	MyKUnit	MyKDist	MyUncertainty
Anonymity Set Size	implemented as binary (known or unknown)	binary distance	not needed
Individual Anonymity Degree	implemented as any types	difference between probabilities	conditional probabilities compared
Entropy Anonymity Degree	implemented as any types	any distance metric	entropies compared

object mapping (e.g., Entropy). Therefore, users can implement metrics on the adversary's knowledge using the *MyKUnit* and *MyKDist* functions, while implementing uncertainty metrics using the *MyUncertainty* function.

6. SUMMARY

In this work, we address how to analyze and control the privacy and utility tradeoff, in general, for network sanitization efforts. For this, we propose NetSANI, a network trace sanitization and anonymization framework, which consists of built-in classes and extensible user-defined functions for the analysis and control of the tradeoff in sanitization evaluation. The NetSANI framework can work on both wireless and wired network traces, and it can accommodate most of the currently available privacy and utility metrics, either collectively or separately, by providing the metrics as user-defined functions. Ultimately, NetSANI should make it easier for wireless-network researchers to share traces with the broader research community.

Acknowledgements

This paper results from a research program in the Institute for Security, Technology, and Society (ISTS), supported by DHS award 2006-CS-001-000001 and by NSF award CNS-0831409. The views and conclusions contained herein are those of the authors and should not be interpreted as necessarily representing the official policies of DHS or NSF.

7. REFERENCES

[1] M. Balazinska and P. Castro. Characterizing mobility and network usage in a corporate wireless local-area network. In *Proceedings of the International Conference on Mobile Systems, Applications, and Services (MobiSys)*, pages 303–316, 2003.

[2] T. Brekne, A. Årnes, and A. Øslebø. Anonymization of IP traffic monitoring data: Attacks on two prefix-preserving anonymization schemes and some proposed remedies. In *Proceedings of the International Symposium on Privacy Enhancing Technologies (PET)*, volume 3856 of *Lecture Notes in Computer Science*, pages 179–196, 2005.

[3] J. Brickell and V. Shmatikov. The cost of privacy: destruction of data-mining utility in anonymized data publishing. In *Proceedings of the ACM SIGKDD International Conference on Knowledge Discovery and Data Mining (KDD)*, pages 70–78, 2008.

[4] Cooperative Association for Internet Data Analysis (CAIDA). www.caida.org, 2008.

[5] S. Clauß. A framework for quantification of linkability within a privacy-enhancing identity management system. In *Proceedings Emerging Trends in Information and Communication Security*, volume 3995 of *Lecture Notes in Computer Science*, pages 191–205, 2006.

[6] S. Coull, C. Wright, F. Monrose, A. Keromytis, and M. Reiter. Taming the Devil: Techniques for evaluating anonymized network data. In *Proceedings of the Annual Symposium on Network and Distributed System Security (NDSS)*, February 2008.

[7] S. E. Coull, F. Monrose, M. K. Reiter, and M. D. Bailey. The Challenges of Effectively Anonymizing Network Data. In *Proceedings of the Cybersecurity Applications & Technology Conference For Homeland Security (CATCH)*, pages 230–236, March 2009.

[8] Community Resource for Archiving Wireless Data At Dartmouth (CRAWDAD). www.crawdad.org, 2010.

[9] Internet measurement data catalog (DatCat). www.datcat.org, 2010.

[10] D. J. Kelly, R. A. Raines, M. R. Grimaila, R. O. Baldwin, and B. E. Mullins. A survey of state-of-the-art in anonymity metrics. In *Proceedings of the ACM Workshop on Network Data Anonymization (NDA)*, pages 31–40, 2008.

[11] D. Koukis, S. Antonatos, and K. G. Anagnostakis. On the privacy risks of publishing anonymized IP network traces. In *Proceedings of the International Conference on Communications and Multimedia Security (CMS)*, volume 4237 of *Lecture Notes in Computer Science*, pages 22–32, 2006.

[12] D. Koukis, S. Antonatos, D. Antoniades, E. P. Markatos, and P. Trimintzios. A generic anonymization framework for network traffic. In *Proceedings of the IEEE International Conference on Communications (ICC)*, volume 5, June 2006.

[13] K. Lakkaraju and A. Slagell. Evaluating the utility of anonymized network traces for intrusion detection. In *Proceedings of the International Conference on Security and Privacy in Communication Networks (SecureComm)*, pages 1–8, 2008.

[14] C. Y. Ma, D. K. Yau, N. K. Yip, and N. S. Rao. Privacy vulnerability of published anonymous mobility traces. In *Proc. of the International Conference on Mobile Computing and Networking (MobiCom)*, pages 185–196, 2010.

[15] R. Pang, M. Allman, V. Paxson, and J. Lee. The devil and packet trace anonymization. *ACM SIGCOMM Computer Communication Review*, 36(1):29–38, 2006.

[16] Protected Repository for the Defense of Infrastructure against Cyber Threats (PREDICT). www.predict.org, 2010.

[17] A. Serjantov and G. Danezis. Towards an information theoretic metric for anonymity. In *Proceedings of the International Symposium on Privacy Enhancing Technologies (PET)*, volume 2482 of *Lecture Notes in Computer Science*, pages 41–53, 2002.

[18] K. Tan, G. Yan, J. Yeo, and D. Kotz. Privacy analysis of user association logs in a large-scale wireless LAN. In *Proceedings of the 30th Annual Joint Conference of the IEEE Computer and Communications Societies (INFOCOM) mini-conference*, April 2011.

[19] K. Tan, J. Yeo, M. E. Locasto, and D. Kotz. Catch, clean, and release: A survey of obstacles and opportunities for network trace sanitization. In *Privacy-Aware Knowledge Discovery: Novel Applications and New Techniques*. Chapman and Hall/CRC Press, December 2010.

[20] M. Woo, J. P. Reiter, A. Oganian, and A. F. Karr. Global measures of data utility in microdata masked for disclosure limitation. *Journal of Privacy and Confidentiality*, 1:111–124, 2009.

[21] J. Yeo, K. Tan, and D. Kotz. User survey regarding the needs of network researchers in trace-anonymization tools. Technical Report TR2009-658, Dartmouth College, 2009.

Epidemic Data Survivability in Unattended Wireless Sensor Networks

Roberto Di Pietro[*]
Università di Roma Tre
L.go S. L. Murialdo, 1
00149-Roma Italy
dipietro@mat.uniroma3.it

Nino Vincenzo Verde
Università di Roma Tre
L.go S. L. Murialdo, 1
00149-Roma Italy
nverde@mat.uniroma3.it

ABSTRACT

A recent research thread focused on Unattended Wireless Sensor Networks (UWSNs), that are characterized by the intermittent presence of the sink. An adversary can take advantage of this behavior trying to erase a piece of information sensed by the network before the sink collects it. Therefore, without a mechanism in place to assure data availability, the sink will not ever know that a datum has been compromised.

In this paper, we adopt data replication to assure data survivability in UWSNs. In particular, we revisit an epidemic model and show that, even if the data replication process can be modelled as the spreading of a disease in a finite population, new problems that have not been discovered before arise: optimal parameters choice for the model do not assure the intended data survivability. The problem is complicated by the fact that it is driven by two conflicting parameters: On the one hand the flooding of the datum has to be avoided—due to the sensor resource constraints—, while on the other hand data survivability depends on the data replication rate. Using advanced probabilistic tools we achieve a theoretically sound result that assures at the same time: Data survivability, an optimal usage of sensors resources, and a fast and predictable collecting time. These results have been achieved in both the full visibility and the geometrical model. Finally, extensive simulation results support our findings.

Categories and Subject Descriptors

C.2.0 [**Computer-Communication Networks**]: [General—Security and protection]; C.2.1 [**Computer-Communication Networks**]: [Network Architecture and Design—Wireless communication]

General Terms

Security, Design

---

[*] He is also with CNR-IIT Security Group, Pisa, Italy.

Keywords

Unattended Wireless Sensor Network, Epidemic Models, Data Survivability

1. INTRODUCTION

A Wireless Sensor Network (WSN) is composed by a collection of sensors organized into a cooperative network. Each sensor possesses a certain processing capability, multiple types of memory, and a power source. They use one or more microcontrollers connected to various sensor devices, actuators, and to small transceiver chips. Sensors self-organize in an ad hoc fashion, and communicate with other sensors or with a trusted entity that performs data collection, i.e., a sink. In traditional scenarios, the sink is always on-line and alive, therefore sensors can send to it the sensed information almost instantaneously. Indeed, it is preferable to get the data off the sensor as quickly as possible to better preserve the information. In such a way, even though the sensor is destroyed, data will survive. The persistent presence of the sink is fundamental in many high failure-rate environments (e.g., fire or evacuation system), where there might be very little time between detection of the event and the destruction of the sensor [3]. In this setting, an adversary has only few chances to erase or to compromise a sensed data before it is received by the sink.

An emerging paradigm of wireless sensor networks is the so called Unattended Wireless Sensor Network (UWSN) [6]. In these kinds of networks there is no real-time communication with the sink; indeed, it performs data collection sporadically. UWSNs are needed in place of traditional WSNs in all those cases where the sink cannot be present because the sensors are deployed in hostile environment, or when it has the need to hide himself from an adversary. As an example, consider a monitor system to detect poaching in a national park. The size of the protected area, and the difficulty of hiding a sink, can motivate the requirement for an itinerant sink [18]. Another example could be a submarine sensor network to detect the presence of individuals or animals, and to track their movements. The inaccessibility of the monitored area, and the technical problems that arise to connect the sink with the sensors do not allow the use of a traditional sink. Other application cases involve the monitoring of critical infrastructures like oil pipelines [2]. It is required to monitor that the pumps are working correctly and that leakages of oil are not present. Usually, these pipelines are built underground or under the sea, where the presence of a persistent sink is prohibitive. The itinerant sink, in this case, could be a feeler that roams within the pipeline.

In the above scenarios, the UWSN is used to keep tabs on an infrastructure that cannot be monitored by traditional systems, and its aim is to report alarm events to a monitoring system. While the transmission from the sink to the monitoring system can be on real time, the time required by the sink to collect the datum inside the UWSN is the weak point: Alarms must be received as soon as possible, even though the sink cannot gain direct access to the sensor that rose the alarm. Because the sink cannot collect data on real time, sensors have to accumulate information and provide a mechanism that assure a fast collecting time. Note that in the meanwhile an adversary can compromise the sensors, delete an information and disappear without being detected. For example, in the case of pipeline monitoring an adversary can steal oil from the pipeline, compromise data collected by the nearest monitoring sensors and then disappear without leaving evidences of its illegal behavior. Since the adversary do not want to be detected, it does not destroy or capture sensors. If a security mechanism is not provided, the sink, and therefore the monitoring system, will not ever know that a piece of information has been deleted or compromised by an adversary.

In data centric storage models, network coding techniques have been used to limit the bandwidth usage and the power consumption [11, 15, 17, 22]. However, these techniques introduce an additional time delay and a computational overhead that must be avoided in quasi-real time settings. Often they are motivated by applications where only historical information or digest data, not real-time or quasi real-time data, are of interest [22]. Further, secret sharing or other cryptographic techniques are used to achieve fault tolerance and compromise resilience [25]. However, these techniques are privacy oriented, a feature that is not an issue in some our envisaged scenarios, where sensors are sending event driven data that do not need to be encrypted. Moreover, adopting secret sharing techniques the information must be collected from many sensors, and then it must be rebuilt by someone (the sink or a particular sensor) introducing an additional overhead, and a single point of failure as well. In our case, instead, we are interested in achieving a trade-off between three features: *data survivability*, *collecting time*, and *resources consumption*.

We reach this target through a controlled data replication process that leverages on a well known epidemic model: the SIS — Susceptibles (S), Infected (I), Susceptibles (S) [14] . In epidemic models, a population of n individuals is partitioned into several compartments, and the spreading of a disease is taken into consideration. Given the transition probabilities between any two compartments, it is possible to predict the evolution of these systems as times go by. The SIS model assumes two compartments named Susceptibles (S) and Infected (I). An individual that is susceptible to a disease becomes infected with a certain probability, while an infected individual immediately becomes susceptible once (and *if*) it is cured of an infection. The acronym SIS describes the cycle between the compartments S and I. This model is characterized by the presence of "endemic states". Indeed, when particular conditions are satisfied, the disease never disappears, becoming endemic. For the sequel of this paper, we adopt this model; in our settings the individuals correspond to the sensors, while the disease corresponds to the information to preserve. Note that when the "disease" (that is, information) becomes endemic, information will be available when the sink eventually appears.

We propose a solution to the data survivability problem in UWSN using a simple and effective data replication process based on the SIS epidemic model. This approach is often used in flooding protocols for WSN, to implement broadcast solutions. However, our goal is quite different: we are not interested in having each sensor storing the datum, we are interested in that *at least* one sensor stores it, the waste of bandwidth —and therefore energy consumption— is minimized, and the collecting time is fast and predictable.

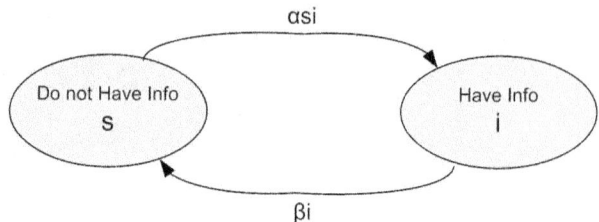

Figure 1: States and Transitions of the SIS model

Contributions

We provide several contributions: (1) We introduce a thorough analysis of the conditions that can assure data survivability in an UWSN. We show that not always the SIS model is able to correctly describe the system evolution. Indeed, factors concerning statistical fluctuations can, in many cases, surprisingly lead to the loss of the information; (2) Rooted on probabilistic theory, we provide the conditions to be satisfied to assure information survivability; and, (3) Taking into account the activity of an adversary, we provide a way to select the replication rate that provides at the same time: Data survivability, energy and bandwidth saving, and a fast and predictable collecting time.

In particular, we investigate these problems in both the full visibility model and the geometrical model. To the best of our knowledge, this is the first contribution to such a realistic setting. All the analytical findings are supported by simulation results.

Organization of the paper

The sequel of this work is organized as follows. Section 2 introduces the models that will be leveraged throughout the paper: The SIS model and the conditions that can generate an endemic state are considered in Section 2.1, while details regarding the network, the attacker and the sink, are respectively reported in Section 2.2, Section 2.3 and Section 2.4. Our epidemic inspired model for information assurance is detailed in Section 3. In particular, a probabilistic bound on the data surviving probability is introduced in Section 3.1. We estimate the expected collecting time in Section 3.2, and then we introduce the trade-off between data survivability, energy and bandwidth saving, and collecting time in Section 3.3. These first results, that assume full visibility among the sensors, are then extended in Section 4, where we introduce several geometrical hypothesis that better describe a realistic UWSN scenario. We simulate the behavior of the epidemic inspired model in Section 5. Finally, Section 6 surveys related work in the area, and Section 7 reports some concluding remarks.

2. REFERENCE MODELS

In this section we introduce the models that will be leveraged throughout this paper.

2.1 The SIS Model

The SIS model was proposed in 1927 by Kermack and Mckendrick to study the mathematical theory of the spread of an infectious disease in a community of susceptible individuals [14]. The traditional epidemic approach does not take into account the details of an infection concerning a *single* individual, but it usually consists in a high level analysis. An individual is considered to be in one of a small number of discrete states. In the SIS model only two of such states are considered: *Susceptible* individuals, that we will indicate with S, and *Infected* individuals, that we will indicate with I. Transitions between these two states are illustrated in Figure 1.

It can be seen that individuals can immediately become susceptible after they recovered from a viral infection. In each instant of time t, the number of infected individuals will be indicated with $I(t)$, while the number of susceptible ones with $S(t)$. We also use $i(t) = I(t)/n$ and $s(t) = S(t)/n$ to indicate the quantity representing the fraction of infected or susceptible subjects. A healthy individual can contract a disease if it is in contact with a sick one. Thus, the fraction of individuals that can contract the disease at time t is proportional to $\alpha i(t)s(t)$, where α indicates the contact rate: It takes into account the probability of getting the disease in a contact between a susceptible and an infectious individual. A sick subject simply recovers from the disease with a rate β, therefore, at time t the fraction of recovering individual is equal to $\beta i(t)$. Thus, the evolution of this system is completely described by the following two differential equations:

$$i'(t) = \alpha s(t)i(t) - \beta i(t) \qquad (1)$$
$$s'(t) = \beta i(t) - \alpha s(t)i(t) \qquad (2)$$

Note that, since we are considering that the population does not change during time, $s'(t) = 1 - i'(t)$. Therefore, equations 1 and 2 are not independent, and to study their behavior it is enough to study only one of them. In the following, we will consider only Equation 1. A steady state is reached when $i'(t) = 0$: The rate of infected individuals will remain indefinitely constant. In our case, there are two steady states that we will indicate with STEADY$_0$ and STEADY$_1$. STEADY$_0$ is reached when $i(t) = 0$, while STEADY$_1$ is reached when $i(t) = 1 - \frac{\beta}{\alpha}$. Studying the behavior of these two steady states, it can be seen that STEADY$_0$ is not "asymptotically stable" when $\beta < \alpha$. A steady state is "asymptotically stable" when not only do initial conditions close to the steady state stay close to the steady state (stable), but they also approach these state asymptotically. When $\beta < \alpha$, a "little" fluctuation from STEADY$_0$ will cause the system to migrate toward STEADY$_1$. Note that this is not the case when $\beta \geq \alpha$, but in that case the disease will die, and so it is not relevant for us. Also, as defined above steady state STEADY$_1$ could be negative, however, since $i(t)$ can range from 0 to 1, when $\beta > \alpha$ we assume that STEADY$_1$ is reached when $i(t) = 0$, in this case STEADY$_0$ = STEADY$_1$. Unlike STEADY$_0$, STEADY$_1$ is asymptotically stable; perturbing it will not produce any long term effect: The system self-stabilizes to $i(t) = 1 - \frac{\beta}{\alpha}$ (or to 0 if $\beta > \alpha$). Equation 1 has the following general solution:

$$i(t) = -\frac{(\alpha - \beta)}{e^{t(\beta - \alpha) + c(\alpha - \beta)} - \alpha} \qquad (3)$$

where c is a constant that depends on the initial conditions:

$$c = \frac{\log\left(\frac{\beta - \alpha}{i(0)} + \alpha\right)}{\alpha - \beta}$$

Using Equation 3, it is possible to predict the number of sick individuals at time t, and thereby the number of healthy individuals.

2.2 The Network Model

Our network model consists of an Unattended WSN composed by a set of homogeneous low-cost sensor randomly distributed over a certain geographical area. The term "unattended" means that the network is not under constant supervision. Sensors sense data from the field, and want to send event driven alarms to the sink. To simplify the analysis, we consider the survivability of a single datum initially sensed by a little subset of sensors. However, all our results can be easily extended considering several different pieces of information generated periodically by the sensors. The evolution

time is partitioned in rounds: In each round both the sensors and the attacker play their game. Sensors will use a pure replication approach to preserve the information, while the attacker will try to compromise them with the final target to completely erase the information from the network before the sink collects it. We will consider two scenarios: In Section 3 we will study the case of a network that enjoys full visibility; then, in Section 4 we will narrow the communication range of each sensor, focusing on the more realistic multi-hop message passing network. Note that, the full visibility case assumes that in one hop each sensor can exchange a message with any other sensor in the network (we can think that the sensor transmission range covers all the network, or that they rely on some underlying routing protocol); while, in the second case, in one hop sensors can exchange only messages with their neighbors.

2.3 The attacker model

As for the attacker, we consider the *Search-and-erase* mobile adversary (μADV) introduced in [18]. The aim of this adversary is to prevent certain target data from reaching the sink without being detected. It could be the case, for example, of a sensor network monitoring a pipeline: sensors must raise an alarm if they report changes in the pressure, or if they detect some oil leakage. The μADV wants to delete the evidence of its illegal behavior, therefore it wants to find and erase all the sensed data that are detecting its action, before they ever reach the sink.

One important feature of the μADV regards the mobility: It is able to move inside the monitored area, and to compromise a subset of sensors within a given time interval. When we say that μADV *compromises* a sensor, we mean that it erases some data contained in its memory, but without changing the sensor behavior or destroying it. Indeed, both these actions would be easily detectable [23], and then alarms and recovering mechanisms could be used. It can erase all the data stored inside the sensor, or just a subset of them. However, since its interest is to delete a particular datum, the attack is successful only if it erases that datum. Therefore, our analysis will be focused on the survivability of that single datum.

We make the following two assumptions about the adversarial capabilities, giving it a strong compromising power:

- In each round, μADV can migrate and compromise a different subset of sensors. Therefore, compromised sensors might not be clustered or physically contiguous.
- The adversary knows which sensors contain the target datum at the end of a round. This hypothesis is not restrictive, indeed the adversary can easily track the route of a datum by simply eavesdropping on the traffic. It then compromises a subset of those sensors during the next round.

In opposition to the attacker knowledge, sensors do not know anything about other sensors, for instance whether a certain neighbor already possesses the information. Better performances can be achieved relaxing this hypothesis. However, we will show that it is possible to achieve extremely good results even in this case.

2.4 The Sink Model

UWSNs are characterized by the presence of an intermittent trusted collection point, also called *intermittent sink*. Several reasons to prefer an intermittent sink instead of a traditional one can be identified. In particular:

- If the scale (in terms of number of sensors) and/or the coverage (in terms of geographical area) of the WSN is very large, the sink cannot serve the whole network.
- The sink, as a centralized and trusted collection point, represents a critical resource. It is a single point of failure and a very attractive attack target. Its destruction essentially "kills" the entire

network, whereas, compromising the sink yields a collection of potentially valuable data. An intermittent or itinerant sink can be monitored in a stronger way, and therefore it can be better protected from an adversary.

- As a computationally powerful entity involved in massive data processing and communication with a multitude of sensors, the sink requires a lot of energy. Thus, although the sink may be physically present at all times, it might need to be switched off periodically in order to preserve its energy budget.
- The operating environment can preclude sink's constant presence. In addition to collecting data from the sensors, the sink often serves as the WSN's gateway to the outside. However, if a WSN operates in a location which is too remote, communication between the sink (if it were on-site) and the rest of the world might be impossible.
- Bandwidth constraints can force the sink to retrieve data only from a subset of sensors per unit of time. In this case, from the sensors perspective the sink is intermittent.

For the above reasons, we consider an intermittent sink that in each round is able to contact and to download data from only a subset of all the sensors belonging to the network. We can assume that sink and sensors use an authentication mechanism, avoiding the impersonation of the sink by the attacker, however this is not strictly relevant for our protocol. Moreover, we take into account two models that differ on the covering power: the *global intermittent sink* and the *itinerant intermittent sink*. The global intermittent sink is able to collect data from any sensor, covering the whole monitored area. However, its collecting power is limited: it can exchange information only with a subset of sensors in each round. The itinerant intermittent sink can retrieve data only from sensors that are positioned in its limited communication range, and for this reason it has to be itinerant. It moves inside the monitored area following a random jump model: it sets its speed so that it can reach any point of the monitored area in one round [10]. The more realistic case of a local itinerant sink will be used when we introduce some geometrical constraints in our model—that is, we relax the assumption that sensors enjoy full visibility. Instead, we will use the global intermittent sink in a first stage, to better describe the relevant phenomenon it is subject to.

3. EPIDEMIC DATA SURVIVABILITY (WITH FULL VISIBILITY)

To assure data survivability we use a pure replication approach, inspired by the SIS epidemic model. However, we will see that in our settings the SIS does not capture the conditions required to assure information survivability, and that stronger hypothesis are needed.

The behavior of the sensors belonging to the UWSN is simple: Data is transmitted by the subset of sensors possessing it, to sensors randomly selected among the whole network. Because of energy and bandwidth constraints characterizing sensors, it is preferable not to flood the network, but to keep the number of messages to the bare minimum necessary to meet information survivability requirements. Indeed, we would like to replicate the datum to be preserved to the minimum extent that allows the information to survive. The μADV goal is to delete a specific datum from the UWSN. To pursue its objective it can compromise each sensor— among the ones that have the information at the beginning of any given round— with probability at most β. Since sensors are not aware neither of the datum targeted by μADV, nor about the state of other sensors, they will always adopt a conservative stance, assuming to face an adversary that effectively corrupts, at each round, each sensor with

Table 1 Sensors, attacker and sink behavior in each round

1: **Sensors Behavior**
2:     **for** Each Datum **do**
3:         **for** each neighbor s **do**
4:             Send the datum to s with probability $\frac{\alpha}{n}$
5:         **end for**
6:     **end for**
7: **end Sensors Behavior**
1: **Attacker Behavior**
2:     **for** each sensor s that has the datum **do**
3:         Attack s with probability β
4:     **end for**
5: **end Attacker Behavior**
1: **Sink Behavior**
2:     **for** each sensor s under my coverage **do**
3:         Collect data possessed by s with probability γ
4:     **end for**
5: **end Sink Behavior**

probability β. When a sensor senses a datum from the field, using a replication approach it will forward the datum to other sensors randomly selected, and the sink will collect such a datum as soon as it contacts one of the sensors possessing it. In this first stage, we assume the presence of a global intermittent sink, that (when eventually showing up) can retrieve the information from any sensor belonging to the network. In each round, it collects the datum from each sensor with probability γ.

The behavior of the sensors in each round, as well as the one of the attacker and the sink, are listed in Table 1. As for the sensor behavior, it can be seen that in each round, each datum is forwarded to a neighbor with probability α/n, where n is the number of sensors belonging to the network. Note that the sensor sends the datum without knowing whether the receiver already has it. As for the attacker, at the beginning of a round it knows who has the datum to erase, and it compromises each one of these sensors with probability β. Note that if a sensor receives the information during the current round, eavesdropping the traffic the attacker can be aware of this event, and it can attack the sensor at the beginning of the next round. The sink behavior is quite simple: In each round it collects data from a sensor that is under its communication range with probability γ.

The described system (composed by n sensors and one adversary that behaves as above) can be modeled with the SIS epidemic model. Indeed, the datum corresponds to a disease. Each healthy subject (sensor) can contract the disease (the datum) from a sick individual (a sensor that already has the datum) with a certain probability. The adversary, instead, corresponds to the process of healing from the disease. A healed subject (that is, a sensor that has been in the compromised status in a previous round) can then re-contract the same disease (that is, re-acquire the datum). As described in Section 2.1, in this model we have two compartments, S and I. S contains the sensor susceptible to learn the information (their number at time t is indicated with $S(t)$), I contains the sensors that currently know the datum (their number at time t is indicated with $I(t)$). Moreover, we use the notation $i(t)$ to indicate the fraction of sensors possessing the datum at the tth round ($i(t) = I(t)/n$), and $s(t)$ to indicate the fraction of sensors that does not have it ($s(t) = S(t)/n$). In the following, when the context is clear, we write i or s instead of $i(t)$ or $s(t)$.

A sensor obtains the information during round t if it did not possess it before, and if at least one of its neighbors forwarded the

14

datum to it during that round. Therefore, assuming full visibility among the sensors, the probability that a sensor receives the datum is equal to $s*\left(1-\left(1-\frac{\alpha}{n}\right)^{in}\right)$, and using the binomial approximation this is equal to: $s*\left(1-\left(1-in\frac{\alpha}{n}\right)\right)=s*i*\alpha$. Note that the approximation introduced, for a network of only 100 sensors, and $\alpha=0.1$, is only of $1.25*10^{-7}$. The probability that a sensor possessing the datum will be compromised by the adversary is equal to βi. Thus, the evolution of the system is well described by the two differential equations of the SIS model: equations 1 and 2.

It can be verified that for any $\alpha > \beta$, $i(t)$ is always greater than 0. Thus, it seems that forecasting the maximum compromising power β of an adversary, it is possible to choose an α ($\alpha > \beta$), to assure data survivability. Indeed, once reached the steady state, at least a fraction correspondent to $1 - \frac{\beta}{\alpha}$ sensors will possess the datum. However, note that this solution requires a high number of replicas. Our aim is to minimize the value α, while preserving datum survivability. In fact, this can avoid to flood the network with too many messages, optimizing bandwidth and energy consumption, and therefore assuring a longer life time to the sensor network. A counter-intuitive result that will be shown in the following, is that selecting the minimum α such that $\alpha > \beta$, is not the best choice. In fact, a fundamental aspect that has to be taken into account is that, after the first round, STEADY_0 is an "absorbing" state: the transition probability to move away from the state STEADY_0 is 0. Indeed, it is possible to move away from it only in the first round, that is $t = 0$ (only in this round the datum is generated). If at any time a statistical fluctuation forces the system to enter in STEADY_0, the endemic prediction will be violated. In the sequel of this paper we are interested in investigating the conditions to be enforced to assure an effective data survival.

To better understand the dynamics of the problem we now analyze the behavior of a network composed by 100 sensors. Figure 2 compares the forecast of the SIS model (Equation 3) with those produced by a simulation that ran for $t = 300$ rounds. The line indicated with "Simulator Mean" represents the mean over 100 measurements, while a single simulation is shown with a cross. In Figure 2(a), the replication rate α is set to 0.95, so that each sensor forwarded the datum to a neighbor with a probability of $\alpha/n = 0.0095$. We simulated the behavior of the network for different values of β ranging from 0 to 1. It is possible to notice that when β is less than 0.6, the simulation and the forecast of the SIS model perfectly match. Then, when β grows approaching to α, there are many simulations ending with $i(t) = 0$. In all these cases μADV won even if its compromising power is still less than α. This problem is mainly due to the proximity of STEADY_1 to STEADY_0. In fact, when $i(t)$ is close to 0, statistical fluctuations can force the system to enter into STEADY_0. Figure 2(b) shows what happens when the power of the adversary is fixed to 0.2, and α varies from 0 to 1. From the figure it is clear that to choose the minimum α greater than β does not assure datum survivability. Indeed, when $\alpha = 0.3$ the datum is lost forever in many simulations. In Section 3.1, we will introduce a probabilistic bound that can be used to estimate values of α that assure data survivability. The graphical representation of such a bounds is reported in Figure 2(b). It can be seen that $i(t)$ unlikely assumes values outside those bounds.

3.1 A probabilistic lower bound on the data survivability

Let us assume that $I(t)$ sensors possess the datum ($I(t) = i(t)*n$) in a certain round t. In the next rounds, the quantity $i(t)$ should fluctuate depending on the parameters of the model, eventually reaching steady state STEADY_1 (for $\alpha > \beta$). However, when just few

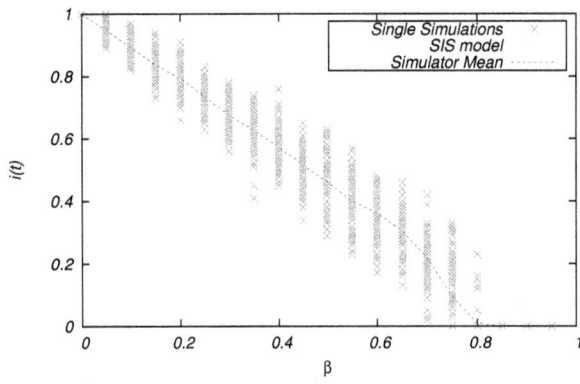

(a) Forecast of the SIS model compared with results of our simulations. Here α is set to 0.95. When $i(t)$ approaches to 0, simulations do not fit the model. It depends on statistical fluctuations of $i(t)$.

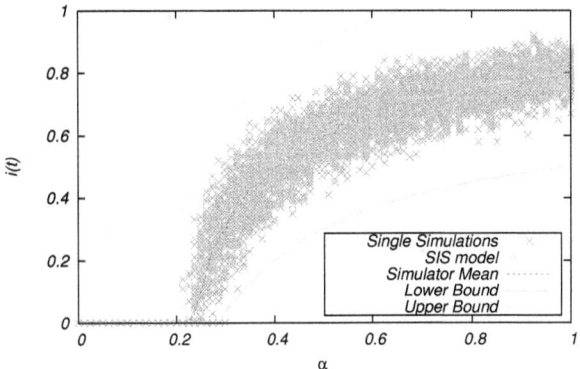

(b) Using the minimum α greater than β introduces a high risk to lose the datum. In the simulations reported in this figure, β is equal to 0.2. However, it can be seen that in some cases the datum is lost even if α is equal to 0.3. Indeed, many simulations terminated with $i(t) = 0$. The bounds showed in the figure are relative to Theorem 3.1: the probability that a single simulation is outside the bounds is less than the 4% considering $\epsilon = 0.25$.

Figure 2: When $i(t)$ is close to 0, the SIS model does not describe well the behavior of the system. Fluctuations from STEADY_1 cause the system to reach STEADY_0, losing the datum forever.

sensors possess the datum, statistical fluctuations can cause the system to enter into the steady state STEADY_0, as shown in previous subsection. Since STEADY_0 is an absorbing state, from that moment onwards the datum is completely lost, and there is no chance to leave this state. In the following, we introduce a bound, based on system parameters and rooted on sound probabilistic tool, that limits the probability to move to the absorbing state due to statistical fluctuations. To prove that the bound holds, we first show that in each round the sum of those sensors that receive the datum and those sensors that loose the datum is concentrated around the mean, and that this mean is equal to $i'(t)$. Later, we show that this implies that the datum—for an appropriate choice of parameters—is lost with negligible probability. In the proof, we will use the Method of Bounded Differences, a very powerful and useful generalization of the Chernoff bound [12]:

[Method of Bounded Differences.] *If f satisfies the Lipschitz property with constants d_j, $j \in [n]$, and $X_1, \dots, X_n$ are independent* random variables, then $\Pr[f > \mathbb{E}[f] + \epsilon] \le \exp\left(-\frac{2\epsilon^2}{d}\right)$ and $\Pr[f < \mathbb{E}[f] - \epsilon] \le \exp\left(-\frac{2\epsilon^2}{d}\right)$, where $d = \sum_{j=1}^n d_j^2$.

Note that a function $f(X_1, \ldots, X_n)$ satisfies the Lipschitz property with constants d_j, if

$$\left| f(X_1, \ldots, X_j, \ldots, X_n) - f(X_1, \ldots, \overline{X_j}, \ldots, X_n) \right| \le d_j$$

with $j \in [n]$. The reader that is not familiar with these tools can refer to [12] for other details.

THEOREM 3.1. *Considering a network composed by n sensors that reached steady state STEADY$_1$ at round $t-1$ ($t > 0$), let $\Phi(t)$ be the subset of sensors—not informed at round $(t-1)$—that receive the datum during round t, and let $\Psi(t)$ be the subset of sensors that are compromised during round t. Assuming full visibility among sensors, we have that:*

$$\Pr\left[g(t) > \epsilon\right] \le \exp\left(-\frac{\epsilon^2 n}{2}\right)$$
$$\Pr\left[g(t) < -\epsilon\right] \le \exp\left(-\frac{\epsilon^2 n}{2}\right) \tag{4}$$

where $g(t) = \frac{|\Phi(t)| - |\Psi(t)|}{n}$.

PROOF. Fixed a round $t > 0$, let $X_1, \ldots, X_n$ be a set of n random variables, such that

$$X_j := \begin{cases} \frac{1}{n}, & \text{if sensor } j \text{ is not informed at round } (t-1) \text{ and} \\ & \text{it receives the datum at round } t; \\ -\frac{1}{n}, & \text{if sensor } j \text{ is compromised during round } t; \\ 0, & \text{otherwise.} \end{cases}$$

Note that a sensor cannot receive a datum it has not (that is, moving from $\mathcal{S}$ to $\mathcal{I}$) and be compromised during the same round. Indeed, at round t the μADV tries to compromise only the sensors that were already in $\mathcal{I}$ at round $(t-1)$. In other words, if a sensor is informed during the current round, it can be attacked only at next round. Further, note that the X_j can be practically considered independent random variables. The intuition is that the probability that a sensor is compromised during round t does not depend on the event that others sensors are compromised or not. Let us consider the function:

$$f(X_1, \ldots, X_n) = \sum_{j=1}^n X_j. \tag{5}$$

It satisfies the Lipschitz property [12] with constant $d_j = 2/n$ for any $j \in [n]$, indeed

$$\left| f(X_1, \ldots, X_j, \ldots, X_n) - f(X_1, \ldots, \overline{X_j}, \ldots, X_n) \right| \le \frac{2}{n}$$

where $X_1, \ldots, X_j, \ldots, X_n$ and $X_1, \ldots, \overline{X_j}, \ldots, X_n$ differ just in the jth coordinate, $j \in \{1 \ldots n\}$. In the full visibility case, the expected value of f is:

$$\mathbb{E}[f] = \mathbb{E}\left[\sum_j^n X_j\right] = n\,\mathbb{E}[X_j] = n\left(\frac{1}{n}\alpha i(t-1)s(t-1) - \frac{1}{n}\beta i(t-1)\right)$$
$$= \alpha s(t-1)i(t-1) - \beta i(t-1) = i'(t-1) = 0 \tag{6}$$

Last equation is true because of the assumption that the system reached steady state at time $t-1$. Moreover, we have that $f(X_1, \ldots, X_n) = g(t)$. Indeed, $\Phi(t) \cap \Psi(t) = \emptyset$, and the following conditions are satisfied:

- when a new sensor obtains the datum during the tth step, then the value of $g(t)$ is increased by $1/n$;
- when a new sensor is compromised during the tth step, then the value of $g(t)$ is decreased by $1/n$.
- otherwise the value of $g(t)$ is unchanged.

Since f satisfies the Lipschitz property with constants $d_j = 2/n$ for any $j \in [n]$, and since $X_1, \ldots, X_n$ are independent random variables, it is possible to use the Method of Bounded Differences, stating that:

$$\Pr[f > \mathbb{E}[f] + \epsilon], \Pr[f < \mathbb{E}[f] - \epsilon] \le \exp\left(-\frac{2\epsilon^2}{d}\right)$$

where $d = \sum_{j=1}^n \left(\frac{2}{n}\right)^2$. It immediately follows that:

$$\Pr\left[g(t) > \epsilon\right], \Pr\left[g(t) < -\epsilon\right] \le \exp\left(-\frac{\epsilon^2 n}{2}\right)$$

$\square$

Note that this result, that assumes full visibility among the sensors, does not depend on any variables but n, that is the number of sensors belonging to the network. The higher is n, the tighter is the bound. For instance, considering a network composed by 100 sensors, the probability that the outcome of our protocol is far from its expected value more than $\epsilon = 0.2$ is less than or equal to 13%; it becomes 4.54×10^{-5} when the number of sensor scales to 500.

Theorem 3.1 provides a lower bound and an upper bound regarding the effect of the statistical fluctuations. In particular, it can be used to estimate such fluctuations, and to provide the hypothesis that assure the data survivability inside an UWSN. The following Lemma is based on this result.

LEMMA 3.2. *With the hypothesis of Theorem 3.1 being satisfied, the probability to lose the datum, is less than or equal to $\exp\left(-\frac{\epsilon^2 n}{2}\right)$ if $\alpha > \frac{\beta}{1-\epsilon}$.*

PROOF. Since $\alpha > \frac{\beta}{1-\epsilon}$, it holds true that $i(t-1) > \epsilon$. Taking into account that $g(t) = \frac{|\Phi(t)| - |\Psi(t)|}{n}$, that is the fraction of sensors that gain the information minus the ones that loose the information, the network completely lose the information if $g(t) < -\epsilon$. Applying Theorem 3.1, $\Pr\left[g(t) < -\epsilon\right] \le \exp\left(-\frac{\epsilon^2 n}{2}\right)$. $\square$

In other words, Lemma 3.2 states that, assuring a sufficiently high replication rate, it is unlikely that statistical fluctuations can force the system to lose the datum. As an example, with the same setting as before, and considering an adversary that can compromise up to 20% of the sensors, the probability to lose the datum is less than or equal to 13% if $\alpha > 0.25$, but it becomes only 3.73×10^{-6} if $\alpha > 0.4$. Lemma 3.2 relies on the knowledge of the value of the parameter β, that is the compromising power of the attacker. This value can be both an upper bound of the expected maximal compromising power of the attacker, than an estimation of the compromising power that it is currently using. For example, it can be estimated using a control mechanism, where each node evaluates the number of neighbors that currently posses the information (they can use a sampling technique to reduce the overhead as well). However, from now on, without loosing in generality we will consider the restrictive hypothesis that β is the maximal compromising power of the attacker.

Table 1 reports the probability to loose the information detected by our simulations for different settings of β and α ($n = 100$, while the results are averaged over 1,000 trials). Once fixed β, without the knowledge of Lemma 3.2, one could haven choose the minimum α greater than β: For example, the values reported in the columns indicated with α_1 or α_2 could have been chosen. However, this would have not been a good choice. Indeed, choosing values from α_1 implies to loose the information with probability 1, in contradiction with the prediction of the SIS model. Choosing values from α_2 allows the data to survive, but with a small probability when compared to values from α_3. In particular, if we want to assure a probability of loose the datum less than or equal to 0.01, Lemma 3.2 states that $\frac{\alpha}{\beta}$ must be greater than 1.42. It can be seen that α_3—matching the constraint on the ratio between α and β ($\frac{\alpha}{\beta} = 1.43$)—enjoys the prediction of the lemma. Indeed, we never detected an information loose greater than 0.01.

3.2 Global Intermittent Sink Collecting Time

To estimate the number of rounds that are needed before the sink finds a given datum is of paramount importance, for instance to assure quality of service, or to provide a bound on the required presence of the sink—relevant in case the sink does not want to disclose its presence in the network deployment area. The following Lemma provides such a bound, under the hypothesis of an UWSN monitored by a global intermittent sink.

LEMMA 3.3. *Once reached STEADY$_1$, considering a global intermittent sink, and assuming full visibility among the sensors, if $\beta \leq \alpha$, the expected time before the sink collects a given datum is equal to $\left(n\gamma\left(1 - \frac{\beta}{\alpha}\right)\right)^{-1}$, where n is the number of sensors belonging to the network.*

PROOF. Let X be the number of rounds needed to collect a sensed datum. We want to evaluate $\mathbb{E}(X)$. If $\beta \leq \alpha$, the probability that the sink collects the datum at a time t is equal to $\gamma n \left(1 - \frac{\beta}{\alpha}\right)$. Indeed, at steady state STEADY$_1$, there are $n\left(1 - \frac{\beta}{\alpha}\right)$ sensors possessing the datum, and the sinks retrieves the information from each of them with probability γ. Therefore:

$$\mathbb{E}(X) = \sum_{i=0}^{\infty} \left(1 - \left(\gamma n \left(1 - \frac{\beta}{\alpha}\right)\right)\right)^i = \frac{1}{n\gamma(1 - \frac{\beta}{\alpha})}$$

$\square$

Lemma 3.3 gives an estimation of the collecting time, assuming that the attacker uses all its compromising power, erasing the memory of up to $\beta * n$ sensors. However, also in this case, the statistical fluctuations that we highlighted in Section 3 have to be taken into account. In Section 5, we will show experimentally that they can (slightly) increase the mean collecting time.

3.3 Trade-off between Energy Consumption, Data Survivability and Collecting time

The following theorem introduces a trade-off between data survivability, bandwidth and power consumption, and collecting time.

THEOREM 3.4. *Once reached STEADY$_1$, considering a global intermittent sink, and assuming full visibility among the sensors, if $\frac{\beta}{1-\epsilon} < \alpha < \beta + \frac{1}{x}$ with $1 < x < n$, the following three conditions will hold:*

- *in each round the expected number of sent messages is less than $\frac{n}{x}$;*
- *the probability to lose the datum is less than or equal to: $\exp\left(-\frac{\epsilon^2 n}{2}\right)$;*
- *the expected collecting time will be equal to $\left(n\gamma\left(1 - \frac{\beta}{\alpha}\right)\right)^{-1}$.*

PROOF. The proof will be split in three parts, proving each one of the three points independently. We will first prove the bound on the expected number of sent messages per round. Since $\alpha < \beta + \frac{1}{x}$, it holds true that $\left(1 - \frac{\beta}{\alpha}\right) < \frac{1}{\alpha x}$, and therefore $n\alpha\left(1 - \frac{\beta}{\alpha}\right) < \frac{n}{x}$. Now, let X be the random variable that indicates the number of sent messages per round. Indicating with *Sensors* the set of the sensors, $\mathbb{E}(X) = \mathbb{E}(\sum_{i,j \in Sensors} Y_{ij})$, where Y_{ij} is equal to 1 if the sensor i forwards the message to the sensor j, and 0 otherwise. $\mathbb{E}(Y_{ij}) = \left(1 - \frac{\beta}{\alpha}\right)\frac{\alpha}{n}$, that is the probability that the sensor i has the message times the probability that it forwards the message to the sensor j. Therefore, for the linearity of the expectation it holds true that $\mathbb{E}(X) = n^2\left(1 - \frac{\beta}{\alpha}\right)\frac{\alpha}{n} = \left(1 - \frac{\beta}{\alpha}\right)\alpha n$, and we can state that $\mathbb{E}(X) < \frac{n}{x}$, concluding the first part of the proof.
Leveraging on the fact that $\alpha > \frac{\beta}{1-\epsilon}$, using Lemma 3.2 it follows that the probability to lose the datum is less than or equal to $\exp\left(-\frac{\epsilon^2 n}{2}\right)$, concluding the second part of the proof.
Finally, Lemma 3.3 can be used to prove the third part of the theorem. In fact, it is enough to prove that $\beta < \alpha$. Since $\frac{\beta}{1-\epsilon} < \alpha$, it follows that $\beta < \alpha(1 - \epsilon) < \alpha$. $\square$

Theorem 3.4 can be used to set the optimal replication rate α, that is able to provide at the same time data survivability, a limited bandwidth and power consumption, and a predictable collecting time. Note that such an α do not always exist. It exists for reasonable values of β, in particular when $\beta < \frac{1-\epsilon}{x\epsilon}$.

4. EPIDEMIC DATA SURVIVABILITY (GEOMETRICAL MODEL)

In Section 3, we have shown that assuring a sufficiently high replication rate, the probability to have the datum destroyed by μADV can be made arbitrarily small. In that setting, we considered a network composed by n sensors, assuming full visibility among them. However, in both WSN and UWSN, the visibility of two sensors is constrained by their transmission range. With this in mind, in this section we reconsider our previous results, introducing the transmission range (r_n)—sensor A can communicate with sensor B if and only if B is inside $A's$ transmission range. We assume that sensors are randomly scattered over a unit square. This implies that all sensors have a number of neighbors concentrated around the mean density with high probability—this fact that will be leveraged in the following to ease calculation. Further, the transmission range r_n is equal for all the sensors, and $r_n \ll 1$. With these new additional hypothesis, we have to revisit Equation 1 and Equation 2. In fact, even if the probability to compromise a sensor that owns the datum is still equal to βi, the probability that the sensor receives the datum is changed, due to the adoption of the geometrical model. Indeed, it corresponds to the probability that it does not possess the datum, times the probability that one of its neighbors decided to forward it to him. Under the above hypothesis, this probability can be expressed as: $sI\pi r_n^2\alpha/n = si\pi r_n^2\alpha$. Equations 1 and 2 now become:

$$i'(t) = \alpha\pi r_n^2 s(t)i(t) - \beta i(t) \qquad (7)$$
$$s'(t) = \beta i(t) - \alpha\pi r_n^2 s(t)i(t) \qquad (8)$$

The general solution of $i'(t)$ is:

$$i(t) = -\frac{(\alpha\pi r_n^2 - \beta)}{e^{t(\beta-\alpha\pi r_n^2)+c(\alpha\pi r_n^2-\beta)} - \alpha\pi r_n^2} \qquad (9)$$

This system has still two steady states: STEADY$_0$ reached when $i(t) = 0$, and STEADY$_1$ reached when $i(t) = 1 - \frac{\beta}{\alpha\pi r_n^2}$. Theorem 3.1

Table 1: Fixed the value of β, three different configurations for α are reported. The first two of them (Table 1(a)) are set in accordance to the SIS model, but do not satisfy the conditions of Lemma 3.2. Instead, α is set according to Lemma 3.2 in Table 1(b). Columns *Probability*$(\cdot, \beta)$ report the probability to loose the datum detected in our experiments. Only with the settings proposed in Table 1(b) we are able to achieve the intended data survival probability ($\geq 99, 99$).

(a) Parameter choice in accordance to the SIS model

β	α_1	$\frac{\alpha_1}{\beta}$	Probability(α_1, β)	α_2	$\frac{\alpha_2}{\beta}$	Probability(α_2, β)
0.1	0.101	1.01	1	0.11	1.1	0.378
0.2	0.202	1.01	1	0.22	1.1	0.648
0.3	0.303	1.01	1	0.33	1.1	0.759
0.4	0.404	1.01	1	0.44	1.1	0.849
0.5	0.505	1.01	1	0.55	1.1	0.888

(b) Parameter choice in accordance to Lemma 3.2

β	α_3	$\frac{\alpha_3}{\beta}$	Probability(α_3, β)
0.1	0.143	1.43	0.003
0.2	0.286	1.43	0.005
0.3	0.429	1.43	0.007
0.4	0.572	1.43	0.008
0.5	0.715	1.43	0.008

and Lemma 3.2 have to be revised to consider the introduced geometrical model:

THEOREM 4.1. *Let us consider a network composed by n sensors, randomly scattered over the unit square, that reached steady state STEADY$_1$ at round $t-1$. Let $\Phi(t)$ be the subset of sensors that receive the datum during round t, and let $\Psi(t)$ be the subset of sensors that are compromised during round t. Assuming transmission range r_n, we have that:*

$$\Pr[g(t) > \epsilon] \leq \exp\left(-\frac{\epsilon^2 n}{2}\right) \qquad (10)$$

$$\Pr[g(t) < -\epsilon] \leq \exp\left(-\frac{\epsilon^2 n}{2}\right) \qquad (11)$$

where $g(t) = \frac{|\Phi(t)| - |\Psi(t)|}{n}$.

PROOF. The proof is identical to the proof of Theorem 3.1. The only difference is in Equation 6, that is the expected value of the function f, defined as in Equation 5. Indeed, it becomes:

$$
\begin{aligned}
\mathbb{E}[f] &= \mathbb{E}\left[\sum_{j=1}^n X_j\right] = n\,\mathbb{E}[X_j] = \\
&= n\left(\frac{1}{n}\alpha\pi r_n^2 s(t-1)i(t-1) - \frac{1}{n}\beta i(t-1)\right) = \\
&= \alpha\pi r_n^2 s(t-1)i(t-1) - \beta i(t-1)
\end{aligned} \qquad (12)
$$

Also in this case $\mathbb{E}[f] = i'(t-1)$, and the proof can continue exactly as in Theorem 3.1. □

LEMMA 4.2. *With the hypothesis of Theorem 4.1 being satisfied, the probability to loose the datum is less than or equal to $\exp\left(-\frac{\epsilon^2 n}{2}\right)$ if $\alpha > \frac{\beta}{\pi r_n^2(1-\epsilon)}$.*

PROOF. The proof is similar to the proof of Lemma 3.2. □

4.1 Local Intermittent Sink Collecting Time

To complete the characterization of the geometrical model, we now consider the presence of an *itinerant intermittent sink*—being in an UWSN, the presence of the sink cannot be predicted, the only assumption is that when it shows up, a steady state has already been reached. The *itinerant intermittent sink* is a sink that moves around the network collecting data from the sensors that are within its communication range. It moves inside the network according to the random jump mobility model: its speed is set so that he can reach each point of the network in one round. The sink is intermittent, so that its behavior is described in the following: it turns off the transceiver, moves to another point of the network, and then it turns on the transceiver again.

LEMMA 4.3. *Once reached STEADY$_1$, considering an itinerant intermittent sink with communication range r_s, and sensors with communication range r_n, the expected time before the sink collects a given datum is equal to $\left(n\gamma\left(1 - \frac{\beta}{\pi r_n^2 \alpha}\right)\pi r_s^2\right)^{-1}$, where n is the number of sensors belonging to the network.*

PROOF. The proof follows the same line of Lemma 3.3. In this case, the steady state is reached when $i(t) = \left(1 - \frac{\beta}{\alpha\pi r_n^2}\right)$, and the probability to find the datum is equal to: $\left(n\gamma\left(1 - \frac{\beta}{\pi r_n^2 \alpha}\right)\pi r_s^2\right)$. Therefore, if X denotes the number of rounds needed by the sink to find a given datum,

$$\mathbb{E}(X) = \left(n\gamma\left(1 - \frac{\beta}{\pi r_n^2 \alpha}\right)\pi r_s^2\right)^{-1}$$

□

4.2 Trade-off between Energy Consumption, Data Survivability and Collecting time

As in the full visibility case, also in the geometrical model it is possible to achieve a trade off between data survivability, bandwidth and power consumption, and collecting time.

THEOREM 4.4. *Once reached STEADY$_1$, considering an itinerant intermittent sink, if $\frac{\beta}{\pi r_n^2(1-\epsilon)} < \alpha < \frac{\beta}{\pi r_n^2} + \frac{1}{x}$ with $1 < x < n$, the following three conditions will hold:*

- *in each round the expected number of sent messages per sensor is less than $\frac{n\pi r_n^2}{x}$;*
- *the probability to lose the datum is less than or equal to: $\exp\left(-\frac{\epsilon^2 n}{2}\right)$;*
- *the expected collecting time will be equal to $\left(n\gamma\left(1 - \frac{\beta}{\pi r_n^2 \alpha}\right)\pi r_s^2\right)^{-1}$, where r_s is the sink's communication range, and r_n is the communication range of the sensors.*

PROOF. The proof is similar to the proof of Theorem 3.4, and comes from the direct application of Lemma 4.2 and Lemma 4.3.

□

Note that when $\beta < \frac{\pi r_n^2(1-\epsilon)}{x\epsilon}$, it always exists an α that respects the hypothesis of Theorem 4.4.

5. EXPERIMENTAL RESULTS

In this section we report our experimental results. Since we were interested in a simulation environment able to undertake hundreds or thousands of sensors, and we were not interested in details like the transmission channel noise, etc., we implemented an ad-hoc

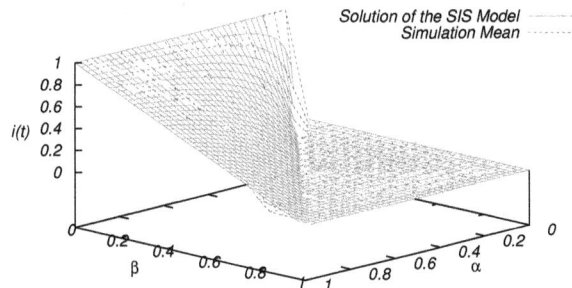

(a) Information survivability in the biologically inspired model.

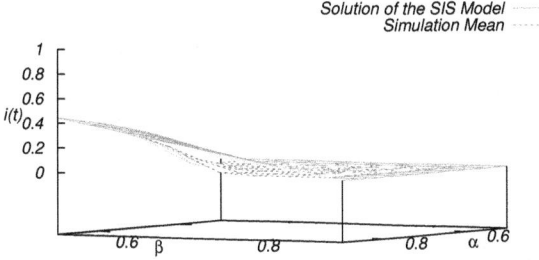

(b) Zoom of Figure 3(a). When β is less than α, but close to it, statistical fluctuations can cause the datum loss.

Figure 3: Full visibility Model. Comparing the biological inspired model forecasting with our experimental results.

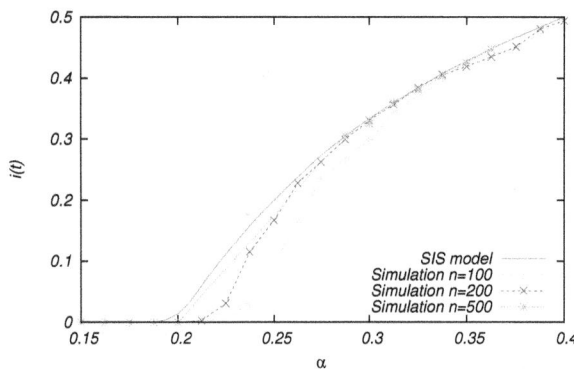

Figure 4: Simulations considering networks of different size. Simulations ran for $t = 300$ rounds with full visibility among sensors and $\beta = 0.2$

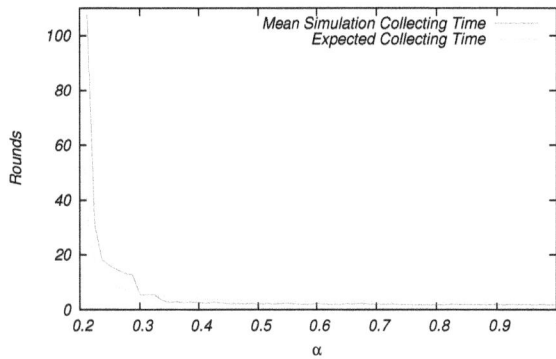

Figure 5: Collecting time considering a Global Intermittent Sink and full visibility among sensors. Here: $\beta = 0.2$ and $\gamma = 0.001$.

simulator instead of using an existing one like NS2, J-sim, Castalia, etc. It does not compete with these simulators in the area of network stack simulation, but scalability and support for extremely large networks are its main qualities. We implemented both the models introduced in this paper: first, we report the results of our biological inspired model where sensors enjoy full visibility, then the results regarding the geometrical model. In both cases, we considered the sensors to be deployed in a unit square area. In the case of the geometrical model, there is the supplementary assumption that sensors are randomly scattered over the unit square. All the following simulations have been obtained as the mean of 200 different experiments.

Figure 3 shows the result of a simulation conducted over a network composed by 100 sensors. As in our biologically inspired model, we considered that the communication range of the sensors allows them to communicate with any other sensor deployed inside the monitored area. The z-axis indicates the size of the subset of sensors possessing the datum normalized by the total number of sensors, while the x and the y-axis indicate different values for α and β respectively. Those values correspond to the replication rate used by the sensors, and the compromising power of the attacker, respectively. Note that, in our protocol, sensors transmit the datum with probability α/n, so that a sensor transmits the datum with a very low probability ($\alpha/100$). Remind that when β is greater than α the datum is lost, so that in those cases $i(t) = 0$. Note that the forecast of the SIS model and the results of the simulation match in almost all the cases. However, for the reasons exposed in Section 3, when $i(t)$ is close to 0, statistical fluctuations cause the loss of the datum. This is confirmed also in Figure 3(a): When β approaches to α, the difference between the two surfaces is more significant. Figure 3(b) is a zoom of Figure 3(a), highlighting a subset of values for

α and β. Here, the surface concerning the experimental simulation is always under the surface that represents the solution of the SIS model. It means that for those values of α and β there is a high risk to lose the datum, even if α is higher than β.

We showed that the effect of statistical fluctuations vanish as the size of the network increases (Theorem 3.1). Figure 4 highlights this aspect. Here, β is fixed to 0.2, and we analyzed the behavior of three networks respectively composed by 100, 200, and 500 sensors. It can be seen that the simulation concerning the network with 500 sensors is much closer to the expected value predicted by the SIS model. In particular, as stated in Theorem 3.1 statistical fluctuations are less and less likely when n grows.

Statistical fluctuations described in Section 3, not only cause the loss of the datum, but can also increase the time required by the sink to collect the datum. In Figure 5, we considered an UWSN of 100 sensors, and a global intermittent sink that collects information with a rate γ set to 0.001. It means that it performs in each round data collection from each sensor with that probability. Here, β is assumed equal to 0.2. The figure compares the expected collecting time introduced in Lemma 3.3, and the output of our experiments. It can be noticed that until α is less than 0.3 the collecting time reported by the simulations is much greater than the expected one. Theorem 3.1 affirms that fluctuations are unlikely in certain cases. From there it can be derived that considering $\beta = 0.2$ as in this

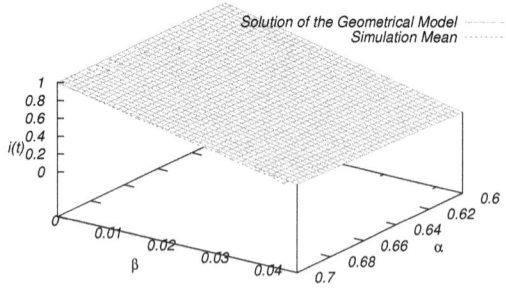

(a) Data survivability in the geometrical model. Theoretical prediction Vs. experimental results. Simulations ran for $t = 4000$ rounds, $n = 100$, and $r = 0.2$.

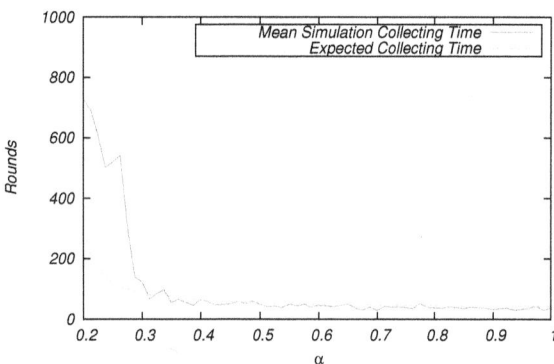

(b) Collecting time considering a Local Intermittent Sink. Sensors and sink transmission ranges are set to 0.3, $\beta = 0.05$. The sink moves inside the network following the random jump model.

Figure 6: Geometrical Model. Theoretical prediction Vs. experimental results.

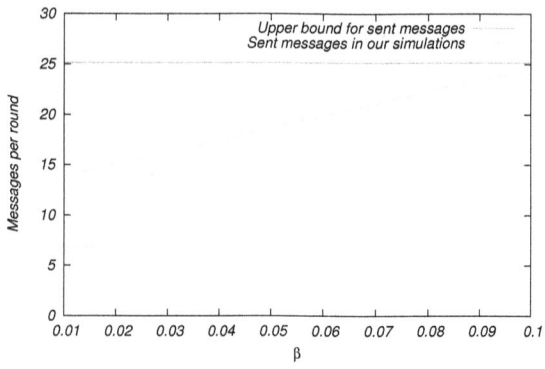

(a) Number of sent messages per round when the hypothesis of Theorem 4.4 are satisfied

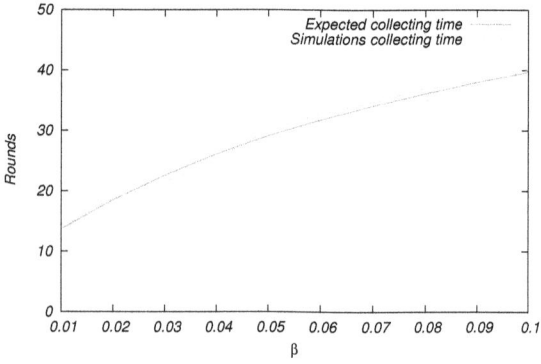

(b) Collecting time when the hypothesis of Theorem 4.4 are satisfied

Figure 7: Geometrical Model.

simulation, for α greater than 0.28, fluctuations of more than $\epsilon = 0.2$ happens only with a probability of 1%. This is confirmed by the figure: when α becomes greater than 0.28, fluctuations are much more unlikely, and we can be sure that the real collecting time and the expected collecting time match.

Previous simulations have been executed using the biological model that does not consider the geometrical aspects of an UWSN. Instead, in the following experiments we simulated the behavior of a network modeled as in the geometrical model introduced in Section 4. In Figure 6(a), we reported the number of sensors possessing the datum after 4,000 rounds. The sensors communication range and the compromising power are both equal to 0.2. The two surfaces match, confirming the correctness of the model. Figure 6(b) shows the collecting time needed in the case of an itinerant intermittent sink. Here, $\gamma = 0.001$ and the communication range of both the sink and the sensors is set to 0.3. Also in this case it can be noticed that statistical fluctuations raise up the real collecting time when α is close to β.

Theorems 3.4 and 4.4 provide a trade-off between data survivability, sent messages, and collecting time in the full visibility and geometrical model respectively. The latter is the most realistic and relevant one, therefore we will now focus on it. In the following simulation, the replication rate α has been set according to Theorem 4.4, while the other parameters have been set in the following way: $n = 1000$, $x = 5$, $\epsilon = 0.2$, $\gamma = 0.001$, $r_s = 0.2$, $r_n = 0.2$. The

results of the simulation are shown in Figure 7. In particular, the number of sent messages is reported in Figure 7(a), while the collecting time is reported in Figure 7(b). In both cases we compared the results of the simulations with the theoretical results provided by the theorem, providing an experimental support to our findings. As for the probability to loose the datum, theorem states that it should be less than $2,06 \times 10^{-9}$, and indeed it has never been lost.

All the performed simulations showed the correctness of our theoretical results, as well as the issues related to the tuning of relevant system parameters. Bandwidth and energy constraints could lead an UWSN's administrator to choose the minimal replication rate (α) to assure information survivability while optimizing resources. However, we proved that this solution could jeopardize datum survivability, and provided a fully fledged framework to trade-off information assurance with replication rate.

6. RELATED WORK

Since the seminal work of Kermack and Mckendrick [14], mathematical models have been extensively used to predict the spreading of diseases within a population. The mathematics of epidemics have been widely used to model the mathematics of gossip communication in WSN too. Gossip based protocols propagate the information in a manner rather similar to the way a viral infection spreads in a biological population. The work of Demers et al. [4] is the first that recognized the power of these protocols, and proposed a formal treatment of gossip. Later, many broadcasting and flooding protocols strongly rooted on those assumptions have been proposed and a comparison of them can be found in [1]. The study of epidemics has often been performed by treating the population as a network graph, with the sensors representing each individual and the edges their interaction, modeling the social network as a scale free topology. Several works have been proposed following this formulation [20, 21, 16], while other approaches use epidemic model to analyze virus spreading in wireless sensor networks [24, 13].

In all the previously cited papers, the focus is on information spreading, and in almost all of them attention is on either broadcasting or flooding. Indeed, data dissemination in the context of WSN is critical. For example, reliable data dissemination to all sensors is absolutely necessary for the propagation of queries, code updates, and other sensitive information. However, in this paper we are not interested in providing the whole network with a given information. We want to assure the information survivability in UWSNs using the less possible waste of energy and without considering which sensors possess the datum. In data centric protocols, the problem has been studied in similar settings using *network coding*: instead of simply relaying the packets sensors receive, they take several packets and combine them together for transmission [11, 15, 22]. These techniques are more performing than simple data replication when bandwidth and sensor buffers are limited, but they introduce a time delay and a computational overhead that must be avoided in quasi-real time scenarios. Further, it should be taken into account that bandwidth requirement is not such a limiting issue in event driven networks, should data be generated only sporadically. On the contrary, our replication scheme allows the careful selection of the replication rate that assures at the same time data survivability, a fast and predictable collecting time, and limited power consumption and bandwidth usage.

UWSNs are an emerging paradigm that is attracting many researchers. The initial work of Di Pietro et Al. [6] introduced the UWSN scenario. The authors defined the mobile adversary and investigated simple techniques to counter attacks focused on erasing specific data. This work has been then extended in [7] to face up with an adversary that indiscriminately erase all sensor data. Another recent result introduced simple cryptographic techniques to prevent the adversary from recognizing data that it aims to erase [8]. Sensor cooperation to achieve self-healing in stationary UWSNs has been explored in [5] and [19]. Note that almost all these works require some cryptographic ability from the sensors. Instead, we propose a straightforward non-cryptographic technique that use a simple replication approach without assuming such a prerequisite. Only in [6] cryptography is not required, but there the geometrical constraints of an UWSN are not taken into account.

To the best of our knowledge, the work most close to our are [3] and [9]. As for the former one, the authors do not consider the presence of an attacker; assuming link and sensor fault probabilities, they focus on the information survival threshold in sensors and P2P networks. In particular, they analyze the conditions that lead to a quick spread or quick extinction of the datum. However, they do not analyze the problems of statistical fluctuation, geometrical modeling, power consumption and collecting time that we highlight in this paper. As for the latter one, the authors just introduce the idea to leverage epidemic modelling to assure information survivability, and show some limitations of current models. However, a complete characterization of information survivability in epidemic models, as well as sink expected collecting time is missing.

7. CONCLUDING REMARKS

In this paper we proposed a data replication approach to assure datum survivability in an UWSN. We modeled the process as the SIS epidemic model, and we showed that using the original SIS model may lead to lose the datum, in contrast with the theoretical results provided in the literature. This risk—due to statistical fluctuations that were overlooked in past research—is sensitive especially when plugging in values to system parameters with the aim to optimize sensors resources usage.

We provided a novel probabilistic analysis for such a model, highlighting the conditions to be satisfied to assure a replication rate that at the same time: Minimizes resources consumption, assures data survivability, and provides a fast collecting time. We also discussed how this model affects the time required by the sink to collect the datum of interest. Note that the above results were discussed in both the full visibility and geometrical model for UWSN. Extensive simulation results confirmed all of our findings.

The introduced model, other than being viable for UWSN and applicable to other fields as well, paves the way for further investigations in the UWSN domain. For instance, assessing how these results are influenced by sensors mobility.

Acknowledgements

The authors would like to thank Riccardo Mariani for his contribution to numerical simulations.

This work has been partially supported by: 1) the EU FP7-ICT project NESSoS (Network of Excellence on Engineering Secure Future Internet Software Services and Systems) under the grant agreement n.256980; and, 2) the Prevention, Preparedness and Consequence Management of Terrorism and other Security-related Risks Programme - European Commission - Directorate-General Home Affairs, under the ExTraBIRE project, HOME/2009/CIPS/AG/-C2-065.

8. REFERENCES

[1] AKDERE, M., BILGIN, C., GERDANERI, O., KORPEOGLU, I., ULUSOY, O., AND CETINTEMEL, U. A comparison of epidemic algorithms in wireless sensor networks. *Computer Communications 29*, 13-14 (Aug. 2006), 2450–2457.

[2] ALBANO, M., CHESSA, S., AND DI PIETRO, R. A model with applications for data survivability in critical infrastructures. *Journal of Information Assurance and Security 4*, 6 (2009), 629–639.

[3] CHAKRABARTI, D., LESKOVEC, J., FALOUTSOS, C., MADDEN, S., GUESTRIN, C., AND FALOUTSOS, M. Information Survival Threshold in Sensor and P2P Networks. *IEEE INFOCOM 2007 - 26th IEEE International Conference on Computer Communications* (May 2007), 1316–1324.

[4] DEMERS, A., GREENE, D., HAUSER, C., IRISH, W., LARSON, J., SHENKER, S., STURGIS, H., SWINEHART, D., AND TERRY, D. Epidemic algorithms for replicated database maintenance. In *PODC '87: Proceedings of the sixth annual ACM Symposium on Principles of distributed computing* (New York, NY, USA, 1987), ACM, pp. 1–12.

[5] DI PIETRO, R., MA, D., SORIENTE, C., AND TSUDIK, G. POSH: Proactive co-Operative Self-Healing in Unattended Wireless Sensor Networks. In *SRDS '08: Proceedings of the 2008 Symposium on Reliable Distributed Systems* (Washington, DC, USA, 2008), IEEE Computer Society, pp. 185–194.

[6] DI PIETRO, R., MANCINI, L. V., SORIENTE, C., SPOGNARDI, A., AND TSUDIK, G. Catch Me (If You Can): Data Survival in Unattended Sensor Networks. *2008 Sixth Annual IEEE International Conference on Pervasive Computing and Communications (PerCom)* (Mar. 2008), 185–194.

[7] DI PIETRO, R., MANCINI, L. V., SORIENTE, C., SPOGNARDI, A., AND TSUDIK, G. Data Security in Unattended Wireless Sensor Networks. *IEEE Transactions on Computers 58*, 11 (2009), 1500–1511.

[8] DI PIETRO, R., MANCINI, L. V., SORIENTE, C., SPOGNARDI, A., AND TSUDIK, G. Playing hide-and-seek with a focused mobile adversary in unattended wireless sensor networks. *Ad Hoc Networks 7*, 8 (Nov. 2009), 1463–1475.

[9] DI PIETRO, R., MARTINELLI, F., AND VERDE, N. V. Introducing epidemic models for data survivability in unattended wireless sensor networks. In *The 2nd IEEE International Workshop on Data Security and PrivAcy in wireless Networks (D-SPAN'11), in press.*

[10] DI PIETRO, R., OLIGERI, G., SORIENTE, C., AND TSUDIK, G. Intrusion-Resilience in Mobile Unattended WSNs. In *Proceedings IEEE INFOCOM* (San Diego, California, USA, Mar. 2010), IEEE Press, pp. 1–9.

[11] DIMAKIS, A. G., PRABHAKARAN, V., AND RAMCHANDRAN, K. Decentralized erasure codes for distributed networked storage. *IEEE/ACM Trans. Netw. 14* (June 2006), 2809–2816.

[12] DUBHASHI, D. P., AND PANCONESI, A. *Concentration of Measure for the Analysis of Randomized Algorithms.* Cambridge University Press, Cambridge, 2009.

[13] GRIFFIN, C., AND BROOKS, R. A note on the spread of worms in scale-free networks. *Systems, Man, and Cybernetics, Part B: Cybernetics, IEEE Transactions on 36*, 1 (2006), 198–202.

[14] KERMACK, W. O., AND MCKENDRICK, A. G. A Contribution to the Mathematical Theory of Epidemics. *Royal Society of London Proceedings Series A 115* (1927), 700–721.

[15] KRISHNAMACHARI, B., ESTRIN, D., AND WICKER, S. Modelling data-centric routing in wireless sensor networks. In *Proceedings of IEEE INFOCOM* (2002).

[16] LI, X., PARKER, T. P., AND XU, S. Towards an analytic model of epidemic spreading in heterogeneous systems. In *The Fourth International Conference on Heterogeneous Networking for Quality, Reliability, Security and Robustness* (New York, NY, USA, 2007), QSHINE '07, ACM.

[17] LIN, Y., LI, B., AND LIANG, B. Stochastic analysis of network coding in epidemic routing. *IEEE Journal on Selected Areas in Communications 26*, 5 (June 2008), 794–808.

[18] MA, D., SORIENTE, C., AND TSUDIK, G. New adversary and new threats: security in unattended sensor networks. *IEEE Network 23*, 2 (Mar. 2009), 43–48.

[19] MA, D., AND TSUDIK, G. DISH: Distributed Self-Healing. In *SSS '08: Proceedings of the 10th International Symposium on Stabilization, Safety, and Security of Distributed Systems* (Detroit, MI, 2008), Springer-Verlag, pp. 47–62.

[20] NEWMAN, M. Spread of epidemic disease on networks. *Physical Review E 66*, 1 (July 2002), 1–11.

[21] PASTOR-SATORRAS, R., AND VESPIGNANI, A. Epidemic Spreading in Scale-Free Networks. *Physical Review Letters 86*, 14 (Apr. 2001), 3200–3203.

[22] REN, W., ZHAO, J., AND REN, Y. Network coding based dependable and efficient data survival in unattended wireless sensor networks. *JCM 4*, 11 (2009), 894–901.

[23] SESHADRI, A., LUK, M., PERRIG, A., VAN DOORN, L., AND KHOSLA, P. K. Scuba: Secure code update by attestation in sensor networks. In *Workshop on Wireless Security'06* (2006), pp. 85–94.

[24] TANG, S., AND MARK, B. L. Analysis of virus spread in wireless sensor networks: An epidemic model. *2009 7th International Workshop on Design of Reliable Communication Networks* (Oct. 2009), 86–91.

[25] Z., R., SUN, X., LIANG, W., SUN, D., AND XIA, Z. Cads: Co-operative anti-fraud data storage scheme for unattended wireless sensor networks. *Inform. Technol. J. 9*, 7 (2010), 1361–1368.

Short Paper: PEPSI: Privacy-Enhanced Participatory Sensing Infrastructure

Emiliano De Cristofaro
Computer Science Department
University of California, Irvine
Irvine, CA, 92617, U.S.A.
edecrist@uci.edu

Claudio Soriente
Distributed Systems Laboratory
Universidad Politécnica de Madrid
28660 Boadilla del Monte (Madrid), Spain
csoriente@fi.upm.es

ABSTRACT

Participatory Sensing combines the ubiquity of mobile phones with the sensing capabilities of Wireless Sensor Networks. It targets the pervasive collection of information, e.g., temperature, traffic conditions, or medical data. Users produce measurements from their mobile devices, thus, a number of privacy concerns – due to the personal information conveyed by reports – may hinder the large-scale deployment of participatory sensing applications. Prior work has attempted to protect privacy in participatory sensing, but it relied on unrealistic assumptions and achieved no provably-secure guarantees. In this paper, we introduce PEPSI: Privacy-Enhanced Participatory Sensing Infrastructure. We explore realistic architectural assumptions and a minimal set of formal requirements aiming at protecting privacy of both data producers and consumers. We also present an instantiation that attains privacy guarantees with provable security at very low additional computational cost and almost no extra communication overhead. Finally, we highlight some problems that call for further research in this developing area.

Categories and Subject Descriptors

C.2.0 [**Computer-Communication Networks**]: General—*Security and Protection*; K.4.1 [**Computers and Society**]: Public Policy Issues—*Privacy*

General Terms

Algorithms, Security

Keywords

Participatory Sensing, Privacy, Security

1. PRELUDE

Participatory sensing is an emerging paradigm that targets the seamless collection of data from a large number of user-carried devices. By embedding a sensor to a mobile phone, participatory sensing (also called *opportunistic* or *urban* sensing) enables harvesting dynamic information about

environmental trends, such as ambient air quality [21], urban traffic patterns [20], health-related information [15], parking availabilities [19], sound events [16], etc. To allow large-scale deployment, researchers are proposing platforms for application developers [7] and devising innovative business models, based on incentive mechanisms for the capitalization on sensed data [14].

Participatory sensing combines the ubiquity of mobile phones with sensing capabilities typical of Wireless Sensor Networks (WSNs). However, it differs in several aspects. *Sensors* are high-end devices, such as smartphones, with much greater resources than traditional WSN sensors. Their batteries can be easily recharged and production cost constraints are not as tight. They are extremely *mobile*, as they leverage the ambulation of their carriers. Moreover, in traditional WSNs, the network operator is assumed to own and query all sensors, while this assumption does not apply to most participatory sensing scenarios. Indeed, mobile devices are *tasked* to participate into gathering and sharing local knowledge; thus, different entities co-exist and might not trust each other.

A typical participatory sensing infrastructure involves (at least) the following parties:

- **Sensors:** Installed on smartphones or other wireless-enabled devices, they emit data reports and form the basis of the participatory sensing infrastructure.

- **Carriers:** Usually envisioned as the people carrying their smartphones, they could also be vehicles, animals or any other entity carrying the mobile sensing device. In the rest of the paper, we refer to a sensor and its carrier as a **Mobile Node**.

- **Network Operators:** They manage the network used to collect and deliver reports, e.g., maintaining WiFi, GSM, or 3G network infrastructure.

- **Queriers:** They subscribe to specific information collected in a participatory sensing application (e.g., "*temperature readings in Irvine, CA*") and obtain corresponding data reports.

Motivation. The number and the heterogeneity of entities involved in participatory sensing prompts a range of new challenges. Unlike in WSNs, sensing devices are not "dull" gadgets, owned by the network operator; they are personal devices that follow users at all time, and their reports often expose personal information. Thus, not only traditional security but also privacy issues must be taken into account, as concerns on personal information disclosure may constitute a fundamental obstacle to large-scale deployment.

Contributions. Prior work has focused on privacy issues in participatory sensing and proposed a few solutions that, however, introduce unrealistic assumptions and provide no *provable* guarantees. On the contrary, we aim at a *cryptographic treatment* of privacy protection in participatory sensing.

We investigate realistic architectural assumptions and a minimal set of formal privacy definitions, intended to protect privacy of both data producers (i.e., mobile nodes) and data consumers (i.e., queriers). Finally, we provide an instantiation that attains privacy guarantees with provable security, at very low additional computational cost and almost no extra communication overhead.

Organization. The next section reviews previous privacy-enhancing solutions and highlights their limitations. Section 3 presents the PEPSI infrastructure and its privacy requirements, while Section 4 yields an efficient instantiation with provable security. Section 5 concludes the paper with a list of open problems.

2. RELATED WORK

In the last years, research interest in participatory sensing has ramped-up. Many researchers have highlighted security and privacy challenges [24], [13], [5], but without proposing actual solutions. Recent proposals in [6] and [12] are—to the best of our knowledge—the only results to address privacy-related problems, hence, they are most related to our work. They aim at protecting anonymity of users, using Mix Network techniques [4], and provide either k-anonymity [25] or l-diversity [18]. They rely on statistical methods to protect privacy and do not achieve provably-secure guarantees. Both proposals only provide limited confidentiality, as reports are encrypted under the public key of a *Report Service* (RS), a trusted party responsible for collecting reports and distributing them to queriers. That is, the RS learns both sensors' reports and queriers' interests.

Additional research work focuses on somewhat related problems. [3] argues that privacy issues can be addressed if each user has access to a private server and uses it as a proxy between her *sensors* and the application requesting her data. However, given the number of contributors in a participatory sensing application, the requirement of *per-user* proxies would severely limit the feasibility of this approach. [23] studies privacy-preserving data aggregation, e.g., computation of sum, average, variance, etc. Similarly, [10] presents a solution for community statistics on time-series data while protecting anonymity (using data perturbation in a closed community with a known empirical data distribution). Other proposals, such as [9] and [11], aim at guaranteeing integrity and authenticity of user-generated contents by employing Trusted Platform Modules (TPMs).

2.1 Limitations of prior work

We now discuss in detail limitations and open problems of prior work on security and privacy in participatory sensing.

Assuming an ubiquitous WiFi infrastructure. One common feature of existing proposals is the assumption of an ubiquitous WiFi infrastructure used to collect and deliver reports [6, 12, 23]. In particular, [6, 12] use standard MAC-IP address recycling techniques to guarantee user unlinkability between reports with respect to WiFi access points. Such an assumption imposes severe limitations on the scope of par-

ticipatory sensing applications, as an ubiquitous presence of open WiFi networks is not realistic today nor anticipated in the next future.

Actually, the majority of existing participatory sensing applications operate from smartphones and use the cellular network to upload reports [22, 21, 19]. Thus, one cannot use WiFi-based anonymization techniques and, in particular, cannot leverage MAC-IP address recycling to guarantee unlinkability. In cellular networks, devices are identified through their International Mobile Subscriber Identity (IMSI), and ID recycling—besides being impossible with current technologies—would lead to denial of service (e.g., the device would not receive incoming calls for its original ID). Thus, it seems not possible to protect privacy of user locations with respect to the network operator. In fact, the regular usage of cellular networks (e.g., including incoming/outgoing phone calls), as well as heartbeat messages exchanged with the network infrastructure, irremediably reveal device's location to the operator.

Using Mix Networks. Another limitation of prior work, such as [6], concerns the use of Mix Networks [4] – anonymizing channels used to de-link reports submitted by sensors before they reach the applications. In other words, Mix Networks act as proxies to forward user reports only when some system-defined criteria are met. Several metrics, such as k-anonymity [25] or l-diversity [18] have been defined to characterize privacy through Mix Networks. Observe that a Mix Network may wait to receive k reports before forwarding them to the application, e.g., to guarantee k-anonymity. However, the anonymity level directly depends on the number of reports received and "mixed" by the Mix Network. They rely on statistical methods to protect privacy and do not guarantee provably-secure privacy. Moreover, there could be scenarios where a relatively long time could pass before the desired level of anonymity is reached (when "enough" reports have been collected). As a result, Mix Networks may remarkably decrease system throughput and cannot be used in settings where *timely* reports are required.

Multiple Semi-Trusted Parties. Available techniques to protect privacy in participatory sensing often involve many semi-trusted independent parties, that are always assumed not to collude. The solutions in [6, 12], besides Mobile Nodes, Registration Authority, and WiFi Access Points, also assumes the presence and the non-collusion of a Task Service (used to distribute tasks to users), a Report Service (to receive reports from sensors), and several Mix Network nodes (i.e., a trusted anonymizing infrastructure). It is not clear how to deploy the Task and the Report services as two separate entities having no incentive to collude. Whereas, we aim at minimizing the number of needed semi-trusted parties (and, in general, the number of involved entities), and propose a participatory sensing infrastructure that can be deployed with formal privacy guarantees.

3. PRELIMINARIES

In this section, we formalize: (i) the entities involved in a privacy-enhanced participatory sensing infrastructure, (ii) involved operations, and (iii) privacy requirements.

3.1 Infrastructure

We envision a participatory sensing infrastructure composed by the following entities:

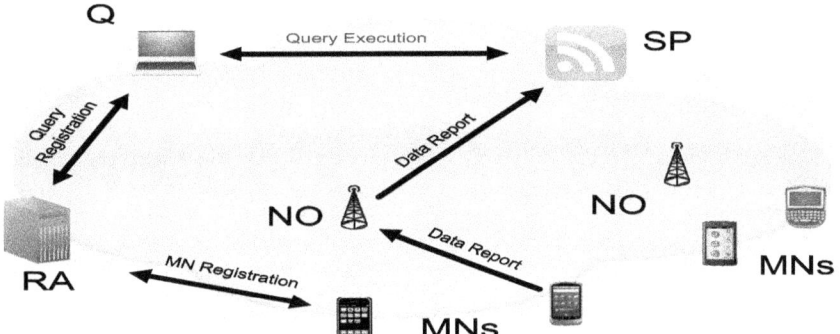

Figure 1: Privacy-Enhanced Participatory Sensing Infrastructure: Mobile Nodes (MNs) register to the Registration Authority (RA) and, subsequently, report sensed data to a Service Provider (SP). Queriers, after registering to RA, subscribe to queries offered by the SP and receive corresponding reports.

Mobile Nodes (MNs). They are computing devices with sensing capabilities (i.e., equipped with one or more *sensors*) and with access to a cellular network. They are carried by people or attached to mobile entities. We assume that MNs run on smartphones and that users voluntarily engage into participatory sensing. We denote with $\mathcal{N}$ a generic mobile node of a participatory sensing application.

Queriers. Queriers are end-users interested in receiving sensor reports in a given participatory sensing application. A generic querier is denoted with $\mathcal{Q}$.

Network Operator (NO). The Network Operator is responsible for the communication infrastructure. We assume that the NO maintains, and provides access to, a cellular network infrastructure (e.g., GSM or 3G).

Registration Authority (RA). The Registration Authority handles the application setup, as well as the registration of participating parties. In our solutions, the RA also contributes to privacy protection, by generating cryptographic public parameters, handling the registration of MNs, and managing queriers' subscription.

Service Providers (SP). The Service Provider acts as an intermediary between the nodes reporting readings and queriers subscribed to them. We envision one or more SPs running participatory sensing applications that offer different query types. (For example, a national service provider might run a pollution monitoring application and define queries to retrieve reports of pollution levels in different cities). Service provider's duties may include listing available sensing services, micropayment, data collection, and notification to queriers.

3.2 Operations

We now describe the common operations performed within participatory sensing applications.

Setup. In this phase, the RA generates all public parameters and its own secret key.

MN Registration. Users register their sensor-equipped device to the RA and install participatory sensing software.

Query Registration. Queriers approach the appropriate RA and request an *authorization* to query the participatory sensing application to obtain a specific type of data

reports, e.g., *"Pollution level in Madrid, Spain"*. (A public list of available sensing services and query syntax may be available from the SP or the RA). Next, they may subscribe to one or more queries, by submitting a request to the SP and awaiting for the responses containing the desired readings. Ideally, only queriers authorized by the RA should receive the desired reports. Also, no information about query interests should be revealed to the SP.

Data Report. MNs report to the SP their readings, using the network access provided by the NO. Ideally, this operation should not reveal to the SP, the NO, or unauthorized queriers any information about reported data, such as type of reading (e.g., pollution) or quantitative information (e.g., $35mg/m^3$ carbon oxide). Also, the SP and any querier should not learn the identity of the source MN.

Query Execution. With this operation, the SP matches incoming data reports with query subscriptions. Ideally, this should be done *blindly*, i.e., the SP should learn nothing beyond the occurrence of an (unspecified) match, if any.

In Figure 1, we illustrate our participatory sensing infrastructure. In the depicted scenario, one may envision that a phone manufacturer (e.g., Nokia) acts as the RA and embeds a given type of sensor (e.g., air pollution meter) in one or more of its phone models, operated by smartphone users, i.e., the MNs. A service provider (such as Google, Microsoft, Yahoo, or a non-profit/academic organization) offers participatory sensing applications (used, for instance, to report and access pollution data), and acts as an intermediary between queriers and mobile nodes. Finally, queriers are users or organizations (e.g., bikers) interested in obtaining readings (e.g., pollution levels).

Observe that—similar to related work—we do not address the problem of encouraging mobile phone users to run participatory sensing applications, nor we focus on business incentives for phone manufacturers or for service providers. Nonetheless, it is reasonable to envision that queriers are willing to pay small fees (or receive advertisement) in return to obtaining measurements of interest.

3.3 Privacy Requirements

Before entering the details of our privacy requirements, observe that the main purpose of a participatory sensing application is to allow queriers to obtain MNs reports. While our main goal is to protect the privacy of both data producers and consumers, entities registered as a querier should still be able to subscribe to a query and receive desired measurements, thus, techniques to identify legitimate parties before registering them are beyond the scope of our work.

We now define the requirements of a Privacy-Enhanced Participatory Sensing Infrastructure (PEPSI). Our definitions are concise due to space limitation, whereas, adversarial games can be found in paper's full version [8].

Soundness. We say that PEPSI is *sound* if, upon subscribing to a query, a querier in possession of the appropriate authorization obtains the desired readings (if any).

Node Privacy. We say that PEPSI is *node-private* if neither the NO, the SP, nor any unauthorized querier, learn any information about the type of reading or the data reported by the MN. Also, other mobile nodes should not learn any information about a given node's reports. In other words, only queriers in possession of the corresponding authorization obtain MN's readings.

Query Privacy. We say that a PEPSI is *query-private* if neither the NO, the SP, nor any mobile node or any other querier, learn any information about the query subscribed by a querier. We leave as part of future work how to guarantee query privacy also w.r.t. the RA.

Report Unlinkability. Report unlinkability prevents any party from linking two or more reports as originating from a given mobile node. PEPSI provides report unlinkability if different reports originating by the same MN cannot be linked to the source by the RA, the SP, the queriers or any other MN[1].

As discussed earlier, it seems unlikely to provide node location privacy w.r.t. NO, as the NO knows phone's position at any time. We still consider node location privacy as for the RA, the SP, or unauthorized queriers.

4. PEPSI

We now present our PEPSI instantiation, in accordance with the architectural design in Figure 1 and that complies with privacy definitions of Section 3.3. We also discuss arguments of its provable security and estimate its performance.

4.1 PEPSI Instantiation

In PEPSI, data reports are always labeled using keywords that identify the nature of the information announced by mobile nodes. Similarly, queriers subscribe to given queries by specifying the corresponding keywords. In the rest of the paper, we use the term *identifier*, and the notation ID (or ID^*) to identify the data report/query type. Examples of such identifiers include: "*Temperature in Irvine, CA*" or "*Pollution in Madrid, Spain*". The list of identifiers – depending on the application – can be obtained either from the SP or the RA. In particular, the RA defines which services (i.e., queries) will be available for mobile nodes to contribute and for users to query. However, as these identifiers can be public, they can be downloaded from the SP or any bulletin board. For ease of presentation, in the rest of the paper, we assume that query identifiers are available at the RA.

---

[1]Observe that we cannot guarantee user anonymity and report unlinkability with respect to the NO, thus, we do not consider the NO in our definition.

4.1.1 High Level Description

PEPSI works as follows. The RA runs the *Setup* algorithm to generate public parameters and secret keys. In order to pose a query, e.g., identified by ID, queriers first need to register to the RA and obtain the corresponding authorization (*Query Authorization*). Then, they subscribe their queries to the SP (*Query Subscription*): in PEPSI, this process reveals nothing about queriers' interests.

At the same time, before starting reporting data, MNs need to authenticate to the RA, and obtain: (i) the identifier ID corresponding to the type of their reports, and (ii) a token that allows them to announce data (*MN Registration*).

The *on-line* part of PEPSI includes two operations: *Data Report* and *Query Execution*. With the former, MNs upload encrypted reports to the SP. In the latter, the SP *blindly* matches received reports with queries and forwards (matching) reports to all subscribed queriers. Only authorized queriers obtain query responses, can decrypt data reports, and retrieve original measurements. Finally, we let the RA run a *Nonce Renewal* procedure to evict malicious MNs from the participatory sensing application. This procedure is run periodically and the new nonce is securely delivered to honest MNs using broadcast encryption [2].

Our main cryptographic building block is Identity-Based Encryption (IBE), specifically, the construction in [1]. The main advantage in using IBE, as opposed to standard public-key cryptography, is to enable non-interactivity in our query protocol design. This is crucial in participatory sensing scenarios, where MNs and queriers have no direct communication nor mutual knowledge.

4.1.2 Algorithms Specification

Setup. The Registration Authority, given a security parameter λ, generates a prime q, two groups $\mathbb{G}_1, \mathbb{G}_2$ of order q, a bilinear map $e : \mathbb{G}_1 \times \mathbb{G}_1 \to \mathbb{G}_2$.[2] Next, a random $s \in \mathbb{Z}_q^*$ and a random generator $P \in \mathbb{G}_1$, are chosen; Q is set such that $Q = P^s$. (P, Q) are public parameters. s is RA's private master key. Also, a nonce $z \in \mathbb{Z}_q^*$ is selected and R is set such that $R = P^z$. Finally, three cryptographic hash function, $H_1 : \{0,1\}^* \to \mathbb{G}_1$, $H_2 : \{0,1\}^{\mathbb{G}_2} \to \{0,1\}^\lambda$, and $H_3 : \{0,1\}^{\mathbb{G}_2} \to \{0,1\}^\lambda$ are chosen.

MN Registration. The MN registration is run between MN and RA. We assume that, after being identified by RA, the Mobile Node $\mathcal{N}$ obtains the pair (z, ID), where z is the nonce generated by RA during setup, and ID identifies the nature of the readings for which $\mathcal{N}$ provides reports.

Query Registration. The query registration is as follows:

1. **Query Authorization:** Querier $\mathcal{Q}$ registers to RA to get an authorization to receive readings for a given query, identified by ID^*. $\mathcal{Q}$ obtains:

$$sig = H_1(ID^*)^s.$$

2. **Query Subscription:** Querier $\mathcal{Q}$—subscribing to readings identified by ID^*—sends to the SP:

$$T^* = H_2[e(R, sig)].$$

Data Report. Mobile node $\mathcal{N}$ periodically submits data reports to SP, using NO's infrastructure. In our protocol,

---

[2]Recall that the map e is *bilinear* if $e(U^a, V^b) = e(U, V)^{ab}$.

to upload a reading, $\mathcal{D}$, related to query ID, $\mathcal{N}$ sends SP (using NO's infrastructure) the pair $\langle T, CT \rangle$, such that:

$$T = H_2[e(Q, H_1(ID)^z)], \quad CT = ENC_k(\mathcal{D})$$

for $k = H_3[e(Q, H_1(ID)^z)]$.

Query Execution. The query execution is as follows:

1. `Blind Matching`: The Service Provider matches T with stored T^*'s and returns $\mathcal{Q}$ all matching T's, alongside associated CT's.

2. `Notification`: On receiving (T, CT), $\mathcal{Q}$ computes $k^* = H_3[e(R, sig)]$ and obtains:

$$\mathcal{D} = Dec_{k^*}(CT)$$

Nonce renewal. We assume a dynamic set of subscribed MNs where new sensors can register and malicious ones are evicted. In order to ban misbehaving sensors, the RA periodically generates and distributes a fresh z to sensors and $R = P^s$ to queriers. The former can be securely distributed to honest sensors using broadcast encryption [2].

4.2 Privacy Analysis

We now consider privacy properties of PEPSI. Due to space limitation, we only provide concise proofs at this stage and defer detailed proofs to [8]. We assume that the system is immune to eavesdropping. In fact, 3G networks encrypt communication between mobile phones and the network operator. Communication between other parties (i.e., $RA \leftrightarrows MN$, $Querier \leftrightarrows SP$, etc.) are encrypted using standard techniques, e.g., using SSL.

Soundness. Our PEPSI solution is *sound*, since: for any (ID^*, sig) held by a querier $\mathcal{Q}$, and ID held by a node $\mathcal{N}$, if: (1) $sig = H_1(ID^*)^s$, where s is RA's secret key, and (2) $ID^* = ID$, we obtain :

$$\begin{aligned} T &= H_2[e(Q, H_1(ID)^z)] = H_2[e(P^z, H_1(ID^*)^s)] \\ &= H_2[e(R, sig)] = T^* \end{aligned}$$

and, similarly, also $k = k^*$. Therefore, (1) SP correctly matches $\mathcal{Q}$'s (authorized) request T^* with the appropriate sensor report $\langle T, CT \rangle$, and (2) $\mathcal{Q}$ can correctly decrypt CT and recover $\mathcal{D}$.

Node Privacy. Our PEPSI solution is *node-private* since only authorized queriers in possession of a valid sig can learn any information about the report $\langle T, CT \rangle$. Privacy w.r.t. the NO, the SP, other MNs and non-authorized queriers, stems from the security of the underlying Identity-based Encryption scheme [1]. The main intuition is that this kind of adversary could obtain information about a node's report only if she was in possession of the appropriate sig or—assuming that ID's have low entropy—the nonce z. Assuming a CPA-secure and key-private IBE system, the resulting PEPSI scheme is trivially *node-private* w.r.t. the NO, the SP, and non-authorized queriers. We sketch a prove of this claim by contradiction. Assuming our claim is not true, then there exists a polynomial-bounded adversary $\mathcal{A}$ that violates node privacy of PEPSI. $\mathcal{A}$ is given ID and the IBE-encryption of $\mathcal{D}$ under the key ID but not the corresponding $sig = H_1(ID)^s$. If $\mathcal{A}$ decrypts $\mathcal{D}$ with non-negligible probability, then we can construct a polynomial-bounded adversary $\mathcal{B}$ which uses $\mathcal{A}$ to break the CPA-security of IBE. This contradicts our assumption.

Note that the RA could use its secret key to "test" an arbitrary ID^* against an eavesdropped report $\langle T, CT \rangle$. That is, the RA could learn whether $ID^* = ID$ and violate node privacy. However, assuming that reports $\langle T, CT \rangle$ are super-encrypted under SP's public key, the RA can access nodes' reports only if it colludes with the SP.

Query Privacy. PEPSI is *query-private* since neither the NO, the SP, other queriers, nor any mobile node, learn any information about query interests of a querier $\mathcal{Q}$. Query privacy stems from the security of the underlying Identity-based Encryption scheme [1]. Arguments behind this claim mirror those outlined above for node privacy, thus, we do not repeat them here.

Observe that the privacy of a querier $\mathcal{Q}$, subscribed to ID^* (i.e., in possession of $sig = H_1(ID^*)^s$), could be violated by a malicious party, subscribed to ID' (i.e., in possession of $sig' = H_1(ID')^s$), only if: (1) she obtains $T = H_2[e(R, sig)]$ sent from $\mathcal{Q}$ to the SP during *Query Subscription* and (2) $ID^* = ID'$. Since the communication between $\mathcal{Q}$ and the SP is encrypted, (1) happens only if such a malicious party colludes with the SP.

Report Unlinkability and Location Privacy. As argued above, it is not possible to guarantee report unlinkability with respect to the network operator. However, one could trust the NO to remove privacy-sensitive metadata from each report (such as mobile nodes' identifiers, the cell from which the report was originated, etc.), before forwarding it to the SP. Nonetheless, this would not require the NO to act as a Mix Network. Also, the NO never delays message forwarding, e.g., until "enough" reports to protect privacy are collected, but forwards "the payload" of each report (i.e., $\langle T, CT \rangle$) as soon as it is received.

Trust Assumptions. The security of PEPSI only relies on the assumption that the SP is not colluding with either the RA or queriers — on the contrary, prior work assumed the presence of *several* non-colluding and/or fully-trusted parties [6, 12, 9, 11]. Specifically, if the RA and the SP colluded, they could violate node privacy using RA's secret key, s, and pairs $\langle T, CT \rangle$ received by the SP. Also, recall that any party registered as a querier could potentially collude with the SP and try violating query privacy: it could test a given sig (obtained during the *Query Authorization*) against messages sent by the victim querier to the SP (during *Query Subscription*). We argue that assuming a non-colluding SP is realistic since in participatory sensing, SPs often capitalize on the services they provide, thus, they have no incentive to deviate from an honest-but-curious behavior.

Furthermore, PEPSI needs to trust the NO to remove sensitive MN information from reports before forwarding to the SP. Recall that this assumption is essential since anonymity w.r.t the NO is not achievable in 3G networks.

4.3 Performance Evaluation

Even if resources in participatory sensing are not as constrained as in WSNs, we aim at minimizing the overhead incurred at mobile nodes. This section provides preliminary figures on the cost of cryptographic operations used to achieve intended privacy features.

We implemented protocol operations executed by MNs on a Nokia N900 (equipped with a 600 MHz ARM processor and 256 MB RAM) running the `libpbc` cryptographic library [17]. We selected Type-A pairings and 160-bit prime q. Computation overhead is due to the computation of T, the encryption key k, and the encrypted report CT. Note that the first two values can be computed off-line, independently of the sensed data. Communication overhead is merely due to the transmission of T, which is the output of a hash function (e.g., SHA-1), and can be as small as 160-bit. Indeed, using available symmetric-key cryptosystems (e.g., AES), the length of CT is almost the same as a reading $\mathcal{D}$.

Without leveraging off-line precomputation, we measured the time to compute and transmit $\langle T, CT \rangle$, using integers as data reports. Over 100 experiments, we experienced an average time of $93.47ms$ to compute $\langle T, CT \rangle$ and around $80ms$ for transmission over the 3G network. Note that a naïve (non-private) solution would save in computation (since data would not be encrypted) but would spend roughly the same transmission time to send the report. Finally, remark that the SP incurs no communication nor computational overhead: its task is limited to hash comparison and forwarding. Similarly, the only additional operation that queriers perform during query execution is the symmetric decryption of received readings, which incurs a negligible overhead.

5. CONCLUSION

The participatory sensing paradigm bears an irrefutably great potential. However, its success depends on the number of users willing to report measurements from their mobile devices. Clearly, a wide-scale user participation is bound to effective protocols that preserve privacy of both data producers (i.e., mobile nodes) and data consumers (i.e., queriers). In this paper, we highlighted shortcomings of previous solutions and we embarked towards a cryptographic treatment of privacy in participatory sensing. To this aim, we analyzed which are the privacy features that can be guaranteed with provable security and introduced a participatory sensing protocol that attains them. Finally, we provided figures of the incurred overhead at mobile nodes.

As often happens, deploying actual solutions based on our proposal requires addressing additional (potential) security issues, such as authentication, data integrity, DoS prevention, active attacks, Sybil attacks, etc. Our next step is to deploy testing applications using the PEPSI infrastructure, as well as to devise a large-scale evaluation of its global overhead. Our future work also includes extending the protocols to efficiently support query privacy w.r.t. the RA (i.e., queriers can register without the RA learning their interests). Interesting open challenges remain in how to provide location privacy with respect to cellular network operator, addressing potential collusion between different parties, and supporting more complex queries (e.g., aggregate and conjunctive queries).

Acknowledgments. This research has been partially funded by US Intelligence Advanced Research Projects Activity (IARPA) under grant FA8750-09-2-0071, the Madrid Regional Council – CAM under project CLOUDS (S2009TIC-1692), the Spanish Research Agency – MICINN under project CloudStorm (TIN2010-19077), and the European Commission under projects MASSIF (FP7-257475) and STREAM (FP7-216181). We are also grateful to Nokia for the devices used in our experiments.

6. REFERENCES

[1] D. Boneh and M. Franklin. Identity-based encryption from the Weil pairing. In *Crypto*, 2001.

[2] D. Boneh, C. Gentry, and B. Waters. Collusion resistant broadcast encryption with short ciphertexts and private keys. In *Crypto*, 2005.

[3] R. Cáceres, L. P. Cox, H. Lim, A. Shakimov, and A. Varshavsky. Virtual individual servers as privacy-preserving proxies for mobile devices. In *MobiHeld Workshop*, 2009.

[4] D. L. Chaum. Untraceable electronic mail, return addresses, and digital pseudonyms. *Communications of ACM*, 24(2), 1981.

[5] D. Christin, M. Hollick, and M. Manulis. Security and Privacy Objectives for Sensing Applications in Wireless Community Networks. In *IEEE ICCCN*, 2010.

[6] C. Cornelius, A. Kapadia, D. Kotz, D. Peebles, M. Shin, and N. Triandopoulos. AnonySense: Privacy-aware people-centric sensing. In *Mobisys*, 2008.

[7] T. Das, P. Mohan, V. Padmanabhan, R. Ramjee, and A. Sharma. PRISM: Platform for Remote Sensing using Smartphones. In *Mobisys*, 2010.

[8] E. De Cristofaro and C. Soriente. PEPSI: Privacy-Enhanced Participatory Sensing Infrastructure. http://sprout.ics.uci.edu/PEPSI, 2011.

[9] A. Dua, N. Bulusu, W. Feng, and W. Hu. Towards trustworthy participatory sensing. In *HotSec*, 2009.

[10] R. Ganti, N. Pham, Y. Tsai, and T. Abdelzaher. PoolView: stream privacy for grassroots participatory sensing. In *SenSys*, 2008.

[11] P. Gilbert, L. Cox, J. Jung, and D. Wetherall. Toward trustworthy mobile sensing. In *HotMobile*, 2010.

[12] K. Huang, S. Kanhere, and W. Hu. Preserving privacy in participatory sensing systems. *Computer Communications*, 33(11), 2010.

[13] A. Kapadia, D. Kotz, and N. Triandopoulos. Opportunistic sensing: Security challenges for the new paradigm. In *COMNETS*, 2009.

[14] J. Lee and B. Hoh. Sell Your Experiences: A Market Mechanism based Incentive for Participatory Sensing. In *PerCom*, 2010.

[15] B. Longstaff, S. Reddy, and D. Estrin. Improving activity classification for health applications on mobile devices using active and semi-supervised learning. In *PervasiveHealth*, 2010.

[16] H. Lu, W. Pan, N. Lane, T. Choudhury, and A. Campbell. SoundSense: scalable sound sensing for people-centric applications on mobile phones. In *Mobisys*, 2009.

[17] B. Lynn. PBC: The Pairing-Based Cryptography Library. http://crypto.stanford.edu/pbc/, Last Accessed, 2011.

[18] A. Machanavajjhala, D. Kifer, J. Gehrke, and M. Venkitasubramaniam. l-diversity: Privacy beyond k-anonymity. *ACM Transactions on Knowledge Discovery from Data (TKDD)*, 1(1), 2007.

[19] S. Mathur, T. Jin, N. Kasturirangan, J. Chandrasekaran, W. Xue, M. Gruteser, and W. Trappe. ParkNet: drive-by sensing of road-side parking statistics. In *MobiSys*, 2010.

[20] P. Mohan, V. Padmanabhan, and R. Ramjee. Rich monitoring of road and traffic conditions using mobile smartphones. In *Sensys*, 2008.

[21] E. Paulos, R. Honicky, and E. Goodman. Sensing atmosphere. In *SenSys Workshops*, 2007.

[22] S. Reddy, K. Shilton, G. Denisov, C. Cenizal, D. Estrin, and M. Srivastava. Biketastic: sensing and mapping for better biking. In *CHI*, 2010.

[23] J. Shi, R. Zhang, Y. Liu, and Y. Zhang. PriSense: Privacy-Preserving Data Aggregation in People-Centric Urban Sensing Systems. In *Infocom*, 2010.

[24] K. Shilton. Four billion little brothers?: Privacy, mobile phones, and ubiquitous data collection. *Communications of the ACM*, 52(11), 2009.

[25] L. Sweeney. k-Anonymity: A model for Protecting Privacy. *Int. J. Uncertain. Fuzziness Knowl.-Based Syst.*, 2002.

Thwarting Inside Jamming Attacks on Wireless Broadcast Communications

Sisi Liu
Dept. of Electrical and
Computer Engineering
University of Arizona
Tucson, AZ, USA
sisimm@ece.arizona.edu

Loukas Lazos
Dept. of Electrical and
Computer Engineering
University of Arizona
Tucson, AZ, USA
llazos@ece.arizona.edu

Marwan Krunz
Dept. of Electrical and
Computer Engineering
University of Arizona
Tucson, AZ, USA
krunz@ece.arizona.edu

ABSTRACT

We address the problem of jamming-resistant broadcast communications under an *internal threat model*. We propose a time-delayed broadcast scheme (TDBS), which implements the broadcast operation as a series of unicast transmissions, distributed in frequency and time. TDBS does not rely on commonly shared secrets, or the existence of jamming-immune control channels for coordinating broadcasts. Instead, each node follows a unique pseudo-noise (PN) frequency hopping sequence. Contrary to conventional PN sequences designed for multi-access systems, our sequences exhibit high correlation to enable broadcast. Moreover, their design limits the information leakage due to the exposure of a subset of sequences by compromised nodes. We map the problem of constructing such PN sequences to the 1-factorization problem for complete graphs. Our evaluation results show that TDBS can maintain broadcast communications in the presence of inside jammers.

Categories and Subject Descriptors

C.2.0 [**Computer - Communication Networks**]: General—*Security and Protection*

General Terms

Security, reliability, algorithms, design

Keywords

Jamming, broadcast communications, denial-of-service, wireless networks, graph factorization, security.

1. INTRODUCTION

Wireless communications are vulnerable to intentional interference attacks, typically referred to as jamming. In the simplest form of jamming, the adversary interferes with the signal reception by transmitting a continuous jamming waveform [24] or several short jamming pulses [18]. Conventional anti-jamming techniques rely extensively on spread spectrum (SS) communications, such as direct sequence spread

spectrum (DSSS) and frequency hopping spread spectrum (FHSS) [1, 24]. SS provides bit-level protection by spreading bits according to a secret pseudo-random noise (PN) code, known only to the communicating parties. In the case of broadcast communications, the sender's PN code must be shared by all (potentially non-trustworthy) receivers. The disclosure of such a secret due to the compromise of any receiver nullifies the gains due to SS [16, 20].

Several researchers have studied the problem of anti-jamming broadcast communications under an internal threat model [4, 8, 9, 14, 16, 20, 21, 25, 26]. Methods in [4, 14, 16, 21] eliminate the dependency of broadcast on shared secrets. Baird et al. proposed the encoding of "indelible marks" at specific locations within each broadcasted message [4]. Assuming that an active jamming attack cannot flip a bit '1'to a bit '0', it was shown that a jammer cannot erase packets from the wireless channel (but can inject arbitrary packets). Pöpper et al. [20] proposed a method called Uncoordinated DSSS (UDSSS), in which broadcast transmissions are spread according to a PN code, randomly selected from a public codebook. At the receiving end, nodes decode received messages by exhaustively applying every PN code in the public codebook. Liu et. al. proposed RD-DSSS, a randomized differential DSSS scheme that also relies on randomly selected PN codes [16]. Compared to UDSSS, the RD-DSSS scheme provides resilience to reactive jammers.

Note that when the spreading PN code is not known a priori, broadcast transmissions must be repeated several times to synchronize the receiver [20]. Moreover, DSSS exhibits a threshold behavior to interference. It rejects the interfering signal as long as the interference remains below the jamming margin, but the throughput becomes practically zero if this margin is surpassed [19, 24]. On the other hand, FHSS exhibits a graceful degradation in performance with the increase of interference. Due to this dual behavior, DSSS and FHSS find applications on different domains. The former is typical in the commercial domain (e.g., [12]) where moderate interference levels are caused by users operating on the same spectrum, while the latter finds applications in adversarial settings where the interference is likely caused by a powerful jammer. Because the adversarial model assumed in this work is of a powerful jammer, we develop anti-jamming methods that adopt a FHSS design.

Our Contributions: We study the problem of anti-jamming broadcast communications in the presence of inside jammers. We propose the *Time-Delayed Broadcast Scheme* (TDBS) for anti-jamming broadcast communications, based on FHSS communications. TDBS differs from classical FHSS designs in that two communicating nodes do not follow the same FH sequence, but are assigned unique ones that have high correlation properties. Unlike the typical broadcast operation where every receiver is eventually tuned to a common broadcast channel, TDBS implements the broadcast operation as a series of unicast transmissions spread both in frequency and time. To ensure resilience to inside jammers, the locations of the unicast transmissions, defined by a frequency band/slot pair, are only partially known to any subset of receivers. Because the jammer can only interfere with a limited set of frequency bands per time slot, a subset of the unicast transmissions are interference-free, thus propagating broadcast messages.

The problem of FH sequence design, is mapped to a 1-factorization problem in complete graphs. While a broad class of scheduling algorithms are known to employ 1-factors (perfect matchings) (e.g., [7, 11, 22, 23, 27]), they are, in general, concerned with unicast communications in a benign setting. They also typically require coordination via the exchange of broadcast messages [7, 11]). TDBS is specifically designed to facilitate broadcasting in the presence of jammers and in the absence of a coordination channel.

Note that TDBS is not meant to be a permanent replacement of the conventional broadcast mechanism in a benign setting. Broadcasting on a common frequency band achieves the optimal communication efficiency (one slot) in the absence of any jammer. TDBS is designed as an emergency mechanism for temporarily restoring communications until the jammer is physically removed from the network. Therefore, its primary focus is resilience to inside jammers.

Paper Organization: The remainder of the paper is organized as follows. In Section 2, we state the system and adversarial model assumptions. In Section 3 we present an overview of TDBS. Section 4 describes TDBS for single-hop networks. In Section 5, we extend the TDBS operation to multi-hop networks. The security and performance of TDBS are evaluated in Section 6. In Section 7, we present related work, and in Section 8, we conclude the paper.

2. SYSTEM AND ADVERSARIAL MODELS

Network Topologies: We consider two types of network topologies. In the topology of figure 1(a), a set of nodes form a single-hop broadcast group. Any node may initiate a broadcast transmission to its neighbors. This single-hop topology is typical in wireless LAN and wireless personal area networks, where a group of devices is assumed to be in close range (e.g., bluetooth devices), and in military scenarios where a set of mobile nodes move in a team-coordinated fashion. In figure 1(b), we consider a multi-hop network connected in ad hoc mode. To make TDBS scalable with the network size, we assume that the network is partitioned to clusters which form cliques [13, 28]. Broadcast transmissions occurring under this architecture may be limited within a cluster, or may propagate to other clusters.

System Model: Nodes communicate over a set $\mathcal{C} = \{f_1, \ldots, f_K\}$ of K distinct frequency bands (e.g., $K = 79$ for the bluetooth standard). Each node is equipped with a single half-duplex transceiver. Hence, a node can only listen to or transmit over one band at a time. We assume that all nodes are synchronized to a time-slotted system. Nodes are capable of hopping between frequency bands. Without loss

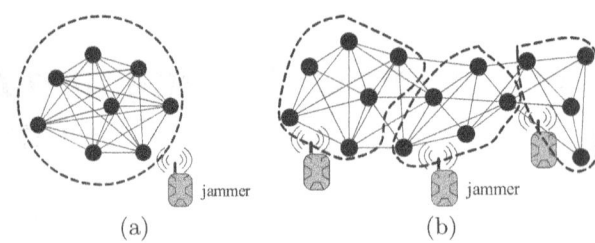

Figure 1: (a) A WPAN architecture in which devices located within one-hop form a broadcast communication group, (b) a multi-hop architecture in which communicating nodes span several hops.

of generality, we assume that frequency hopping occurs on a per-slot basis. For simplicity, the duration of one time slot is assumed sufficient for the transmission of one message unit.

The network is initialized by a trusted authority, which is responsible for pre-loading relevant parameters such as PN FH sequences and other cryptographic secrets. For multi-hop topologies, we assume a static network topology, known to the trusted authority. Broadcast communications can be either public (transmitted in an unencrypted form) or private. In the latter case, confidentiality and authenticity of the communication is achieved via resource-efficient public key operations. Once the network is initialized, the trusted authority is no longer needed.

Adversary Model: The goal of the adversary is to prevent the sender(s) from communicating with all, or a subset of the intended receivers. For this purpose, the adversary deploys a set of jamming devices at locations of his own choosing, which can be centrally coordinated. These devices are capable of collectively jamming any J frequency bands of the adversary's choosing, by adding interfering signals to the selected frequencies. Wireless transmissions over any of the jammed frequency bands are assumed to be "irrecoverably" corrupted. We do not impose any particular power constraint on the adversary, but assume that the jammed frequency bands become unavailable in the entire network (single-hop, or multi-hop). The jamming devices can switch between frequency bands on a per-slot basis.

The adversary is capable of physically compromising network devices and recovering stored information including cryptographic keys, PN codes, certificates, etc. Moreover, the adversary is aware of the methods used to protect broadcast transmissions (in our case the specifics of the PHY layer implementation and the TDBS algorithm). Note that similar adversary models have been considered in [14–16, 20].

3. OVERVIEW OF TDBS

To achieve jamming-resistant communications in the presence of insiders, TDBS realizes broadcast as a series of unicast transmissions distributed in frequency and time, thus avoiding the convergence of all nodes to a common frequency band. The locations of the unicast transmissions, defined by a frequency band/slot pair (f, s), are only partially known to each node (every node is aware of his own schedule). Therefore, the compromise of a node reveals only the set of locations assigned to that node, while keeping the locations of other communicating nodes secret.

For this purpose, nodes are divided into pairs scheduled to communicate over frequency bands which are selected at random. It is possible to partition the set of nodes to

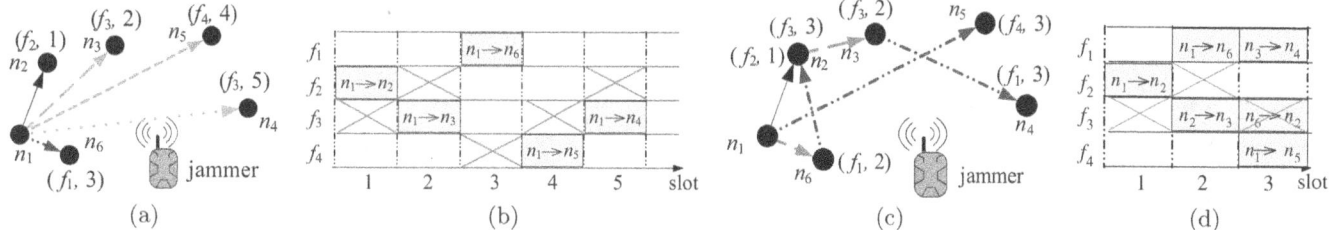

Figure 2: (a) Operation in the SU mode. Broadcast is realized as a series of unicasts. The pair (f, s) denotes the frequency band and time slot where the unicast takes place, (b) the timeline of the unicast transmissions of n_1 for the SU mode. The "x" marks denote frequencies jammed by the adversary, (c) operation in the AB mode. A broadcast transmission is relayed by several nodes at separate frequency bands, (d) the timeline of the unicast transmissions for the AB mode.

groups of size larger than two for more efficient broadcast communication at the expense of reduced resilience to node compromise. Because we are primarily concerned with the jamming-resistance property, we consider the case of node pairs. The communicating pairs and assigned frequency bands change on a per-slot basis thus realizing a FH system. TDBS differs from traditional FH designs in that: (a) communicating nodes do not synchronize to the same FH sequence, but follow unique hopping patterns and, (b) these patterns have a high correlation to lower the number of slots required to complete a broadcast transmission. Moreover, TDBS differs from rendezvous systems that have been proposed for coordinating multi-channel access (e.g. [3, 5]), in that it focuses on the broadcast operation as opposed to rendezvous for unicast communications.

Two modes of operation are proposed for TDBS: the sequential unicast mode (SU) and the assisted broadcast mode (AB). In the SU mode, the sender sequentially relays information to intended receivers. This more inefficient mode is appropriate when receivers do not have relaying capabilities, or are not trusted to relay the broadcast message. In the AB mode, any node that receives a broadcast message can act as a relay for that message.

Figure 2 shows an example of the two modes. In figure 2(a), node n_1 operates in the SU mode. It sequentially unicasts a broadcast message to nodes $n_2 - n_6$. Figure 2(b), depicts the timeline of transmissions of figure 2(a). The broadcast is completed after five slots. The "x" marks denote the frequency band jammed by the adversary at each time slot. Figure 2(c), shows the operation in the AB mode. Node n_1 initiates a broadcast in slot 1, by transmitting a message m to n_2. In slot 2, n_1 and n_2 relay m to n_6 and n_3, respectively, using frequency bands f_1 and f_3 in parallel. In slot 3, the broadcast is completed with the relay of m from n_1, n_3 and n_6 to n_5, n_4 and n_2, respectively. The timeline of the transmissions taking place in the AB mode is shown in figure 2(d). Observe that in this scenario the broadcast is completed despite the jamming of the transmission between n_6 and n_2 in slot 3.

The main challenge of TDBS is to design the FH sequences of individual nodes such that the following requirements are met: (a) hopping sequences are pseudo-random, (b) compromise of a subset of nodes (insiders) limits the information leakage relevant to the sequences of uncompromised nodes, and (c) every node has the same opportunity to perform a broadcast (fairness). In the next section, we develop algorithms for constructing hopping sequences for TDBS-SU and TDBS-AB that satisfy the above requirements. We first

illustrate our algorithms for single-hop topologies and then extend our results to multi-hop topologies.

4. TDBS FOR SINGLE-HOP TOPOLOGIES

To achieve resilience to jamming, we randomly distribute unicast transmissions both in frequency and in time. This problem can be viewed as a link scheduling problem for avoiding collisions in multi-channel networks, under the node-exclusive interference model. A large body of literature treats this type of scheduling as various instances of a matching problem in general graphs [7, 11, 22, 23, 27]. However, pre-existing methods are not immediately applicable to our setup for the following reasons.

In link scheduling problems, the goal is to maximize the aggregate network throughput, realized as the sum of individual traffic flows. We are concerned with the dissemination of one message to a specified set of receivers (the members of a broadcast group) over unpredictable frequency band/slot locations, and in the presence of adversaries. This desired property is not necessarily satisfied by maximum throughput designs, which optimally schedule link transmissions in the entire network (centralized approaches) [27]. Moreover, decentralized solutions implementing distributed matching algorithms require the local exchange of coordination messages between nodes, over a commonly agreed channel [7,11]. Clearly, such a channel cannot be available in our setup due to the presence of an inside jammer.

To ensure the broadcast property, we map the problem of constructing FH sequences to the problem of producing 1-factorizations in complete graphs. 1-factorizations realize a series of perfect matchings (1-factors), which span the all edges of a complete graph [30]. Hence, a broadcast from any node will be communicated to all other nodes. We first present relevant preliminaries from graph theory. Interested readers are referred to [17,30] for an in-depth treatise of the problem of 1-factorization.

4.1 Definitions and Useful Theorems

Consider a graph $\mathcal{G}(\mathcal{V}, \mathcal{E})$, where $\mathcal{V}$ denotes the vertex set and $\mathcal{E}$ denotes the edge set. Assume that $|\mathcal{V}| = 2n$ where n is a positive integer (a dummy node can be added otherwise).

DEFINITION 1. **Complete graph:** $\mathcal{G}(\mathcal{V}, \mathcal{E})$ *is said to be complete if each pair of vertices is connected by an edge. We denote such a graph by* K_{2n}, *where* $|\mathcal{V}| = 2n$.

DEFINITION 2. **1-factor:** *A 1-factor or a perfect matching F of a graph $\mathcal{G}$ is a subset of $\mathcal{E}$ that partitions $\mathcal{V}$, i.e., F*

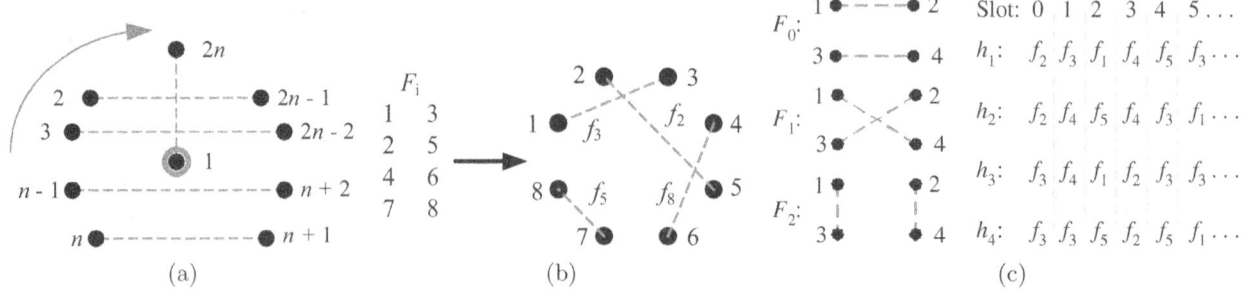

Figure 3: (a) Algorithm for constructing a 1-factorization $\mathcal{F} = \{F_0, \ldots, F_{2n-2}\}$. To obtain a factor F_i, every node is rotated by i positions to the left. Node 1 remains fixed, (b) mapping of a 1-factor to unicast transmissions. Paired nodes concurrently communicate on separate frequency bands, (c) construction of hopping sequences for sequential unicast based on 1-factorization for a group of four nodes.

is a set of pairwise disjoint edges of $\mathcal{G}$ that covers all vertices of $\mathcal{V}$.

DEFINITION 3. **1-factorization:** *A 1-factorization* $\mathcal{F}_{2n} = \{F_0, F_1, \ldots, F_{2n-2}\}$ *of a graph* $\mathcal{G}$ *is a partition of its edge set* $\mathcal{E}$ *to* $(2n-1)$ *1-factors.*

THEOREM 1. **1-factorization of** K_{2n}**:** *A complete graph* K_{2n} *is 1-factorable [30].*

Construction of 1-factorizations of K_{2n}: 1-factorizations of K_{2n} can be systematically constructed using well-known algorithms (e.g., [10, 17, 29, 30]). These methods typically rely on the selection of a "starter" 1-factor, based on which the entire 1-factorization can be derived. A simple method for constructing a 1-factorization of K_{2n} is to select a starter 1-factor and apply a shift-and-rotate operation to it [30]. This method is illustrated in figure 3(a). A 1-factorization is initialized by the 1-factor F_0. Node 1 remains fixed. To obtain the 1-factor F_i, nodes in the perimeter are rotated clockwise by i steps.

4.2 Mapping to the 1-factorization Problem

In this section, we map the problem of constructing hopping sequences for TDBS into the problem of generating 1-factorizations of complete graphs. In our mapping, the vertex set $\mathcal{V}$ of K_{2n} represents the node set $\mathcal{N}$ of the single-hop network, and an edge $(x, y) \in \mathcal{E}$ represents a unicast transmission between nodes x and y. A 1-factor corresponds to partitioning of the $2n$ nodes into n communicating pairs. These pairs are scheduled to communicate in parallel over separate frequency bands. A 1-factorization $\mathcal{F}_{2n}$ partitions the set of edges $\mathcal{E}$ into $(2n-1)$ disjoint 1-factors, where each edge appears exactly once. In a schedule constructed according to $\mathcal{F}_{2n}$, every node has the opportunity to communicate with all remaining $(2n-1)$ nodes, thus achieving the sequential relay of a broadcast message.

An example of the mapping to the 1-factorization problem is shown in figure 3(b). A group of eight nodes is partitioned into four pairs, which are scheduled to communicate over four frequency bands. According to the 1-factor F_i, the communicating pairs during slot i are $\{(1, 3), (2, 5), (4, 6), (7, 8)\}$, communicating over frequency bands f_3, f_2, f_8 and f_5, respectively. Figure 3(c) shows a feasible set of hopping sequences h_j for four nodes, $j = 1, \ldots, 4$, based on the 1-factorization of K_4. Communication of all pairs of nodes is completed in three slots. We now present algorithms for constructing FH sequences.

Algorithm 1 TDBS-SU: Sequential Unicast Mode
1: Generate $\mathcal{F}_{2n}$ of K_{2n}
2: **repeat**
3:   **for** $i = 0$ to $(2n-2)$ **do**
4:     **for** $j = 1$ to $\lceil \frac{n}{K} \rceil$ **do**
5:       $\pi = rand(perm(\mathcal{C}))$
6:       **for** $w = 1$ to $\min\{n, K\}$ **do**
7:         $h_{F((j-1)K+w,1)} = h_{F((j-1)K+w,2)} = \pi(w)$
8:       **end for**
9:     **end for**
10:   **end for**
11: **end repeat**

4.3 TDBS-SU: Sequential Unicast Mode

In the SU mode, a sender sequentially unicasts the broadcast message to $(2n-1)$ intended receivers. The hopping sequences are constructed as follows.

Step 1: Construct a 1-factorization $\mathcal{F}_{2n}$ of K_{2n}, where $\mathcal{F}_{2n} = \{F_0, F_1, \ldots, F_{2n-2}\}$.
Step 2: For all $F_i \in \mathcal{F}_{2n}$, $0 \leq i \leq 2n - 2$, repeat Steps 3-5.
Step 3: Obtain a random permutation π of the set of frequency bands $\mathcal{C}$.
Step 4: Assign frequency bands in π to $\min\{n, K\}$ edges of F_i in the order of occurrence of the edges.
Step 5: Repeat Steps 3 and 4 until all pairs in F_i are assigned a frequency band.
Step 6: Repeat Steps 1-5.

The pseudo-code of the hopping sequence construction for the SU mode is shown in Algorithm 1. In figure 3(c), we show an example of the application of Algorithm 1 to a group of four nodes. The set of available channels is $\mathcal{C} = \{f_1, \ldots, f_5\}$, $(K = 5)$. Because $K \geq n$, the n pairs corresponding to a 1-factor can communicate in parallel in one slot. In slot 0, pairs communicate according to factor F_0. The random permutation of $\mathcal{C}$ is $\pi = \{f_2, f_3, f_5, f_1, f_4\}$. Pair $(1, 2)$ is assigned band $\pi(1) = f_2$ and pair $(3, 4)$ is assigned band $\pi(2) = f_3$. The process is repeated for factors F_1, and F_2. Note that condition $K \geq n$ is not necessary for the correct operation of our algorithm. When the number of frequency bands is smaller than the pairs of communicating nodes, transmissions corresponding to one factor are split in multiple slots, as shown in Steps 3-5. However, for single hop networks, it is expected that $K >> n$. We now show that Algorithm 1 constructs random FH sequences.

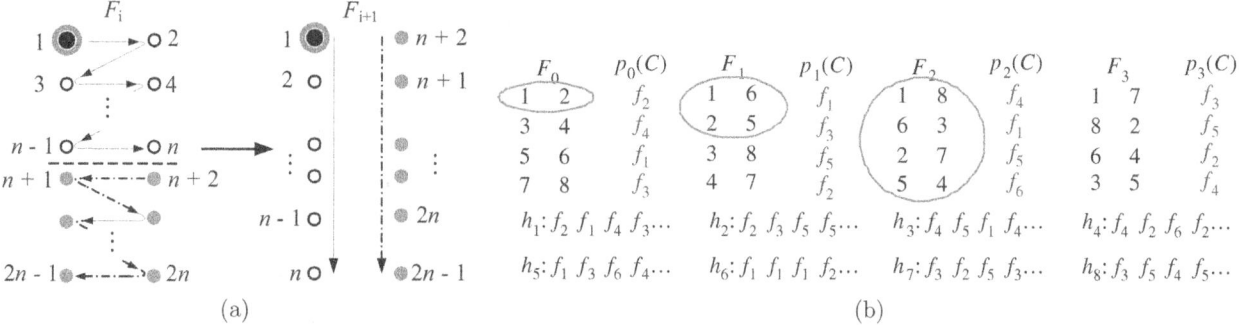

Figure 4: (a) Splitting algorithm used to obtain the 1-factor F_{i+1} from the 1-factor F_i. The first n nodes of F_i are obtained in a "zigzag" fashion and are placed on the first column of F_{i+1}. The last n nodes of F_i are obtained in an "inverse zigzag" fashion and are placed in the second column of F_{i+1}, (b) the first four 1-factors for a group of eight nodes and the corresponding hopping sequences.

PROPOSITION 1. *The FH sequences constructed by Algorithm 1 are random.*

PROOF. Let $h_j = \{X_1, X_2, \ldots\}$ denote a FH sequence constructed by Algorithm 1 for a node j, where X_i is a random variable denoting the frequency band used at slot i. Random variables X_i form an i.i.d. with each variable being randomly distributed (frequency bands at Step 4 are randomly and independently selected). Hence, h is random. $\square$

4.4 TDBS-AB: Assisted Broadcast Mode

Algorithm 2 TDBS-AB: Assisted Broadcast Mode

1: Generate random F_0 of K_{2n}
2: initialize $i = 0$
3: **repeat**
4: **for** $j = 1$ to $\lceil \frac{n}{K} \rceil$ **do**
5:     $\pi = rand(\text{perm}(\mathcal{C}))$
6:     **for** $w = 1$ to $\min\{n, K\}$ **do**
7:        $h_{F_i((j-1)K+w,1)} = h_{F_i((j-1)K+w,2)} = \pi(w)$
8:     **end for**
9: **end for**
10: $F_{i+1} = \text{split}(F_i)$
11: $i{+}{+}$
12: **end repeat**

In the AB mode, any node that has already received a broadcast message operates as a broadcast relay. To construct hopping sequences for the AB mode, the 1-factors F_i are selected and arranged in such a way that the *number of nodes that can relay a broadcast transmission in each 1-factor is maximized*. This property minimizes the delay until the broadcast is completed, while increasing resilience to jamming. We first define the notion of the *relay set*.

DEFINITION 4. The Relay Set R_j^i *of node j in a 1-factor F_i is defined as the set of nodes that can relay a transmission that originated from j.*

The main idea of our hopping sequence construction algorithm is to maximize the size of the relay set R_j^i, for every node j and in every 1-factor F_i. Note that in the AB mode, it is not necessary that the series of 1-factors form a 1-factorization (i.e., that all pairs of nodes communicate directly), because nodes can receive the broadcast transmission via multiple hops. The hopping sequences assigned to each node are constructed as follows.

Algorithm 3 Splitting Algorithm `split`

1: $F_{i+1}(1,1) = F_i(1,1)$
2: **if** n even **then**
3:     $F_{i+1}(1,2) = F_i(\frac{n}{2}+1, 2)$
4: **else**
5:     $F_{i+1}(1,2) = F_i(\lceil \frac{n}{2} \rceil, 2)$
6: **end if**
7: **for** $j = 2$ to n **do**
8:     $F_{i+1}(j,1) = F_i(\lceil \frac{j}{2} \rceil, 2)$, if j even
9:     $F_{i+1}(j,1) = F_i(\lceil \frac{j}{2} \rceil, 1)$, if j odd
10:     **if** n even **then**
11:        $F_{i+1}(j,2) = F_i(\lceil \frac{n+j}{2} \rceil, 1)$, if j even
12:        $F_{i+1}(j,2) = F_i(\lceil (\frac{n+j}{2}) \rceil, 2)$, if j odd
13:     **else**
14:        $F_{i+1}(j,2) = F_i(\lceil \frac{n+j}{2} \rceil, 2)$, if j even
15:        $F_{i+1}(j,2) = F_i(\lceil (\frac{n+j}{2}) \rceil, 1)$, if j odd
16:     **end if**
17: **end for**

Step 1: Obtain an arbitrary 1-factor F_0 of K_{2n}. Set $i = 0$.
Step 2: Obtain a random permutation π of the set of frequency bands $\mathcal{C}$.
Step 3: Assign frequency bands in π to $\min\{n, K\}$ edges of F_i in the order of occurrence of the edges.
Step 4: Repeat Steps 2 and 3 until all pairs in F_i are assigned a frequency band.
Step 5: Construct 1-factor F_{i+1} according to the *splitting algorithm*. Set $i = i + 1$.
Step 6: Repeat Steps 2 and 5.

The pseudo-code of TDBS-AB is shown in Algorithm 2. The pseudo-code of the splitting algorithm employed to generate F_{i+1} from F_i is shown in Algorithm 3, and illustrated in figure 4(a). Every pair of nodes that communicate according to the 1-factor F_i are placed in adjacent rows in the 1-factor F_{i+1}. The propagation of this property in subsequent 1-factors minimizes the broadcast delay by maximizing the size of the relay set R_j^i for any j and for every 1-factor.

To illustrate the application of Algorithm 2, consider a network of eight nodes. The first four 1-factors that are generated by our algorithm and the corresponding hopping sequences assigned to various nodes are shown in figure 4(b). Node 1 initiates a broadcast transmission of message m following the 1-factor F_0. The circles mark the nodes that receive message m after the completion of the unicasts corresponding to various 1-factors. In fact, one can verify from the 1-factors shown in Fig. 4(b) that any broadcast transmission initiated under 1-factor F_0 is completed by 1-factor $F_{\log_2(8)-1} = F_2$. In section 6, we prove that this property holds for any broadcast initiated at any time slot. Note that TDBS-AB uses the same mechanism as TDBS-SU (Steps 2-4) for assigning frequency bands to communicating pairs. Therefore, Proposition 1 holds for the hopping sequences generated by TDBS-AB. These sequences are uniformly distributed over the set of available channels, thus minimizing the success of an external jammer in guessing the frequency bands of future communications based on past observations. Moreover, compromise of sequences limits the information leakage regarding other sequences.

5. TDBS IN MULTI-HOP NETWORKS

In this section, we extend the operation of TDBS to multi-hop networks. In this scenario, the FH sequence design can be viewed as a global scheduling problem. While several distributed methods have been proposed for distributed scheduling (e.g., [7,11]), we note that these methods require coordination via a commonly accessible channel. However, such a channel can be blocked by an inside jammer. We, therefore, develop a scalable solution based on clustering, that does not require node coordination.

We partition the network into clusters where each cluster forms a clique [13,28]. Clique clustering produces a network partition where every node belongs to a single cluster and the members of each cluster are within one hop. We then divide the broadcast operation into two phases: (a) the intra-cluster phase, and (b) the inter-cluster phase. During the intra-cluster phase, communication is limited within each cluster. In the inter-cluster phase, messages are exchanged between border nodes of adjacent clusters. The two phases are interleaved in time.

5.1 Intra-cluster Phase

In the intra-cluster phase, a broadcast message propagates to all nodes within a cluster. Because the nodes of a cluster form a clique, the SU or AB operation modes for single-hop networks are employed. To avoid interference between adjacent clusters, the set of available frequency bands $\mathcal{C}$ is divided into four mutually exclusive sets which are assigned to each cluster according to the four color theorem [2].

One such assignment is shown in figure 5(a). The shading pattern of each cluster denotes a separate set of frequency bands. In this example, 10 frequency bands are assigned to each cluster, yielding a $K = 40$. Note that the number of available frequency bands K is expected to be be much larger than the number of nodes within the same collision domain (i.e., cluster size). In any case, the algorithms outlined in Sections 4.3 and 4.4, produce FH sequences for any relation between K and n. The steps for deriving FH sequences for the intra-cluster phase are as follows.

Step 1: Color each cluster based on the four-color theorem.
Step 2: For each distinct cluster size $2n$, construct a 1-factorization $\mathcal{F}_{2n}$ of K_{2n}.
Step 3: For each cluster, pick the 1-factorization corresponding to its cluster size and construct FH sequences for the cluster nodes following the SU mode or the AB mode.
Step 4: Repeat Steps 2 and 3 until all clusters are processed.

In Step 2, it is sufficient to produce distinct 1-factorizations for every possible cluster size. Two clusters of the same size can use the same 1-factorization, dictating the rendezvous of its cluster members, respectively. However, due to the random permutation assignment of frequency bands in Step 3, the pairs of nodes of each cluster will communicate at different frequency bands, thus ensuring the randomness of the pairwise communication among pairs.

5.2 Inter-cluster Phase

In the inter-cluster phase, border nodes in adjacent clusters relay broadcast messages that are intended to propagate beyond the boundaries of each cluster. To do so, while avoiding collisions between adjacent transmissions, we exploit the cluster labeling produced by the application of the four-color theorem. During this phase, every time-slot is marked with one of the four colors indicating the set of clusters that are allowed to transmit on that slot. As an example, in figure 5, clusters A and D are allowed to transmit on slot 0, clusters C and F on slot 1, clusters B and E on slot 2 and cluster G on slot 3, with this sequence repeating modulo four (slot numbers indicate assignment before the interleaving with the intra-cluster phase) . After the slot coloring, the FH sequences of individual nodes are generated as follows.

Step 1: For each cluster x, find the nodes in x bordering adjacent clusters. Place this nodes to a set $\mathcal{A}$.
Step 2: For each node $i \in \mathcal{A}$, find the neighbors of i in adjacent clusters. If a neighbor is common to two nodes in x, assign it to the node with the fewer neighbors. Break ties arbitrarily (e.g., considering the node with the lowest id). Merge nodes assigned to the same i to a single vertex and place vertices to set $\mathcal{B}$. Create a bipartite graph $G(\mathcal{A} \cup \mathcal{B}, \mathrm{E})$, where an edge (x,y) exists if nodes corresponding to y are assigned to x. G forms a 1-factor F_x.
Step 3: For each slot colored with x's color, obtain a random permutation π of the set of frequency bands $\mathcal{C}$.
Step 4: Assign frequency bands in π to $\min\{n, K\}$ edges of F_x in the order of occurrence of the edges.
Step 5: Repeat Steps 3 and 4 until all pairs in F_x are assigned a frequency band.
Step 6: Repeat Steps 1-5, until all clusters are processed.

The inter-cluster phase is illustrated in Figure 5(b). According to their color, clusters A and D are scheduled to broadcast during slot 0. Nodes 2,3, and 4 belong to set $\mathcal{A}$ of cluster A since they can communicate with nodes of adjacent clusters. For slot 0, the communicating pairs are $\{2 - 9, 10\}$ $\{3 - 11, 12\}$ and $\{4 - 7, 8\}$, and are assigned frequency bands f_{11}, f_{22}, and f_2, respectively. Similarly, for cluster D and slot 0, the communicating pairs are $\{5 - 6, 13\}$ $\{14 - 15\}$ and $\{16 - 17\}$, and are assigned frequency bands f_8, f_{33}, and f_{25}, respectively. Note that during the inter-cluster phase, all channels in $\mathcal{C}$ are available for assignment to the communications of adjacent pairs of nodes.

The intra-cluster and inter-cluster slots are interleaved in the FH design, to allow for both single hop and multi-hop broadcast transmissions are achieved.

6. PERFORMANCE AND SECURITY EVALUATION

In this section, we evaluate the performance of TDBS and

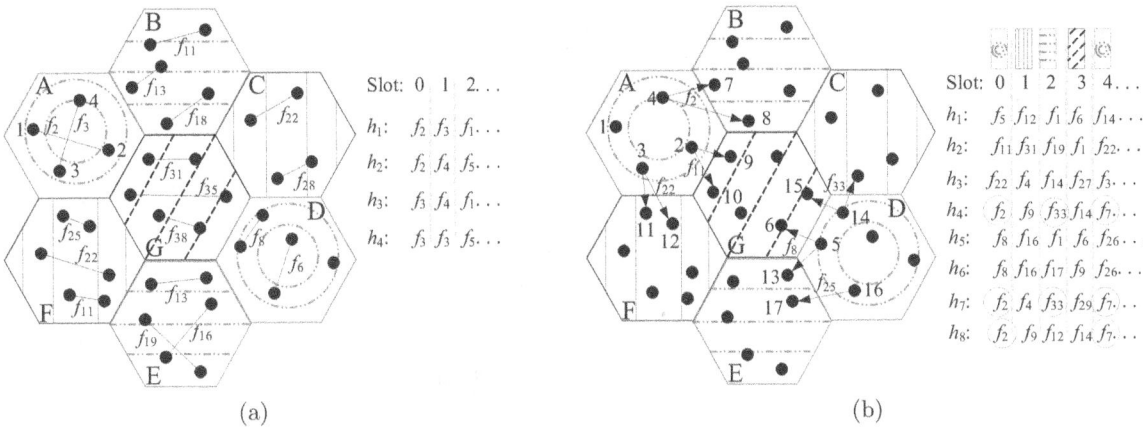

Figure 5: (a) The intra-cluster phase, (b) the inter-cluster phase.

analyze its security properties. As a performance/security metric, we use the broadcast delay, defined as follows.

DEFINITION 5. **The Broadcast Delay** D *is the number of slots required for the completion of a broadcast operation, i.e., until all intended recipients have received a copy of the broadcasted message.*

6.1 Performance in the Absence of Jammers

In this section, we evaluate the broadcast delay for the two TDBS modes in the absence of jammers. This analysis is provided to facilitate the evaluation of the broadcast delay when jammers are assumed to be present.

PROPOSITION 2. *The broadcast delay of TDBS-SU is* $D = \lceil \frac{n}{K} \rceil (2n - 1)$ *slots.*

PROOF. The proof is provided in Appendix A. $\square$

Next, we evaluate the broadcast delay in the AB mode.

PROPOSITION 3. *The broadcast delay for TDBS-AB is* $D = \lceil \frac{n}{K} \rceil \lceil \log_2(2n) \rceil$ *slots.*

PROOF. The proof is provided in Appendix B. $\square$

6.2 Security Analysis

We first analyze the resilience of TDBS to external and internal jammers for single-hop networks.

6.2.1 Resilience to External Jammers

Under an external threat model, the hopping sequences assigned to various nodes remain secret. For this scenario, we assume that the adversary deploys multiple jamming devices that can jam up to J frequency bands per time slot, with $J < K$. For convenience, we assume $K \geq n$ so that all node pairs corresponding to a 1-factor can communicate in parallel in one time-slot. This is typical in wideband communications where K is much larger than the expected number of nodes within the same collision domain. Our results can be extended to the $K < n$ case in a straightforward manner. Suppose that a jammer attempts to jam the broadcast of a single node j. To compute D, we evaluate the average number of 1-factorizations needed to complete the broadcast, in the presence of the external jammer, and for each mode.

PROPOSITION 4. *In the presence of an external jammer, the expected number* $\mathrm{E}[Z]$ *of 1-factorizations needed to complete a broadcast operation in the SU mode is*

$$
\mathrm{E}[Z] = (1-p)^{2n-1} + \sum_{i=2}^{\infty} i(1-p^{i-1})^{2n-1} \times \\
\sum_{k=1}^{2n-1} \binom{2n-1}{k} \left(\frac{p^{i-1}(1-p)}{1-p^{i-1}} \right)^k, \tag{1}
$$

where $p = \frac{J}{K}$ *denotes the jamming probability.*

PROOF. The proof is provided in Appendix C. $\square$

In figure 6(a), we compare the theoretical value of $\mathrm{E}[Z]$ with the simulated one. For our simulations, we generated sequences of size $1,000$ hops for different values of n and K according to Algorithm 1. We also randomly selected J channels to be jammed per time-slot. All results were averaged over 100 runs. We measured $\mathrm{E}[Z]$ as a function of the jamming probability $p = \frac{J}{K}$. We observe that the simulation values agree with the theoretical ones.

Based on Proposition 4, the expected broadcast delay $\mathrm{E}[D]$ is equal to the expected number of 1-factorizations needed for the completion of a broadcast, times the number of slots needed for the completion of each 1-factorization. The first $(\mathrm{E}[Z] - 1)$ 1-factorizations require $(2n - 1)$ slots, while the last 1-factorization requires, on average, $\frac{2n-1}{2}$ slots (the last successful transmission takes place on any of the 1-factors of the last 1-factorization with equal probability). Therefore, $\mathrm{E}[D] = (2n-1)\left(\mathrm{E}[Z] - \frac{1}{2}\right)$.

Figure 6(b), shows the theoretical and simulated value of $\mathrm{E}[D]$ as a function of the jamming probability p. We observe that even when the adversary jams 80% of the available channels, nodes are still capable of completing their broadcast transmissions at the expense of some delay. Nevertheless, the broadcast communication is maintained. In figure 6(c), we show $\mathrm{E}[D]$ as a function of the number of available channels K for various values of J. $\mathrm{E}[D]$ decreases with K, approaching the asymptotic value of K, obtained in the absence of a jammer, i.e., $\mathrm{E}[D] = 2n - 1$.

For the AB mode, $\mathrm{E}[D]$ does not have a simple closed-form expression but involves complex summation formulas. However, we can derive a useful formula for $J = 1$.

PROPOSITION 5. *After the first successful relay of a broadcast message* m, *the broadcast delay until* m *is received by*

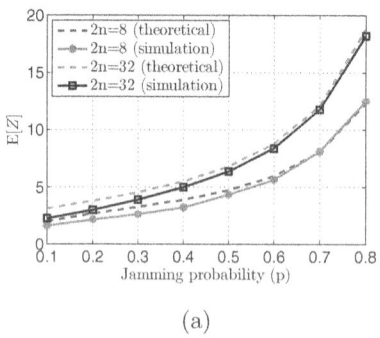 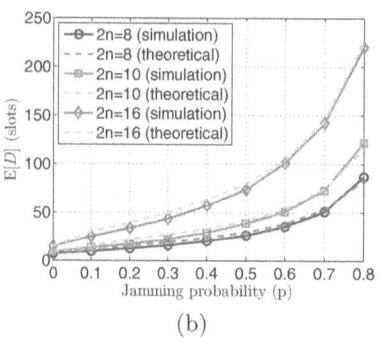 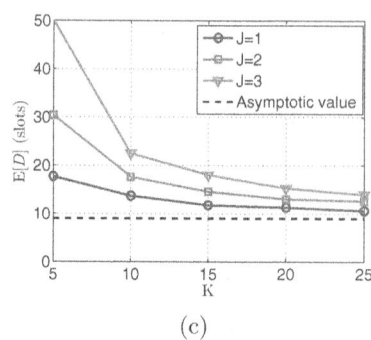

(a)   (b)   (c)

Figure 6: (a) $\mathrm{E}[Z]$ as function of the jamming probability p, (b) $\mathrm{E}[D]$ as a function of jamming probability p. (c) $\mathrm{E}[D]$ as a function of K when $2n = 10$.

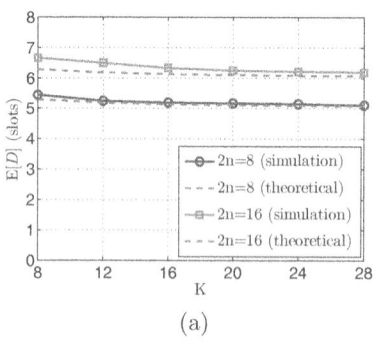 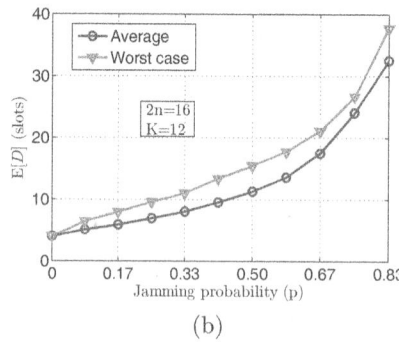 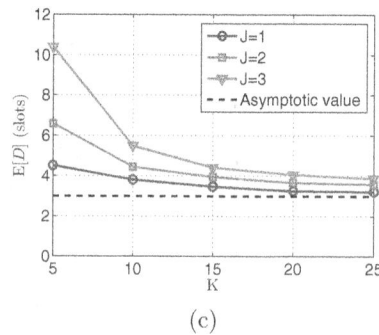

(a)   (b)   (c)

Figure 7: (a) $\mathrm{E}[D]$ as a function of K when $J = 1$, for the AB mode of the worst case. The theoretical value is computed based on (3), (b) $\mathrm{E}[D]$ as a function of p, for the AB mode. The average and worst case are shown, (c) $\mathrm{E}[D]$ as a function of K and for various J. The asymptotic value is equal to $\lceil \log_2(2n) \rceil$.

$(2n - 2)$ nodes (all nodes, but one) is bounded by

$$\lceil \log_2(2n) \rceil - 1 \leq D \leq \lceil \log_2(2n) \rceil. \tag{2}$$

PROOF. The proof is provided in Appendix D. □

Proposition 5 allows us to estimate the expected broadcast delay for the AB mode. Let D_1 denote the expected delay until the first success, D_2 the delay until $(2n-2)$ nodes receive message m and D_3 the delay until the last node receives m. The expected broadcast delay is bounded by

$$\begin{aligned}
\mathrm{E}[D] &= \mathrm{E}[D_1 + D_2 + D_3] \\
&\leq \frac{K}{K-1} + \lceil \log_2(2n) \rceil + \frac{K}{K-1}. \tag{3}
\end{aligned}$$

In (3), we have used the fact that it takes, on average, $\frac{K}{K-1}$ slots for the first successful relay when $p = \frac{1}{K}$. Moreover, after the first success, $\lceil \log_2(2n) \rceil$ slots are needed in the worst case until $2n - 2$ nodes receive m. The last node receives m after $\frac{K}{K-1}$ slots, on average.

We also studied the performance of the AB mode via simulations. For our simulations, we generated sequences of size $1,000$ hops for different values of n and K according to Algorithm 2. We also randomly selected J channels to be jammed per time-slot. All results were averaged over 100 runs. Figure 7(a) shows $\mathrm{E}[D]$ as a function of K for $J = 1$. We observe that the theoretical value derived using Proposition 5 agrees with the simulation. In figure 7(b), we show the average and worst-case broadcast delay, as a function of p. We observe that even when $p = 0.83$, the average and worst-case delays differ by less than six slots. This is due to the "relay explosion" effect of the splitting algorithm. The AB

mode is significantly more resilient to jamming than the SU mode, due to the larger number of broadcast relays. Even when 83% of the frequency bands are jammed, the AB mode requires only 38 slots to complete a broadcast, compared to 228 slots needed with the SU mode. In figure 7(c), we show $\mathrm{E}[D]$ as a function K for different values of J. We observe that with the increase of K, $\mathrm{E}[D]$ asymptotically approaches the performance of the AB mode in the absence of jammers.

6.2.2 Resilience to Internal Jammers

Assume now that the adversary has compromised r nodes and recovered their FH sequences. We are interested in determining the broadcast delay until the remaining $(2n-r-2)$ *legitimate* nodes receive a broadcast message m. Knowledge of the r FH sequences reduces the adversary's uncertainty with respect to the frequency locations of legitimate unicasts. This is because the space of $\mathcal{C}$ for the selection of the uncompromised FH sequences is reduced. The exact value of $\mathrm{E}[D]$ depends on the selection of the 1-factorization that is used to construct the hopping sequences and the specific arrangement of the compromised nodes on that 1-factorization. The jamming probability p varies on a slot-by-slot basis and is given in the following proposition.

PROPOSITION 6. *Under the compromise of r nodes, the jamming probability p is bounded by*

$$\min\{1, \frac{J}{K - \lceil \frac{r}{2} \rceil}\} \leq p \leq \min\{1, \frac{J}{K - r}\}. \tag{4}$$

PROOF. The proof is provided in Appendix E. □

We further used simulation to investigate the impact of

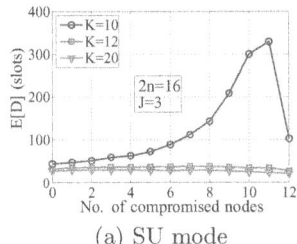

(a) SU mode

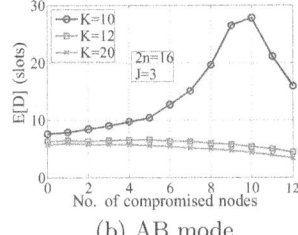

(b) AB mode

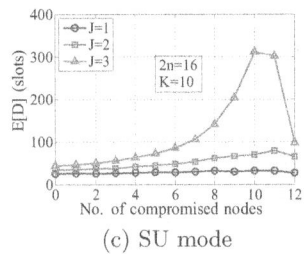

(c) SU mode

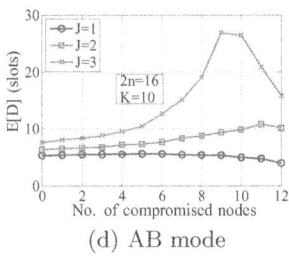

(d) AB mode

Figure 8: (a), (b) $\mathrm{E}[D]$ **as a function of the number of compromised nodes for various values of** K, **when** $J = 3$, (c), (d) $\mathrm{E}[D]$ **as a function of the number of compromised nodes for various values of** J, **when** $K = 10$.

node compromise on the broadcast delay. For our simulations, we generated FH sequences of length $1,000$ hops for different values of n and K. We randomly selected r of these sequences to be exposed to the adversary. At each time slot, the adversary randomly jammed J bands, excluding the exposed ones. A broadcast was deemed successful, when all legitimate nodes obtain a message copy. All results were averaged over 100 runs. Figures 8(a) and 8(b) show $\mathrm{E}[D]$ as a function of the number of compromised nodes when $J = 3$ and $K = 10, 12, 20$, for the SU and AB modes, respectively. We observe that legitimate nodes complete their broadcast transmissions even when more than 50% of the nodes are compromised. The AB mode exhibits significantly lower delay compared to the SU mode, due to the use of multiple relays. Note that when K is small and several nodes are compromised, the jammers have a high chance of jamming legitimate pairs. This fact can be seen from the sharp increase of $\mathrm{E}[D]$ when $K = 10$.

In figure 8(c) and 8(d), we show $\mathrm{E}[D]$ as a function of the number of compromised nodes when $K = 10$ and for various values of J, under the SU and AB modes, respectively. Even with the increase of J, legitimate nodes are able to complete their broadcast transmissions in both modes, with the AB mode being the most efficient. Note that $\mathrm{E}[D]$ decreases when a large number of nodes is compromised, since fewer legitimate nodes need to receive a unicast message for completing a broadcast transmission.

6.3 Evaluation of Multi-hop Scenarios

In this section, we evaluate TDBS for multi-hop networks. We focus on the jamming-resistance of the inter-cluster phase, since for the intra-cluster phase, the security analysis for single-hop networks holds. We define the following performance metrics for the inter-cluster phase:

- **Flooding Delay** D_f: the number of slots needed until all clusters adjacent to a cluster i, have received a broadcast that originated in i, directly from a node in i.

- **Escape Delay** D_e: the number of slots needed until a broadcast message m originating at a cluster i, reaches any node in any adjacent cluster.

  Escape diversity DIV: the fraction of adjacent clusters that receive a broadcast m directly from a cluster i, when some border nodes in i are compromised.

We first analytically evaluate the average flooding delay $\mathrm{E}[D_f]$ in the presence of external jammers. Assume a cluster with N_C adjacent clusters. Let N_L denote the number of "bridge links" between two adjacent clusters.

PROPOSITION 7. *In the presence of an external jammer,*

$\mathrm{E}[D_f]$ *is equal to*

$$\mathrm{E}[D_f] = (1 - \tilde{p})^{N_C} + \sum_{i=2}^{\infty} i(1 - \tilde{p}^{i-1})^{N_C} \times$$
$$\sum_{k=1}^{N_C} \binom{N_C}{k} \left(\frac{\tilde{p}^{i-1}(1 - \tilde{p})}{1 - \tilde{p}^{i-1}} \right)^k, \quad (5)$$

where $\tilde{p} = \left(\frac{J}{K} \right)^{N_L}$ *denotes the probability that all* N_L *links to an adjacent cluster are jammed at a particular slot*

PROOF. The proof of Proposition 7 follows the same steps as the proof of Proposition 4, by substituting $p = \frac{J}{K}$ with $\tilde{p} = \left(\frac{J}{K} \right)^{N_L}$. Due to space limitations we refer to the proof provided in Appendix C. □

We also verified Proposition 7 via simulations. In our setup, we generated a multi-hop topology consisting of 50 nodes, organized in clusters. We then generated FH schedules for all nodes in the network for the inter-cluster phase, according to the algorithm described in Section 5.2. At each time slot, the jammer was assumed able to block J random frequency bands across the entire network. Results were averaged over all clusters in the network. Figure 9(a) shows $\mathrm{E}[D_f]$ as a function of the jamming probability p. We denote the number of "bridge links" between two adjacent clusters to be N_L. We observe that, even when 80% of the available frequency bands are jammed, only 13 inter-cluster slots are needed until all neighboring clusters directly receive a broadcast. Once the message propagates to adjacent clusters, the intra-cluster phase follows. We also evaluate the expected escape delay $\mathrm{E}[D_e]$ under the compromise of r border nodes.

PROPOSITION 8. *Under the compromise of* r *border nodes of a cluster* i, $\mathrm{E}[D_e]$ *is given by*

$$\mathrm{E}[D_e] = \frac{1}{1 - \left(P_c^{N_L} + \sum_{i=1}^{N_L} \binom{N_L}{i} \left(\frac{J(1 - P_c)}{K - r} \right)^i \right)^{N_C}}, \quad (6)$$

where $P_c = \frac{r}{N_C \times N_L}$ *denotes the compromise probability.*

PROOF. The proof is provided in Appendix F. □

The expected escape diversity $\mathrm{E}[DIV]$ is evaluated in the following proposition.

PROPOSITION 9. *Under the compromise of* r *nodes,* $\mathrm{E}[DIV]$ *is given by*

$$\mathrm{E}[DIV] = 1 - P_c^{N_L}. \quad (7)$$

PROOF. The proof is provided in Appendix G. □

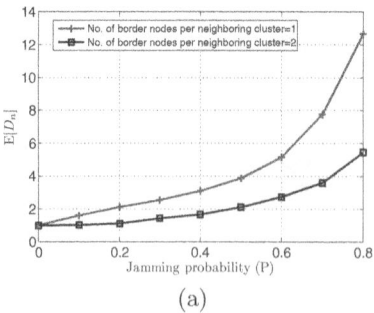 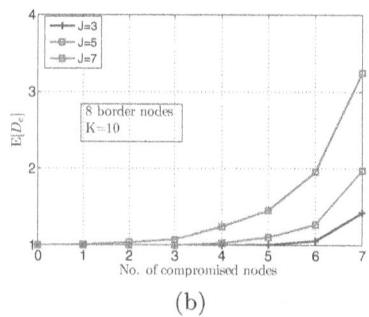 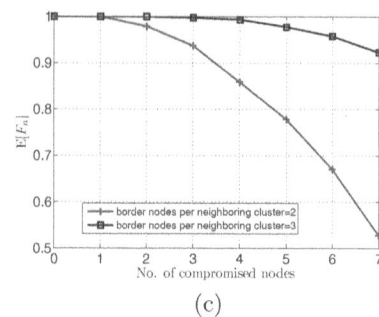

|(a)|(b)|(c)|

Figure 9: (a) $E[D_f]$ **as a function of the jamming probability** p, (b) $E[D_e]$ **as a function of the number of compromised nodes** r **for various** J, (c) $E[DIV]$ **as a function of** r **for various** N_L.

Figures 9(b) and 9(c) evaluate $E[D_e]$ and $E[DIV]$ as a function of the number of compromised border nodes. In our simulation, compromised border nodes do not relay messages and their FH sequences are assumed exposed. From figure 9(b), we observe that a small number of slots is sufficient for the first copy of a broadcast message to reach one adjacent cluster. From figure 9(c), we observe that more than 90% of neighboring clusters are guaranteed to receive the message when $N_L = 3$, while this value being reduced to 50% when $N_L = 2$.

7. RELATED WORK

The problem of jamming in wireless communications has been extensively studied under an external threat model (for example, see [1, 24] and the references therein). Jamming is typically mitigated by spreading the transmitted signal to a larger bandwidth following a secret PN code. Without knowledge of this code, the jammer has to expend several orders of magnitude more energy (typically 20-30 dB gain) to interfere with ongoing transmissions. However, in the case of broadcast communications, compromise of commonly shared PN codes suppresses the advantages of SS.

Recently, several researchers have considered the problem of jamming under an inside threat model. Chan et al. showed that a jammer that targets the broadcast control channel in GSM networks can reduce the required power for performing a DoS attack by several orders of magnitude [6]. Desmedt et al. proposed an anti-jamming scheme that protects broadcast communications from a small number of inside and colluding jammers [9]. Their method relies on combinatorial block designs to allow for partial sharing of secret information with respect to the location of the broadcast frequency bands. To protect control-channel traffic, the replication of broadcast transmissions over multiple channels whose location are cryptographically protected, was suggested in [6, 25, 26].

Alternative methods eliminate the dependence on shared secrets [4, 14, 16, 20]. Baird et al. proposed a keyless anti-jamming technique based on encoding of indelible marks at specific locations within each broadcasted message [4]. Pöpper et al. proposed a solution called Uncoordinated DSSS (UDSSS) [20]. In UDSSS, broadcast transmissions are spread according to a PN code, randomly selected from a public set of codes. Liu et. al. proposed RD-DSSS, a randomized differential DSSS scheme also relying on randomly selected PN codes [16]. Compared to UDSSS, the RD-DSSS scheme provides resilience to reactive jammers.

Several methods attempt to identify the compromised nodes that leaked information to the jammer. Lazos et al. proposed the assignment of unique frequency hopping sequences to each receiver, overlapping in a fixed subset of hops [14]. Using the uniqueness of the assigned sequences, compromised nodes whose sequences are used for jamming are identified. Tague et al. proposed the GUIDE scheme for identifying compromised nodes based on the set of control channels that are jammed. They formulated the identification problem as a maximum likelihood estimation problem [26]. Chiang and Yih-Chun Hu, developed a code-tree based approach for identifying compromised PN codes [8].

8. CONCLUSION

We proposed TDBS, a scheme for jamming-resistant broadcast communications in the presence of inside jammers. In TDBS, broadcast is realized as a series of unicast transmissions distributed in frequency and time. Because the adversary is limited in the number of channels he can jam, several unicast transmissions remain interference-free. We mapped the problem of constructing hopping sequences for TDBS to the problem of 1-factorization of complete graphs. We analytically evaluated the security properties of TDBS under an external and an internal threat model and showed that TDBS maintains broadcast communications even when multiple nodes are compromised. We verified our theoretical analysis using extensive simulations.

Acknowledgments

Part of this work was conducted while M. Krunz was a visiting researcher at the University of Carlos III, Madrid, and IMDEA Networks, Spain. This research was supported in part by NSF (under grants CNS-0844111, CNS-0721935, CNS-0904681, CNS-1016943, IIP-0832238), Raytheon, and the Connection One center. Any opinions, findings, conclusions, or recommendations expressed in this paper are those of the author(s) and do not necessarily reflect the views of the National Science Foundation.

9. REFERENCES

[1] D. Adamy. *EW 101: A first course in electronic warfare.* Artech House Publishers, 2001.

[2] K. Appel and W. Haken. Every planar map is four colorable: Part I. *Illinois Journal of Mathematics,* 21(3):491–567, 1977.

[3] P. Bahl, R. Chandra, and J. Dunagan. SSCH: slotted seeded channel hopping for capacity improvement in

IEEE 802.11 ad-hoc wireless networks. In *Proc. of MOBICOM*, pages 216–230, 2004.

[4] L. C. Baird, W. L. Bahn, M. D. Collins, M. C. Carlisle, and S. C. Butler. Keyless jam resistance. In *Proc. of the IEEE Workshop on Information Assurance United States Military Academy*, 2007.

[5] K. Bian, J. Park, and R. Chen. A quorum-based framework for establishing control channels in dynamic spectrum access networks. In *Proc. of MOBICOM*, pages 25–36, 2009.

[6] A. Chan, X. Liu, G. Noubir, and B. Thapa. Control channel jamming: Resilience and identification of traitors. In *Proc. of ISIT*, 2007.

[7] P. Chaporkar, K. Kar, X. Luo, and S. Sarkar. Throughput and fairness guarantees through maximal scheduling in wireless networks. *IEEE Transactions on Information Theory*, 54(2):572–594, 2008.

[8] J. T. Chiang and Y.-C. Hu. Dynamic jamming mitigation for wireless broadcast networks. In *Proc. of INFOCOM*, pages 1211–1219, 2008.

[9] Y. Desmedt, R. Safavi-Naini, H. Wang, C. Charnes, and J. Pieprzyk. Broadcast anti-jamming systems. In *Proc. of the IEEE International Conference on Networks (ICON)*, pages 349 – 355, 1999.

[10] J. H. Dinitz and D. R. Stinson. A hill-climbing algorithm for the construction of one-factorizations and room squares. *SIAM J. Algebraic Discrete Methods*, 8(3):430–438, 1987.

[11] A. Gupta, X. Lin, and R. Srikant. Low-complexity distributed scheduling algorithms for wireless networks. *IEEE/ACM Transactions on Networking (TON)*, 17(6):1846–1859, 2009.

[12] IEEE. IEEE 802.11 for wireless local area networks. http://www.ieee802.org/11/.

[13] H. Ishii and H. Kakugawa. A self-stabilizing algorithm for finding cliques in distributed systems. In *Proc. of the 21st IEEE Symposium on Reliable Distributed Systems (SRDS'02)*, pages 390–395, 2002.

[14] L. Lazos, S. Liu, and M. Krunz. Mitigating control-channel jamming attacks in multi-channel ad hoc networks. In *Proc. of WiSec*, pages 169–180, 2009.

[15] A. Liu, P. Ning, H. Dai, Y. Liu, and C. Wang. Defending DSSS-based broadcast communication against insider jammers via delayed seed-disclosure. In *Proc. of the Annual Computer Security Applications Conference (ACSAC'10)*, 2010.

[16] Y. Liu, P. Ning, H. Dai, and A. Liu. Randomized differential DSSS: Jamming-resistant wireless broadcast communication. In *Proc. of INFOCOM*, 2010.

[17] E. Mendelsohn and A. Rosa. One-factorizations of the complete graph-a survey. *Journal of Graph Theory*, 9(1):43–65, 1985.

[18] G. Noubir and G. Lin. Low-power DoS attacks in data wireless LANs and countermeasures. *Mobile Computing and Communications Review*, 7(3):29–30, 2003.

[19] R. Poisel. *Modern communications jamming principles and techniques*. Artech House on Demand, 2004.

[20] C. Popper, M. Strasser, and S. Capkun. Jamming-resistant broadcast communication without

shared keys. In *Proc. of the USENIX Security Symposium*, 2009.

[21] C. Popper, M. Strasser, and S. Capkun. Anti-jamming broadcast communication using uncoordinated spread spectrum techniques. *IEEE Journal on Selected Areas in Communications*, 28(5), 2010.

[22] S. Sarkar and L. Tassiulas. End-to-end bandwidth guarantees through fair local spectrum share in wireless ad-hoc networks. *IEEE Transactions on Automatic Control*, 50(9):1246–1259, 2005.

[23] G. Sharma, C. Joo, and N. Shroff. Distributed scheduling schemes for throughput guarantees in wireless networks. In *Proc. of the 44th Annual Allerton Conference on Communications, Control, and Computing*, 2006.

[24] M. K. Simon, J. K. Omura, R. A. Scholtz, and B. K. Levitt. *Spread Spectrum Communications Handbook*. McGraw-Hill, 2001.

[25] P. Tague, M. Li, and R. Poovendran. Probabilistic mitigation of control channel jamming via random key distribution. In *Proc. of IEEE PIMRC*, pages 1–5, 2007.

[26] P. Tague, M. Li, and R. Poovendran. Mitigation of control channel jamming under node capture attacks. *IEEE Transactions on Mobile Computing*, 8(9):1221–1234, 2009.

[27] L. Tassiulas and A. Ephremides. Stability properties of constrained queueing systems and scheduling policies for maximum throughput in multihop radio networks. *IEEE Transactions on Automatic Control*, 37(12):1936–1948, 2002.

[28] P. Tosic and G. Agha. Maximal clique-based distributed group formation for autonomous agent coalitions. In *Proc. of the Third International Joint Conference on Autonomous Agents and Multiagent Systems (AAMAS 2004)*, 2004.

[29] W. Wallis. One-factorizations of complete graphs. *Contemporary Design Theory: A Collection of Surveys*, pages 692–731, 1992.

[30] W. Wallis. *One-factorizations*. Kluwer Academic Publishers, 1997.

APPENDIX

A. Proof of Proposition 2: To complete a broadcast in the SU mode, the sender must unicast the broadcast message to $(2n-1)$ receivers. The $(2n-1)$ transmissions correspond to the $(2n-1)$ 1-factors of $\mathcal{F}_{2n}$. Each factor requires $\lceil \frac{n}{K} \rceil$ time slots to be completed (here, all transmissions of a 1-factor are completed before transmissions of other 1-factors can proceed, in order to avoid schedule conflicts). Hence, the broadcast delay is equal to $\lceil \frac{n}{K} \rceil$ times the number of factors of $\mathcal{F}_{2n}$.

B. Proof of Proposition 3: We first prove that any broadcast transmission in the AB mode is completed after $\lceil \log_2(2n) \rceil$ 1-factors. Without loss of generality, assume that a broadcast is initiated by node $F_i(k,1)$, located in the kth row of F_i. With the completion of F_i, the relay set is $R_i^j = \{F_i(k,1), F_i(k,2)\}$. After the execution of Algorithm 3, nodes $F_i(k,1)$ and $F_i(k,2)$ appear in adjacent rows (due to the cyclic nature of Algorithm 3, rows 1 and 8 are considered adjacent) on the 1-factor F_{i+1}. This can be easily verified by reversing the mapping from F_{i+1} to F_i in lines 8-15 of Algorithm 3. Because the pair $(F_i(k,1), F_i(k,2))$ appears on separate rows on F_{i+1}, each node will relay a broadcast to two new nodes, thus increasing R_{i+1}^j to four.

Further execution of Algorithm 3 divides the nodes in the relay set R_{i+1}^j to four adjacent rows. Since none of the nodes in R_{i+1}^j appears on the same row, the relay set after the completion of factor F_{i+1} increases to eight nodes. Following the recursive application of the splitting algorithm, the relay set after the completion of $\lfloor \log_2(2n) \rfloor$ 1-factors has a size of $2^{\lfloor \log_2 2n \rfloor}$. If $\lfloor \log_2(2n) \rfloor = \log_2(2n)$, the broadcast is complete since $2^{\log_2(2n)} = 2n$. Otherwise, one extra 1-factor is needed to relay the broadcast to the remaining $2n - 2^{\lfloor \log_2(2n) \rfloor}$ nodes. Because $2^{\lfloor \log_2(2n) \rfloor} > n$, the splitting algorithm places n nodes from the relay set into the n rows of the $\lfloor \log_2 2n \rfloor + 1 = \lceil \log_2(2n) \rceil$th 1-factor. These n relays complete the broadcast operation. Combining the two cases yields a required number of 1-factors that is equal to $\lceil \log_2(2n) \rceil$. Proposition 3 follows by noting that every 1-factor requires $\lceil \frac{n}{k} \rceil$ slots to be completed.

C. Proof of Proposition 4: Suppose that an arbitrary node j attempts a broadcast transmission in the presence of an external jammer. This broadcast is completed in a single 1-factorization if the jammer is unsuccessful in jamming the communication of j for $2n-1$ consecutive slots. Because h_j is random, a transmission of node j is successful with probability $\left(1 - \frac{J}{K}\right)$. Moreover, the events of a successful transmission of node j at slot i and slot w, $i \neq w$ are independent. Hence,

$$\Pr[Z = 1] = \left(1 - \frac{J}{K}\right)^{2n-1} = (1-p)^{2n-1}.$$

The broadcast is completed in two 1-factorizations if every receiver is jammed at most one time, and at least one receiver is jammed on the first 1-factorization. Taking into account all possible combinations,

$$\Pr[Z = 2] = \sum_{k=1}^{2n-1} \binom{2n-1}{k}(1-p)^{2n-1-k}p^k(1-p)^k.$$

Generalizing to the case of $Z = i$, it follows that

$$\Pr[Z = i] = \sum_{k=1}^{2n-1} \binom{2n-1}{k}(1-p^{i-1})^{2n-1-k}$$
$$p^{(i-1)k}(1-p)^k,$$
$$= (1-p^{i-1})^{2n-1} \sum_{k=1}^{2n-1} \binom{2n-1}{k}$$
$$\left(\frac{p^{i-1}(1-p)}{1-p^{i-1}}\right)^k.$$

Proposition 4 follows from the definition of the expectation, i.e., $\mathrm{E}[Z] = \sum_i i \Pr[Z = i]$.

D. Proof of Proposition 5: The lower bound immediately follows from Proposition 3. The broadcast delay in the absence of a jammer is equivalent to the delay in the presence of an external jammer who is unsuccessful in jamming any communicating pair for $\lceil \log_2(2n) \rceil - 1$ slots. Hence, after the first successful relay, the lower bound on D follows.

To compute the upper bound on D, assume that an arbitrary node j wants to broadcast a message m to the re-

maining $(2n-1)$ nodes. Let a_i denote the size of the relay set in slot i. Initially, $a_0 = 2$, i.e., node j has completed its first successful relay. Once $a_i \geq 2$, the adversary can jam at most one of the pairs relaying m. The size of the relay set in this worst-case scenario grows according to the formula.

$$a_i = 2a_{i-1} - 1 = 2^i + 1, \quad i \leq \lceil \log_2(2n) \rceil - 1, \quad (8)$$

where a_i is computed recursively with $a_0 = 2$. To show the validity of (8), we refer to the proof of Proposition 3, where we showed that for $a_i \leq n$, the size of the relay set doubles with the increment of i. Because the adversary jams at most one frequency band per time slot, in the worst case, $a_i = 2a_{i-1} - 1$. This is true until $a_i \geq n$, in which case the size of the relay set can no longer double. In slot i, $i \leq \lceil \log_2(2n) \rceil - 1$, the relay set becomes larger than n for the first time. That is, it takes $i = \lceil \log_2(2n) \rceil - 1$ slots until more than half the nodes can relay message m. These $a_i \geq n$ relay nodes communicate with the remaining $2n - 2^i - 1 \leq n$ nodes that have not yet received m. Since only one frequency band is jammed, the number of nodes that have received m at the end of slot $(i+1)$ is equal to $(2n-2)$. In this worst case, only one node has not received m after $\lceil \log_2(2n) \rceil$ slots.

E. Proof of Proposition 6: Let x be the number of frequency bands over which the r compromised nodes are scheduled to communicate according to the 1-factor F. The number of bands over which legitimate communications take place in each slot is reduced to $K - x$. Hence, the jamming probability is increased to $p = \frac{J}{K-x}$. To derive bounds on p, we consider the lowest and highest values of x. If the compromised nodes are scheduled to communicate with each other at 1-factor F, then $x = x_{\min} = \lceil \frac{r}{2} \rceil$, where the ceiling function is used to account for an odd r. This value of x yields the lower bound on p. On the other hand, if all r nodes are scheduled to communicate with legitimate ones (appear on separate rows in F), then $x = x_{\max} = r$, and p attains its maximum value. Note that $p \leq 1$ and hence, $r \leq K - J$. When r is larger than $K - J$, there are 1-factors where all transmissions are jammed with certainty.

F. Proof of Proposition 8: At each time slot, the probability that an adjacent cluster fails to receive a broadcast is due to: (a) all N_L links are shared with compromised border nodes, and (b) the links shared with uncompromised border nodes are jammed by the adversary. So the probability that a neighboring cluster fails to receive a broadcast is

$$P_{fail} = P_c^{N_L} + \sum_{i=1}^{N_L} \binom{N_L}{i} \left(\frac{J(1-P_c)}{K-r}\right)^i.$$

The probability that at least one of the neighboring clusters successfully receive the broadcast at a time slot is

$$P_{success} = 1 - P_{fail}^{N_C}.$$

The broadcast among adjacent nodes forms a Bernoulli trial with a success probability $P_{success}$, so the average delay until the first success is $1/P_{success}$, which leads to our result.

G. Proof of Proposition 9: For any neighboring cluster, the probability that it can not receive a broadcast is that all N_L links are shared with compromised border nodes. This probability is $P_c^{N_L}$. So the expected number of neighboring clusters that can get a broadcast is $N_C \cdot (1 - P_c^{N_L})$. Dividing this value with N_C, yields $\mathrm{E}[DIV]$.

Short Paper: Jamming-Resilient Multipath Routing Leveraging Availability-Based Correlation

Hossen Mustafa[a], Xin Zhang[b], Zhenhua Liu[a], Wenyuan Xu[a], Adrian Perrig[b]

[a] Dept. of CSE, University of South Carolina, Columbia, SC 29208, USA
{mustafah,liuz}@email.sc.edu, wyxu@cse.sc.edu
[b] CyLab, Carnegie Mellon University, Pittsburgh, PA 15213, USA
xzhang1@cs.cmu.edu, adrian@ece.cmu.edu

ABSTRACT

Jamming attacks are especially harmful to the reliability of wireless communication, as they can effectively disrupt communication. Existing jamming defenses primarily focus on repairing connectivity between adjacent nodes. In this paper, we address jamming at the network level and focus on restoring the end-to-end data delivery through multipath routing. As long as all paths do not fail concurrently, the end-to-end path availability is maintained. Prior work in multipath selection improves routing by choosing node-disjoint paths or link-disjoint paths. However, through our experiments on jamming effects using MicaZ nodes, we show that topological disjointness is insufficient for selecting fault-independent paths. Thus, we address multipath selection based on the knowledge of a path's *availability history*. Using Availability History Vectors (AHVs) of paths, we present an AHV-based Link-State (ALS) algorithm to select fault-independent paths. Our extensive simulation results validate that the ALS algorithm is effective in overcoming the jamming impact by maximizing the end-to-end availability of the selected paths.

Categories and Subject Descriptors: C.2.0 [Computer-Communication Networks]: General-Security and Protection

General Terms: Reliability, Security.

Keywords: Wireless Networks, Routing Algorithms, Jamming.

1. INTRODUCTION

Wireless networks communicate through a shared medium and thus are vulnerable to jamming or radio interference. To cope with jamming, much research effort has focused on local repairing, i.e., restoring communication between adjacent nodes. Those anti-jamming measures include the conventional physical-layer techniques that rely on advanced transceivers [7] (e.g., frequency hopping) and MAC-layer mechanisms [5, 10] that adjust error correcting codes, channel adaptation [10], or physical location [3]. Although those

techniques are important to defend against jamming, we take a different viewpoint and focus on defending against jamming at the network level, i.e., restoring reliability of end-to-end data delivery.

In this study, we examine multipath routing protocols that will react to communication disturbance on-demand. Particularly, a source node selects multiple paths for reaching the destination. When one of the paths fails, other working paths will be used to deliver packets and thereby maintain end-to-end availability, *as long as not all paths between the source and destination fail concurrently*. Such end-to-end availability provided by multiple paths between a pair of nodes is referred to as *multipath availability*. A crucial component of multipath routing is *multipath selection*, as the selection tactic and resulting path qualities will directly influence the effectiveness of multipath routing. In this study, we design multipath selection algorithms that optimize multipath availability even when one or more jammers disrupt network communication occasionally or continuously.

Most existing multipath selection algorithms [4, 9] choose node-disjoint paths or link-disjoint paths, i.e., paths without common nodes or shared links, in an attempt to minimize the probability that paths fail simultaneously. While such an approach is simple and intuitive, it relies on the assumption that the topological disjointness among multiple paths is sufficient to guarantee failure-independence. However, in a wireless network, disjoint paths can still be failure-correlated, especially in the presence of multiple interference sources. We illustrate this by two examples. Consider the two wireless ad hoc networks shown in Figure 1, where three paths between the source node S and the destination node D are disjoint. In Figure 1 (a), a stationary interferer J with an irregular jamming area becomes active occasionally. Upon turning on, J disturbs routes $Rt2$ and $Rt3$ and causes those two paths to fail concurrently. In Figure 1 (b), two interferers J_1 and J_2 are far away from each other but turning on or off synchronously. As a result, J_1 and J_2 turn routes $Rt1$ and $Rt3$ to be fault-correlated. In both cases, the disjointness is necessary but not sufficient to guarantee fault-independence between paths.

To address the failure correlation between disjoint paths in the presence of jamming, one natural way is to mathematically model the impact of jamming on the network links. However, electromagnetic signals propagate in complex environments full of absorption, reflection, scattering and diffraction, and the resulting jamming impact on the network is highly irregular [2]. Figure 2 shows packet delivery contours of a sender in the presence of a jammer

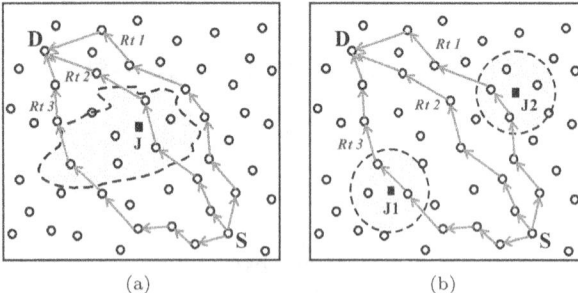

(a)   (b)

Figure 1: An illustration that disjoint paths are still correlated with regard to jamming (shaded areas represent jamming regions): (a) one non-isotropic jamming area and (b) two jamming areas far apart.

obtained using MicaZ nodes, and the pink (darker shades) areas within which a receiver can successfully receive messages exhibits high irregularity. This indicates that even given accurate information of jammers' locations and jamming power levels, it is still difficult, if even possible, to quantify their impacts with reasonable accuracy.

Rather than relying on inaccurate models, our key insight is to address multipath selection based on the knowledge of a path's *availability history*, granted that failure correlation between paths can be automatically derived from their availability history. Specifically, if two paths tend to exhibit a history of concurrent failures, we regard them as failure-correlated, otherwise failure-independent. Admittedly, by using the historical failure correlation to predict future correlation, our scheme is most resilient to the types of failures that can repeat themselves in the future, while we will show that it is still effective in improving network reliability when new types of failures emerge in the future. Our underlying rationale for leveraging availability history to exploit failure-correlation lies in the following: given the intricate causes to failure-correlation between different paths, the best we can do is to derive such correlation *after* the failures take place, while it is an open challenge to detect failure-correlation *before* failures happen. In our prior work [11], we have proposed the availability history approach for the Internet. In this paper, we demonstrate that availability history is particularly effective to defend against jamming attacks in wireless networks.

The rest of this paper is organized as follows. We specify our network and threat model in Section 2. Then, we present an Availability-History-Vector (AHV)-Based Link-State (ALS) algorithm that selects multiple paths based on AHVs in Section 3, and we evaluate the ALS algorithm in our customized simulator in Section 4. Finally, we conclude the paper in Section 5.

2. NETWORK AND THREAT MODELS

In this section, we summarize the network model and the threat model for our study, and overview our approach.

2.1 Network Model

To focus our effort in examining the resilience of multipath selection against jamming and radio-interference, we consider multi-hop wireless ad hoc networks with limited mobility (e.g., wireless mesh networks). That is, the link state is primarily affected by jamming but not by the mobility of network nodes. Further, we assume that each node will

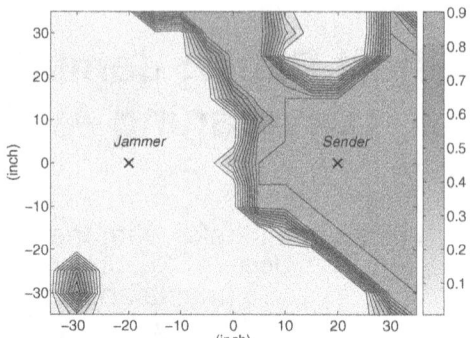

Figure 2: PDR contours of a sender located at (20,0) in the presence of a jammer located at (-20,0) to illustrate the irregularity of jamming effect in a real system. To obtain the PDR contours, a receiver was placed at the grid with a grid size of 5 inches in an indoor environment. The sender, receiver, and the jammer are all implemented on MicaZ nodes with the same transmission power levels.

maintain a neighbor table recording the link states between its neighbors and itself. Such a neighbor table is supported by most routing protocols and can be easily implemented by periodically broadcasting beacons.

2.2 Threat Model

Besides jamming, our scheme is resilient to other types of failures or network dynamics that can change disjoint paths into fault-dependent ones. For instance, network nodes belonging to the same carrier may be far apart but leave/join the network at the same time. Nevertheless, we focus on studying the multipath selection problem under the threat of jamming. In particular, we examine the following representative jammers to mimic radio interference sources and malicious jammers.

- **Stationary Jammers.** One or more stationary jammers alternate between on and off mode but do not move around. Specifically, when interferers are active, they emit energy to the channel without following the MAC protocol implemented by the network. When multiple interferers are present, they can start to emit signals simultaneously, independently, or in a manner such that at least one of them is active at any time instant. Regardless of their activation patterns, they will disturb the network communication occasionally.

- **Mobile Jammers.** A mobile jammer will move around in the network while emitting signals continuously, and it will disrupt the network communication in its vicinity. A mobile jammer can travel following a specific pattern or can walk randomly in the network. The distinction between this model and the stationary one is that a mobile jammer, especially the jammer moving randomly, affects a wider range of links but not at the same time. As a result, it is challenging to predict the future link states with the history information when a mobile jammer is present.

3. AHV-BASED LINK-STATE ALGORITHM

The success of multipath selection necessitates two components, namely, (a) a *metric* that can accurately reflect failure correlation between different paths, and (b) a *selec-*

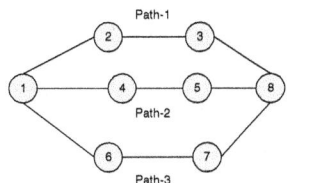

(a) A simplified topology

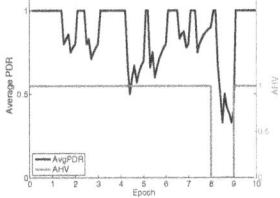

(b) PDR to AHV for the link 1→2

Figure 3: An illustration of converting PDR to AHV with topology.

tion algorithm that can effectively leverage the metric to rule out failure-correlated paths from being selected together.

In Section 3.1 we present a new mechanism which not only can evaluate individual path availability, but can also derive a multipath availability metric even in the presence of failure correlation between links. Then in Section 3.2, we describe how our mechanism helps to select multiple paths based on AHVs.

We use the following standard notations: (a) "∧" is the logical AND bit-operation; (b) "∨" stands for the logical OR bit-operation; (c) "$|\mathcal{X}|$" operation returns the cardinality of the set $\mathcal{X}$; and (d) "$\|\mathcal{X}\|$" operation returns the norm of the vector $\mathcal{X}$.

3.1 Modeling Availability History

To bypass the complexity caused by precisely predicting or modeling the correlation between different paths while still capturing the failure correlation between them, we propose a new mechanism called an *Availability History Vector* (AHV), to record path availability histories, from which the failure correlation between different paths can be learned. We first define an AHV on a per-link basis, from which path (multipath) availability can be then easily derived.

AHV of A Single Link. One natural metric to determine the availability of a wireless link is the Packet Delivery Ratio (PDR), i.e., the percentage of packets successfully delivered over the link. Recording the PDR time series directly requires at least 1 byte for each data point, and calculating the aggregated PDR of a path requires multiplication. To store and compute availability history efficiently, we utilize a binary vector for recording, and bitwise operations for calculating path availability.

In particular, we map a PDR to a 0-1 value, where '1' corresponds to the time instant when the link is *available* (acceptable PDR), while '0' corresponds to the time instant when the link is *unavailable* (unacceptable PDR). A threshold γ_0 is predefined to determine whether a PDR is acceptable. Furthermore, we divide time into epochs with fixed duration. At the lth epoch, let PDR_{ij}^l be the average PDR between node i and j, then the availability record of the link between node i and j at the lth epoch is

$$r_{ij}^l = \begin{cases} 1 & \text{if } PDR_{ij}^l \geq \gamma_0, \\ 0 & \text{otherwise.} \end{cases}$$

and the AHV of this link for e epochs is $\mathbf{a}_{ij} = [r_{ij}^1, r_{ij}^2, \ldots, r_{ij}^e]$.

To facilitate observation, we depict an AHV as a continuous line and illustrate an example of converting the PDR between node 1 to 2 (as shown in Figure 3 (a)) into the AHV with γ_0 being 0.6 in Figure 3 (b); except for Epoch 9, the availability of other epochs are '1'.

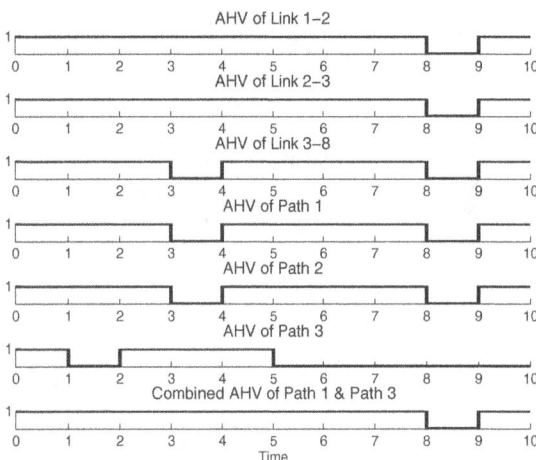

Figure 4: The AHVs for the network in Figure 3(a).

So far, AHV is used to characterize individual links. Now we present how to derive an AHV for an entire path consisting of concatenating links or sub-paths, using the following *series combination* operation.

AHV of One Path. The AHV of a complete path is computed as the logical AND bit operation of all AHVs of the links or sub-paths. The AHV of path p_i can be formulated as

$$\mathcal{A}_i = \mathbf{a}_{I_1 I_2} \wedge \mathbf{a}_{I_2 I_3} \wedge \ldots \wedge \mathbf{a}_{I_q I_{q+1}},$$

where I_q is the qth node ID on the path p_i.

For example, recall that Path-1, shown in Figure 3(a), consists of links 1→2→3→8. Figure 4 illustrates the series combination for calculating its AHV. The top three lines present the AHVs of links 1→2, 2→3, and 3→8, and the fourth line is the AHV of Path-1, computed as the AND bit operation of the first three AHVs.

AHV of Multiple Paths. Recall that in multipath routing, we aim at selecting multiple paths that provide the highest multipath availability; thus we derive the AHV of a given set of k paths using the following *parallel combination* operation.

Let M be the set of k paths between a source-destination pair. The AHV of M is computed as the logical OR bit operation of all AHVs of the paths, denoted as

$$\mathcal{A}_M = \mathcal{A}_1 \vee \mathcal{A}_2 \vee \ldots \vee \mathcal{A}_k.$$

Figure 4 shows an example of the AHVs of three paths along with the combined AHV of Path-1 and Path-3, obtained by a logical OR bit operation on Path-1 and Path-3's AHVs.

3.2 AHV-Based Multipath Selection

The AHV-Based Link-State (ALS) algorithm selects a few failure-independent paths utilizing the individual path AHV information. Specifically, each node maintains a history table recording the AHVs between its neighbors and itself, and such history tables for every link are accessible by the ALS algorithm. One challenge facing the ALS algorithm is that a huge number of possible paths may exist between nodes in multi-hop wireless networks. As the number of nodes increases, the number of paths will increase exponentially. Selecting multiple paths from a large number of candidate paths can be computationally prohibitive. To address this issue, we propose a two-stage framework to select multiple paths, (a) the *path pre-selection* stage and (b) the *greedy multipath selection* stage.

In particular, we model the network as a weighted graph $G = (N, E, W)$ with N being the node set, E being the link set, and W being the map from edges to weights. Given the network graph G, h paths are selected as the candidates in the *path pre-selection* stage. Out of h candidate paths, k paths are chosen in *greedy multipath selection* stage that produce a high level of availability according to the AHVs.

3.2.1 Path Pre-Selection

The quality of the h candidate paths directly affects the achievable multipath availability to be obtained in the greedy multipath selection stage. Denote the quality of path p_i as $w(p_i)$ and denote $\mathcal{N}_i$ as the node set on the path p_i, the candidate path set H will satisfy the following requirements:

1. $|H| \leq h$,

2. $\forall p_j, p_i \in H, \frac{|\mathcal{N}_i \cap \mathcal{N}_j|}{\min(|\mathcal{N}_i|, |\mathcal{N}_j|)} \leq \rho$,

3. $\forall p_u \notin H, p_i \in H, w(p_i) \geq w(p_u)$ OR $\frac{|\mathcal{N}_i \cap \mathcal{N}_u|}{\min(|\mathcal{N}_i|, |\mathcal{N}_u|)} \geq \rho$,

where ρ is a threshold and $\rho \in [0, 1]$.

The second condition requires that any pair of paths belonging to H should have less than ρ percent of shared nodes. The parameter ρ controls the level of overlapping between paths in H. When $\rho = 0$, H only contains node-disjoint paths, while when $\rho = 1$, H consists of any paths without the disjointness restriction. Setting $\rho = 0$ may sound appealing at first glance, but strictly choosing h disjoint paths can filter out 'good' candidates, some of which in combination can be highly failure-independent. At the other extreme, setting $\rho = 1$ can include several candidate paths that are highly correlated with each other, reducing the diversity of H. Thus, ρ serves as a tunable value to strike the balance between those extreme cases. In our study, we choose $\rho = 0.8$.

The third condition requires that a top-ranked candidate path should be selected, unless many of its nodes overlap with higher ranking ones. The paths are ranked with regard to the link quality. We continue to use PDR as the link quality indicator, and the PDR of a path that connects node i and node j by q links is,

$$PDR_{ij} = \prod_{i=1}^{q} PDR_{I_i I_{i+1}}$$

To obtain h paths, we utilized Yen's ranking algorithm [6], a classic algorithm to determine the K shortest paths. A few issues arise when applying Yen's ranking algorithm to obtain H: (a) it assumes the end-to-end weight of two consecutive links equals the *sum* of individual link weight while the end-to-end PDR is the *product* of individual $PDRs$; (b) it returns paths with the top *minimum* weight while we are interested in top *maximum* weighted ones, and (c) it returns paths regardless of the number of shared nodes among them. To address those issues, we define the weight of a path from nodes i to j as

$$w_{ij} = -\log(PDR_{ij}) = -\sum_{i=1}^{q} \log(PDR_{I_i I_{i+1}})$$

and simply discard a path from H if it shares more than ρ percent of nodes with a higher ranking path.

3.2.2 Greedy Multipath Selection

From the availability history carried by AHVs, we can infer that two paths are highly correlated if they tend to fail at the same time in their AHVs, and vice versa. Several algorithms have been proposed to leverage such history records to cluster correlated links into groups [8]. For our purpose of selecting failure-independent routing paths, we derive a multipath availability metric from AHVs and employ a selection scheme that can preclude failure-correlated paths from being selected together without additional clustering efforts.

Multipath Availability Metric (MAM). It is computed as the number of 1-epochs (i.e., availability bit equals '1' in that epoch) in the AHV of multiple paths between a source-destination pair. Specifically, the availability of a multipath set M is denoted by $\theta(M) = |\mathcal{A}_M|$. Accordingly, our algorithm will select the k AHVs that can produce the largest MAM, by which it can ensure that failure-correlated paths are bound to be less likely chosen together.

Formally, let H be the output of path pre-selection stage. The multipath selection problem can be defined as the following:

DEFINITION 1.

$$\underset{M}{maximize} \quad \theta(M)$$
$$subject\ to \quad |M| \leq k, M \subseteq H.$$

The multipath selection problem in Definition 1 is NP-complete, according to our prior work [11]. Thus, rather than designing an algorithm to search for the optimal solution, we use an approximation algorithm (as shown in Algorithm 1) to solve the multipath selection problem. Essentially, **AHVSelect()** is a greedy algorithm. In each iteration, the algorithm greedily selects the path that can maximize the multipath availability accumulated so far, and it has a time complexity of $O(hk)$.

To illustrate, recall the example topology shown in Figure 3(a) with the AHV of each path given in Figure 4. Suppose Path-1 has already been selected. If we further select Path-2 which is failure-correlated with Path-1, the resulting combined AHV gains no increase in the total number of 1-epochs. In contrast, if we parallel-combine Path-3, which is failure-independent with Path-1, the resulting combined AHV benefits from a significant increase in MAM; thus it is chosen over Path-2 in our selection mechanism.

Algorithm 1 AHVSelect: AHV-Based Multipath Selection

Require: INPUT:
  $H, k, \{\mathcal{A}_i\}_{i \in H}$
  OUTPUT:
  M;
  PROCEDURES:
1: $M = \emptyset$, $\theta(M) = 0$
2: **while** $|M| \leq k$ **do**
3:   *select* a path $p \in H$ that maximizes $\theta(M \cup p)$
4:   *add* p to M, *update* $\theta(M) = \theta(M \cup p)$
5: **end while**

---

4. ALGORITHM EVALUATION

In this section, we evaluate the performance of the AHV-based Link-State algorithm in our customized simulator, which provides the flexibility of adopting various physical propagation models and hardware models for decoding pack-

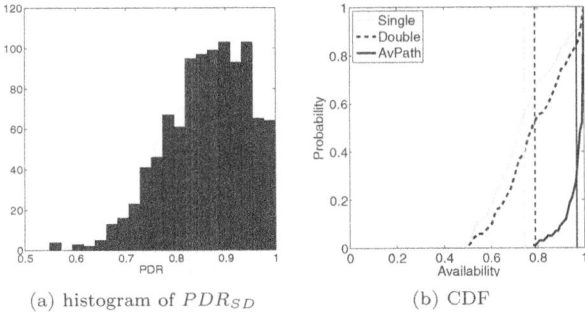

(a) histogram of PDR_{SD} (b) CDF

Figure 5: The end-to-end PDR and availability in the no-jammer case.

ets. The focus is to validate the algorithm performance without the influence of network traffic.

4.1 Simulation Methodology

Propagation Model. To prepare for the extensive performance study, we chose a simple yet representative model that captures the essence of signal propagation without using computer-aided modeling tools, i.e., log-normal shadowing model [1]. Our model captures both path loss versus distance and the random attenuation due to blockage from objects in the signal path, and it has the following form,

$$PL(d) = PL(d_0) - 10 \cdot \eta \cdot \log(\frac{d}{d_0}) + X_\sigma,$$

where $PL(d)$ is the path loss at distance d, $PL(d_0)$ is the known path loss at a reference distance d_0, η is the Path Loss Exponent, and X_σ is a Gaussian zero-mean random variable with standard deviation σ. To emulate a real environment, we tune the variables obtained from our prior empirical study [2]: $\eta = 2.11$, $\sigma = 1.8$, and $PL(d_0) = 33$dB.

Essentially, the link quality (PDR) between a pair of directly connected nodes is determined by the physical-layer metric, i.e., signal-to-noise ratio (SNR) at the receiver. When the SNR is larger than a threshold value ξ_o, a message can be decoded and will be received successfully, otherwise it will not. We measured the PDRs by examining the SNR for each link periodically while setting ξ_o to 0dB.

Network Setup and Scenarios. We simulated a random wireless network consisting of 1000 nodes in a 700-by-700m square. The nodes were deployed with a uniform density and each node had a transmission range of about $40m$, which resulted in approximately 10 neighbors per node.

We evaluated our ALS algorithm with $k = 2$ and compared it with two other baseline algorithms: (a) single path: selecting the path with the highest average end-to-end PDR; (b) double disjoint paths: selecting two paths that are disjoint and have the top $PDRs$. We denote those three algorithms as AvPath, single, and double, respectively.

We studied the following scenarios: no jammer, one stationary jammer, two stationary jammers, and a mobile jammer with two types of moving patterns. For each scenario, we ran our experiment 100 times to collect the statistical characteristics. For each simulation run, the nodes built their neighbor tables and history tables prior to time $t_1 = 600s$. At time t_1, all algorithms selected paths based on the link information observed so far. Then the average availability between a pair of nodes (S and D) that were approximately 20 hops apart was measured for 600 seconds, and the normalized availability is depicted.

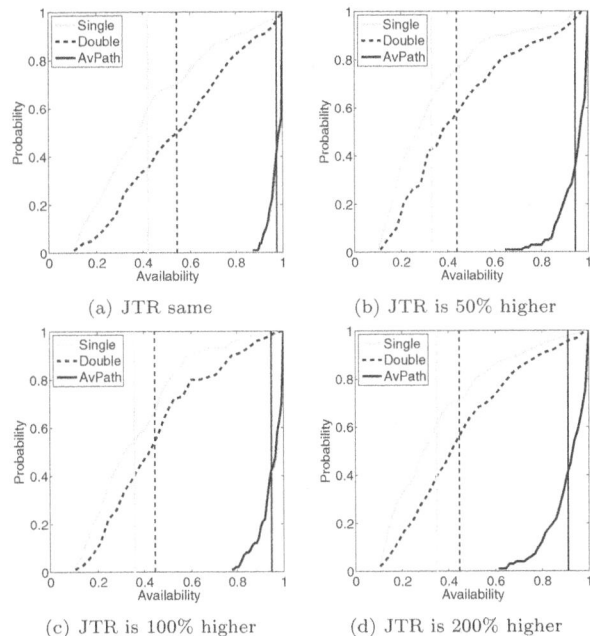

(a) JTR same   (b) JTR is 50% higher

(c) JTR is 100% higher   (d) JTR is 200% higher

Figure 6: CDF of Availability for one jammer with different Jammer Transmission Range(JTR).

4.2 Results

No Jammer. Figure 5 shows the histogram of the end-to-end PDR and CDF (Cumulative Distribution Function) of the normalized availability between node S and node D with no active jammers. The vertical lines are the average normalized availabilities for the three cases. Overall, selecting two disjoint paths did increase the average availability slightly: by 4%. However, by selecting two fault-independent paths, our ALS algorithm boosted the average availability more: from 75% to 98%.

Stationary Jammers. In this set of experiments, we studied two scenarios: a one-stationary-jammer scenario and a two-stationary-jammer scenario. In both scenarios, the stationary jammers were present at the beginning of the simulations, and they alternated between ON and OFF for random amount of time, e.g., a random duration uniformly distributed between 5 and 20 seconds. The jammers were placed somewhere on the shortest path between nodes D and S, so that it would affect the shortest path between the source and the destination. We assumed that the jammers were capable of transmitting at a higher power level than the network nodes, and we evaluated cases when the jammer had (i) the same, (ii) 50% more, (iii) 100% more, and (iv) 200% more transmission range than the network nodes. The average availability between S and D for the one jammer case is depicted in Figure 6, and two jammer case is depicted in Figure 7. In all cases, the ALS algorithm outperforms the other two baseline algorithms by $60\% - 70\%$.

Additionally, the average availability of all algorithms decreases as the transmission range of the jammer increases, since a larger jamming range will affect more paths and will reduce the end-to-end availability.

Mobile Jammers. In our experiment, we studied two types of mobile jammers: one traveling in a circle (CW) and the other moving randomly (RW), as illustrated in Figure 8(a) and (c). Regardless of their moving patterns, both mobile jammers' transmission range is 100% more than net-

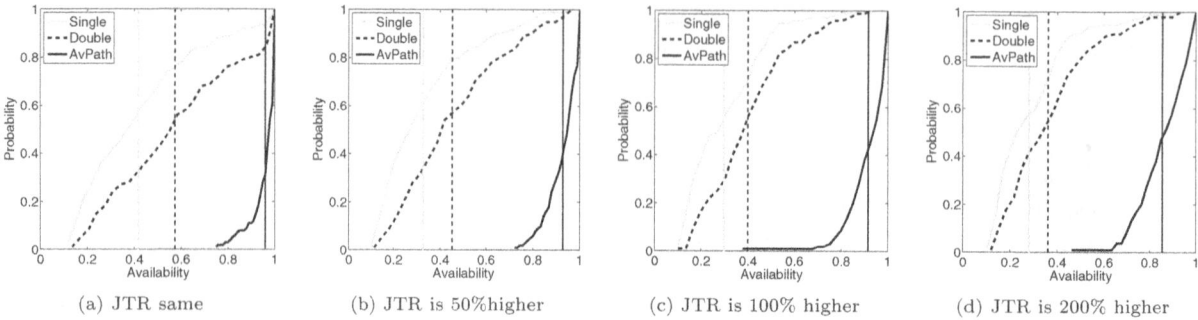

| (a) JTR same | (b) JTR is 50%higher | (c) JTR is 100% higher | (d) JTR is 200% higher |

Figure 7: CDF of Availability for two jammers with different Jammer Transmission Range(JTR).

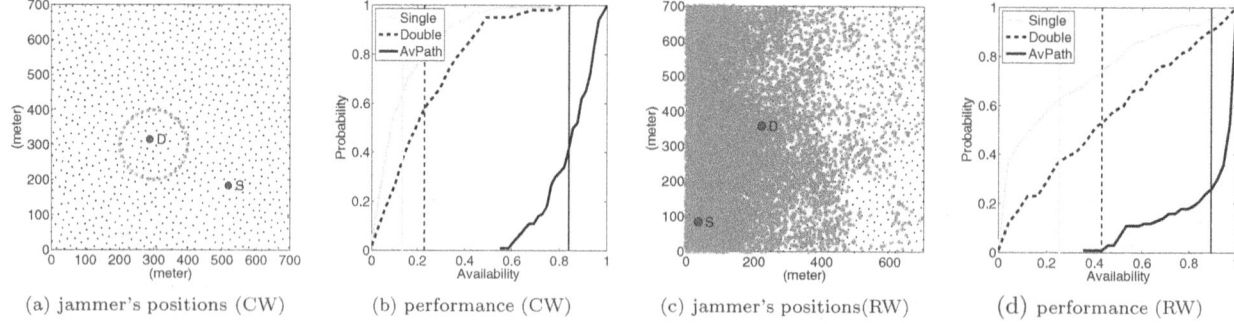

| (a) jammer's positions (CW) | (b) performance (CW) | (c) jammer's positions(RW) | (d) performance (RW) |

Figure 8: Two types of mobile jammers: a circular-walk jammer (CW) and a random-walk jammer (RW).

work nodes, and both jammers remained active throughout the simulation. Specifically, the circular-walk jammer constantly disturbed communication between node D and node S, as it hovered around the destination node D (affecting node D about 40% of the time). As a result, the single-path algorithm generated a path that is only available 18% of the time, on average. The double-disjoint-path algorithm selected two paths that in combination have slightly higher availability than the single path, even though twice the number of paths were used. In comparison, the `AvPath` also selected two paths but two fault-independent paths, and thus the availability of those paths is 60% more than the other two algorithms. Finally, the RW-mobile jammer represents a jammer whose behavior is not fully captured in the availability history prior to multipath selection, i.e., it creates new 'future' failures. The simulation results in this case show that the ALS algorithm can improve the availability even when unexpected new faults may appear after multipath selection is done. This is because that both failure-dependence and the impact of jamming are partially affected by wireless network factors, such as network topologies and radio propagation environments. Although the 'future' failure has not occurred yet, its impact has already been partially encoded in the historical failure correlation implicitly.

5. CONCLUSION

We have addressed the problem of multipath selection with the goal of improving jamming resilience in wireless networks. Our key insight is to select multiple paths that are unlikely to fail concurrently, based on the knowledge of paths' availability histories. The availability histories of paths are efficiently recorded and calculated via availability history vectors (AHVs). Leveraging AHVs, we have presented AHV-based Link-State multipath selection algorithms. Our extensive simulation results have validated that (1) selecting disjoint paths is insufficient to improve end-to-

end availability in the presence of jamming; and (2) AHV-based algorithms can effectively identify multiple paths that provide high end-to-end availability, even in the presence of a new jammer that has not yet affected the AHVs prior to path selection.

In summary, our AHV-based algorithms can greatly improve the end-to-end message delivery in the presence of a wide variety of jamming attacks.

6. REFERENCES

[1] A. Goldsmith. *Wireless Communications*. Cambridge University Press, New York, USA, 2005.

[2] Z. Liu, H. Liu, W. Xu, and Y. Chen. Exploiting jamming-caused neighbor changes for jammer localization. *Accepted to IEEE Transactions on Parallel and Distributed Systems (TPDS)*.

[3] K. Ma, Y. Zhang, and W. Trappe. Mobile network management and robust spatial retreats via network dynamics. In *Proceedings of workshop on Resource Provisioning and Management in Sensor Networks (RPMSN05)*, 2005.

[4] S. Mueller, R. Tsang, and D. Ghosal. Multipath routing in mobile ad hoc networks: Issues and challenges. In *Performance Tools and Applications to Networked Systems*, 2004.

[5] G. Noubir and G. Lin. Low-power DoS attacks in data wireless lans and countermeasures. *SIGMOBILE Mob. Comput. Commun. Rev.*, 7(3):29–30, 2003.

[6] M. Pascoal and E. Martins. A new implementation of yen's ranking loopless paths algorithm. *4OR: A Quarterly Journal of Operations Research*, 1(2):121–133, 2003.

[7] J. Proakis. *Digital Communications*. McGraw-Hill, Columbus, OH, 2000.

[8] A. Tachibana, S. Ano, T. Hasegawa, M. Tsuru, and Y. Oie. Locating congested segments on the internet by multiple paths' delay performance clustering. In *IEEE International Conference on Communications*. IEEE, 2007.

[9] K. Wu and J. Harms. On-demand multipath routing for mobile ad hoc networks. In *Networks EPMCC*, pages 1–7, 2001.

[10] W. Xu, W. Trappe, and Y. Zhang. Channel surfing: defending wireless sensor networks from interference. In *Proceedings of conference on Information Processing in Sensor Networks (IPSN)*, pages 499–508, 2007.

[11] X. Zhang and A. Perrig. Correlation-resilient path selection for multi-path routing. In *IEEE Globecom*, 2010.

Short Paper: Reactive Jamming in Wireless Networks— How Realistic is the Threat?

Matthias Wilhelm, Ivan Martinovic,* Jens B. Schmitt, and Vincent Lenders[‡]
Disco Labs, TU Kaiserslautern, Germany   [‡]Armasuisse, Switzerland
{wilhelm,martinovic,jschmitt}@cs.uni-kl.de   vincent.lenders@armasuisse.ch

ABSTRACT

In this work, we take on the role of a wireless adversary and investigate one of its most powerful tools—radio frequency jamming. Although different jammer designs are discussed in the literature, reactive jamming, i.e., targeting only packets that are already *on the air*, is generally recognized as a stepping stone in implementing optimal jamming strategies. The reason is that, while destroying only selected packets, the adversary minimizes its risk of being detected. One might hope for reactive jamming to be too challenging or uneconomical for an attacker to conceive and implement due to its strict real-time requirements. Yet, in this work we disillusion from such hopes as we demonstrate that flexible and reliable *software-defined* reactive jamming is feasible by designing and implementing a reactive jammer against IEEE 802.15.4 networks. First, we identify the causes of loss at the physical layer of 802.15.4 and show how to achieve the best performance for reactive jamming. Then, we apply these insights to our USRP2-based reactive jamming prototype, enabling a classification of transmissions in real-time, and reliable and selective jamming. The prototype achieves a reaction time in the order of microseconds, a high precision (such as targeting individual symbols), and a 97.6 % jamming rate in realistic indoor scenarios for a single reactive jammer, and over 99.9 % for two concurrent jammers.

Categories and Subject Descriptors

C.2.0 [**Computer Communication Networks**]: General— *Security and protection (e.g., firewalls)*

General Terms

Security, Experimentation, Performance

Keywords

Reactive jamming, software-defined jammer, 802.15.4, WSN

*This work was partially funded by the Carl-Zeiss Foundation Fellowship.

1. INTRODUCTION

The simplicity of deployment and administration as well as low-cost hardware result in an increased reliance on wireless communication systems. However, the blocking of wireless communication, i.e., jamming, is one of the major security threats and understanding the impact and complexity of such attacks and their countermeasures is of great interest to the networking community (see, e.g., [2, 11, 16, 17]), as this physical attack against the availability is unique to wireless networks and hard to mitigate on higher layers.

In the literature, several jammer categories have been identified [11, 17] according to their channel-awareness and statefulness. Constant and random jammers are the prevalent form of jammers as they are easy to implement, but lack channel-awareness. On the other end of the spectrum, reactive jammers base their jamming decisions on both the current and previous channel states. This is very desirable from the attacker's point of view since it has several benefits: *(i)* it allows for effective and efficient jamming [6], as only short jamming bursts are required to destroy complete packets; *(ii)* reactive jamming is challenging to detect [15], because only limited interference with other nodes is experienced, which minimizes the risk of exposure; and *(iii)* it enables the implementation of optimal jamming strategies, since channel-awareness is a major factor for such strategies. For example, Bayraktaroglu et al. [1] show that a smart jammer that takes the sender's state into account can be four orders of magnitude more efficient than a constant jammer. On the other hand, reactive jamming is challenging to accomplish due to the strict real-time requirements for detection and subsequent jamming. The form of jamming signals and the jamming precision become crucial for a successful destruction of packets. Hence, the question arises: Is reactive jamming a realistic threat in wireless networks in terms of technical feasibility and economic viability?

In this work, we deliver the bad news that, indeed, flexible reactive jamming is feasible in 802.15.4 networks by using low-cost software-defined radios (SDR), which are easy to configure and adapt to different application scenarios. Thus, research efforts in jamming detection and countermeasures should assume more sophisticated, yet economical, adversaries. To assist in the experimental evaluation of the main factors in reactive jammer designs, we provide a USRP2-based flexible experimental platform to the research community.[1] To achieve the best jamming performance, we analyze the causes of loss at the physical layer of 802.15.4

---

[1]Visit `http://disco.cs.uni-kl.de` or contact the main author for the necessary resources.

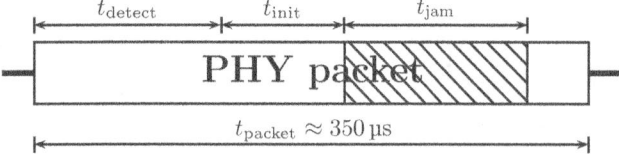

Figure 1: Time constraints: the reactive jammer must detect a transmission, initiate the jamming process and interfere with the transmission to prevent a packet reception.

and derive guidelines for successful reactive jamming against ZigBee-based networks. We assess the applicability of our approach by systematically evaluating the performance of our prototype system in several experimental settings. The results justify that reactive jamming should be considered a real threat with a low entry barrier.

2. DESIGN CHALLENGES

We set several goals for a reactive jamming platform: an accurate detection of RF transmissions as well as reliable and precise jamming, all while a packet is still on the air. Additionally, the aim is to achieve 100 % transmission cancelation even in challenging conditions often found in indoor wireless sensor networks (WSNs), e.g., assuming multipath fading and strong signals at the receiver due to short distances.

To get an impression of the timing requirements, see Fig. 1. The system must detect a transmission and decide whether it must be jammed or not (with the required time t_{detect}), schedule and initialize the sending of a jamming signal (with delay t_{init}), and send a short, yet sufficient jamming burst to destroy the packet (t_{jam}), all while it is being transmitted.[2] The concurrent jamming must exceed the shortest interference time t_{jam}^{min} to cause a packet loss. Therefore, we require

$$t_{\mathrm{detect}} + t_{\mathrm{init}} + t_{\mathrm{jam}}^{min} \leq t_{\mathrm{packet}},$$

i.e., to react quickly enough to hit the packet for the minimal required jamming duration. In the case of IEEE 802.15.4, the shortest packets are ACKs, with a duration of $t_{\mathrm{packet}} = 352\,\mu s$. Despite these tight requirements, the system design should still be flexible and reconfigurable, so a fully programmable reactive jammer based on the software-defined radio paradigm is what we aim for.

Challenge 1: How can we ensure successful jamming? Our goal is to destroy all selected packets while keeping the jamming duration as short as possible. This poses a quite different problem compared to proactive jamming performance evaluations in the literature [1, 5]. The reactive jammer must be able to destroy transmissions at the receiver even if a sender has already started a transmission. In §3, we provide an overview for causes of loss on the physical layer and identify the jamming signal that causes the minimal packet reception ratio (PRR). In §5.1 we evaluate the minimal jam duration and show that the required jamming burst can be as short as $t_{\mathrm{jam}}^{min} = 26\,\mu s$ to ensure a PRR of 0 %.

Challenge 2: How do we achieve real-time performance? Nychis et al. [9] show that the host-based SDR architecture (where the processing is done by a PC) introduces additional latency (e.g., 2 ms on average in case of

the USRP2) into the system. We mitigate this problem by implementing our system on the USRP2's FPGA, which enables a high-speed detector design and deterministic timing (see §4 for details). Our experimental results show that we achieve a jamming initialization time of $t_{\mathrm{init}} \approx 15\,\mu s$, while still keeping the flexibility of SDR-based systems.

Challenge 3: How do we react to 802.15.4 packets only? Our goal is a high detection accuracy, but with a minimal introduced delay t_{detect}. Along this way, different implementation choices can be made, e.g., a simple power detector is easy to implement and offers a short reaction time, but cannot classify transmissions accurately (e.g., it may not discriminate between different wireless technologies). Therefore, the detector of our prototype is designed to search for modulated 802.15.4 PHY headers, thus restricting our jamming to 802.15.4 packets only. The detector adds an additional delay of less than 4 μs. Overall, the experiments in §5 show that our prototype reacts quickly enough to detect and reliably destroy ZigBee transmissions.

3. EFFECTIVE REACTIVE JAMMING

We concentrate on physical layer attacks against 802.15.4 instead of jamming approaches against MAC mechanisms [5, 7] such as attacking the clear channel assessment (CCA). In this section, we identify the causes of packet loss on the physical layer of 802.15.4, as well as which jamming signals and timings are consequently the most effective ones against such transmissions. The results are verified through systematic experiments in a WSN testbed with MICAz motes. We identify the factors that influence the jamming performance, and select the optimal jamming signal, which we subsequently implement as part of the reactive jamming system.

3.1 802.15.4 Background

Before going into details, we briefly cover aspects of the 802.15.4 physical layer that are necessary for the later discussion of jamming against such networks. Although IEEE Std. 802.15.4-2006 [4] defines four different physical layers for the wireless interconnection of devices in wireless personal area networks (WPANs), we limit ourselves here to the 2.4 GHz PHY because of its widespread use. The standard defines 16 channels labeled Channel 11–26, with a bandwidth of 2 MHz each and a 5 MHz interspacing. Bytes in the PHY protocol data unit (PPDU) are transmitted at a rate of 250 kbps. They are divided into groups of 4 bit, which are then mapped to a set of 16 symbols. These symbols are spread with the corresponding 32 bit pseudo-noise (PN) chipping sequence, i.e., 802.15.4 uses direct sequence spread spectrum (DSSS) with a spreading factor of eight. This stream of chips is then modulated onto the carrier using O-QPSK with half-sine pulse-shaping, and transmitted over the wireless medium to the receiver.

Reception process. The reception process can be explained in terms of the PPDU headers (SHR and PHR), shown in Fig. 2. The essential components are shown in more detail, and ellipses show the required reception steps for these components. When a carrier is detected, the receiver synchronizes with the predefined preamble sequence (eight "0" symbols in the standard) to compensate the phase and frequency offset of the incoming transmission. This is necessary as the sender and receiver are not synchronized; with this step, the receiver recovers the timing of both chips and symbols, and the symbol clock adjusts to the symbol

---

[2]We do not consider the propagation delay in our analysis, we assume short distances between all devices.

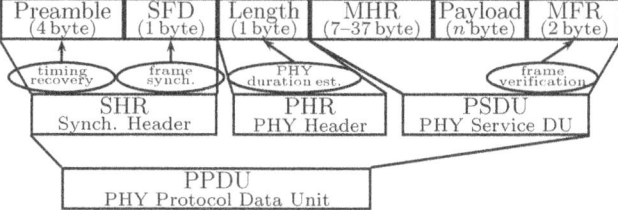

Figure 2: The structure of IEEE 802.15.4 packets.

boundaries. The receiver then expects a specific two symbol sequence, the Start-of-Frame Delimiter (SFD) that marks the beginning of the PHY header (PHR) and the following MAC layer frame. This process is called frame synchronization. The PHR consists of 7 bit containing the length of the following PHY service data unit (PSDU), which allows for duration estimation of the transmission. At each symbol clock tick, a decision is made as to which of the 16 possible symbols was the one most likely transmitted during the last period. At the end of the PSDU, the MAC footer (MFR) contains a 16 bit integrity checksum (frame check sequence, FCS) using CRC16 that verifies whether the frame is received without errors. If this is the case, the received frame is passed to the higher layers. We refer the reader to [10, 14] for a more detailed treatment of the 802.15.4 PHY and the properties of different transceiver designs.

3.2 Causes of Loss on the 802.15.4 PHY

To understand the underlying reasons for the effectiveness of different jamming approaches, we need to identify the causes of packet loss on the 802.15.4 physical layer. For a study focused on the IEEE 802.11 physical layer, refer to the work of Gummadi et al. [3].

Symbol misdetection and integrity errors. Once a frame is detected, the most likely symbol that has recently been transmitted is chosen on each symbol clock tick. Strong jamming transmissions concurrently with a symbol cause a symbol misdetection if a sufficient number of chips are flipped, consequently generating bit errors on higher layers. Integrity checks such as the CRC16 check of 802.15.4 detect these errors, resulting in a packet drop as no forward error correction (FEC) is used in 802.15.4. Thus, a single symbol error is sufficient to destroy a complete packet. Similarly, the MHR contains addressing information and the frame type, which can trigger packet drops if damaged even before the integrity of the frame is checked.

Failed timing recovery. If a jammer interferes with the preamble at the beginning of the transmission, it can cause the timing recovery to fail. A corrected phase and frequency offset are crucial for a successful packet reception, as otherwise symbol decisions are based on sub-optimal (non-peak) sampling times that decrease the SNR dramatically. This makes the symbol decisions more prone to errors, even if the jammer interfered during the preamble only. Additionally, a failure to lock onto a transmission can also cause the frame synchronization (discovering the SFD) to fail, such that a packet is overheard completely even if the incoming signal is strong.

Frame sync and damaged PHY headers. With this strategy, a jammer interferes with the SFD or PSDU length field. After the SFD is detected, the receiver knows that a frame is arriving and starts to interpret a number of incoming symbols determined by the frame length. A proactive

jammer can insert SFDs on the channel to trigger frame detection events at a receiver. The receiver then fails to detect any further transmission for a period of time as it is already occupied with decoding channel noise. In addition, a reactive jammer is able to selectively block the SFD symbols such that a receiver does not detect a frame, or to introduce an error in the frame length field that also results in a misinterpretation of the frame's fields.

Limited dynamic range. Common commercial receiver designs use mechanisms that make receivers more robust in regular situations, but have a jamming amplification effect, such as Automatic Gain Control (AGC). AGC is a control loop that adjusts the amplification of incoming baseband signals to fill the complete dynamic range of the analog-to-digital converter (ADC). This enables transceiver designers to use cheap ADCs with low resolution, such as 4–6 bit [10]. However, on the downside, an adversary can exploit the AGC mechanism in two ways: either through a pre-emptive locking of the receiver to low amplification, which makes other signals too weak to receive (causing failed timing recovery or frame synchronization), or by reactively sending a strong jamming signal to the receiver that uses a high gain setting (causing clipping in the ADC and therefore symbol misdetection). Interestingly, both of these strategies affect following symbols after the jamming has ceased, as the control loop does not react instantaneously.

3.3 Effectiveness of Jamming Waveforms

Based on the previous discussion, we want to identify jamming waveforms that are the most effective against 802.15.4. By waveform, we refer to the shape of the RF signal transmitted on the channel, specified by a sequence of I/Q samples. We check the susceptibility to three different jamming waveforms that trigger the causes presented in the previous section: symbol, timing, and frame sync errors. The signals we consider are *(i)* wideband noise, *(ii)* a narrowband continuous wave (single-tone jamming), and *(iii)* 802.15.4 modulated signals with different content, such as random symbols, preambles or SFDs to interfere with the PHY packet reception process.

3.3.1 Experimental Setting

We conduct the experiments in a room with a surface area of 4 m × 3 m, with two MICAz motes programmed as sender and receiver placed at 2 m apart, and a USRP2 as the jammer in the same room. The USRP2 is equipped with an XCRV2450 board with a maximum transmit power of 100 mW (20 dBm), and 3 dBi omnidirectional antennas. The jamming waveforms are generated on a host PC using GNU Radio. We use constant jamming and deactivate the clear channel assessment functionality of the sender such that it transmits irrespective of the channel state to ensure that we only observe physical layer effects. We do not use reactive jamming at this point because this would introduce new uncertainties into the experiment, however, the results also apply to reactive jamming. We vary the transmission power of the jammer (denoted as *jammer gain*) and measure the resulting PRR at the receiver, i.e., packets that successfully passed the CRC check despite jamming.

3.3.2 Results

A comparison of the jamming effectiveness for different waveforms is given in Fig. 3a for waveforms that mainly

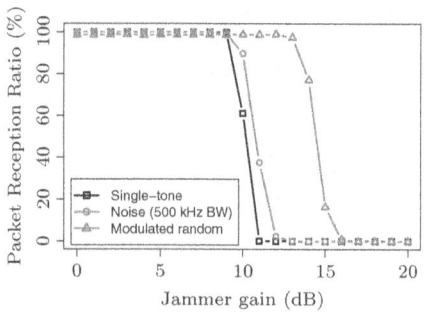
(a) Impact of waveforms that interfere with the symbol decision.

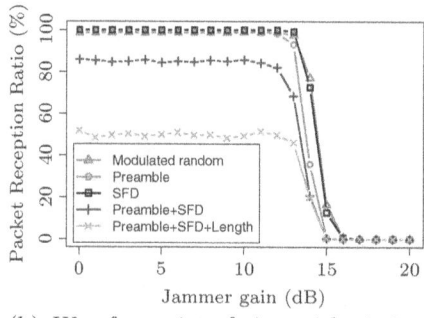
(b) Waveforms interfering with timing recovery and frame synchronization.

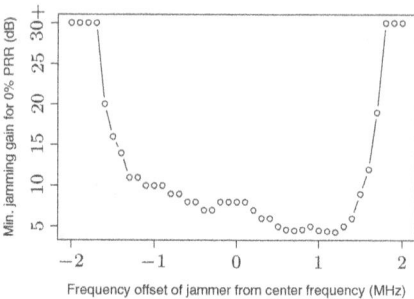
(c) Impact of relative position of the tone jamming signals in the channel.

Figure 3: The results of the jamming experiments to identify the most effective jamming waveform.

cause symbol misdetection, and Fig. 3b for those waveforms that interfere with the 802.15.4 PHY reception process. The results for the different waveforms are analyzed below.

Noise jamming. Wideband interference is always present in wireless communications, such that the receivers are specifically designed to withstand its influence. Its main effect is chip flipping that increases the likelihood of symbol misdetection. However, for a limited power budget (e.g., 20 dBm for the USRP2) the jamming signal's power is spread over a wider spectrum, depending on the bandwidth of the signal. This is the main factor why noise jamming has a limited efficiency in our tests; we achieved the best results with a BW of 500 kHz, yet it was always a few dB less efficient in comparison to single-tone jamming to achieve a PRR of 0 %.

Single-tone jamming. We used a constant signal that is modulated on the carrier, resulting in a continuous wave. This very narrowband signal may be expected to perform badly as only a small portion of the 802.15.4 channel bandwidth is affected. However, several effects cause a superior jamming efficiency in our experiments. First, this waveform interferes with timing recovery, the receiver detects the jamming signal as a second carrier signal, and the frequency mismatch makes a phase correction impossible. The second effect is that it has the largest signal amplitude of the tested waveforms; it offers more power per Hertz with a limited power budget as the signal is more concentrated on the channel. This causes AGC to react faster, which results in chip misdetection on smaller power levels in comparison to other jamming waveforms.

Because of the first effect, the relative position of the tone in the channel is an important factor. We experimented with different offset values from the channel's center frequency, and the results are shown in Fig. 3c.[3] We observe that the channel filter of the MICAz transceiver has a width of 3 MHz, which cancels out-of-band interference. Additionally, a jamming signal directly on the center frequency is less effective in comparison to a 1 MHz frequency offset (on the corner frequency of the modulation), which complies with results in the literature [12]. Surprisingly, this effect is not symmetric. We can only speculate why this is the case, but an artifact from either the USRP2's behavior (nonlinearities in the transmitter chain) or the receiver chip is a potential explanation.

802.15.4 modulated jamming. We generated the modulated signals using the UCLA ZigBee implementation [14]. We evaluated five patterns: random symbols, preamble (0x00), SFD (0xA7), synchronization header SHR (preamble+SFD), and SHR+PHR headers (preamble+SFD+length). Each of the sequences has a different effect on the receiver. Random symbols interfere with the symbol recognition and can therefore flip symbols (Fig. 3a). We expected the preamble or SFD symbols to interfere with the timing recovery, but these two waveforms are comparable to random symbols in their jamming efficiency. The reason is that the receiver locks onto stronger preambles (the *radio capture* effect), and that SFDs without preambles are not detected by the receiver because of lacking timing recovery.

Network degradations with weaker jamming transmissions are observed for the SHR and SHR+PHR waveforms. The receiver can lock onto such jamming signals even if they are weaker than the legitimate signal. Thus, even with a smaller jammer power a severe reduction in the PRR is possible as the receiver is busy decoding noise (see the comparison in Fig. 3b). This effect can be amplified further through the use of a valid length field after the SFD, forcing the receiver to stay longer in the reception state. For a proactive jammer this attack is attractive, because even weak signals at the receiver can still cause severe reductions in the PRR.

3.4 Guidelines for Effective Reactive Jamming

Considering reactive jamming, 802.15.4 modulated symbols are not as effective, since the receiver is already locked on the transmission. Due to the design choices of the transceiver in the MICAz sensor motes, single-tone jamming proves more efficient for reactive jamming than actual 802.15.4 waveforms with a limited power budget. This waveform reliably jams transmissions of the sensor motes in our experiments, and it is easily generated in software. The most efficient placement of the tone is at 1 MHz above the center frequency of the channel.

4. IMPLEMENTATION DETAILS

In this section, we explain how the widely used USRP2 can be turned into a reactive jammer.

USRP2 integration. The USRP2 platform is equipped with a Xilinx Spartan-3 FPGA running with a clock speed of 100 MHz, which provides sufficient performance and a fine-grained timing resolution of 10 ns/cycle. Additionally, the USRP2 has enough free resources (only 40 % of the FPGA is occupied) to add our prototype while reusing the function-

---

[3]Note that the measurements result from a different experimental setup and the jammer gain values are not directly comparable to the other results.

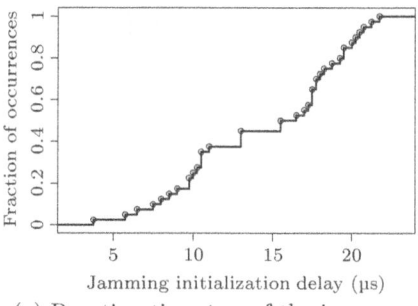

(a) Reaction time t_{init} of the jammer.

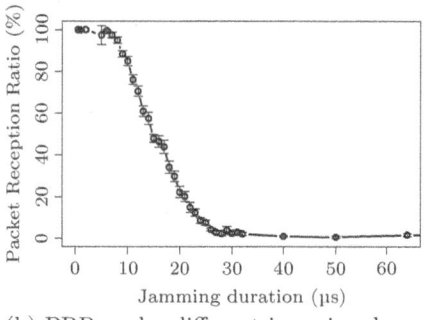

(b) PRR under different jamming durations (t_{jam}).

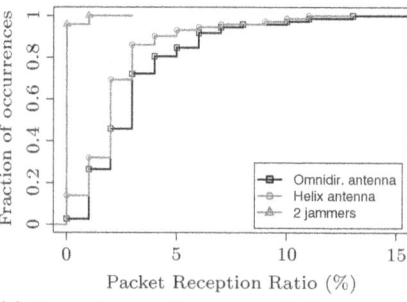

(c) Jamming performance of the system in the indoor grid scenario.

Figure 4: The results of the system performance evaluation.

ality of the original system. We modified the UHD FPGA code and firmware from Ettus Research. The operation of the USRP2 is controlled by a softcore processor in FPGA logic that executes firmware code written in C. This offers an easy integration path for our system and a maximum of reuse. However, the sequential program execution of the firmware may introduce larger time deviations into the system. The magnitude of these effects are evaluated in the next section. We added a detection module in FPGA logic that receives complex samples from the RX DSP pipeline and interrupts the firmware on a detection event. We altered the firmware to await such interrupts and to initiate the jamming process, which causes the USRP2 to start sending a ready-made jamming waveform on the channel.

Detector implementation. For every clock cycle, a new complex RF sample is available as input to the detector module. Considering the symbol duration of 16 µs in 802.15.4, we have 1600 clock cycles per symbol available, which enables complex detector designs. We implemented a PHY header (preamble+SFD) detector in our prototype. First, we perform an MSK demodulation on the signal (as explained in [14]), and feed the resulting stream of chips into a correlating receiver that detects a SHR on the channel accurately.[4] Once a SFD is detected, an interrupt is triggered at the programmable interrupt controller. Our detector adds a 4 µs delay after the SFD because of the time needed for correlation.

5. EXPERIMENTS

5.1 Micro-Benchmarks

Reaction delay. First, we determine the jamming initialization time after a packet is detected (t_{init}). More precision enables a "surgical" jamming where we can operate on a (sub-)symbol level. Further, we evaluate whether the firmware-based approach with its indeterministic timing is sufficient for our strict timing requirements. For this experiment, we place a MICAz mote close to the RX antenna of the jammer and start detecting its transmissions. The jammer schedules a jamming request as soon as an SFD is detected and initiates the transmission of the jamming signal. Using a second USRP2, we monitor and collect samples from the channel and measure the time from the end of the SFD and the beginning of the jamming signal. We use power envelope detection to identify the start of the packet and the start of

the jamming signal; the resulting t_{init} is the elapsed time between these two events, minus 4 µs from the detector.

The empirical CDF (ECDF) of the experimental results is shown in Fig. 4a. We observe a delay of $t_{\mathrm{init}} = 14.4$ µs on average, which is mainly caused by the firmware latency. For the summary of delay components, the RX/TX turnaround from the daughterboard accounts for 1 µs, a small number of FPGA cycles is spent in the TX DSP pipeline, the rest (and the deviations) is caused by the interrupt handling and the additional processing in the firmware.[5]

Necessary jamming durations. Another interesting parameter is the shortest duration t_{jam}^{min} necessary to achieve reliable jamming. Two MICAz motes are programmed as sender and receiver. To ensure that the jamming duration is the only factor in this performance measurement, the receiver is placed close to the jammer's TX antenna. For each jam duration we consider, we transmit 100 packets and measure the PRR at the receiver, with 10 repetitions each. We use a single-tone as the jamming waveform.

The experimental results are shown in Fig. 4b, 95 % confidence intervals are provided for the PRR means. The experiments show that a duration of approximately 26 µs is sufficient to reliably jam 802.15.4 transmissions. In theory, the destruction of a single symbol (16 µs) should be enough to cause a dropping probability of 93.75 % (there is still a 1 in 16 chance that the correct symbol is chosen), but due to symbol misalignments we require a slightly longer jamming duration to ensure interference with a complete symbol.

5.2 System Performance Evaluation

We evaluate our entire system in an indoor scenario to show that the system operates reliably even in challenging propagation environments.

Setting and methodology. The experiments are conducted in a 6 m × 6 m room. We measure the PRR in the presence of our reactive jammer for different positions of the receiver; here, we consider 72 positions arranged on a grid. We transmit 100 frames per position, giving an overall number of 7200 packets to jam in each experiment.

We use tone jamming, and several antenna configurations for the USRP2 jammer: for RX, an omnidirectional antenna is used, for TX we evaluate two antenna setups: *(i)* a second omnidirectional antenna, and *(ii)* a 13 dBi directional helix antenna. The helix antenna is expected to increase the

---

[4]In recent work, we extended this design to demodulate complete packets to get real-time access to their content.

[5]An improved implementation (that was available only after the review process) achieves faster and more deterministic results by using the softcore processor's internal interrupt handler instead of interrupt polling.

signal power at the receiver with its directional characteristics and to reduce the influence of antenna misalignments. The antennas are placed on one side of the room. We use two MICAz motes as sender and receiver, which are moved simultaneously with a constant distance of 1 m to provide them with excellent reception conditions.

Results. The ECDF of the different experiments is shown in Fig. 4c. For the omnidirectional TX antenna, 227 packets out of 7200 arrived at the receiver; the jammer has an average success rate of 96.85 %. The helix TX antenna boosts the success rate further; 168 arrived at the receiver, making an average success rate of 97.67 %. This shows that the antenna choice increases the jamming performance, yet not dramatically. Only few positions can be considered as problematic with a PRR of more than 5 % (18 % resp. 8 % of the positions in the experiments). Our analysis of missed packets showed that a jamming process can prevent a subsequent packet detection because of self-interference, because only a single board is used for both transmitting and receiving.

Two reactive jamming systems can be used concurrently to achieve better results, as this helps to minimize jamming opportunities missed by the system, and enables a better positioning of the TX antenna. No coordination is used, and both reactive jammers act independently when they detect incoming SFDs. The second TX antenna is placed on the other end of the room. This setup allowed only the reception of single packets at 3 different positions, a total of 3 packets was received in 7200 tries, resulting in a successful jamming rate of 99.96 %. This shows that redundancy is more powerful than the antenna choice in our scenario.

6. DISCUSSION

Our experimental results show that effective reactive jamming is in reach for an adversary. While our implementation presented here is specifically designed for 802.15.4, adaptations for different technologies are mainly a matter of exchanging the detector for different standards, and choosing an effective jamming waveform. Probably, the most crucial factor remains the reaction time. Nevertheless, when considering other technologies, the duration of an ACK frame for 802.11g (without legacy devices) is $t_{packet} \approx 30\,\mu s$, while our current prototype implementation reacts in $20\,\mu s$. This shows that even high-speed communication standards such as WLAN can be targeted with the system described here.

Turning bad news into good ones, we remark that our results also support recent research activities, which discuss that jamming does not only belong to an attacker but can also protect devices in the network from receiving malicious transmissions [11]. In previous work [8], we showed that injection attacks against WSNs can be mitigated in a cooperative manner by jamming packets with suspicious signal fingerprints. As we considered standard sensor motes in our experiments, a special admission frame prior to the actual data frames was necessary to relax the timing constraints in order to decouple the jamming decision from the actual jamming process. With a reactive jammer, such a protection scheme is conceivable for unmodified systems. By using different detectors, various jamming triggers can be defined, such as a full demodulation of the transmission to access the packet's content. This would also allow for a sophisticated real-time classification of packets [13], e.g., by address fields, ACKs only, or by the signal's physical properties such as the direction of arrival, device location, or RF fingerprints.

7. CONCLUSION

In this work we justified that real-time reactive jamming based on the software-defined radio paradigm is feasible and must be considered a realistic threat. Our analysis is based on a prototype implementation, which achieves a high precision of reactive jamming even if using low-cost COTS hardware such as the USRP2. Using this prototype, we provided insights to the causes for loss, and offered guidelines for successful reactive jamming against WSNs with an experimental study on physical layer effects. We evaluated the performance of our prototype system in a realistic MICAz testbed, and showed that the proposed system design offers not only a high precision but also the possibility of adapting the system to new requirements, such as reactively jamming 802.11 networks. In summary, the goal of this work was to practically demonstrate that reactive jamming should be considered as a weapon in the arsenal of the attacker. Thus research in jamming countermeasures becomes an even more important and delicate research issue in the future.

8. REFERENCES

[1] E. Bayraktaroglu, C. King, X. Liu, G. Noubir, R. Rajaraman, and B. Thapa. On the performance of IEEE 802.11 under jamming. In *Proc. of IEEE INFOCOM*, pages 1265–1273, Apr. 2008.

[2] J. T. Chiang and Y.-C. Hu. Cross-layer jamming detection and mitigation in wireless broadcast networks. *IEEE/ACM Transactions on Networking*, 19(1):286–298, Feb. 2011.

[3] R. Gummadi, D. Wetherall, B. Greenstein, and S. Seshan. Understanding and mitigating the impact of RF interference on 802.11 networks. In *Proc. of ACM SIGCOMM*, pages 385–396, Aug. 2007.

[4] IEEE Computer Society. IEEE Standard 802.15.4-2006: Wireless medium access control and physical layer (PHY) specifications for low-rate wireless personal area networks (WPANs). http://www.ieee802.org/11/, Sept. 2006.

[5] Y. W. Law, M. Palaniswami, L. V. Hoesel, J. Doumen, P. Hartel, and P. Havinga. Energy-efficient link-layer jamming attacks against wireless sensor network MAC protocols. *ACM Transactions on Sensor Networks*, 5(1):6:1–38, Feb. 2009.

[6] M. Li, I. Koutsopoulos, and R. Poovendran. Optimal jamming attacks and network defense policies in wireless sensor networks. In *Proc. of IEEE INFOCOM*, pages 1307–1315, May 2007.

[7] G. Lin and G. Noubir. On link layer denial of service in data wireless LANs. *Wireless Communications and Mobile Computing*, 5(3):273–284, May 2005.

[8] I. Martinovic, P. Pichota, and J. B. Schmitt. Jamming for good: a fresh approach to authentic communication in WSNs. In *Proc. of ACM WiSec*, pages 161–168, Mar. 2009.

[9] G. Nychis, T. Hottelier, Z. Yang, S. Seshan, and P. Steenkiste. Enabling MAC protocol implementations on software-defined radios. In *Proc. of USENIX NSDI*, pages 91–105, Apr. 2009.

[10] N.-J. Oh and S.-G. Lee. Building a 2.4-GHz radio transceiver using IEEE 802.15.4. *IEEE Circuits and Devices Magazine*, 21(6):43–51, Nov. 2005.

[11] K. Pelechrinis, M. Iliofotou, and S. V. Krishnamurthy. Denial of service attacks in wireless networks: The case of jammers. *IEEE Communications Surveys & Tutorials*, PP(99):1–13, second quarter 2011 (to appear).

[12] R. A. Poisel. *Modern communications jamming principles and techniques*. Artech House Publishers, Boston, MA, Nov. 2003.

[13] A. Proaño and L. Lazos. Selective jamming attacks in wireless networks. In *Proc. of IEEE ICC*, pages 1–6, May 2010.

[14] T. Schmid. GNU Radio 802.15.4 en- and decoding. Technical Report TR-UCLA-NESL-200609-06, UCLA NESL, Sept. 2006.

[15] M. Strasser, B. Danev, and S. Čapkun. Detection of reactive jamming in sensor networks. *ACM Transactions on Sensor Networks*, 7(2):16:1–29, Aug. 2010.

[16] A. D. Wood and J. A. Stankovic. Denial of service in sensor networks. *IEEE Computer*, 35(10):54–62, Oct. 2002.

[17] W. Xu, W. Trappe, Y. Zhang, and T. Wood. The feasibility of launching and detecting jamming attacks in wireless networks. In *Proc. of ACM MobiHoc*, pages 46–57, May 2005.

Short Paper: Security Evaluation of IEEE 802.11w Specification

Md. Sohail Ahmad
R&D, AirTight Networks
Pinnac House 2, S.No: 7, Kothrud,

Pune - 38, Maharashtra, India
+91-20-66407009

md.ahmad@airtightnetworks.com

Shashank Tadakamadla
R&D, AirTight Networks
Pinnac House 2, S.No: 7, Kothrud,

Pune - 38, Maharashtra, India
+91-20-66407011

shashank.t@airtightnetworks.com

ABSTRACT
The IEEE 802.11w amendment for protected management frame has been finalized. The main purpose of this new amendment is to reduce the susceptibility of Wi-Fi networks to various DoS attacks. In this paper, we scrutinize the resilience of 802.11w amendment against known disconnection based DoS attacks. Our analysis of the IEEE 802.11w reveals that new attributes introduced in this amendment can be misused to cause serious disruption in 802.11 wireless networks. We present results to verify our analysis and discuss possible remediation of the reported problems.

Categories and Subject Descriptors
C.2.1 [**Computer – Communication Networks**]: Network Architecture and Design - Wireless Communication

General Terms
Security, Reliability.

Keywords
IEEE 802.11w, IEEE 802.11i, IEEE 802.1x, DoS, Jamming attack, Deadlock.

1. INTRODUCTION
Wireless Fidelity (Wi-Fi) technology that we are using today is not same as it was a decade ago. It has undergone several amendments over the last few years and one of such amendments is 802.11i. Wired Equivalent Privacy (WEP), which was the only security configuration present in the original standard, was found to be broken. Hence, IEEE made an amendment in the year 2004 to enhance the data security and user authentication mechanism. But, it was not designed to solve disruptions created by unauthorized or malicious wireless device present in the network [3]. Soon it was realized that such disruptions in wireless networks could also facilitate succeeding various other attacks e.g. Man-in-the-Middle (MITM) attack or dictionary attack.

Initially, management frames did not contain sensitive information and hence their protection was less desired. But with new fast handoff, radio resource measurement, discovery and wireless network management schemes (provided in the upcoming 802.11r, 802.11k and 802.11v drafts), new and more sensitive information about wireless networks is being exchanged in management frames. The IEEE task force proposed a new amendment 802.11w, which was targeted to protect wireless connections and network sensitive information exchanged in management frames. The 802.11w amendment was ratified in 2009.

Security evaluations and results presented in this paper are based on the final approved version of the IEEE 802.11w specification [1] and its open source software [2] implementation. In this paper, we include the test results from our experiments of Denial-of-Service (DoS) attacks against 802.11w.

The rest of the paper is organized as follows. In Section 2, we present the details of 802.11w which are most relevant to DoS attack mitigation. In Section 3, we briefly discuss about known DoS attacks on pre-802.11w wireless networks and then present our analysis of new DoS vulnerabilities in 802.11w. In Section 4, information related to the experiment test bed and its results are presented. In Section 5, we briefly discuss the possible remediation of DoS attacks on 802.11w networks. Finally, we conclude with a summary of our findings and provide directions for future research.

2. IEEE 802.11w
Before 802.11w, only data frames could be protected in Wi-Fi and all other frames such as management and control frames were used without any protection. 802.11w amendment has allowed the use of a few management frames with protection. These are called Robust Management (RM) frames. RM frames include *Deauthentication, D*isassociation and *Action m*anagement frames. The 802.11w ratified standard assigns three key security properties to RM frames - *Data Origin Authenticity, Replay Detection,* and *Management Frame Protection (MFP)*.

The *Data Origin Authenticity* defines a mechanism by which a station that receives an RM frame can determine which station has transmitted that frame. This property is required to prevent one station from masquerading as another station. Data origin authenticity is only applicable to unicast Robust Management Frames. The 802.11w does not guarantee data origin authenticity for broadcast/multicast RM frames. The *Replay Detection*

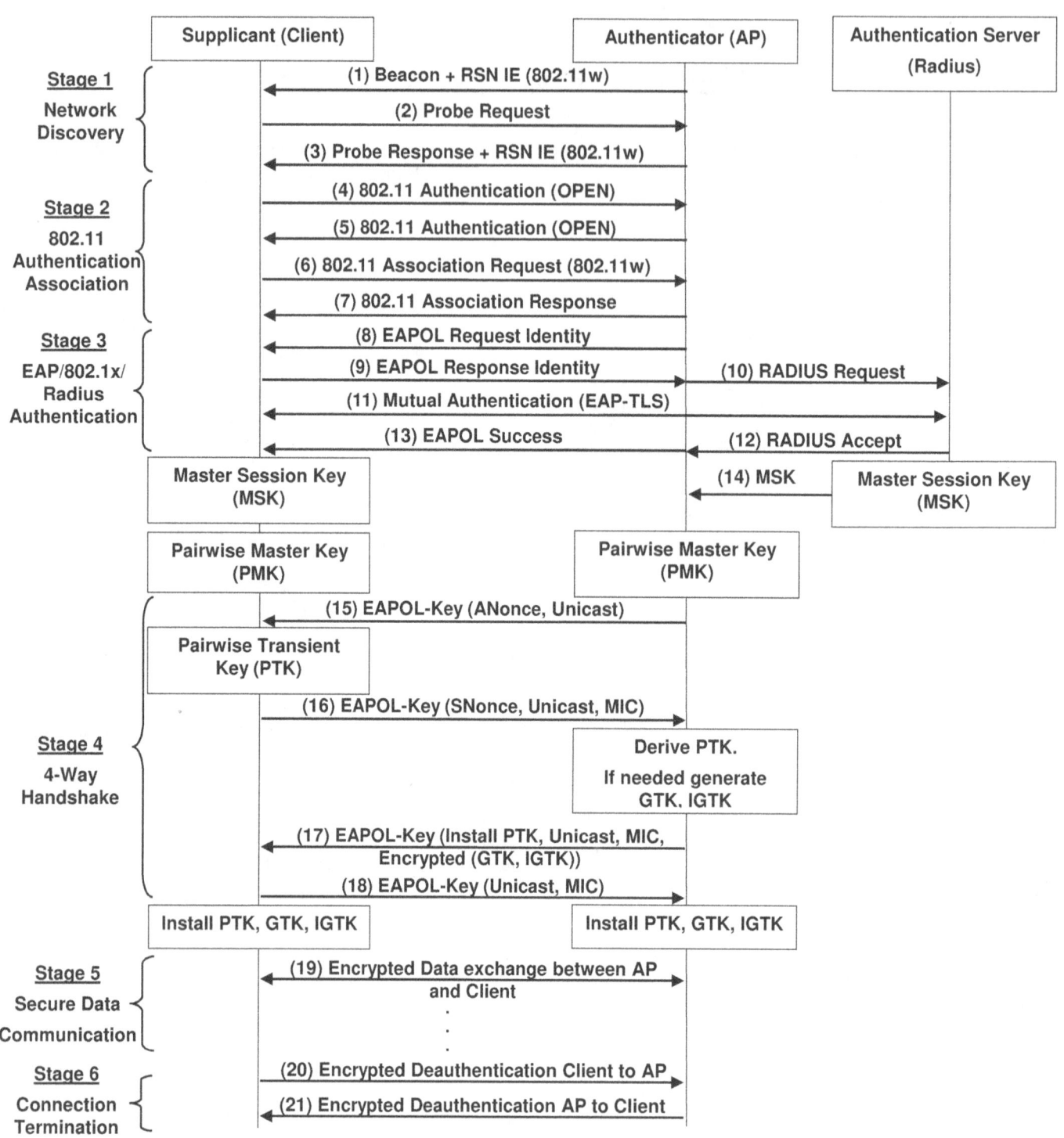

Figure 1. RSNA Connection Establishment, Authentication and Termination Procedure

mechanism defines a means by which a station that receives an RM frame can detect whether the received frame is a replayed transmission or not. *MFP* is required in the Robust Security Network Association (RSNA) to protect against data forgery and eavesdropping. MFP rules are applied only after the Pairwise Transient Key (PTK) for protection of unicast frames is established. The rules are applied to broadcast/multicast frames only after the group keys to protect broadcast/multicast frames are installed. A new encryption key called Integrity Group Transient Key (IGTK) has been introduced in 802.11w to provide message integrity protection for group addressed RM frames. IGTK is generated by an AP and is shared among all associated clients. RM frames transmitted or received by a client before security keys are installed are unprotected. Below, we briefly describe key properties of 802.11w protocol.

All 802.11i capable devices advertise Robust Security Network (RSN) Information Element (IE) in selective management frames. AP advertises its 802.11i capability in Beacon, Probe Response frames while client advertises in (Re)Association Request and EAPOL frames. 802.11w capability of a device is advertised in the RSN capabilities field of RSN IE which is two bytes field. Two reserved bits of RSN capabilities have been chosen to advertise following two new 802.11w specific parameters:

(a) Management Frame Protection Required (MFPR) - Bit number 6 of RSN capabilities is assigned to announce MFPR. A wireless device sets this bit to 1 to advertise that protection of RM frames is mandatory.

(b) Management Frame Protection Capable (MFPC) - Bit number 7 of RSN capabilities is assigned to announce MFPR. A wireless device sets this bit to 1 to advertise that protection of RM frames is enabled.

Figure 1 illustrates complete RSNA establishment and termination procedure in an 802.11w enabled Wi-Fi network. Frames numbered (1) to (3) represent 11w specific network and security capability discovery phase. AP advertises its 11w capability in frame number (1) and (3). Frames numbered (4) to (7) depict 802.11 authentication and association phase. Client advertises its 11w capability in frame number (7). Remaining all frame exchange is similar to 802.11i as explained in [5] except frame number (17) in which AP also sends IGTK along with GTK to the client and frame number (20), (21) in which connection termination is done using protected RM frames.

Broadcast/Multicast Integrity Protocol (BIP) is used in 802.11w to provide data integrity and replay protection of broadcast/multicast RM frames. BIP uses AES-128 in Cipher-based MAC (CMAC) mode. All group addressed RM frames include Management MIC Information Element (MMIE). MMIE is used to provide message integrity and replay protection. All clients present in an 802.11w enabled BSS, receives IGTK, Packet Number (IPN), Key ID, and IGTK at the end of 4-way EAPOL handshake. IPN is a monotonically increasing 6 bytes number. AP inserts a new IPN into the MMIE IPN field every time it generates a group addressed RM frame. IPN field is used by clients to detect replayed frames.

Unicast RM frames are protected similar to unicast data frames using PTK which is unique for each client and is generated per session. When RM frame protection is enabled and the 4-Way handshake is completed, all the RM frames that are transmitted are encrypted.

Broadcast/Multicast RM frames are protected by BIP as explained in paragraph above. It uses IGTK to encrypt the content of management frame.

(Re)Association Request frame based DoS attack in an 802.11i enabled wireless network is a known problem [7]. It has also

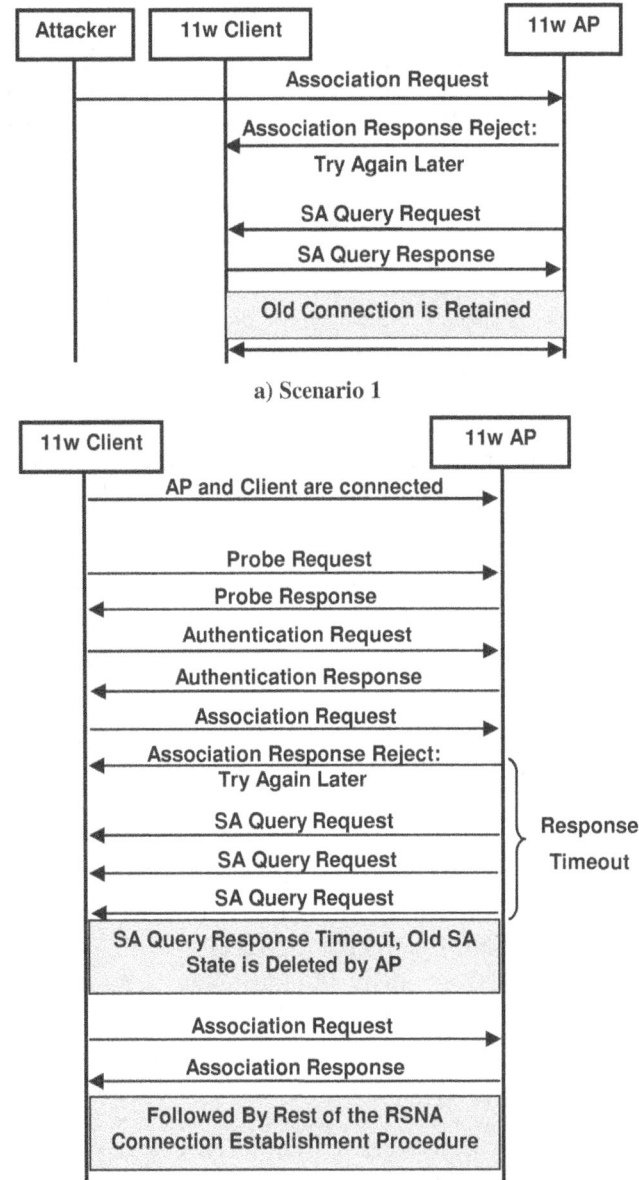

a) Scenario 1

b) Scenario 2

Figure 2. Possible Scenarios of SA Query

been studied in the context of 802.11w. It has been found that more severe DoS attacks can be launched in 802.11w networks as it creates a deadlock condition also known as Security Association *(SA) termination* problem [1]. In order to solve SA termination problem, a new security state verification procedure has been introduced in 802.11w, which is known as SA Query procedure. SA Query procedure uses two newly introduced action management frames called *SA Query Request* and *SA Query Response*. These are RM frames; hence they are always protected using PTK.

SA Query Request is sent by an AP whenever there is a need to synchronize the SA state with an associated client. An AP sends

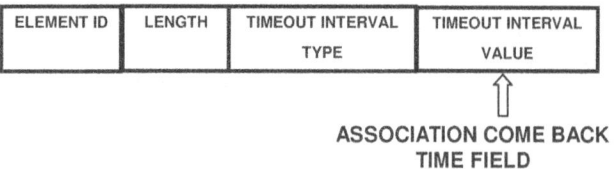

ELEMENT ID	LENGTH	TIMEOUT INTERVAL TYPE	TIMEOUT INTERVAL VALUE

ASSOCIATION COME BACK
TIME FIELD

Figure 3. Time Information Element (TIE)

SA Query Request upon receiving a (Re)Association Request frame for a client whose SA state is present in the AP. If the client is active and its SA state is still valid, then client decrypts SA Query Request message using its PTK. The client transmits SA Query Response to the AP. This helps the AP in two scenarios as shown in Figure 2. In scenario 1, an attacker tries to delete legitimate client's SA state by sending spoofed (Re)Association Request frame. In scenario 2, a wireless client re-starts and tries to re-establish a fresh security association with the AP.

A new IE called Time Information Element (TIE) has been introduced in 802.11w. TIE is shown in figure 3. TIE is present in all (Re)Association Response frames which are sent with status code 30 (0x1E). This is an indication for the connecting client that association is rejected temporarily and it should try again after sometime. Timeout Interval Value (TIV), also known as *Comeback Time* is 4 octets field and the value is interpreted in milliseconds (ms). Default value present in TIV is 1000ms. Maximum value that TIV can hold is 4294967295ms which is equivalent to approximately 50 calendar days.

3. ANALYSIS OF DoS ATTACK RESILIENCE OF IEEE 802.11w

In the simplest scenario, a DoS attack can be launched by continually injecting disconnection frames e.g. Deauthentication and Disassociation frames. Apart from these two types of frames, a few 802.11w implementations have been found vulnerable to other types of frames as well. These are spoofed management or data frames and that desynchronize the state machine of a victim wireless device resulting into connection termination or loss of data service [3][4][6].

3.1 Known Disconnection Based DoS Attacks

Authentication attack is launched by listening to the traffic and learning the MAC addresses of a victim AP and an associated client. Thereafter, an attacker forges an Authentication frame and transmits it either from the client to the AP or from the AP to the client to cause disconnection. 802.11w does not provide any protection to the Authentication frame.

(Re)Association Request/Response frame based attack is launched by listening to the traffic and learning the MAC addresses of a victim AP and an associated client. Thereafter, an attacker forges a (Re)Association Request/Response frame and transmit it either from the client to the AP or from the AP to the Client to cause disconnection. As we have mentioned earlier in section 2, 802.11w provides a mechanism to deal with spoofed (Re)Association Request frame based attack.

Deauthentication/Disassociation attack is launched by listening to the traffic and learning the MAC addresses of an AP and an

associated client. Thereafter, an attacker forges a Deauthentication or a Disassociation frame and transmits it either to the client or to the AP to cause disconnection. Deauthentication attack is more efficient than Disassociation attack because it requires more work for the station to return back to the associated state. 802.11w has introduced protection for Deauthentication/Disassociation management frame to prevent this attack.

EAPOL frames are exploited to launch DoS attack in an 802.11i enabled BSS. An adversary forges EAPOL-Start messages and injects it repeatedly to prevent 802.1x authentication from succeeding or forges EAPOL-Logoff message and sends to an AP in order to delete 802.1x authentication state of an already authenticated and associated client.

Jamming attack can also be launched by physically (RF) or virtually (NAV) [3][6] jamming the channel. The attack is very disruptive in nature as it affects wireless devices present on affected channels regardless of their BSSID. 802.11w does not provide any fix for this type of attack.

3.2 New DoS Attacks against 802.11w

During our 802.11w evaluation, we identified a few weaknesses in the protocol which can be exploited by an attacker to disrupt or break the wireless connections of legitimate users. In this section, we present three such weaknesses of 802.11w:

First type of vulnerability that is present in 802.11w enabled BSS is **BIP vulnerability**. BIP only provides data integrity and replay protection to broadcast and multicast addressed RM frames. It uses IGTK, which is shared by all clients associated to an AP. All broadcast and multicast addressed RM frames are only transmitted by an AP. Since all radio communication from client to AP is unicast, hence, in a normal protocol operation, clients do not use IGTK for broadcast RM frame encryption and transmission. A malicious wireless client having knowledge of IGTK can misuse it to create protected broadcast Deauthentication or Disassociation frames and launch insider DoS attack.

Second type of attack is **SA Query Manipulation** attack. The attack desynchronizes the SA state of an associated client and an AP and thereby ceases the data service operation. In this attack, an attacker artificially triggers SA Query procedure on an AP by injecting spoofed (Re)Association Request frame on behalf of an associated and authenticated client. The attacker jams the client to prevent it from sending SA Query Response. By doing this attacker is able to delete the SA state of the associated client. This is achieved by launching virtual jamming or NAV attack [2]. The AP remains unaffected from the attack and is able to transmit all SA Query Request frames as receiver address (RA) of NAV attack frames contains AP's hardware address. Since the attacker knows the time needed by the AP to complete the SA Query procedure, the client is jammed slightly more than SA Query procedure timeout period to ensure that replies from the client never reaches to the AP. Figure 4 depicts SA Query manipulation attack. Deletion of SA state on the AP creates *Deadlock* condition as the AP is unable to decrypt encrypted data packets coming from the client. The AP attempts to notify client by sending Deauthentication frames with a reason code 7 *(Class 3 frame received from non-associated STA)*. These notification frames are sent unprotected due to the absence of

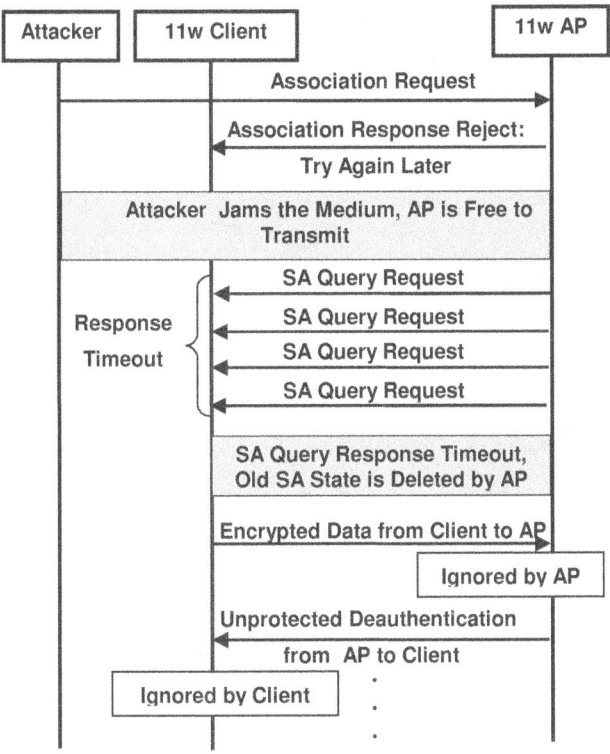

Figure 4. SA Query Manipulation Attack

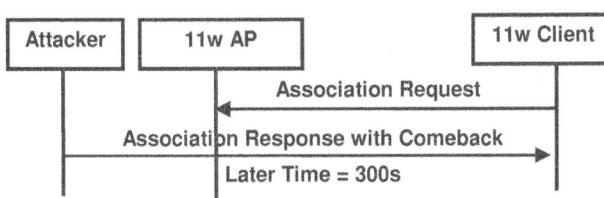

Figure 5. Association Starvation Attack

security key on the AP and hence they get ignored by the victim client. Hereafter, there is no way left for the client and the AP to re-synchronize their state. This situation of the AP and the client is referred as Deadlock.

The weakness of SA query procedure has also been discussed in [4] and the use of RF jamming has been suggested to achieve the end effect. While devising the above mentioned attack, it is important to ensure that client does not disconnect and delete its SA state which is hard to achieve by launching RF jamming attack as client immediately disconnects from the AP due to loss of *Beacon* frames from the AP.

Third type of attack that is possible in 802.11w based BSS is **Association Starvation** attack. This attack exploits the TIE field introduced in (Re)Association Response frames. TIE transmitted in (Re)Association Response frames serves the purpose of informing the connecting client that the AP requires some time to complete the SA Query procedure and after how long the AP will be ready to accept the association from the same client. Since (Re)Association Response frame is unprotected, an

attacker creates a fake (Re)Association Response frame with failure status code (30) and TIE containing very high comeback time and send it to the legitimate client. The client honors TIE value and does not try to associate with the AP for the duration mentioned in the TIE. Figure 5 depicts the association starvation attack.

4. EXPERIMENT SETUP

All attacks discussed in this paper were implemented using off-the-shelf hardware and freely available software. We have selected *Hostapd, Wpa_supplicant,* and *ath9k* software which implements 802.11w to evaluate its resilience against known and newly identified DoS attacks.

4.1 Test Setup

Two Fedora 11 running laptops and Atheros chipset based client cards (D-link DWA-645 and DWA-652) were used to setup 11w AP and 11w client. Hostapd software version 0.7.3 and wpa_supplicnat software version 0.7.3 were used to create 802.11w capable BSS. Cisco Aironet a/b/g client adapter (AIR-CB21AGE- K9) and a Backtrack 2 running laptop were used to launch DoS attack. We have used wireshark-inject version 0.99.4 to inject attack frames. All experiments were conducted in 2.4 GHz band in 11g mode. The only legitimate traffic on the wireless network was ICMP Ping traffic flowing between 11w AP and 11w client.

Table 1. Results of Known DoS Attacks

Attack Frame Type	Open Source 802.11w
Deauthentication	No
Disassociation	No
Authentication	No
Association Request	No
Re-association Request	No
Association Response	No
Re-association Response	No
EAPOL-Start	No
EAPOL-Logoff	Yes
Jamming Attack	Yes

Table 2. Results of IEEE 802.11w Specific DoS Attacks

Attack Frame Type	Open Source 802.11w
BIP Vulnerability	Yes
SA Query Manipulation Attack	Yes (Deadlock)
Association Starvation Attack	Yes

4.2 Test Results

In Table 1, we have presented the test results of known DoS attacks. In Table 2, test results of newly discovered attacks are presented. "Yes" indicates that the client either gets disconnected from the AP or data service offered to associated clients stop when an attack is launched. "No" indicates that there is no effect on AP-client association state or data service offered to associated clients when an attack is launched.

5. DISCUSSION

The results from theoretical analysis and experiments in the previous sections show that an 802.11w enabled wireless network is still vulnerable to two known and three new DoS attacks presented in this paper. RF jamming and EAPOL – Logoff are known DoS attacks which are not addressed in 802.11w. We identified three new weaknesses/vulnerabilities in the 802.11w. The same was experimentally verified using open source implementation of 802.11w and results are presented in Table 2. Below, we briefly discuss the plausible solution of DoS attacks on 802.11w networks:

EAPOL-Logoff frame based wireless DoS attack is quite old yet 802.11w specification does not say anything about it. The attack can be avoided by not honoring unencrypted EAPOL-Logoff frames received from clients whose SA state is valid on the AP.

BIP vulnerability gives rise to an insider DoS attack. The problem can be addressed by disallowing the use of BIP for Deauthentication and Disassociation frames.

SA Query Manipulation attack creates deadlock between an AP and an associated client and ceases data service operation. This occurs when an AP deletes PTKSA and changes the SA state of an associated client without sending protected disconnection notification to the client. This desynchronizes the state of the AP and the client. The deadlock problem can be resolved by making it mandatory to send protected Deauthentication or Disassociation notification frame even if no SA Query Response is received and SA Query procedure indicates that the client has already deleted PTKSA.

In case of **Association Starvation** attack, 802.11w specification does not provide any guidelines to client when it receives Association Response frame with TIE. By honoring the TIE field, a client becomes vulnerable to Association Starvation attack as discussed in section 3. To fix this problem, 802.11w implementation of client should be such that association rejection sent by the AP is honored by the client but the comeback later value present in TIE is not used to control the client's re-try of connection handshake with the same AP. This will at least ensure that the client is not starved for long and the connection handshake succeeds with the AP at the end of SA Query procedure.

6. CONCLUSION AND FUTURE WORK

In this paper we analyzed and tested the tolerance of 802.11w amendment against known disconnection based DoS attacks. We also identified three new weaknesses in 802.11w and verified against a real 802.11w enabled wireless network. We believe that these weaknesses could be exploited in future to create disruptions in a Wi-Fi network and hence would defeat the purpose of the amendment.

BIP vulnerability based insider DoS attack is similar to conventional DoS attack and hence there is no difference in the number of frames required to run a DoS attack, for, say one minute. For SA Query manipulation attack to succeed, jamming attack frame needs to be injected for SA query timeout interval which is by default one second. Association starvation attack requires injection of a few attack frames at the time of 802.11 association phase as attack frames need to reach client before legitimate association response from an AP.

Conventional wireless DoS attacks typically require continual injection of disconnection frames, but the newly identified association starvation attack, presented in this paper, has potential to drastically reduce injection rate of disconnection frames, as the successful starvation attack puts client to sleep mode for several seconds.

The good news is that all three new weaknesses of 802.11w and EAPOL-Logoff attack presented in this paper can be addressed by software modification. Solution to SA Query manipulation attack presented in this paper only addresses deadlock problem. It does not try to solve the SA termination. We believe that retaining SA of a client with an AP in presence of RF jamming or Virtual jamming is of great importance even though no data service can be made available to the client. The reason is that once a client is disconnected, various other attacks can be launched, in fact unprotected Deauthentication and Disassociation frames can be continually injected to completely knockout the client from an 802.11w enabled wireless network.

In future, we plan to work on the SA retaining strategies in an 802.11w enabled wireless network in the presence of jamming attack.

7. REFERENCES

[1] IEEE Standard for Information Technology – Telecommunications and information exchange between systems – Local and metropolitan area networks – Specific requirements. Wireless LAN Medium Access Control (MAC) and Physical Layer (PHY) Specifications. Amendment 4: Protected Management Frames. IEEE Std. 802.11w-2009, September 2009.

[2] http://hostap.epitest.fi/hostapd/

[3] John Bellardo, Stefen Savage, "*802.11 Denial-Of-Service attacks: Real Vulnerabilities and Practical Solutions,*" In Proceedings of the 12th conference on USENIX Security Symposium – Volume12, Pages 15-28, 2003.

[4] Matrin Eian, "*Fragility Of Robust Security Network: 802.11 Denial Of Service*", ACNS 2009, LNCS 5536, Pages 400–416, 2009

[5] Changhua He, John C Mitchell, "*Security Analysis and Improvements for IEEE 802.11i*", In Proceedings of the 12th Annual Network and Distributed System Security Symposium, Pages 90-110, 2005

[6] Wenyuan Xu, Wade Trappe, Yangyong Zhang, Timothy Wood, "*The Feasibility Of Launching and Detecting Jamming Attacks in Wireless Networks*", In ACM MobiHoc, Pages 46-57, 2005.

[7] Md Sohail Ahmad, JVR Murthy, and Amit Vartak, "*Autoimmunity Disorder in Wireless LANs*", Defcon 16, 2009.

Inferring Users' Online Activities Through Traffic Analysis

Fan Zhang[1,3], Wenbo He[1], Xue Liu[2] and Patrick G. Bridges[4]
Department of Electrical Engineering, University of Nebraska-Lincoln, NE, USA[1]
School of Computer Science, McGill University, Montreal, Quebec, Canada[2]
Department of Electronics and Information, Huazhong University of Sci. & Tech., Wuhan, China[3]
Department of Computer Science, University of New Mexico, Albuquerque, NM, USA[4]
fzhang2@unl.edu, wenbohe@engr.unl.edu, xueliu@cs.mcgill.ca, bridges@cs.unm.edu

ABSTRACT

Traffic analysis may threaten user privacy, even if the traffic is encrypted. In this paper, we use IEEE 802.11 wireless local area networks (WLANs) as an example to show that inferring users' online activities accurately by traffic analysis without the administrator's privilege is possible during very short periods (e.g., a few seconds). The online activities we investigated include web browsing, chatting, online gaming, downloading, uploading and video watching, etc. We implement a hierarchical classification system based on machine learning algorithms to discover what a user is doing on his/her computer. Furthermore, we conduct experiments in different network environments (e.g., at home, on university campus, and in public areas) with different application scenarios to evaluate the performance of the classification system. Results show that our system can distinguish different online applications on the accuracy of about 80% in 5 seconds and over 90% accuracy if the eavesdropping lasts for 1 minute.

Categories and Subject Descriptors

C.2.0 [**Information Systems Applications**]: General—*Security and Protection*

General Terms

Experimentation, Security

Keywords

Traffic Analysis, Privacy, Users' Online Activities, Machine Learning

1. INTRODUCTION

Traffic analysis attacks on encrypted traffic are often referred to as *side-channel information leaks*. Although the privacy threat of side-channel information leaks has been discovered in various applications, including web browsing [1,

2], secure shell (SSH) [3], keystroke dynamics [4], video-streaming [5] and voice-over-IP (VoIP) [6, 7], these investigations are based mostly on an implicit assumption that the adversary knows a user's online activity (i.e., the particular network application or service that a user is running). Actually, a user's online activity is highly private and sensitive information. Users usually do not want strangers, their parents, guardians, supervisors, bosses or peers to track their online activities. Furthermore, it is more risky if the technique inferring users' online activities is combined with the previous study on side-channel information leaks.

Nowadays, due to the shared-medium of wireless links and the ease of eavesdropping in WLANs, traffic traces that users sent over wireless links are almost exposed to adversaries. In this paper, we investigate the user privacy breach on *users' online activities* by analyzing *encrypted MAC-layer* traffic. We attempt to infer users' online activities in real time by using no more information than packet size, timing and direction. It is a challenging task to do this accurately with such limited information, especially among a wide range of network applications, such as web browsing, online chatting, online gaming, downloading, uploading, online video and BitTorrent. Although traffic features (e.g., average packet size, frequency of a frame and average interval-arrival time) between low bandwidth consumption and high bandwidth consumption applications are identifiable (e.g., chatting vs. downloading), similar applications have very fine distinction, especially under time-varying network environments, different users' online habits and software. In our work, we show that traffic, even from the same application, varies largely among different environments. We also consider *concurrent* online activities. In this case, traffic features in one application may be submerged by another application; and the changeable features make the accurate identification of users' online activities even more difficult.

To overcome the above challenges, we explore an *online hierarchical classification system* based on machine learning (ML) techniques to map traffic features to the online activities and show that an adversary is able to infer and track what the user is doing during very short periods (e.g. a few seconds) without any information about the protocols, software and servers the user is using. Specifically, our classification system performs *multiclass classification* by taking advantage of both the efficient computation of decision tree structure and the high classification accuracy of Support Vector Machine (SVM) and Neural Network (NN) algorithms. Traffic features adopted in the classification system are only based on packet-level statistical values, such as average packet size and average interarrival time etc., in the MAC layer. We conduct experiments in different network environments (e.g., at home, on university campus and in public areas) with different application scenarios to evaluate the classification system. Results show that the proposed classification system achieves good accuracy in noisy environments, distinguishes online activities with around 80% accuracy in 5 seconds, and with over 90% accuracy if the eavesdropping duration lasts for 1 minute. We hope that our work will alert LAN users, network designers, and administrators that there is a serious privacy breach of users' online activities.

The rest of this paper is organized as follows. We summarize the related work in Section 2. Section 3 overviews the background and challenges. We present the design of the online hierarchical classification system in Section 4. Then we demonstrate the experiments conducted at home, on campus and in public networks to evaluate the accuracy of our classification system in Section 5. Section 6 discusses the implication issues. Finally, we conclude the paper in Section 7.

2. RELATED WORK

Side-channel Information Leaks: Side-channel information leaks have been researched widely. Encrypted traffic does not prevent traffic analysis attacks, thus user privacy is still vulnerable. Liberatore, et al. [8] present a straightforward traffic analysis attack against encrypted HTTP streams to identify the source of the traffic, and the authors in [2, 9] do similar webpage fingerprinting. Chen, et al. [1] find that significant traffic distinctions of different webpages help an adversary to wiretap what the user is browsing. Moreover, the lengths of encrypted VoIP packets can be used to identify the phrases spoken within a call [7]. In addition, adversaries may adopt wireless signal strength in multiple monitoring locations to obtain an accurate estimation of a user's location and motion behind walls [10, 11]. Srinivasan, et al. [12] show that a Fingerprint And Timing-based Snooping (FATS) attack can observe private activities, such as cooking, showering, and using the toilet, by eavesdropping on the wireless transmissions of sensors in a home. However, the above research rarely concerns the privacy regarding users' online activities.

Traffic Classification: Traffic classification is mostly employed by network administrators to monitor network traffic and identify Internet applications. These applications are mostly described based on protocol behaviors, such as HTTP, SMTP, FTP, SSH and DNS, etc. But nowadays, many applications are able to run over one protocol. For example, web browsing, chatting, online gaming, downloading, watching online video, etc., can be executed in HTTP protocol. Hence, we focus on the users' online activities which may have more sensitive information than protocol behaviors.

In addition, traffic classification usually uses traffic features in or beyond the IP layer, such as IP address, TCP port, protocol fingerprinting, etc. Few are implemented only by features in the MAC layer. But compared with the difficulty of getting traffic from the routers, gateways or servers without the administrator's privilege, the easy way is for an adversary to eavesdrop on the traffic in the MAC layer. Thus in this paper, we investigate traffic classification on encrypted traffic in the MAC layer.

The traditional identification techniques, the *port-based approach*, *payload-based approach* and *host-behavior-based approach* [13] are no longer valid in the MAC layer. The *port-based approach* relies on the well-known ports registered by the Internet Assigned Numbers Authority (IANA) [14], and the *payload-based approach* is based on features of the payload [15]. But this information is undetectable in the MAC-layer due to the MAC-layer encryption. Similarly, the *host-behavior-based approach* [16, 17] can not be used without end-to-end information about host connections, such as port, IP address, etc. Instead, we employ a *flow-feature-based approach* which is based on *machine learning (ML)* techniques for the MAC-layer traffic classification.

Recently, Wright, et al. [18, 19] and Dainotti, et al. [20] propose packet-level classification approaches based on the features, packet interarrival time and payload size. Our classification approach is different from the above approaches in a few important ways. (1) The evaluation in [18, 19, 20] is based on traffic flows, which means that packets in a flow belong to an application. In contrast, we do not know which flow or application an encrypted frame belongs to in the MAC layer. (2) In terms of different time-varying wireless environments, the traffic varies largely. Thus, we evaluate our classification system at home, on campus and in a public area. (3) Our classification system, which is based on different machine learning algorithms and features, gives an identification in real time (every 5 seconds). Nowadays, online classification methods [21, 22, 23, 24] rely on features of TCP/UDP and IP traffic. These features are unavailable in the MAC layer and can not be applied to the MAC-layer classification.

Machine Learning: Recently, researchers have adopted ML technologies in the flow-feature-based traffic classification. Nguyen et al. conduct a survey [13] in this area focusing on ML techniques, such as Bayesian techniques [25], k-nearest neighbor algorithm, decision tree (e.g., C4.5), NN and SVM [26]. Hidden Markov Model (HMM) is also employed in traffic analysis [7, 18, 20]. In this paper, we use two intelligent ML algorithms, SVM and NN, to identify seven popular online activities.

3. BACKGROUND AND CHALLENGES

3.1 Adversary Model

The shared-medium nature of WLANs poses privacy vulnerabilities on users' online activities. To track the traffic from and to a user, the adversary only needs to install sniffer software (e.g. Wireshark, Aircrack-ng). In this case, the network adapter passes all packets it receives to the adversary rather than just frames addressed to it. In this paper, we act as an adversary and use the *Intel Wireless WiFi Link 4965AGN* network cards with the *Libpcap* library to intercept specific users' traffic. The adversary does not know any information about the software and encryption schemes adopted by the users.

Figure 1 shows the working scenario of an adversary who adopts traffic classification to infer users' online activities. The adversary sniffs the WLAN in the same channel as the Access Point (AP). The classification system collects traffic samples of the whole network and knows how many users are in this WLAN. Then after the adversary inputs the MAC address of the user he wants to eavesdrop on, the classifica-

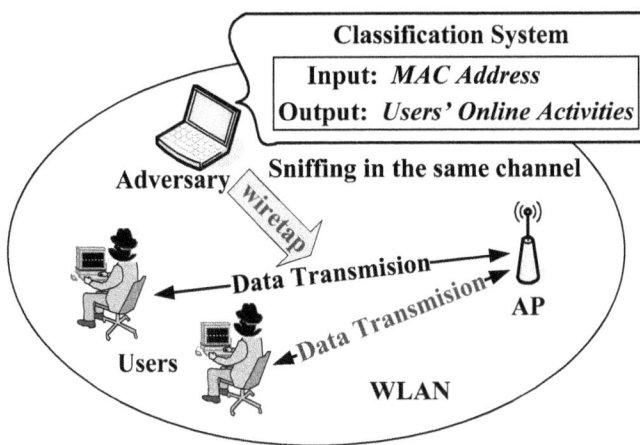

Figure 1: Adversary Model

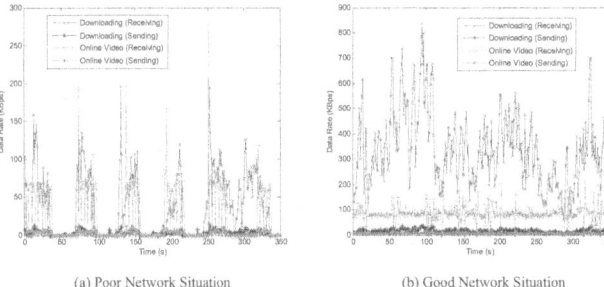

Figure 2: Data rate of the same applications in different network situations

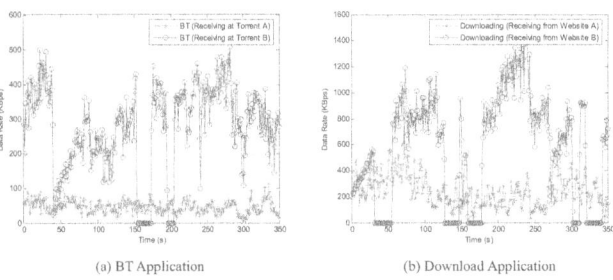

Figure 3: Data rate of the same applications from different servers

tion system identifies which online applications the user is running.

3.2 Challenges

Challenges for the MAC-layer traffic classification come from the following factors.

3.2.1 Limited Flow Features

Features for traffic classification in TCP/UDP and the IP layer can be obtained from packet headers, including the TCP port and IP address, payload information, SYN packet and protocol fingerprinting [13]. In contrast, valid information from the MAC layer is very limited, since MAC layer frames are usually encrypted. From the MAC header, we can find the MAC address, SSID (Service Set Identifier), directions of the traffic (receiving or sending), RF signal strength and frame types. Besides the header, we only get the packet-level data, such as frame size and its timestamp.

3.2.2 Noises in Traffic Features

Traffic patterns, even from the same application, can be easily affected by network situations, such as signal strength, available bandwidth, and service provider. Therefore, a MAC-layer flow of a given application may exhibit different features in different time slots, locations and network situations. From Figure 2, we can see that the data rate of the same applications (e.g., downloading or online video) fluctuates tremendously (even from 0 to 1MBps) in a very short time and differs markedly in different network situations. The data rate in Figure 2(b) with better network situations is much larger than that in Figure 2(a). In addition, the flow features may be affected by the attributes of an application, such as "who is running the application"; "which software is used by a user"; "the target content server (websites)",·etc. We download the same contents by BitTorrent (BT) and HTTP from different servers at the same time. As shown in Figure 3, the data rates widely diverge. This noise makes a highly accurate traffic classification difficult to achieve. Hence, it is hard to find standard or uniform parameters for classifiers in different situations.

3.2.3 Existence of Concurrent Applications

A user may open multiple application windows and perform multiple tasks on the Internet simultaneously. By wire-tapping on the traffic in the MAC layer, we only observe the aggregated traffic to and from a given user. Hence, using traffic analysis, it is very hard to know how many applications are running by a specific user and what bandwidth portion is allocated to individual applications. In addition, because the frames in the MAC layer are transmitted over the last hop, the end-to-end information, such as the relationship of frames between sending and corresponding responses is undetectable.

3.2.4 Dynamic Task Switch by Users

Because a user may continually switch his/her applications and each application may last for a short period of time, tracking users' activities requires that the system should map the traffic patterns to specific applications quickly and accurately without complete knowledge about the traffic. In addition, the classification model must be updated dynamically according to the time-varying network environments.

4. CLASSIFICATION METHODOLOGY

4.1 Data Collections

4.1.1 Data Set

We investigate seven popular network applications, including web browsing, chatting, online gaming, downloading, uploading, online video and BT, which are labeled from ① to ⑦. We list the applications and their variations in Table 1.

Multiple concurrent applications are also studied in this paper. In most of the cases, users do not run more than two applications in each short time (e.g., 5 seconds). Even if users run more than two, we can identify two main applications which have larger traffic loads in the concurrent traffic.

Table 1: Attributes of network applications

Applications	Software	Server (Website)
Browsing ①	IE, Mozilla Firefox	Yahoo, CNN, Amazon, Google, etc.
Chatting ②	MSN, QQ, Google Talk	MSN, Tencent, Google
Online Game ③	QQ Three Kingdoms, World of Warcraft	Tencent, WoW Servers
Downloading ④	HTTP	Ubuntu, Microsoft, Sun, etc.
Uploading ⑤	HTTP	YouTube, Facebook, Google, etc.
Online Video ⑥	HTTP or specific client	YouTube, MSN, etc.
BitTorrent ⑦ (Typical P2P File-sharing)	Bitcomet, Flashget, Xunlei, Linux BitTorrent Client	http://torrent.ubuntu.com, Xunlei, http://www.verycd.com/, etc.

Table 2: Features used in classification

data frames, control frames, management frames	data rate (receiving and sending)
	frame size (categories, mean, median, variance, ...)
	frame interarrival time (mean, median, variance, ...)
	frame size distribution ($> m$ bytes or $< m$ bytes) ($m = 100, 500, 1000, ...$)
	number of frames (receiving and sending)

Table 3: Features of seven applications (from AP to the user)

Applications	Average frame size (byte)	Average interarrival time (s)	Frame size distribution (>500bytes)
Browsing ①	1013.20	0.0284	64.617%
Chatting ②	269.06	0.9901	9.357%
Online Game ③	459.53	0.3084	34.501%
Downloading ④	1575.3	0.0028	99.951%
Uploading ⑤	132.76	0.0301	0.0307%
Online Video ⑥	1547.6	0.0119	99.560%
BitTorrent ⑦	962.04	0.0247	60.650%

Hence, we consider only two concurrent applications in this paper. They can be divided into three types: a large bandwidth consumption application plus a low bandwidth consumption application (e.g., downloading and chatting), two large bandwidth consumption applications (e.g., downloading and online video) and two small bandwidth consumption applications (e.g., browsing and chatting). The *six typical* combinations of the concurrent applications we selected in our experiments are browsing and chatting {①,②}, browsing and BT {①,⑦}, browsing and uploading {①,⑤}, chatting and downloading {②,④}, downloading and video {④,⑥}, video and BT {⑥,⑦}.

The traffic samples we collected in the experiments are divided into the training set and the testing set. The former is used to train the classification system to build the model, and the latter is used to evaluate classification accuracy.

4.1.2 Scenarios

We consider three dominant WLAN deployments: public network, home network, and university campus (or enterprise) network. The traffic in public networks is usually not encrypted at the link layer [27]. Hence, it is very easy to obtain the identifying features of a specific user's traffic in such an environment. We carry out tests in airports, cafe houses, McDonald's, etc. Home and small business networks are small and more likely to adopt link-layer encryption, such as Wired Equivalent Privacy (WEP) or WiFi Protected Access (WPA). We conduct the experiments in a home environment with *Comcast Internet* as the Internet Service Provider. Campus networks usually support a large population of users and employ the link-layer encryption. We also conduct experiments on the university campus.

To achieve better accuracy, the classification system must adapt to dynamic network conditions and tolerate the noises caused by variant versions of applications, users' habits and interferences among concurrent applications.

To evaluate the network condition, we collect traffic data samples in different *received signal strength indication (RSSI)*, with various *channel utilization*, in different time slots (morning, afternoon and evening, respectively) and networks. In this way, the training data in a certain network condition indicated by RSSI and channel utilization are used to build the classifier models under different network conditions. The system will select the most appropriate classifier model, which is under similar network conditions as the testing data.

To tolerate noise, we consider various attributes of applications in our data collection efforts. We select commonly used applications and their attributes listed in Table 1. More than 10 people participate in the test with their choices of different operating systems, software and laptops.

4.2 Feature Extraction and Selection

4.2.1 Feature Extraction

The observed traffic traces are time-series data. Individual frames contain very little information, but they are correlated with their neighboring frames in a certain pattern for a given application. Therefore, the statistical features of frames may disclose information leaks. For example, chatting and gaming have a small number of frames with relatively small size for both sending and receiving. Browsing contains bursty traffic. Downloading and uploading are both high bandwidth consumption applications with large frame size in downlink and uplink, respectively. Online video demonstrates a relatively stable data rate which is usually between BT and downloading. BT may be a high bandwidth consumption application in bidirectional directions. Its traffic variance is also very large.

For statistical analysis, we need to demarcate traffic flows into a series of measurements. We use an *"observation window"* to represent a segment of a flow and extract the flow features in each individual window. The window size, W, can be either expressed in time domain or measured by events. Intuitively, if the window size reflects the periodic

Table 4: Similarity distances of seven applications

D_M	①br.	②ch.	③ga.	④do.	⑤up.	⑥vo.	⑦bt.
①br.	-	1854.3	361.14	374.48	767.63	21.707	**3.7258**
②ch.	1854.3	-	**8.9232**	4258.1	1556.3	1625.1	1439.3
③ga.	361.14	**8.9232**	-	55341	33480	2176.9	205.03
④do.	374.48	4258.1	55341	-	100037	**93.777**	576.74
⑤up.	767.63	1556.3	33480	100037	-	5699.2	**189.79**
⑥vo.	21.707	1625.1	2176.9	93.777	5699.2	-	**15.852**
⑦bt.	**3.7258**	1439.3	205.03	576.74	189.79	15.852	-

components of the traffic trace, it will be useful for feature extraction. We have attempted to find the periodicity of the traffic traces by the *fast Fourier transform*. Unfortunately, the periodicity is fuzzy and undetectable. In our experiments, we use a fixed time domain to describe W. For example, the traffic is a time series denoted as $\{T_1, T_2, \cdots, T_W, T_{W+1}, \cdots, T_N\}$. Without using a sliding window, the traffic data will be divided into *flow segments*: $\{T_1, T_2, \cdots, T_W\}\{T_{W+1}, \cdots, T_{2W}\}, \cdots$. But with the sliding window technique, the flow segments to be considered will be $\{T_1, T_2, \cdots, T_W\}, \{T_2, \cdots, T_{W+1}\}, \cdots$. In this way, we can obtain more instances of features.

We list the features used in our classification in Table 2. Therein, "frame size distribution (>500bytes)" means the percentage of frames which are larger than 500 bytes in each window size. Table 3 illustrates features in home scenarios with *RSSI* around 55, which is equivalent to -50dBm of RF Signal Strength according to Cisco Standard [28]. We can see that different applications have very different features.

4.2.2 Feature Selection

Since the flow features are not equally important for inferring specific applications, we need to identify representative features and remove irrelevant and redundant ones to improve classification accuracy. We use a *best first search* to generate candidate sets of features, since it provides higher classification accuracy than *greedy search* [29]. We also use the correlation-based filter (CFS) to examine the relevance of each feature, i.e., those highly correlated to a specific class but with minimal correlation to each other [26]. CFS is practical and outperforms the other filter method (consistency-based filter) in terms of classification accuracy and efficiency [29]. For every trace, the CFS selected three categories of features: frame size, number of frames and frame distribution information. The aptness of the feature selection is evaluated in Section 5.

4.3 ML Algorithms

In our classification system, the relationships of frames in the MAC layer are vaguely understood and difficult to describe adequately with conventional approaches, so straightforward classification methods, such as k-nearest neighbor algorithm, decision tree (e.g., C4.5) and Naive Bayes, etc., may not yield high classification accuracy. HMM is a powerful statistical technique based on the Markovian assumption. But the number of parameters that need to be set in an HMM is huge. As a result, the amount of data that is required to train an HMM is also very large. Hence, we use SVM and NN algorithms, which are widely used in intelligent data mining applications [26], to design the classifiers. These two methods can model complex relationships between inputs and outputs and find patterns in data. NN is a universal approximation tool and able to tolerate noise. SVM performs better with small training sets, which is very useful for online classification. Kim et al. present in [26] that SVM outperforms other classification methods with more than 98% overall accuracy. Considering that the relationships between features seem to be nonlinear, we choose radial basis function (RBF) for both SVM and NN algorithms to achieve non-linear classification. RBF is one of the most commonly used in SVM. Similarly, we also use a popular artificial NN, radial basis function network (RBFN), to do the classification.

4.4 Hierarchical Classification Structures

Classifying seven applications in aggregated traffic belongs to the category of multiclass classification. The main technique for multiclass classification is to decompose the multiclass problem into several binary problems, especially for SVM. The common methods to build such binary classifiers are (i) one of the classes to the rest (one-versus-all, OVA) (ii) between every pair of classes (one-versus-one, OVO), or (iii) directed acyclic graph SVM (DAGSVM) [30]. For a K-class problem ($K = 7$ in our classification for seven popular online applications), the disadvantage of OVA is that it needs K classifiers and each classifier needs to be trained by training samples of all the classes. OVO and DAGSVM have to construct $K(K - 1)/2$ classifiers, which incur large computational overhead.

To decrease the number of classifiers and improve the accuracy, we use the decision tree structure [31, 32, 33] in our classification system. We present hierarchical classification structures, which take advantage of both the efficient computation of the tree structure and the high classification accuracy of SVM and RBFN, in Figure 4 and 5, respectively. We use K ($K = 7$) classifiers for SVM and $K - 1$ classifiers in the RBFN model. Each classifier only needs to be trained to a subset of the training samples, and the hierarchical classification allows individual classifiers in the structure to be updated flexibly and independently. This is a notable improvement when the number of classes is large. At each node of the tree, a decision is made to assign the input to several possible groups which are the subtrees. Each of these groups may contain multiple classes. This is repeated down the tree until the sample reaches a leaf node that represents the class it has been assigned to.

In the design of the classification system, the basic rule we obey is to separate the most different and independent groups or classes first and distinguish the most similar classes last. We measure the similarity of different applications by using the *Mahalanobis distance*. It is a multivariate distance measure for several modeling algorithms, such as k-nearest

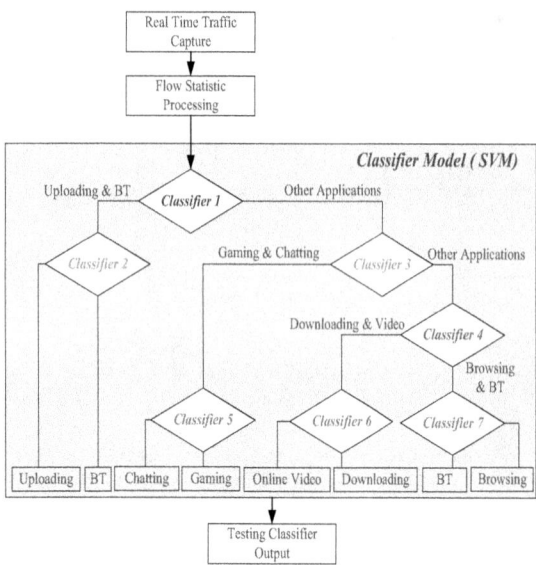

Figure 4: The hierarchical classification structure of SVM algorithms

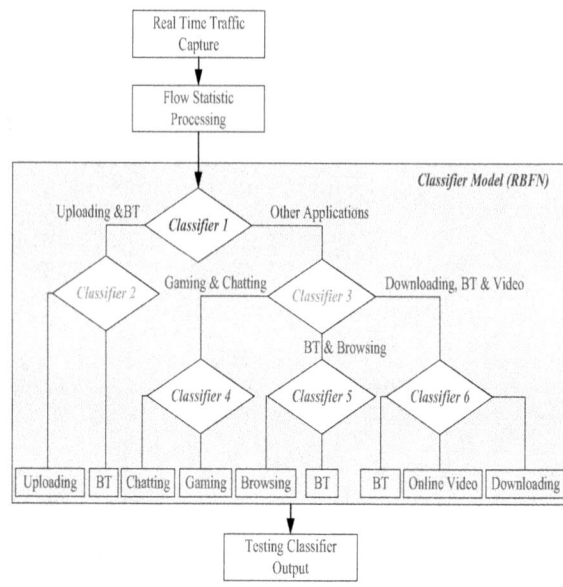

Figure 5: The hierarchical classification structure of RBFN algorithms

neighbors and RBFN. The Mahalanobis distance from a multivariate matrix Y to X is shown as follows:

$$D_M(Y) = \sqrt{(Y - \mu)^T S^{-1} (Y - \mu)}$$

where μ and S are the mean and covariance of X.

For example, to calculate the Mahalanobis distances between *browsing* and *chatting*, we use the data rate in downlink and uplink as the multivariate matrix Y for *browsing* and denote X for *chatting*. $D_M(Y)$ is the Mahalanobis distance from *browsing* to *chatting*. Similarly, $D_M(X)$ is the Mahalanobis distance from *chatting* to *browsing*. After that, we utilize, $E(D_M(X) + D_M(Y))$, the *average* of these two distances as the distance between *browsing* and *chatting*. We show the similarity in distances of seven applications in Table 4 (in home scenarios with *RSSI* around 55).

Among seven applications, only *upload* and *BT* may have continuous large traffic in uplink. Hence, we adopt *Classifier 1* to distinguish *upload* and *BT* from the rest of the applications in Figure 4 and Figure 5. From Table 4, we notice that the following application pairs have relatively small distances: *browsing* and *BT*, *chatting* and *online gaming*, and *downloading* and *online video*. Therefore, we group each pair and design *Classifiers 3* and *4* to separate the application pairs in SVM algorithms in Figure 4, where *Classifiers 2, 5, 6* and *7* are leaf nodes in the binary classification tree. The output of the system is an application for the input flow segment.

Likewise, the hierarchical classification structure of RBFN is shown in Figure 5. A major difference between RBFN and SVM is that a RBFN classifier is able to separate more than two classes. Therefore, we use *Classifiers 3* and *6* for multiple class separation in order to reduce the number of classifiers. *Classifiers 2, 4* and *5* are binary classifications. Because *BT* has a large range of data rates, sometimes it looks like *downloading* with a large data rate, and sometimes it is like *browsing*. In order to improve the accuracy of detection *BT*, we identify the BT application by *Classifiers 2*

and *7* in SVM algorithms, and by *Classifiers 2, 5* and *6* in RBFN algorithms.

4.5 Classification for Concurrent Applications

A user may open multiple windows and run multiple online applications simultaneously. In this case, the traffic we observe in the MAC layer is a mixture of frames from multiple applications. However, it is hard to separate frames of one application from the others when the frames are encrypted.

Our strategy is to use the proposed hierarchical structure in Section 4.4 to identify the dominating application at first. Then we classify the possible concurrent applications. We denote the window size as W and give a classification result of concurrent applications after L window sizes. For each W, we identify the flow segment of the application it belongs to. Then we get L identified sub-flows to compute the proportion that each application occupied in the L subflows. The application with the highest proportion will be the dominating application. Similarly, we can get the application which is the second largest proportion. At the same time, we need to set a threshold for an application to identify its existence. Only if the proportion of the application is larger than its threshold, the application may be regarded as a concurrent application. According to the above strategy, we may infer the possible concurrent applications in the aggregated traffic.

However, the low traffic applications (e.g., chatting and online gaming) are hardly detected. They may be inundated by the dominating applications. In this case, we adjust features to tell if the aggregated traffic includes low bandwidth applications. For example, we adopt *the frame size distribution* and *the number of frames* in small size (e.g., ≤ 400bytes) as features to tell if the downloading frames are mixed with chatting. The reason is that downloading has few frames smaller than 400 bytes, and most chatting frames are smaller than 400 bytes. To efficiently identify multiple online applications, we have to reduce the window size W.

Table 5: Overall accuracy for seven applications ($W = 5s$)(%)

Overall accuracy of SVM algorithms: *The Same Location, User in One Day*								
Scenarios	①br.	②ch.	③ga.	④do.	⑤up.	⑥vo.	⑦bt.	Mean
Home	42.690	79.935	98.017	91.285	95.969	91.283	81.734	**82.987**
Public	65.934	70.450	74.041	94.052	87.172	64.319	91.054	**78.146**
University	45.623	66.967	84.399	85.526	91.901	83.984	70.172	**75.510**
Overall accuracy of RBFN algorithms: *The Same Location, User in One Day*								
Home	37.767	77.932	88.181	99.877	95.922	93.321	89.683	**83.240**
Public	48.738	61.488	81.031	94.005	84.748	96.227	91.381	**79.657**
University	28.533	64.442	61.160	95.703	91.901	71.584	90.847	**72.024**
Overall accuracy: *Similar RSSI, Totally Different Location, User and Time*								
Mixed (SVM)	53.164	61.108	67.873	92.740	91.866	72.402	58.218	**71.053**
Mixed (RBFN)	36.362	68.367	58.901	95.386	93.827	90.894	56.023	**71.394**

Table 6: Accuracy and FP in Different Window Sizes (%)

Metrics	Window Sizes	①br.	②ch.	③ga.	④do.	⑤up.	⑥vo.	⑦bt.	Mean
Accuracy	$W = 5s$ (SVM)	42.690	79.935	98.017	91.285	95.969	91.283	81.734	**82.987**
Accuracy	$W = 5s$ (RBFN)	37.767	77.932	88.181	99.877	95.922	93.321	89.683	**83.240**
Accuracy	$W = 60s$ (SVM)	53.571	99.427	100.000	100.000	95.969	100.000	99.692	**92.666**
Accuracy	$W = 60s$ (RBFN)	72.936	85.293	93.742	100.000	95.922	100.000	95.137	**91.861**
FP	$W = 5s$ (SVM)	2.583	1.815	2.930	1.257	0.773	2.621	7.871	**2.836**
FP	$W = 5s$ (RBFN)	2.734	2.212	3.287	0.932	0.020	1.047	9.322	**2.793**
FP	$W = 60s$ (SVM)	0.055	0.734	0.662	0.131	0.000	0.000	6.975	**1.222**
FP	$W = 60s$ (RBFN)	1.507	1.448	1.861	0.129	0.000	0.297	4.255	**1.356**

Thus, the majority of the frames in individual windows are from a single application, and we have more chances to detect concurrent applications in a fixed time duration.

As a user usually does not actively run more than two online applications at the same time, we test our classification system based on two concurrent applications. We show in Section 5 that we can successfully detect the two concurrent applications (the main application and the hidden application) in the aggregated traffic.

5. EVALUATION

Our prototype classification system has been tested at a home, on a university campus, and in public areas. Wireless LANs in these environments all support 802.11a/b/g modes, and the data rate may fluctuate from 1Mbps to 54Mbps. The encryption scheme of WLANs at home and on campus is WPA/WPA2, and the traffic collected in public areas is unencrypted. More than 10 volunteers run the same applications on different devices, operating systems or laptops. An application runs for about 10 minutes each time. In total, we get more than 50 hours of traffic data. In our experiments, we measure the traffic and collect features when the RSSI is larger than 40 (i.e., RF Signal Strength > -70dBm) and the maximum data rate is larger than 50KB/s. Otherwise, users will suffer from poor network quality. We divide the collection data into many groups according to similar RSSI values or scenarios. A similar RSSI means ±10dBm, and scenarios are determined by many factors, such as location, user and time duration of measurement. For each group of data, the training data is randomly selected from the collected data and the rest are used for evaluation, called testing data. In the experiments, the testing data set is a factor of 3 to 10 times larger than the training data set.

5.1 Performance Metrics

A key criterion of performance evaluation for classification techniques is the accuracy (i.e., how accurately the technique or model classifies the flows) [13], which can be measured by three metrics: *overall accuracy*, *true positive (TP)*, and *false positive (FP)*. The *overall accuracy* is defined as the percentage of correctly classified instances among the total number of instances, and *true positive* means the percentage of members of a given class $\mathcal{X}$ is correctly classified to class $\mathcal{X}$. FP reflects the percent of non-class $\mathcal{X}$ packets incorrectly classified as belonging to class $\mathcal{X}$.

5.2 Overall Accuracy in Different Scenarios

The overall accuracy of different applications and scenarios is listed in Table 5. We set the window size to $W = 5$ seconds. The overall accuracy of classification for seven applications in different scenarios is around 80% when we select the same location and user in one day. We achieve the best accuracy in the home scenario, 82.987%, and the lowest accuracy in the university scenario, 75.510%. The relatively low accuracy in the university environment is caused by traffic interference and collision, which lead to large jitters in the data rate. In contrast, the number of users is very limited in the home scenario, so the interference and collision caused by sharing wireless bandwidth is less than in the public and university scenarios. Public networks likely have a low and restricted data rate. This rate limiting reduces the classification accuracy. The mixed scenario is only distinguished by the similar RSSI. It may include the traffic trace from home, public area, and university. Hence, it has much noise and different traffic patterns in different environments. Therefore, the accuracy in the mixed scenario is the lowest, about 71%, among all scenarios.

Among different applications, browsing has the lowest ac-

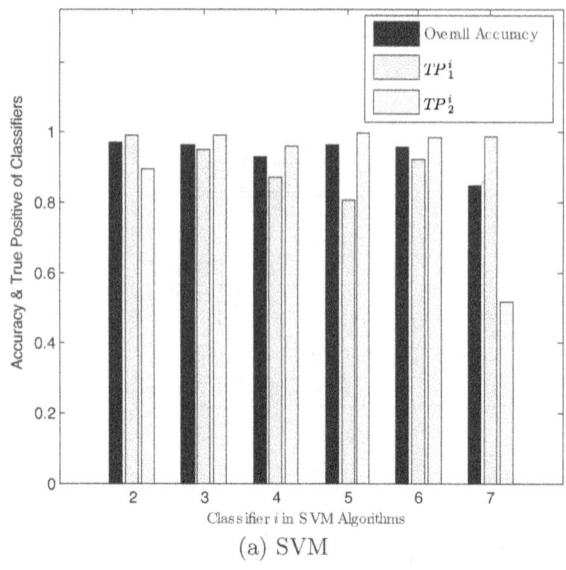

(a) SVM

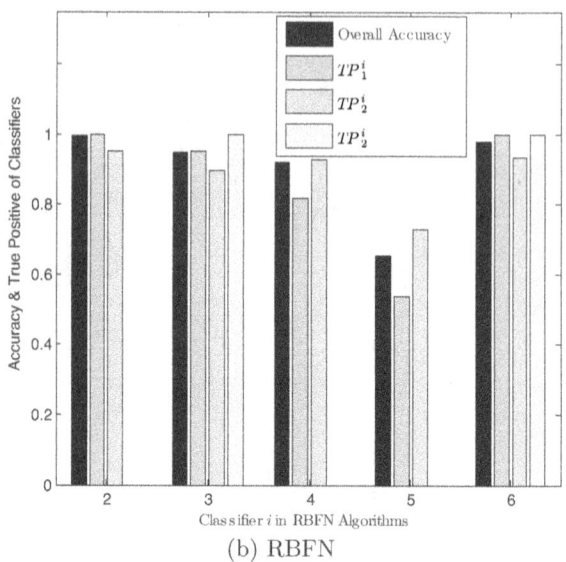

(b) RBFN

Figure 6: Overall accuracy and TP of classifiers

curacy. This is caused by two factors. First, browsing applications have a large variance in the data rate. Flash, GIF and video files of advertisements are embedded in many websites which may generate bursty traffic. Second, in a hierarchical classification structure, browsing is in the lowest layer of the classifier model, shown in Figure 4 and 5. Errors from previously layers have accumulated to the classifier of browsing. In summary, high bandwidth applications have better accuracy than low bandwidth applications.

SVM algorithms achieve similar overall accuracy to RBFN algorithms. For high traffic applications, RBFN performs better than SVM, such as downloading, online video and BT. On the contrary, SVM gets better accuracy in low traffic applications, especially in browsing and chatting.

5.3 Accuracy and False Positive in Different Window Sizes (W)

Changing the window size from 5 to 60 seconds, the classification accuracy of each application is presented in Table 6. The accuracy increases simultaneously with the rise in W. This is because the features extracted from a larger window can tolerate more noise. If we collect features every 60 seconds, it achieves more than 90% accuracy; and five applications can be classified with almost 100% accuracy. SVM is more sensitive to increasing window size and performs better than RBFN.

The FP of each application is also listed in Table 6. We can see that the FPs of low traffic applications are mostly higher than those of high traffic applications. BT always has the largest FP in both SVM and RBFN algorithms. That means other applications are misclassified as belonging to BT, especially for browsing. The reason is that the traffic of BT varies very much. It may resembles low traffic applications, or looks like high traffic applications according to network resources.

5.4 Overall Accuracy and True Positive of SVM and RBFN Classifiers

We give the overall accuracy and TP of each classifier

for SVM and RBFN in Figure 6. The features are generated according to Section 4.2, and W is set as 5 seconds. The classification systems of SVM and RBFN algorithms are shown in Figure 4 and 5. Note that, for simplicity, *Classifier 1* does not use either SVM or RBFN but only employs a threshold of data rate. For example, if the sending data rate is beyond 40KB/s and the average sending rate is above 60KB/s in consecutive 5 seconds, we regard the traffic as probably uploading and then pass it to *Classifier 2*, otherwise to *Classifier 3*. The classifiers, except *Classifier 1*, are shown in Figure 6. TP_j^i indicates the TP of the jth class which is under *Classifier i* in Figure 4 and 5. For example, *Classifier 3* ($i = 3$) of RBFN, TP_1^3 indicates the TP of low traffic applications "chatting & gaming," TP_2^3 shows the TP of "browsing and BT" and TP_3^3 describes the TP of large traffic applications "downloading, online video and BT."

For SVM algorithms, the overall accuracies of the classifiers are beyond 80%; and the TPs are above 85% except browsing, the lowest at 51.534%. This fact is also observed in Section 5.2. Figure 6(b) shows the overall accuracy and TP of RBFN classifiers. All classifiers perform well with high accuracy over 85%, except for *Classifier 5* at 65.380% and the TP of browsing at only 53.946%. It shows TPs are close to accuracies both in SVM and RBFN algorithms. That means our classification system is very balanced. We also observe that RBFN algorithms are good at multiclass classification, since the two triple-category classifiers perform well.

5.5 Feature Selection

Figure 7 compares the overall accuracy of classifications when we use the same hierarchical structure but different features. Note that, classifier 1 is not included because it does not use ML algorithms. For SVM algorithms, we use two pairs of features in one case, *(receiving data rate, sending data rate)* and *(number of receiving frames, number of sending frames)*. In the second case, we adopt one pair of features *(mean receiving frame size, mean sending frame size)*. The

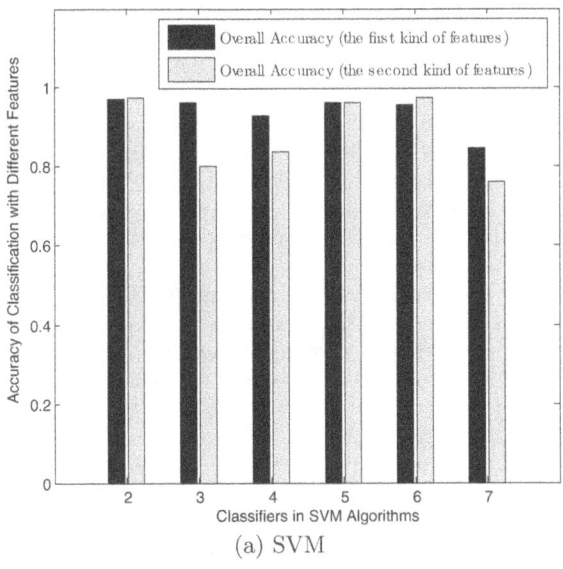

(a) SVM

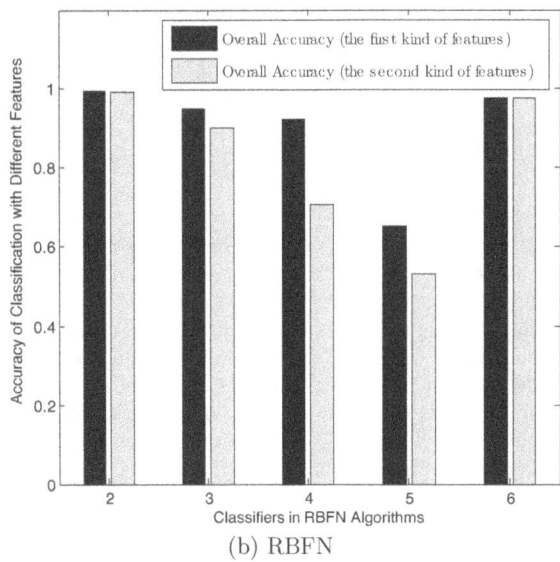

(b) RBFN

Figure 7: Overall accuracy by using different feature selection

Table 7: Detection probability for concurrent applications (%)

Applications	SVM	RBFN
{①br., ⑤up.}	{41.4, 100.0}	{47.8, 100.0}
{①br., ⑦bt.}	{75.7, 100.0}	{54.2, 100.0}
{①br., ②ch.}	{100.0, 36.5}	{100.0, 41.0}
{②ch., ④do.}	{100.0, 100.0}	{100.0, 100.0}
{④do., ⑥vo.}	{100.0, 98.2}	{100.0, 100.0}
{⑥vo., ⑦bt.}	{100.0, 63.7}	{100.0, 65.3}

classification with two pairs of features yields better accuracy.

For RBFN algorithms, we use multiple features, *(mean receiving frame size), the number of frames* and *frame size distribution*, in the first case. The second case only uses one feature, *(mean receiving frame size)*. Figure 7 shows that classifiers using the first kind of features achieve higher accuracy. In summary, more appropriate features will benefit the performance of classification and improve the accuracy.

5.6 Classification for Concurrent Applications

To verify the ability to identify multiple concurrent online applications, we let aggregated traffic (six combinations of two concurrent applications) pass through the proposed classification system. Because we can not be certain that frames from each application will appear in each flow segment, the classification result of each flow segment can not be used to judge the accuracy of concurrent applications. Instead, we use the detection probability to evaluate the performance of our classification system. The result is given every 1 minute when $L = 60$ and $W = 1$ second. If the dominating application is the right aggregated application, we give a detection probability of 100%. Then we compute the detection probability of the second application by dividing its proportion by all applications except the dominating application. Using these methods, we give the detection probability of six combinations in Table 7. We see that our system separates

two large bandwidth consumption applications, downloading and online video, with 100% accuracy. A large bandwidth consumption application plus a low bandwidth consumption application (e.g., downloading and chatting) also perform well with 100% accuracy. Because browsing is hard to separate from BT, other combinations have a lower probability of being classified accurately. Chatting has the lowest probability, about 36.474%, when identified from browsing. The performance of SVM algorithms is similar to that of RBFN algorithms.

6. DISCUSSIONS

6.1 Impact of Rate Limiting

For fairness and security, rate limiting software may be used to control the traffic rate of individual users in LANs. Hence, a user can not send or receive frames beyond a specified rate. With such a restriction, if the traffic rate is too low, the rate-related features can not be used to separate high traffic applications from original low traffic applications. However, if the specified rate is not too low (e.g., above 50KBps), the feature-based classification presented in this paper is still valid. In addition, we have examined our classification approach in public networks, where the data rate is limited, and our approach performs well.

6.2 Resistance to Current Defense Methods

Our system can thwart *pseudonyms* [10], because all packets sent under one pseudonym are trivially linkable. Moreover, pseudonym schemes only change MAC addresses each session or when idle. The infrequent change of MAC addresses can not defend the monitoring of an adversary in a few seconds. A link protocol [34] has implemented the function to obscure identifiers; but it can not obscure the traffic features, such as frame interarrival time and frame size distribution. In addition, high-level mitigation policies, such as packet padding, are likely to be ineffective or incur prohibitively high communication overhead [1, 2]. Traffic morphing [35] defends against traffic analysis in VoIP and web browsing applications by modifying packet sizes. However, other features (e.g., *data rate*) may still be sufficient for classification. Therefore, efficient defense against side-channel information leaks is a future research topic with strong practical relevance.

7. CONCLUSIONS

In this paper, we propose an online hierarchical classification system to identify users' online activities with high accuracy just by peeping at MAC-layer traffic. The classification system is implemented by using ML algorithms, including SVM and RBFN, and achieves high accuracy in different network situations, such as at home, in university and public network environments. The results show that it can distinguish different online applications with around 80% accuracy in just 5 seconds, and the accuracy is over 90% if the eavesdropping duration lasts for 1 minute. At the same time, our classification system can discover the combination of multiple concurrent online applications. Our work shows that the privacy leak of users' online activities is a severe threat in WiFi networks. We expect that our classification system will invoke public attention to user privacy in online activities.

8. REFERENCES

[1] S. Chen, R. Wang, X. Wang, and K. Zhang. Side-channel leaks in web applications: A reality today, a challenge tomorrow. In *Proceedings of IEEE Symposium on Security and Privacy*, pages 191–206, 2010.

[2] Q. Sun, D.R. Simon, Y. Wang, W. Russell, V.N. Padmanabhan, and L. Qiu. Statistical identification of encrypted web browsing traffic. In *Proceedings of IEEE Symposium on Security and Privacy*, 2002.

[3] P. Haffner, S. Sen, O. Spatscheck, and D. Wang. ACAS: automated construction of application signatures. In *Proceedings of the 2005 ACM SIGCOMM workshop on mining network data*, pages 197–202. ACM, 2005.

[4] X. Song, D. Wagner, S. David, and X. Tian. Timing analysis of keystrokes and timing attacks on SSH. In *Proceedings of USENIX Security Symposium*, 2001.

[5] T.S. Saponas, J. Lester, C. Hartung, S. Agarwal, and T. Kohno. Devices that tell on you: Privacy trends in consumer ubiquitous computing. In *Proceedings of USENIX Security Symposium*, 2007.

[6] C.V. Wright, L. Ballard, F. Monrose, and G. M. Masson. Language identification of encrypted VoIP traffic: Alejandra y roberto or alice and bob. In *Proceedings of USENIX Security Symposium*, 2007.

[7] C.V. Wright, L. Ballard, S. E. Coull, F. Monrose, and G. M. Masson. Spot me if you can: Uncovering spoken phrases in encrypted VoIP conversations. In *Proceedings of IEEE Symposium on Security and Privacy*, 2008.

[8] M. Liberatore and B. Levine. Inferring the source of encrypted http connections. In *Proceedings of Computer and Communications Security*, 2006.

[9] D. Herrmann, R. Wendolsky, and H. Federrath. Website fingerprinting: attacking popular privacy enhancing technologies with the multinomial naive-bayes classifier. In *Proceedings of the 2009 ACM workshop on Cloud computing security*, pages 31–42. ACM, 2009.

[10] T. Jiang, H.J. Wang, and Y. Hu. Preserving location privacy in wireless LANs. In *Proceedings of MobiSys*, pages 246–257, 2007.

[11] J. Wilson and N. Patwari. See through walls: Motion tracking using variance-based radio tomography networks. *IEEE Transactions on Mobile Computing*, 2010.

[12] V. Srinivasan, J. Stankovic, and K. Whitehouse. Protecting your daily in-home activity information from a wireless snooping attack. In *Proceedings of the 10th international conference on Ubiquitous computing*, pages 202–211. ACM, 2008.

[13] T.T. Nguyen and G. J. Armitage. A survey of techniques for internet traffic classification using machine learning. *IEEE Communications Surveys and Tutorials*, 10(1-4):56–76, 2008.

[14] Internet Assigned Numbers Authority (IANA), August, 2008. http://www.iana.org/assignments/port-numbers.

[15] T. Karagiannis, A. Broido, and M. Faloutsos. Transport layer identification of P2P traffic. In *Proceedings of the 4th ACM SIGCOMM conference on Internet measurement*, pages 121–134. ACM, 2004.

[16] T. Karagiannis, K. Papagiannaki, and M. Faloutsos. BLINC: multilevel traffic classification in the dark. *ACM SIGCOMM Computer Communication Review*, 35(4):229–240, 2005.

[17] K. Xu, Z.L. Zhang, and S. Bhattacharyya. Profiling internet backbone traffic: behavior models and applications. *ACM SIGCOMM Computer Communication Review*, 35(4):169–180, 2005.

[18] C.V. Wright, F. Monrose, and G. Masson. HMM Profiles for Network Traffic Classification (Extended Abstract). In *Proceedings of Workshop on Visualization and Data Mining for Computer Security (VizSEC/DMSEC)*. Citeseer, 2004.

[19] C.V. Wright, F. Monrose, and G.M. Masson. On inferring application protocol behaviors in encrypted network traffic. *The Journal of Machine Learning Research*, 7:2745–2769, 2006.

[20] A. Dainotti, W.D. Donato, A. Pescape, S. Rossi, et al. Classification of network traffic via packet-level hidden Markov models. In *Proceedings of GLOBECOM*, pages 1–5. IEEE, 2008.

[21] J. Erman, A. Mahanti, M. Arlitt, I. Cohen, and C. Williamson. Offline/realtime traffic classification using semi-supervised learning. *Performance Evaluation*, 64(9-12):1194–1213, 2007.

[22] D. Bonfiglio, M. Mellia, M. Meo, D. Rossi, and P. Tofanelli. Revealing skype traffic: when randomness plays with you. *ACM SIGCOMM Computer Communication Review*, 37(4):37–48, 2007.

[23] L. Bernaille, R. Teixeira, I. Akodkenou, A. Soule, and K. Salamatian. Traffic classification on the fly. *ACM SIGCOMM Computer Communication Review*, 36(2):23–26, 2006.

[24] M. Tavallaee, W. Lu, and A.A. Ghorbani. Online Classification of Network Flows. In *Proceedings of Seventh Annual Communication Networks and*

Services Research Conference, pages 78–85. IEEE, 2009.

[25] A. Moore and D. Zuev. Internet traffic classification using Bayesian analysis techniques. *ACM SIGMETRICS Performance Evaluation Review*, 33(1):50–60, 2005.

[26] H. Kim, K. Claffy, M. Fomenkov, D. Barman, M. Faloutsos, and K. Lee. Internet traffic classification demystified: myths, caveats, and the best practices. In *Proceedings of the 2008 ACM CoNEXT conference*, pages 1–12. ACM, 2008.

[27] J. Pang, B. Greenstein, R. Gummadi, S. Seshan, and D. Wetherall. 802.11 user fingerprinting. In *Proceedings of MobiCom*, pages 99–110. ACM Press, 2007.

[28] J. Bardwell. Converting signal strength percentage to dBm values. *WildPackets*, 2002.

[29] N. Williams, S. Zander, and G. Armitage. A preliminary performance comparison of five machine learning algorithms for practical IP traffic flow classification. *ACM SIGCOMM Computer Communication Review*, 36(5):5–16, 2006.

[30] C.W. Hsu and C.J. Lin. A comparison of methods for multiclass support vector machines. *Neural Networks, IEEE Transactions on*, 13(2):415–425, 2002.

[31] S. Cheong, S.H. Oh, and S.Y. Lee. Support vector machines with binary tree architecture for multi-class classification. *Neural Information Processing-Letters and Reviews*, 2(3):47–51, 2004.

[32] B. Fei and J. Liu. Binary tree of SVM: a new fast multiclass training and classification algorithm. *Neural Networks, IEEE Transactions on*, 17(3):696–704, 2006.

[33] G. Madzarov and D. Gjorgjevikj. Multi-class classification using support vector machines in decision tree architecture. In *Proceedings of EUROCON 2009*, pages 288–295. IEEE.

[34] B. Greenstein, D. Mccoy, J. Pang, T. Kohno, S. Seshan, and D. Wetherall. Improving wireless privacy with an identifier-free link layer protocol. In *Proceeding of MobiSys*, 2008.

[35] C.V. Wright, S.E. Coull, and F. Monrose. Traffic morphing: an efficient defense against statistical traffic analysis. In *Proceedings of NDSS*, 2009.

Interactive decryption of DECT phone calls

Patrick McHardy
kaber@trash.net

Andreas Schuler
dect@badterrorist.com

Erik Tews
TU Darmstadt
Hochschulstrasse 10
64289 Darmstadt, Germany
e_tews@cdc.informatik.tu-darmstadt.de

ABSTRACT

DECT[3] is a widely deployed standard mostly used for short range wireless phones. So far, no method has been published which is able to recover the audio signal in a call that is encrypted and lasts only for a few minutes.

In this paper, we present a method that recovers the audio signal sent from the phone to its base station in an encrypted call. To do so, we use a replay-attack against the phone to recover the key streams, which were used to encrypt the call. The method is applicable to short calls too, where not enough keystreams are available to recover the ciphers key using a key recovery attack[8] on DSC. The method is fast and practical and can be executed at very low cost.

Categories and Subject Descriptors

C.2.1 [**Network Architecture and Design**]: Wireless communication; D.4.6 [**Security and Protection**]: Metrics, Cryptographic controls; E.3 [**DATA ENCRYPTION**]: Code breaking

Keywords

DECT, DSC, Replay attacks, Keystream recovery

1. INTRODUCTION

With more than 800 million devices sold worldwide[1], Digital Enhanced Cordless Telecommunications (DECT)[3] is one of the most common standards for short range cordless telephones. Besides for phones, DECT is used for many other applications like wireless payment systems, traffic control, access control and room monitoring. DECT networks usually consists of a single or multiple base stations named DECT Fixed Part (FP) in the standard and phones named DECT Portable Part (PP) linked with these base stations. For most residential use cases, only a single base station is operated with a small number of phones. A single base

---

[1] http://www.etsi.org/WebSite/NewsandEvents/201004_CATIQ.aspx

station can cover a single house or up to a few hundred meters in the open field. European systems operate at 1880 to 1900 MHz and have a maximum transmit power of 250 mW, while the North American version operates at 1920 to 1930 MHz and just uses a maximum transmit power of 100 mW. DECT systems can scale to many base stations and phones, and also support roaming as GSM does.

To protect sensitive data transmitted over DECT, the standard provides authentication (DECT Standard Authentication Algorithm, DSAA) as well as confidentiality (DECT Standard Cipher, DSC). Both algorithms were specially designed for DECT and are only available to DECT device manufactures who sign a non-disclosure agreement. DSAA is responsible for the initial pairing of a new phone with its base station. It is also used for authentication of phones and base stations and for key derivation to generate a session key (Cipher Key (CK)) for DSC from the User Authentication Key (UAK).

DSC is used for encryption. It is a stream cipher, which takes an Initialization Vector (IV) and a session key (cipher key, CK) to generate a key stream (cipher stream, CS) from it. Besides the actual payload (voice data), parts of the the control traffic (C-channel traffic) are also encrypted, which for example contain the dialed number.

1.1 Previous attacks on DECT

First attacks on DECT were made public at the end of 2008 and the first paper *Attacks on the DECT authentication mechanism*[5] by Lucks, Schuler, Tews, Weinmann and Wenzel was published at CT-RSA 2009. They reverse engineered DSAA and implemented a low-cost DECT sniffer, which uses a DECT PCMCIA card. Many combinations of phones and base stations on the market did not use DSC at all, always sending their communications in clear. This can be easily be eavesdropped on using their passive DECT sniffer.

All other devices examined did not request authentication of the base station, but the base station did request authentication of the phones and enabled encryption. To attack these phones, they implemented a rogue base station impersonating the original base station. When a phone was connected to their base station, the base station did not request encryption, so the phone did send it's data in clear. Because no phone requested authentication of the base station or enforced encryption, none of the phones noticed that the base station was not in possession of the correct UAK. However, this method can only be used to intercept calls originating from the phone, but not from the original base station. These methods were later improved by [7] and [6].

To counter these attacks, new phones were developed, which always require encryption. If a base station does not enable encryption when a new call is established, the call will be automatically dropped. Such phones are immune against these attacks.

In 2009, the DECT Standard Cipher was reverse engineered by Nohl, Tews, and Weinmann[8, 9]. They also presented a key recovery attack on the DSC, which recovers the key in a few minutes to hours using a fast computer. However, this attack needs about 2^{15} key streams produced with the same key and different Initialization Vectors, which must be available to the attacker. They proposed two methods to recover that many key streams:

- If only silence is transmitted from the base station to the phone (for example a voice mail system is being called and the caller leaves a long message on the system), then the plaintext of the payload will be known and these key streams can be extracted in about 10-11 minutes. Also this method does not recover the first 40 bits of these key streams, which are only used to encrypt control traffic (see Figure 3). This renders the attack less efficient on these key streams.

- Some phones show a call duration counter on their display, which is implemented on the base station. This counter is updated once per second using C-channel messages. Because the plaintext of those messages is mostly constant, this can be used to recover about 5 key streams per second. This makes the recovery of 2^{15} key streams in about two hours possible.

So far, no method has been published to decrypt a short DECT call, without iterating over all 2^{64} possible keys for the DSC, which is made on a phone, where encryption and authentication are enforced, and no other implementation flaws are present.

1.2 Our contribution

In this paper, we propose a practical and efficient method to recover the audio data sent from a phone to the base station during an encrypted DECT call. We use a replay attack against the phone to recover the keystreams which were used to encrypt the call. These keystreams can be used to decrypt the call. Our method requires nearly no computational power and can recover the data from an x seconds phone call in about $2.8 * x$ seconds. This value is based on experiments, and depends on the implementation of the attack and the phone being attacked.

Because some phones have bad echo cancellation, this may also include the audio sent from the base station to the phone, which is played by the phone speaker and recorded by the phone microphone again.

2. DECT PROTOCOL

To understand our attack, we give a brief overview of the DECT protocol. The DECT standard allows a wide variety of features, which can be implemented, however just a small subset of them is usually implemented in a standard consumers phone. A DECT network consists of a single or multiple base stations, named **DECT Fixed Part (FP)**, and a number of phones, named **DECT Portable Part (PP)**.

2.1 Radio protocol

The DECT protocol can be divided into 5 layers: Physical Layer, MAC Layer, Data Link Control Layer, Network Layer and the actual speech and audio coding. Encryption takes place in the MAC Layer, however encryption is negotiated at the Network Layer.

To allow multiple devices to transmit on the same frequency, DECT uses TDMA (Time Division Multiple Access), a period of 10 ms, as known as **frame**, is divided into 24 **time slots**. In every frame, one of the first 12 time slots is used for transmissions from the base station to the phone (FP → PP), and the time slot 12 time slots later is used for transmissions from the phone to the base station (PP → FP). In every time slot, 480 bits could be transmitted. A single DECT **full slot packet (P32)** has a total length of $32+64+320+4+4 = 424$ bits and is divided into an S-, A-, B-, X- and an optional Z-Field. The remaining 56 or 60 bits are a guard period between the time slots.

- The S-field is only a static preamble of a packet, which is used by the receiver to synchronize on the signal.

- The A-field contains the packet header and can transport control traffic. Control traffic is separated into different logical channels, namely the C, M, N, P, and Q channels. A tag in the A-field header determines which channel is embedded in the packet, and for example C-channel messages are usually split over several packets, because they usually don't fit in a single A-field.

- The B-field contains the actual payload, for example the voice data, when a phone call is made over DECT.

- The X and Z fields are checksums to detect transmission problems.

An overview of the particular fields is given in Figure 1 and Figure 3. Base stations usually broadcast a beacon once per period. Phones synchronize their timer on this beacon.

Most of the time, a phone only passively listens to the broadcasts of a base station. When there is traffic, for example a call is active or the base station needs to update the display of the phone, the phones establish a connection with the base station. A base station can request a new connection from the phone by broadcasting an `LCE-PAGE-REQUEST` message.

The DECT standard makes heavy use of timers, to specify how long certain procedures may take. Only one timer, namely the `LCE.01` timer is of importance for the attack. When a connection is not needed anymore by any upper protocol layers, the `LCE.01` timer is started, which runs for 5 seconds. If there is no more activity on the connection within these 5 seconds, the connection is terminated.

An existing connection between a phone and a base station does not necessarily mean that a call is active. Instead, a base station might, for example, establish a connection just to update a phone display state to indicate that a new voicemail has arrived or a text has been received by the base station. All phones we examined so far send packets with all bits set to 1 (**0xff** in hex) in the B-field when there is no audio data present in the connection.

DECT supports sending shorter packets (the standards also specifies the P00 format), if no payload present, but this is an optional feature, the base station and the phone

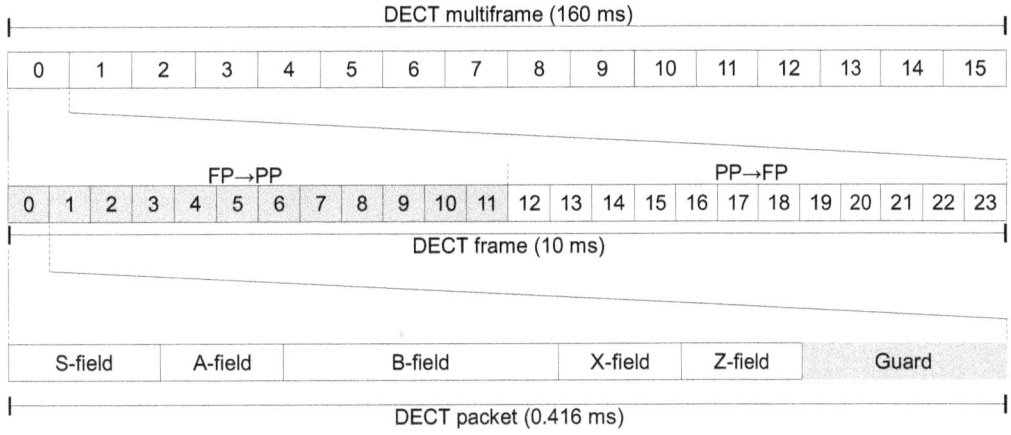

Figure 1: DECT TDMA structure

must support. Even if the phone would be able to send shorter packets, the base station could indicate that it is not capable of processing such packets and the phone would need to switch to P32 packets with B-fields.

2.2 Authentication and key derivation

Usually, phone and base station share a 128 bit symmetric key named UAK. For authentication, two different procedures are defined:

2.2.1 Authentication of a phone by base station

First, a base station can request authentication from a phone. To do so, the base station chooses two random numbers RS and RAND_F and sends them in an AUTHENTICATION-REQUEST message to a phone. Now the phone computes a response to this challenge using the DSAA algorithms A11 and A12 with the UAK and these two random numbers as input. The result RES1 is transmitted in an AUTHENTICATION-RESPONSE message to the base station, which performs the same computations and compares the received RES1 with the locally computed result XRES1. In addition to that a 64 bit cipher key CK is also generated by A12, which can be used for encryption later on. See Figure 2 for details.

2.2.2 Authentication of a base station by a phone

A phone can also request authentication from a base station. To do so, it picks just a single 64 bit random number RAND_P and sends it to the base station. The base station picks another 64 bit random number RS, and computes a response RES2 to the challenge sent by the phone using the DSAA algorithms A21 and A22 with UAK, RAND_P and RS as input. RES2 and RS are transmitted to the phone, which compares it to the locally computed result. No cipher key is generated and the procedure does not affect the generated cipher key from the previous paragraph.

None of the devices examined [5, 6] used this feature, so it has no importance for the rest of this paper. We will discuss this in Section 6.2 as a countermeasure.

2.3 Encryption

Even when there is no encryption in use, a base station continuously broadcasts a multiframe number embedded in a Q-channel message. Every packet sent and received by the base station has a frame number, which is a function

depending on the last broadcasted multiframe number and the time elapsed since this event. Every packet in the same frame shares the same frame number.

For encryption, DECT defines a stream cipher, the DECT Standard Cipher (DSC). DSC takes a 64 bit initialization vector IV and a 64 bit cipher key (CK) as input and generates a key stream (cipher stream, CS) of arbitrary length from it. The IV used is the frame number zero-padded to 64 bit length. Usually, 720 bits of key stream ($cs0 \ldots cs719$) are generated for each IV. The first 360 bits ($cs0 \ldots cs359$) are used to encrypt the packet sent from the base station to the phone (FP $\rightarrow$ PP). The remaining 360 bits ($cs360 \ldots cs719$) are used to encrypt the packet sent from the phone to the base station (PP $\rightarrow$ FP) in the same frame. To encrypt a packet, the first 40 bits of key stream ($cs0 \ldots cs39$) are used to encrypt C-channel messages in the A-field, if the A-field contains C-channel traffic. If no C-channel traffic is present in the packet, the first 40 bits ($cs0 \ldots cs39$) are silently discarded. The remaining 320 bits ($cs40 \ldots cs359$) are XORed with the B-field to encrypt the payload present in the B-field. An overview of the process is given in Figure 3.

To enable encryption, the base station sends a CIPHER-REQUEST message to the phone, indicating that it requests ciphering. The phone either confirms that using a mac layer message, or sends a CIPHER-REJECT message back to the base

Figure 2: Authentication of a DECT PP

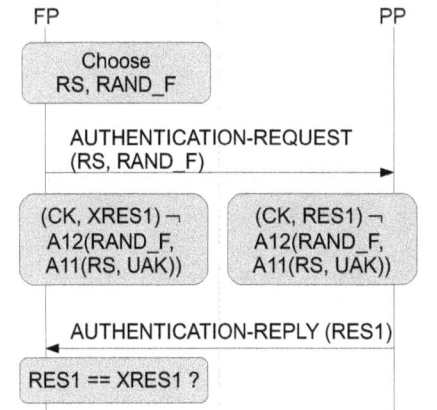

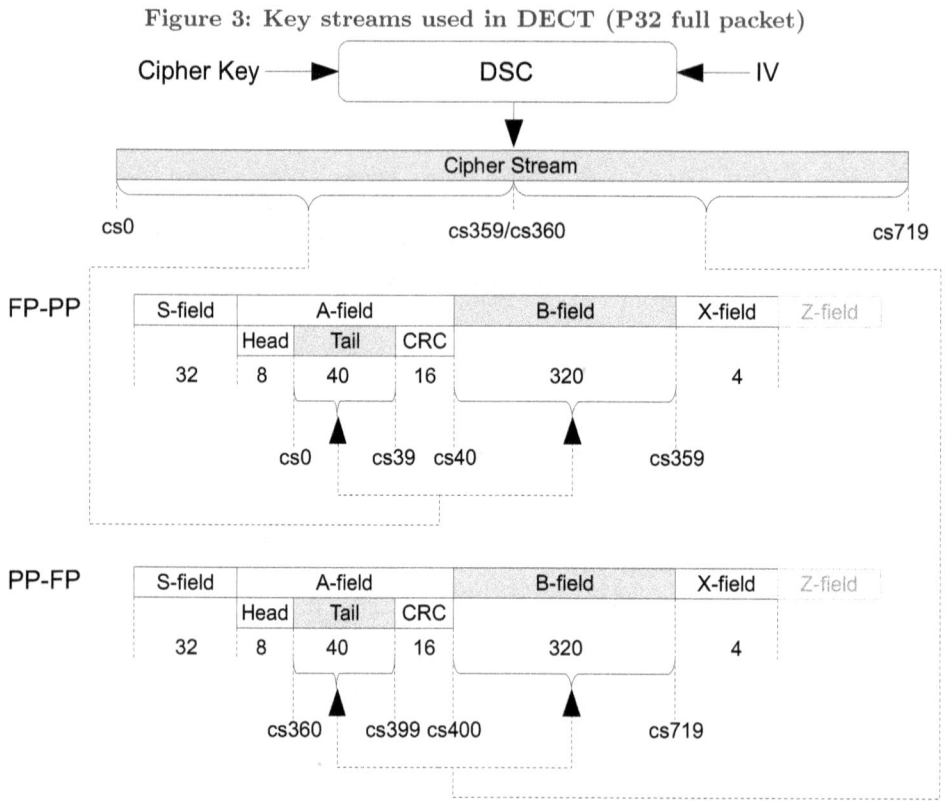

Figure 3: Key streams used in DECT (P32 full packet)

station, indicating that it is not capable of enabling ciphering. After ciphering has been confirmed by the phone, the base station sends a mac layer message back to the phone to confirm. The next packet send or received will be encrypted.

3. EXECUTION OF THE ATTACK

The attack is executed in two phases: In the first phase outlined in Section 3.1, the call is passively recorded. If the call would be unencrypted, the attack would be finished after this step. For encrypted calls, a second phase outlined in Section 3.2 is executed, which decrypts the call.

3.1 Recording the encrypted call

In the first phase, a call is recorded in its encrypted form. To do so, the attacker needs to be in communication range of the victim's phone and base station. If he is able to receive signals from multiple base stations, he needs to pick the right one, or just record all calls originating from any base station. To pick the right one, he might call the victim's land line, and see which base stations signal an incoming call to their phones. It is not required that the victim takes the call, only that the base station signals to at least one of the phones that there is an incoming call. Repeating this procedure should narrow down the set of possible base stations to a single one. Alternatively the attacker could use a directional antenna pointing at the victim's base station and pick the one with the strongest signal.

The attacker now records all packets send between the base station and the phones. We decided to use the tools written by the authors of [5] for this purpose. For simplification, we assume that only one phone is present, however

the attack could also be carried out if multiple phones are present at the victim's base station.

After the call has been completed, the attacker is ready to execute the second phase of the attack. Because the second phase of the attack will disrupt communication between the phone and it's base station, the attacker may decide to delay the second phase to a later time, if he expects more calls to be made in the next time he is interested in.

3.2 Decryption of the call

The key idea in the second phase of the attack is, to use a replay attack against the phone to recover all keystreams, which were used to encrypt the original call. We first set up our base station impersonating the original base station of the victim.

3.2.1 Jamming the base station

To make the victim's phone loose communication with its original base station, one can use a utility named *hijack*, that is part of *libdect*, which broadcasts frames in the same channel and time slot as the original base station suggesting that the phone should change it's frequency and time slot. When the phone has received such a packet, it will switch to the frequency and time slot we suggested and switch to our base station. Checking whether the phone has locked on our base station can be done by periodically broadcasting a `LCE-PAGE-REQUEST` message from our base station. When the phone answers to the `LCE-PAGE-REQUEST`, it has locked on our base station.

DECT base stations are usually built in a way that they can detect another base station broadcasting on their frequency in their time slot. They do that by periodically skipping some of their broadcast packets and instead switching to listen mode in this time slot. If a signal is received there, another system must be broadcasting on the same frequency and time slot and the time slot or the frequency is changed. When we broadcast a request that the phone should switch to the frequency and time slot of our faked base station, our packet will not collide with the packed send by the base station and will very likely be received by the phone correctly.

3.2.2 Recovering the key streams

In the next step, we need to set the correct cipher key on the phone, which was used in the call we would like to decrypt. If no further call has been made and the phone was not switched off in the meantime, we could skip this step. Executing the step will only cost less than a second of additional attack time. Of course we do not know the key, otherwise, we could easily decrypt the call from our capture ourselves. However, the key was derived from the UAK and two random numbers RAND_F and RS using the A11 and A12 algorithms at the begin of the recorded call. We simply send again the AUTHENTICATION-REQUEST message, which was exchanged at the beginning of the recorded call. The phone will respond with an AUTHENTICATION-REPLY message containing the response of the challenge we send.

If the response, which is included, is not equal to the response in our recording, we might have picked the wrong phone, recorded incorrect data or the UAK on the phone has been altered. Therefore, the following steps would be unlikely to succeed:

We now repeat the following procedure: Let n be the multiframe number of the first packet in our capture that we have not decrypted so far. We wait just before our base station broadcasts the next update of our multiframe number using a Q-channel message and set the multiframe number of our base station to $n - (t_d/16)$. Here, t_d is the time it takes from sending a CIPHER-REQUEST message to the phone until ciphering is enabled in the MAC layer and the first encrypted packet from the phone is sent in 10^{-2} seconds.

Then we broadcast our multiframe number update and send a CIPHER-REQUEST message to the phone. The phone will receive our multiframe number update and update its multiframe number accordingly. After having received our CIPHER-REQUEST message, the phone will respond with an encryption control MAC layer message stating that it is ready to enable encryption. We now confirm that using a MAC layer message and the phone will signal that it will enable encryption now. The next packet sent by the phone will be encrypted using the same key as the original call and the same initialization vectors (frame numbers) will be used. From now on, we do not send any payload to the phone and wait until the LCE.01 timer on the phone has expired and the link is released. Because we have not established a phone call on the link or did run any other application on it, the B-fields of all frames sent by the phone just contained **0xff** as plaintext. XORing all B-fields of the received frames with **0xff** reveals the key streams used to encrypt the frames in the original call. XORing these key streams with the B-fields in the original call decrypts these B-fields, revealing the audio data sent from the phone to the base station in the original call. We now repeat that procedure until all original call frames have been decrypted.

After the call has been decrypted, we shut down our base

station and the phone starts scanning for the original base station and locks on it again.

Choosing t_d too small when implementing the attack results in some keystreams at the beginning of the call not being recovered. Choosing t_d too large results in a small performance decrease of the attack, so one might choose a slightly larger value for t_d in this step.

Figure 4: Attack overview

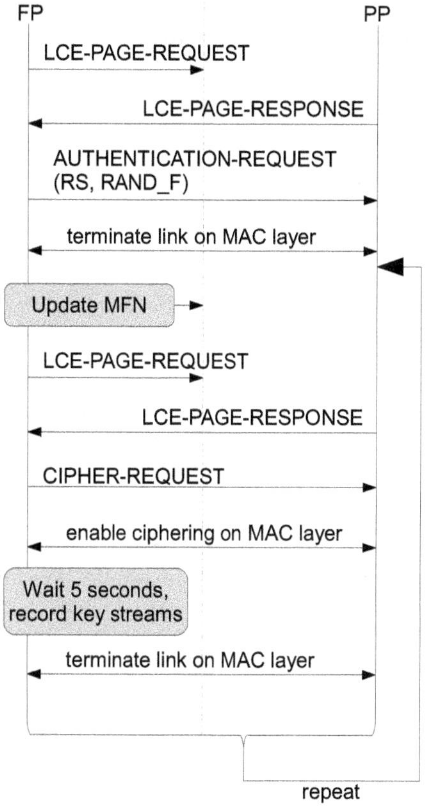

4. IMPLEMENTATION

We implemented a proof-of-concept of our attack. As basis, we used a DECT stack for the Linux kernel, which is available on http://dect.osmocom.org/. We needed to tweak three parts of the stack:

kernel We made a small change to the kernel code, that makes it possible to update the multiframe number in the kernel from the userland.

libnl We added another function, that passes a new multiframe number from the userland to the kernel.

libdect This library implements all higher level functionality of the kernel stack. We added a small change to libdect so that a program using libdect can pass a new multi frame number to the kernel, using libnl. We also wrote a new program that uses libdect to implement the attack tool. Because libdect already implemented much of the functionality we needed, we were able to implement the tool in 222 lines of C-code.

To enable encryption on the link, we used a cipher key CK with all bytes set to zero (**0x00 0x00 0x00 0x00 0x00 0x00 0x00 0x00**), so that the kernel decrypted all the encrypted traffic with this key. To capture the encrypted frames, we used libpcap, which is also part of the DECT stack, which we did not need to modify. To reveal the keystream, we decrypted the received B-field with the cipher key **0x00 0x00 0x00 0x00 0x00 0x00 0x00 0x00** again, which revealed the original B-field received and then XORed the B-field with **0xff** to reveal the keystreams.

We used a Siemens Gigaset AS150 phone to test our code. During implementation and execution, we observed the following effects:

- The phone did accept changes of the multiframe number without any problems, when the phone was in idle mode. However, it sometimes took the phone a few seconds until it was responsive again, after having changed the multiframe number.

- Changing the multiframe number after having established a connection, but before sending the **CIPHER-REQUEST** message did cause the phone to drop the connection.

- Sometimes, the phone lost the connection with our base station and became unresponsive. Stopping our base station and starting it again a few seconds later solved the problem. Restarting the phone or any other kind of interaction with the phone was never required, so this would only cause a delay in the execution of the attack, but not render it impossible. We are not entirely sure yet, whether this is a problem on the phone DECT stack or on our side.

- Sometimes, we received a few bits in the B-field incorrectly, resulting in some bits of the keystream recovered incorrectly. However, this only creates minor variations in the recovered audio stream, which usually will not be noticed.

  If this method would be used to recover a data-call (for example wireless internet access over DECT), this might be a problem. One could execute the attack multiple times to spot and correct variations in the keystreams recovered.

We also tested the attack successfully against a *Siemens Gigaset 4000 Classic* and a *T-Sinus 501* phone. Another test against an *AVM FritzFon* failed, due to genereal problems with our DECT stack, not related to the attack.

4.1 Performance

We were able to establish a connection with the phone about once every 14 seconds. A single connection lasted for 5 seconds, until the phones LCE.01 timer expired. (In fact our fake base station implements a 5 seconds LCE.01 timer, so our base station closes the connection just before the phone would have closed it. Disabling this timer on our base station makes the phone close the connection a few moments later, because it also implements the timer.) As a result, we were able to recover about 500 key streams in 14 seconds. The exact attack speed depends on the timing parameters chosen for the implementation and on the attacked phone.

As we did not send any call related messages on the C-channel, the phone did never ring or play any other sounds. Also, the content of the phone display did not change during the attack. Only when we had to restart our base station, the phone display indicated that it has lost the link to its base station and was now scanning for the base station. This makes it very unlikely that the attack is detected by a user by looking at the phone. Of course a user with a DECT sniffer could detect the presence of an attacker.

5. VARIATIONS AND FUTURE WORK

The attack is also applicable if the start of the call we would like to decrypt has not been recorded or has been recorded incorrectly. If so, the attacker does not know the random numbers used at the beginning of the call, and cannot replay them to the phone. But the attacker would still be able to send the **CIPHER-REQUEST** command to the phone, and as long as no subsequent call has been made on the phone, execute the attack anyway.

At the moment, we are just able to hold the connection to the phone for about 5 seconds, until the phones LCE.01 timer has expired. Setting up the connection again takes some time and slows down the attack from a theoretical maximal speed of 100 key streams per second to about 33 key streams per second. If one could find a way to send messages to the phone while the link is open to prevent the phones timer from expiring, this could speed up the attack. At the moment, we are not able to send C-channel messages over the link, because we cannot properly encrypt such messages, because we do not have a way to generate or recover the needed key streams.

The attack only recovers the parts of the key streams used by the phone to encrypt the B-field of frames, which are transmitted from the phone to the base station, more precisely bits 400 to 719 of the output of DSC (cs400...cs719). If one could recover other parts of the output of DSC, one could decrypt parts of the data sent from the base station to the phone (bits 0 to 359 are used here), or parts of the C-channel traffic send from the phone to the base station (bits 360 to 399). Besides the full frame (named P32 in the DECT standard), the DECT standard also defines the *half frame format* (named P08j). Here, only 80 instead of 320 bits are used for the B-field. So bits 160 to 199 are used to encrypt the B-field send from the phone to the base station. If one would request the usage of half slots from the phone, one could recover bits 160 to 199 of the output of DSC and use these bits to decrypt parts of the voice-data send from the base station to the phone in the original call.

5.1 TETRA and GSM

TETRA (Terrestrial Trunked Radio)[2] is a digital radio protocol mostly used by government agencies to replace analog walkie-talkies. GSM (Global System for Mobile Communications)[3] is a radio protocol for digital cell phones). TETRA and GSM use a similar radio protocol. We think that the attack techniques used here might be applicable to these protocols too. A similar protocol level attack against GSM is known[1], but no attack on GSM or TETRA using our method has been published so far.

---

[2] http://www.etsi.org/website/Technologies/TETRA.aspx
[3] http://www.etsi.org/WebSite/technologies/gsm.aspx

6. COUNTERMEASURES

We think the attack is hard to counter. The attack uses no implementation specific problems and just relies on the standard. However, we discuss countermeasures in this section:

6.1 Forbidding the reuse of random numbers

In our attack, we negotiate the same key again as in the original call. A phone could keep a record of the last used keys and/or random numbers in the key exchange messages to prevent renegotiation of an old key. First of all, the standard does not prohibit the reuse of random numbers, so this could lead to compatibility problems with base stations, which tend to reuse keys. In addition, this will be hard to implement on low-cost consumer phones, with very limited memory. One could store the list of old keys in RAM, which would be erased when the phone is turned off. Storing the list in the EEPROM would also be unwise, because the EEPROM can only do a limited amount of write-cycles, before the memory gets permanently damaged. The attacker could also negotiate a lot of random keys with the phone first, so that the key the attacker is targeting for would be erased from that list.

In addition, cipher keys should be erased from the phone memory, after a link using that cipher key has been terminated.

6.2 Requiring authentication of the base station first

In contrast to GSM, DECT also supports authentication of base stations. So far, we have not seen a phone in the real world, that uses this feature[6]. This feature is defined in the standard and could easily be implemented. A phone could request that a base station authenticates itself first, before being allowed to enable encryption on a link or to request authentication. However, a skilled attacker could relay these requests to the original base station, impersonating the phone. As a result, the attack would still be possible, however the base station would be able to report the abnormal high rate of authentication requests. Because this authentication procedure does not affect the cipher key, the base station and the phone cannot alter the cipher key by choosing different random numbers for every authentication.

6.3 Checking for changes in the multiframe number broadcasted by the base station

Setting the multiframe number used by our base station back to a value used in the original call is vital to our attack. In practice, a base station should never change their multiframe number, except for a base station, which has just been started or restarted. Frequent changes in the multiframe number of a base station can be detected by a phone and should be seen as in indicator of an attack. A phone could, for example, put a base station that changes their multiframe number frequently on a temporary blacklist. This could be used to render the attack less effective, but not impossible, because a base station has to be allowed to reset its multiframe number when it has been restarted.

6.4 Rekeying

To counter key recovery attacks on the DSC, a new update of the DECT GAP (Generic Access Profile) Standard[2] was published in 2010[4], which allows rekeying during a call. Because current attacks on DSC need a lot of keystreams and a single cipher key is only used for 60 seconds and thus generates 6000 keystreams at most, making key recovery attacks impractical. For rekeying, a new `AUTHENTICATION-REQUEST` message is being sent during an encrypted call, negotiating a new key. Our attack relies on the fact that we can see the random numbers embedded in that message and replay them later. As a result, we would only be able to decipher the first 60 seconds of a call, until the first rekeying event. The `AUTHENTICATION-REQUEST` message cannot be decrypted using our method because it is sent from the base station to the phone, but not in the reverse direction. Also, we would be able to decipher the last seconds of a call, if no subsequent call has been made, and the key is still present in the phone memory.

To attack such phones, attempts to change the multiframe number during a call could be made, so that the `AUTHENTICATION-REQUEST` message sent from the base station in its encrypted form can be replayed. However, we are at the moment not in possession of a phone, which implements this updated DECT GAP standard, and therefore we cannot perform tests on such a phone.

6.5 Disabling B-field encryption, when unused

Another countermeasure would be to send the B-field unencrypted, when it is not used to transport payload. Alternatively, the B-field could be filled with random data instead.

7. CONCLUSION

We have shown that calls made with DECT phones, which do not allow unencrypted calls and have no other implementation flaws, can be decrypted. This works even for very short calls, where a key recovery attack against DSC is not (currently) possible. Weak spots are the missing replay protection and that the cipher key is only derived from the UAK and random numbers chosen only by the base station, but not by the phone. The attack is practical and can be executed at very low cost.

We are confident, that these problems and all other known problems in the DECT standard will be fixed by ETSI in a new release of the DECT standard with a new version of the security algorithms namely DSAA and DSC and the corresponding changes in the DECT protocol. We have contacted DECT device manufacturers so that they can evaluate our results and implement countermeasures. Today, DECT is still a great standard for cordless phones, which outperforms WIFI-phones when it comes to implementation costs and energy efficiency, but cannot provide the same level of security as an WPA2 protected wireless network.

We would like to thank the DECT Forum and ETSI. We notified both of them in advance, so that they can start to incorporate countermeasures against the attack in the next release of the DECT standard.

8. REFERENCES

[1] E. Barkan, E. Biham, and N. Keller. Instant ciphertext-only cryptanalysis of GSM encrypted communication. *Advances in Cryptology-CRYPTO 2003*, pages 600–616, 2003.

[2] European Telecommunications Standards Institute. ETSI EN 300 444 V2.1.1: Digital Enhanced Cordless Telecommunications (DECT); Generic Access Profile (GAP), Oct 2008.

[3] European Telecommunications Standards Institute. Digital Enhanced Cordless Telecommunications (DECT); Common Interface (CI); Part 1: Overview, June 2010.

[4] European Telecommunications Standards Institute. ETSI EN 300 444 V2.2.1: Digital Enhanced Cordless Telecommunications (DECT); Generic Access Profile (GAP), June 2010.

[5] S. Lucks, A. Schuler, E. Tews, R. Weinmann, and M. Wenzel. Attacks on the DECT authentication mechanisms. *Topics in Cryptology–CT-RSA 2009*, pages 48–65.

[6] A. Mengele. Digital Enhanced Cordless Telecommunication (DECT) devices for residential use. Diploma thesis, Technische Universität Darmstadt, 2009.

[7] H. Molter, K. Ogata, E. Tews, and R. Weinmann. An Efficient FPGA Implementation for an DECT Brute-Force Attacking Scenario. In *2009 Fifth International Conference on Wireless and Mobile Communications*, pages 82–86. IEEE, 2009.

[8] K. Nohl, E. Tews, and R. Weinmann. Cryptanalysis of the DECT standard cipher. In *Proceedings of the 17th international conference on Fast software encryption*, pages 1–18. Springer-Verlag, 2010.

[9] M. Weiner, E. Tews, B. Heinz, and J. Heyszl. Fpga implementation of an improved attack against the dect standard cipher. In *ICISC 2010 - 13th Annual International Conference on Information Security and Cryptology*, LNCS. Springer, Nov 2010.

APPENDIX

A. ACRONYMS

Name	Description	Section
A11	Algorithm in DSAA	2.2
A12	Algorithm in DSAA	2.2
A21	Algorithm in DSAA	2.2
A22	Algorithm in DSAA	2.2
AUTHENTICATION-REQUEST	Message to request authentication	2.2
AUTHENTICATION-RESPONSE	Response to an authentication request	2.2
C-Channel	A channel for control traffic	2.1
CIPHER-REQUEST	Message to request start of ciphering	2.3
CK	Cipher Key	2.2
DSAA	DECT Standard Authentication Algorithm	1, 2.2
DSC	DECT Standard Cipher	1, 2.3
FP	DECT base station	1
frame	Time period of 10 ms	2.1
LCE.01	Timer which starts when a connection is not required anymore	2.1
LCE-PAGE-REQUEST	Message to request a phone to start a connection	2.1
multiframe number	Most significant bits of a frame number	2.1
P00	Packet format with no B-field	2.1
P08j	Packet format with 80 bits B-field	5
P32	Standard packet format with 320 bits B-field	2.1
packet	A single data burst	2.1
PP	DECT phone	1
RAND_F	Random number chosen by a base station	2.2
RAND_P	Random number chosen by a phone	2.2
RES1	Response to a challenge during authentication of a phone	2.2
RES2	Response to a challenge during authentication of a base station	2.2
RS	Random number chosen by a DECT network	2.2
UAK	User Authentication Key (shared by phone and base station)	2.2

Cryptographic Link Signatures for Spectrum Usage Authentication in Cognitive Radio*

Xi Tan, Kapil Borle, Wenliang Du and Biao Chen
Dept. of Electrical Engineering & Computer Science, Syracuse University
Syracuse, New York, USA
{xtan, kmborle, wedu, bichen}@syr.edu

ABSTRACT

It was shown that most of the radio frequency spectrum was inefficiently utilized. To fully use these spectrums, cognitive radio networks have been proposed. The idea is to allow secondary users to use a spectrum if the primary user (i.e., the legitimate owner of the spectrum) is not using it. To achieve this, secondary users should constantly monitor the usage of the spectrum to avoid interference with the primary user. However, achieving a trustworthy monitoring is not easy. A malicious secondary user who wants to gain an unfair use of a spectrum can emulate the primary user, and can thus trick the other secondary users into believing that the primary user is using the spectrum when it is not. This attack is called the Primary User Emulation (PUE) attack. To prevent this attack, there should be a way to authenticate primary users' spectrum usage.

We propose a method that allows primary users to add a cryptographic link signature to its signal so the spectrum usage by primary users can be authenticated. This signature is added to the signal in a transparent way, such that the receivers (who do not care about the signature) still function as usual, while the cognitive radio receivers can retrieve the signature from the signal. We describe two schemes to add a signature, one using modulation, and the other using coding. We have analyzed the performance of both schemes.

Categories and Subject Descriptors

K.6.5 [**Management of Computing and Information Systems**]: Security and Protection—*Authentication, Physical security, Unauthorized access*

General Terms

Security

---

*This work was supported in part by AFOSR Award No. FA9550-09-1-0224 and by a subcontract from ANDRO Computational Solutions under the AFOSR STTR program contract FA9550-10C0179.

Keywords

Cognitive Radio Networks, Primary User Emulation Attack, Physical-layer Authentication

1. INTRODUCTION

Recently, there has been a growing interest in cognitive radio. In general, cognitive radio refers to a wireless device that can change its transmission or reception parameters to achieve efficient communication [13]. One of the promising applications of cognitive radio is to enable the current fixed spectrum channels assigned by Federal Communications Commission (FCC) to be utilized by new users.

In a recent study, FCC has found that most of the radio frequency spectrum was inefficiently utilized [22]: some spectrum is overloaded, while other spectrum is rarely used. This is because spectrum is statically assigned by FCC; only the FCC-designated owners can use the spectrum assigned to them. With cognitive radios, FCC is considering allowing unlicensed users to utilize licensed bands provided it would not cause any interference (by avoiding transmission whenever licensed user's presence is sensed). This is a new paradigm for wireless communication. The licensed user is called *primary user*, and the unlicensed user is called *secondary user*.

Threat in cognitive radio network: To avoid interfering with primary users, secondary users should conduct primary user detection, i.e. to detect whether a primary user is using its spectrum or not. There are two main approaches for primary user detection: *energy detection* and *feature detection* [14]. In energy detection, secondary users use energy strength to identify a primary user's signal, whereas in feature detection, secondary users find some specific features of a signal, and use these features to identify a primary user. Examples of features include pilot, synchronization word, and cyclostationarity [10, 19, 20].

Unfortunately, neither energy detection nor feature detection can produce a trustworthy result. If a malicious secondary user wants to gain an unfair use of the primary user's idle spectrum, it can emulate the primary user's behavior or energy strength when sending its own signals. This attack is called Primary User Emulation (PUE) attack. In cognitive radio networks, it is essential to be able to detect whether the legitimate primary user is using the spectrum or not even if the network is under PUE attacks.

Existing approaches: The problem is actually an authentication problem, i.e., when a receiver has detected signals at a particular spectrum, how can the receiver be sure that the signal is indeed sent by the primary owner of the spectrum? In general, this is a solved problem, as we can simply ask the primary user to attach a digital signature in its signals. Unfortunately, we are facing three constraints.

First, in cognitive radio networks, it is impractical to conduct authentication at layers other than the physical layer. As we know, authentication can be done at various levels, including data-link layer (e.g. wireless access point), network layer (e.g. IPSec), transport layer (e.g. SSL), and application layer (e.g. SSH). Unfortunately, conducting authentication above the physical layer does not seem practical in the cognitive radio applications. The reason is the following. For two devices to be able to authenticate each other at Layer N, these devices normally need to have a common component at Layer N. For example, to use IPSec for authentication purpose, both devices must run the IP and IPSec protocols. In the Internet, most of the computers are running IP, so this is not an issue. Unfortunately, in the wireless world, devices are so diversified, many of them differ significantly above the physical layer. For example, a cognitive radio receiver may be able to receive signals from TV stations, process them at the physical layer, but it may lack the component to understand the data in the signals. Therefore, if the authentication depends on the correct understanding of the data (done at upper layers), the cognitive radio receiver will be unable to authenticate the primary user.

Second, the authentication scheme should be transparent to the existing receivers, i.e., after the authentication information is added to signals, the existing devices should still be able to work as usual, although they may not be able to authenticate the signals. This requirement is extremely important. For example, when a TV station adds some authentication information to its signals for cognitive radio receivers, if all the existing television sets (which are not cognitive radios) need to be recalled and modified, no TV station will add the authentication information. Therefore, it is essential for the authentication scheme at the physical layer to be transparent to the existing devices.

Third, to further complicate the problem, FCC made another rule, stating that "no modification to the incumbent system (i.e., primary user) should be required to accommodate opportunistic use of the spectrum by secondary users" [5].

Several solutions have been proposed to solve the authentication problem. One approach is to use location detection [4]. Namely, secondary users detect whether a signal is indeed from the primary user's location. Such an approach either needs to use sophisticated antenna or collaboration of multiple nodes; both are expensive.

Recently, Liu et al proposed an interesting solution to solve the authentication problem while complying to the FCC regulation [16]. In this scheme, a helper node is placed close to a primary user. The idea is to put necessary mechanisms on the helper node, which then conveys the authentication information to the secondary users. While this scheme complies with the FCC restriction, the cost is quite significant. For example, establishing such a node is not easy or cheap. To cover the same area as its primary user, the helper node needs to use the same level of energy when transmitting (a typical Digital TV tower covers over 50 miles radius). Although the helper node does not need to transmit at all the time, its overall energy usage is significant, as it

needs to wake up quite frequently to serve the newly joined secondary users, who can join at any arbitrary time.

Our approach. We have a different take on the FCC regulation. The main reason for this regulation is the cost induced on the primary users. If the cost is too high, primary users will be reluctant to participate. The cost can be measured from three aspects: the existing receiver's equipment update costs, the primary user's equipment update costs, and the operation cost. Since the existing receivers are often in a large quantity for most primary users, any solution that requires the update on the existing receivers will never be adopted. Therefore, the main concern of the FCC regulation boils down to the cost on the primary users, including the operating costs and an one-time equipment update cost.

The ideal solution is to follow the FCC rule while paying no cost or minimal cost. Such a solution has yet to be discovered and will be definitely an interesting direction to pursue. The state-of-art solution proposed by Liu et al. [16] complies with the FCC rule, but pays a heavy cost on both operation and equipment. If the FCC's real concern is the cost, a solution with lower cost should become promising even if the FCC rule is not followed. Unlike the other FCC rules, there is no negative impact on the community if this rule is violated. We strongly believe that if we can demonstrate significant benefit, FCC may consider lifting this rule. After all, by allowing cognitive radios to use primary users' spectrum, FCC is actually lifting a pre-existing rule. Moreover, FCC rules only apply to the U.S., other counties may not have such a rule.

For this technical paper, we have no intention of arguing whether FCC should lift that rule (the decision is more political than scientific). Our objective is to show the research community as well as to FCC the followings using scientific evidences (instead of political arguments): (1) the FCC regulation can be lifted without affecting the existing receivers, and (2) without this FCC regulation, the cost of authenticating primary users can be significantly reduced by using the ideas proposed in the paper.

Our problem, constraints, and challenges. Summarizing the above discussion, we formulate the following objective for this paper:

> Our objective is to develop low-cost physical-layer schemes for authenticating primary users' spectrum usage. The schemes should be transparent to the existing receivers.

We have developed two techniques, one based on the QPSK modulation, and the other based on error-correcting codes. We have conducted comprehensive analysis to demonstrate the effectiveness of our schemes.

2. PHYSICAL-LAYER SPECTRUM USAGE AUTHENTICATION

The problem we are addressing in this paper seems like a broadcast authentication problem [18]; however, compared to the existing broadcast authentication problem, our problem has the following unique properties. First, the goal of our problem is to authenticate the *spectrum usage*, i.e., to verify whether the primary user is indeed using a specific spectrum; we do not need to verify whether the *contents* sent by the primary user are authentic or not. On the other hand, verifying the authenticity of the contents is exactly the objective of broadcast authentication.

Second, there are two types of receivers in our problem. One is the cognitive radio receivers (called *CR Receivers* in short). They need to be able to authenticate the spectrum usage from the signals sent by the primary users. Because this type of receivers is not the dedicated "listener" of a primary user, they may not have the capabilities (e.g. circuit or software) to understand the primary user beyond the physical layer. Therefore, the authentication has to be done at the physical layer. The solutions to the broadcast authentication problem do not have such a constraint, so they are mostly developed in the upper layers.

The other type of users is the existing receivers. They are, in many cases, not cognitive radios. They have no interest to verify whether a spectrum is actually used by a primary user or not. We call this type of receivers the *non-CR* receivers. Because the physical-layer functionalities are usually built into the hardware for these receivers, it is difficult and costly to modify these receivers. Therefore, the solution to our problem should not require any change to the non-CR receivers. The traditional broadcast authentication problem does not have such a constraint.

Based on the unique features of our problem, we decompose our problems into two independent problems:

- **Problem 1 (Tag Generation):** What kind of information should be used for authenticating spectrum usage? Namely, how can primary users generate authentication tags (we refer to the authentication information as *authentication tag* in this paper), so CR receivers can use the tag to verify whether a spectrum is currently being used by its legitimate owner or not?

- **Problem 2 (Tag Transmission):** How can primary users transmit authentication tags, so the tags can be retrieved by CR receivers from the signal at the physical layer, while the tags do not interfere with non-CR receivers' functionalities. In other words, authentication tags should be *transparent* to non-CR receivers.

2.1 Authentication Tag Generation

Problem 1 can be solved using one-way hash chains. We describe the solution in the following.

Preparation: The primary user generates the following one-way hash chain:

$$h_n \to h_{n-1} \to \ldots \to h_1 \to h_0,$$
$$\text{where } h_i = hash(h_{i+1}).$$

The end of the hash chain, h_0, should be published beforehand so all CR receivers can get it. For example, h_0 can be published on a web site [1]. Each number on the hash chain is only valid in a specific time window. We use $[t_{i-1}, t_i]$ to represent the effective time window for the hash value h_i. The hash chain has to be used reversely, i.e., h_1 will be used first (during $[t_0, t_1]$), then h_2 (during $[t_1, t_2]$), and so on. Because of the way how the one-way hash chain is generated, disclosing h_i does not lead to the disclosure of h_j for $j > i$.

Authentication Tag. For the primary user, between time t_{i-1} and t_i, the authentication tag is simply h_i, i.e., the

---

[1]The web site should use `https` to protect the authenticity of h_0.

primary user simply embeds h_i to its signals (how to embed the value to signals will be discussed later). An example is shown in Figure 1. In this example, during $[t_1, t_2]$, h_2 is embedded in the signals, and sent out repeatedly. The repetition is necessary because CR receivers may tune in to this spectrum at any arbitrary moment.

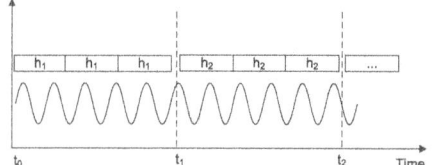

Figure 1: Authentication Tags

Tag Verification. Once a CR receiver receives the signals from a particular spectrum, it retrieves the authentication tag h_i from the signals; then using the current time and the spectrum owner's h_0 value[2], the receiver can verify the validity of h_i. It should be noted that only loose time synchronization is needed in this scheme.

Replaying Attacks. At first sight, this solution seems problematic, because a malicious receiver can replay the authentication tag in its own signals once the valid h_i is disclosed by the primary user. This is actually not a big problem. Recall the goal of h_i is to prove to the receivers that the primary user is using the current spectrum at time t, where $t \in [t_{i-1}, t_i]$. If the primary user is still using the spectrum, then replaying h_i has no negative effect, because whatever the attack says is still the truth. However, if the primary user stops using the spectrum, then the attacker's replaying of h_i will have a negative effect, as the attacker can successfully fool the receivers. Nevertheless, such attack is only effective within the $[t_{i-1}, t_i]$ time window. When the time window expires, attackers need h_{i+1} to continue to fool the receivers. However, if the primary user is not using the spectrum, h_{i+1} will not be sent out.

Therefore, the maximum advantage that a malicious user can take is the length of a time window, i.e., they can unfairly use the rest of a time window if the primary user stops. As we will show later, the actual time window can be set to quite to a small value, thus minimizing the impact of such an attack. For example, for Digital TV broadcasting, our results show that the time to transmit one 128-bit tag is only 3.2 ms. If we allow 5 seconds of error (in both directions) in clock synchronization, an 11-second window will be sufficient.

When the time window gets smaller, the hash chain will be longer for a fixed period of time. If a primary user stops using a spectrum for a long period of time, receivers need to do many hash functions to verify an authentication tag when the primary user becomes active. This is not a major problem, because hash operations are quite efficient. However, if such a cost is a concern for CR receivers, we can use multiple hash chains. For example, we can use a different hash chain each day, so every day, we start with a new h_0 value. All these h_0 values can be distributed together.

---

[2]Spectrum assignments are public knowledge, and can be obtained beforehand.

81

2.2 Authentication Tag Transmission

After the authentication tag is generated, we need to find a way to embed the tag in the signals. Generally speaking, this should not be very difficult; however, we are bounded by two constraints. First, tags have to be added at the physical layer. This is because most primary users differ quite significantly above the physical layer. For a CR receiver to authenticate different primary users at upper layers require the CR receiver to be equipped with the corresponding hardware or software to understand the protocols at upper layers. This is expensive and unrealistic. Our second constraint is the transparency requirement. In order not to disrupting service to existing receivers, the added authentication tag should not require any modification for the non-CR receivers.

The question is whether any information can be added to the physical layer without changing the physical-layer behaviors of the non-CR receivers. The answer is yes. Actually, in wireless communication, extra data are constantly "added" to the existing signals; these data are called *noise*. During the transmission of wireless signals, noise are always present in the received signals. Therefore, the physical-layer logic has to be designed to tolerate noise up to certain degree.

Our idea is to treat the authentication tag as noise ("man-made" noise), and then intentionally add the noise to the signals. If we can keep the noise level low enough, the physical-layer logic of the non-CR receiver will naturally filter out the noise. On the other hand, if we can keep the noise level above certain threshold, the CR receivers will be able to retrieve the "man-made" noise (i.e. tags) from the signals.

Our main challenge is to find a place in the physical layer, where the "man-made" noise can be added. There are two main components in the physical layer: coding and modulation. For coding, there are two different types: one is source coding, the goal of which is to increase the efficiency of transmission; the other is channel coding, the goal of which is to improve the reliability of transmission. We focus on the channel coding component. For modulation, its goal is to transform a message signal (e.g. a digital bit stream or an analog audio signal) into suitable format that can be physically transmitted. Authentication tags can be added to both coding and modulation components (see Figure 2). We will discuss them separately in the following two sections.

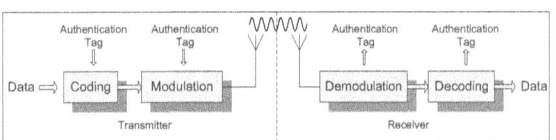

Figure 2: Process

3. ADDING TAGS TO MODULATION

In this section, we describe how authentication tags can be transparently added to modulation schemes at the physical layer. There are many modulation schemes, and the way how tags are added will be quite different, although the essence is the same, i.e., tags are added as noise. In this paper, to present a concrete method, we have chosen a popular modulation scheme, called QPSK (Quadri-Phase-Shift Key-

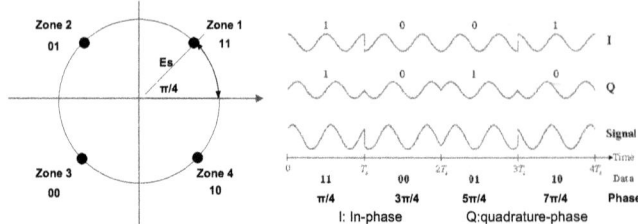

Figure 3: QPSK Modulation

ing). We describe how tags can be added to this particular scheme. The technique can be easily generalized to broader classes of modulations, such as PSK (Phase Shift Keying), of which QPSK is a special case.

3.1 QPSK Background

QPSK [12] is one of the digital modulation techniques used for transmission of digitally represented data. This modulation scheme uses phases in the transmitted wave to carry information. In QPSK, four phases are used: $\frac{\pi}{4}$, $\frac{3\pi}{4}$, $\frac{5\pi}{4}$ and $\frac{7\pi}{4}$. These four phases can carry two bits of information. Therefore, in the input data, which is a sequence of binary data stream, each two bits are treated as a pair. There are four combination of pairs: 00, 01, 10 and 11, and each of these unique combinations is called a *dibit*. Each dibit is mapped to one phase. For example, if we choose the Gray encoded set of dibits, 11, 01, 00 and 10 are mapped to phases $\frac{\pi}{4}$, $\frac{3\pi}{4}$, $\frac{5\pi}{4}$ and $\frac{7\pi}{4}$, respectively. This mapping is called a *dibit-phase mapping*.

With this dibit-phase mapping, we can modulate the signal using the following signal modulation equation:

$$S_i(t) = \sqrt{\frac{2E_s}{T}} \cos(2\pi f_c t + (2i-1)\frac{\pi}{4}) \quad i = 1, 2, 3, 4.$$

A QPSK signal can actually be represented by a two-dimensional signal constellation, which is a common representation of signal in digital modulation schemes. QPSK constellation is considered as a diagram for dibits-phase mapping. The diagram is divided into four zones by the x-axis and y-axis. There are four message points in the constellation diagram, each falling into one zone. These points represent messages 11, 01, 00 and 10; their corresponding phases are $\frac{\pi}{4}$, $\frac{3\pi}{4}$, $\frac{5\pi}{4}$, and $\frac{7\pi}{4}$, respectively. These points' signal strength is the same (equal to E_s), so they are placed on the same circle. Figure 3 depicts the constellation diagram.

In QPSK modulation, the digital data stream is transformed to the resulting QPSK signal and then the transmitter would send it out. When a receiver gets the signal, it generates a QPSK constellation from the received signal. Then, depending on which zone a signal falls into, the receiver can determine the dibit information in the signal.

3.2 QPSK Tagging Scheme

Because of noise, when receivers receive a signal, and convert the signal into the QPSK constellation diagram, the message points may not fall exactly on their original positions, i.e. at $\frac{\pi}{4}$, $\frac{3\pi}{4}$, $\frac{5\pi}{4}$ or $\frac{7\pi}{4}$. They may scatter around the original positions, i.e., noise may have perturbed the positions. That is why in the demodulation, receivers will use the zone, instead of the positions, to get the data carried by the signals. As long as the positions are not perturbed

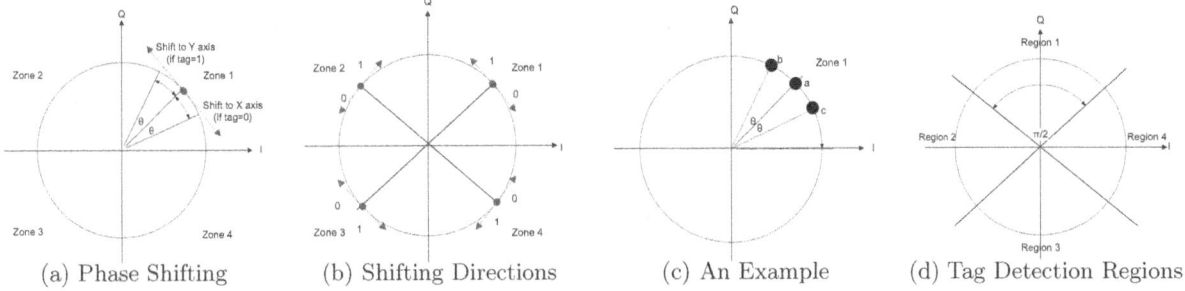

| (a) Phase Shifting | (b) Shifting Directions | (c) An Example | (d) Tag Detection Regions |

Figure 4: The QPSK Tagging Scheme

too much, the data carried by the signals can still be correctly retrieved. In other words, QPSK can tolerate noise to certain degree.

We can take advantage of this noise tolerance. We can treat our tag as a man-made noise, and intentionally perturb the message points during modulation based on the tag information. When the receiver gets the signal, it can get the tag information based on how the message points are perturbed. We discuss this process in more details in the following modulation and demodulation parts.

Adding Tags in Modulation. The basic idea to add man-made noise (i.e. tags) to QPSK is to perturb the position of the phase in the constellation diagram, just like what natural noise does to the phase positions. There are many different ways to perturb the positions, we will only describe a simple perturbation method in the following (our analysis will be based on this method):

- When the tag is 1, we shift the phase by θ degree towards the y-axis, where $0 < \theta < \frac{\pi}{4}$. The final position stays on the circle to maintain the same signal energy.

- When the tag is 0, we shift the phase by θ degree towards the x-axis.

Figures 4(a) and 4(b) illustrate the tagging scheme. Figures 4(c) shows an example of adding tag information to signals in Zone 1. In this example, the data is 11. If the tag is 1, the final phase position will be at point b; otherwise, it will be at point c.

Retrieving Tags in Demodulation. When demodulating, we need to retrieve both data and tag. As we have already discussed, data can be retrieved based on which zone in the constellation diagram the signal falls into. As for the tag, we divide the constellation into four *regions*. Different from zones, the boundary of regions are the two cross lines in Figure 4(d). Based on zones and regions, receivers can detect both data and tag.

- Data detection: this is the same as the original QPSK scheme, i.e., data are detected based on the zones. Keeping data detection scheme the same is essential for the transparency for the non-CR receivers.

- Tag detection: if data fall into Region 1 and Region 3, the carried tag bit is 1; otherwise, it is 0.

Obviously, due to the natural noise and our man-made noise, there will be errors in both data and tag detections. We will present the detailed analysis results in Section 5.

4. ADDING TAGS TO CODING

In this section, we describe how authentication tags can be transparently added to the coding module at the physical layer. In particular, we focus on the coding module that tries to enhance the error tolerance of communication systems. A common scheme used in this module is the Error Correcting Code (ECC).

4.1 ECC Background

Error correcting codes provide a mechanism for improving the error performance of communication systems. This is achieved by adding redundancy. For example, in order to transform a message of k symbols, we can use an encoding scheme to add redundant information in a particular way to map this message into an n-symbol codeword ($n > k$), such that the codeword can tolerate up to t corrupted symbols. Such a code is referred to as a (n, k) block code. We call t the error correction capability of this code i.e., it can correct up to t symbol errors per n-symbol codeword.

One of the most common class of ECC code is the Reed-Solomon code. For example, The digital TV broadcast uses the $(207, 187)$ Reed-Solomon code [1], i.e. each 187-symbol input block is turned into a 207-symbol block, where each symbol consists of 8 bits. In Reed-Solomon code, error correction capability t equals to $\frac{n-k}{2}$. Therefore this code can tolerate up to 10 corrupted symbols in the communication ($t = \frac{207-187}{2} = 10$ in the $(207, 187)$ code).

4.2 ECC Tagging scheme

Our main idea of adding authentication tags in the ECC module is to take advantage of the error correction capability t of the code. Basically, to embed a tag, we intentionally corrupt symbols at certain particular positions in the transmitted codeword. As long as the total number of errors (our "injected" errors plus the errors naturally incurred) in each codeword are still less than t, the error correction code module at the receiver side will be able to recover all the symbols correctly in the codeword. Therefore, non-CR receivers can receive the signals as usual, i.e., the tags are transparent to this type of receivers. In our scheme, we embed the tag information in certain position of the codeword such that the receiver can extract the tag information before the receiver decodes the codeword. The explanation of our scheme is given in below.

Consider a communication system that uses an (n, k) linear block code to improve its error performance, where each symbol consists of M bits. Let $(\mathbf{c_1}, \ldots, \mathbf{c_L})$ be a sequence of codewords that need to be transmitted. Our goal is to

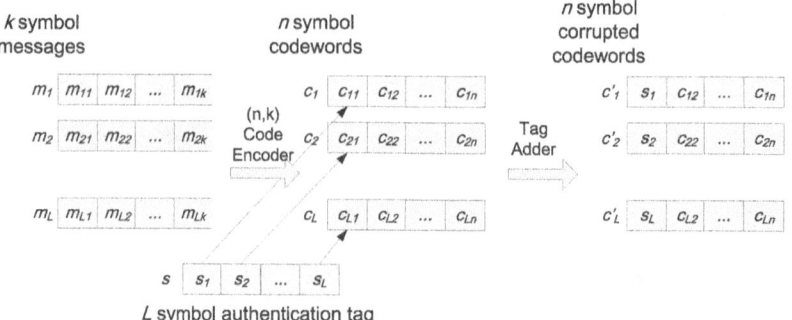

k symbol messages | n symbol codewords | n symbol corrupted codewords

Figure 5: The ECC Tagging Scheme

embed an authentication tag in this sequence. Let $\mathbf{s}$ be our tag, it is divided into L symbols, each with M bits, i.e., $\mathbf{s} = (s_1, \ldots, s_L)$. To encode the authentication tag $\mathbf{s}$ in the codeword sequence $(\mathbf{c_1}, \ldots, \mathbf{c_L})$, we replace the first symbol in $\mathbf{c_i}$ with s_i (for $i = 1, 2, \ldots, L$). The process is illustrated in Figure 5.

In the above description, we only corrupt one symbol in each codeword. We can corrupt more than one symbols in each codeword to embed more tag information. There is a tradeoff. By adding authentication tag in our described manner, we are effectively reducing the error correcting capability of the code. Namely, if the transmitter intends to insert q tag symbols (i.e., corrupting q symbols) in a codeword with error correction capability of t symbols, then we are effectively reducing its actual capability to $(t - q)$. Finding a right balance between q and t is very important.

Moreover, it should be noted that our tag can also be corrupted due to the errors incurred in the communication. Therefore, receivers may be unable to get the tag with 100 percent accuracy. We will analyze this error probability in the next section.

5. ANALYSIS

The objective of this section is to understand the performance of the QPSK and ECC tagging schemes. In particular, we would like to study how the tagging schemes affect data transmissions (i.e., the data error rate), and how well receivers can recover the tag (i.e., the tag error rate). The following parameters are relevant to our scheme:

- The length L of each tag: Each tag is basically a hash value. In our analysis, we assume that MD5 is used, i.e., each tag has 128 bits. Similar analysis can be done for other hash functions.

- Signal-to-noise ratio (SNR), E_b/N_0: It is defined as the power ratio between a signal (meaningful information) and the background noise (unwanted signal), and measured by dB.

In this section, we first analyze the following error rates. These analytical results will be used as the basis for our more comprehensive analysis in Sections 6 and 7.

- Signal symbol error rate P_s: This probability indicates how accurately receivers can retrieve the data sent in the signal. P_s is defined upon *symbol*. In QPSK,

a symbol consists of two bits. In the ECC tagging scheme, a symbol is made of M bit. The value of M depends on what error correcting code is used.

- Bit error rate for tag detection P_t: This probability indicates how accurately cognitive radio receivers can retrieve each bit of the tag information.

5.1 Analysis of the QPSK Approach

In QPSK, the offset to the signal constellations affects the signal symbol error probability. To be more specific, when the shifting angle offset becomes larger, the error performance for the data becomes worse, but the error on detecting the tags will decrease. Therefore, it is a tradeoff between the signal symbol error rate and the tag bit error rate. We would like to analyze and understand this tradeoff.

Let us analyze the situation in Figure 4(a) (because of symmetry, it is sufficient to analyze only one zone): Assume that the modulated signal $S(t, \theta)$ consists of two parts: signal symbol (dibit) 11 and authentication tag 1. Since the tag is 1, the shifting direction is to the Y-axis. Let the shifting angle be $\theta \in (0, \pi/4)$. After the transmission, the received signal $\bar{S}(t, \theta)$ is the following: (We assume the Additive White Gaussian Noise (AWGN) model in our analysis)

$$\bar{S}(t, \theta) = S(t, \theta) + W(t) = \sqrt{\frac{2E_s}{T_s}} \cos(2\pi f_c t + \frac{\pi}{4} + \theta) + W(t),$$

where $W(t)$ is the sample function of a white Gaussian noise process of zero mean and power spectral density $N_0/2$; A detailed analysis of $S(t, \theta)$ is in Appendix $A.1$.

According to its received signal $\bar{S}(t, \theta)$, the observation vector s of a coherent QPSK receiver has two elements:

$$x_1 = \sqrt{\frac{E_s}{2}}(\cos\theta - \sin\theta) + w_1,$$

$$x_2 = \sqrt{\frac{E_s}{2}}(\cos\theta + \sin\theta) + w_2.$$

Thus, x_1 and x_2 are sample values of independent Gaussian random variables with mean values equal to $\sqrt{E_s/2}(\cos\theta - \sin\theta)$ and $\sqrt{E_s/2}(\cos\theta + \sin\theta)$, respectively, and with a common variance equal to $N_0/2$. These two elements together decide the positions of the received signal $\bar{S}(t, \theta)$ in the QPSK constellation.

Based on our decision rules in the QPSK tagging scheme, we can calculate the signal symbol error rate P_s and the tag bit error rate P_t:

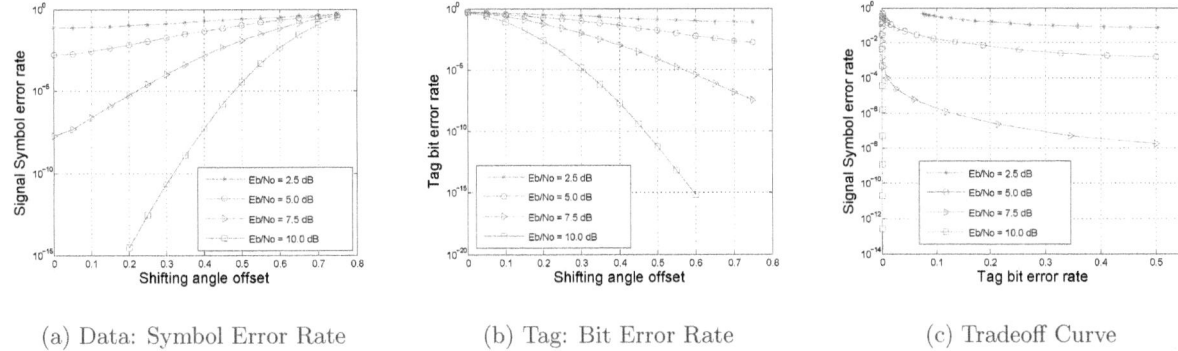

| (a) Data: Symbol Error Rate | (b) Tag: Bit Error Rate | (c) Tradeoff Curve |

Figure 6: Performance of the QPSK Tagging Scheme

THEOREM 1. *Let the angle offset be θ. Let E_b/N_0 be the signal-to-noise ratio (SNR), where $E_b = E_s/2$. The signal symbol (2 bits per symbol in QPSK) error rate P_s is given in the following formula:*

$$P_s \simeq \frac{1}{2} \operatorname{erfc}(\sqrt{\frac{E_b}{N_0}}(\cos\theta - \sin\theta)) +$$
$$\frac{1}{2} \operatorname{erfc}(\sqrt{\frac{E_b}{N_0}}(\cos\theta + \sin\theta)),$$
$$where, \quad \operatorname{erfc}(x) = \frac{2}{\sqrt{\pi}} \int_x^\infty e^{-t^2}\, dt$$

To prove the theorem, we simply need to compute the following probability (a proof is given in Appendix A.2):

$$P_s = 1 - Pr(s \text{ falls inside Zone 1}).$$

We plot the results of P_s in Figure 6(a). From the curves, we can see that when the shifting angle increases, P_s also increases, i.e., the performance of data detection gets worse. If we fix the shifting angle, and compare the three curves, we can see that the larger the SNR is, the lower the P_s is; therefore increasing SNR can reduce data errors.

The next theorem gives the bit error rate for tags.

THEOREM 2. *Let the angle offset be θ. Let E_b/N_0 be the signal-to-noise ratio (SNR), where $E_b = E_s/2$. The bit error rate P_t for tag is the following:*

$$P_t \simeq \frac{1}{2} \operatorname{erfc}(\sqrt{\frac{E_b}{N_0}}(\cos\theta)) + \frac{1}{2} \operatorname{erfc}(\sqrt{\frac{E_b}{N_0}}(\sin\theta)),$$
$$where \quad \operatorname{erfc}(x) = \frac{2}{\sqrt{\pi}} \int_x^\infty e^{-t^2}\, dt.$$

To prove the theorem, we simply need to compute the following probability (a proof is given in Appendix A.3):

$$P_t = 1 - Pr(s \text{ falls inside Region 1 or Region 3}).$$

We plot the results of P_t in Figure 6(b). Each curve indicates that as the angle offset increases, P_t decreases, i.e., the performance of QPSK tagging scheme gets better. It seems that Figure 6(a) and Figure 6(b) are quite similar in shapes; that is because the functions used to calculate both signal symbol error rate and tag error rare are essentially the same for QPSK, only with different parameters.

To understand the relationship between data errors and tag errors, we plot them together in Figure 6(c). We can clearly see the tradeoff between these two errors. We can also see that increasing SNR can achieve a better performance for our tagging scheme. When SNR equals 10 dB, the curve is a straight line. That's because the tag bit error rate is very low at that SNR.

5.2 Analysis of the ECC Approach

To perform the analysis for the ECC tagging scheme, we assume a binary symmetric channel (BSC) with channel error rate p. A Binary Symmetric Channel is one where the input symbol to the channel is 1 bit and the probability of receiving erroneous symbol is p. This means, if the input to the channel is 1(0), we receive 0(1) with probability p. The purpose of using a BSC is to hide the underlying modulation schemes, interleaving and other communication blocks, so as to make the analysis independent to any of them. To compute the bounds for the error probabilities we assume that hard decision [3] is made by the receiver.

The three important metrics that we are going to show are signal symbol error rate P_s after decoding codeword, codeword error rate P_{cw}, and tag bit error rate P_t. The codeword error rate P_{cw} for a given code is the probability that the transmitted codeword and the decoded codeword are not the same. Similarly, the symbol error rate P_s is the probability that the transmitted symbol and the received symbol are not the same. Tag bit error rate P_t is the probability that the received tag bit is in error.

We would like to analyze our tagging scheme using a specific type of linear block code. We choose the Reed-Solomon (RS) codes, which are a very important class of error correcting codes; it finds application in a large number of digital communication systems. Let an (n, k) RS code encode a k-symbol input message into a n-symbol output message. Let each symbol be M bits wide. This (n, k) RS code can correct up to $t = \frac{n-k}{2}$ symbol errors per codeword [2].

Now, if we corrupt q $(q < t)$ symbols in each codeword, the codeword error rate P_{cw} and symbol error rate P_s are

---

[3]We say a receiver makes a *hard decision* when each received analog symbol at modulation layer is quantized and decoded to the respective bits independently of other received symbols.

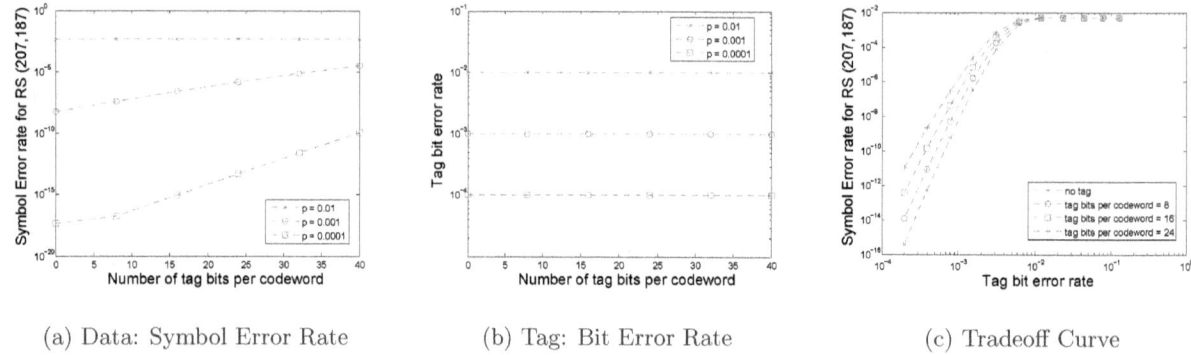

| (a) Data: Symbol Error Rate | (b) Tag: Bit Error Rate | (c) Tradeoff Curve |

Figure 7: Performance of the ECC Tagging Scheme

bounded by the followings [2]:

$$P_{cw} \leq \sum_{i=(t-q)+1}^{n} \binom{n}{i} p_s^i (1-p_s)^{n-i},$$

$$P_s \leq \frac{1}{n} \sum_{i=(t-q)+1}^{n} i \binom{n}{i} p_s^i (1-p_s)^{n-i},$$

where, $p_s = 1 - (1-p)^M$.

By the nature of our scheme, corrupting q symbols in a codeword is equivalent to replacing that many symbols in the codeword with q symbols of the authentication tag, with each symbol consisting of M bits.

Regarding the tag bit error P_t, since the tag bits in a received codeword are checked before being handed to the error correction code decoder, the bit error rate for the tag is the same as the channel bit error p of the BSC channel under consideration. Therefore,

$$P_t = p.$$

To plot the performance of this scheme we use the (207,187) Reed Solomon code. Each symbol in a codeword of this code is 8 bits wide. A plot of symbol error rate P_s against the number of tag bits per codeword is shown in Figure 7(a). It can be seen that as we embed more bits in a codeword, the error performance of the code decreases. The behavior of tag bit error rate P_t against the number of tag bits per codeword is shown in Figure 7(b). Because the way we receive tag bits is independent of the decoding of codeword, we can see that the tag bit error remains constant even if we add more bits per codeword. The fact that tag bit error rate is equal to the channel error rate and it is constant results in its positive correlation with the symbol error rate as shown in Figure 7(c).

6. REDUCING TAG ERROR RATE

The authentication tag is formed using cryptographic hash functions, so, even a single bit error in the tag will make the tag invalid. In order to transmit the tag reliably, its error probability needs to be brought down to a fairly small value. However, the analysis in the last section show that to achieve a reasonably low error rate on data, the bit error rate of tag is not so low. Therefore, for a 128-bit MD5 hash, having at least one bit of error in the tag is quite possible. We use P_e^{tag} to represent the error rate for the entire L-bit tag, i.e. P_e^{tag} is the probability of having at least one bit error in the L-bit tag. This is different from the bit error rate P_t discussed in the previous section.

We need to keep P_e^{tag} fairly low (e.g., below 10^{-10}), even if the bit error rate P_t is not low. There are two approaches to do so. One is the repetition approach, i.e., we repeat each tag for many times. This way, even if some bits of a tag are corrupted during the transmission, receivers can still re-construct the correct tag with high probability by combining all the copies of the tag together (e.g. using majority voting for each bit). Another approach is to use error correcting code on the tag. Error correcting code can be used to correct the error bit in the tags and bring down tag error rate. Because our tag is quite short (e.g. 128 bits for MD5), we can afford to use a long code to keep P_e^{tag} significantly small. We will discuss and analyze this approach in this section.

Let the L-bit authentication tag be encoded using an (n^{tag}, k^{tag}) linear block code, which can correct up to t errors. Let each symbol in the code be 1 bit wide. Let P_t be the tag bit error probability, which is already given in Section 5 for both QPSK and ECC tagging schemes. In our analysis, if we assume a binary symmetric channel for tag transmissions, P_t is essentially the channel error rate. For most of the linear block codes it is very difficult to find the exact codeword error rate or bit error rate. Therefore, they are upper bounded by the following inequality [2]:

$$P_{cw}^{tag} \leq \sum_{i=t^{tag}+1}^{n^{tag}} \binom{n^{tag}}{i} P_t^i (1-P_t)^{n-i}.$$

$$P_b^{tag} \leq \frac{1}{n^{tag}} \sum_{i=t^{tag}+1}^{n^{tag}} i \binom{n^{tag}}{i} P_t^i (1-P_t)^{n-i}.$$

Since the tag is encoded by ECC code, we are interested in finding the whole L-bit tag error rate. It is given by the following theorem.

THEOREM 3. *Let L be the length of the tag. Let (n^{tag}, k^{tag}) be the linear block code that we use to encode this tag. Let D be the desired upper bound for the codeword error rate P_{cw}^{tag}.*

The probability (P_e^{tag}) that there is at least one bit of error in the tag can be upper bounded by the following inequality:

$$P_e^{tag} \leq 1 - (1-D)^{\frac{L}{k^{tag}}}.$$

The proof is given in Appendix A.4. It should be noted that D is selected by users, and it decides n^{tag}, i.e. which RS code we need to choose. The smaller the D is, the larger the n^{tag} will be.

7. EVALUATION

Now, we are going to answer the question that are essential to primary and secondary users, i.e., given a bound on P_e^{tag}, what are the impacts of our tagging schemes on them? For primary users, they worry about how much error performance (mostly reliability) may be affected by the proposed scheme, or how much power they need to increase to keep the same level of performance. For secondary users, they worry about how long it takes them to verify a tag. Because secondary users need to monitor a quite large spectrum range (i.e., many primary users), they cannot afford to spend too long on one primary user: the shorter, the better. Formally speaking, primary users concern about their transmission powers (i.e., the signal to noise ratio) and data error rate (i.e., signal symbol error rate in our analysis), while secondary users concern about the time for receiving a complete tag.

To facilitate our evaluation, we define the tag to data ratio W as the ratio of tag rate over data rate, which is used for calculating how long it takes to transmit a single authentication tag. We also define the ratio of k to n for any (n,k) linear block code, which is called code rate. Therefore, for the (n^{tag}, k^{tag}) code used to encode our tag, its code rate is $R_c^{tag} = \frac{k^{tag}}{n^{tag}}$.

The following two theorems give the tag to data ratio W for QPSK and ECC schemes respectively.

THEOREM 4. *In the QPSK tagging scheme, let R_c^{tag} be the code rate for the encoded tag, if encoding tags by a (n^{tag}, k^{tag}) linear block code. The tag to data ratio W for QPSK scheme is given by the following (the proof is given in Appendix A.5):*

$$W = \frac{R_c^{tag}}{2}.$$

THEOREM 5. *In the ECC tagging scheme, let R_c^{data} be the code rate for the encoded data. Let R_c^{tag} be the code rate for the encoded tag. If q is the number of encoded tag bits we embed in each n bit data codeword, then the tag to data ratio W is given by the following (the proof is given in Appendix A.6):*

$$W = \frac{q R_c^{tag}}{n R_c^{data}}.$$

This tag to data ratio W decides how long it takes a cognitive radio receiver to get a complete tag. Since the verification of a tag is quite fast (computing a few one-way hash functions), we will not include the tag verification time in our evaluation. Based on the tag to data rate W, the time T^{tag} required to transmit one L-bit authentication tag can be computed using $T^{tag} = \frac{L}{W \cdot r}$, where r is the data rate (bits per second) in a communication system.

Now, we are ready to find out two important relationships among signal to noise ratio (SNR), data error rate (i.e. signal symbol error rate in our analysis), and tag to data ratio. The first is the relationship between the data error rate and the tag to data ratio W, if the primary users decide to keep the same transmission power (i.e. SNR) as that without the authentication tag. The second relationship is the one between the transmission power and the tag to data ratio W, if the primary users decide to keep the data error rate the same as that without the tag.

For both QPSK and ECC tagging schemes, the essential issue is to choose a proper (n^{tag}, k^{tag}) code to keep the tag error rate below a threshold. Namely, when SNR and data error rate are fixed, the length of tag is decided by the tag's error correcting code that we select to achieve our threshold goal. The bigger the code rate is, the bigger the tag to data ratio, so the smaller the tag transmission time T^{tag} becomes.

Based on the theorems derived in this paper, we are able to find a group of suitable (n^{tag}, k^{tag}) codes to bring the error rate of a 128-bit tag down to the threshold ε. Assuming ε is 10^{-10} (i.e., $P_e^{tag} < 10^{-10}$), we are able to plot Figures 8(a) and 8(b) for the QPSK tagging scheme, and Figures 8(c) and 8(d) for the ECC tagging scheme.

Since it is difficult to test all the (n^{tag}, k^{tag}) codes, the code we use is not guaranteed to be the optimal one. These four figures only show the basic relationship between SNR, data error rate, and tag to data ratio; they are not precisely the boundary or optimal solution. Solution using the optimal codes can achieve a better result. Finding the optimal solution is one of the directions in our future research.

QPSK tagging scheme evaluation. Figure 8(a) shows that W increases as the data error rate increases (Symbol Error Rate in QPSK), when the transmission power is kept the same (assuming that the noise power does not change, increasing SNR means increasing signal power). This means that if the primary users want to achieve a higher tag to data ratio with the same power, they have to sacrifice data reliability, that is, increasing data error rate.

Figure 8(b) shows, in each curve, if the primary users want to keep the same data error rate, W will increase if the SNR increases. Therefore, if we augment the signal power, the tag to data ratio is going to increase, and therefore less time is required to send a tag.

On both Figures 8(a) and 8(b), the largest value of tag to data ratio W is 0.5. That is because the best case (i.e., tags do not need to be encoded with error correcting codes) in QPSK is to embed one bit of tag for each two data bits.

An Example. There are many applications of QPSK in reality. Consider the Digital Video Broadcasting Satellite, to which we can apply the QPSK Tagging scheme. Suppose we would like to keep our 128-bit tag error rate below 10^{-10} and keep the symbol error rate for a receiver below 10^{-5}. We also assume SNR = 8 dB and tag bit error rate P_t is 5×10^{-3}. In this situation, as showed in Figure 8(b), tag to data ratio W is 0.15. Since the data rate for the QPSK is 39Mbps due to DVB-S [17], the time required to transmit one authentication tag is $\frac{128}{0.15 \times 39M} = 2.18 \times 10^{-2}$ms.

ECC tagging scheme evaluation. As for ECC tagging scheme, to have a common basis for comparison between the tagging schemes, we assume that QPSK modulation is used to transmit the bits in the ECC tagging scheme too. Assuming the channel to be memoryless i.e., the data errors are independent of each other, the channel error rate, p, for

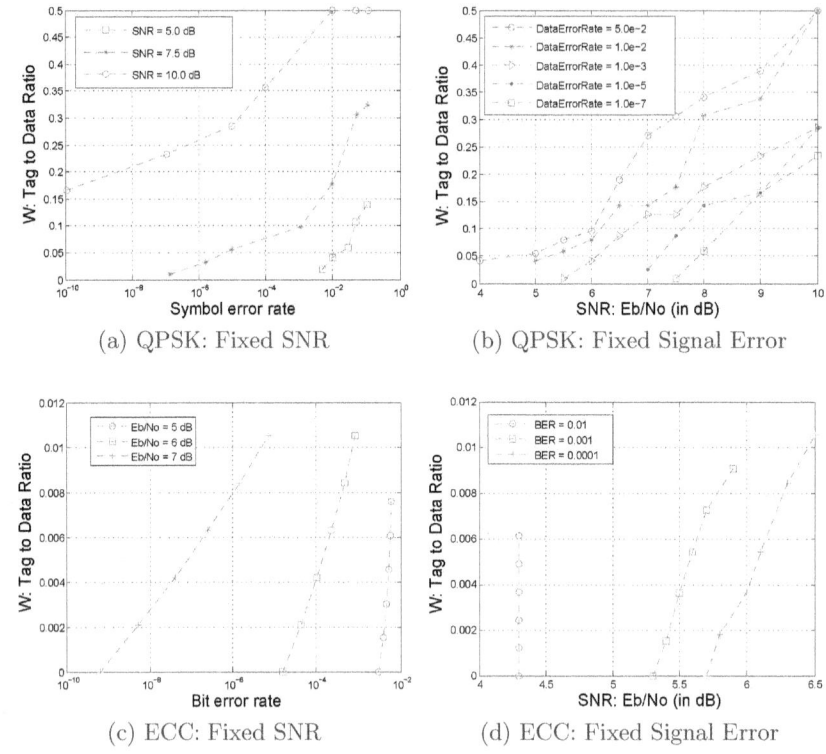

(a) QPSK: Fixed SNR

(b) QPSK: Fixed Signal Error

(c) ECC: Fixed SNR

(d) ECC: Fixed Signal Error

Figure 8: Comprehensive Analysis Of QPSK and ECC Tagging Schemes

a AWGN channel is given by [2], $p = \frac{1}{2}erfc\left(\sqrt{\frac{E_b}{N_0}}\right)$, where E_b/N_0 = Signal to Noise ratio (SNR). From this expression we can see that for a constant SNR, the channel error rate p is constant.

A look at Figure 7(a) tells us that by corrupting bits in a codeword we effectively reduce the error performance of the code. Therefore, to maintain the same error performance at the receiver we need to increase SNR; if SNR is fixed, the error performance will degrade. Figure 8(c) shows the relationship between the tag to data ratio W and the data error rate at a constant SNR for the RS (207, 187) code. Figure 8(d) shows the relationship between the tag to data ratio W against SNR at a constant data error (for the same RS code).

An Example. Error correcting codes are used in Digital TV broadcasting. Suppose the channel error rate at a DTV receiver is 10^{-3}. Since it uses RS (207,187) code with symbol width of 8 bits, each codeword contains $207 \times 8 = 1656$ bits. If we encode the 128-bit tag using (127,50) BCH code (One kind of Error-correcting Code), which has symbol width of 1 bit, the length of encoded tag will be $127 \times 128/50 = 326$ bits. Afterwards, every 8 bits of encoded tag are embedded into each 1656-bit codeword, the tag to data ratio can be calculated to be, $W = 2.044 \times 10^{-3}$. Since, the data rate for the regular terrestrial DTV transmission is 19.39 Mbps [1], the time required to transmit one authentication tag is $\frac{128}{2.044 \times 10^{-3} \times 19.39 \times 10^6} = 3.2$ms.

8. RELATED WORK

Numerous work has been conducted to derive the signal features that are unique to a transmitter or primary user,

so these features can be used as signatures to identify a particular transmitter [3, 8, 11] or detect legitimate primary users [10, 14, 19–21, 24]. Although this approach has been successful in certain scenarios, recently, it was pointed out by Danev et al. that the features are not completely trustworthy, and most features can be spoofed [7].

A recent attempt concerns adding secure signatures to transmitter signals for authentication. Wang et al. [23] proposed a scheme to add a low-power signal as the identity in television broadcast. Yu et al. proposes a physical-layer authentication scheme [25]. Their idea is to superimpose a tag signal with the original signal in order to prove its legitimacy to receivers. However, the authentication scheme described in the paper is based on a secret key; this is not practical for broadcasting authentication. Moreover, the tag in the paper is generated from the signal and the secret key; this makes the authentication quite sensitive to errors: if there is an error in the data (which is quite common in the physical layer), it will be hard to verify the authentication tag. Furthermore, the way how tags are added to signals in our work is different from that in [25]. As for the solution proposed by Liu et al. [16], we have already discussed it in the introduction section.

Other related work includes water marking [6,9,15], which also discuss how to embed tags inside signals. Their objective is different from ours; their goal is to use the tag for the copyright protection purpose.

9. CONCLUSION

In this paper, we present a method to solve the primary emulation attack in cognitive radio networks. In our scheme, primary users use a one-way hash chain to authenticate its legitimate use of spectrum. To ensure that the existing non-CR receivers can properly receive signals, the authentication tag must be transparent to them. Thus, we present two schemes, one conducting tagging in QPSK modulation, the other in the error-correcting coding. We have analyzed the performance of two schemes, and our evaluation results indicate that the scheme is quite practical for cognitive radio.

10. REFERENCES

[1] ATSC Digital Television Standard Part 2: RF/Transmission System Characteristics (A/53, Part 2:2007. www.atsc.org.

[2] J. G. Proakis and M. Salehi, *Digital Communications*. New York, McGraw-Hill, 2007, p. 192, 434, 472-474.

[3] V. Brik, S. Banerjee, M. Gruteser, and S. Oh. Wireless device identification with radiometric signatures. In *Proceedings of the ACM MobiCom*, September 14–19 2008.

[4] R. Chen, J. Park, and J. H. Reed. Defense against primary user emulation attacks in cognitive radio networks. *IEEE Journal on Selected Areas in Communications*, (1):25–37, 2008.

[5] Federal Communications Commission. Facilitating opportunityies for flexible, efficient, and reliable spectrum use employing spectrum agile radio technologies. *ET Docket, (03-108)*, December 2003.

[6] I. J. Cox, M. L. Miller, and A. L. McKellips. Watermarking as commnications with side information. *Proceedings of the IEEE*, (7):1127–1141, July 1999.

[7] B. Danev, H. Luecken, S. Čapkun, and K. E. Defrawy. Attacks on physical-layer identification. In *Proceedings of the 3rd ACM Conference on Wireless Network Security*, 2010.

[8] B. Danev and S. Čapkun. Transient-based identification of wireless sensor nodes. In *Proceedings of the 8th IEEE/ACM Information Processing in Sensor Networks*, pages 25–36. IEEE/ACM, 2009.

[9] C. Fei, D. Kundur, and R. H. Kwong. Analysis and design of secure watermark-based authenticaiton systems. *IEEE Transactions on Information Forensics and Security*, (1):43–55, March 2006.

[10] L. P. Goh, Z. Lei, and F. Chin. Dvb detector for cognitive radio networks. In *Proceedings of the International Conference on Communications 2007*, pages 6460–6465, 2007.

[11] J. Hall, M. Barbeau, and E. Kranakis. Detecting rogue devices in bluetooth networks using radio frequency fingerprinting. In *Proceedings of Communications and Computer Networks*, pages 108–113, October 4–6 2006.

[12] S. Haykin. Book: Digital communications.

[13] J. Mitola III and G. Q. Maguire, Jr. Cognitive radio: making software radios more personal. *IEEE Personal Communications Magazine*, (4):13–18, August 1999.

[14] H. Kim and K. G. Shin. In-band spectrum sensing in cognitive radio networks: energy detecion or feature detection? In *Proceedings of the 14th ACM international conference on Mobile computing and networking*, pages 14–25, 2008.

[15] J. E. Kleider, S. Gifford, S. Chuprun, and B. Fette. Radio frequency watermarking for ofdm wireless networks. *IEEE International Conference on Acoustics, Speech, and Signal Processing*, May 2004.

[16] Y. Liu, P. Ning, and H. Dai. Authenticating primary users' signals in cognitive radio networks via integrated cryptographic and wireless link signatures. In *Proceedings of 2010 IEEE Symposium on Security and Privacy*, May 2010.

[17] Introduction of DVB-S. Website: http://www.complextoreal.com/tdvbs.htm.

[18] A. Perrig and J. D. Tygar. *Secure Broadcast Communication: in Wired and Wireless Networks*. Kluwer Academic Publisher, 2003.

[19] Y. Qi, T. Peng, W. Wang, and R. Qian. Cyclostationarity-based spectrum sensing for wideband cognitive radio. In *Proceedings of the 2009 WRI International Conference on Communications and Mobile Computing*, pages 107–111, 2009.

[20] A. Sahai and D. Cabric. Cyclostationary feature detection. *Tutorial presented at the IEEE DySPAN 2005 (Part II)*, November 2005.

[21] S. ShellHammer, S. Shankar N., R. Tandra, and J. Tomcik. Performance of power detector sensors of dtv signals in ieee 802.22 wrans. In *TAPAS '06: Proceedings of the first international workshop on Technology and policy for accessing spectrum*, 2006.

[22] G. Staple and K. Werbach. The end of spectrum scarcity. *IEEE Spectrum*, March 2004.

[23] X. Wang, Y.Wu, and B. Caron. Transmitter identification using embedded pseudo random sequences. *IEEE Transactions on Broadcasting*, (3):244–252, September 2004.

[24] W. Xia, S. Wang, W. Liu, and W. Cheng. Correlation-based spectrum sensing in cognitive radio. In *CoRoNet: Proceedings of the 2009 ACM workshop on Cognitive radio networks*, pages 67–72, 2009.

[25] P. L. Yu, J. S. Baras, and B. M. Sadler. Physical-layer authentication. *IEEE Transactions on Information Forensics and Security*, (1), March 2008.

APPENDIX

A. PROOFS

A.1 Detaild Analysis of QPSK

Without authentication tags, the original modulated signal is the following:

$$S(t) = \sqrt{\frac{2E_s}{T_s}} \cos(2\pi f_c t + \pi/4).$$

After adding the tag, the new modulated signal becomes

$$S(t, \theta) = \sqrt{\frac{2E_s}{T_s}} \cos(2\pi f_c t + \pi/4 + \theta)$$

$$= \sqrt{\frac{E_s}{2}}(\cos\theta - \sin\theta)\phi_1(t) - \sqrt{\frac{E_s}{2}}(\cos\theta + \sin\theta)\phi_2(t),$$

where, $\phi_1(t)$ is the in-phase component basis function, and $\phi_2(t)$ is the quadrature-phase component basis function:

$$\phi_1(t) = \sqrt{\frac{2}{T_s}} \cos(2\pi f_c t), \quad \phi_2(t) = \sqrt{\frac{2}{T_s}} \sin(2\pi f_c t).$$

A.2 Proof of Theorem 1

PROOF. In this QPSK Tagging Scheme, signal symbol error probability is the following:

$$
\begin{aligned}
P_t &= Pr(\text{s falls inside any regions except Region 1}) \\
&= 1 - Pr(\text{ s falls inside Region 1}) \\
&= 1 - Pr(\text{ } x_1 \text{ falls inside Region 1 }) * \\
&\quad Pr(\text{ } x_2 \text{ falls inside Region 1 }),
\end{aligned}
$$

where x_1 and x_2 are sample values of independent Gaussian random variables with mean values equal to $\sqrt{E_s/2}(\cos\theta - \sin\theta)$ and $\sqrt{E_s/2}(\cos\theta + \sin\theta)$, respectively, and with a common variance equal to $N_0/2$. Moreover, x_1 and x_2 are independent of each other.

Therefore,

$$
P_t = 1 - \int_0^\infty \frac{1}{\sqrt{\pi N_0}} exp[-\frac{(x_1 - \sqrt{\frac{E_s}{2}}(\cos\theta - \sin\theta))^2}{N_0}] dx_1 *
$$
$$
\int_0^\infty \frac{1}{\sqrt{\pi N_0}} exp[-\frac{(x_2 - \sqrt{\frac{E_s}{2}}(\cos\theta + \sin\theta))^2}{N_0}] dx_2
$$

Let

$$
\frac{x_1 - \sqrt{\frac{E_s}{2}}(\cos\theta - \sin\theta))}{\sqrt{N_0}} = z_1
$$
$$
\frac{x_1 - \sqrt{\frac{E_s}{2}}(\cos\theta + \sin\theta))}{\sqrt{N_0}} = z_2
$$

Then changing the variables from x_1 to z_1, and x_2 to z_2, we can have

$$
P_t = 1 - \{1 - \frac{1}{2}\,\mathrm{erfc}(\sqrt{\frac{E_s}{2N_0}}(\cos\theta - \sin\theta))\} *
$$
$$
\{1 - \frac{1}{2}\,\mathrm{erfc}(\sqrt{\frac{E_s}{2N_0}}(\cos\theta + \sin\theta))\}
$$
$$
= \frac{1}{2}\,\mathrm{erfc}(\sqrt{\frac{E_s}{2N_0}}(\cos\theta - \sin\theta))
$$
$$
+ \frac{1}{2}\,\mathrm{erfc}(\sqrt{\frac{E_s}{2N_0}}(\cos\theta + \sin\theta))
$$
$$
- \frac{1}{4}\,\mathrm{erfc}(\sqrt{\frac{E_s}{2N_0}}(\cos\theta - \sin\theta)) * \mathrm{erfc}(\sqrt{\frac{E_s}{2N_0}}(\cos\theta + \sin\theta)).
$$

In the region where $(E_s/N_0) \gg 1$, we may ignore the second term on the right side of *Eq.* 1, so approximate the formula for average signal symbol error probability as

$$
\begin{aligned}
P_s &\simeq \frac{1}{2}\,\mathrm{erfc}(\sqrt{\frac{E_s}{2N_0}}(\cos\theta - \sin\theta)) + \\
&\quad \frac{1}{2}\,\mathrm{erfc}(\sqrt{\frac{E_s}{2N_0}}(\cos\theta + \sin\theta)),
\end{aligned}
$$
$$
where, \quad \mathrm{erfc} = \frac{2}{\sqrt{\pi}}\int_x^\infty e^{-t^2}\,dt
$$

In QPSK, two bits per symbol, which means the signal energy per bit is half of signal energy per symbol, that is,

$$
E_b = \frac{1}{2}E_s
$$

Thus, we may write:

$$
\begin{aligned}
P_s &\simeq \frac{1}{2}\,\mathrm{erfc}(\sqrt{\frac{E_b}{N0}}(\cos\theta - \sin\theta)) + \\
&\quad \frac{1}{2}\,\mathrm{erfc}(\sqrt{\frac{E_b}{N0}}(\cos\theta + \sin\theta))
\end{aligned}
$$

□

A.3 Proof of Theorem 2

The proof is similar to the proof of Theorem 1, so we omit it here.

A.4 Proof of Theorem 3

PROOF.

$$
\begin{aligned}
P_e^{tag} &= Pr\{\text{at least 1 error in tag}\} \\
&= 1 - Pr\{\text{no error in any tag codeword}\} \\
&= 1 - (1 - P_{cw}^{tag})^{\frac{L}{k^{tag}}} \\
&\leq 1 - (1 - D)^{\frac{L}{k^{tag}}}
\end{aligned}
$$

□

A.5 Proof of Theorem 4

PROOF. Suppose, we encode the tag using a (n^{tag}, k^{tag}) code to bring down the tag error probability below a certain threshold. Then, the code rate for the tag is

$$
R_c^{tag} = \frac{k^{tag}}{n^{tag}}.
$$

In case of QPSK, we superimpose 1 bit of encoded tag on every symbol, which represent 2 bits. So, the ratio of tag rate to data rate is:

$$
W = \frac{R_c^{tag}}{2}.
$$

□

A.6 Proof of Theorem 5

PROOF. Let, the communication system use an (n, k) code. Then the code rate in this case is

$$
R_c^{data} = \frac{k}{n}.
$$

Suppose, we encode the tag using a (n^{tag}, k^{tag}) code to bring down the tag error probability below a certain threshold. Then, the code rate for the tag is

$$
R_c^{tag} = \frac{k^{tag}}{n^{tag}}.
$$

If, we embed q bits of encoded tag in n bits of a codeword, then the number of tag bits per n bit codeword is qR_c^{tag}

Then, the ratio of tag rate to data rate is given by

$$
W = \frac{qR_c^{tag}}{k} = \frac{qR_c^{tag}}{nR_c^{data}}.
$$

□

Short Paper: ACE - Authenticating the Channel Estimation Process in Wireless Communication Systems

Rob Miller
Wireless Information Network Laboratory
(WINLAB), Rutgers University
New Brunswick, NJ
rdmiller@winlab.rutgers.edu

Wade Trappe
Wireless Information Network Laboratory
(WINLAB), Rutgers University
New Brunswick, NJ
trappe@winlab.rutgers.edu

ABSTRACT

Accurate channel estimation is essential to modern wireless communication. Pilot waveforms are susceptible to attacks that can severely degrade performance. Thus, it is important to protect channel estimation. Related research focuses on transmitter authentication rather than channel estimate authentication, and results rely heavily upon correlated estimates that occur within the channel coherence time in multipath-rich environments and/or sacrifice system throughput. We propose a methodology to authenticate channel estimation by leveraging physical layer properties of the wireless channel without any coherence time dependence or overhead. Our methods inherently provide data authentication, work in any environment, and provide error inference. We focus on general multi-antenna, multicarrier communication schemes and relate our results to existing protocols such as 802.11g/n and WiMAX.

Categories and Subject Descriptors

C.2.0 [**Computer-Communication Networks**]: General—*Security and Protection*

General Terms

Security, Reliability, Experimentation

Keywords

Authentication, Channel Estimation, MIMO, OFDM

1. INTRODUCTION

Reliable wireless communication is often hampered by the effects of the channel. Transmitted waveforms interact with reflectors and scatterers resulting in multiple distorted copies of the signal arriving at the receiver. Modern wireless systems mitigate these effects by using channel estimates to remove the distortion. Specific known waveforms are often transmitted within data packets so that a receiver can obtain the channel estimates — such waveform segments are referred to as *pilots*.

Pilots used in wireless systems are often simple waveforms (e.g. tones) and are unencrypted and unencoded

— therefore they are vulnerable to attack. Research has shown that current software defined radios (SDR) and limited protocol knowledge can be used to perform practical channel estimation attacks that greatly hamper performance [1, 4]. It is thus vital to protect the channel estimation procedure. Encoding or encrypting the pilots is impractical, as it overly complicates the detection process. Existing literature focuses on transmitter authentication rather than channel estimate authentication, or requires undesirable constraints such as timing, throughput, or environmental limitations [2, 8–11]. Our techniques work as a physical (PHY) layer overlay to existing channel estimation procedures and also provide channel estimation error inference. Moreover, our protection procedure works in any channel environment, without coherence time constraints, and without sacrificing any data throughput.

In Section 2 we overview channel estimation. Section 3 gives a description of related work. We then introduce our general framework for protecting channel estimation in Section 4. Section 5 details specific channel state information (CSI) protection techniques, and Section 6 follows with practical extensions. In Section 7, we demonstrate our techniques using real-world SDR platforms. We continue with a security discussion in Section 8, and conclude the paper in Section 9.

2. CHANNEL ESTIMATION OVERVIEW

Wireless communication is complicated by the effects of the channel since waveforms experience changes in amplitude and phase due to propagation loss, interaction with reflectors and scatterers, and channel noise. Over the timespan of a single packet, most channels are modeled as linear, time-invariant (LTI) systems, so that if Alice transmits $x(t)$, then Bob receives $y(t) = h(t) * x(t) + n(t)$, where $n(t)$ is additive noise, $*$ is convolution, and $h(t)$ represents the channel response. For an LTI channel with D distinct multipath components, $h(t) = \sum_{d=0}^{D-1} a_d e^{j\theta_d} \delta(t - \tau_d)$, where a_d represents the amplitude, θ_d the phase shift, and τ_d the time-delay induced by the channel for the dth signal path.

Pilots are used to estimate the above effects of the channel, but after a short amount of time (the coherence time), the channel decorrelates with itself, and pilots must be reissued. Similarly, the range of frequencies that experience comparable fading effects is referred to as the coherence bandwidth. The wireless channel also rapidly decorrelates with itself in space for distances larger than one half of the waveform's wavelength [5]. While spatial diversity can result from mobility, it also results from the use of multiple antennas — which is prominent in emerging wireless systems (e.g. 802.11n, WiMAX, and LTE).

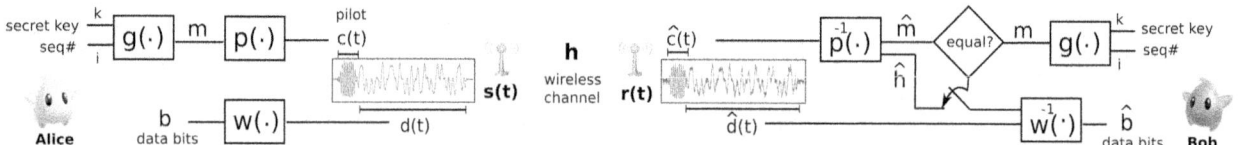

Figure 1: The general CSI protection procedure is depicted. Alice and Bob use a secret key, k, and a sequence number, i, to achieve CSI authentication by encoding messages into the pilot waveform.

Receivers repeatedly estimate the channel from the *pilots*. Classical results on piloting are listed in [3, 7], but only consider time and frequency in a basic repetitive manner, and do not provide the channel estimate authentication or error inference that our techniques provide. For this paper, we consider packet-based protocols, however all principles and techniques can be directly applied to streaming data. Since most future wireless systems are multi-antenna (e.g. MIMO) and multi-carrier (e.g. OFDM), this is where we concentrate. We note that applying our techniques to single-antenna, single-frequency systems can be achieved by merely simplifying the methods.

3. RELATED WORK

Physical layer authentication has received recent attention. In [11], the authors investigate and implement techniques that embed power-based authentication messages (referred to as tags) into data transmissions. The technique requires accurate CSI estimates, which can be attacked as the pilot transmissions remain unaltered and unprotected. Further, the implementation lowers the overall system throughput as the tag is within the data itself. One security flaw of the approach in [11] is that the tags may be recorded and reused in a replay attack at a later time.

In [2], the authors also use the entire transmission to send an authentication message, resulting in throughput degradation similar to [11]. The scheme involves sending the authentication message by embedding a channel response into the message and relying on equalization at the receiver to resolve the authentication message. Richly scattering environments complicate processing, and the technique itself relies heavily upon successive messages within the coherence time of the channel. In [8–10], the authors leverage statistically similar channel estimates over time to authenticate the transmitter. The techniques rely upon reliable successive CSI estimates in richly scattering environments, and [10] assumes a burst structure not emulative of current systems.

Our work provides a practical method of CSI estimate authentication that is computationally simple and does not depend upon successive reliable estimates within the channel coherence time. Our techniques are also applicable to *any* channel, not just richly scattering environments. Further, our techniques do not lower data throughput since the authentication messages are solely embedded within the pilots. Data authentication is inherently part of our techniques because rogue data packets will not share the same CSI as the authenticated pilots, thus resulting in demodulation errors at the receiver. Our techniques give error inference, which is important to drive mitigation decisions.

4. CSI PROTECTION FRAMEWORK

We assume that Alice and Bob share a secret key, k. Regardless of how the key is bootstrapped, using k, Alice and Bob can embed authentication messages into the physical attributes of the pilots. A new authentication message, m_i, will be created by $m_i = g(k, i)$, where k is the secret

key, i is the message sequence number, and $g(\cdot)$ is a one-way function. To prevent replay attacks, we use a sequence number and require that different keys are used for each direction of the communication. The one-way function allows for quick recovery from authentication errors. The following procedure, illustrated in Figure 1, describes how CSI estimate authentication can be achieved by using the pilot waveform to embed authentication messages:

(1) Alice computes an authentication message, m_i, using the packet number, i, secret key, k, and cryptographic one-way function [?], $g(\cdot)$, via $m_i = g(k, i)$.

(2) The authentication message is mapped to a physical pilot waveform via $c_i(t) = p(m_i)$.

(3) Given L data bits, $\underline{b}_i^L = \{b_0, b_1, \cdots b_{L-1}\}$, Alice generates the data waveform via $d_i(t) = w(\underline{b}_i^L)$.

(4) Alice prepends the pilot to the data waveform[1], and transmits $s_i(t) = [c_i(t) \ d_i(t)]$.

(5) The transmission is affected by the wireless channel, so that Bob receives $r_i(t) = \hat{s}_i(t) = [\hat{c}_i(t) \ \hat{d}_i(t)]$.

(6) Bob decodes the authentication message, $\hat{m}_i$, and estimates the CSI, $\hat{h}_i$ via $(\hat{m}_i, \hat{h}_i) = p^{-1}(\hat{c}_i(t))$.

(7) If the authentication message is correct, then Bob trusts the CSI estimate to recover the bits. Otherwise, Bob may sound an alert and/or demodulate the data *without* the CSI estimate.

$$\underline{\hat{b}}_i^L = \begin{cases} w^{-1}(\hat{d}_i(t), \hat{h}_i) & \text{if } \hat{m}_i = m_i \\ w^{-1}(\hat{d}_i(t)) & \text{if } \hat{m}_i \neq m_i \end{cases}$$

Using *only* the pilot waveform for the authentication message increases the authentication bit-rate, does not degrade data throughput, and prevents an eavesdropper from using the channel estimates to directly demodulate the data. To maintain valid CSI estimates, we require that the message bearing pilots be transmitted within the coherence bandwidth of the traditional non-authenticated pilot.

5. CSI PROTECTION PROTOCOLS

Our protocols rely on the basic premise that signals transmitted within the same channel coherence bandwidth, Δ_{BW}, will experience comparable channel effects [5]. Thus, if a pilot is transmitted at a nominal frequency of $\tilde{f}$, then the same pilot transmitted at frequency f_0 will experience similar fading effects if $|\tilde{f} - f_0| < \Delta_{BW}$. Thus, referring to our LTI channel model, $a_d^{\tilde{f}} \approx a_d^{f_0}$, $\theta_d^{\tilde{f}} \approx \theta_d^{f_0}$, and $\tau_d^{\tilde{f}} \approx \tau_d^{f_0}$ for each of the D multipath components of $h(t)$. For microcellular environments, the coherence bandwidth typically does not go below 80 KHz [6] — later we use this value in our validation experiments.

Suppose, for simplicity of discussion, that Alice has a single transmit antenna, then she can embed an authentication message into the *frequency* of the pilot without

---

[1]The concatenation of the pilot and data waveforms should be done to avoid phase discontinuities, such as through Savitzky-Golay smoothing.

sacrificing CSI validity so long as the transmission remains within Δ_{BW}. By quantizing Δ_{BW} into N distinct levels surrounding the frequency, $\tilde{f}$, that Alice would *normally* use to transmit the pilot, she can send an authentication message by transmitting her pilot in the appropriate frequency interval. We emphasize that the pilot is transmitted at the offset frequency, f_0, while the data is still transmitted at the nominal frequency, $\tilde{f}$. Since Bob expects the authentication message at f_0, he can still properly demodulate the data transmitted at the nominal frequency, $\tilde{f}$, by accounting for the known frequency offset in his data recovery routines. Further, since f_0 is within the coherence bandwidth of $\tilde{f}$, the CSI estimate for f_0 is nearly identical to the original estimate for $\tilde{f}$. Using the above Frequency Quantization (FQ) methodology, we now introduce three practical channel estimate authentication schemes: (1) Relative Frequency Codebook (RFC), (2) Binary Frequency Codebook (BFC), and (3) Joint Frequency-Power Codebook (FPC). Figure 2 (a) depicts the three methods.

5.1 Relative Frequency Codebook (RFC)

Alice and Bob will experience timing instabilities and drifts because they are using independent local oscillators (LOs) [4], therefore *absolute* frequency is not a suitable choice for CSI authentication in the real world. Consider the 802.11g protocol, which requires oscillator accuracy within 25ppm. For signals at 2.4 GHz, this equates to a 60 KHz frequency offset. Since LO offsets and drift pose a problem, we propose the use of *relative* frequency. Given a MIMO scenario with M transmit antennas, Alice should transmit a baseline pilot using her first physical transmit antenna. She can then use the remaining $M - 1$ antennas to transmit authentication messages using the relative frequency offsets from the baseline pilot transmission. Frequency drifts are *not* an issue in this scenario, because all M antennas are driven by the same local oscillator (at Alice or Bob). Given N frequency quantization levels and M antennas, Alice can achieve b authentication bits per packet, where $b = (M - 1) \log_2 N$.

As an example, suppose Alice has $M = 2$ transmit antennas and uses $N = 8$ quantization levels over 80 KHz to provide CSI authentication. By frequency shifting the pilot for the second antenna, Alice sends 3-bit ($=\log_2 8$) authentication messages by using 10 KHz frequency offset increments [2]. Consider that Alice uses a nominal carrier frequency, $\tilde{f}$, and encodes her messages using a frequency offset that is proportional to the two's complement form of her message, m. Denoting the two's complement operator as †, Alice transmits her message bearing tone at $f_0 = \tilde{f} + (\Delta f)(m^\dagger)$, where $\Delta f = 10$ KHz.

The RFC authentication scheme offers error inference by pilot observation. For instance, channel noise simply increases the noise floor. Co-channel interference does the same, but in a sporadic manner since transmissions are asynchronous. For interfering devices, invalid authentication messages would be seen at unexpected times. While an adversary can mimic both channel noise and co-channel interference, truly smart attacks will target the pilots in a synchronous fashion. But because Eve is not aware of the authentication message to send, she does not know where in frequency to transmit her rogue, attack pilots. And even if Eve is equipped with perfect knowledge of the the

proper frequency intervals, it is extremely probable that there are frequency offsets between Eve's pilots and Alice's pilots (due to independent LOs). If this frequency error is resolvable, then Bob can detect Eve's presence. The RFC scheme is amenable to current CSI estimation methods such as 802.11n, where sequential transmissions from each antenna are used in the beginning of every packet to estimate the channel.

5.2 Binary Frequency Codebook (BFC)

If Alice transmits multiple pilots within a given channel coherence bandwidth using identical power, then *all* of the pilots will experience the same channel effects. Alice may thus send an authentication message by utilizing *all* of the N frequency quantization bins in a binary fashion (i.e. on/off). One of the bins should be used as a frequency reference, thus she can send an $(N - 1)$-bit authentication message using a single antenna. When using multiple antennas, Alice can achieve an additional N-bit message per antenna because the frequency reference from the first antenna can be re-used due to the fact that all of her antennas share a common LO. Key to the success of this technique is pilot resolvability, and thus protocol parameters such as the pilot length and tone frequency separation must be chosen to ensure frequency resolvability. Relying on a single frequency reference per packet, the BFC scheme achieves $b = (N - 1) + (M - 1)N$ authentication bits per packet.

Error inference for the Binary Frequency Codebook scheme is similar to RFC's, but with a major enhancement regarding smart adversarial detection. If Alice transmits several pilots from a given antenna using identical power and within the same coherence bandwidth then the pilots will arrive at Bob with the same power. Any significant variations in the power associated with different pilots within a coherence bandwidth would immediately reveal that an adversary was attempting to disrupt channel estimation by inserting their own pilots. The astute reader may recognize that Eve may be able to target the reference pilot if it is known a priori, and thus there is a chance that her rogue pilot arrives at the reference pilot within the power deviation threshold, but with a random phase. In such a scenario, the authentication message will be correct, however the CSI estimate for the reference pilot will be perturbed. We mitigate any potential harm due to this attack by requiring that Bob only use CSI estimates based upon non-reference pilots for the BFC scheme. MIMO operation results in more reliable adversarial detection.

5.3 Joint Frequency-Power Codebook (FPC)

Further leveraging properties of the coherence bandwidth, Alice can add *transmission power* to her arsenal for authentication. By transmitting relative power within Δ_{BW}, Alice increases the authentication bit rate. Now, Alice transmits pilots at *every* frequency quantization level, using Q *power* quantization levels. Because Alice is using relative power, a pilot reference power is needed in addition to the pilot frequency reference. Since different antennas will experience different fading effects, Alice needs a pilot reference for each transmit antenna. Thus, Alice can achieve $b = (N - 1) \log_2 Q$ authentication bits per transmitter. Again, the CSI estimates remain valid, and we require that Bob only use CSI estimates from non-reference pilots due to possible attacks against the reference pilots. Adversarial detection is even more reliable as Eve is less likely to guess the proper power levels to transmit.

---

[2]Recalling our discussion earlier, 80 KHz is used in this paper as a conservative value for the coherence bandwidth.

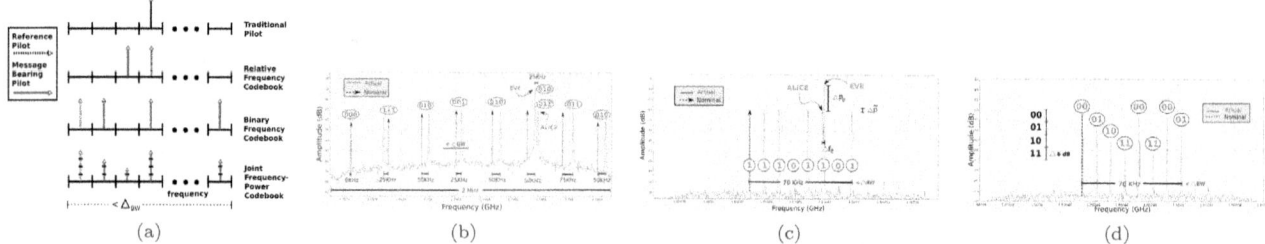

(a)   (b)   (c)   (d)

Figure 2: The three Frequency Quantization schemes are depicted in (a). Real-world experiments were conducted using each of the methods, and results are illustrated in: (b) RFC, (c) BFC, (d) FPC.

5.4 Selective Usage (SU)

In OFDM, carrier frequencies are selected carefully to minimize inter-carrier interference, and thus they may not be readily adaptable. In order to accommodate these operational scenarios, we propose a lower bit-rate alternative that we refer to as Selective Usage (SU). Without altering the actual frequency of the pilots, Alice *selectively* omit the pilot for a given transmit antenna. While CSI information cannot be directly estimated by Bob for the omitted antenna, he may utilize estimates from neighboring pilots that lay within the coherence bandwidth, or he may develop an appropriate estimate based upon previous measurements. Additionally, Bob can always use the data itself to perform timing, frequency, and phase recovery when the pilot is absent. While this is less efficient from a processing perspective, it does allow for CSI authentication without loss of accuracy due to CSI estimate interpolation. Selective omission of pilots will effectively transmit the authentication message to Bob in a binary fashion using each nominal pilot frequency. For instance, Alice can send a 1 to Bob by transmitting a pilot, and a 0 by remaining idle. Given M transmit antennas, Alice can send b authenticated bits per packet, where $b = \log_2 M$. Under SU, transmissions from antennas that should remain silent would indicate smart adversarial activity.

6. EXTENSIONS

We now explore extensions that enhance the authentication bit rate further and/or deal with system constraints.
Multiple Frequency Extensions: By using K carrier frequencies (i.e. by looking at K different bands of frequencies, where each band has bandwidth equally governed by the channel coherence bandwidth), the Frequency Quantization schemes can all achieve increased authentication bit rates. For the RFC scheme, only a single reference is needed per packet. Thus, the authentication bit rate becomes $b_{RFC} = (M-1)\log_2 N + (K-1)M\log_2 N$. The BFC scheme also only requires a single reference per packet, resulting in an authentication bit rate of $b_{BFC} = KMN - 1$. For the FPC scheme, a reference is needed at *each* carrier, thus achieving an authentication bit rate of $b_{FPC} = KM(N-1)\log_2 Q$. For the SU scheme, the authentication bit rate per packet is similar to the BFC scheme in that each carrier operates independently, thus resulting in $b_{SU} = K\log_2 M$. Note that these multiple frequency extensions hold for a single antenna, where the authentication bit rate can be calculated by using $M = 1$.
OFDM Extensions: Popular standards, such as 802.11n and WiMAX, utilize OFDM and are Fast Fourier Transform (FFT) based, thus restricting the use of user-defined frequencies as called for in our Frequency Quantization scheme. OFDM can utilize Frequency Quantization for CSI authentication by incorporating a larger FFT size. As

an example, 802.11 uses a 64-point FFT during channel estimation. By increasing the FFT to 256 points, Alice can achieve 4 authentication bins per pilot (and hence convey 2 authentication *bits* per pilot). With this minor modification, the data transmission may resume the legacy FFT size thus maintaining efficient use of the transmission device. Note that WiMAX implementations already utilize a 256-point FFT (with 8 carriers set aside as pilots). Further, some carriers are often idle during pilot transmission. In 802.11g, the training sequence (TS) portion of the pilot only modulates on every 4th carrier. By altering this carrier allocation (e.g. via a straight-forward modification to device driver firmware), Alice can incorporate CSI authentication into 802.11g.

7. EXPERIMENTAL VALIDATION

Our real-world experiments used GNU Radio and Universal Software Radio Peripheral (USRP) devices.
RFC Experiment: In the RFC experiment, Alice uses two transmit antennas to send 8 authentication messages (by using 8 carriers) across 2 MHz in the 1800 MHz band. The carriers are each separated by 200 KHz. At a given carrier, Alice embeds an authentication message by transmitting the pilot at a frequency that is appropriately offset from nominal. She uses the same pilot message mapping function discussed in Section 5.1, but with a frequency quantization interval (Δf) of 25 KHz. Each authentication message conveys 3-bits, hence valid frequency offsets are: $\{-100, -75, -50, -25, 0, 25, 50, 75\}$ KHz, which equate to $\{100, 101, 110, 111, 000, 001, 010, 011\}$ in bits. In the experiment, Alice transmits an authentication bit sequence of $\{000, 111, 010, 001, 010, 011, 011, 010\}$, resulting in frequency offsets of $\{0, -25, 50, 25, 50, 75, 75, 50\}$ KHz. Figure 2(b) depicts the spectrum received by Bob due to transmissions from Alice's second antenna during pilot activity. The nominal pilot frequencies (as transmitted by Alice's first antenna) are depicted with the dashed lines. Also present is an adversary, Eve, who attacks the CSI. For illustrative purposes, Eve is only active on a single carrier. Ample attacker transmit power allows Eve to trick Bob into decoding the wrong CSI pilot at the sixth carrier. Because Eve does not know the authentication message, she cannot predict exactly where to transmit the rogue CSI pilot tone. Since the rogue pilot is offset by -25 KHz (Δf_e) from Alice's, Bob decodes: $\{000, 111, 010, 001, 010, 0\underline{1}0, 011, 010\}$, where $\underline{0}$ indicates the bit received in-error. Since the authentication message is incorrect, Eve's presence is revealed.
BFC Experiment: In the BFC experiment, we isolate activity at a single carrier frequency to focus on a particular authentication message. Using a single antenna, Alice sends an 8-bit authentication message, $m = \{11101101\}$, in the 1800 MHz band over 80 KHz ($< \Delta_{BW}$). Figure 2 (c) shows the spectrum as seen by Bob. Again, Eve is present,

and tries to disrupt channel estimation– she transmits her own pilot, which corrupts the sixth bit in the authentication message. Note that if Eve attacks an inactive bit, then the authentication message will fail and her presence is revealed. However, if she is close enough in frequency to an active bit (i.e. Δf_e is not resolvable), then the authentication message will be correct despite an inaccurate CSI estimate. Such is the case for this experiment, but because Alice and Bob are using BFC, Bob can still detect Eve's presence as the transmissions all occur within the coherence bandwidth of the channel and power deviations are a clear indicator of an attacker. We see that Eve's power deviation from Alice's is quite large ($\Delta p_e \approx 10\ dB >> \Delta \tilde{p}$).

FPC Experiment: In the FPC experiment, we isolate activity at a single carrier frequency to focus on a specific authentication message m. Using a single antenna, Alice transmits a 14-bit $m = \{00101100110001\}$, in the 1800 MHz band over 80 KHz. Like BFC, it is essential that the authentication message be sent within the coherence bandwidth of the channel (i.e. $< \Delta_{BW}$). Using this scheme, a power reference is necessary for every message carrier. Alice chooses to use the lowest frequency carrier to transmit the nominal reference. To provide a better graphical illustration of the FPC technique, Alice incorporates power backoffs in 6 dB increments. In order to send authentication bits $\{00,01,10,11\}$, Alice uses relative power attenuations of $\{0,6,12,18\}$ dB from nominal. To send the desired 14-bit authentication message, Alice transmits $\{00, 01, 10, 11, 00, 11, 00, 01\}$ by transmitting her pilot carriers at levels of $\{0, -6, -12, -18, 0, -18, 0, -6\}$ dBm. Figure 2 (d) shows the spectrum as seen by Bob for this authentication message. As can be seen, the message is fully recovered by analyzing the relative powers of the received pilot signals.

8. SECURITY ANALYSIS & DISCUSSION

We assume that our adversary, Eve, knows the physical layer protocol used by Alice-Bob, the basic channel estimation procedure, and that she transmits her own "jammer" pilots similar to [4]. We consider a very strong adversary, where Eve is perfectly synchronized in both time and frequency with Alice-Bob. Consequently, we assume that Eve has a priori knowledge of when Alice and Bob are about to communicate and can perfectly time her attack pilots so as to maximally disrupt the Alice-Bob channel estimation. Although this assumption is powerful, it is plausible as evidenced by research efforts by the software radio and electronic warfare communities. We also assume that Eve is computationally limited in the sense that she cannot break any underlying cryptographic algorithms, and that Alice and Bob share cryptographic keys that are unknown to Eve. We now examine the underlying security and reliability issues of our CSI protection schemes.

8.1 Cryptographic Protocol Aspects

A cryptographic one-way function $g(\cdot)$ is used to compute an authentication message m_i for the i-th packet via $m_i = g(k, i)$. Regardless of how this message is transmitted, if $g(\cdot)$ is an appropriately chosen cryptographic one-way function (such as SHA-256/512), then even if Eve knows the sequence number, it will be hard for her to invert and find the key k shared by Alice and Bob. Further, as the sequence number increments during each transmission, Eve will not be able to record a previous authentication message m_i (or, equivalently, the pilot tones associated with m_i) to launch a replay attack as future transmissions will inherently have a different sequence number and au-

thentication message associated with them. One practical issue is the size of the authentication message. In practice, the 256 bits associated with SHA-256 output is reasonable for an authentication message. For example, using the FPC method, one can embed a 384-bit authentication message in a single 802.11g transmission, which uses $K = 64$ OFDM subcarriers, $N = 4$ frequency quantization bins, $Q = 4$ power quantization levels, and only a single transmission antenna ($M = 1$). A second practical issue is protocol synchronization between Alice and Bob. Initial protocol bootstrapping involves the distribution of k and a starting counter i. Synchronization between Alice and Bob requires that they be at the same value for i and, although unlikely, it may be possible that Alice's counter i_A is not the same as Bob's i_B. This desynchronization could occur, for example, due to a poor communication link, but can be easily detected by declaring synchronization failure when there are more than a fixed amount of authentication failures. Desynchronization can also be dealt with by making $m_i = i \| g(k, i)$ (similar to how S/KEY copes with synchronization in Lamport's one-time password scheme).

8.2 Probability Analysis

Destructive Interference: Constructive interference results in enhanced energy and is a result of signals arriving at a common antenna with the same frequency and phase. Contrarily, if a signal arrives with the same frequency but opposite phase, destructive interference will result, and the overall energy will be decreased. Consider the baseband representation of two signals arriving at Bob from Alice and Eve, respectively. Both Alice and Eve transmit $x(t)$ to Bob, and the signals are assumed to be perfectly frequency matched so that Bob sees $x_A(t) = a_A x(t) e^{j\Theta_A} + n_A(t)$, and $x_E(t) = a_E x(t) e^{j\Theta_E} + n_E(t)$. The cumulative arriving signal at Bob is $r(t) = x_A(t) + x_E(t) = x(t) e^{j\Theta_A}(a_A + a_E e^{j\Theta_\Delta}) + n(t)$, where we define $\Theta_\Delta = \Theta_E - \Theta_A$, and $n(t) = n_A(t) + n_E(t)$. Thus, perfectly constructive interference results in $r(t) = x(t) e^{j\Theta_A}(a_A + a_E) + n(t)$ for $\Theta_A = \Theta_E$. For the perfectly destructive scenario, we have $r(t) = x(t) e^{j\Theta_A}(a_A - a_E) + n(t)$ for $\Theta_A = -\Theta_E$.

As an attacker, Eve can never be certain of the phase, frequency, and amplitude of her signal arriving at Bob relative to the signal transmitted by Alice. We consider her additive effect as normally distributed in-phase and quadrature components, $\Re(x_E(t)) \sim N(0, \sigma_E^2)$ and $\Im(x_E(t)) \sim N(0, \sigma_E^2)$. Thus, Eve's effective magnitude perturbation is a Rayleigh random variable, $|x_E(t)| \sim \mathcal{R}(\sigma_E)$, with a uniformly random phase effect, $\arg(x_E(t)) \sim U(0, 2\pi]$. In high jammer-to-signal (J/S) scenarios, Eve's transmission dominates regardless of Alice's transmission, while the opposite is true for low J/S scenarios. In our analysis, we assume the worst case scenario: where Eve is equipped with ample jammer power such that the J/S $>> 0$ dB.

RFC Probability Analysis: We calculate two distinct probabilities: the probability of false alarm, PFA, and the probability of missed detection, PMD. We define a false alarm as the case where we mistakenly declare an authentication sequence as invalid (a.k.a. only Alice transmitted, but we declare Eve as present). We define a missed detection as the scenario where we accept an authentication message even though adversarial activity has corrupted our CSI estimate. For ease of analysis, we define an authentication message to be encompassed by a single antenna using a single carrier (i.e 1 pilot using the RFC scheme, and N pilots using the BFC and FPC schemes). For our analysis, we assume a powerful adversarial model where Eve is equipped with ample transmitter (jammer) power and is capable of perfect timing and frequency synchronization. We note that such an adversarial model provides a lower bound on protocol performance (and is increasingly more plausible given recent advancements in SDR architectures).

For the RFC scheme, a false alarm occurs when noise causes the true pilot to not be detected at all, or when a pilot is mistakenly detected in another frequency quantization bin. We model the additive noise component, $n(t)$, as complex Gaussian, $(n(t) \sim CN(0, \sigma_n^2))$, again resulting in a Rayleigh distributed magnitude perturbation $(|n(t)| \sim \mathcal{R}(\sigma_n))$ at a uniform phase $(\arg(n(t)) \sim U(0, 2\pi])$. A false alarm thus occurs when the noise is large enough to surpass a power detection threshold, P_τ, in at least 1 of the $N - 1$ non-active frequency quantization bins, or when the noise destructively interferes with the true pilot in such a way as to drop it below the power detection threshold. Hence,

$$PFA = P_{N-1}(|n(t)| \geq P_\tau) + P_1(|x_A(t) + n(t)| < P_\tau)$$
$$\leq P_{N-1}(|n(t)| \geq P_\tau) + P_1(|n(t)| > (|x_A(t)| - P_\tau))$$
$$= 1 - (1 - e^{\frac{-P_\tau^2}{2\sigma_n^2}})^{(N-1)}(1 - e^{\frac{-(|x_A(t)| - P_\tau)^2}{2\sigma_n^2}}),$$

where the inequality occurs due to the random phase effect of the additive noise. A missed detection occurs when Eve selects the exact message bearing frequency interval to send her rogue pilot, thus giving $PMD = \frac{1}{N}$.

BFC Probability Analysis: For the BFC scheme, a false alarm occurs when one or more of the true pilots are not detected within an appropriate power deviation, P_Δ, or when a silent bin is detected as active. Our PFA assumes η of N active frequency quantization bins (i.e. pilots).

$$PFA = P_\eta(|n(t)| \geq P_\tau) + P_{(N-\eta)}(|n(t)| > P_\Delta)$$
$$= 1 - (1 - e^{\frac{-P_\tau^2}{2\sigma_n^2}})^{(N-\eta)}(1 - e^{\frac{-P_\Delta^2}{2\sigma_n^2}})^{\eta}$$

A missed detection occurs when Eve correctly guesses the N-bit authentication sequence, and hence $PMD = \frac{1}{2^N}$.

FPC Probability Analysis: For the FPC scheme, a false alarm occurs when the power from any of the N transmitted pilots deviate into another power quantization interval. Remember that for the FPC scheme, Q power quantization levels are used per pilot. Thus is it sensible to define the power deviation threshold, P_Δ, as half of a power quantization interval. Regardless of power deviation threshold selection, $PFA = P_N(|n(t)| > P_\Delta) = 1 - (1 - e^{\frac{-P_\Delta^2}{2\sigma_n^2}})^N$. A missed detection occurs when Eve correctly guesses the proper quantization level to use at each of the N pilot tones. Hence, $PMD = \frac{1}{Q^N}$.

Performance Analysis: Further illustrating the feasibility of our methods for real wireless systems, we present performance evaluation for a typical 802.11g implementation. Using $K = 64$ pilot carriers (one per 802.11g subcarrier), we consider $N = 4$ frequency quantization bins and $Q = 4$ power quantization levels per pilot, with single antenna operation ($M = 1$). Our analysis assumes an SNR of 35 dB, which is equivalent to 3 to 4 signal quality bars out of 5 (i.e. good, but not excellent, signal quality). For ease of presentation we assume a nominal signal magnitude reception of 1 volt, and use reception magnitudes of $\{1.0, 0.8, 0.6, 0.4\}$ volts to decode our power quantization bits. Accordingly, we select a power detection threshold, P_τ, of 0.3 volts, and a power deviation threshold, P_Δ, of

Table 1: CSI Protection Performance Analysis for Typical WiFi Authentication with SNR=35 dB, N= 4, Q= 4, M= 1, and $K \in \{1, 2, 64\}$.

Method	K	PFA	PMD	# Auth Bits
RFC	2	0	6.25e-2	2
	64	0	2.94e-39	126
BFC	1	2.72e-7	6.25e-2	3
	64	1.74e-5	8.64e-78	255
FPC	1	5.44e-7	3.9e-3	6
	64	3.48e-5	7.46e-155	384

0.1 volt. Table 1 lists the PFA and PMD results for $K = 1$ and $K = 64$ pilot carriers. As can be seen, implementing any of our schemes in realistic operating conditions results in reasonable PFA and PMD.

9. CONCLUSION

Accurate channel estimation is imperative for current and emerging wireless communication systems. Invalid estimates can result from channel noise, co-channel interference, or adversarial activity. It is thus important to not only authenticate the channel estimation procedure, but also infer the cause of bad estimates. Unlike existing techniques, we have proposed various authentication schemes that operate reliably across coherence time intervals, provide error inference, can be applied in any channel environment, and do not incur additional system overhead. Our techniques were demonstrated in real-world experiments.

10. REFERENCES

[1] T. Clancy and N. Goergen, *Security in Cognitive Radio Networks: Threats and Mitigation*, Third International Conference on Cognitive Radio Oriented Wireless Networks and Communications (CrownCom) (2008).

[2] N. Goergen, W.S. Lin, K.J.R. Liu, and T.C. Clancy, *Authenticating MIMO Transmissions Using Channel-Like Fingerprinting*, IEEE Global Communications Conference (GLOBECOM) (2010).

[3] M. Hsieh and C. Wei, *Channel Estimation for OFDM Systems Based on Comb-Type Pilot Arrangement in Frequency Selective Fading Channels*, IEEE Transactions on Consumer Electronics (1998), 217–225.

[4] R. Miller and W. Trappe, *Subverting MIMO wireless systems by jamming the channel estimation procedure*, Proceedings of the third ACM conference on Wireless network security (2010), 19–24.

[5] T.S. Rappaport, *Wireless Communications: Principles and practice*, Prentice Hall, Upper Saddle River, NJ, 2002.

[6] S.Y. Seidel, T.S. Rappaport, S. Jain, M.L. Lord, and R. Singh, *Path Loss, Scattering, and Multipath Delay Statistics in Four European Cities for Digital Cellular and Microcellular Radiotelephone*, IEEE Transactions on Vehicular Technology **40** (1991), no. 4, 721–730.

[7] R. Tesi, M. Hamalainen, and J. Iinatti, *Channel Estimation Algorithms Comparison for Multiband-OFDM*, The 17th Annual IEEE International Symposium on Personal, Indoor and Mobile Radio Communications (2006).

[8] L. Xiao, L. J. Greenstein, N. B. Mandayam, and W. Trappe, *MIMO-Assisted Channel-Based Authentication in Wireless Networks*, IEEE Conf. on Information Sciences and Systems (CISS) (2008), 642–646.

[9] L. Xiao, L.J. Greenstein, N. Mandayam, and W. Trappe, *Using the Physical Layer for Wireless Authentication in Time-Variant Channels*, IEEE Transactions on Wireless Communications (2008), 2571–2579.

[10] L. Xiao, L.J. Greenstein, N.B. Mandayam, and W. Trappe, *A Physical-Layer Technique to Enhance Authentication for Mobile Terminals*, IEEE International Conference on Communications (ICC) (2008), 1520–1524.

[11] P. Yu, J. Baras, and B. Sadler, *An Implementation of Physical Layer Authentication Using Software Radios*, Report No. ARL-TR-4888 (2009).

On the Robustness of IEEE802.11 Rate Adaptation Algorithms against Smart Jamming [*]

Guevara Noubir
College of Computer and
Information Science
Northeastern University
Boston, MA 02115
noubir@ccs.neu.edu

Rajmohan Rajaraman
College of Computer and
Information Science
Northeastern University
Boston, MA 02115
rraj@ccs.neu.edu

Bo Sheng
Dept. of Computer Science
University of Massachusetts
Boston, MA 02125
shengbo@cs.umb.edu

Bishal Thapa
College of Computer and
Information Science
Northeastern University
Boston, MA 02115
bthapa@ccs.neu.edu

ABSTRACT

We investigate the resiliency of IEEE802.11 rate adaptation algorithms (RAA) against smart jamming attacks. We consider several classes of state-of-the-art RAAs that include the SampleRate, ONOE, AMRR, and the RAA used in Atheros Microsoft Windows XP driver. We model the behavior of these algorithms, and show the existence of very efficient attacks that exploit RAA-specific vulnerabilities as well as the inherent weaknesses that exist in the design of IEEE802.11 MAC and link layer protocol: in particular the overt packet rate information being transmitted, predictable rate selection mechanism, performance anomaly caused by the equiprobability of transmissions among all nodes regardless of the data rates being employed, and the lack of interference differentiation from poor link quality by IEEE802.11 RAAs. In this work, we present algorithms that determine optimal jamming strategies against RAAs for a given jamming budget, and experimentally demonstrate the efficiency of these smart jamming attacks, which can be orders of magnitude more efficient than naive jamming. For example, in the case of SampleRate, eight reactive jamming pulses every second are sufficient to achieve the same network throughput degradation achieved by a periodic jammer with the jamming energy cost 100 times higher. Some of the RAAs react even worse to smart jamming attacks; ONOE in particular suffers from the phenomenon of *congestion collapse* where the nodes fail to recover from the lowest data rate even after the jammer stops jamming. At the end, we summarize fundamental reasons behind such RAA vulnerabilities and propose a preliminary set of mitigation techniques. We leave the experimental demonstration of the efficiency of the proposed mitigation mechanisms for future work.

[*]This work was partially supported by NSF grant 0915985.

Categories and Subject Descriptors

C.2.1 [**Computer-Communication Networks**]: Network Architecture and Design —*Wireless Communication*

General Terms

Security, Algorithms

Keywords

IEEE802.11, Rate Adaptation, Smart Jamming, USRP, GNU Radio, Experimentation

1. INTRODUCTION

With rapid advancement and standardization of wireless technology, wireless LANs (WLANs) are now ubiquitous, providing the last mile access to the Internet. Security issues in WLANs, however, remain a serious concern and have attracted a lot of attention in the research community. Among various security attacks, jamming continues to be an effective exploit that can deny or degrade service to legitimate WLAN users. A knowledgeable attacker can intermittently inject signals into the medium and occupy wireless channels, interfere with regular traffic and disrupt WLAN operations effectively at minimal jamming cost. Existing jammers rely on high transmission power and frequent injection of jamming signals to disrupt communication. Such a strategy is inefficient in terms of jamming power consumption; furthermore, increases the risk of trivial jammer detection due to high power jamming and/or frequent packet injections into the communication medium.

In this paper, we study the resiliency of IEEE802.11 rate adaptation algorithms (RAAs) against smart jamming attacks. To this end, we first consider the design of an optimal jammer targeting the vulnerabilities of IEEE802.11 RAAs. The function of the RAA is to enable WLAN users to adaptively choose the best transmitting rate according to current wireless link conditions in order to achieve the maximum throughput possible. Intuitively, lower rates are more reliable and suitable for poor channel conditions and the higher data rates for good channel conditions. It is well known that most common implementations of RAA in use today cannot distinguish between the causes of packet failures due to the poor link quality and due to the interference/collisions. If a jammer injects

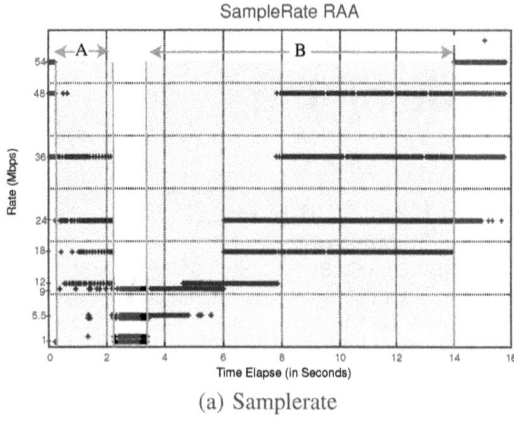

(a) Samplerate

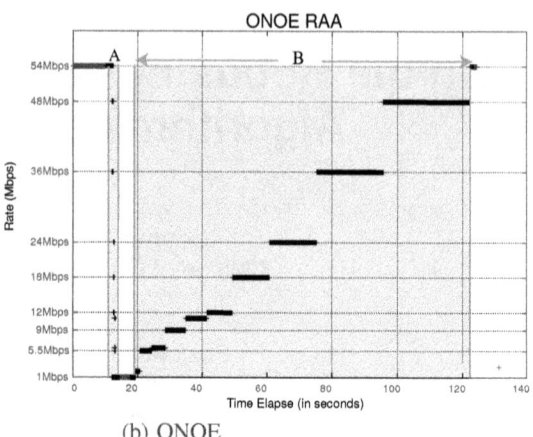

(b) ONOE

Figure 1: (a) Time it takes to drop the rate to the lowest value, (b) Time it takes to recover to the optimal data rate.

pulses so as to interfere with the regular packets, the legitimate user will assume that the link quality is poor for the current transmission rate, and will decrease the rate to a lesser value. What makes it worse is that once the jamming stops, the recovery period before attaining the optimal data rate for communication in these RAAs are much longer than the time it takes for them to adaptively lower the data rate due to collision or malicious interference. Figure 1 shows such a phenomenon that is predominant in the case of two of the most commonly used RAAs: SampleRate and ONOE. Overall, this is one of the reasons that the IEEE802.11 wireless network suffers from significant performance degradation even with an oblivious jammer injecting small pulses intermittently into the channel.

IEEE-802.11 WLAN also suffers from a performance anomaly where the poorest link dictates the throughput of the whole network sharing a common channel. This phenomenon was first reported in [11]. The reason for this is because all participating nodes have the same probability of transmitting at any instant of IEEE802.11 communication independent of the data rates being used at different links. However, this behavior leads to an efficient adversary attack called the *reflection attack* where the jammer targets one particular link and jams to bring down its data rate, while in effect causing the whole network throughput to suffer heavily as shown in Figure 2. Figure 2(a) depicts an experimental setting with multiple links sharing a common channel and a reactive jammer present in the medium that selectively jams all the non-1Mbps traffic of some link, l_i. Without the loss of generality, we pick D as the victim link for the experiment. Figure 2(b) clearly shows that the impact of jamming victim link D trickles down to non-victim links (A, B, C, D) in terms of the average throughput degradation and ultimately the whole network throughput is affected even though only a single link is being targeted by the jammer.

Hence, in this paper, we carefully analyze the vulnerabilities inherent to IEEE802.11 MAC and RAAs, and design optimal jammer exploits to maximize the throughput reduction at a minimal jamming cost. The main contributions of our work are as follow:

- We first analyze three widely-used RAAs – ONOE, AMRR, SampleRate and derive the cost of jamming in each case to achieve a desired throughput reduction (Section 5).

- We then classify RAAs based on their rate selection strategies and use that framework to design optimal jamming strategies that exploit the RAA-specific behavior. We show that our jamming cost analysis can be used to efficiently design a

smart jammer that targets specific packets and optimize the reduction in throughput when subjected to a jamming energy budget. We also present a technique that applies to the case when jamming costs cannot be estimated (Section 4).

- We analyze the weaknesses inherent in the IEEE802.11 MAC and Link layer protocols that allow jammers to be extremely efficient with their jamming.

- We build a testbed comprising of the USRP/GNURadio platform and present a comprehensive experimental evaluation of three RAAs mentioned above and the RAA used in Microsoft Windows XP in the presence of smart jamming. Our experimental results confirm that a smart reactive jammer can maintain links at a low data rate (1 Mbps) at a minimal jamming cost (jamming only $5 - 8$ packets/s) (Section 6).

- Finally, we propose a set of preliminary mitigation mechanisms with their implementation left for future work (Section 7).

Paper Outline: In Section 2, we review the related work. In Section 3, we provide the background for our work and discuss inherent weaknesses of IEEE802.11. Subsequently, we discuss our system model and the framework for cost analysis of IEEE802.11 RAA jamming in Sections 4 and 5. Finally, in Section 6, we evaluate the proposed smart jamming attacks using a carefully designed real-world experimentation test-bed. We present the details of the implementation and evaluation methodology. At the end, we conclude with the discussions on the mitigation techniques and future work in Sections 7 and 8.

2. RELATED WORK

Anti-jamming techniques have been studied extensively for decades [30]. Most of the earlier mechanisms focused on protecting physical layer of the wireless communication and made use of spread-spectrum techniques, directional antennas, and coding schemes. At the time, most of the wireless communication were not packetized nor networked. Reliable communication in the presence of adversaries have regained significant interest in the last few years. New attacks and thus the need for more complex applications and deployment environments have emerged. Several specifically crafted attacks and counter-attacks have been proposed for: packetized wireless data networks [20, 22], multiple access resolution in the presence of adversaries [1–3], multi-hop networks [20,

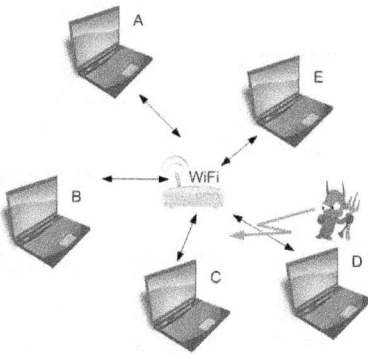

(a) Reflection Attack

	Victim Link	Non-victim Links
Avg. Throughput (Pre-jamming)	16.1 Mbps	15.4 Mbps
Avg. Throughput (Post-jamming)	1.02 Mbps	0.96 Mbps
Data Rate (Pre-jamming)	54 Mbps	54 Mbps
Data Rate (Post-jamming)	1 Mbps	54 Mbps

(b) Performance Anomaly

Figure 2: Smart Jamming Strategy that exploits the IEEE802.11 Performance Anomaly.

33,43], broadcast communication [8,10,32], cross-layer attacks [21], and navigation information broadcast systems [27]. However, very little work has been done on protecting rate adaptation algorithms against adversarial attacks. Rate adaptation plays an important role in IEEE802.11 as the link quality in a WLAN is often highly dynamic. In recent years, a number of algorithms for rate adaptation have been proposed in literature [7, 12, 14, 17, 25, 26, 41, 42], and few have been used in Commercial Off-The-Shelf (COTS) products as well [5, 19]. Their main idea is to estimate channel quality and adjust the transmission rate accordingly. Most of the existing mechanisms estimate channel quality using some metrics, such as statistics of packet successes and failures, PHY metrics like the SNR, probe packets etc. Based on where this information is collected, we can classify RAAs into two main categories: the first category is *sender-based* where the RAAs determine the rates solely based on the metrics collected and calculated at the sender side (irrespective of the receiver feedback/information) [5, 15, 19, 26, 42] and the second category is *receiver-based* where the algorithm explicitly uses feedbacks from the receiver to select a data transmission rate [9, 12, 17, 28, 29]. Regardless, most of these algorithms are vulnerable to even the simplest of jamming attacks mainly because these algorithms fail to differentiate between interference caused by link quality and collisions/fading/malicious interference, and therefore causing the collected statistical information to be biased by the interference making them an inaccurate assessment of the link quality. [17] tries to differentiate between the losses due to collision and link conditions using RTS/CTS exchange. The basic intuition in their work is that with the RTS/CTS enabled, the packet loss is certainly caused by the link quality. Robust Rate Adaptation Algorithm in [42] adopts a similar idea to obtain more accurate statistics of packet loss. However, these approaches cannot mitigate the issue of (malicious) interference caused by jamming because the adversary may not obey the RTS/CTS policy, e.g., the jammer can jam the data packet following an RTS/CTS exchange.

[28] proposes to let the receiver send corrupted packets back to the sender to help determine the cause of the packet failure. However, it does not help the WLAN under jamming attacks either because, (a) the interference caused by jamming may have different characteristics from the interference caused by the channel noise. So it is difficult for the proposed scheme to detect the existence of the jamming signals, and (b) the adversary may jam the feedback packets from the receiver so that the sender has no sufficient information for analysis.

To the best of our knowledge, [23] is the first work to consider RAA jamming. They demonstrate that in fact existing RAAs are highly vulnerable to jamming. They show that fixed data rate network outperforms most of the rate-adaptive network in the presence of naive jamming. Their work, however, assumes an unconstrained jammer and does not consider the case where the jammers, similar to the senders and receivers, are resource constrained. In contrast, our paper focuses on the robustness of RAAs against attacks that specifically target the specific rate adaptation vulnerabilities and IEEE802.11 weakness and efficiently reduce the network throughput within their limited jamming budget. Furthermore, their anti-jamming mechanism depends on figuring out correct threshold to distinguish between scenarios of jamming and no-jamming, and hence to be able to switch between using RAA and fixed data rate as triggered by their threshold cutoff. This scheme of calculating the appropriate threshold can easily be exploited by a smart jammer. Their work, therefore, only provides resiliency against naive jamming. Our work, on the other hand, discusses the mitigation of vulnerabilities at the IEEE802.11 MAC and Link Layer to keep smart jammers from launching efficient denial of service attacks.

Lastly, [6] considers intelligent jamming that exploits the performance anomaly in IEEE802.11 WLAN. They propose ways to detect and alleviate the impact of such jamming under their setup. Their work, however, like [23] only considers inefficient jammers that blindly send intermittent or periodic signals without exploiting the publicly known protocol information. Therefore, their jammer requires being physically placed in the vicinity of the victim node such that it does not jam a region and instead jams only the targeted victim node. Jamming a region is detrimental to the jammer's performance not only in terms of jamming cost but also it would lead to easy detection. In contrast, our work considers reactive jammers that are not only channel aware but specifically filter out the victim nodes traffic, and focus all of their jamming on the packets of the victim node as shown in Figure 2.

3. IEEE802.11 MAC AND RAAS

In this section, we briefly introduce the specific RAAs that we analyze in this paper, and discuss the inherent weaknesses of IEEE-802.11 MAC and RAAs that allow for smart jamming attacks.

3.1 Background

We have examined four RAAs in our experiments. The first three are included in MadWifi driver with source codes and the fourth one is the Atheros Windows XP driver for which details are not available. The following is a brief description of the Madwifi (most popular open source driver) implementation of the RAAs [36]:

SampleRate: SampleRate is the default RAA used in Madwifi driver [5, 35, 36]. It maintains the statistical information for each data rate which includes the average transmitting time (ATT) (considering the retries) and the number of consecutive failures. The algorithm picks the rate with the lowest ATT for transmission. After every 10 packets, SampleRate randomly picks a different data rate for probing to update its packet rate statistics. This allows for rate update even when the current rate is performing with no failures. The ratesbe with more than 3 consecutive failures are not eligible for probing (black-listed). After a 2 second period, all the black-listed rates are reconsidered for probing if their theoretical

ATT with no retransmissions is better than the ATT of the current rate in use. In non-malicious environment, SampleRate quickly converges to the optimal data rate.

ONOE: ONOE is the RAA developed by the Madwifi developers [37]. ONOE monitors the history of packet successes and failures within a window of 1 second, and uses a credit system where it increases the credit value by 1 if more than 90% of packets have succeeded during the last window, otherwise decreases the credit by 1. When the credit reaches 10, the sender increases the transmitting rate to the next higher rate. If all the packets succeed during the last monitor window, then the sender directly increases the rate. If each packet fails at least once on average, then the sender decreases the rate to the next lower rate. Therefore, Onoe is more conservative in its step-ups as it takes at least 10 seconds before it decides to increase the data rate, whereas, it steps down pretty quickly if the link quality deteriorates.

AMRR: Adaptive Multi Rate Retry is a two-stage RAA, which is basically an extension of ARF (Auto Rate Fallback) with multi-rate retransmissions [19]. The main idea behind this RAA is that the short-term fluctuations are dealt via multi-rate retries (MRR) implemented at the driver, and the long term rate adaptation is taken care of by applying a basic mechanism where the sender adjusts the rate upwards after 10 consecutive ACKs, and adjusts the rate downwards after 2 consecutive failures. The MRR is defined as a tuple $(r_0/c_0, r_1/c_1, r_2/c_2, r_3/c_3)$, where the retry rates (r_0, r_1, r_2, r_3) are set to $(the\ current\ rate,\ one\ level\ lower\ rate,\ two\ level\ lower\ rate,\ the\ lowest\ base\ rate)$ and the retry counts (c_0, c_1, c_2, c_3) are set to $(1, 1, 1, 1)$ respectively. The more details on the multi rate retries for AMRR, ONOE and SampleRate can be found in [18].

3.2 Weaknesses of IEEE802.11 MAC and RAAs

There are four major weaknesses in existing rate adaptation algorithms used in combination with IEEE802.11 Link and MAC layer protocols for WiFi communication:

- *Overt Packet Rate Information:* The IEEE802.11 standard makes the rate of the current packet being transmitted explicitly available in the SIGNAL field of the PLCP header (encoded and modulated with a robust base rate). This allows an adversary equipped with a smart radio to quickly identify the current packet rate and jam it before the end of the transmission. Even without the PLCP header information, a smart jammer can recover the rate of a packet by (1) analyzing the I and Q signal constellation to derive the current modulation of the packet (e.g., BPSK, QPSK, 16QAM, 64QAM for 802.11ag), and (2) attempting the error correction schemes (e.g., 1/2, 2/3, 3/4 for 802.11g). The combination of modulation and coding scheme uniquely identifies the packet rate in a 802.11 communication. Furthermore, distinguishing between DSSS and OFDM are even easier when using the spectrum signature of the frame preamble. This allows for an easy detection of current data rate in use by an adversary.

- *Predictable rate selection rules:* The behavior of existing rate adaptation algorithms is very predictable. SampleRate, for example, sends probes periodically at the interval of every ten packets with a different data rate. Furthermore, the Madwifi (most widely used linux driver) implementation of SampleRate makes it even more predictable by using deterministic rules to pick data rates for probing. Similarly, the credit mechanisms of ONOE is easily track-able by an adversary, and so is the exponential backoff mechanism of AMRR.

- *Equi-probable transmissions:* The IEEE802.11 standard gives equal opportunity to all the nodes to transmit, independent of their link quality (therefore the data rates). This allows adversaries to mount *reflection attack*, where a victim node is targeted for attack and forced into selecting a low data rate. The victim now monopolizes the channel, therefore indirectly blocking/delaying other nodes from transmitting. This can transform moderate load into saturation traffic load, and possibly a self-sustaining low-rate selection phenomenon as seen in the case of ONOE. We call this jammer-triggered *congestion collapse*. We discuss this in detail in Section 5.

- *Lack of Interference Differentiation:* Radio receivers are incapable of differentiating between *malicious interference* (e.g., jamming) and *non-malicious interference* such as direct collisions (two nodes' MAC backoff timer expiring at the same time), hidden terminal problem, or noise from spatial reuse of channels. This gets even harder to do for moving nodes with dynamic link quality due to multi-path fading and environmental changes.

All these weaknesses in IEEE802.11 MAC and RAAs allow for very efficient and effective attacks by an adversary spending minimum jamming cost.

4. IEEE802.11 RAA JAMMING

In this section, we present our model for studying RAA jamming attacks and devise optimal attack against rate adaptation given a fixed energy budget for the jammer.

4.1 System Model and Problem Formulation

4.1.1 Network Model

We consider a WLAN with a set U of users who share the same wireless channel and are all within one another's communication range. We assume there are n directional communication links given by the set $L = \{l_1, l_2, \ldots, l_n\}$ among all users. Let $D = \{d_i > 0 | 1 \leq i \leq n\}$ denote the set of expected traffic demands on links L. For a saturated network, $d_i = d$ for all links l_i. Let m represent the available number of transmitting data rates for each user and R denote the set of data rates in ascending order:

$$R = \{r_1, r_2, \ldots, r_m\}\ \forall i, j, i < j \Rightarrow r_i < r_j.$$

Now, we use $t_i \in R$ to represent the transmission rate used on the link l_i (i.e, by the sender). Thus, $T = \{t_1, \ldots, t_n\}$ represents the array of rates used on the n links respectively. The overall throughput of the WLAN can be approximately expressed as

$$\Gamma(D, T) = \frac{\sum_i d}{\sum_i \frac{d}{t_i}}.$$

$$\Longleftrightarrow \Gamma(D, T) = \frac{1}{\sum_i \frac{1}{t_i}}$$

Note that L, D and T may vary over time. Here, we assume that they are stable for an epoch t.

4.1.2 Adversary Model

We assume the adversary is equipped with a radio device operating on the 802.11 frequency band that can receive signals from the air and inject signals to it. Under our model, the jammer uses a fixed transmission power to generate a short pulse signal that is strong enough to jam a packet if hit. During our experimental evaluation, we observed that a jamming pulse as small as $22\mu s$ in length

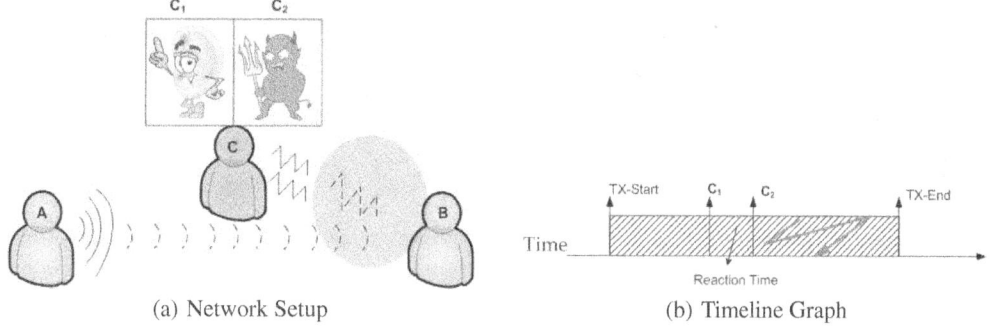

(a) Network Setup (b) Timeline Graph

Figure 3: Block Diagram: A is the sender, B is the receiver, C is the jammer (C_1 and C_2 are its sensing and jamming counterparts).

can make the concurrently transmitted packet undecodable even if it is being sent using the most reliable rate by the sender. Additionally, we assume that the adversary has a bounded energy source which limits it to injecting at most B jamming packets during any epoch. Thus, the objective of the adversary is to jam the WLAN with at most B packets and alter the transmitting rates, T, to a new set T' such that $\Gamma(D, T')$ is minimized.

Figure 3 depicts the network and the adversary model of our system.

4.2 Sketch of an Attack

We divide each jamming attack into two phases, an *initial phase* and a *maintenance phase*. The first phase is to bring down the transmitting rates on some links and the second phase is to keep those links at the low rate for the duration of the epoch given a fixed jamming budget.

4.2.1 Initial Phase

This phase is a short period compared to the maintenance phase and the epoch. We assume that prior to the start of the initial phase the adversary has monitored the traffic in the air and obtained some information about the WLAN, such as the identifier of each user and data link, traffic demands (length of the payload in each link), and current rates. In this initial phase, the adversary first selects a set of victim links and calculates a target rate for each of them that is no more than the current rate. Then, if the target rate for a victim link is smaller than the current rate, the adversary intensively jams the packets transferred on the victim link to trigger the RAA to decrease the data rate. The jamming in this phase stops when the rate on each victim link reaches the target level. Our goal in this phase is to bring down the transmitting rates on the victim links to the target rates in a quick and efficient way. As we will see later, it may not be necessary to jam all the packets on the victim links to achieve this phenomenon.

4.2.2 Maintenance Phase

After the initial phase, each victim link's rate has already been decreased to the adversary's target rate. However, additional jamming is needed to prevent those links from recovering to their previous higher rates as more packets are being delivered. We call this the maintenance phase. In this phase, the adversary selectively jams the packets transferred on the victim links so that the RAA does not increase the rates. Compared to the initial phase, the jamming in the maintenance phase is less frequent, but it lasts for a longer period (the remainder of the epoch) depending on the budget and the goal of the jammer.

In this two-phase attack design, the challenge is to determine which victim links to invest the energy on and achieving their cor-

responding target rates. In the rest of this section, we present algorithms to solve this problem. We look at two scenarios differentiated based on the awareness or the oblivion of the adversary regarding the RAA being employed by communicating links.

Fig. 4 shows the performance of RAA jamming in terms of above described phase costs for each of the four RAAs (SampleRate, ONOE, AMRR, Windows RAA).

4.3 Optimal Algorithm for Known RAA

We first consider the case where the jammer is aware of the RAA being used for each link in the network.[1] With the RAA information, we can derive two important parameters of the jamming cost spent in the initial phase and maintenance phase. We call them *initial cost* and *maintenance cost*, which are defined as the number of jamming pulses needed in the initial and maintenance phases under our model respectively. Let $ic(r, r', k)$ denote the initial jamming cost of degrading the transmitting rate on link l_k from r to r' ($ic(r, r', k) = 0$ if $r \leq r'$). Let $mc(r, k)$ denote the maintenance cost of keeping link l_k at rate r for the duration of an epoch. In the next section, we will show how to calculate them $ic(r, r', k)$ and $mc(i, k)$ for a particular RAA. Here, we assume that they are given parameters for the problem.

Given the demand D, and the set of initial transmission rates T, our goal is to find the best jamming strategy to yield a new set of rates T' and maintain it for the epoch t within the jammer budget B.[2] Thus, our problem can be formulated as

$$\text{minimize } \Gamma(D, T') \Rightarrow \text{maximize } \sum \frac{1}{r_i'}$$

$$s.t. \quad \sum_{\forall k} (ic(t_k, t_k', k) + mc(t_k', k)) \leq B$$

We propose Algorithm 1 to find the best victim links and their target rates. In the algorithm, $Opt(x)$ represents the maximum objective we can achieve with cost budget x and $T^x = \{t_1^x, t_2^x, \ldots, t_k^x\}$ is the corresponding resulting set of rates, i.e., link l_k uses rate t_k^x in the optimal result.

Initially, Opt is set to the current value of $\sum \frac{1}{t_i}$. The algorithm is a dynamic program that incrementally fills the array $Opt(x)$. Lines 4-17 enumerate all possible choices for the last jamming action which can be represented as a $< l_k, r, r' >$ tuple, i.e., the last jamming to decrease the rate on l_k from r to r'. In line 7, y represents the budget cost for all the previous jamming actions. $< l_k, r, r' >$ is valid only if $y > 0$ and given that the jamming link l_k was using rate r. Among all possibilities for the last jamming action, we

---

[1]Note each link may use a different RAA.

[2]Note that while demands might be difficult to predict, it can be assumed to be uniform in saturated conditions.

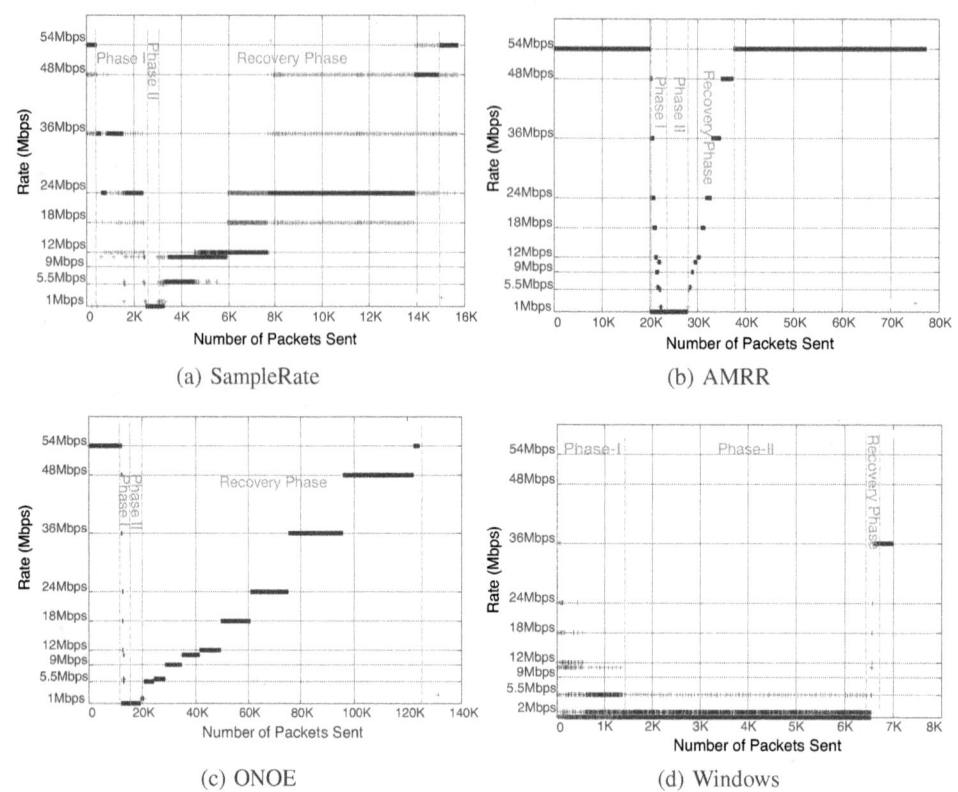

(a) SampleRate

(b) AMRR

(c) ONOE

(d) Windows

Figure 4: Performance of RAAs under Jamming

Algorithm 1 Optimal Jamming for Known RAA

1: $Opt(0) \leftarrow \frac{\sum d_i}{\Gamma(D,T)}, T^0 \leftarrow T$
2: **for** $x = 1$ to B **do**
3:     $Opt(x) \leftarrow Opt(x-1), T^x \leftarrow T^{x-1}$
4:     **for all** link l_k **do**
5:         **for** r in R such that $r \leq t_k$ **do**
6:             **for** r' in R such that $r' < r$ **do**
7:                 $y \leftarrow x - ic(r, r', k) - mc(r', k)$
8:                 **if** $y > 0$ **then**
9:                     $ty \leftarrow Opt(y) - \frac{1}{r} + \frac{1}{r'}$
10:                    **if** $t_k^y = r$ and $ty > Opt(x)$ **then**
11:                        $Opt(x) \leftarrow ty$
12:                        $T^x \leftarrow T^y$ and set $t_k^x \leftarrow r'$
13:                    **end if**
14:                **end if**
15:            **end for**
16:        **end for**
17:    **end for**
18: **end for**
19: Output $Opt(B)$ and $T' \leftarrow T^B$

---

pick the one that can maximize the objective and record the maximum value in $Opt(x)$ (lines 11-12). T^x is also updated to keep track of the victim links and their target rates. Finally, T^B contains the best target rates for each victim link and $Opt(B)$ is the optimal value of the objective function. The complexity of Algorithm 1 is $O(B \cdot n \cdot m^2)$.

4.4 Greedy Algorithm for Unknown RAA

If the RAA in the WLAN is unknown, the adversary may not be able to calculate the initial cost and maintenance cost. An alternative way is to run a short training session where the adversary conducts jamming trials on each link at different rates and estimates the initial cost and maintenance cost based on the observation. If the training session cannot provide a consistent and accurate estimation, we propose the following greedy heuristic for the reactive jammer.

At all times, for each link l_i the adversary maintains an estimate gmc_i of the cost of maintaining the link at its current rate for the duration of the epoch. It also maintains the total cost gic incurred thus far in bringing the rates of the victim links down to the current rates. Initially, gmc_i for all i and gic are set to zero.

To determine the next victim link, the adversary computes, for each link l_i, the degradation in throughput, $GD(i)$, when its rate is decreased by a level (assuming it is not already at the lowest level).

$$GD(i) = d \cdot \left(\frac{1}{p(t_i)} - \frac{1}{t_i} \right),$$

where for a given rate r, $p(r)$ is the largest rate smaller than r in R; if r equals r_1, then $p(r)$ is also r_1. If $gic + \sum_i gmc_i < B$, the adversary selects the link l_i with the maximum value of $GD(i)$ as a victim link and jams the link until l_i starts to use $p(t_i)$. The cost gic is accordingly updated to include the number of packets used in the preceding step. Then, the adversary updates the estimate gmc_i by simply jamming packets higher than the current rate and extrapolating the cost over the epoch duration.

The adversary repeats this process to identify multiple victim links for the epoch until the budget is exhausted. The greedy algorithm is summarized below.

Algorithm 2 Greedy Algorithm for Unknown RAA

1: $gic = 0, \forall i \; gmc_i = 0, J = \{\}$
2: **while** $B - gic - \sum_i gmc_i > 0$ **do**
3:    Pick link l_i where $i = \arg \max GD(i)$; if no such link exists, then exit the loop
4:    $J \leftarrow J + \{l_i\}$
5:    Jam l_i until B' packets are injected or rate of l_i reduced by one level (assume x packets are injected)
6:    Monitor a time unit to update the cost estimate gmc_i for maintaining l_i at current rate for epoch
7:    $gic \leftarrow gic + x$
8: **end while**
9: Launch maintenance jamming on all links in J

We can prove that the greedy algorithm is, in fact, optimal if the following two conditions hold true:

1. RAA satisfies a special property: the *forward difference*[3] of rate reciprocal sequence (in increasing order) is non-decreasing, i.e.,

$$\frac{1}{r_i} - \frac{1}{r_{i+1}} \geq \frac{1}{j} - \frac{1}{r_{j+1}} \; where \; 1 \leq i \leq j \leq n$$

2. The maintenance cost is uniform across all links and rate levels.

The first condition implies that the incremental performance degradation increases with a decrease in rate level. This applies to all the IEEE802.11 variants studied in this paper. In the next section, we show that the second condition also approximately holds for all of the RAAs studied in this paper.

5. JAMMING COST FOR KNOWN RAA

In this section, we analyze the initial and maintenance costs for jamming RAAs. As discussed in the preceding section, an adversary equipped with such an analysis can efficiently design an optimal jammer. Here we only consider the three RAAs – ONOE, AMRR, and SampleRate – used in our experiments. For other RAAs, similar analysis can be conducted. AHence, in this paper, we carefully analyze the vulnerabilities inherent to IEEE802.11 MAC and RAAs, and design optimal jammer exploits to maximize the throughput reduction at a minimal jamming cost. The main contributions of our work are as follow:

- We first analyse three widely-used RAAs – ONOE, AMRR, SampleRate and derive the cost of jamming in each case to achieve a desired throughput reduction (Section 5).

- We then classify RAAs based on their rate selection strategies and use that framework to design optimal jamming strategies that exploit the RAA-specific behaviour. We show that our jamming cost analysis can be used to efficiently design a smart jammer that targets specific packets and optimizes the reduction in throughput subject to a jamming energy budget. We also present a technique that applies to the case when jamming costs cannot be estimated (Section 4).

- We carefully analyze the weaknesses inherent in the IEEE802.11 MAC and Link layer protocols that allows jammers to be extremely efficient with their jamming.

---

[3]Sequence of differences between two successive rate reciprocals.

- We build a testbed comprising of the USRP/GNURadio platform and present a comprehensive experimental evaluation of four RAAs (mentioned above) in the presence of smart jamming. Our experimental results confirm that a smart reactive jammer can maintain links at a low data rate (1 Mbps) at a minimal jamming cost (Jam only $5 - 8$ packets/s) (Section 6).

- Finally, we propose a set of preliminary mitigation mechanisms with their implementation left for future work (Section 7).

fter analyzing the costs, we also study the impact of "self-collisions" – collisions arising due to contention among the transmitting stations. The phenomenon where self-collisions cause the network throughput to degrade (or even cause zero throughput – collapse) is called *congestion collapse* [16]. We show that in some cases, the adversary can take advantage of self-collisions and smart-jam to trigger congestion collapse, which in turn significantly reduces the Phase-II maintenance cost.

5.1 Initial Cost

For the initial phase cost analysis, we assume that the adversary's goal is to quickly bring down the rates on the victim links. Thus, the general strategy would be to intensively jam all the packets whose rates are higher than the target rate. We analyze the initial cost for the three specific RAAs as follows.

ONOE: To make ONOE decrease the current rate to the next lower rate, the average number of transmissions per packet (including retransmissions) needs to be more than 1 during a monitor window (1 second). Therefore, in order to decrease the rate by L levels, the adversary has to jam an average of one transmission per packet for each of the L windows. Hence, the cost would be L packets within a monitor window. Note that ONOE counts the total number of retries, thus jamming the retransmissions is also effective.

AMRR: AMRR decreases the rate when it encounters two consecutive failures. Thus, the initial cost for AMRR to decrease the rate by L levels is $2 \cdot L$.

SampleRate: The analysis for SampleRate is more complicated as its behavior is less predictable compared to ONOE and AMRR. When decreasing the rate, SampleRate does not always decrease to the next lower rate. Here, we estimate an upper bound on the initial cost. SampleRate has a black-list policy that any rates with more than 3 consecutive failures will not be considered as a candidate for a period of 2 seconds. Therefore, an effective way for the initial phase is to black-list all the rates higher than the target rates. Assuming there are L' rates higher than the target rate, the initial cost for SampleRate is at most $4 \cdot L'$.

5.2 Maintenance Cost

In general, the value of t depends on the type and value of jammer budget. In Section 6, we will discuss budget types when describing the evaluation metrics. For now, we assume that t is infinite.

ONOE: In the case of ONOE, the low data rate can be maintained by keeping the credit value constant. During a monitor window, if we jam 10% of the packets, the credit will be decreased by 1. Then in the next window, we can jam only one packet (no failure will directly trigger the rate increase), and let the credit increase back to the previous value. By repeating this process, we can prevent ONOE from ever increasing the credit value to 10, thus keeping the rate unchanged. Assuming during each window the sender sends roughly the same amount of packets, the maintenance cost for ONOE is to jam 5% of the packets.

AMRR: In AMRR, the rate is increased after 10 consecutive successes. Thus, jamming one packet after 9 successes will ensure that AMRR continues to use the same rate. So the maintenance cost for AMRR is to jam 10% of the packets.

SampleRate: SampleRate probes other potentially-better rates after every 10 packets and update the statistics for that rate. If we jam all the probes, the transmitting rate stays the same. Therefore, the maintenance cost for SampleRate is also to jam 10% of the packets.

We verify these values later in the evaluation section.

5.3 Impact of Self Collisions on Maintenance Cost

The WLAN's regular traffic also generates self-collision among all the contending stations. These self collisions may keep some RAAs from increasing the transmission rate, especially when traffic demands are high. This would lead to a significant reduction in maintenance cost for the jammer, specifically in some cases, we will see that this may even lead to a zero maintenance cost for the adversary (the jammer triggering the congestion collapse).

In this subsection, we take ONOE as a case study to analyze the impact of the self collisions under saturated traffic conditions. We use PI to indicate the probability of interference caused by self collisions. According to Bianchi's model [4], we can estimate PI given the number of contenting stations, n. Here, we omit the details and list the calculated PI for some values of n in the following table.

n	2	3	5	10
PI	0.057	0.1044	0.1779	0.2894

Recall that ONOE maintains a history of packet successes and failures within a monitor window of 1 second. It increases the credit by 1 if more than 90% of packets succeed; otherwise it decreases the credit by 1. When the credit reaches 10, the sender increases the transmission rate to the next higher rate. Suppose that during a window of a second, the sender has transmitted s packets. The number of successes in this period is a random variable X that follows a binomial distribution $X \sim B(s, 1-PI)$. The probability of increasing the credit is thus $P_{incC} = Pr(X \geq 0.9 \times s)$.

Now, we calculate the probability P_{incR} that the rate increases. There are two events that can cause an increase in data rate: all transmissions succeed during a window, or the credit reaches 10. For a particular window, let us denote the probability of all successes as P_{suc}^s. In practice, s is sufficiently large. Hence, P_{suc}^s is close to 0. Therefore, we focus on calculating P_{credit} defined as the probability that the credit reaches 10. Let $P(t, i)$ be the probability that after t monitor windows, the credit value is $i(\forall i < 10)$. Initially, $P(0, 0) = 1$. For $i \leq 8$,

$$P(t, i) = P(t-1, i-1) \times P_{incC} + P(t-1, i+1) \times (1 - P_{incC})$$

For $i = 9$,

$$P(t, i) = P(t-1, i-1) \times P_{incC}$$

The probability of increasing the rate by the credit value reaching 10 after t windows is,

$$P_{credit}(t) = P(t, 10) = P(t-1, 9) \times P_{incC}$$

Thus, $P_{incR} \simeq P_{credit}(t) = P(t-1, 9) \times P_{incC}$.

Using the values of PI from the table above, we can see that ONOE is highly vulnerable to self collision. Even with only 3 contending nodes in the channel, P_{incR} turns out to be less than 0.1%. Therefore, in a network with size $n \geq 3$, the maintenance cost for ONOE is reduced by at least a factor of 10 due to self collisions.

In summary, this analysis concludes that some RAAs such as ONOE do not perform well under saturated network conditions which allows the adversary to launch more efficient jamming attacks with much smaller maintenance cost.

6. IMPLEMENTATION AND EVALUATION

In this section, we first discuss the details of our novel testbed designed to implement smart jamming attacks against different RAAs: the hardware and software components, test-bed setup, the jammer implementation, evaluation methodology and performance metrics. Then, we evaluate the efficiency of the attacks and validate the claims made in Section 4 and 5 using results from real world experiments.

6.1 Testbed Topology

For our experiments, we only consider a single link network since our earlier study (Figure 2) show that targeting a single victim link for jamming can cause the whole network throughput to degrade effectively with minimal jamming cost (reflection attack).

6.1.1 System Layout

Our testbed consists of two communication nodes, a sender and a receiver, and the adversary as shown in Figure 3. The sender sends UDP traffic to the receiver to saturate the network. The attacker constantly sniffs the channel and when it sees a sender packet destined for the receiver node of interest, it jams the packet before the transmission is over. For this to happen, the jamming packet must overlap with the sender packet at the receiver side as shown in the time line graph (See Figure 3). Figure 5 depicts the actual test-bed setup we use to run experiments.

6.1.2 Basic Hardware and Software Components

The hardware components of our testbed includes two PCs, (A) a sender node and (B) a receiver node, (C) jammer host, (D) jammer radio and RF-cables and splitters/combiners. We chose to use the RF-cabled setup for our experiments because of following two reasons:

- To achieve reproducible results

- To isolate our testbed from the laboratory network (this includes preventing the jammer from affecting lab network)

All of the above would be hard to achieve in an open medium. Note that operating the nodes with antennas in an open medium will only make the jamming more effective because of additional collisions/losses due to the propagation environment and external traffic.

The software components of our testbed include software defined radio (SDR) for signal processing, a traffic generator, a traffic sniffer tool, and the open source wireless card driver. Later, we will see why the use of open source wireless driver is necessary for the implementation of our reactive jammer.

Testbed Hardware Specification: Our jammer radio is a USRP board [38], which consists of a motherboard and two daughter boards. Each of the daughter boards are capable of operating independently as a transceiver. We use the first daughter board to sniff the channel as the jammer's sensing counterpart that triggers the second daughter board used to jam the channel. We chose D-Link WDA-1320 PCI express wireless cards for our experiments. They run on Atheros AR5212 chipsets that are compatible with open source Madwifi driver [36].

Testbed Software Specification: We use open source GNURadio [39] as the Software Defined Radio (SDR) that runs on USRP

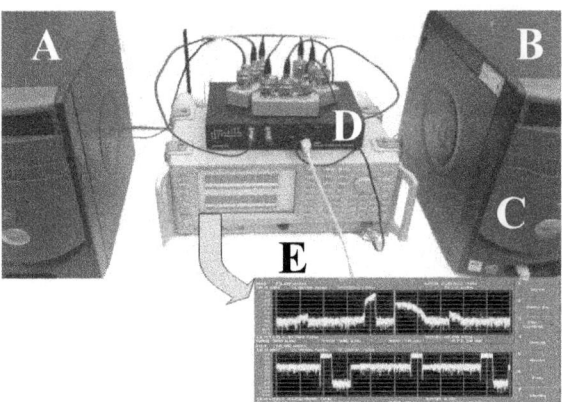

Figure 5: Experimentation Test-bed: (A) Sender, (B) Receiver, (C) Jammer-host, (D) USRP+Splitters+RF-cables, (E) Analyzer.

Component	Version/Model
Host CPUs	Intel Core2 6300
Jammer Radio Motherboard	USRP1
Jammer Radio Daughter boards	RFX-2400
Sender and Receiver Wireless Cards	D-Link WDA-1320 PCI express
Splitter/Combiner	HyperLink SC2402
RF-Cables	L-com RG174 RF-Coaxial Cable

Table 1: Experimental Testbed Hardware Specifications.

to implement fully reactive jammers that are channel aware and can sense and jam the channel within a quick turn around time, if it decides to do so on a per packet basis. Iperf is used as the traffic generator, and Wireshark as the receiver sniffer/analyzer in our testbed.

Component	Version/Model
Host OS	Ubuntu v9.10
Sender Traffic Generator	Iperf v2.0.4
Receiver Sniffer/Analyzer	Wireshark v1.2.7
Jammer SDR	GNURadio v3.3.0
Sender and Receiver Wireless Driver	Madwifi v0.9.4

Table 2: Experimental Testbed Software Specifications.

6.1.3 Types of Jammers

In our experiments, we consider the following four kinds of jammers:

- **Continuous Jammer:** This jammer produces a continuous signal at a specified power level. We use this kind of jammer to introduce channel noise into our testbed.

- **Periodic Jammer:** This jammer produces a periodic pulse of fixed size enough to destroy a packet if hit. The idle interval is the input to this kind of jammer and is based on the jammer budget as well as the desired network throughput.

- **Memoryless Jammer:** This jammer is similar to the periodic jammer, except the length of the period is decided using a memoryless distribution, the mean of which is the input parameter for the jammer.

- **Reactive Jammer:** This jammer is channel aware and jams reactively using the information it decodes from the IEEE802.11 PLCP header. The implementation of this kind of jammer requires more explanation, the details of which is provided below.

6.1.4 Implementation of the Reactive Jammer

The reactive jammer has two counterparts as shown in Figure 3. The main goal of this jammer is to be able to sniff all the packets in the medium (carried out by C_1 counterpart), and jam the packets destined for the receiver node of interest using an optimal jamming strategy (carried out by the C_2 counterpart). The sniffer's job is to sniff all the packets in the channel, decode only the PLCP IEEE802.11 header, which is always sent at the robust rate of 1.0 Mbps (we disable short preambles), and make jamming decisions on a per-packet-basis using the jamming algorithm described in Section 4. The ultimate goal for all the jammers is to keep the victim link at the the lowest data rate possible in the most efficient way which would result in an overall total network throughput reduction (reflection attack) and may even cause congestion collapse making the optimal use of its jamming budget. This jammer is the best of all the jammers described above.

Limitations: USRP has an inherent hardware limitation that only allows USRP to sample at most 8MHz band. This is a problem because IEEE802.11 communication uses 20MHz band. Furthermore, USRP uses USB to communicate with the host, which has a bandwidth limitation of 32MB/sec. This causes a delay in the order of milliseconds between sensing the channel, passing the information up to the host, host making the decision and asking the USRP to send a jamming signal into the channel [38, 39]. This is ultimately the bottleneck in our testbed implementation of a fully reactive jammer.

To mitigate these limitations, we apply following remedies to our experimental setup:

Remedy: First, with the choice of our hardware (USRP), the jammer can only samples 8MHz band out of 20MHz band of WiFi communication, in turn giving up on the quality of the received samples. However, once the preamble (sent at 1 Mbps) is detected, the jammer only have to decode the 802.11 PLCP header to extract rate information needed for the jamming algorithms discussed in Section 4. Note that this does not allow the jammer to differentiate between the receivers (MAC address is not known from the PLCP header). But, for the case of a single link network that we consider in our experiment, this suffices. If we were to run experiments with reactive jamming in a multiple links scenario, we must improve on our testbed hardware to be able to sample a larger band, and decode more information off the packet (such as receiver MAC address) to target the victim node for jamming.

With the setup shown in Figure 5, we can achieve the reaction time (including the turnaround from sensing to jamming plus the USB delay) of around 2ms. Obviously, this is not enough to be able to jam higher rate packets, even if we set the packet size to be 1470 bytes. To alleviate this issue, we modify the Madwifi driver to reduce 20MHz bandwidth of IEEE802.11 transmission to 5MHz. This makes the data packet transmission four times longer than when sent using the normal 20MHz band. This allows us as the jammer to jam high data-rate within our testbed. Note that this modification while allowing to complete our experiments does not impact the IEEE802.11 MAC and RAA behavior. In our future work, we plan on using better hardware that will make this problem go away so that we do not need the narrow band remedy.

6.1.5 Assumptions

We make following assumptions in our experimentation:

1. We use RF-cables and splitters/combiners in our experimentation setup. We use continuous jammers to induce noise into our emulation of a wireless channel. This type of setup is typical for evaluating wireless communication systems and achieve reproducible results using channel emulator [40].

2. We consider a single link scenario for the evaluation of the reactive jammer. We focus on jamming a single node with the idea that this would trigger the reflection attack on the network with multiple links, thus optimizing the use of jamming resources. In Figure 2, we run simple experiments in a multiple link scenario, and show that reflection attack can be easily executed.

6.2 Evaluation

In this section, we evaluate the actual performance of reactive jamming against various RAAs. We also compare them with the performance of an oblivious jammer against the same set of RAAs within the same experimentation setup. We first describe the experimentation methodology, the metrics used to evaluate the performance, and then present the experimentation results at the end.

Experimentation Setup: We run our experiments in an RF-cabled setup as described above and depicted in Figure 5. This allowed us to isolate our testbed from the surrounding interference, hence, we were able to achieve results that show very little variance. Each experiment runs for a specified set of parameters is defined by the sender continuously sending saturated traffic for 50 second period. We repeat each experiment 10 times to eliminate the margin of error, which is already very small for us. Since, the retransmissions from the sender are sent using MRR implemented at the driver level (thus, not captured by the Wireshark running at the sender side), we split the sender RF output and connect it to an extra node that sniffs all the retransmissions and logs all the rates used and number of packets sent (retransmissions included) for analysis.

Parameters: The set of parameters used for experimental evaluation is provided below:

Parameter	Setting
Packet Size	1470 bytes
Frequency	2.462 GHz (Channel 11)
Traffic Type	UDP
Traffic Bandwidth	1MB
Noise Power	-20 dB

Table 3: Parameter Specification

Performance Metrics: In Section 5, we describe Phase-I and Phase-II costs as the initial and maintenance phase costs for the jammer to trigger RAA to drop the data rate to the lowest level and

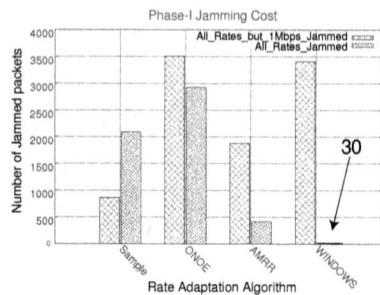

Figure 6: Phase I cost for reactive jammer with (a) not allowing any traffic to go through (b) allowing only 1Mbps traffic to go through, for four different RAAs

keep it there for a certain epoch t. Time parameter t of the maintenance phase depends on the jammer budget. There are two possible scenarios for the jammer budget assigned to the jammer, one that sets the budget as the rate (X Joules per second), and another that assigns total energy (Y Joules) to be used regardless of the time period. Phase-I depends on this definition of the budget. If time is the constraint, it make sense for the jammer to blindly jam all packets and bring down the data rate abruptly, otherwise, it can optimize the jamming energy used when there is no constraint on time spent in achieving the Phase-I goal. This is why, we evaluate the Phase-I cost in both scenarios (See Figure 6). Note that jamming all packets may trigger easier jammer detection than jamming only the non-1 Mbps data traffic.

In the following, we measure the performance of the jammer in terms of packets jammed during Phase-I and Phase-II.

Evaluation Results:

1. Phase-I cost: This is the cost for the reactive jammer to bring down the link to the lowest data rate (1Mbps). Figure 6 illustrates the cost for the two scenarios described above, one that allows only 1Mbps to go through, and another that jams all data-rate packets. As we can see, for the SampleRate, jamming all but 1Mbps packets performs better than jamming all the packets. This can be explained by the fact that in SampleRate, the multi rate retry parameters $(r_0, r_1, r_2, r_3) = (r, 1Mbps, 1Mbps, 1Mbps)$, and the total number of tries is 8 per packet. So, if the jammer jams all the packets, it has to jam 9 packets per transmission. However, if the jammer jams only non-1Mbps packets, it won't have to jam so many packets before SampleRate decides that 1Mbps data packets are the only ones succeeding. For ONOE, it does not seem to differ much either way, and for AMRR jamming all packets performs better than jamming only the non-1Mbps packets. These can be explained by the fact that ONOE counts retransmission failures the same way as it counts the original transmission failure, and the MRR count for AMRR (4 retransmissions) is much smaller than SampleRate and ONOE. For windows RAA, it seems that jamming all packets abruptly brings the link down to 1Mbps.

2. Phase-II cost: This is the cost to maintain the link at 1Mbps. Figure 7 illustrates Phase-II cost for the reactive jammer to maintain RAAs at 1Mbps. This effectively supports our claim that smart jammers can efficiently keep the network at a low throughput with minimal jamming. As we can see, jamming 8, 5, and 6 packets per second can cause SampleRate, ONOE, and AMRR to maintain the network at the lowest data-rate. We do not show the histogram for Windows RAA

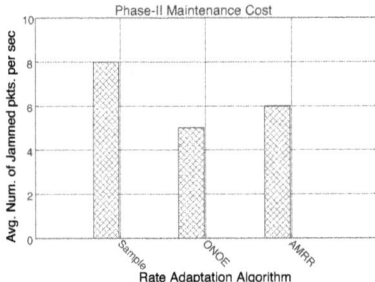

Figure 7: Phase II maintenance cost for reactive jammer for three different RAAs

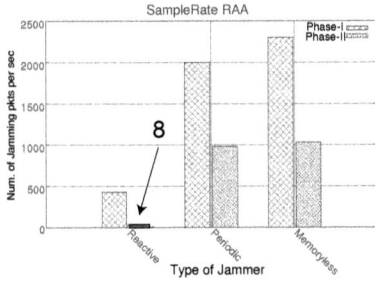

Figure 8: Phase I and Phase II cost comparision for three different kinds of jammers

because, we observed that it is impossible to maintain Windows RAA at 1Mbps. Even if the 2Mbps packet transmission continuously fails, it attempts sending packet at 2Mbps after each 1Mbps successful attempt.

3. Cost comparison among different types of jammers: Finally, we compare the efficiency of reactive jammer in terms of Phase-I and Phase-II costs against oblivious jammers. Figure 8 illustrates the comparison between the performance of periodic jammer, memoryless jammer, and the reactive jammer for the case of SampleRate. As we can see, reactive jammer needs only half the energy that the periodic or the memoryless jammer requires to achieve the same end-goal.

To this end, we have demonstrated that existing rate adaptation algorithms for IEEE802.11 are highly vulnerable to smart jamming attacks, which can result in a significant degradation of the network capacity at an extremely low jamming cost for the adversary.

7. PRELIMINARY MITIGATION TECHNIQUES

In the following, we sketch several mitigation techniques that can prevent smart jamming by severely limiting the amount of key information that can be inferred by an adversary. This lack of information then forces the adversary to operate as a memoryless jammer. In the future, we plan to design full fledged mitigation mechanisms, analyze them, and carry a detailed evaluation of their performance.

Concealing explicit and implicit rate information: The rate information can be protected using post-coding encryption. The encryption should not conflict with the decoding process to preserve the properties of the error correction code. This can be achieved by generating a cryptographic stream based on a shared secret key and a random initialization vector. The initialization vector is sent in the clear as the first sequence following the frame preamble and before

the PLCP header. The PLCP header and the packet are XORed with the cryptographic stream. The secret key should either be pre-shared or established using an appropriate authentication and key establishment protocol [13, 24, 31]. This technique will allow to protect the SIGNAL field from being eavesdropped by an adversary and also from guessing the implicit error correction code being used.

To further protect against implicit rate guessing using modulation constellation analysis, we propose to use the same high-order QAM and provide robustness through a larger set of coding rates. This can be achieved with Trellis Coded Modulation [34].

Finally, IEEE802.11g and IEEE802.11a should not be mixed with IEEE802.11b as it would be easy to distinguish between the two physical layers (i.e., OFDM vs. DSSS/CCK).

An adversary might still be able to guess partial information about the rate from the duration of a transmission. This can be protected by using constant duration transmissions through packet length adjustments. However, this is not necessary in practice, since when monitoring the duration, the adversary only knows if a higher rate or a lower rate is being used at the end of the transmission. For example, an adversary can only guess if the rate is 54Mbps by examining the duration of the packet when the transmission is over and whence too late to jam the high rate packets.

Unpredictable rate selection rules: While for a protocol such as ONOE, it might be hard to make it resilient against smart-jamming because of its highly predictable rate selection rules, the popular SampleRate protocol can easily be protected through randomized probing. Instead of sending a probe every ten packets, the probing order should be randomized, furthermore the probed rates should not be sequential but randomly selected unlike the Madwifi implementation.

Interference differentiation: Differentiation between malicious and non-malicious interference, in general, is a difficult problem. Some mechanisms can be used to detect the presence of a reactive jammer. For example, interrupting the transmission for a short period of time within the packet (the location is cryptographically derived) or placing a training sequence at a cryptographic location within the packet allowing the receiver to detect if a jamming signal is present.

8. CONCLUSION AND FUTURE WORK

In this paper, we investigated the robustness of IEEE802.11 RAAs against smart jamming attacks. We consider several classes of RAAs, and specially analyze three state-of-the-art RAAs: SampleRate, ONOE, and AMRR. We evaluate these three RAAs and Windows RAA using our carefully designed GNURadio/USRP aided testbed. We present optimal jamming strategies that exploit the weaknesses found in IEEE802.11 MAC and RAAs. Finally, we discuss the mitigation techniques to alleviate the vulnerabilities that allows the jammer to execute very smart and efficient jamming attacks. In the future, we plan on implementing those mitigation techniques and carry a detailed evaluation of their performance. Our future work also includes studying performance of more current RAAs against smart jamming attacks.

9. REFERENCES

[1] B. Awerbuch, A. Richa, and C. Scheideler. A jamming-resistant mac protocol for single-hop wireless networks. In *ACM PODC*, 2008.

[2] E. Bayraktaroglu, C. King, X. Liu, G. Noubir, R. Rajaraman, and B. Thapa. On the performance of IEEE 802.11 under jamming. In *Proceedings of IEEE INFOCOM*, 2008.

[3] M. A. Bender, M. Farach-Colton, S. He, B. C. Kuszmaul, and C. E. Leiserson. Adversarial contention resolution for simple channels. In *SPAA*, 2005.

[4] G. Bianchi. Performance analysis of the IEEE 802.11 distributed coordination function. *IEEE Journal on Selected Areas in Communications*, 2000.

[5] J. Bicket. Bit-rate selection in wireless networks. *MIT Master's Thesis*, 2005.

[6] I. Broustis, K. Pelechrinis, D. Syrivelis, S. V. Krishnamurthy, and L. Tassiulas. Fiji: Fighting implicit jamming in 802.11 wlans. *SecureComm*, 2009.

[7] J. Camp and E. Knightly. Modulation rate adaptation in urban and vehicular environments: Cross-layer implementation and experimental evaluation. *MobiCom*, 2008.

[8] A. Chan, X. Liu, G. Noubir, and B. Thapa. Control channel jamming: Resilience and identification of traitors. In *IEEE ISIT*, 2007.

[9] C. C. Chen, H. Luo, E. Seo, N. Vaidya, and X. Wang. Rate-adaptive framing for interfered wireless networks. In *INFOCOM*, 2007.

[10] J. Chiang and Y.-C. Hu. Cross-layer jamming detection and mitigation in wireless broadcast networks. In *MobiCom*, 2007.

[11] M. Heusse, F. Rousseau, G. Berger-Sabbatel, and A. Duda. Performance anamoly of 802.11b. *INFOCOM*, 2003.

[12] G. Holland, N. Vaidya, and V. Bahl. A rate-adaptive mac protocol for multihop wireless networks. *ACM MOBICOM*, 2001.

[13] T. Jin, G. Noubir, and B. Thapa. Zero pre-shared secret key establishment in the presence of jammers. In *MobiHoc*, 2009.

[14] G. Judd, X. Wang, and P. Steenkiste. Efficient channel-aware rate adaptation in dynamic environments. *MobiSys*, 2008.

[15] A. Kamerman and L. Monteband. Wavelan ii: A high-performance wireless lan for the unlicensed band. *Bell Labs Technical Journal*, 1997.

[16] G. Keiser. *Local Area Networks*. McGraw-Hill, 2002.

[17] J. Kim, S. Kim, S. Choi, and D. Qiao. Cara: Collision-aware rate adaptation for IEEE 802.11 wlans. *IEEE INFOCOM*, 2006.

[18] N. Koci and M. K. Marina. Understanding the role of multi-rate retry mechanism for effective rate control in 802.11 wireless lans. *IEEE Conferene on Local Computer Networks*, 2009.

[19] M. Lacage, M. H. Manshaei, and T. Turletti. IEEE 802.11 rate adaptation: A practical approach. *ACM MSWiM*, 2004.

[20] M. Li, I. Koutsopoulos, and R. Poovendran. Optimal jamming attacks and network defense policies in wireless sensor networks. In *INFOCOM*, 2007.

[21] G. Lin and G. Noubir. On link layer denial of service in data wireless lans. *Wirel. Commun. Mob. Comput.*, 5(3):273–284, 2005.

[22] G. Noubir and G. Lin. Low-power dos attacks in data wireless lans and countermeasures. *ACM SIGMOBILE*, 7(3):29–30, 2003.

[23] K. Pelechrinis, S. V. Krishnamurthy, C. Gkantsidis, and I. Broustis. Ares: An anti-jamming reinforcement system for 802.11 networks. *CoNEXT*, 2009.

[24] C. Pöpper, M. Strasser, and S. Čapkun. Anti-jamming broadcast communication using uncoordinated spread spectrum techniques. *IEEE Journal on Selected Areas in Communications*, 28(5):703–715, 2010.

[25] H. Rahul, F. Edalat, D. Katabi, and C. Sodini. Frequency-aware rate adaptation and mac protocols. *MobiCom*, 2009.

[26] K. Ramachandran, R. Kokku, H. Zhang, and M. Gruteser. Symphony: Synchronous two-phase rate power control in 802.11 wlans. *MobiSys*, 2008.

[27] K. B. Rasmussen, S. Capkun, and M. Cagalj. Secnav: secure broadcast localization and time synchronization in wireless networks. In *MobiCom*, 2007.

[28] S. Rayanchu, A. Mishra, D. Agrawal, S. Saha, and S. Banerjee. Diagnosing wireless packet losses in 802.11: Separating collision from weak signal. In *INFOCOM*, 2008.

[29] B. Sadeghi, V. Kanodia, A. Sabharwal, and E. Knightly. Opportunistic media access for multirate ad hoc networks. *ACM MOBICOM*, 2002.

[30] M. K. Simon, J. K. Omura, R. A. Scholtz, and B. K. Levitt. *Spread spectrum communications; vols. 1-3*. Computer Science Press, Inc., NY, 1986.

[31] M. Strasser, C. Popper, S. Capkun, and M. Cagalj. Jamming-resistant key establishment using uncoordinated frequency hopping. In *ISSP*, 2008.

[32] P. Tague, M. Li, and R. Poovendran. Probabilistic mitigation of control channel jamming via random key distribution. In *Proceedings of International Symposium on Personal, Indoor and Mobile Radio Communications*, 2007.

[33] P. Tague, D. Slater, G. Noubir, and R. Poovendran. Linear programming models for jamming attacks on network traffic flows. In *WiOpt*, 2008.

[34] G. Ungerboeck. Channel coding with multilevel/phase signals. *IEEE Transactions on Information Theory*, pages 55–67, 1982.

[35] http://madwifi-project.org/wiki/UserDocs/RateControl. Rate control in madwifi.

[36] http://madwifi.org/. Multiband atheros driver for wifi.

[37] http://madwifi.org/browser/trunk/ath_rate/onoe. Onoe rate control.

[38] https://www.ettus.com. Universal software radio peripheral.

[39] http://www.gnuradio.org. Gnuradio.

[40] http://www.home.agilent.com/agilent/product.jspx?pn=11759C. Agilent technologies rf channel simulator.

[41] M. Vutukuru, H. Balakrishnan, and K. Jamieson. Cross-layer wireless bit rate adaptation. *SIGCOMM*, 2009.

[42] S. H. Wong, H. Yang, S. Lu, and V. Bharghavan. Robute rate adaptation for 802.11 wireless networks. *ACM MobiCom*, 2006.

[43] W. Xu, K. Ma, W. Trappe, and Y. Zhang. Jamming sensor networks: attack and defense strategies. *IEEE Network*, 20(3):41–47, 2006.

Short Paper: Lightweight Remote Attestation using Physical Functions

Ahmad-Reza Sadeghi
TU Darmstadt (CASED)
& Fraunhofer SIT
Darmstadt, Germany
ahmad.sadeghi@trust.cased.de

Steffen Schulz
TU Darmstadt (CASED)
& Macquarie University (INSS)
Darmstadt, Germany
steffen.schulz@cased.de

Christian Wachsmann
TU Darmstadt (CASED)
Darmstadt, Germany
christian.wachsmann@cased.de

ABSTRACT

Remote attestation is a mechanism to securely and verifiably obtain information about the state of a remote computing platform. However, resource-constrained embedded devices cannot afford the required trusted hardware components, while software attestation is generally vulnerable to network and collusion attacks.

In this paper, we present a lightweight remote attestation scheme that links software attestation to remotely identifiable hardware by means of Physically Unclonable Functions (PUFs). In contrast to existing software attestation schemes, our solution (1) resists collusion attacks, (2) allows the attestation of remote platforms, and (3) enables the detection of hardware attacks due to the tamper-evidence of PUFs.

Categories and Subject Descriptors

K.6.5 [**Security and Protection**]: Physical security, invasive software (e.g., viruses, worms, Trojan horses)

General Terms

Design, Security

Keywords

Remote Attestation, Software-based Attestation, Physically Unclonable Functions (PUFs), Embedded Devices

1. INTRODUCTION

One of the major challenges in computer security is how to gain assurance that a local or remote computing platform behaves as expected. Various approaches have been proposed that aim to assure the correct and secure operation of computer systems (*attestation*) [15]. Common to all existing approaches is that the platform to be evaluated (*prover*) sends a status report of its current configuration to a *verifier* to demonstrate that it is in a known and thus

---

*Full version available upon request.

WiSec'11, June 14–17, 2011, Hamburg, Germany.

trustworthy state. Since malicious hard- or software on the prover's platform may forge this report, its authenticity is typically assured by a secure co-processor [5, 12] or trusted software [1].

A recent industrial initiative towards the standardization of attestation was brought up by the Trusted Computing Group (TCG) by specifying the Trusted Platform Module (TPM) [22] as a trust anchor for authentic reporting of a platform's software state. Today, TPMs are typically implemented as secure co-processors and are available in many PCs, laptops, and server systems. The TCG also specifies the Mobile Trusted Module (MTM) [23], which is a TPM for mobile and embedded devices. However, the integration of security hardware in low-cost embedded devices (e.g., wireless sensor nodes) is often infeasible. in this context, *software attestation* [20] was proposed, requiring neither trusted hardware nor a secure software core.

Software attestation exploits the computational limits of the prover to ensure that only a specific algorithm can be executed within a certain time frame. Within this algorithm, the prover computes a *checksum* of its software state, e.g., its program memory content, and sends it to the verifier. The verifier computes a reference checksum using a reference software state and accepts the prover only if (1) the checksum reported by the prover matches the reference checksum and (2) the prover answered within the same time an honest device would have needed. The first check guarantees that the expected software is present at the prover, while the second ensures that the prover has not performed additional computations, e.g., to hide malicious software.

Unfortunately, software attestation schemes require strong assumptions to be secure, namely (1) the absence of network attacks (such as impersonation or collusion with other devices) and (2) the hardware of the prover was not modified to increase its performance or memory capacity. As a result, the existing software attestation schemes are unsuitable for remote attestation or in scenarios where the adversary can modify the prover's hardware, such as sensor networks.

To overcome these problems the checksum must be linked to the prover's platform. One possible solution links the checksum computation to hardware-specific side-effects, such as CPU states and caching effects that are considered to be expensive to simulate [9]. However, it has been shown that these side-effects are not appropriate to achieve a strong link to the underlying hardware [21, 11] as they only bind the software computation to *classes* of devices instead of individual provers.

Contribution.

In this paper, we propose a lightweight remote attestation scheme that combines software attestation with device-specific hardware functions. Specifically, we show how Physically Unclonable Functions (PUFs) can be integrated into the software attestation s.t. a compromised device is unable to efficiently outsource the software checksum computation to colluding parties and propose practical optimizations to facilitate the verification of the PUF.

In contrast to plain software attestation, our scheme (1) is secure against a collusion of malicious provers, (2) allows for the authentication and attestation of remote provers, and (3) enables the detection of hardware attacks on the prover. We present different solutions for the efficient and practical verification of PUFs by the verifier and discuss their trade-offs. The proposed scheme is applicable to any current (and likely future) software attestation protocol.

2. Physically Unclonable Functions (PUFs)

A Physically Unclonable Function (PUF) is a noisy function that is embedded into a physical object, e.g., an integrated circuit [14]. Today, there are already several PUF-based security products aimed for the market, e.g., PUF-enabled RFID chips and proposals for IP-protection and anti-counterfeiting solutions [26, 8]. When queried with a *challenge* x, a PUF generates a *response* $y \leftarrow \text{PUF}(x)$ that depends on both, x and the unique device-specific intrinsic physical properties of the object containing PUF. Since PUFs are subject to noise (e.g., thermal noise), they typically return slightly different responses when queried with the same challenge multiple times. However, these output variations can be eliminated by using *fuzzy extractors* [4], which can be efficiently implemented on resource-constrained devices [24]. Hence, PUFs can be used as deterministic functions.

Based on [2, 18], we consider PUFs that have the following properties, where PUF and PUF$'$ are two different PUFs:

- *Robustness:* When queried with the same challenge x, PUF always returns the same response y.

- *Independence:* When queried with the same challenge x, PUF and PUF$'$ return different responses y and y'.

- *Pseudo-randomness:* It is infeasible to distinguish a PUF from a pseudo-random function PRF.

- *Tamper-evidence:* Any attempt to physically access the object containing PUF irreversibly changes PUF, i.e., PUF cannot be evaluated any more but is turned into a random PUF$' \neq$ PUF.

Independence and pseudo-randomness imply that $\mathcal{A}$ cannot predict PUF responses to unknown challenges, which means that $\mathcal{A}$ cannot simulate a PUF based on its challenge-response behavior. Moreover, tamper-evidence ensures that $\mathcal{A}$ cannot obtain any information on the PUF by physical means, e.g., hardware attacks. Hence, $\mathcal{A}$ cannot simulate or clone a PUF.

3. PUF-BASED ATTESTATION

Our PUF-based attestation scheme extends existing software attestation protocols. A software attestation protocol is a two-party protocol between a *prover* $\mathcal{P}$ and a *verifier* $\mathcal{V}$, where $\mathcal{V}$ should be convinced that $\mathcal{P}$ is in a trusted software *state* S. Typically, $\mathcal{P}$ is an embedded device with constrained computing capabilities (e.g., a sensor node), whereas $\mathcal{V}$ is a more powerful computing device (e.g., a base station). On a high level, all known software attestation protocols exploit the computational limits of $\mathcal{P}$ to assure that nothing else than a specific trusted algorithm can be executed within a specific time frame.

In contrast to existing software attestation schemes, our solution assures the verifier $\mathcal{V}$ that the attestation result has actually been computed by the original hardware of a specific prover $\mathcal{P}$. We propose to use a *hardware checksum*[1] based on PUFs to include device-specific properties of $\mathcal{P}$'s hardware into the attestation protocol. Our design exploits the limited throughput of external interfaces to prevent an adversary from outsourcing the computation of the software checksum to a more powerful computing device.

Trust model and assumptions.

The adversary $\mathcal{A}$ controls the communication between the verifier $\mathcal{V}$ and the prover $\mathcal{P}$, i.e., $\mathcal{A}$ can eavesdrop, manipulate, reroute, and delete all messages sent by $\mathcal{V}$ and $\mathcal{P}$. Moreover, $\mathcal{A}$ knows all algorithms executed by $\mathcal{P}$ and can install malicious software on $\mathcal{P}$. However, due to the unclonability of the PUF (Section 2), $\mathcal{A}$ cannot simulate the hardware checksum, while the tamper-evidence of the PUF ensures that $\mathcal{A}$ cannot physically access or manipulate the internal interfaces between CPU, memory, and PUF of $\mathcal{P}$. Further, we assume that external interfaces of $\mathcal{P}$ are significantly slower than the internal interface that is used by the CPU to access the hardware checksum. All provers $\mathcal{P}$ are initialized in a secure environment before deployment. The verifier $\mathcal{V}$ is trusted to behave according to the protocol. Moreover, $\mathcal{V}$ can simulate any algorithm that can be executed by $\mathcal{P}$ in real time and maintains a database D containing the identity I and the exact hard- and software configuration of each $\mathcal{P}$.

Protocol description.

Figure 1 shows the proposed PUF-based attestation protocol, consisting of a generalized software-attestation protocol with additional inclusion of a device-characteristic hardware checksum function HwSum() at the prover $\mathcal{P}$ and EmulateHwSum() at the verifier $\mathcal{V}$. By careful integration of this hardware checksum into the software attestation algorithm, we bind the software attestation to the respective hardware platform, enabling true remote attestation.

The main protocol is the generalization of a typical software attestation protocol: The verifier $\mathcal{V}$ starts the protocol by sending a random challenge r to the prover $\mathcal{P}$ and then measures the time $\mathcal{P}$ takes to reply with the checksum σ_k computed over its current software state S (e.g., its program memory). In detail, on receipt of r, $\mathcal{P}$ sets up the initial checksum value σ_0 and Pseudo-Random Number Generator (PRNG) state r as required by the under-

---

[1]For the purpose of this paper, we consider HwSum() to be a PUF to gain tamper evidence, however, simpler implementations are possible, e.g., an HMAC with a hard-wired key.

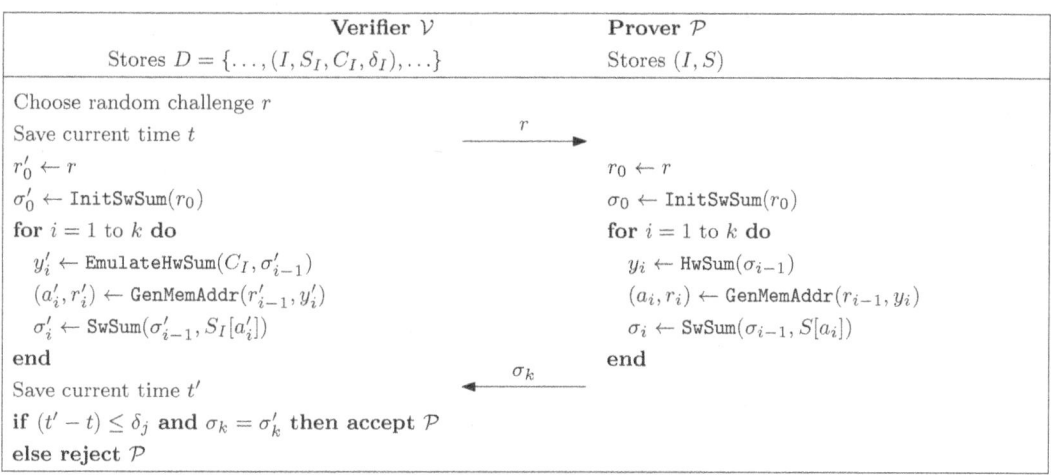

Verifier $\mathcal{V}$	Prover $\mathcal{P}$
Stores $D = \{\ldots, (I, S_I, C_I, \delta_I), \ldots\}$	Stores (I, S)
Choose random challenge r	
Save current time t	
	$\xrightarrow{\quad r \quad}$	
$r'_0 \leftarrow r$	$r_0 \leftarrow r$
$\sigma'_0 \leftarrow \mathtt{InitSwSum}(r_0)$	$\sigma_0 \leftarrow \mathtt{InitSwSum}(r_0)$
for $i = 1$ to k **do**	**for** $i = 1$ to k **do**
$\quad y'_i \leftarrow \mathtt{EmulateHwSum}(C_I, \sigma'_{i-1})$	$\quad y_i \leftarrow \mathtt{HwSum}(\sigma_{i-1})$
$\quad (a'_i, r'_i) \leftarrow \mathtt{GenMemAddr}(r'_{i-1}, y'_i)$	$\quad (a_i, r_i) \leftarrow \mathtt{GenMemAddr}(r_{i-1}, y_i)$
$\quad \sigma'_i \leftarrow \mathtt{SwSum}(\sigma'_{i-1}, S_I[a'_i])$	$\quad \sigma_i \leftarrow \mathtt{SwSum}(\sigma_{i-1}, S[a_i])$
end	**end**
Save current time t'	
	$\xleftarrow{\quad \sigma_k \quad}$	
if $(t' - t) \leq \delta_j$ **and** $\sigma_k = \sigma'_k$ **then accept** $\mathcal{P}$	
else reject $\mathcal{P}$	

Figure 1: Remote attestation based on physical functions

lying software attestation scheme. $\mathcal{P}$ then iteratively computes σ_k by taking i random measurement samples out of S. Specifically, in each iteration i of the checksum computation $\mathcal{P}$ invokes three procedures: $\mathtt{GenMemAddr}()$, $\mathtt{SwSum}()$, and $\mathtt{HwSum}()$. $\mathtt{GenMemAddr}(r_{i-1}, y_i)$ is used to generate an output r_i and a memory address a_i, which determines the next memory block $S[a_i]$ of S to be included into the software checksum as $\sigma_i \leftarrow \mathtt{SwSum}(\sigma_{i-1}, S[a_i])$. Note that $\mathtt{SwSum}()$ is the same function as in plain software attestation, while we require only a minor modification of $\mathtt{GenMemAddr}()$ to include the hardware checksum output y_i. Typically, modern software attestation schemes implement $\mathtt{GenMemAddr}()$ as a Pseudo-Random Number Generator (PRNG) to prevent efficient pre-computation or memory mappings attacks. However, neither the PRNG nor the $\mathtt{SwSum}()$ are required to be cryptographically strong [20]. Hence, it is usually straightforward to integrate y_i into $\mathtt{GenMemAddr}()$ by using it as an additional seed to the PRNG.

In contrast to plain software attestation, our attestation scheme integrates a hardware checksum $\mathtt{HwSum}()$ into each iteration i, yielding the previously mentioned additional input $y_i \leftarrow \mathtt{HwSum}(\sigma_i)$ to the $\mathtt{GenMemAddr}()$ procedure. As a result, every iteration of the software checksum additionally depends on the result of the device-characteristic hardware checksum, thus binding the attestation response σ_k to the prover's hardware. Similarly, each iteration of $\mathtt{HwSum}()$ depends on the previous intermediate software checksum σ_{i-1}, s.t. $\mathtt{HwSum}()$ cannot be executed independently of $\mathtt{SwSum}()$. However, we emphasize that the depicted algorithm can be optimized to execute $\mathtt{HwSum}()$ and $\mathtt{SwSum}()$ in parallel in all but the very first iteration.

After every memory block $S[a_i]$ has been included into the checksum at least once, $\mathcal{P}$ sends σ_k to $\mathcal{V}$. While waiting for the response of $\mathcal{P}$, $\mathcal{V}$ can compute a reference checksum σ'_k by simulating the computation of $\mathcal{P}$ using the known trusted software state S_I recorded in database D and emulate $\mathtt{HwSum}()$ using $\mathtt{EmulateHwSum}()$ with some verification data C_I, which is secret information only available to $\mathcal{V}$. $\mathcal{V}$ accepts only if (1) $\mathcal{P}$ replied within a certain time frame δ_I and (2) σ_k matches σ'_k. The first check ensures that $\mathcal{P}$ computed σ_k in about the same time δ_I an honest device would have needed and has not performed additional computations, e.g., to hide the presence of malware. The second

check verifies whether the software state S measured by $\mathcal{P}$ corresponds to the known trusted software state S_I. If either of these checks fails, $\mathcal{P}$ is assumed to be in an unknown software state and is rejected.

Note that the verification of the PUF-based hardware checksum by $\mathcal{V}$ is not straightforward: $\mathcal{V}$ must be able to predict the outputs of the PUF, while this must be infeasible for $\mathcal{A}$. This is further complicated by the large amount of hardware checksum responses required by our construction and the closely parallelized execution of software and hardware checksum. Hence, the integration of PUFs into software attestation requires careful consideration and we discuss possible instantiations in Section 4

Security objectives.

In contrast to existing software attestation schemes, our PUF-based attestation scheme additionally achieves the following security goals:

- *Correctness:* A prover in a known trusted state must always be accepted by the verifier.

- *Unforgeability:* A prover in an unknown state must be rejected by the verifier. Note that this also includes attacks, where the adversary makes the sensor node to collude with more powerful devices to forge the attestation.

- *Prover authentication:* A prover pretending to be another prover must be rejected by the verifier.

- *Prover isolation:* A prover colluding with other (malicious) provers must be rejected by the verifier.

- *Tamper-evidence:* A prover that is not in its original hardware state must be rejected by the verifier.

4. INSTANTIATION

In this section, we show how existing software attestation schemes can be used to instantiate software checksum $\mathtt{SwSum}()$ and the memory address generator $\mathtt{GenMemAddr}()$ with only minor modifications. Moreover, we discuss different instantiations of the hardware checksum $\mathtt{HwSum}()$ and, in particular, the corresponding secret verification data C_I and $\mathtt{EmulateHwSum}()$ algorithm.

4.1 Memory Address Generation and Software Checksum

The memory address generator GenMemAddr() and the software checksum SwSum() components of our PUF-based attestation scheme can be instantiated using any of the existing software-based attestation schemes (e.g., [19, 27, 3]) with only minor modifications to GenMemAddr() for the integration of the hardware checksum HwSum(). In all modern software attestation designs, GenMemAddr() is implemented as a PRNG with internal state r that is used to generate pseudorandom outputs a_i. We can thus integrate the output y_i of HwSum() simply by merging it with the current state r in each iteration. Due to the unpredictability property of the PUF (Section 2), this is equivalent to (partly) reseeding the PRNG, which effectively prevents the PRNG from repeating its sequence.

4.2 Hardware Checksum

We present two alternative instantiations of the hardware checksum HwSum() based on emulatable and non-emulatable PUFs. In general, emulatable PUFs yield more efficient protocols. However, since PUFs are not expected to be emulatable by design (Section 2), we focus on solutions for different approaches based on non-emulatable PUFs.

4.2.1 Emulatable PUFs

One approach to implement HwSum() are emulatable PUFs, which allow the manufacturer of the PUF to set up a mathematical model that enables the prediction of PUF responses to unknown challenges [13, 16]. Typically, the creation of this model requires extended access to the PUF hardware, which is only available during the manufacturing process of the PUF and permanently disabled before deployment [13].

More detailed, during the production of the hardware of prover $\mathcal{P}$, the trusted hardware manufacturer sets up a secret mathematical model C_I of PUF(). Before deployment of $\mathcal{P}$, the interface for modelling the PUF() is then disabled s.t. any attempt to reactivate it leads to an irreversible change of PUF(). During deployment of $\mathcal{P}$, C_I and an algorithm EmulateHwSum() for emulating HwSum() is given to the verifier $\mathcal{V}$. In the attestation protocol, $\mathcal{P}$ computes $\text{HwSum}(\cdot) = \text{PUF}(\cdot)$, whereas $\mathcal{V}$ emulates $\text{HwSum}(\cdot) = \text{EmulateHwSum}(C_I, \cdot)$.

In practice, emulatable PUFs can be realized by most delay-based PUFs (e.g., Arbiter PUFs [10, 7] and Ring Oscillator PUFs [6]), which allow for creating precise mathematical models based on machine learning techniques [17]. However, the security properties of practical instantiations of emulatable PUFs still need further evaluation. Hence, in the following section, we present different solutions based on non-emulatable PUFs.

4.2.2 Non-emulatable PUFs

For non-emulatable PUFs, the verifier $\mathcal{V}$ typically maintains a secret database D of PUF challenges and responses, called Challenge Response Pair (CRP) database. Note that our attestation scheme requires PUFs that ideally have an exponentially large CRP space, such that an adversary $\mathcal{A}$ with direct access to the PUF cannot create a complete CRP database and then emulate the PUF. However, this means that the verifier $\mathcal{V}$ can also store a subset of the CRP space. We thus have to deterministically limit the CRP subspace used during attestation without allowing the adversary to exploit this to simulate the PUF in future attestation runs.

In the following, we describe two different approaches of how non-emulatable PUFs can be used to instantiate HwSum().

Commitment to procedure.

One approach is creating a database D of attestation challenge messages (q, r) and the corresponding checksums σ_k in a secure environment before the prover $\mathcal{P}$ is deployed. In the attestation protocol, the verifier $\mathcal{V}$ can then use D to obtain the reference checksum σ_k instead of emulating the PUF.

Specifically, before deployment, $\mathcal{V}$ runs the attestation protocol several times with $\mathcal{P}$. For each protocol run, $\mathcal{V}$ records in D the attestation challenge (r, q) sent to $\mathcal{P}$ and the corresponding checksum σ'_k returned by $\mathcal{P}$. When running the attestation protocol after deployment, $\mathcal{V}$ chooses a random set $(I, (r, q), \sigma'_k) \in D$ and sends (r, q) to $\mathcal{P}$, which then computes σ_k using $\text{HwSum}(\cdot)$. $\mathcal{V}$ accepts $\mathcal{P}$ only if $\mathcal{P}$ replied with $\sigma_k = \sigma'_k$ in time δ_I.

The solution allows for very efficient verification of σ_k by $\mathcal{V}$, however, the number of attestation protocol runs of each $\mathcal{P}$ is limited by the size of D. Moreover, this approach does not allow to update the software state of $\mathcal{P}$ after deployment, e.g., to fix bugs that allow runtime compromise.

Commitment to challenge.

Since updates to the software of the prover $\mathcal{P}$ are usually developed after deployment of $\mathcal{P}$, the software state S and thus the inputs to HwSum() are not known before deployment of $\mathcal{P}$ and the final checksum value σ_k cannot be computed in advance.

Our solution to this problem is to reduce the amount of challenges x_i generated by the intermediate checksum results σ_i, s.t. it becomes feasible to create a CRP database independently of σ_i, and thus S. To prevent the adversary from exploiting this to simulate the attestation procedure, we use a random offset q to determine this reduced CRP space within the overall CRP space of HwSum(), such that the adversary cannot generate the required CRPs before the actual attestation protocol starts. The offset q is sent from the verifier $\mathcal{V}$ to $\mathcal{P}$ together with the random attestation challenge r in the first message of the attestation protocol (see Figure 1).

More detailed, we chose $f(\cdot)$ to be a function that maps intermediate checksum results σ_i to bitstrings of length n and derive the challenges as $x_i \leftarrow \text{HwSum}(q||f(\sigma_i))$. Before deployment, the verifier $\mathcal{V}$ then evaluates $y_j \leftarrow \text{HwSum}(q||j)$ for $j \in \{0, \ldots, 2^n - 1\}$, and records $(q, y_0, \ldots, y_{2^n-1})$ in $C_{I,q}$ for a number of randomly chosen offsets q.

After deployment, $\mathcal{V}$ chooses a random nonce r and an offset $q \in C_I$ to start an attestation. The prover $\mathcal{P}$ then computes the checksum σ_k using $\text{HwSum}(q||\sigma_{i-1})$. While waiting for the response of $\mathcal{P}$, $\mathcal{V}$ computes the reference checksum σ'_k using $\text{EmulateHwSum}(C_{I,q})$ and the current reference software state S_I. $\mathcal{V}$ accepts only if $\mathcal{P}$ replied with $\sigma_k = \sigma'_k$ in time δ_I.

In this approach, the number of attestations are limited by the amount of random offsets q for which a CRP subspace has been generated in advance and by the storage available at the verifier $\mathcal{V}$. The offsets cannot be re-used since they cannot be encrypted and are potentially disclosed to the adversary.

On-demand CRP generation.

As a final modification, we propose a method to reduce the storage requirements at the verifier $\mathcal{V}$ and to allow a theoretically unlimited number of attestation protocols runs, by generating additional CRP subspaces on demand once an attestation succeeded.

Specifically, $\mathcal{V}$ and $\mathcal{P}$ can establish a mutually authenticated and confidential channel after successful attestation to exchange additional CRPs for future attestation runs. For this purpose, σ_k is treated as a common shared secret and the last message shown in the attestation protocol in Figure 1 is replaced with explicit key confirmation.

$\mathcal{V}$ can then send a new random offset q to $\mathcal{P}$, who responds with a response vector $y_j \leftarrow \mathrm{PUF}(q||j)$ for $j \in \{0, \ldots, 2^n - 1\}$ sorted by j. Finally, $\mathcal{P}$ deletes q and y_j from its memory and $\mathcal{V}$ updates $C_I \leftarrow (q, y_0, \ldots, y_{2^n-1})$ accordingly.

Note that this approach doubles the computational load of $\mathcal{P}$ and increases the communication load, so that it may not be suitable for, e.g., sensor networks.

5. SECURITY CONSIDERATIONS

In the following, we show that our PUF-based attestation protocol presented in Section 3 achieves prover authentication and prover-isolation. Hereby, we assume the underlying software attestation schemes and PUFs to fulfill their security properties.

Correctness and unforgeability of attestation.

Our solution preserves the security of existing software attestation schemes, consisting of the GenMemAddr() and SwSum() procedures. Our modifications are limited to GenMemAddr(), where we add the pseudo-random PUF responses y_i as an additional input to the PRNG state update procedure. Done properly, additional input to the PRNG state update will, in the worst case, not increase but keep the entropy of the internal PRNG state when compared with the regular PRNG state update. The required modifications thus do not affect correctness and unforgeability since the output distribution of the original and the modified GenMemAddr() procedure remain computationally indistinguishable as long as the original PRNG is secure.

Prover identification.

The main security goal of our design is to link the checksum to the hardware of the prover $\mathcal{P}$. Our solutions achieves this goal by identifying $\mathcal{P}$ based on the outputs of the hardware checksum HwSum(). The implementation of this requirement is straightforward: We must ensure that a sufficient amount of identifying information is generated by HwSum() and incorporated into the attestation checksum σ_k to prevent simple guessing attacks.

Prover isolation.

Our design runs the software and hardware checksums SwSum() and HwSum() in parallel and creates a strong algorithmic dependence on the output of both checksums in the respective previous iteration. To detach the computation of SwSum() from the hardware of the prover $\mathcal{P}$, the adversary $\mathcal{A}$ must thus simulate the function $y_{i-1} \leftarrow$ HwSum() for each iteration i of the software checksum to generate the correct input to the memory generator GenMemAddr(). Furthermore, the intermediate checksum results σ_i are used as input to the next iteration of HwSum(). Hence, there are three major obstacles for $\mathcal{A}$: (1) the performance of HwSum() cannot be increased due to the tamper-evidence of the PUF, (2) $\mathcal{A}$ must involve the original hardware of $\mathcal{P}$ due to the unclonability of the PUF, and (3) the minimum *additional* delay incurred by transferring the HwSum() input and output bytes to a remote device is dictated by the throughput of the external communication interfaces of $\mathcal{P}$, since $\mathcal{A}$ cannot access the significantly faster internal interface between the CPU and HwSum(), which can be protected by the PUF.

Hence, any attempt to run HwSum() and SwSum() on separate devices will significantly increase the time required for all HwSum() iterations, regardless of the gained performance improvement on the SwSum() computation.

6. CONCLUSION

We presented a novel approach to attest both the software and the hardware configuration of a remote platform for embedded devices, which do not possess trusted hardware components. Our solution combines existing software attestation with cost-efficient physical security primitives, Physically Unclonable Functions (PUFs). In contrast to existing software attestation protocols, our scheme does not require an authenticated channel between the prover and the verifier and reliably prevents remote provers from colluding with other systems to forge the software checksum. We are currently working on an prototype implementation.

Acknowledgement

This work has been supported in part by the European Commission under grant agreement ICT-2007-238811 UNIQUE and ICT-2007-216676 ECRYPT NoE phase II.

7. REFERENCES

[1] W. A. Arbaugh, D. J. Farber, and J. M. Smith. A secure and reliable bootstrap architecture. In *Proceedings of the IEEE Symposium on Research in Security and Privacy*, pages 65–71, Oakland, CA, May 1997. IEEE Computer Society, Technical Committee on Security and Privacy, IEEE Computer Society Press.

[2] F. Armknecht, R. Maes, A.-R. Sadeghi, B. Sunar, and P. Tuyls. Memory leakage-resilient encryption based on physically unclonable functions. In M. Matsui, editor, *Advances in Cryptology - ASIACRYPT 2009*, volume 5912, chapter 40, pages 685–702. Springer Berlin Heidelberg, Berlin, Heidelberg, 2009.

[3] Y.-G. Choi, J. Kang, and D. Nyang. Proactive code verification protocol in wireless sensor network. In *Computational Science and Its Applications – ICCSA 2007*, pages 1085–1096. Springer, August 2007.

[4] Y. Dodis, L. Reyzin, and A. Smith. Fuzzy extractors: How to generate strong keys from biometrics and other noisy data. In *Advances in Cryptology – EUROCRYPT '2004*, Lecture Notes in Computer Science. Springer-Verlag, Berlin Germany, 2004.

[5] J. Dyer, M. Lindemann, R. Perez, R. Sailer, L. van Doorn, S. W. Smith, and S. Weingart. Building the IBM 4758 Secure Coprocessor. *IEEEC*, 34(10):57–66, 2001.

[6] B. Gassend, D. Clarke, M. van Dijk, and S. Devadas. Silicon physical random functions. In *ACM Conference on Computer and Communications Security*, pages 148–160, New York, NY, USA, 2002. ACM Press.

[7] B. Gassend, D. Lim, D. Clarke, M. van Dijk, and S. Devadas. Identification and authentication of integrated circuits: Research articles. *Concurr. Comput. : Pract. Exper.*, 16(11):1077–1098, 2004.

[8] Intrinsic ID. Intrinsic id — product page. `http://www.intrinsic-id.com/products/`, November 2010.

[9] R. Kennell and L. H. Jamieson. Establishing the genuinity of remote computer systems. In *Proceedings of the 12th USENIX Security Symposium*, pages 295–308. USENIX, Aug. 2003.

[10] J. W. Lee, D. Lim, B. Gassend, G. E. Suh, M. van Dijk, and S. Devadas. A technique to build a secret key in integrated circuits for identification and authentication application. In *Proceedings of the Symposium on VLSI Circuits*, pages 176–159, 2004.

[11] Y. Li, J. McCune, and A. Perrig. SBAP: Software-based attestation for peripherals. In A. Acquisti, S. Smith, and A.-R. Sadeghi, editors, *Trust and Trustworthy Computing*, volume 6101 of *Lecture Notes in Computer Science*, chapter 2, pages 16–29. Springer Berlin / Heidelberg, Berlin, Heidelberg, 2010.

[12] J. Nick L. Petroni, T. Fraser, J. Molina, and W. A. Arbaugh. Copilot - a coprocessor-based kernel runtime integrity monitor. In *Proceedings of the 13th USENIX Security Symposium* [25], pages 179–194.

[13] E. Öztürk, G. Hammouri, and B. Sunar. Towards Robust Low Cost Authentication for Pervasive Devices. In *Proceedings of the 2008 Sixth Annual IEEE International Conference on Pervasive Computing and Communications (PERCOM'08)*. IEEE Computer Society, March 2008.

[14] R. S. Pappu, B. Recht, J. Taylor, and N. Gershenfeld. Physical one-way functions. *Science*, 297:2026–2030, 2002.

[15] B. Parno, J. M. McCune, and A. Perrig. Bootstrapping Trust in Commodity Computers. In *Proceedings of the IEEE Symposium on Research in Security and Privacy*, pages 414–429, Oakland, CA, May 2010. IEEE Computer Society, Technical Committee on Security and Privacy, IEEE Computer Society Press.

[16] U. Rührmair. SIMPL systems: On a public key variant of physical unclonable functions. Cryptology ePrint Archive, Report 2009/255, 2009.

[17] U. Rührmair, F. Sehnke, J. Sölter, G. Dror, S. Devadas, and J. Schmidhuber. Modeling attacks on physical unclonable functions. In *ACM CCS 2010*, 2010.

[18] A.-R. Sadeghi, C. Wachsmann, and I. Visconti. PUF-Enhanced RFID Security and Privacy. In *2nd Workshop on Secure Component and System Identification (SECSI 2010), Cologne, Germany, April 26-27, 2010*, April 2010.

[19] A. Seshadri, M. Luk, A. Perrig, L. van Doorn, and P. Khosla. SCUBA: Secure code update by attestation in sensor networks. In *WiSe '06: Proceedings of the 5th ACM workshop on Wireless security*, pages 85–94, New York, NY, USA, 2006. ACM.

[20] A. Seshadri, A. Perrig, L. van Doorn, and P. K. Khosla. SWATT: SoftWare-based ATTestation for embedded devices. In *Proceedings of the IEEE Symposium on Research in Security and Privacy*, pages 272–, Oakland, CA, May 2004. IEEE Computer Society, Technical Committee on Security and Privacy, IEEE Computer Society Press.

[21] U. Shankar, M. Chew, and J. D. Tygar. Side effects are not sufficient to authenticate software. In *Proceedings of the 13th USENIX Security Symposium* [25], page 7.

[22] Trusted Computing Group (TCG). *TPM Main Specification, Version 1.2*, February 2005.

[23] Trusted Computing Group (TCG). *Mobile Trusted Module (MTM) Specifications*, May 2009.

[24] P. Tuyls and L. Batina. RFID-Tags for Anti-Counterfeiting. In *Proceedings of the Cryptographers' Track at the RSA Conference 2006 (CT-RSA'06)*, volume 3860 of *LNCS*, pages 115–131. Springer Verlag, February 2005.

[25] USENIX. *Proceedings of the 13th USENIX Security Symposium*, Berkeley, CA, USA, Aug. 2004.

[26] Verayo, Inc. Verayo website — product page. `http://www.verayo.com/product/products.html`, November 2010.

[27] Y. Yang, X. Wang, S. Zhu, and G. Cao. Distributed software-based attestation for node compromise detection in sensor networks. In *SRDS '07: Proceedings of the 26th IEEE International Symposium on Reliable Distributed Systems*, pages 219–230, Washington, DC, USA, 2007. IEEE Computer Society.

Accelerometers and Randomness: Perfect Together

Jonathan Voris
Polytechnic Institute of NYU
jvoris@isis.poly.edu

Nitesh Saxena
Polytechnic Institute of NYU
nsaxena@poly.edu

Tzipora Halevi
Polytechnic Institute of NYU
thalev01@students.poly.edu

ABSTRACT

Accelerometers are versatile sensors that are nearly ubiquitous. They are available on a wide variety of devices and are particularly common on those that are mobile or have wireless capabilities. Accelerometers are applicable in a number of settings and circumstances, including important security and privacy domains. In this paper, we investigate the use of accelerometers for the purpose of *true random number generation*. As our first contribution, we discover that an accelerometer possesses two unique and appealing properties when used as an entropy source. First, contrary to intuition, an accelerometer can derive sufficient entropy even when it is stationary (i.e., not subject to perceivable acceleration). Next, and more importantly, the entropy of a stationary accelerometer can not be reduced in the presence of a variety of environmental variations or even under adversarial manipulations. This means that, unlike other sensors, accelerometers are resistant to changing environments, benign or otherwise. To support this claim, we develop a thorough experimental adversarial model for accelerometers that supply a system with entropy. To the authors' knowledge, this is the first real world model in the context of entropy collection.

As our second contribution, we demonstrate the validity of accelerometer based random number generation on an RFID tag, which is a highly resource constrained device. We present the design and implementation of our method on an Intel WISP tag and conduct several novel experiments to evaluate its feasibility. Our results indicate that a high quality 128-bit random number can be extracted using an accelerometer in about 1.5 seconds even when the sensor is in a stationary state. To our knowledge, this is the first random number generation technique that is known to be viable for RFID devices based on general-purpose hardware.

Categories and Subject Descriptors

K.6.5 [**Security and Protection**]: Miscellaneous

General Terms

Security

Keywords

Random number generation, sensors, ubiquitous computing, computational RFID

1. INTRODUCTION

In this paper, we consider the difficult problem of *true random number generation* (RNG). RNG is a fundamental component of several cryptographic and security primitives, such as key generation, strong password generation, encryption, and authentication. It is also a necessary building block of randomized algorithms used in other areas of computer science. Our focus is specifically on hardware RNG rather than pseudo RNG which does not draw randomness from any external properties or occurrences. When constructing a random number generator, the most critical design choice is deciding which type of hardware, input interface, or sensor to use. Traditional desktop computers have many interfaces available to them from which they may draw entropy. Each of these interfaces comes with its own set of weaknesses, however. As an example, sensors such as microphones and wireless interfaces draw entropy from sources that are susceptible to environmental variations or are easy for a malicious entity to manipulate or monitor.

The problem of finding a satisfactory source of entropy is exacerbated by the resource constraints imposed by inexpensive devices such as Radio Frequency Identification (RFID) tags. The manufacturers of these wireless appliances often can not afford to include any hardware that serves a unary purpose such as the collection of entropy. As a result, they are forced to rely on whatever forms of input and sensory data collection are already presently available. The low memory, power, and computational abilities of RFID enabled devices further complicate the RNG endeavor. For an RNG solution to be applicable to RFID tags it must not consume much power, be highly computationally efficient, and require little storage space.

Given their utility, accelerometers are becoming increasingly ubiquitous, especially on mobile and wireless devices. Accelerometers are inexpensive, costing less than $1 [1], and can be added to devices which typically do not have them at little extra cost. For example, one can be added to a desktop or laptop computer using a USB dongle. They are also available on RFID tags [33, 37] and have already been utilized for RFID security and privacy primitives (e.g., see the Secret Handshakes work on context recognition [12]). Given these appealing features and multiple use cases, we set out to investigate whether accelerometers can be used as viable sources of randomness, and to determine how their entropy collection performance and capabilities compares to existing solutions.

An important metric on which an entropy source must be judged is its sensitivity. A sensor must be capable of picking up more detailed information about its environment than an adversary can detect. If this is not the case, then it would be trivial for such an adversary to simply monitor the underlying physical phenomenon in order to predict the generator's output. We discover that accelerometers perform better than other types of sensors in this regard. They are more sensitive than intuitively expected, being capable of picking up even minute vibrations from afar. These devices are so perceptive that models in laptops and USB sticks have been repurposed by Cochran et al. to monitor early indications of earthquakes [9].

As our results demonstrate, *even stationary* accelerometers provide a satisfactory amount of entropy. That is, they are capable of providing sufficient randomness to enable the efficient generation of random numbers on computational RFID tags (such as Intel's WISP tags [33, 37]) and other computing devices. Despite this high sensitivity threshold, we find that accelerometers are resistant to several environmental changes and different types of manipulations by adversarial parties. Besides those that involve tampering with the sensor or the use of specialized equipment such as a centrifuge or vibration isolator, any benign changes or adversarial manipulations only increase the amount of entropy that is available to an accelerometer. These two key insights make accelerometers a unique RNG solution that is easily deployable on many platforms.

Overview of Contributions and Paper Outline.

In this paper, we make the following technical contributions. We present two unique and appealing properties of an accelerometer when used as an entropy source. *First*, contrary to intuition, an accelerometer can derive sufficient entropy even when it is stationary, i.e., not subject to perceivable acceleration. *Second*, and more importantly, accelerometers are resistant to a variety of environmental variations and even to adversarial manipulation. To substantiate these claims, we develop an adversarial model for an accelerometer being used as an entropy source (*Section 3*). Our results demonstrate that most benign or adversarial changes that an accelerometer can be subject to will *increase* the entropy it provides. The best approach an attacker could take to interfering with the amount of accelerometer generated entropy would be to place the accelerometer equipped device in as stable an environment as possible.

As our second contribution, we demonstrate the practicality of our proposal. We design and implement an accelerometer based random number generator on an RFID tag (WISP), which is a highly constrained device (*Section 4*). We also report on the detailed results regarding the novel experiments we performed to measure the amount of randomness one can expect to derive from an accelerometer while it is undergoing a variety of motions and circumstances. Our results indicate that a high quality 128-bit random number can be extracted using an accelerometer on a WISP tag in about 1.5 seconds in a stationary state and much faster when an accelerometer equipped device is used and carried during daily activities.

Additionally, we show that accelerometer based RNG compares favorably to existing RNG solutions in terms of many metrics. Accelerometers are universal and capable of functioning irrespective of how they are stowed since they function when placed inside of other objects. Due to these features, accelerometer based RNG can work on routers and servers that lack traditional interfaces, and on RFID enabled devices that are often kept inside wallets or purses. We corroborate our results with a thorough comparison with related work on alternative sources of randomness (*Section 6*).

2. BACKGROUND AND PRELIMINARIES

2.1 Random Number Generation Theory

Cryptographic applications demand "strongly" uniform numbers. The bits of the number must be independent and uniformly dis-

tributed, or as close to this as attainable. If this type of random value was naturally occurring, utilizing it would be a relatively simple matter of recording it and handing it to the cryptographic application. Unfortunately, this type of strong randomness is unlikely to be available in practice. While the naturally occurring phenomena that sensors capture are unpredictable, they necessarily contain some bias rather than being distributed uniformly.

Extraction functions have been created to address the above problem. An extractor is a function that takes a string of unpredictable but biased, or "weakly" random, bits as input and returns a string of close to uniform, or "strongly" random, bits as output. One example of such an extractor is the "independent sources" extraction of Barak, Impagliazzo, and Wigderson [5], which simply works by multiplying two independent values and adding the result to a third in a recursive fashion. Along the same lines, a second type of extractor was described by Barak, Shaltiel, and Tromer [6]. This extraction technique utilizes a Toeplitz matrix as a seed, which is multiplied against the column matrix containing the input to the hash function. Both of these extractors produce streams of output that are provably close to uniform when provided with inputs which possess sufficiently high min-entropy. Min-entropy, a mathematical property of a distribution, is defined as follows:

DEFINITION 1. *The min-entropy of a given distribution X on $\{0,1\}^n$ is:*

$$min\text{-}entropy(X) = \min_{x \in \{0,1\}^n} \log_2 \frac{1}{Pr[X = x]}$$

In words, the min-entropy of a distribution is equal to the probability of the most likely element in X being drawn from X. Phrased somewhat differently, if a distribution X has a min-entropy of k, the likelihood of drawing any single element x from X does not exceed $1/2^k$ for all $x \in X$.

Min-entropy is an important measurement of a distribution because it captures the amount of randomness a distribution is capable of supporting. Despite the fact that elements of X are n bits in length, due to the bias of the distribution, X may not contain enough entropy to actually support the extraction of n unbiased bits. Only k "strongly" random bits can be derived from a distribution that has a min-entropy of k regardless of the distribution's element length n.

With the concept of min-entropy established, the definition of an extraction function can be expanded in more detail.

DEFINITION 2. *A (k, ϵ)-extractor is a function of the form:*

$$F : \{0,1\}^n * \{0,1\}^d \rightarrow \{0,1\}^m$$

where, for every distribution X over $\{0,1\}^n$ with min-entropy $\geq k$, the output of $F(X, s)$ is statistically ϵ-close to the uniform distribution over $\{0,1\}^m$ when s is chosen uniformly at random, $s \in_R \{0,1\}^d$.

Thus, a (k, ϵ)-extractor is nothing more than a function that accepts n bits of input with min-entropy k and a d bit seed and outputs m bit long values that are nearly uniform. Here, "strongly" random numbers have been described as being "ϵ-close" to uniform.

2.2 WISP Tags

To investigate how to meet the RNG needs discussed above, we mainly utilized a special type of RFID tag designed by Intel Research known as a Wireless Identification and Sensing Platform (WISP) [33, 37]. WISPs are passively-powered RFID tags that are compliant with the Electronic Product Code (EPC) protocol. Specifically, we utilized the 4.1 version of the WISP hardware, which partially implements Class 1 Generation 2 of the EPC standard. Where the WISP differs from standard tags, however, is in its inclusion of an onboard Texas Instruments MSP430F2132 microcontroller and sensors such as the ADXL330 three-axis ±3g accelerometer. This 16-bit MCU features an 8 MHz clock rate, 8 kilobytes of flash memory, and 512 bytes of RAM. WISPs are the first programmable passive RFID devices. They have seen use in studies on a variety of topics, from the energy harvesting experiments [24, 23] to monitoring animal behavior [21, 35]. Unlike standard RFID tags, which are fixed function and state machine based, the flexibility of the WISP allowed us to implement novel security solutions on a live, passive RFID device. The mass manufacturing cost of a WISP tag is expected to be close to $1 [8].

3. ADVERSARIAL MODELING

A prerequisite to building a secure RNG system is to understand how the underlying entropy source behaves in the presence of benign or malicious changes in the context the system is deployed in. In particular, it is important to determine whether or not the min-entropy of the output distribution of the source is affected under different operating conditions, and if so, to what level. If the min-entropy can be reduced to less than a predetermined value (or, in the worst case, brought down to zero), then the extraction function will not be able to guarantee a near uniform distribution for the numbers generated, thus undermining the system's security. For example, the distribution of a microphone or other audio sensor's output will be influenced by the sound produced by users in close proximity, among other environmental factors. Thus, if an adversary can supply a constant audio input or loud noise to the microphone, the system can be forced into a zero entropy state.

In this paper, we develop an experimental adversarial model for an accelerometer being used as an entropy source. In order to achieve this, we analyze what factors, malicious or otherwise, affect the output – and therefore the min-entropy – of the accelerometer, and to what extent this occurs.

The values that are output by an accelerometer are a function of the following variables: *acceleration, noise, sampling rate* and *temperature*. Our model is driven by the question: *can an adversary who tries to manipulate these variables reduce the min-entropy to a level lower than an expected value?*. As our test sensor, we use an onboard WISP accelerometer, model ADXL330 [2], which is also commonly used on other low-end devices. We also perform some experiments with a mobile phone accelerometer (specifically model LIS302DL) which can be found on Nokia N97 cell phones [28, 38]. We analyze different accelerometer input variables and their affect on min-entropy generation below.

1. Acceleration: Clearly, an accelerometer's output depends on what external acceleration the sensor is subject to. Acceleration is defined as a change in velocity. The output of an accelerometer typically varies linearly with acceleration, as is the case for the ADXL330 accelerometer. Our experiments for common and benign movement and acceleration scenarios also confirm that min-entropy increases with the amount of motion applied to an accelerometer equipped device, and that, out of all potential motions, stationary state samples yield the lowest min-entropy. More details on this are provided in Sections 4.1 and 4.6.

We further test some specialized scenarios where an RFID tag may experience either a very low or a constant acceleration that may affect the amount of min-entropy its onboard accelerometer produces (refer to Section 4.3). Both sets of experiments attempt to explore the possibility for an intruder to significantly reduce the amount of min-entropy that is being derived. Our results show that the min-entropy level can not be lowered considerably.

2. Noise: Another important parameter that impacts the randomness of accelerometer output is the sensor's noise. This includes intrinsic noise generated from within the accelerometer circuitry as well as that induced by the environment (typically referred to as seismic noise). As specified in [2], this noise follows a Gaussian distribution. This was also confirmed by means of a set of our stationary state samples (Figure 1). Note that the peak of this distribution is what corresponds to the min-entropy; the flatter the curve, the higher the min-entropy.

We note that an accelerometer's noise is random and its overall level can only be lowered by reducing the bandwidth of the accelerometer, which would in turn increase the resolution of the sensor. This can only be performed by changing the capacitances on the accelerometer circuitry [2], which requires physical access to the device. Therefore, it would not be possible for an adversary to manipulate the amount of noise present in order to cull the min-entropy. The WISP schematic depicts the default bandwidth to be 50 Hz, which corresponds to a capacitance value of 0.1 μF for each of the three axes [13]. All of our experiments reported in this paper were performed at this default setting.

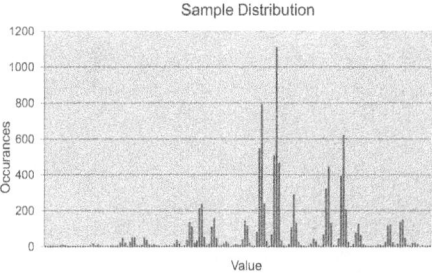

Figure 1: A Stationary State Sample Distribution taken from the WISP's Accelerometer

3. Sampling Rate: The sampling rate of an accelerometer's analog-to-digital converter (ADC) is an important measure of the sensor's output. Our experiments indicate that the rate at which an acceleration sensor is sampled does not have a significant effect on the min-entropy of its output (see Section 4.4 for details). Notice that in certain applications, such as a passive RFID system, a malicious reader can control the sampling rate in an attempt to undermine the level of randomness that is produced from a tag's accelerometer.

4. Temperature: We review the effect of temperature on an accelerometer's output and on the min-entropy level. According to the ADXL330 specification, the effect of temperature on the accelerometer's sensitivity is very low. It is only ±0.015% per °C, or 1% for 70°C. Further, the bias change is ±1 mg/°C with a maximum of 70 mg for 70°C. In addition, our tests confirm that temperature does not have a considerable impact on the level of accelerometer min-entropy (see Section 4.5). The default temperature for experiments was the room temperature in our lab.

Our experiments show that an adversary who tries to manipulate an accelerometer's input can not reduce the min-entropy level. No matter how these inputs are modified, it does not seem possible to reduce the min-entropy found in the sensor's output beneath what is present in a stationary sample taken from the sensor. In other words, our model establishes a safe rough lower-bound for the min-entropy of accelerometer readings. We note that this bound is an essential parameter for the extraction approach and model that is presented in [6], which is what we employ for our extraction needs.

To summarize, according to our experimental model, accelerometers turn out to be resilient to adversarial control. The best approach an attacker could take in terms of interfering with the amount of min-entropy generated by one of these sensors would be to place the accelerometer equipped device in as stable an environment as possible, as anything else will only serve to increase the min-entropy of its readings rather than reduce it.

It may be possible to perform a more sophisticated form of attack to reduce the amount of randomness in an accelerometer's output by ensuring that the device is constantly undergoing precisely the same or a very high amount of force. For example, an adversary could place an RFID tag in a centrifuge that spins the tag at a very high speed, pinning the accelerometer readings to the same maximum value. On the other extreme, a perfect vibration shield could be used to completely cut a device's accelerometer off from the external phenomena which it draws its entropy from. An intermediate possibility that we experimented with in Section 4.7 involves inducing a resonance effect [3]. If an accelerometer is exposed to a sustained force at a particular frequency, known as its "resonant frequency", the amplitude of the output signal will grow significantly, causing the signal to "clip" or saturate. This will cause the accelerometer to constantly output same maximum output value, yielding zero min-entropy. We could not, however, successfully exploit this phenomenon with the LIS302DL accelerometer by using its specified resonance frequency of 2000 Hz [22]. (This experiment is further detailed in Section 4.7).

While these types of attack may succeed, they are not very practical. First, to perform them, physical access to the device for an extended period of time is needed, at which point an adversary could instead physically decompose the tag to compromise the integrity of the entropy collection process as well as any secrets that are stored on the device. Second, these attacks may be easily detected. Third, it might be hard to design a true vibration shield that can shield an accelerometer from all vibrations.

4. ACCELEROMETER RNG ON RFID

Like most devices, RFID tags are in need of RNG. One motivating example is that random values are a prerequisite for executing RFID tag-to-reader authentication protocols, such as HB+ and HB# [25, 14]. Privacy-preserving authentication protocols also require unpredictable numbers [29]. In this section, we discuss the design, implementation, and experimental analysis of an accelerometer based random number generator for RFID devices.

As discussed in Section 1, RNG is beyond the capacity of today's average RFID tag. As a result, alternative approaches to the creation of random values must be considered. One such proposal is proposed by Holcomb et al. [19, 20]. This technique utilizes onboard RAM as a source of true randomness. This technique is quite promising as any device, regardless of its constraints, will contain some amount of onboard memory from which randomness can be drawn.

Unfortunately, previous work has illustrated that practical considerations prevent the FERNS approach to random number generation from reaching its full theoretical potential [34]. Since FERNS relies on pre-existing memory circuitry as a source of entropy, it must compete with other system functionalities for use of this shared resource. Other code running on an RFID tag will necessarily be occupying the device's memory at any given point during execution. As such, the amount of uninitialized RAM available for utilization as a randomness generator may be restricted to a fraction of such a device's overall memory.

Furthermore, RAM is subject to a phenomenon known as *data remanence*. While it is still volatile in the traditional sense, due to properties of the underlying hardware such memory retains its contents while receiving power and for a duration of several seconds

afterwards, as discussed by Skorobogatov and Halderman et al. [36, 17]. This means that after a portion of memory has been used for entropy collection once, it will require a relatively extended period of time without power before it can again be used in this capacity. In a usable RFID based security application which requires multiple random numbers this may lead to unacceptably high delays. As an alternative, we instead turn to entropy collection techniques which rely on onboard sensors. While not as general purpose as RAM, sensors have many uses outside of security and privacy applications. Note that not all sensors qualify to serve this purpose. RFID devices are often stowed inside other objects. For instance, access cards are often stored inside of a wallet or purse. This rules out the use of sensors such as microphones, cameras, or light sensors. See Section 6 for a more thorough sensor comparison. Accelerometers, on the other hand, appear to be a promising foundation for performing RNG on RFID tags.

4.1 Min-Entropy Estimation

To investigate the viability of generating cryptographic quality random numbers using accelerometer readings on mobile hardware, several experiments were performed. First, we needed to approximate the min-entropy of the accelerometer samples intended for extraction. Accelerometer samples were taken over a 10 minute interval while a variety of different movements were performed with the tags. In all cases, min-entropy was calculated by applying the following process. After collecting a sample of accelerometer readings, the number of occurrences of the most common value in the sample was counted. The probability of choosing this element is calculated by dividing this number by the total number of elements in the sample. The min-entropy of the sample distribution was computed by applying Definition 1 to this value.

Movement	Min-Entropy
Stationary #1	3.4
Stationary #2	3.6
Hand	10.8
Arc Swipe	11.3
Drop	9.1
Triangle	11.0
Alpha	11.0
Key Twist	11.7
Circle	11.4

Table 1: Min-entropy Estimates of Accelerometer Sample Distribution for 10 Minute Motion Samples

The sample with the least amount of motion involved was the stationary sample, where the WISP tag was simply left sitting on a desk. This test was meant to model a scenario where a tag is placed in front of an RFID reader's antenna without actually being held by a user. The hand test measured the min-entropy of the accelerometer readings while the WISP tag was held in the palm of a hand. This test was meant to model a scenario where a tag is presented in front of an RFID reader's antenna while being held as still as possible by a user. The arc swipe sample involved moving the WISP tag in an arc like half circle pattern from the middle left hand side of the reader's antenna, to the center top of the antenna, then to the middle right hand side of the antenna, and then back again. This test was meant to model a scenario where a tag is swiped in front of an RFID reader's antenna while being held by a user.

For the drop test, the WISP tag was repeatedly picked up and vertically dropped in front of the antenna. This test was meant to stimulate items being deposited in front of a RFID reader as they move down a conveyor belt in a factory or retail checkout. In

Movement	Sample Size	Min-Entropy
Overnight #1	1,231,095	3.5
Overnight #2	2,778,113	3.9

Table 2: Min-Entropy Estimates of Accelerometer Sample Distribution for Overnight Samples

the triangle test, the WISP tag was moved in a triangular pattern from the bottom left hand corner of the reader's antenna, to the top center of the reader's antenna, then to the bottom right hard corner, before being moved back to the bottom left. For the alpha sample, the tag was moved in a loop resembling a lower-case Greek letter alpha. Both the alpha and triangle tests were also meant to model a scenario where a tag is swiped in front of an RFID reader's antenna in a certain manner while being held by a user.

Instead of moving the tag parallel to the reader surface, for the key twist test, the tag was held in place relative to the antenna but spun in circles around its central axis, similar to the motion performed when a key is used to open a door. This test represents the motion underwent by an RFID tag embedded in a key while unlocking a door. Finally, the circle test saw the WISP tag moved roughly in a circle in front of the antenna, once again to model a scenario where a tag is swiped in front of an RFID reader's antenna in a certain manner while being held by a user. The arc swipe, triangle, alpha, key twist, and circle motions were first suggested in the study of Secret Handshakes [12] and were included to provide a basis for comparison with this work.

The results of these tests are given in Table 1. Out of all these patterns, the stationary option yielded the lowest min-entropy with a value of 3.4. To verify the accuracy of this result, a second 10 minute stationary sample was taken. The min-entropy of this sample was found to be slightly higher than the first, 3.6. Thus it was concluded that a min-entropy level of approximately 3.4 should be assumed for accelerometer outputs, since it is unknown how much motion, and therefore how much additional min-entropy, will be captured by the samples at any given time. Note that the min-entropy of a sample distribution captures an estimate of the amount of randomness that can be expected to be derived from a single sensor reading rather than the entire distribution sample. That is, a stationary accelerometer can support the creation of 3.4 random bits per one 30-bit accelerometer sample. Due to the limitations of our sample sizes, these values should be regarded as min-entropy lower bounds rather than definitive min-entropy estimations.

Our tests determined that the min-entropy of the RFID tagŠs accelerometer samples is at its lowest when the tag is still. This was further confirmed by a series of specialized experiments reported in Section 4.3 to 4.7). To further ensure an accurate estimate of the sensor value's min-entropy for this (worst-case) scenario, a sizeable sample was needed. To achieve this, a tag was programmed to transmit its raw accelerometer values upon receipt of a query from a reader. The reader was left to query the tag overnight twice. The results of these tests are given in Table 2. The 1,231,095 readings collected in the first sample yielded a min-entropy of 3.5 while the second batch's 2,778,113 readings had a min-entropy of 3.9. These values confirmed that the original min-entropy estimate was accurate and not due to a chance in the smaller sample.

4.2 Extraction

In order to produce a uniformly distributed random value, we utilized known extractor functions. However, since the extraction was to be implemented on a WISP tag, which has limited resources, special considerations were necessary. Extractor functions, reviewed previously in Section 2.1, were used to achieve this goal. Specif-

ically, we used the independent sources extractor presented in [5] and the matrix extractor presented in [6], as described below. (Although we concentrate on generating a 128-bit random number, our approach presented in this section can be generalized to produce an arbitrarily long random number).

Chained Extraction: For efficiency purposes (due to the resource limitations), we decided to implement the extraction using a two-stage process, where the output of the independent sources extractor was fed into the matrix extraction function as input. The first (independent sources) extractor was utilized to create a compressed output and allowed us to minimize the amount of input for the second (matrix) extractor, which was then used to generate a 128-bit random output. The primary advantage of this approach includes reducing the input for the second extractor, which in turn significantly reduces the computation required. Another benefit of this approach is that it can be easily generalized to create random output that is longer than 128-bits (even on limited computation devices).

Extractor Function Details: As mentioned above, for the first stage in our extraction process, we implemented the independent extraction technique. We used as input the three axes of an accelerometer sample (which were 10-bits long each), resulting in a total 30-bit input which produced a 10-bit output. A core advantage of this extractor lies in its simplicity. Since it only involves one multiplication step and one addition step, it can be readily deployed on platforms that lack the computational resources. Unfortunately, the independent sources extractor can not be used on its own to craft 128-bits of randomness. Since each input to this function is only 10-bits in our case (i.e., we only had three axes of accelerometer output acting as three independent sources), it can only be used to generate a 10-bit long random number.

For the second stage, we applied the matrix extractor. For example, to produce a 128-bit random output corresponding to our stationary state samples, a 50 sample input to the extractor was used that had a min-entropy equivalent to about 198, which was necessary for the matrix extractor [6]. Since the extractor input consisted of the first stage output, this resulted in 500 bits input length.[1]

This entropy extraction technique is more flexible than others since it provides a method to control its input length, the size of its output, and how close to uniform its results will be [6]. Unfortunately, it has larger input requirements than its alternatives (when used alone), which makes the matrix extractor harder to use, as a single-stage process, on resource constrained devices.

Implementation Details: To implement the two-stage or double extractor on a WISP tag, several changes had to be made. These changes were necessary, in particular, for the matrix extractor to work within the constraints of the tag. Only the top row and leftmost column of the Toeplitz matrix seed are permanently stored on the tag. When performing matrix multiplication operations, each row of the matrix was generated as needed from the seed and discarded afterwards in order to minimize the amount of memory needed to store the seed. Furthermore, all binary values are stored in byte arrays rather than arrays of boolean values. While this adds complexity to the manipulation of individual bits, it reduces the required storage space. In addition, rather than buffering accelerometer samples prior to applying the extraction, the matrix operations were done on a piecemeal, sample-by-sample basis, saving both memory as well as computation.

NIST Test Results: To confirm the randomness of our double extractor output, this approach was further implemented on a laptop computer and applied to each of the motion samples described in Section 4.1 as well as the two overnight samples which were taken. The movement samples were run through the National Institute of

---

[1]The extractor seed was 627-bit long.

Standards and Technology (NIST) "Statistical Test Suite for the Validation of Random Number Generators and Pseudo Random Number Generators for Cryptographic Applications" [32] both prior to and following extraction. The frequency, frequency within a block, cumulative sums, runs, longest-run-of-ones in a block, binary matrix rank, non-overlapping template matching, overlapping template matching, Maurer's "Universal Statistical," approximate entropy, serial, and linear complexity tests from the NIST suite were applied to the sample data[2]. The results of these tests are provided in Table 3.

Movement	% of NIST Tests Passed
Overnight #1	100.0%
Overnight #2	99.4%
Stationary #1	98.8%
Stationary #2	96.9%
Hand	98.8%
Arc Swipe	98.8%
Drop	97.5%
Triangle	93.8%
Alpha	98.1%
Key Twist	98.1%
Circle	97.5%

Table 3: NIST Test Suite Results for Double (Independent, then Matrix) Extracted 10 Minute Motion Samples and Overnight Samples

We find that the longer input samples passed a very high percentage of the test (with the overnight samples passing either all or 99.4% of the attempted tests). Since a relatively large number of samples are needed for proper statistical results, the smaller samples (such as the triangle data which only included 250 samples) returned lower results but still passed at least 93.8% of the tests. We therefore conclude that the NIST test indicate that our double extractor generated data with a sufficient level of randomness.

4.3 Effect of Vibration Shielding and Specialized Motion

We conducted several tests using commercial anti-vibration pads to garner insight into the effect of vibration shielding on the min-entropy of accelerometer readings. The pads used in our tests are rubber blocks that were originally designed to absorb distracting motion caused by large appliances such as washers and dryers. The intention behind these experiments was to isolate a WISP tag, and therefore its accelerometer, from external vibrations. We anticipated that this would prevent the sensor from picking up any external vibrations and that the min-entropy estimate of its readings would consequentially be lower.

The results of these tests, shown in Table 4 above, were surprising, however. The min-entropy reported by the WISP when the first sample was taken with it placed on the pad, 3.3, was only 0.1 lower than the baseline value taken with the tag placed directly on a desk. The second sample taken with a WISP on top of these pads revealed a slightly lower min-entropy value of 2.5. This is still within the range of usual values for the tag when it is at rest, however. The anti vibration pads thus had little impact on the min-entropy levels exhibited by the accelerometer readings. There are several possible explanations for this unexpected result. Since the pads were intended to dampen the impact of large vibrations from household appliances, perhaps they do not shield against the minute motion that the accelerometer we employ is capable of detecting.

---

[2]Using the default NIST test variables and parameters.

Test	Min-Entropy
WISP Stationary on Desk	3.4
WISP Stationary on Pad #1	3.3
WISP Stationary on Pad #2	2.5
WISP Stationary under Pad	3.0
WISP Stationary Pad Sandwich	2.0
WISP Dropped on Pad	7.4
WISP Slid Down Inclined Plane on Pad	6.2
N97 Stationary on Pad	1.4
N97 Stationary under Pad	1.4
N97 Stationary Pad Sandwich	1.3
WISP Salad Spinner	10.2

Table 4: Min-entropy Estimates of Accelerometer Sample Distribution for Shielding and Specialized Motion Tests

Alternatively, this could indicate that the bulk of the randomness output by the accelerometer comes from internal sources of noise rather than external vibrational motion. Finally, the accelerometer may have still been picking up vibration from the air above the tag rather from the surface and ground beneath it.

To refine these results, we took several samples with the WISP tag positioned differently relative to the anti vibration pads. To see if the device's accelerometer was being influenced by subtle motion from above, we "sandwiched" a tag between two pads. This resulted in a more dramatic min-entropy estimate decrease, as this value fell to 2.0. Yet, we were uncertain as to whether this effect was caused by the isolation of the tag from external movement or simply because the weight of the pad kept the WISP tag pinned down. To determine which was the case, we conducted a test where the tag was placed under a pad but did not have a pad underneath it as well. This resulted in a reading of 3.0, representing a higher amount of min-entropy. It therefore appears that the anti vibration pads did indeed shield the WISP tag from external motion, but this must be applied from all sides for the impact to be discernible.

To ensure that our results were generalizable to all devices and not simply limited to WISP tags or devices with an ADXL330 accelerometer model, we also ran tests with a Nokia N97 phone's LIS302DL accelerometer (a comparison between the min-entropy contained in the output of the LIS302DL and ADXL330 acceleration sensors is provided in Section 5.2, the former being lower). The results of this trial largely mirrored those performed with a WISP tag. Placing the phone under or on top of a pad diminished the min-entropy of the sensor's samples to identical values of 1.4, which represented the lower end of the phone's accelerometer while at rest. Placing the phone between two pads again had a larger impact, bringing the min-entropy level of the phone's accelerometer values down to 1.3.

The drop test listed in Table 3 was also reproduced, only in this variant the tag was dropped on to an anti-vibration pad. Although the tag was observed to bounce upon impact with this rubber surface, the results indicate that the pads did reduce the impact at the end of the fall somewhat, as the min-entropy estimate of the sample taken without padding, 9.1, was higher than the 7.4 obtained when the anti vibration pads were utilized. All these experiments indicate that commercial vibration pads are unlikely to shield a large fraction of movement from being read by an accelerometer. This substantially limits possibilities for adversarial action on an accelerometer based RNG system.

We also conducted an inclined plane test in order to study the performance of the tag under different constant force circumstances, as mentioned in Section 3. The goal was to have the device sustain constant accelerations in order to cause its accelerometer readings to remain similar, thus lowering the min-entropy. A book was propped up adjacent to a rubber pad and a WISP tag was repeatedly slid down this surface. The positions of the book, rubber pad, and reader antenna were fixed from sample to sample. The amount of force applied to the tag's accelerometer was controlled by repeatedly picking the tag up, placing it at the top of the book, and allowing it to slide down along the book's front cover. One ten minute sample was taken. This motion sample yielded a min-entropy of 6.2, which is slightly beneath that of the free fall trials.

Finally, we took readings with a WISP tag placed inside of a swirling salad spinner. This kitchen tool was used as an impromptu budget friendly centrifuge. The purpose of this test was to provide constant acceleration by keeping the spinner running at a close to constant speed. The tag was taped to the inside of the moving portion of the spinner and read while the device was in motion. The spinner was regularly pumped to prevent the tag from slowing down during the test. As was the case for the inclined plane tests, the placement of the reader antenna and salad spinner was not altered during the tests. The variable element in this experiment was the location of the tag as it rotated along the inside walls of the salad spinner. A single ten minute trial was also conducted for this test. The resultant min-entropy estimate of the tag's accelerometer values was found to be 10.2. This is comparable to the results observed during the motion tests without specialized equipment rather than being indicative of any adversarial ability to reduce the randomness inherent in the accelerometer output.

Contrary to our intuition, the scenarios that were intended to feed constant force in to the accelerometer resulted in an increase in the min-entropy of its output. This seems to indicate that noise contributes significantly to the randomness contained within accelerometer samples. These experiments provide an initial estimation as to the degree of influence an adversary is capable of exerting over the output of an accelerometer. However, it must be noted that these results should not be taken as conclusive proof that a potential attacker would not be able to do better.

4.4 Effect of Sampling Rate and Method

Our experiments indicate that the rate at which an accelerometer is sampled does not have a significant impact on the min-entropy of its outputs. A function estimating the impact of the sampling speed is portrayed in Figure 2, which was moved to the Appendix. This figure implies that even at a sampling rate of infinity (i.e., when the time interval between successive reads is 0), the min-entropy of the sensor's output distribution would stand at around 3. The most feasible explanation for this behavior is that the entropy present in accelerometer samples comes mostly from noise. If the sampling rate used is smaller than the accelerometer's bandwidth, which should be the case to allow the ADC to work, then each reading is affected by a different noise level. This is because the state of the accelerometer always changes between each reading.

The next element that we looked at as a potential contributing factor to the accelerometer's min-entropy level was the sampling method employed. The WISP firmware has two separate techniques for taking readings from the acceleration sensor. One is a "quick" technique that does not allow the accelerometer to fully settle before taking readings, but instead takes a fast reading and then attempts to compensate for the error in the hasty sample. The other allows the accelerometer to settle completely instead. The "quick" reading technique is used by default, so all samples taken thus far have utilized this sampling technique. To see if the "slow" sampling technique resulted in a distribution with significantly different min-entropy from the default "quick" technique, an overnight test was conducted again, this time with the WISP firmware set to

use the "slow" technique. The resultant min-entropy estimate of this sample was 3.4.

4.5 Effect of Temperature

We then set out to determine if temperature plays a role in determining the amount of randomness contained in these values. In order to see if temperature had any impact on the min-entropy of the accelerometer values whatsoever, we first used a blow dryer to cause a WISP tag to warm up and a freezer to cool it down. The tag was programmed to transmit the output of both its accelerometer and its internal thermometer to the RFID reader through its EPC ID. For the "hot" test, the WISP tag was placed in front of a polling reader's antenna while a blow dryer was aimed directly at the tag. The blow dryer was placed on the highest setting that we could use. For the "cold" test, the tag was placed in a plastic bag in the freezer section of a mini-refrigerator overnight. Immediately upon removing the tag, it was interrogated by an RFID reader. Both samples were taken for a period of 10 minutes as with the movement tests. The results of these tests are shown in Table 6 in the Appendix.

Since the min-entropy of the preliminary "hot" test sample was dramatically different from that of the stationary tag samples we previously encountered, we could not rule out the possibility that temperate did indeed have an impact on the randomness of the accelerometer samples. However, in both the cases of the "hot" and "cold" test, we were not able to exert as careful control over the temperate as we would have liked. This is because the temperature of the "cold" tag began to rise as soon as it was removed from the freezer, while the heightened min-entropy of the "hot" tag could have been caused either by the increase of temperature from the blow dryer or the buffeting of the air being blown at the tag by the blow dryer. Thus, as a follow up, we performed 3 additional temperature tests. In the first two, an electric heater was used in place of the blow dryer.

In one of these tests, the heater was set only to blow air on the tag, allowing us to isolate the effect of the force of air on the tag's accelerometer readings without simultaneously warming the tag. In the second, the heater was set to produce warmth in order to replicate the outcome of the blow dryer test with a different device. As a third test, to obtain a more stable cold temperature reading, the WISP tag was placed in a plastic bag and sealed in a thermos full of ice. After waiting several seconds to allow the tag's temperature to cool to that of the thermos, the thermos containing the tag was placed in front of the antenna of our RFID reader and queried for a 10 minute interval.

The min-entropy did not change much for the freezer test. This is because there was the least variation in its temperature out of all of the temperature tests performed. The heater and thermos tests each saw drastic changes in temperature, yet only saw modest increases in their min-entropy level. The fan test saw a substantial increase yet did not involve any temperature change at all, while the blow dryer test had the largest net gain of all the temperature tests performed. Since all tests in this group were performed with the WISP tags at rest, we can conclude that while temperature does indeed have an effect on the min-entropy level of an accelerometer's readings, this effect is dwarfed by the effect of physical movement on the sensor, even if this movement is as subtle as a stream of air from a fan, blow dryer, or other source.

4.6 Effect of Context and Users

All of the previous motion tests were conducted by directly handling WISP tags. In practice, however, many users do not directly manipulate their RFID tags. They instead leave their tags in their wallets, bag, purses, or other containers. These items are presented to the RFID reader's antenna, allowing the tags to be read through the material of the container. Thus, we took an additional round of samples with the WISP tag placed inside different objects. First, the WISP tag was wrapped in bubble wrap and placed inside a cardboard box. Next, the tag was placed inside of a wallet. The wallet was tested both while placed open on a desk and held open while in front of the reader's antenna. The scenario where a tag is placed loose inside a purse or backpack was also tested.

The min-entropy measurements of these samples are provided in Table 5. In the case of the box, wallet, and backpack tests, the observed min-entropy estimates were actually 0.1 or 0.2 lower than the lowest min-entropy observed for the stationary samples that we recorded. This can be partially attributed to random differences between the two sample sets. However, the shielding tests conducted with vibration dampening pads discussed in Section 4.3 suggest that accelerometers are affected not only by small movements in adjacent solid objects but also by airborne vibration. We therefore conclude that these types of enclosures reduce the amount of detectable motion derived from both these sources by a small degree.

Movement	Min-Entropy
Box	3.3
Wallet	3.1
Hand Wallet	7.3
Purse	4.3
Backpack	3.3

Table 5: Min-entropy Estimates of Accelerometer Sample Distribution for 10 Minute Container Samples

Finally, several samples were also taken to test for variations between different users. All of the samples taken thus far were performed by the same test subject. While little variation was anticipated in the non-interactive samples, such as the stationary ones where a tag was left sitting on a desk, we wanted to make sure our tests captured any differences that might exist between the motions when performed by different volunteers. We therefore repeated the hand held and arc swipe tests with four different volunteers. These tests shed some light on the randomness of accelerometer readings under different circumstances. The min-entropy of these samples is given in Table 7 in the Appendix. The average value across all "volunteer hand" samples was 5.2 and the standard deviation of these measurements was 0.7. For the "volunteer swipe" samples, the average value was 8.8 while the standard deviation came to 0.3.

4.7 Effect of Resonance

We conducted a set of tests where an accelerometer was subjected to various types of tones in an attempt to cause resonance, as discussed in Section 3. To this end, we utilized a Creative Inspire 5.1 5300 speaker system [11] to output sounds of different frequencies. Since these speakers feature a 40 to 20,000 Hz operating range [10] they were well suited to subjecting acceleration sensors to different kinds of forces. We desired to use this audio equipment in conjunction with a WISP and its onboard ADXL330 accelerometer, but unfortunately the Impinj RFID reader interfered with the sound hardware when in use.

As an alternative, we utilized the LIS302DL accelerometer that is found on Nokia N97 mobile phones [38]. Recall that this model has a lower min-entropy than the ADXL330 accelerometer (refer to Section 5.2 for more details). Since this sensor has a resonance frequency of 2000 Hz [22], multiples of this frequency are the most likely to provoke feedback. We therefore attempted to create a resonance effect by playing tones with frequencies that were multiples

of 500 Hz. Each tone was played at medium volume and a sample was taken for a duration of ten minutes.

The results of these tests showed no discernible correlation between the pitch of the tone being played and the min-entropy level exhibited by the device's accelerometer samples. These tests do not completely rule out the possibility of reducing the min-entropy of an accelerometer's output by inducing a resonance effect because it is certainly possible that we simply did not achieve the correct frequency. While we did produce the specified resonance frequency for the N97's accelerometer, perhaps this value was altered in practice by external elements such as the casing of the phone. Nonetheless, this result underscores the difficulty of creating such an effect even under ideal laboratory conditions.

5. DISCUSSION AND EXTENSIONS

5.1 Efficiency

While RFID read rates are notoriously difficult to measure in a reproducible fashion due to the number of variables involved, in the absence of a more standardized metric they will be used to gauge the plausibility of utilizing the approaches presented in this paper in a practical RFID deployment. The time between WISP reads over the course of our study was 31.2 milliseconds. 50 samples were needed to generate 128 random bits using the chained double extraction mechanism. It therefore takes $50 * 31.2$ milliseconds $= 1.6$ seconds to generate a single 128 bit random value using the chained double extraction mechanism. More generally, assuming an average accelerometer min-entropy contribution of 3.5 per sample, $k/3.5 + 20.2$ samples are required to produce a k bit output 2^{-35} close to uniform value. Combined with the observed sampling rate, this yields an execution time of $9.0k + 631.2$ milliseconds to generate a k random bits.

5.2 Mobile Phone RNG

We also took samples from an accelerometer on a mobile phone in order to demonstrate the applicability of this entropy collection technique to devices besides computational RFID tags. More specifically, we ran our tests on a Nokia N97 phone with a STMicroelectronics LIS302DL accelerometer. This is the same model that was utilized in our resonance experiments (see Section 4.7). We accessed this sensor using the J2ME Mobile Sensor API. We attempted to take overnight stationary samples using this device's accelerometer much as was done with our WISP tags, but for unknown reasons the phone consistently ceased logging after three hours. We therefore initially took two 3 hour LIS302DL samples.

The min-entropy of the first sample was estimated to be 1.1, while the second was 1.7. These estimates were significantly below those derived from our computational RFID tag samples. This is due to the reduced resolution of the LIS302DL in comparison with the ADXL330. The amount of min-entropy that accelerometers, and sensors in general, are capable of producing is a function of the device's resolution as we explain in Section 3. More sensitive devices are capable of picking up more minute variations in external phenomena and their readings will therefore capture more randomness. As a result, it makes sense that the N97's LIS302DL, with a resolution of $0.15328125\ m/s^2$, produces less entropy per reading than the WISP's ADXL330, which features a resolution of $0.05748046875\ m/s^2$. A complementary explanation of the reduced level of randomness experienced on the N97 is that its accelerometer is held steady by the other components surrounding it in the casing of the phone, while the WISP accelerometer component was left out in the open, exposing it to more variations in movement as a result.

As a final test of the N97's accelerometer, one of the authors performed a test where he carried the phone with him while performing his daily activities. The phone was set to log its accelerometer reading for the three hour limit while the tester treated it in precisely the same way as his actual cell phone. He kept the phone in his pocket while at his desk, eating a meal, and riding on mass transportation, lifted the phone to his ear when he received an incoming call on his actual phone, and held it under his real phone when sending text messages or surfing the web. The min-entropy of the phone's accelerometer readings did indeed increase dramatically when the tester used it to mimic daily usage. The estimate came to 6.3, a 4.5 time increase over the average of our stationary estimates. This proves that accelerometer based RNG is viable not only for highly constrained devices such as RFID tags, but also more general purpose wireless appliances such as cell phones.

6. COMPARISON: ACCELEROMETERS VS. OTHER ENTROPY SOURCES

We now argue that accelerometer based random generation is superior when weighed against prior state-of-the-art solutions. We accomplish this via a comparison with existing work on traditional and sensor based methods of entropy collection. See Figure 3 in the Appendix for a side-by-side comparison summary of the advantages and disadvantages of each entropy collection possibility.

6.1 Traditional Sources

In [15], Gutterman et al. establish that the Linux kernel collects entropy from four distinct sources: keyboard inputs, mouse gestures, hard drive use, and interrupt events.

Manual or Automatic? In order to register randomness, keyboards and mice must be moved in an unpredictable manner by a human user for the duration of the entropy creation process. Since humans are notoriously bad at behaving in a random fashion [18], this results in an unexpectedly high burden for users of RNG systems that utilize these interactive types of input. Hard drive events seem like a more promising RNG source than either mice or keyboards since they do not require explicit user involvement. Similarly, the use of radio events does not require any user interaction either. Interrupt events are vague and on many systems do not yield much entropy [15].

Found Where? While, as shown in Figure 3 of the Appendix, mice, keyboards, and hard drives are ubiquitous on desktop and laptop computers, they are uncommon on devices with a smaller form factor or more constraints such as RFID tags. Radio frequency noise is a natural choice as an entropy source for wireless devices since they are necessarily equipped with a radio receiver that could be used in this capacity.

Adversarial Control? Unfortunately, the susceptibility of wireless transmissions to outside manipulation makes them a poor choice for gathering entropy, as an adversary could easily overwhelm any existing radio noise by jamming the signal. A similar shortcoming of mice and keyboards is that the range of inputs that they register during normal operation is driven by the application in use at any given time. This means that they may contain much less entropy than expected or, even worse, potentially be predictable by an attacker. For example, when using a distributed application via a web browser, the information sent between the user's machine and the application server can provide detailed information about the locations of buttons and input fields that will be utilized. On web servers, we expect there to be a high volume of network traffic, and thus corresponding hard disk reads and writes, present. This is a good thing from the perspective of harvesting sufficient entropy.

Unfortunately, much like mouse motion, the fact that this activity is driven by network traffic provides adversarial entities some level of control over disk activity.

Works When Stored? A device's mouse and keyboard cannot be used when the device is placed in a wallet or other type of storage, as shown in Figure 3 in the Appendix. Since mice and keyboards require constant user involvement to be able to craft entropy, they clearly cannot be used to this end while stowed. On the other hand, hard drives and radios do not require any user manipulation to function and are thus capable of achieving normal operation when placed in a bag, purse, or wallet.

Indefinite Reuse? Due to their limited use by a single individual the drives of standard desktop systems will be idle more often than not. Gutterman et al. found that an idle system generated only 16-bits of entropy every 15 minutes based on hard drive activity [15].

6.2 Microphones

Microphones are used to create randomness by the service provided at random.org [16].

Manual or Automatic? As Morrison [30] points out, microphones are preferable to mice due to the fact that mice require the devoted attention of a user while audio sensors do not. Like microphones, accelerometers are also sensors that require an analog to digital converter. However, microphones still require some user involvement because they must be set to a viable source of noise prior to use. Unlike microphones, accelerometers are ready for RNG without any user involvement whatsoever.

Found Where? Since microphones are a necessity for all mobile phones and are the most commonly encountered optional peripheral for desktop computers, they seem like a natural choice for use as a fount of entropy. This concept was further explored by Morrison in [30], where he points out that mice and microphones are the two common computer interfaces that utilize analog to digital converters. These are useful for RNG because the process of turning an analog signal into a digital value always introduces entropy into a system irrespective of the physical phenomenon that is actually captured by a sensor. A potential issue with sound based solutions is that they require the raw storage of sound files, which might take up too much storage space on constrained devices such as cell phones and RFID tags.

Adversarial Control? As shown in the Appendix's Figure 3, a random number generation technique that relies on a microphone is vulnerable to control, for example, by making loud noises. Morrison's work exposes this critical flaw with the use of microphones in the context of RNG. The output of his audio based randomness generator failed to pass statistical tests in cases where the sampling rate was too low as well as situations where the environment was either very quiet or noisy enough to cause the ADC to "clip," that is, exceed the range of the analog to digital converter.

Works When Stored? Microphones do not work when placed in a storage item due to the fact that any enclosure they are placed in will muffle ambient sound.

Indefinite Reuse? In general, as shown in Figure 3 which is found in the Appendix, microphones can be sampled repeatedly and indefinitely. The main problem Morrison found with using audio to derive entropy is that sound samples are correlated when sampled at a high rate, though. In order to avoid this, microphone samples can be added and sampled at a higher period. This decreases the correlation between consecutive samples, but unfortunately also reduces the output rate or the resultant random number generator.

6.3 Cameras

The next group of sensors that we turn our attention to are cameras. Bouda et al. elaborate on this intuitive choice [7].

Manual or Automatic? Like many of the other sensors listed in Figure 3 in the Appendix, cameras do not need manual intervention in order to take samples. If reliant on external data, however, an administrator must ensure that the camera in use is pointed at source that contains sufficient entropy, such as a lava lamp [31]. If, on the other hand, the camera based RNG technique does not require any external stimulus to operate, as is the case with the work of Bouda et al. [7], then no initial setup is required to instantiate a camera based random number generator.

Found Where? As listed in Figure 3 of the Appendix, cameras are found on a wide variety of devices.

Adversarial Control? If the external images captured by a camera were utilized as part of the entropy collection process, cameras would be vulnerable to manipulation. Bouda et al. sidestep this issue by relying solely on the mechanics of the camera for entropy rather than any external phenomenon. This is accomplished by sampling the camera while its shutter is closed. This scenario has limited applicability, however, as most web, laptop, and phone cameras do not have a shutter. The authors of this work show that one of the advantages of using a camera is that its samples yield a min-entropy of approximately 4.0. This is comparable to the accelerometer min-entropy estimates which are provided in Section 4. In addition, all of the sequences they tested pass 15/16 of the tests in the NIST battery, which is also comparable to our results.

Works When Stored? A camera can not collect external data when stored in a wallet or purse. Thus, if reliant on external data, a camera cannot be used for RNG when stored. If not, then it can be.

Indefinite Reuse? Similar to other sensors, cameras can be used indefinitely.

6.4 Other Sensors

In this subsection, we complete our analysis of alternative entropy sources by discussing the use of the remaining four sensors listed in Figure 3 in the Appendix. These are thermometers, photometers, proximity sensors, and magnetometers.

Manual or Automatic? As listed in the Appendix's Figure 3, all of these sensors are automatic with the exception of photometers which, like cameras, must be pointed at a light source with suitable variability to achieve RNG.

Found Where? Thermometers are frequently found on desktop and laptop machines as well as on some RFID tags, e.g., WISPs. Photometers are similar to cameras in that they are sensors of light, but unlike cameras, photometers are not found on any commercially available devices that we are aware of. Proximity sensors and magnetometers are starting to be deployed on cell phones and video game systems.

Adversarial Control? It is possible for adversarial control on all four of these sensor types to result in a loss of entropy. Thermometers can be exposed to a source of heat or cold that pushes their temperature beyond their operation range, for example. Along the same lines, photometers could be covered up and blocked from their randomness producing source of light. An item placed near a proximity sensor would cause it to constantly register the same value. Finally, a magnetometer could simply be moved to output a value of an adversary's choosing.

Works When Stored? The only miscellaneous sensor that works when stored is a magnetometer. Placing this device in an enclosure does not impact its ability to perceive magnetic fields.

Indefinite Reuse? The most beneficial part of these four entropy sources is that, as sensing hardware, they can be queried indefinitely for readings without any limitations.

6.5 Special Purpose Hardware

The generation of true randomness can be achieved by harvesting entropy from electrical and material processes within a device's own circuitry as opposed external phenomena [4]. This activity manifests itself in various forms, including thermal, shot, flicker, generation, and burst noise [4, 26, 27].

While hardware harbors internal unpredictability in the form of numerous varieties of noise, capturing this entropy and converting it into usable digital data is a non-trivial task. Devices require a mechanism through which they can sample minute and transient variations present in their own circuitry. Several different techniques for accomplishing this have been proposed, such as direct amplification and discrete-time chaos [4].

Random number generators that operate solely on internal entropy have some desirable characteristics. Since they do not need to perform any environmental sampling, their design is simpler than solutions involving sensors. This implies that their form factor can be smaller and their cost can be lower when compared to similar external techniques. Additionally, since they do not explicitly rely on sampling contextual phenomena, they have the potential to be more robust in the face of adversarial interference. On the other hand, since they do not involve any environmental monitoring, this class of techniques requires hardware that is necessarily single purpose in nature. As such, they may not be affordable for a given hardware design in terms of cost or space. Another downside to disregarding external entropy is that any randomness originating from beyond the device itself is forfeited, which may limit the amount of available entropy. Finally, throughput considerations may be an issue for users of internal random number generators. For example, while it is unlikely to suffer from protracted delays in practice, it is not possible to know whether or not the Intel random number generator will produce any output in a given time frame [4]. While useful when present, the specialized hardware needed to harvest internal entropy may not be available on any particular computing system. This is particularly true of low cost devices with small form factors, such as RFID tags. An accelerometer on an RFID tag, on the other hand, can be used for other tasks besides random number generation, such as context recognition as developed in [12].

7. CONCLUSIONS

In this paper, we established that an accelerometer is a source of entropy which possess some unique and appealing properties. Most importantly, we demonstrated that accelerometers, unlike other sensors, are resistant to a variety of environmental variations and even to adversarial manipulation. To support this claim, we developed a thorough experimental adversarial model for accelerometers when used as an entropy source. We also demonstrated that accelerometers compare positively to other entropy sources with respect to their universality and usability through a thorough comparative analysis. Furthermore, we showed that deriving entropy from an accelerometer should work on many devices by designing, implementing, and evaluating an accelerometer based RNG solution on the WISP computational RFID tag, which is a constrained device. Our experiments indicate that accelerometers generate sufficient entropy to meet some cryptographic needs even while stationary and produce even more when in motion. The best approach an attacker could take to interfering with the amount of min-entropy generated by an accelerometer would be to place one in as stable an environment as possible, as anything else will only serve to increase the min-entropy of the readings rather than reduce it.

Acknowledgments: We are thankful to our shepherd René Mayrhofer and WiSec'11 anonymous reviewers for their thoughtful feedback.

8. REFERENCES

[1] Mouser Electronics MMA7660FCR1 Freescale Semiconductor Board Mount Accelerometers. Available at `http://www.mouser.com/search/ProductDetail.aspx?qs=uDmhV2jwPReFrqFV70kRUw==`, 2009.

[2] Analog Devices. Adxl330 small, low power, 3-axis ±3 g imems accelerometer. Available at `http://www.sparkfun.com/datasheets/Components/ADXL330_0.pdf`, 2006.

[3] B. Crowell. Vibrations and Waves. Available at `http://www.lightandmatter.com/html_books/3vw/ch02/ch02.html`, 2009.

[4] B. Jun and P. Kocher. The Intel Random Number Generator. Available at `http://www.cryptography.com/public/pdf/IntelRNG.pdf`, 1999.

[5] B. Barak, R. Impagliazzo, and A. Wigderson. Extracting Randomness Using Few Independent Sources. In *SIAM Journal on Computing*, 2006.

[6] B. Barak, R. Shaltiel, and E. Tromer. True Random Number Generators Secure in a Changing Environment. In *Cryptographic Hardware and Embedded Systems*, 2003.

[7] J. Bouda, J. Krhovjak, V. Matyas, and P. Svenda. Towards True Random Number Generation in Mobile Environments. In *Nordic Conference on Secure IT Systems: Identity and Privacy in the Internet Age*, 2009.

[8] M. Buettner, R. Prasad, M. Philipose, and D. Wetherall. Recognizing Daily Activities with RFID-Based Sensors. In *UbiComp*, 2009.

[9] E. Cochran, J. Lawrence, and C. Christensen. Quake-Catcher Network. Available at `http://qcn.stanford.edu/`, 2008.

[10] Creative Asia. Creative inspire m5300 5.1 speakers. Available at `http://asia.creative.com/products/product.asp?category=4&subcategory=25&product=15999&nav=1&listby`, 2010.

[11] Creative Worldwide Support. Technical specifications of creative 5.1 speakers. Available at `http://support.creative.com/kb/ShowArticle.aspx?sid=47175`, 2010.

[12] A. Czeskis, K. Koscher, J. Smith, and T. Kohno. RFIDs and Secret Handshakes: Defending Against Ghost-and-Leech Attacks and Unauthorized Reads with Context-Aware Communications. In *ACM Conference on Computer and Communications Security*, 2008.

[13] D. Yeager and A. Sample. WISP 4.1DL Schematic v8. Available at `http://wisp.wikispaces.com/file/view/WISP4.1DL_Schematic_v8.pdf`, 2010.

[14] H. Gilbert, M. Robshaw, and Y. Seurin. HB#: Increasing the Security and Efficiency of HB+. In *EuroCrypt*, 2008.

[15] Z. Gutterman, B. Pinkas, and T. Reinman. Analysis of the Linux Random Number Generator. In *Symposium on Security and Privacy*, 2006.

[16] M. Haahr. RANDOM.ORG - True Random Number Service. Available at `http://www.random.org/`, 2010.

[17] J. Halderman, S. Schoen, N. Heninger, W. Clarkson, W. Paul, J. Calandrino, A. Feldman, J. Apelbaum, and E. Felten. Least We Remember: Cold Boot Attacks on Encryption Keys. In *USENIX Security Symposium*, 2008.

[18] R. Halprin and M. Naor. Games for Extracting Randomness. In *Symposium On Usable Privacy and Security*, 2009.

[19] D. Holcomb, W. Burleson, and K. Fu. Initial SRAM State as a Fingerprint and Source of True Random Numbers for RFID Tags. In *Conference on RFID Security*, 2007.

[20] D. E. Holcomb, W. P. Burleson, and K. Fu. Power-up SRAM State as an Identifying Fingerprint and Source of True Random Numbers. *IEEE Transactions on Computers*, 2009. to appear.

[21] J. Holleman, D. Yeager, R. Prasad, J. Smith, and B. Otis. NeuralWISP: An Energy-Harvesting Wireless Neural Interface with 1-m Range. In *BioCAS*, 2008.

[22] ICBuy.com. LIS302DL Accelerometer Specifications. Available at `http://tec.icbuy.com/product/productView/id/162826.html`, 2008.

[23] B. Jiang, S. Roy, K. Sundara-Rajan, M. Philipose, J. Smith, and A. Mamishev. Energy Scavenging for Inductively Coupled Passive RFID Systems. In *IEEE Instrumentation and Measurement Technology Conference*, 2005.

[24] B. Jiang, J. Smith, M. Philipose, S. Roy, K. Sundara-Rajan, and A. Mamishev. Energy scavenging for inductively coupled passive RFID systems. In *IEEE Transactions on Instrumentation and Measurement*, 2007.

[25] A. Juels and S. Weis. Authenticating Pervasive Devices with Human Protocols. In *CRYPTO*, 2005.

[26] K. Lundberg. Noise Sources in Bulk CMOS. Available at `http://web.mit.edu/klund/www/papers/UNP_noise.pdf`, 2002.

[27] M. Tormanen. Analog IC Design 2010: Lecture 9 - Noise. Available at `http://framtiden.eit.lth.se/fileadmin/eit/courses/eti063/lectures2010/AnalogIC_F9.pdf`, 2010.

[28] MEMS Industry Group. Nokia Beats Apple to Compass-in-Phone. Available at `http://memsblog.wordpress.com/2009/12/03/nokia-beats-apple-to-compass-in-phone/`, 2009.

[29] D. Molnar and D. Wagner. Privacy and Security in Library RFID: Issues, Practices, and Architectures. In *ACM Computer and Communications Security*, 2004.

[30] R. Morrison. Design of a True Random Number Generator Using Audio Input. In *Journal of Craptology*, 2001.

[31] L. Noll, S. Cooper, and M. Pleasant. LavaRnd. Available at `http://www.lavarnd.org`, 2003.

[32] A. Rukhin, J. Soto, J. Nechvatal, M. Smid, E. Barker, S. Leigh, M. Levenson, M. Vangel, D. Banks, A. Heckert, J. Dray, and S. Vo. A Statistical Test Suite for Random and Pseudorandom Number Generators for Cryptographic Applications. In *Special Publication 800-22*, Available at `csrc.nist.gov/groups/ST/toolkit/rng/documentation_software.html`, 2008.

[33] A. Sample, D. Yeager, P. Powledge, and J. Smith. Design of a Passively-Powered, Programmable Sensing Platform for UHF RFID Systems. In *IEEE International Conference on RFID*, 2007.

[34] N. Saxena and J. Voris. We Can Remember It for You Wholesale: Implications of Data Remanence on the Use of RAM for True Random Number Generation on RFID Tags. In *Conference on RFID Security*, 2009.

[35] N. Segawa. Behavior Evaluation of Sika Deer (Cervus Nippon) by RFID System. In *WISP Summit*, 2009.

[36] S. Skorobogatov. Low Temperature Data Remanence in Static RAM. Available at `www.cl.cam.ac.uk/techreports/UCAM-CL-TR-536.html`, 2002.

[37] J. Smith, A. Sample, P. Powledge, A. Mamishev, and S. Roy. A Wirelessly-Powered Platform for Sensing and Computation. In *8th International Conference on Ubiquitous Computing*, 2006.

[38] STMicroelectronics. LIS302DL MEMS motion sensor 3-axis - 2g/8g smart digital output "piccolo" accelerometer. Available at `http://www.st.com/stonline/products/literature/ds/12726/lis302dl.pdf`, 2008.

APPENDIX: Additional Tables and Figures

Figure 2: Effect of Altering the WISP Read Rate on the Min-Entropy of its Accelerometer Samples

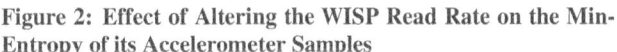
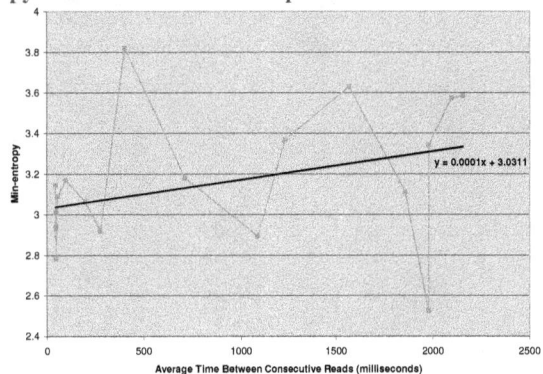

Figure 3: Comparison Table (highlighted cells represent positive features)

Sensor or traditional?	Entropy source	Manual or automatic?	Found where?	Adversarial control?	Works when stored?	Indefinite reuse?
Sensor	Accelerometer	Automatic	Cell phones, certain laptop models, certain video game remote control models, fitness aids, WISPs	Can only increase entropy	Yes	Yes
Traditional	Mouse	Manual	All laptops, all desktops, certain cell phone models, and certain gaming system models	Can decrease entropy	No	No
	Keyboard	Manual	All laptops, all desktops, certain cell phone models, certain gaming system models	Can decrease entropy	No	No
Traditional	Hard Drive	Automatic	All desktops, most laptop models, most gaming system models	Can decrease entropy	Yes	No
	Radio	Automatic	Cell phones, laptops, video game remote controls, portable gaming systems, optional desktop peripheral, routers, WISPs	Can decrease entropy	Yes	No
Sensor	Microphone	Requires initial setup	Cell phones, portable gaming systems, optional desktop peripheral	Can decrease entropy	No	Yes
	Camera	Requires initial setup (if reliant on external data)	Cell phones, certain laptop models, certain monitor models, certain gaming system models, optional desktop peripheral	Can decrease entropy (if reliant on external data)	No if reliant on external data, yes otherwise	Yes
	Thermometer	Automatic	Desktops, laptops, WISPs	Can decrease entropy	No	Yes
	Photometer	Requires initial setup	Uncommon on commercial devices	Can decrease entropy	No	Yes
	Proximity	Automatic	Certain cell phone models, certain gaming system models	Can decrease entropy	No	Yes
	Magnetometer	Automatic	Certain cell phone models	Can decrease entropy	Yes	Yes

Table 6: Temperatures (in degrees Celsius) and Min-Entropy Estimates for Temperature Control Samples

Control Method	Min. Temp.	Average Temp.	Max. Temp.	Min-Entropy
Blow Dryer	40.5	69.8	81.4	6.6
Freezer	14.9	26.3	27.7	3.8
Fan	21.1	22.4	22.7	6.0
Heater	28.1	32.3	35.1	4.8
Thermos	-1.2	-0.9	0.0	4.7

Table 7: Min-entropy Estimates of Accelerometer Sample Distribution for Multiple Volunteer Tests

Movement	Min-Entropy
Volunteer Hand #1	5.5
Volunteer Hand #2	3.9
Volunteer Hand #3	5.4
Volunteer Hand #4	5.8
Volunteer Swipe #1	8.5
Volunteer Swipe #2	9.1
Volunteer Swipe #3	8.7
Volunteer Swipe #4	9.1
Sitting Still	4.7
Sitting Shaking	8.5
Walking	10.9
Jogging	11.1

Address Space Randomization for Mobile Devices

Hristo Bojinov
Stanford University
Stanford, CA, USA
hristo@cs.stanford.edu

Dan Boneh
Stanford University
Stanford, CA, USA
dabo@cs.stanford.edu

Rich Cannings
Google, Inc.
Mountain View, CA, USA
richc@google.com

Iliyan Malchev
Google, Inc.
Mountain View, CA, USA
malchev@google.com

ABSTRACT

Address Space Layout Randomization (ASLR) is a defensive technique supported by many desktop and server operating systems. While smartphone vendors wish to make it available on their platforms, there are technical challenges in implementing ASLR on these devices. Pre-linking, limited processing power and restrictive update processes make it difficult to use existing ASLR implementation strategies even on the latest generation of smartphones. In this paper we introduce *retouching*, a mechanism for executable ASLR that requires no kernel modifications and is suitable for mobile devices. We have implemented ASLR for the Android operating system and evaluated its effectiveness and performance. In addition, we introduce *crash stack analysis*, a technique that uses crash reports locally on the device, or in aggregate in the cloud to reliably detect attempts to brute-force ASLR protection. We expect that retouching and crash stack analysis will become standard techniques in mobile ASLR implementations.

Categories and Subject Descriptors

D.4.6 [**Operating Systems**]: Security and Protection

General Terms

Security, Experimentation, Performance

Keywords

ASLR, control flow hijacking, return-to-libc, mobile devices, smartphones, Android

1. INTRODUCTION

Over the last few years Address-Space Layout Randomization (ASLR) has become mainstream, with various levels of support in Linux [25], Windows [20], and Mac OS X

[19]. ASLR randomizes the base points of the stack, heap, shared libraries, and base executables. The goal of ASLR is to make certain classes of control-hijacking attacks more difficult: with executable code residing at unknown locations, garden variety buffer or stack overflow attacks are made significantly harder to develop and execute [14]. In conjunction with OS mechanisms that only allow writing to non-executable memory (e.g. DEP in Windows), ASLR prevents many network-based native code control hijacking attacks from completing [24].

Implementation challenges.

Although there has been much work on implementing and evaluating ASLR for general-purpose PCs, none of the major smartphones currently use it. In principle, the same ASLR techniques should carry over to mobile devices, however there are several practical obstacles that make this difficult. Smartphone operating systems spend considerable effort to minimize boot and application launch time, power consumption, and memory footprint. These optimizations make existing ASLR implementation strategies insufficient. We give two examples for challenges in implementing ASLR in Android:

- The Android OS prelinks shared libraries to speed up the boot process. Prelinking takes place during the build process and results in hard-coded memory addresses written in the library code. This prevents relocating these libraries in process memory. Android also uses a custom dynamic linker that cannot self-relocate at run-time (unlike *ld.so*). Recent attack techniques against ASLR clearly demonstrate the need to randomize the whole process address space, including base executables and shared libraries [18].

- During normal operation the filesystem on the device is mounted read-only for security reasons. This prevents binary editing tools [12] from modifying images on the device or in file-backed memory.

Our contributions.

We propose *retouching*, a novel mechanism for randomizing prelinked code for deployment on mobile devices. Retouching can randomize all executable code including libraries (and prelinked libraries), base executables, and the linker. Unlike traditional ASLR implementations, retouching requires no kernel modifications. We implement the mechanism for Android, evaluate its effectiveness, and measure its impact on performance at build and runtime and on memory footprint. Our conclusion is that retouching is an effective approach to ASLR and is particularly well-suited in situations where performance is an issue, or when there are incentives to avoid kernel changes.

Our second contribution is a cloud-based approach to detecting and preventing ASLR brute-forcing [23]. We introduce *crash stack analysis*, a technique that analyzes crash reports from mobile devices and reliably detects attempts to bypass ASLR by guessing the random offset used on each device. We evaluate crash stack analysis using real crash data as well as simulated attacks, and conclude that the approach can effectively detect attacks and, in addition, can help pinpoint the OS code being targeted.

Brute forcing mobile ASLR can be very effective and difficult to detect locally. By making a *single* attempt on every mobile user the attacker can compromise 1/256 of mobile devices (assuming 8 bits for ASLR randomness as in Windows). Given the billions of phones in use, this fraction gives the attacker control of a large number of devices.

In the rest of the paper, Sections 2 and 3 give some background information on ASLR and the Android OS, Section 4 presents the threat model that we address with our design and implementation in Section 5. Section 6 evaluates the implementation and discusses it in the context of other related and future work. Section 7 introduces crash stack analysis and evaluates its effectiveness. Sections 8 and 9 discuss future and related work, and Section 10 concludes.

2. OVERVIEW OF ADDRESS-SPACE RANDOMIZATION

Before discussing our system we first survey traditional strategies for implementing ASLR and their limitations on Android. The first ASLR implementation, PaX [25], was designed for Linux. Subsequently, ASLR was implemented in Windows Vista and Mac OS X. We briefly describe these implementations focusing primarily on user-space randomization (as opposed to kernel randomization, which is a separate topic).

2.1 PaX

PaX implements ASLR by generating three different random offsets (delta values) that apply to different areas of the address space:

- **delta_mmap** controls the randomization of areas allocated via mmap(), which includes shared libraries, as well as the main executable when compiled and linked as an ET_DYN ELF file

- **delta_exec** is the offset of the base executable, followed by the heap, when the base executable is of type ET_EXEC (not position-independent)

- **delta_stack** is the offset for the user-space stack

PaX ASLR is complemented by data and stack execution prevention logic. While several elements of PaX are applicable to Android, the technique for randomizing the location of shared libraries and the dynamic linker is not: most shared libraries are prelinked and mapped to specific locations when built, and the dynamic linker is unable to self-relocate.

2.2 Windows

Following the implementation of DEP (Data Execution Prevention: marking the stack and heap as non-execute) in Windows XP SP2, Microsoft implemented ASLR in Windows Vista. The two mechanisms work together to prevent control-flow hijacking attacks (such as return-to-libc), as well as injected code from being executed on the stack or heap. In the Windows ASLR implementation, executable code randomization happens on every reboot, when a global image offset is selected randomly out of 256 possibilities. Additionally, every process is launched with an individually randomized stack, heap, and Process Environment Block (PEB) [26]. The 8 bits of entropy used for selecting the offsets renders the Windows ASLR implementation vulnerable to guessing attacks [23], but is still better than no randomization at all.

Adopting the Windows ASLR approach directly in Android would increase boot time of the device substantially by eliminating library prelinking.

2.3 Mac OS X

Apple introduced ASLR in the Leopard release of Mac OS X. Currently, OS X only randomizes the offsets of shared libraries. This randomization is performed at the time libraries are prelinked, effectively prelinking them at a different address on each system. In addition to ASLR, the operating system protects stack and heap data from being executed (heap protection is only available for 64-bit binaries) [19, 15].

Retouching, the technique we have developed, is conceptually similar to randomization during prelinking. The additional benefits of retouching are in significantly reducing the amount of work performed on the target device by performing the prelinking during the build process and retaining the minimum information needed for randomization. Additionally, no ELF manipulation code needs to be installed on the target.

3. OVERVIEW OF ANDROID

Android [1] is an operating system for mobile devices developed by Google, Inc. While Android borrows much platform code from other open-source operating systems, its security model was built from the start with the assumption that the device will be running a variety of untrusted (or partially trusted) applications. A manifestation of this approach is the execution of each installed application in a separate process running under a unique user identifier (UID): any damage that the application can cause will be contained within the resources that are dedicated to this UID—disjoint from those of any other UID or application.

Android is built on top of the Linux kernel. The system includes many device drivers and native system libraries, including a customized implementation of libc. Applications in Android are written in Java and execute in a virtual machine called Dalvik, in the form of Dalvik bytecode. After boot, the system runs many services (such as the media service, telephony service) each in its own process and having a unique UID.

An important Android process, called *zygote*, is used to speed-up application launch. The zygote is initialized at boot time with commonly used shared libraries, application frameworks, and the Dalvik virtual machine. When the user launches an application the zygote forks and the requested

Relocation Type	Count
local	139837
external	28480

Table 1: Local vs. external relocations in a typical release build of the platform (all prelinked libraries). Removing local relocations by pre-linking saves space and reduces library load time.

Prelinking	Trial 1	Trial 2	Trial 3
enabled	57.2s	57.6s	57.5s
disabled	60.7s	60.9s	60.3s

Table 2: The effect of prelinking on boot time of the HTC Magic (about 3 seconds, or 5% on average).

application runs in the forked process. Since most resources are already loaded in the zygote, the application can immediately begin executing. The zygote architecture implies that with stack and heap randomization during process launch all applications launched on the phone inherit the same randomization parameters.

Prelinking using apriori.

One notable extension at the platform level is the prelinking mechanism implemented by the *apriori* tool. In dynamic linking, relocations are contents (addresses) in a binary object file which need to be adjusted upon loading the binary in memory. Apriori is a Google-built prelinker which resolves local relocations (relocations that refer to code in the same object) in native shared libraries, and pins the libraries to specific memory offsets. The prelinking happens after library objects are compiled and linked, but before they are stripped of unnecessary sections. Apriori looks at the relocations listed for each prelinked library, and resolves those that are local (i.e. not referencing other libraries)—removing them from the relocation section of the library.

Table 1 shows that local relocations comprise the majority of relocation entries in prelinked libraries, and Table 2 demonstrates the impact of prelinking on boot time of the device—a 5% improvement (the Eclair branch of the code base was used for this comparison). While removing relocations also contributes to a reduced filesystem image and relieves demand for main memory, the main goal of prelinking was to speed up the boot process. The impact of prelinking on individual application launch is smaller, because much of that cost is absorbed when the zygote is started.

Prelinking in Android offers clear benefits, but at the same time it prevents standard implementations of ASLR which rely exclusively on randomizing library locations at load time. Prelinked libraries contain hard coded memory addresses and cannot be relocated. When the dynamic linker loads a prelinked file, it uses a provided hard coded address as the location of the library in memory instead of selecting an available address in the regular shared library load area (Table 4). Android does not use the standard Linux dynamic linker (*ld.so*), and instead has a simpler implementation that is mapped to a fixed location in memory.

Software updates.

The Android platform has a built-in mechanism for over-the-air (OTA) software updates, comprising the following components:

- Scripts for packaging over-the-air updates, invoked from *build/ tools/ releasetools/ ota_from_target_files*; the resulting package includes a list of instructions in the Edify language—these instructions are executed during the update on the target device;

- The *updater* binary, which is statically linked, and executed on the handset while in recovery mode; the source code is located under *bootable/recovery/updater*.

4. THREAT MODEL

The primary goal of ASLR is to make remote exploitation difficult. ASLR is not designed to protect against a malicious application already on the phone. To see why, recall that shared libraries are loaded at the same memory location for all processes in the system. Hence, a malicious application can determine the memory location of libc, and use that information to mount a return-to-libc attack on another process. ASLR cannot prevent this. Consequently, in evaluating the security of our proposal we only consider remote attackers who do not already have a foothold on the phone. More precisely, we use the following threat model.

In-scope threats.

Our goal is to prevent network attackers from exploiting vulnerable network-facing services.

- **Network attackers** have the ability to send arbitrary packets to any open port on the device, as well as receive responses. A malicious website and a nearby rogue access point are potential network attackers.

- **Network-facing services** can have exploitable vulnerabilities such as buffer and stack overruns. These can result in either code injection or return-to-libc exploits, and ASLR aims to prevent the latter. Examples of such vulnerabilities would include a rogue SMS packet [16] or a malicious video that targets a codec flaw.

Out-of-scope threats.

In the context of Android we do not address the case of malicious applications (executed by the Dalvik VM) attempting to attack other processes on the system. The UID-based compartmentalization mechanism in Android is specifically intended to sandbox applications and limit the impact they can have on the system overall. We point out that Dalvik applications have access to native libraries (via JNI), and thus to the randomization offsets that have been applied in the system.

5. DESIGN AND IMPLEMENTATION

The Android environment prevents existing approaches to ASLR. Our goal is to design a new light-weight ASLR strategy that is well suited for constrained environments of this type. Our approach applies equally well to other mobile operating systems.

5.1 Background

Modern compilers like GCC can generate code which is position-independent (PIC). PIC object files have all of their location-sensitive offsets listed in *relocation sections*: these lists are later used to "fix" the library to a location at load time. Shared libraries built with PIC code can be linked as ET_DYN ELF objects, which means that they can be loaded at arbitrary addresses. In Linux, *ld.so* is a special shared library (an ET_DYN object itself) which is responsible for dynamically linking any other libraries that must be loaded into a process. Notably *ld.so* is able to relocate itself, which is not trivial to implement.

In contrast to shared libraries, base executable files are often built as ET_EXEC objects, which must be loaded at a specific location known during the link process. On some platforms base executables can also be linked as ET_DYN, which makes it possible to load them at an arbitrary location in the process address space. Such executable objects are referred to as PIE (position-independent executables).

Effects of prelinking.

In the absence of any prelinking, position-independent (ET_DYN) ELF objects can be loaded at arbitrary locations in the process address space: this is the general idea in PaX. In contrast, for Android:

- Shared libraries are PIC, but the majority of them are prelinked to specific addresses.

- Base executables are compiled as PIC, but not linked as PIE.

- The dynamic linker is linked at a fixed address because it is simpler than *ld.so* and is not able to relocate itself.

On the one hand, the extensive use of PIC code in the platform comes at a minimal cost to performance due to the extensive prelinking performed. On the other hand, PIC code allows for easier patching of software: only the modules affected by a bug fix need to be recompiled, and all the rest can simply be prelinked again, lowering the risk of introducing new bugs in an incremental update.

5.2 Design Idea

For a base executable object that was compiled to be PIC, linking to a fixed base address consists of resolving primarily internal relocations (usually in the GOT section) using that fixed address and removing the entries from the relocation table; for shared libraries, prelinking has a similar effect (Figure 1), outlined in Section 3.

We now make three important observations. First, PIC binaries can be rebased even after prelinking. At prelinking time we can save the address of all locations where apriori inserted hardcoded addresses (this is exactly the set of local relocations). Then, to shift the binary to a new location we can loop over the list of addresses and add the ASLR random offset to the contents at each of them.

Second, binaries can be trivially reverted to their original state to support software updates. This is necessary in the case of incremental updates, where the hashes of patched files are checked to ensure the device being updated has the expected build. To revert randomization, we simply overwrite the contents at the known locations in each file with their known, build-time contents.

Third, randomization is possible at software update time (rather than on every boot or process restart). This enables a light-weight, user-space implementation, and in Section 6 we argue that the loss in terms of security is small.

Retouching design.

Based on the observations made earlier, the process of *retouching* is spread over all stages of building and deploying a software update. During a build, we retain some of the relocation data that is normally lost after the build completes (file offsets and, for convenience, a copy of the original contents at those offsets). The data is retained in a separate area at the end of each binary. When packaging OTA updates, the retained relocation data is still in the executable files; in addition, the OTA update script now includes a command which explicitly applies randomization (or derandomization if desired) to all relevant files. Finally, when the OTA update script is run on each target device, randomization (or derandomization) is executed.

During normal device boot there are no execution flow changes: the affected binary objects are simply loaded to their randomized addresses instead of the nominal addresses that were used in the original build.

5.3 Implementation

In order to assess the feasibility of retouching we have implemented ASLR for the Android platform, and contributed the code to the Android Open Source Project (AOSP). We start with a discussion of shared libraries, and then expand to base executables and the dynamic linker.

Shared libraries.

Randomizing libraries during software updates is preferable because it does not eliminate the performance gains offered by prelinking in the first place. In addition, update time randomization is performed in recovery mode in which the main operating system image is not locked and can be safely modified.

The randomization process consists of the following four steps:

Step 1: Keeping track of relocation lists.

Prelinking in the Android platforms involves resolving internal relocations for each shared library (Table 1). Subsequently, during randomization these previously resolved relocations must be adjusted (retouched) by the difference

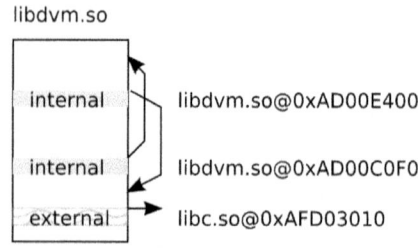

Figure 1: Prelinking resolves internal relocations while leaving external ones intact.

Record Type	Format	Description
2 bytes	$1S_2C_{13}$	2-bit offset (4, 8, 12, 16) 13-bit content delta (signed)
3 bytes	$01S_2C_{20}$	2-bit offset (see above) 20-bit content delta (signed)
8 bytes	$00S_{30}C_{32}$	absolute offset, max $2^{30} - 1$ absolute contents (4 bytes)

Table 3: The three record formats used in retouch file compression.

between the "default" prelink location of the library and the new, randomized location.

By the end of the platform build process, relocations that have been prelinked are stripped from the final shared library files. In order for retouching to succeed during a device update, we must have the list of relocations available at that time. We achieve this by modifying *apriori*, the Android prelinker, to output a list of file offsets that have been prelinked. For each library, this list is stored at the end of the target binary file.

Step 2: Compressing retouch data.

Even though we only need to keep a small amount of data for each prelinked relocation (a file offset, and contents at that offset), the aggregate size of retouch data ends up being substantial. We came up with a simple variable record size encoding in order to minimize the size of the OTA update package and the amount of additional space required on the device.

Each prelinked relocation is nominally eight bytes in size: a four-byte file offset, and four bytes of original contents. In our compression scheme, each relocation corresponds to a 2, 3, or 8-byte record, essentially implementing a form of Huffman encoding based on the following observations:

- Relocation offsets and contents are 4-byte aligned.

- Relocation offsets are output in order and tend to be clustered closely together.

- Relocation contents also tend to exhibit proximity, but to a lesser degree.

Specifically a 2-byte record will be used for a relocation if it is located within 4 to 16 bytes from the previous one, and has contents within $2^{12} - 1$ in absolute value. A 3-byte record will be used if the relocation is located within 4 to 16 bytes, with contents that differ by no more than $2^{19} - 1$. As a fallback, the relocation can use up a full 8 bytes, with the most significant two bits of the offset used to indicate this type of record (limiting the file size of shared libraries to $2^{30} - 1$ bytes). Record formats are specified in Table 3. Compression reduces the amount of space needed for retained relocation data by approximately 60%.

Step 3: OTA update file generation.

After the build is complete, the OTA update file is generated, and we ensure that an instruction to retouch all binaries is always included. Alternatively, the instruction can be to undo retouching (in case derandomization is required for some reason).

Step 4: OTA deployment on target device.

OTA updates are executed on Android phones in the following steps: reboot into recovery mode, check filesystem digest (only in incremental updates), extract files from update package (zip), reboot into the updated main image.

In our implementation, randomization involves on-device modification of all shared library files. As a consequence, for incremental updates we have to mask the randomization so that the filesystem digest check will succeed. This is why every list of retouch entries contains the prelinked relocation offsets **and** original contents at those locations: before computing a digest of the software image the update script can restore in memory each binary to its original state. Another benefit of this approach is evident during randomization: retouch data is never modified, and should randomization be interrupted in the middle, the process can simply be rerun, generating a new randomization offset and overwriting any modified shared library contents. (In reality, this process is a bit more complicated due to flash filesystem unreliability that goes beyond what is normally seen with a hard-disk based filesystems. For brevity, we skip the details here.)

With ASLR, software update proceeds as follows (randomization-related steps are in bold):

- The device is booted in recovery mode.

- (Incremental updates only) **After masking randomization in memory,** a digest of the existing contents of each patched file is checked against the digest included in the update. The update proceeds only if there is a match: this ensures that an incremental update will only be applied to the appropriate build it was created against.

- Files are extracted from the update and copied to their destinations, for example in the */system* directory. (This includes shared libraries about to be retouched.)

- **Retouch data are used to randomize the prelinked relocations in specified binaries (all prelinked shared libraries in the first release of retouching, and eventually all binaries). First, a random offset is generated, then used to shift all the binaries.**

- The device can now be rebooted into the new, updated software build.

Randomizing the base executables and dynamic linker.

Base executable offset randomization is possible by porting existing functionality e.g. from the PaX project, however this is challenging for a number of practical reasons.

Firstly, Android executables are not readily linked as ET_DYN ELF objects, but rather are of the ET_EXEC type (in other words, even though the code is position independent via the "-pic" compiler option, the resulting executables are not position independent); retouching allows us to navigate around this hurdle.

Second, implementing the PaX shadow copy technique for ET_EXEC binaries would require kernel changes difficult to open-source for the ARM architecture, while all the changes we introduce are in user-space and in the platform build system.

The third, and last obstacle is that the Linux dynamic linker *ld.so* is randomized in PaX via changing the mmap base. In contrast, the Android linker is much simpler and must exist at a predefined address in memory, fixed at build time. Here once again retouching comes to the rescue.

Our implementation of retouching for base executable and linker address randomization requires two separate builds of each executable, and proceeds in the following steps:

- Perform a build to the default base address (0x8000 for executables, and 0xB0000100 for the linker).

- Save the output binary.

- Perform a build to a new base address (e.g. 0xFF8000, and 0xB0FF0100 for the linker).

- Run the *retouch-bindiff* tool on the two builds of the same binary, which outputs a list of retouch entries that can be appended to the binary.

- (During OTA update) Retouch using the binary file generated at build time. Same approach as the one used for libraries.

The *retouch-bindiff* tool simply takes two input files and finds the 4-byte file records that differ, outputting their offsets and contents. The tool also performs a sanity check to ensure that the provided base offset difference (0xFF0000 for the examples above) is exactly equal to the difference at each record. In our experiments, out of all the executables present on the Eclair branch of AOSP the sanity check failed only for the *debuggerd* binary, which has some base offset-dependent data compiled in. This executable serves to gather crash data from the device, and can easily be excluded from randomization without introducing vulnerability in the system.

In its current form *retouch-bindiff* cab be impacted by changes in compilation flags or implementation. For example, if different types of relocations are created during compilation, the tool may not be able to generate the correct type of retouch entry. Ideally, base executable and dynamic linker randomization should be implemented by retaining relocation data during the linking stage and converting that to retouch entries, eliminating any guesswork and the inconvenience of double compilation introduced by *retouch-bindiff*.

5.4 Sources of Randomness

When we generate a random offset during the update process, we use two sources of randomness. The first one is /dev/random, which contains random bits saved across reboots. Note that randomization happens during software update, which means that the device has been operational for some period of time and has been able to collect some entropy.

The second source of randomness we use is system time. While time is not truly random, the clock reading during updates will tend to be random across the population of devices (Android phones will not automatically reboot when an update is being deployed by the carrier). This means, that without prior knowledge of the attacked device, the low-order bits of the system time during the last update will look random to the attacker.

The general problem of gathering entropy on mobile devices is a topic that has received attention on its own, and [13] evaluates several approaches. Randomization during device manufacture is also a possibility which can be explored in the future.

6. EVALUATION

To evaluate our new approach to ASLR we discuss the amount of work to mount a brute-force guessing attack, the additional storage requirements on the device, and the negligible impact on performance.

6.1 Guessing Attacks

Existing ASLR implementations randomize offsets at boot or run-time. Our retouching approach randomizes offsets only at system update time. We briefly argue that from the point of view of the attacker this difference has minimal impact — it only makes a brute force guessing attack easier by a factor of 2 in expectation.

Consider a randomization space of size N (in other words, the number of different offsets for the target executable code post-randomization is N). If the randomization offset is constantly updated at boot or run-time then an attacker making random guesses at the randomization value will need N random attempts in expectation before making a correct guess.

With randomization at install time and during software update (which is less frequent than boot-time randomization), the attacker is **guaranteed** to succeed after N attempts, and is expected to succeed in $(N + 1)/2$ attempts. This factor of 2 is the result of the difference between *sampling with replacement* and *sampling without replacement*.

Randomizing during software updates has a number of advantages over run-time randomization. First, it is less likely to corrupt the device because it happens in a simple "recovery boot" environment in which platform executables can be safely written. In addition, the kernel need not get involved in this process, and the boot time savings that prelinking affords can be preserved (i.e., no additional run-time relocation is necessary).

Entropy.

In our initial implementation we limit ourselves to 10 bits of entropy for each base address (executable, prelinked libraries), and 8 bits for the dynamic linker. We do this because of space constraints and to ensure system stability; the number of bits used can be revised in the future. Table 4 shows the default address space layout of an Android process, along with the maximum randomization offset that we add or subtract. In Table 5 we show the significant bits of the offsets generated by the randomization code over several uploads of an ASLR-enabled package. In the actual retouching, these offsets are multiplied by 4096 for shared libraries and base binaries and 256 for the dynamic linker.

6.2 Storage Impact

We require 426KB of space to store randomization data for shared libraries in /system/lib (averaging about 3.3 bytes per relocation entry). For comparison, the actual libraries take up 24.63MB on disk, and thus the storage overhead is less than 2%. Table 6 summarizes these numbers against a non-prelinked, non-retouched baseline build.

Area Purpose	Location	Randomization
executable	0x00000000	+ 0x003FF000
stacks	0x10000000	
mmap	0x40000000	
shared libraries	0x80000000	
prelinked libraries	0x9A100000	- 0x003FF000
linker	0xB0000100	+ 0x0000FF00
thread 0 stack	0xB0100000	
kernel	0xC0000000	

Table 4: Default address space layout in Android. Note that the prelinked library area is offset downward, to avoid overlapping with the linker (we can do this because addresses from 0x90000000 to 0xB0000000 are dedicated to prelinked libraries).

Run #	Value (10 bits)	Run #	Value (10 bits)
1	0011000011	7	1001101001
2	1010010101	8	1000011000
3	1100011100	9	1110100000
4	1101100100	10	1001001011
5	1010000001	11	1010010001
6	0011111101	12	0011110110

Table 5: Randomization offsets generated by using /dev/random and the current time.

The impact of retouching on OTA update package size is smaller than that on the filesystem (250KB added), and incremental updates (which are typically used) will be substantially less impacted because only changed binaries need to have their retouch data patched, and that can also be done incrementally.

We estimate that if base executables and the dynamic linker are to be retouched, there will be about 52K additional retouch entries, which would add approximately 170KB to the space required in the OTA update and the filesystem, bringing the total storage overhead to 0.8MB.

6.3 Performance Impact

The impact of retouch file generation on build time is negligible. OTA updates take 10 additional seconds to retouch (randomize) shared libraries, and after that there is no performance impact at boot or run-time.

7. DETECTING ASLR ATTACKS: CRASH STACK ANALYSIS

The difficulty of brute-forcing ASLR implementations has been studied extensively: Shacham et al. [23] demonstrate

Build Type	/system/lib Size (MB)	OTA Size (MB)
regular	25.63	40.96
prelinked (default)	24.63	40.75
prelinked and retouched	25.35	41.01

Table 6: Storage space impact of prelinking and retouching vs. a regular, non-prelinked build.

No ASLR (@-0)		ASLR (@744)	
Offset	Result	Offset	Result
0	correct	744	correct
1	crash (pc@-28)	745	crash (pc@-28)
2	crash (pc@-1)	746	crash (pc@-1)
3	crash (fr#2@6)	747	crash (fr#2@6)
4	crash (lr@4)	748	crash (lr@4)
5	infinite loop	749	infinite loop
6	crash (lr@-6)	750	crash (lr@-6)
7	stack corrupt	751	stack corrupt
8	crash (pc@-1)	752	crash (pc@-1)
9	crash (pc@-1)	753	crash (pc@-1)
10	crash (pc@9)	754	crash (pc@9)

Table 7: Results of simulated attack attempting to call exit(). The nominal (non-randomized) location was 0xAFD1977D. The crash results indicate the reported location of the PC, LR, or stack frame #2 return address compared to the target address for the exec() function, thus for example "pc@-28" means that at the time of the crash the PC contained the attempted jump address minus 28.

how a process can be derandomized relatively quickly on a 32-bit OS with PaX enabled. While 64-bit address spaces make it harder to crack randomization, the fundamental concern about how much each element of the address space is randomized remains valid. In addition, 64-bit addresses are simply not available on many platforms that are of interest today and in the foreseeable future, including most that run the Android OS.

For massively deployed, networked platforms there is an additional risk. An attacker who chooses to keep a low profile can try to guess the randomization offset of a target device only once. While most of the time the guess will be unsuccessful, about $1/2^n$ of the targets will be compromised, where n is the number of bits of randomness introduced. For example if $n = 8$, one out of every 256 devices will be compromised, which can be a significant number.

We chose to tackle the problem of ASLR brute-forcing by focusing on detection by the OS. In related work, segvguard [21] attempts to do this in a very basic way by throttling the rate at which a process can be restarted on a single machine. The key observation is that brute-forcing inevitably leads to a significant number of process crashes before the attack succeeds. Importantly, we expect that the crash patterns are mostly invariant to relocation: library code crashes in a similar way regardless of where the target library is relocated. This insight leads to a detection algorithm which is much more reliable than the one used by segvguard, and which can also be applied in a centralized manner to detect low-profile brute-forcing attempts.

When a process crashes, it does so at a specific address of the program counter (PC). It is reasonable to expect that during unsuccessful ASLR brute-forcing attempts the address of the crash will be closely related to the guessed address of the jump. For example, if the function being exploited is at the non-randomized address 0xAD000000 and we guess incorrectly that it has been randomized to 0xAD002000, we expect the crash to happen with a PC value close to 0xAD002000. The reasoning is that we can only execute a few instructions at a random position in memory without triggering a segmentation violation. Even more frequently the crash will be immediate due to an attempt to execute instructions from a non-executable memory page. It turns out that this idea is applicable to the ARM architecture if we also take into account the link register (LR) which commonly holds the return address when leaf functions are executed (this optimization avoids having to access the stack when making most leaf function calls). In our tests, during most ASLR brute-forcing crashes one of the two registers contains an address which is very close to the one that was guessed (Table 7).

Crash address traces.

In order to detect ASLR brute-forcing, we collected crash reports, and grouped crash addresses (PC and LR values) by their least significant 12 bits into *traces*. For every trace we counted the number of *distinct* addresses with the intuition that large traces will be present exactly when an attack is in progress. Our experiments confirm this (Section 7.2).

Android tombstones.

The Android runtime environment creates a crash dump file (called a *tombstone*) each time a process in the system exits abnormally. In addition, customer devices can report crashes to central servers, making a limited amount of information available for analysis (this information is retained only for a short time). We use these mechanisms to evaluate our crash stack analysis technique.

no ASLR		ASLR (-2)	ASLR (-8)
0	0xAFD1977D	2	8
1	0xAFD1A77D	3	
2	0xAFD1B77D	4	
3	0xAFD1C77D	5	
4	0xAFD1D77D	6	
5	0xAFD1E77D	7	
6	0xAFD1F77D	8	
7	0xAFD2077D		
8	0xAFD2177D		

Figure 2: **An attack guessing the same address over multiple randomized devices will manifest itself as crashes at the same offset on multiple pages: one long trace due to the frequency of immediate crashes at the called address. In this case, the attacker jumps to address 0xAFD1977D, and crashes at 0xAFD1B77C and 0xAFD2177C are observed on the two randomized devices on the right, after the PC in each report is derandomized. An attack making different guesses will create multiple long traces, each matching a particular crash behavior such as "pc@-28" or "lr@4" (not shown), in addition to the most frequent "pc@-1" behavior.**

7.1 Evaluation via Simulated Attacks

We wrote a small piece of simulated attack code which attempts to execute the `exit()` function from `libc` by guessing its randomization offset. A successful run is one which produces the supplied exit code. We executed the attack code on a non-randomized system as well as on several randomized instances. Representative results are shown in Table 7. Clearly crash address patterns are retained across randomization, yielding identical crash offsets relative to the guessed address during brute-forcing. The pigeonhole principle implies that if a sufficient number of devices are attacked (e.g. a multiple of the size of the randomization space—several thousand in our case), we are guaranteed to see a long crash trace for at least one page offset: an attacker has no apriori information about the randomization at each device, so his guess about the address of the target code will be spread over the whole space of randomization offsets, *when taken relative to the randomization of each device* (see the example in Figure 2, based on the data in Table 7). This holds even when the attacker is making exactly the same guess across all target devices (a "normal" process crash will rarely, if ever, behave this way: the crash location will be consistently offset from the randomization base).

7.2 Evaluation Using Real Crash Reports

In order to estimate the likelihood of false positives generated by our crash analysis algorithm, we used the set of all 6805 crash reports (from close to 5000 different devices), generated by the `system_server` process on a specific build of the Android operating system. These reports did not contain any identifying information—in fact, the only data available was the program counter (PC), link register (LR), and return addresses in all stack frames at the time of the crash.

Our main goal was to confirm that in normal execution (without ASLR or brute-forcing attacks) crash address traces are short, and thus easily distinguished from those expected in attack scenarios. The longest trace we found had a length of 4 (Table 8), while any successful attack that attempts to brute-force the current ASLR implementation will inevitably create a trace of size close to 1024 (the number of different randomization offsets used in our implementation) over a relatively small number of attacked devices. Thus, crash address trace size is an excellent indicator that can be used to detect ASLR derandomization attempts.

7.3 Implementation Notes

In our experiments we have evaluated crash stack analysis deployed as a cloud service which can continually monitor crash reports from user devices, grouping the reports by device ID, process name, and build number, and looking for telltale crash address traces.

Local detection.

Crash stack analysis can be also run locally on a device, in order to detect and immediately block attempted ASLR brute-forcing. Such attempts carry a signature which is distinct from that of a process repeatedly crashing on some error condition. In this context, blocking the attack can involve preventing the automatic restart of the crashing process.

In order to implement local detection, the algorithm for building crash address traces needs to be modified. While it may be sufficient to look for process tombstones that match exactly on their 12 least-significant bits but differ on the next 10, looking at *similar* offsets might yield more accurate

Offset (bits 0-11)	Address	Library
0xCF4	0xAC04CCF4	libskia.so
	0xAD012CF4	libdvm.so
	0xAD035CF4	libdvm.so
	0xAD214CF4	libnativehelper.so
0xCB8	0xAD00ECB8	libdvm.so
	0xAD018CB8	libdvm.so
	0xAD041CB8	libdvm.so
0x95C	0xAD00F95C	libdvm-ARM.so
	0xAD01395C	libdvm.so
	0xAD3EB95C	libandroid_runtime.so
0x260	0xAC072260	libOpenVG_CM.so
	0xAC08A260	libOpenVG_CM.so
	0xAF90B260	libcutils.so

Table 8: Largest crash address traces, listed by tag, obtained from 6805 actual device crash reports for system_server. Small trace size indicates no ASLR brute-forcing (as expected).

detection. The reason for this is that not all crashes happen at exactly the same distance from the guessed function address (Table 7), and at the same time on a single device it is unlikely that a "regular" crash will exhibit a crash pattern with similar page offsets in a number of different memory pages.

Protecting user privacy.

Central reporting of device information such as crash data, always has the potential of violating user privacy. In Android, there are several safeguards: first, crash reports contain only a minimum amount of data necessary to identify the location of the problem: register and stack contents, and minimal memory contents pointed to by *instruction* registers such as LR and PC in ARM. Second, reports are only retained for a small amount of time, on the order of days. Finally, access to reports is highly restricted even within the Android team. Crash stack analysis can work within the existing privacy safeguards, without the need to disclose any additional device or user information.

Reacting to attacks.

The primary use of crash stack analysis is to identify attacks that are in progress—almost in real time. There could be a variety of responses to such attacks: from quickly finding and patching the root cause (the vulnerability which made the brute-force ASLR attack possible in the first place), to restricting device access at the network level with the cooperation of carriers, or even alerting potentially affected users.

8. EXTENSIONS AND LIMITATIONS

We briefly mention a few extensions of the retouch approach and some limitations which may encourage further work.

Same random offset across processes.

A limitation of all major ASLR implementations to date [17] including ours, is that all processes on a single device have the same shared library layout. This is necessary to not

effect system performance. To exploit this limitation, however, the attacker must already have a foothold on the device, which is not the intended threat model for ASLR.

Not using ELF utilities.

Retouching can be performed by retaining all relocation information for shared libraries and prelinking at update time. At that time base executables could also be linked at a randomized address. However, the space overhead of such implementation would be substantial, due to the larger (uncompressed) size of relocation sections and the need to include ELF libraries and a linker in the updater binary. The added complexity would also be significant as there would have to be a method for undoing the randomization to accommodate future incremental updates.

Non-prelinked libraries and mmap randomization.

While our retouching technique is applicable to non-prelinked shared libraries, randomization for this area of memory is best achieved via the PaX approach: by randomizing the mmap base. This protection is already in place, and also extends to file data mapped by processes. Additionally, the majority of shared libraries in Android are already prelinked, and the expectation is that with time non-prelinked libraries will become increasingly rare.

Recent advances in attack techniques, such as JIT spraying [4], have cast new doubts about the effectiveness of ASLR in preventing exploits. We note that randomization of the mmap region in the process address space effectively neutralizes such concerns: the Dalvik VM uses a small mmap'ed area to store executable JIT output, and thus inherits the benefits of randomization.

8.1 Heap and Stack Randomization

So far we focused on randomization of executable memory because the heap and stack areas of a process are already randomized via traditional techniques. For example, the Android kernel already performs stack randomization for each process. Heap randomization is performed by either randomizing the location of brk or by modifying *malloc()* to allocate space randomly. Additional pointer protection features have been available for several years, both in allocator implementations and as compile-time options [6]. Android uses dlmalloc which offers some overflow protection for allocated chunks, and ProPolice [9] which compiles the use of stack canaries into native binaries.

Stack randomization in userspace.

Since retouching requires only userspace OS modifications, we also explored userspace techniques for stack randomization. One approach is to modify the code in bionic/ linker/arch/arm/begin.S used as a prologue in the linker binary. This code normally invokes *linker_init()*, which in turn loads the base executable and returns its address. We modified this prologue code in begin.S to add a random number of harmless additional lines to the process environment strings before invoking the dynamic linker. The resulting executable prologue looks as follows:

```
_start:
        /* BEGIN RANDOMIZATION CODE */
        mov     r0, sp
        mov     r2, sp
```

```
        sub     r2, r2, <RAND>
aslr_args:
        ldr     r1, [r0]
        str     r1, [r2]
        add     r0, r0, #4
        add     r2, r2, #4
        cmp     r1, #0
        bne     aslr_args
        sub     sp, sp, <RAND>
        /* add more env[] strings */
        adr     r1, ASLR_ENV_PAD
aslr_pad:
        str     r1, [r2]
        add     r2, r2, #4
        cmp     r2, r0
        bne     aslr_pad
        /* END RANDOMIZATION CODE */

        /* original code */
        mov     r0, sp
        mov     r1, #0
        bl      __linker_init

        /* linker init returns the
           _entry address in the
           main image */
        mov     pc, r0

        .globl ASLR_ENV_PAD
ASLR_ENV_PAD:
        .ascii "ASLR_ENV_PAD=1\0"
```

Since the environment is on the stack, this has the effect of shifting the process stack by a small, random number of bytes (note that here we don't specify the source of randomness; <RAND> stands for a register that holds a random value, perhaps based on the current time and/or stack contents). We verified that with this change, using an arbitrary 4-byte aligned random offset, the system boots successfully and process stacks are shifted down as expected. The drawback of performing this type of stack randomization is that the added offset can only be relatively small—on the order of hundreds or thousands of bytes, and thus may not prevent some buffer-overrun attacks. The existing kernel implementation is more robust as it randomizes the more significant bits in the stack location while it also does not waste physical memory.

Applicability to other platforms.

Since most code running on Android devices is written in Java, and thus not vulnerable to buffer-overflow attacks, mobile ASLR is even more applicable to platforms that run primarily native applications, such as iOS. While we have used Android to develop and demonstrate our approach, we expect broader adoption across the different smartphone ecosystems.

9. RELATED WORK

For real impact on security, ASLR must be deployed in conjunction with protections against injecting and executing code on the system. Our work is complementary to current work on write-protecting executable pages in Android.

In spirit, retouching is related to Address Space Layout

Permutation (ASLP), proposed in [12]. ASLP performs modifications on base executable files at launch time by using the retained relocation section in each executable. However, for shared libraries, ASLP defaults to the standard kernel-based approach of *mmap()* randomization, without performing any fine-grained permutation of code. This approach cannot work in Android due to prelinking of shared libraries. Our retouching approach can randomize shared libraries and works well with prelinking, without requiring any kernel modifications or executable file editing at runtime; in addition, retouching addresses the randomization of the smaller, non-self-relocating dynamic linker in Android called `linker`.

Retouching is also conceptually similar to the Windows utility `rebase` [2], which allows a user to manually move the starting offset of an executable or DLL file by executing relocation in advance. However `rebase` has no facility for supporting software updates, prelinked libraries, or randomization. The relevance of `rebase` has declined once Windows implemented ASLR.

In related work, *address obfuscation* has been proposed as a way to achieve higher levels of randomization, beyond those achievable in ASLR [3]. Similar to address obfuscation, retouching starts during build time and completes at install. In contrast to it, retouching does not involve any complicated transformations on the code or data sections. This should result in lower overall risk at deployment as well as possibly better performance, since shifting the whole executable object by a multiple of the CPU page size is generally expected to have no impact on caching. A similar technique called *code islands* has been proposed, targeting large multithreaded server deployments [27].

Randomization can reach beyond the layout of a single, user-space process. The kernel stack can be also randomized, as well as system calls [5] and even the CPU instruction set [11]. Retouching is complementary to all of these mechanisms, providing an efficient, effective, and simple way to reduce the attack surface of processes.

A different thread of work has investigated control-flow hijacking prevention in embedded devices lacking modern CPU capabilities such as a MMU [10]. We note that in their architecture smartphones are more similar to desktop PCs than simple microcontroller-based devices. In this sense, desktop-grade protection techniques are more relevant to our work.

Privilege escalation techniques have also been explored in the context of Android inter-process communication via the Intent mechanism [7]. Our work is inherently at a lower level in the stack, however ASLR can still help prevent applications from being exploited through native code vulnerabilities, thus closing some of the possible routes to abuse.

Finally, ASLR has been evaluated in the past, and often found to have limited effectiveness [23], or to be poorly implemented [15, 8]. Shacham's Return-Oriented Programming technique [22] demonstrates that preventing code injection offers little protection on its own; in addition, return-oriented programming can be used when some executable pages are left non-randomized—this highlights the need to randomize all binary code in the system. In Section 7 we show that crash stack analysis can be used to rapidly detect and block ASLR brute-forcing. At the same time, control over all the shipping native code in Android makes complete randomization of the process address space feasible; this will help avoid many of the mistakes or omissions made by early ASLR implementations for the desktop.

10. CONCLUSION

This paper introduces a new technique for implementing ASLR, which is particularly well-suited to the constraints imposed by modern consumer-oriented mobile devices. Our approach, called retouching, can randomize the location of all native executable code without kernel modifications, and without erasing the savings in boot time afforded by pre-linking. We implemented retouching-based ASLR on the Android platform, and evaluated its impact on the system: from building to OTA updates and execution. We also developed and evaluated crash stack analysis, a technique for detecting ASLR brute-forcing attempts which is the only one we are aware of that uses crash address information to reliably detect targeted attacks. We conclude that retouching, in combination with crash stack analysis, is a robust ASLR implementation, resilient to brute-force derandomization.

11. REFERENCES

[1] Android. www.android.com.

[2] Ruediger R. Asche. Rebasing win32 dlls: The whole story, 1995. http://msdn.microsoft.com/en-us/library/ms810432.aspx.

[3] Sandeep Bhatkar, Daniel C. DuVarney, and R. Sekar. Address obfuscation: an efficient approach to combat a broad range of memory error exploits. In *In Proceedings of the 12th USENIX Security Symposium*, pages 105–120, 2003.

[4] Dion Blazakis. Interpreter exploitation: Pointer inference and jit spraying, 2010. http://www.semantiscope.com/research/BHDC2010/BHDC-2010-Paper.pdf.

[5] Monica Chew and Dawn Song. Mitigating buffer overflows by operating system randomization. Technical report, UC Berkeley, 2002.

[6] Crispin Cowan, Steve Beattie, John Johansen, and Perry Wagle. Pointguard™: Protecting pointers from buffer overflow vulnerabilities. In *In Proc. of the 12th Usenix Security Symposium*, 2003.

[7] Lucas Davi, Alexandra Dmitrienko, Ahmad-Reza Sadeghi, and Marcel Winandy. Privilege escalation attacks on android. In *ISC*, pages 346–360, 2010.

[8] Jake Edge. Linux aslr vulnerabilities, 2009. http://lwn.net/Articles/330866/.

[9] Hiroaki Etoh. Gcc extension for protecting applications from stack-smashing attacks, 2005. http://www.research.ibm.com/trl/projects/security/ssp/.

[10] Aurélien Francillon, Daniele Perito, and Claude Castelluccia. Defending embedded systems against control flow attacks. In *SecuCode '09: Proceedings of the first ACM workshop on Secure execution of untrusted code*, pages 19–26, New York, NY, USA, 2009. ACM.

[11] Gaurav S. Kc. Countering code-injection attacks with instruction-set randomization. In *In Proceedings of the ACM Computer and Communications Security (CCS) Conference*, pages 272–280. ACM Press, 2003.

[12] Chongkyung Kil, Jinsuk Jun, Christopher Bookholt, Jun Xu, and Peng Ning. Address space layout permutation (aslp): Towards fine-grained randomization of commodity software. In *ACSAC '06: Proceedings of the 22nd Annual Computer Security Applications Conference*, pages 339–348, Washington, DC, USA, 2006. IEEE Computer Society.

[13] J. Krhovjak, V. Matyas, and J. Zizkovsky. *Generating Random and Pseudorandom Sequences in Mobile Devices*, pages 122–+. Springer, 2009.

[14] David Litchfield. Buffer underruns, dep, aslr and improving the exploitation prevention mechanisms (xpms) on the windows platform, 2005. http://www.ngssoftware.com/papers/xpms.pdf.

[15] Charlie Miller. Owning the fanboys: Hacking mac os x, 2008. http://www.blackhat.com/presentations/bh-jp-08/bh-jp-08-Miller/BlackHat-Japan-08-Miller-Hacking-OSX.pdf.

[16] Charlie Miller. Fuzzing the phone in your phone, 2009. http://www.blackhat.com/presentations/bh-usa-09/MILLER/BHUSA09-Miller-FuzzingPhone-PAPER.pdf.

[17] John Moser. Prelink and address space randomization, 2006. http://lwn.net/Articles/190139/.

[18] Giampaolo Fresi Roglia, Lorenzo Martignoni, Roberto Paleari, and Danilo Bruschi. Surgically returning to randomized lib(c). In *ACSAC '09: Proceedings of the 2009 Annual Computer Security Applications Conference*, pages 60–69, Washington, DC, USA, 2009. IEEE Computer Society.

[19] Clint Ruoho. Aslr: Leopard versus vista, 2008. http://www.laconicsecurity.com/aslr-leopard-versus-vista.html.

[20] Mark Russinovich. Inside the windows vista kernel: Part 3, 2007. http://technet.microsoft.com/en-us/magazine/2007.04.vistakernel.aspx.

[21] segvguard. http://www.daemon-systems.org/man/security.8.html.

[22] Hovav Shacham. The geometry of innocent flesh on the bone: Return-into-libc without function calls (on the x86. In *In Proceedings of the 14th ACM Conference on Computer and Communications Security*, 2007.

[23] Hovav Shacham, Eu jin Goh, Nagendra Modadugu, Ben Pfaff, and Dan Boneh. On the effectiveness of address-space randomization. In *In CCS'04: Proceedings of the 11th ACM Conference on Computer and Communications Security*, pages 298–307. ACM Press, 2004.

[24] Brad Spengler. Pax: The guaranteed end of arbitrary code execution, 2003. http://grsecurity.net/PaX-presentation_files/frame.htm.

[25] The PaX Team. Homepage of the pax team, 2008. http://pax.grsecurity.net/.

[26] Ollie Whitehouse. An analysis of address space layout randomization on windows vista, 2007. http://www.symantec.com/avcenter/reference/Address_Space_Layout_Randomization.pdf.

[27] Haizhi Xu and Steve J. Chapin. Improving address space randomization with a dynamic offset randomization technique. In *SAC '06: Proceedings of the 2006 ACM symposium on Applied computing*, pages 384–391, New York, NY, USA, 2006. ACM.

Short Paper: A new Identity-based DH Key-agreement Protocol for Wireless Sensor Networks Based on the Arazi-Qi Scheme

Isabelle Hang
SAP Research Center
Karlsruhe
Vincenz-Priessnitz-Str. 1
D-76131 Karlsruhe, Germany
isabelle.hang@sap.com

Markus Ullmann
University of Applied Sciences
Bonn Rhine-Sieg & Federal
Office for Information Security
Godesberger Allee 185-189
D-53133 Bonn, Germany
markus.ullmann
@bsi.bund.de

Christian Wieschebrink
Federal Office for
Information Security
Godesberger Allee 185-189
D-53133 Bonn, Germany
christian.wieschebrink
@bsi.bund.de

ABSTRACT

Public key cryptography based on elliptic curves is a promising foundation for energy-scarving pairwise key establishment in wireless sensor networks. Focusing on the Diffie-Hellman key-agreement, identity-based schemes can be applied to provide mechanisms for authentication. The AQ-protocol presented by Arazi et al. introduces such a key establishment supporting fixed as well as ephemeral keys.

In this paper we review two known attacks of the ephemeral key establishment of this protocol. We introduce a new ephemeral key establishment for the AQ-protocol to fix these problems and analyze the proposed approach from a security perspective. We illustrate its feasibility for wireless sensor networks by presenting implementation results for the MICAz platform using TinyOS 2.x.

Categories and Subject Descriptors

E.4 [**Data Encryption**]: Public key cryptosystem

General Terms

Security

Keywords

Wireless sensor networks, identity-based Diffie-Hellman key-agreement, ephemeral key establishment

1. INTRODUCTION

Key-issuing and -agreement are important challenges in wireless sensor networks as preconditions for a confidential and authenticated message exchange. Identity-based procedures pose a very interesting alternative to standard key establishment protocols. Key establishment procedures based on Diffie-Hellman need a separate cryptographic authentication of the involved entities to prevent man-in-the-middle-attacks. This cryptographic authentication goes typically back to certificates. Certificates however require additional computational effort to check their validity. Identity-based schemes avoid explicit certificates and embed the authentication into the key establishment procedure itself. The notion of identity-based public key schemes was introduced by Adi Shamir [16] who presented an identity-based signature scheme. Boneh and Franklin were the first to present an ID-based encryption scheme [5]. Their work is based on bilinear pairings on elliptic curves and lead to a high research activity in this field. In the present paper we only regard pairing-free identity-based schemes.

As certificate verification is avoided ID-based schemes offer the potential to reduce computational overhead compared to standard public key schemes. For the usage in sensor networks two schemes offer a minimal amount of computational effort. One approach was introduced by Benjamin Arazi, Ortal Arazi and Hairong Qi (which we call AQ-protocol in the following) [1], [3]. A second method was proposed by Dario Fiore and Rosario Gennaro, see [11].

For the application of the mentioned schemes a lightweight public key infrastructure is needed. This consists of a third party, a key generation center (KGC). The task of the KGC is to perform the key-issuing which is a precondition for the following key establishment between motes.

In 2009, Schwarz proposed in [15] a man-in-the-middle-attack on the ephemeral key establishment of the AQ-protocol. Assuming that an adversary is physically able to peculate and replace the broadcasted messages of the motes, he can force both motes to agree on the same ephemeral key in each session. We present a further attack, which compromises the ephemeral key-agreement. Thus, we propose a new ephemeral key establishment protocol in this paper and provide a security analysis concerning the new protocol.

We show that our protocol is resilient against the considered attacks and provides perfect forward secrecy. Perfect forward secrecy means, that an adversary cannot reveal established ephemeral keys of past sessions, even if the adversary knows both private keys of the involved motes. If the knowledge of one secret key does not reveal the established ephemeral key generated in past sessions, this characteristic is called partial forward secrecy.

The rest of the paper is organized as follows: Section 2 starts with a description of pairwise key-generation methodology described by Arazi and Qi. The man-in-the-middle attack and an ephemeral key compromise attack is subject of section 3. In the following section 4 our new proposal which counters the mentioned attack is presented. A security analysis is given in section 5 followed by a performance analysis in section 6. Finally, section 7 summarizes the findings of this paper.

2. THE ARAZI-QI PROTOCOL

The pairwise key-generation methodology described by Arazi and Qi contains two steps: Before a pairwise key between two motes can be established, it is necessary that each mote is endowed with an identity, a private key, and a public value. This first step is called key-issuing procedure. The corresponding public key can be computed using the public value and the related identity. The key-issuing procedure can be considered as an identity-based approach according to [9]. Then, in the second step called key establishment a session key between two motes is achieved. This session key can be a fixed or an ephemeral key.

2.1 Identity-based Key-Issuing

It is assumed that a suitable elliptic curve E over some finite field along with a point G of prime order q is given. Furthermore a cryptographic hash function $H : \{0,1\}^* \rightarrow \{1,\ldots,q-1\}$ is needed. The KGC generates a nonce $d \in \{1,\ldots,q-1\}$ as the master private key and calculates the master public key $\mathbf{R}$ as $\mathbf{R} = d \times \mathbf{G}$. The curve parameters, the point $\mathbf{G}$, the order q, and the master public key $\mathbf{R}$ are known to all motes.

During the key-issuing which takes place before the motes of the network are deployed, the KGC endows all motes with a private key and a public value over a secure channel. The private key of a mote is not only known to that mote, but also to the KGC.

First, the KGC generates a nonce $h_A \in \{1,\ldots,q-1\}$ and calculates $\mathbf{U}_A = h_A \times \mathbf{G}$. $\mathbf{U}_A$ is the public value of mote A. Then, the private key $x_A \in \{1,\ldots,q-1\}$ of mote A is generated by the KGC as follows

$$x_A = [H(ID_A, \mathbf{U}_A) \cdot h_A + d] \bmod q.$$

The public value $\mathbf{U}_A$ and the secret key x_A are issued by the KGC to mote A. Mote A can verify the validity of the issued values by checking whether

$$x_A \times \mathbf{G} = H(ID_A, \mathbf{U}_A) \times \mathbf{U}_A + \mathbf{R}.$$

The value $x_A \times \mathbf{G}$ is the public key of mote A. Notice that this value is never used explicitly. As it embeds the identity ID_A of mote A, a randomly chosen public value $\mathbf{U}_A$ for mote A, and the public key $\mathbf{R}$ of the KGC, it is always applied as a calculation using this information.

2.2 Key Establishment

The second step, the key establishment, is usually accomplished after the motes are deployed. Arazi and Qi suggested two different methodologies: the fixed and the ephemeral key establishment. We analyze the running times of the following protocols in terms of the number of required point

multiplications on the elliptic curve E, since these operations are the most expensive from a computational perspective [12].

2.2.1 Fixed Key Establishment

Two motes A and B, which want to establish a fixed key, have to exchange their identities ID_A and ID_B and their public values $\mathbf{U}_A$ and $\mathbf{U}_B$. Mote A computes the key $\mathbf{K}_{AB}$ as follows

$$\mathbf{K}_{AB} = x_A \times [H(ID_B, \mathbf{U}_B) \times \mathbf{U}_B + \mathbf{R}] = x_A x_B \times \mathbf{G}$$

Mote B calculates its session key $\mathbf{K}_{BA}$ respectively.

To confirm that both motes share a joint key, the motes have to encrypt and decrypt a test message. A successful confirmation verifies the key and the identity of the communication partners. The verification of the identity is possible since the identity of a mote together with its public value is embedded in the private and the public key of each mote. Using false information to calculate the session key, either a false public value or a false identity, lead to a failure during the key confirmation.

This fixed key establishment requires two point multiplications on each mote. Arazi and Qi proposed a more efficient implementation in [3]. Here the common key is calculated by mote A as follows

$$\mathbf{K}_{AB} = [x_A \cdot H(ID_B, \mathbf{U}_B) \bmod q] \times \mathbf{U}_B + x_A \times \mathbf{R}.$$

As the point multiplication of the private key of a mote x_A and the master public key $\mathbf{R}$ is used in all fixed key establishments, this computation can be pre-calculated and stored on the mote. So, the above protocol requires only a single point multiplication and the addition of this stored value.

In comparison plain EC-Diffie-Hellman key-agreement requires a single point multiplication on each mote, however as mentioned above the authenticity of the public keys has to be guaranteed by certificates. If we assume that the public keys are signed via ECDSA in such certificates, two additional point multiplications are required to check the signature. Thereby the above AQ-protocol saves two point multiplications.

2.2.2 Ephemeral Key Establishment

The ephemeral key establishment proposed in the AQ-protocol is based on the fixed key establishment described above. Two motes, which agree upon an ephemeral key, establish a variation of the fixed key blended with a random value. The protocol contains the following steps:

1. Mote A and mote B randomly generate the nonces p_A and $p_B \in \{1,\ldots,q-1\}$ respectively. Mote A calculates the point $\mathbf{E}_A = p_A \times \mathbf{G}$ and mote B calculates the point $\mathbf{E}_B = p_B \times \mathbf{G}$.

2. Mote A and mote B interchange $(ID_A, \mathbf{U}_A, \mathbf{E}_A)$ and $(ID_B, \mathbf{U}_B, \mathbf{E}_B)$.

3. A and B respectively compute the session key

$$
\begin{aligned}
\mathbf{K}_{AB} &= p_A \times [H(ID_B, \mathbf{U}_B) \times \mathbf{U}_B + \mathbf{R}] \\
&\quad + (x_A + p_A) \times \mathbf{E}_B \\
&= p_A x_B \times \mathbf{G} + x_A p_B \times \mathbf{G} + p_A p_B \times \mathbf{G} \\
&= p_B \times [H(ID_A, \mathbf{U}_A) \times \mathbf{U}_A + \mathbf{R}] + x_B \times \mathbf{E}_A \\
&\quad + p_B \times \mathbf{E}_A \\
&= p_B \times [H(ID_A, \mathbf{U}_A) \times \mathbf{U}_A + \mathbf{R}] \\
&\quad + (x_B + p_B) \times \mathbf{E}_A = \mathbf{K}_{BA}.
\end{aligned}
$$

4. A key confirmation approves that both motes share the same session key and also verifies their identities.

This ephemeral key establishment requires the total amount of four point multiplications per mote. The AQ-protocol reduces the number of point multiplication during the runtime by calculating the session key as follows:

$$
\begin{aligned}
\mathbf{K}_{AB} &= [p_A \cdot H(ID_B, \mathbf{U}_B) \ mod \ q] \times \mathbf{U}_B \\
&\quad + (x_A + p_A) \times (\mathbf{E}_B + \mathbf{R}) - x_A \times \mathbf{R}
\end{aligned}
$$

The calculation and storage of the point $\mathbf{E}_A = p_A \times \mathbf{G}$ can take place before the key establishment begins.

The values $[p_A \cdot H(ID_B, \mathbf{U}_B) \ mod \ q] \times \mathbf{U}_B$ and $(x_A + p_A) \times (\mathbf{E}_B + \mathbf{R})$ have to be computed during the runtime of the key establishment. As mentioned above, the value $x_A \times \mathbf{R}$ is fixed in each session and can be re-used once it is calculated. So, it is only necessary to compute two point multiplication during the runtime of the key establishment.

In comparison standard DH-based ephemeral key-agreement schemes such as the MQV- or Unified Model protocol [6] require two point multiplications for checking certificates (see above) and at least two point multiplications for the actual key-agreement on each mote. One point multiplication can be precalculated here such that (at least) three point multiplications are required during runtime in these protocols.

3. ATTACKS

3.1 Man-in-the-Middle-Attack by Schwarz

Here we assume a Dolev-Yao like adversary Eve. Eve is able to eavesdrop on the whole communication between two motes. Furthermore she is able to delete messages, reuse old recorded messages or generate and apply new protocol messages, for details see [10].

Schwarz proposed in [15] a man-in-the-middle-attack on the ephemeral key establishment of the AQ-protocol. Assuming that Eve is physically able to peculate and replace the broadcasted messages of the motes, she can force both motes to agree on the same ephemeral key in each session. This constant session key equals the negative value of the fixed key. The attack works as follows:

Eve eavesdrops on the communication of mote A and mote B and peculates the messages $(ID_A, \mathbf{U}_A, \mathbf{E}_A)$ and $(ID_B, \mathbf{U}_B, \mathbf{E}_B)$ and replaces the point $\mathbf{E}_A$ of mote A with

$$
\mathbf{E}_A^* = -(H(ID_A, \mathbf{U}_A) \times \mathbf{U}_A + \mathbf{R}) = -x_A \times \mathbf{G}
$$

and the point $\mathbf{E}_B$ of mote B, with

$$
\mathbf{E}_B^* = -(H(ID_B, \mathbf{U}_B) \times \mathbf{U}_B + \mathbf{R}) = -x_B \times \mathbf{G}.
$$

Mote A receives the compromised message $(ID_B, \mathbf{U}_B, \mathbf{E}_B^*)$ and calculates the session key $\mathbf{K}_{AB}$ as follows

$$
\begin{aligned}
\mathbf{K}_{AB} &= [p_A \cdot H(ID_B, \mathbf{U}_B) \ mod \ q] \times \mathbf{U}_B \\
&\quad + (x_A + p_A) \times (\mathbf{E}_B^* + \mathbf{R}) - x_A \times \mathbf{R} \\
&= [p_A \cdot H(ID_B, \mathbf{U}_B) \ mod \ q] \times \mathbf{U}_B + x_A \times \mathbf{E}_B^* \\
&\quad + x_A \times \mathbf{R} + p_A \times \mathbf{E}_B^* + p_A \times \mathbf{R} - x_A \times \mathbf{R} \\
&= [p_A \cdot H(ID_B, \mathbf{U}_B) \ mod \ q] \times \mathbf{U}_B + p_A \times \mathbf{R} \\
&\quad + x_A \times \mathbf{E}_B^* + p_A \times \mathbf{E}_B^* \\
&= p_A x_B \times \mathbf{G} - x_A x_B \times \mathbf{G} - p_A x_B \times \mathbf{G} \\
&= -x_A x_B \times \mathbf{G}.
\end{aligned}
$$

Mote B also receives the compromised message $(ID_A, \mathbf{U}_A, \mathbf{E}_A^*)$ and calculates the session key $\mathbf{K}_{BA} = -x_A x_B \times \mathbf{G}$ respectively. The key confirmation is successful as mote A and mote B have calculated the same session key $\mathbf{K}_{AB} = \mathbf{K}_{BA}$.

Attacking every ephemeral key establishment performed by mote A and mote B, Eve can force both motes to generate the same key in each session. So, the advantage of the ephemeral key establishment to create a new key value for each session and to conceal the fixed key is lost. Under this attack, the original Arazi and Qi ephemeral key establishment cannot provide neither perfect forward secrecy nor partial forward secrecy.

3.2 Ephemeral Key Compromise Attack

Again, for the attack presented here it is assumed that Eve is physically able to peculate and replace the broadcasted messages of the motes. Moreover, this attack requires that Eve learns the nonce of one of the motes before or while the key establishment takes place. Then, she can force this mote to agree upon a joint secret key.

Although the disclosure of a nonce is a strong assumption, this could be caused by a weak random number generator. As sensor motes are ressource constrained devices it seems reasonable to consider such an attack. It can be described as follows:

Mote A generates a nonce $p_A \in \{1, \ldots, q-1\}$ and computes $\mathbf{E}_A = p_A \times \mathbf{G}$. Without loss of generality, we assume that Eve learns p_A. Mote B also calculates $\mathbf{E}_B = p_B \times \mathbf{G}$ with a nonce $p_B \in \{1, \ldots, q-1\}$.

Then, mote A and mote B exchanges the messages $(ID_A, \mathbf{U}_A, \mathbf{E}_A)$ and $(ID_B, \mathbf{U}_B, \mathbf{E}_B)$. Eve eavesdrops this communication and defrauds the message $(ID_B, \mathbf{U}_B, \mathbf{E}_B)$. She impersonates mote B and sends $(ID_B, \mathbf{U}_B, \mathbf{E}_B^*)$ to mote A with $\mathbf{E}_B^* = p_E \times \mathbf{G} - x_B \times \mathbf{G}$ using her own nonce p_E, the generator point $\mathbf{G}$, and the public key $x_B \times \mathbf{G}$ of mote B. Mote A computes its session key using the compromised value $\mathbf{E}_B^*$ as follows

$$
\begin{aligned}
\mathbf{K}_{AB^*} &= [p_A \cdot H(ID_B, \mathbf{U}_B) \ mod \ q] \times \mathbf{U}_B \\
&\quad + (x_A + p_A) \times (\mathbf{E}_B^* + \mathbf{R}) - x_A \times \mathbf{R} \\
&= [p_A \cdot H(ID_B, \mathbf{U}_B) \ mod \ q] \times \mathbf{U}_B \\
&\quad + p_A \times \mathbf{R} + x_A \times \mathbf{E}_B^* + p_A \times \mathbf{E}_B^* \\
&= p_A x_B \times \mathbf{G} + (x_A + p_A) \times \mathbf{E}_B^* \\
&= p_A x_B \times \mathbf{G} + x_A \times (p_E \times \mathbf{G} - x_B \times \mathbf{G}) \\
&\quad + p_A \times (p_E \times \mathbf{G} - x_B \times \mathbf{G}) \\
&= p_A x_B \times \mathbf{G} + x_A p_E \times \mathbf{G} - x_A x_B \times \mathbf{G} \\
&\quad + p_A p_E \times \mathbf{G} - p_A x_B \times \mathbf{G} \\
&= x_A p_E \times \mathbf{G} + p_A p_E \times \mathbf{G} - p_A x_B \times \mathbf{G}.
\end{aligned}
$$

Eve knows the nonce p_E, the nonce p_A of mote A, the public key $x_A \times \mathbf{G}$ of mote A, and the public key $x_B \times \mathbf{G}$ of mote B. She can easily compute the session key $\mathbf{K}_{AB*}$ as

$$\mathbf{K}_{AB*} = p_E x_A \times \mathbf{G} + p_A p_E \times \mathbf{G} - p_A x_B \times \mathbf{G}.$$

The proposed attack succeed as Eve and mote A share the same session key. This attack enables an adversary to establish a joint secret key with a mote. However, it does not reveal the private key of this mote.

4. THE NEW EPHEMERAL KEY ESTABLISHMENT APPROACH

We suggest a modification of the AQ-protocol to fix the above weaknesses.

In the following we assume that a key-issuing procedure according to Section 2.1 has taken place. This means that mote A and mote B are equipped with secret keys x_A and x_B and public value $\mathbf{U}_A$ and $\mathbf{U}_B$ respectively. The protocol starts with the generation of nonces. A nonce $p_A \in \{1, \ldots, q-1\}$ is generated by mote A and a nonce $p_B \in \{1, \ldots, q-1\}$ is generated by mote B. They calculate the following points

$$\mathbf{E}_A = p_A \times \mathbf{G} \qquad \mathbf{E}_B = p_B \times \mathbf{G}$$

and exchange the messages $(ID_A, \mathbf{U}_A, \mathbf{E}_A)$ and $(ID_B, \mathbf{U}_B, \mathbf{E}_B)$. Mote A checks whether $\mathbf{E}_B \neq \mathcal{O}$, $\mathbf{E}_B \in E$ and then calculates the session key $\mathbf{K}_{AB}$ as

$$\begin{aligned} \mathbf{K}_{AB} &= x_A \times [H(ID_B, \mathbf{U}_B) \times \mathbf{U}_B + \mathbf{R}] + p_A \times \mathbf{E}_B \\ &= x_A x_B \times \mathbf{G} + p_A \times \mathbf{E}_B \\ &= x_A x_B \times \mathbf{G} + p_A p_B \times \mathbf{G}. \end{aligned}$$

Similarly, after a check whether $\mathbf{E}_A \neq \mathcal{O}$ and $\mathbf{E}_A \in E$, the session key $\mathbf{K}_{BA}$ is computed by mote B as

$$\begin{aligned} \mathbf{K}_{BA} &= x_B \times [H(ID_A, \mathbf{U}_A) \times \mathbf{U}_A + \mathbf{R}] + p_B \times \mathbf{E}_A \\ &= x_B x_A \times \mathbf{G} + p_B \times \mathbf{E}_A \\ &= x_B x_A \times \mathbf{G} + p_B p_A \times \mathbf{G}. \end{aligned}$$

The key confirmation succeeds as the communication partners have generated a joint session key.

Notice that this key establishment also requires the total number of four point multiplication. Again, it is possible to reduce the computational effort during run-time. Mote A computes its joint session key with mote B as follows

$$\mathbf{K}_{AB} = [x_A \cdot H(ID_B, \mathbf{U}_B) \mod q] \times \mathbf{U}_B + x_A \times \mathbf{R} + p_A \times \mathbf{E}_B.$$

As the point $\mathbf{E}_A$ can be pre-calculated and the value $x_A \times \mathbf{R}$ is fixed in each session, a mote only has to calculate two point multiplications during the key establishment.

5. SECURITY ANALYSIS

The common key $\mathbf{K}_{AB}$ is the sum of two curve points:

$$x_A x_B \times \mathbf{G} \qquad \text{and} \qquad p_A p_B \times \mathbf{G}.$$

The first point $x_A x_B \times \mathbf{G}$ is the result of the fixed key establishment procedure mentioned in section 2.2.1. Only this part constitutes the authenticated part of the whole key establishment procedure.

The second part $p_A p_B \times \mathbf{G}$ represents an anonymous Diffie-Hellman key-agreement. An attacker can try to exploit the lack of authentication of an anonymous Diffie-Hellman key-agreement. At first view this seems to be a weakness of our approach. We analyze possible attacks in detail in the subsections 5.2 and 5.3.

5.1 Elliptic Curve Attacks

Given the elliptic curve points $\mathbf{G}$ and $\mathbf{E}_A$ the computation of the discrete logarithm p_A of $\mathbf{E}_A = p_A \times \mathbf{G}$ is supposed to be hard if a verified and accepted elliptic curce E is used.

Furthermore it is assumed, that the elliptic curve Diffie-Hellman assumption is valid, too. Given the elliptic curve points $\mathbf{G}$, $\mathbf{E}_A$ and $\mathbf{E}_B$ the computation of the key $\mathbf{K}_{AB} = p_A p_B \times \mathbf{G}$ is supposed to be hard, too.

In addition, to exclude specific elliptic curve subgroup attacks, an elliptic curve E with cofactor 1 should be used.

5.2 Dolev-Yao Adversary

We discuss several attacks where the aim of Eve is to bias the key calculation of the motes A and B in a way that she can take an advantage of the agreed key $\mathbf{K}_{AB}$.

1. Eve tries to reduce the randomness of the established key $\mathbf{K}_{AB}$ by altering the exchanged values. For example she could replace $\mathbf{E}_A$ and $\mathbf{E}_B$ by $\mathcal{O}$ in the messages $(ID_A, \mathbf{U}_A, \mathbf{E}_A)$ and $(ID_B, \mathbf{U}_B, \mathbf{E}_B)$. Since $a \times \mathcal{O} = \mathcal{O}$ for any $a \in \{1, \ldots, q-1\}$ an attacker could easily force A and B to agree upon the (static) key $\mathbf{K}_{AB} = x_A x_B \times \mathbf{G}$. For this reason it has to be checked whether $\mathbf{E}_A, \mathbf{E}_B \neq \mathcal{O}$ after the first protocol step.

2. Eve could replace $\mathbf{E}_A$ and $\mathbf{E}_B$ by values which are not elements of the group generated by $\mathbf{G}$ (or even the curve E). In order to avoid unpredictable protocol outcomes the motes check whether the exchanged values $\mathbf{E}_A$ and $\mathbf{E}_B$ are valid group elements.

3. Eve multiplies $\mathbf{E}_A$ and $\mathbf{E}_B$ with a constant scalar $l \in \{1, \ldots, q-1\}$. She computes

$$\mathbf{E}_A^* = l \times (p_A \times \mathbf{G}) \qquad \mathbf{E}_B^* = l \times (p_B \times \mathbf{G})$$

and replaces the protocol messages by $(ID_A, \mathbf{U}_A, \mathbf{E}_A^*)$ and $(ID_B, \mathbf{U}_B, \mathbf{E}_B^*)$. Mote A checks whether $\mathbf{E}_B^* \neq \mathcal{O}$, $\mathbf{E}_B^* \in E$ and then calculates the session key $\mathbf{K}_{AB}$ as

$$\begin{aligned} \mathbf{K}_{AB} &= x_A \times [H(ID_B, \mathbf{U}_B) \times \mathbf{U}_B + \mathbf{R}] + p_A \times \mathbf{E}_B^* \\ &= x_A x_B \times \mathbf{G} + p_A \times \mathbf{E}_B^* \\ &= x_A x_B \times \mathbf{G} + l p_A p_B \times \mathbf{G}. \end{aligned}$$

After a check whether $\mathbf{E}_A^* \neq \mathcal{O}$ and $\mathbf{E}_A^* \in E$, the session key $\mathbf{K}_{BA}$ is computed by mote B as

$$\begin{aligned} \mathbf{K}_{BA} &= x_B \times [H(ID_A, \mathbf{U}_A) \times \mathbf{U}_A + \mathbf{R}] + p_B \times \mathbf{E}_A^* \\ &= x_B x_A \times \mathbf{G} + p_B \times \mathbf{E}_A^* \\ &= x_B x_A \times \mathbf{G} + l p_B p_A \times \mathbf{G}. \end{aligned}$$

So, $\mathbf{K}_{AB} = \mathbf{K}_{BA}$. By this Eve can alter the common key, but she has no benefit and no information on the established key $\mathbf{K}_{AB}$.

5.2.1 Authentication Attacks

Here, we analyze an attack on the above protocol run by Eve in the role of mote A with mote B.

Eve initializes the protocol run. The protocol starts with the generation of nonces. A nonce $p_E \in \{1, \ldots, q-1\}$ is generated by Eve and a nonce $p_B \in \{1, \ldots, q-1\}$ is generated by mote B. They calculate the following points

$$\mathbf{E}_A = p_E \times \mathbf{G} \qquad \mathbf{E}_B = p_B \times \mathbf{G}$$

and exchange the messages $(ID_A, \mathbf{U}_A, \mathbf{E}_A)$ and $(ID_B, \mathbf{U}_B, \mathbf{E}_B)$. Eve calculates the session key $\mathbf{K}_{AB}$ as

$$\begin{aligned}
\mathbf{K}_{AB} &= x_E \times [H(ID_B, \mathbf{U}_B) \times \mathbf{U}_B + \mathbf{R}] + p_E \times \mathbf{E}_B \\
&= x_E x_B \times \mathbf{G} + p_E \times \mathbf{E}_B \\
&= x_E x_B \times \mathbf{G} + p_E p_B \times \mathbf{G}.
\end{aligned}$$

B computes the session key as follows.

$$\begin{aligned}
\mathbf{K}_{BA} &= x_B \times [H(ID_A, \mathbf{U}_A) \times \mathbf{U}_A + \mathbf{R}] + p_B \times \mathbf{E}_A \\
&= x_B x_A \times \mathbf{G} + p_B \times \mathbf{E}_A \\
&= x_B x_A \times \mathbf{G} + p_B p_E \times \mathbf{G}.
\end{aligned}$$

Thus the keys are not equal.

$\mathbf{K}_{AB}$ and $\mathbf{K}_{BA}$ would be equal if and only if x_E equals x_A. As Eve does not know x_A Eve cannot act in the role of mote A.

5.2.2 Resilience against the Man-In-The-Middle-Attack by Schwarz

This proposal is resilient against the man-in-the-middle-attack mentioned in [15], because the communication partners do not agree upon a joint session key in a compromised session. A compromised key establishment takes the following steps:

1. Mote A generates a nonce $p_A \in \{1, \ldots, q-1\}$ and calculates the point $\mathbf{E}_A = p_A \times \mathbf{G}$.

2. Mote B generates a nonce $p_B \in \{1, \ldots, q-1\}$ and calculates the point $\mathbf{E}_B = p_B \times \mathbf{G}$.

3. Mote A sends $(ID_A, \mathbf{U}_A, \mathbf{E}_A)$ to mote B and mote B sends $(ID_B, \mathbf{U}_B, \mathbf{E}_B)$ to mote A. Both messages are peculated by Eve.

4. Eve calculates

$$\mathbf{E}_A^* = -[H(ID_A, \mathbf{U}_A) \times \mathbf{U}_A + \mathbf{R}] = -x_A \times \mathbf{G}$$

and sends $(ID_A, \mathbf{U}_A, \mathbf{E}_A^*)$ to mote B. She also calculates

$$\mathbf{E}_B^* = -[H(ID_B, \mathbf{U}_B) \times \mathbf{U}_B + \mathbf{R}] = -x_B \times \mathbf{G}$$

and sends $(ID_B, \mathbf{U}_B, \mathbf{E}_B^*)$ to mote A. Neither mote A nor mote B can verify the integrity of the received values $\mathbf{E}_A^*$ and $\mathbf{E}_B^*$. Mote A computes its ephemeral key $\mathbf{K}_{AB}$ as follows

$$\begin{aligned}
\mathbf{K}_{AB} &= x_A \times [H(ID_B, \mathbf{U}_B) \times \mathbf{U}_B + \mathbf{R}] + p_A \times \mathbf{E}_B^* \\
&= x_A x_B \times \mathbf{G} + p_A \times \mathbf{E}_B^* \\
&= x_A x_B \times \mathbf{G} - p_A x_B \times \mathbf{G}.
\end{aligned}$$

Mote B computes its ephemeral key $\mathbf{K}_{BA}$ using $\mathbf{E}_A^*$ as follows

$$\begin{aligned}
\mathbf{K}_{BA} &= x_B \times [H(ID_A, \mathbf{U}_A) \times \mathbf{U}_A + \mathbf{R}] + p_B \times \mathbf{E}_A^* \\
&= x_B x_A \times \mathbf{G} + p_B \times \mathbf{E}_A^* \\
&= x_B x_A \times \mathbf{G} - p_B x_A \times \mathbf{G}.
\end{aligned}$$

5. The key confirmation fails as mote A and mote B do not share the same session key $\mathbf{K}_{AB} \neq \mathbf{K}_{BA}$.

5.3 Strong Adversary

5.3.1 Resilience against the Ephemeral Key Compromise Attack

Even if Eve learns the nonce that generates an actual used point $\mathbf{E}$, she cannot force the corresponding mote to agree upon a joint session key by a straightforward adaption of the attack of section 3.2.

1. Mote A generates a nonce $p_A \in \{1, \ldots, q-1\}$ and computes the point $\mathbf{E}_A = p_A \times \mathbf{G}$. Without loss of generality, it is assumed that the adversary learns p_A. Mote B also calculates the point $\mathbf{E}_B = p_B \times \mathbf{G}$ with a nonce $p_B \in \{1, \ldots, q-1\}$.

2. Mote A sends $(ID_A, \mathbf{U}_A, \mathbf{E}_A)$ to mote B and mote B sends $(ID_B, \mathbf{U}_B, \mathbf{E}_B)$ to mote A. Eve eavesdrops this communication and peculates the message $(ID_B, \mathbf{U}_B, \mathbf{E}_B)$. She impersonates mote B and sends $(ID_B, \mathbf{U}_B, \mathbf{E}_B^*)$ to mote A with

$$\mathbf{E}_B^* = p_E \times \mathbf{G} - x_B \times \mathbf{G}$$

using the generator point $\mathbf{G}$, a nonce p_E generated by Eve, and the public key $x_B \times \mathbf{G}$ of mote B.

3. Mote A computes its session key $\mathbf{K}_{AB}$ as follows

$$\begin{aligned}
\mathbf{K}_{AB} &= x_A \times [H(ID_B, \mathbf{U}_B) \times \mathbf{U}_B + \mathbf{R}] + p_A \times \mathbf{E}_B^* \\
&= x_A x_B \times \mathbf{G} + p_A \times \mathbf{E}_B^* \\
&= x_A x_B \times \mathbf{G} + p_A \times (p_E \times \mathbf{G} - x_B \times \mathbf{G}) \\
&= x_A x_B \times \mathbf{G} + p_A p_E \times \mathbf{G} - p_A x_B \times \mathbf{G}.
\end{aligned}$$

4. As the fixed key $x_A x_B \times \mathbf{G}$ is unknown to Eve, this attack is not successful.

5.3.2 Perfect Forward Secrecy

It is easy to demonstrate that the knowledge of x_A and x_B is not sufficient to disclose $\mathbf{K}_{AB}$ by analyzing the key-agreement formula of $\mathbf{K}_{AB}$. The adversary cannot calculate the second summand $p_A p_B \times \mathbf{G}$ of the expression:

$$\mathbf{K}_{AB} = x_A x_B \times \mathbf{G} + p_A p_B \times \mathbf{G}.$$

In conclusion, the described approach provides perfect forward secrecy as the ephemeral keys $\mathbf{K}_{AB}$ and $\mathbf{K}_{BA}$ cannot be revealed using the knowledge of both private keys.

5.3.3 Resilience against the Jealous Spouse Attack

Moreover, we analyzed the adaptability of the so called jealous spouse attack, published in [7], to our protocol proposal.

Aim of this attack is to reveal a session key between two motes B and C. It makes strong assumptions about the adversary in the sense that Eve has to know the secret key k_A of a third mote A. Furthermore, she has to know two session keys of B and C which are generated after interaction with the adversary. In certain key agreement protocols it is then possible to derive a session key K_{BC} [7].

As well, a straightforward adaptation of this attack to our proposal does not work.

6. PERFORMANCE ANALYSIS AND IMPLEMENTATION

Former implementations of the AQ-protocol only focused on the Intel Mote 2 platform or the Telos B platform, see [4], [2] and [3]. We have implemented the fixed key establishment and the presented ephemeral key establishment on a MICAz platform manufactured by Crossbow Technologies Inc. [13]. Compared to Telos B and Intel 2 platforms, the computational and memory capacities of this platform are more restricted. It is equipped with a 8-bit-microcontroller consuming 8mA, when in the active mode. The unit draws a voltage of approximately 3V.

We used TinyOS 2.x as operating system, see [17]. The implementation of elliptic curve and large number operation was provided by TinyECC. This is a configurable library designed for TinyOS 1.x [14]. We revised parts of the TinyECC code to adapt it to TinyOS 2.x.

Our implementation used the elliptic curve DSECP160R specified in [8]. The cryptographic complexity of an elliptic curve of this size is equivalent to that of 1024-bit RSA.

We implemented a plain EC-Diffie-Hellman key-agreement, the fixed key establishment of the AQ-protocol, and our modified ephemeral key establishments on a MICAz mote and measured the required time to compute the session key.

The plain EC-Diffie-Hellman key-agreement can be calculated with a single point multiplication. This takes 4.1 seconds in our implementation. The fixed key establishment requires one scalar multiplication and one addition. Its computation lasts 5.6 seconds. We implemented the ephemeral key establishment using three point multiplications and two additions during the key establishment. This takes 8.5 seconds.

7. CONCLUSIONS

In this paper we analyzed the key establishment of the AQ-protocol. Our security analysis identified several weaknesses which could be given that an adversary is physically able to manipulate a session communication in the network. We consider these security problems to limit the utility of the AQ-protocol and therefore we presented a new approach to establish an ephemeral key. This key establishment is shown to be resilient against the presented attacks. As the described adversary is only able to manipulate a single communication session with a single mote, future work has to address an extended adversary, able to manipulate a series of communication sessions with one or more arbitrary motes.

Presently our proposal lacks a formal security proof. It is still an open issue which proof model is appropriate.

The presented performance analysis required a partly adaption of the well-known TinyECC library to TinyOS 2.x. Our implementation is again an example for an ECC-based protocol successfully running on the limited MICAz hardware platform. Nevertheless we consider the full adaption of TinyECC to TinyOS 2.x as an important future goal.

Our approach seems to be especially suitable for cluster heads in hierarchical sensor networks with appropriate hardware support for point multiplications on elliptic curves.

8. REFERENCES

[1] B. Arazi. Certification of DL/EC Keys. In *Proceedings of the IEEE P1363 Study Group for Future Public-Key Cryptography Standards*, 1999.

[2] O. Arazi, I. Elhanany, D. Rose, H. Qi, and B. Arazi. Self-Certified Public Key Generation on the Intel Mote 2 Sensor Network Platform. In *2nd IEEE Workshop on Wireless Mesh Networks*, pages 118–120, September 2006.

[3] O. Arazi and H. Qi. Load-Balanced Key Establishment Methodologies in Wireless Sensor Networks. *Int. J. Secur. Netw.*, 1(3/4):158–166, 2006.

[4] O. Arazi, H. Qi, and D. Rose. A Public Key Cryptographic Method for Denial of Service Mitigation in Wireless Sensor Networks. *4th Annual IEEE Communication Society Conference on Sensor, Mesh and Ad Hoc Communications and Networks (SECON)*, pages 51–59, June 2007.

[5] D. Boneh and M. Franklin. Identity based encryption from the weil pairing. In *Proceedings of Advances in Cryptography - Crypto 2001*, pages 213–229. LNCS 2139, Springer Verlag, 2001.

[6] C. Boyd and A. Mathuria. *Protocols for Authentication and Key Establishment*. Springer, 2003.

[7] M. Burmester. On the risk of opening distributed keys. In *Proceedings of Advances in Cryptography - Crypto 1994*, pages 308–317. LNCS 839, Springer Verlag, 1994.

[8] Certicom Research. *Standards For Efficient Cryptography 2 (SEC 2: Recommended Elliptic Curve Domain Parameters)*, January 2010.

[9] Y. Desmedt and M. Burmester. Identity-Based Key Infrastructures. In *IFIP World Computer Congress (WCC2004-SEC)*, pages 167–176, 2004.

[10] D. Dolev and A. C. Yao. On the security of public key protocols. Technical report, Stanford University, 1981.

[11] D. Fiore and R. Gennaro. Making the Diffie-Hellman Protocol Identity-Based. In *CT-RSA*, pages 165–178, 2010.

[12] D. Hankerson, A. Menezes, and S. Vanstone. *Guide to Elliptic Curve Cryptography*. Springer, 2004.

[13] C. T. Inc. MICAz: Wireless Measurement System, 2008.

[14] A. Liu and P. Ning. TinyECC: A Configurable Library for Elliptic Curve Cryptography in Wireless Sensor Networks. In *IPSN '08: Proceedings of the 7th International Conference on Information Processing in Sensor Networks*, pages 245–256, Washington, DC, USA, 2008. IEEE Computer Society.

[15] O. Schwarz. Public-Key-Verfahren in hierarchischen Sensornetzen. Diplomarbeit, Technische Universität Chemnitz, 2009.

[16] A. Shamir. Identity-Based Cryptosystems And Signature Schemes. In *Advances in Cryptology — CRYPTO '84*, volume 196 of *Lecture Notes in Computer Sciences*, pages 47–53. Springer-Verlag, 1984.

[17] TinyOS, 2010.

How Secret-sharing can Defeat Terrorist Fraud

Gildas Avoine
Université catholique de Louvain
ICTEAM Institute
B-1348, Louvain la Neuve, Belgium
gildas.avoine@uclouvain.be

Cédric Lauradoux
Université de Lyon, INRIA,
INSA-Lyon, CITI,
F-69621, Villeurbanne, France
cedric.lauradoux@inria.fr

Benjamin Martin
Université catholique de Louvain
ICTEAM Institute
B-1348, Louvain la Neuve, Belgium
benjamin.martin@uclouvain.be

ABSTRACT

Terrorist fraud is a relay attack against distance bounding protocols where the prover conspires with an adversary to misrepresent the distance between himself and the verifier. In ideal situations, the adversary does not gain any knowledge about the prover's long-term secret. This makes designing a distance bounding protocol resistant to a such fraud tricky: the secrets of an honest prover must be protected, while those of a dishonest one should be disclosed as an incentive not to cheat.

In this paper, we demonstrate that using a secret-sharing scheme, possibly based on threshold cryptography, is well suited for thwarting terrorist fraud. Although such an idea has been around since the work of Bussard and Bagga, this is the first time that secret-sharing and terrorist fraud have been systematically studied altogether. We prove that secret sharing can counter terrorist fraud, and we detail a method that can be applied directly to most existing distance bounding protocols. We illustrate our method on the protocol of Hancke and Kuhn, yielding two variants: the threshold distance bounding (TDB) protocol and the thrifty threshold distance bounding (TTDB) protocol. We define the adversarial strategies that attempt to gain some knowledge on the prover's long-term secret, evaluate the amount of information disclosed, and determine the adversary's success probability.

Categories and Subject Descriptors

K.6.5 [**Management of Computing and Information Systems**]: Security and Protection—*Authentication*

General Terms

Security, design, theory.

Keywords

Authentication, distance-bounding, terrorist fraud, mafia fraud, secret sharing, threshold cryptography.

1. INTRODUCTION

Man-in-the-middle attacks (MITM) are effective against a wide range of protocols.

Two variants are particularly relevant when considering authentication protocols that use distance-bounding for checking proximity: *mafia fraud* and *terrorist fraud* [1].

In mafia fraud, the adversary, Eve, attempts to impersonate a legitimate prover, Alice, to a legitimate verifier, Bob, using MITM. Terrorist fraud, also known as *rental fraud* in [13], is a variant of mafia fraud where Alice helps Eve to impersonate herself to Bob. Many scenarios may justify this singular attack, e.g., Alice pays Eve for getting a perfect alibi during a crime. However, terrorist fraud can be quite hazardous for Alice if Eve is able to (re)impersonate her afterward: Eve could commit crimes pretending to be Alice. Hence, Alice allows terrorist fraud only if Eve is able to achieve a *one-time impersonation*. More precisely, we assume that Alice does not get involved in terrorist fraud if Eve may gain some advantage for future attacks.

Since the seminal works of Desmedt *et al.* on these frauds [5, 13], most of the literature [3, 8, 14, 17, 21, 22, 27, 34, 36, 37] has been dedicated to mafia fraud. Concerning terrorist fraud, the first proposal was made by Bussard and Bagga [10, 11]. Their work was later extended by Reid, Nieto, Tang, and Senadji [30]. Recently, new protocols emerged to defeat terrorist fraud [22, 37]. All these protocols use secret-sharing, even if not explicitly stated by the authors.

This paper attempts to shed more light on terrorist fraud. Our contribution is an examination of secret sharing, and more precisely, (n, k) threshold cryptography. Classical authentication [19] and most distance bounding protocols [8, 17] fail to resist terrorist fraud because all the material needed for the authentication can be supplied to the adversary, as the long-term secret key cannot be retrieved from this material. This problem can be discarded by using a threshold scheme: the authentication material consists in the n shares of an (n, k) threshold scheme. If Alice exposes any combination of k shares to Eve, the long-term secret leaks. Therefore, Eve can only obtained $k - 1$ shares from Alice.

In the following sections, we provide a method based on secret sharing that enforces security against terrorist fraud. To illustrate our method, we suggest two protocols based on Hancke and Kuhn's protocol [17], which are: *threshold distance-bounding* (TDB) and *thrifty threshold distance-bounding* (TTDB). In TDB, Alice uses a different (n, k) threshold scheme in each protocol round to answer Bob. TTDB is more thrifty than TDB in the sense that the same system of shares is used q times ($2 \le q < k - 1$) instead of only once. The success probability of impersonation in mafia fraud and in terrorist fraud are given for both protocols. Particular attention is paid to key recovery attacks which fall into two categories: birthday paradox and divide-and-conquer. The first attack is prevented by choosing carefully the size of the values exchanged at the initialization of the protocol. The second attack depends on the capability of the adversary to observe the protocol success. For this purpose, we define three different classes of adversaries. Against the weakest adversary, TDB with $k = 2$ and TTDB with $k = 3$, $q = 2$ provide the best security level. For stronger adversaries, TDB with $k = 3$ must be considered. For TTDB, the same system of shares cannot be used more than $q = \frac{k-1}{2}$ times.

Our contribution is fourfold: (1) We introduce a method based on (n, k) threshold cryptography that enforces the security of distance bounding protocols against terrorist fraud. (2) We illustrate our method by applying it to Hancke-Kuhn's protocol, yielding two variants of this protocol. (3) We refine the adversary model, introducing three classes of adversaries: BD-ADV, RES-ADV, and RD-ADV. (4) We provide a comprehensive and accurate analysis of key recovery strategies, including bounds on the disclosed information and on the number of shares needed to maintain system security.

The rest of the paper is organized as follows: Section 2 reviews distance bounding protocols, mafia and terrorist frauds, and defines the adversary capabilities. The protocols TDB and TTDB are described in Section 3. Section 4 and 5 analyze the security of our protocols against different adversaries and strategies, including impersonation and key recovery attacks. Section 4 computes the success probabilities of mafia fraud and attacks based on the birthday paradox. Section 5 introduces the post-ask strategy for key-recovery based divide-and-conquer. Finally, the advantages and weaknesses of previous works are discussed in Section 6.

2. THREAT MODEL

We now briefly review the definitions of distance-bounding protocol, mafia fraud, and terrorist fraud. Detailed explanations of these concepts can be found in [1]. Following this review, we refine the adversary model to capture its capability to mount key recovery attacks.

2.1 Definitions

DEFINITION 1 (DISTANCE-BOUNDING PROTOCOL)
A distance bounding protocol *authenticates a prover to a verifier and bounds the distance between them.*

DEFINITION 2 (NEIGHBORHOOD)
In a distance bounding protocol, the distance measurement allows the verifier to define an area, called the neighborhood, *in which the protocol execution is considered genuine.*

Three attacks exist against distance-bounding protocols: distance fraud, mafia fraud, and terrorist fraud. Distance fraud is not covered in this paper as it is not a MITM. Mafia and terrorist frauds, however, are two types of MITM that introduce an interaction between the legitimate prover, Alice, and the adversary, Eve.

DEFINITION 3 (MAFIA FRAUD)
Mafia fraud is an attack where an adversary defeats a distance bounding protocol using a MITM between the verifier and an honest prover located outside the neighborhood.

In mafia fraud, Alice and Bob are unaware of the presence of Eve, while the latter collaborates with Alice in a terrorist fraud.

DEFINITION 4 (TERRORIST FRAUD)
Terrorist fraud is an attack where an adversary defeats a distance bounding protocol using a MITM between the verifier and a dishonest prover located outside the neighborhood. In this situation, the dishonest prover helps the adversary maximize her chances of a successful attack, without providing any advantage for future attacks.

PROPOSITION 1 *Given a distance-bounding protocol, let $P_\mathcal{M}$ and P_T denote respectively the success probabilities of an adversary in the mafia and terrorist frauds. Then, the following inequality holds:*

$$P_\mathcal{M} \le P_T. \tag{1}$$

To justify the previous inequality, the relation between Alice and the device executing the protocol needs to be explored: we can consider a *black-box* [7] model or a *white-box* [31] model. If Alice controls the device executing the protocol at her side (white-box), she can provide Eve with information that she cannot obtain herself in mafia fraud. Otherwise (black-box), Alice can at least authorize Eve to mount a sort of "mafia fraud" in which she is aware of the attack.

DEFINITION 5 (SECURITY REGARDING TERRORIST FRAUD)
If a protocol satisfies Equation 1 with equality and $P_\mathcal{M} < 1$, it is considered secure against terrorist fraud.

REMARK 1 *We stress that the security of a protocol regarding terrorist fraud is strongly related to its resilience to mafia fraud. Indeed, taking into account Proposition 1 and the above definition, security with respect to terrorist fraud cannot be examined as an absolute value. The relevant value is the advantage Eve gains in mounting a terrorist fraud instead of a mafia fraud. Eve will not involve Alice if she cannot provide useful information.*

REMARK 2 *Secret values are involved during the execution of the protocol between Alice and Bob. An important requirement is that they cannot be recovered by Eve, using an attack better than an exhaustive search.*

2.2 Adversary

Eve is a man in the middle adversary with complete control of the channel between the legitimate parties. We consider three classes of adversaries depending on their capabilities to observe the protocol result:

DEFINITION 6 (BD-ADV)
The Blind-Adversary *does not learn whether the protocol succeeds.*

DEFINITION 7 (RES-ADV)
The Result-Adversary *can observe if the protocol succeeds.*

For instance, in a building access control system, the adversary knows that the protocol succeeded if the door opens.

DEFINITION 8 (RD-ADV)
The Round-Adversary has the capability to observe the result of each round, e.g., using a side channel attack.

The BD-ADV case is in fact the hypothesis used in all the existing works related to the terrorist fraud (Section 6). However, distance bounding protocol designers should be aware that the observability of a protocol result is critical when evaluating key information leakage (Section 4 and 5). Hence, the designers should take into account stronger adversaries (RES-ADV and RD-ADV) during the protocol conception and analysis.

3. THRESHOLD DISTANCE-BOUNDING

A brief introduction to secret-sharing and threshold cryptography are reviewed in Appendix A and are a prerequisite to understanding our protocols: TDB and TTDB.

In TDB, each round uses a different part of the long term key s and a given threshold scheme, *i.e.*, one share is used per round. In TTDB, the same part of s and its associated threshold scheme are used for several rounds. The notations used in the paper are summarized in Table 1.

Our protocols assume the use of an (n, k) threshold scheme Λ. From a secret s, n shares are computed such that any combination of k shares can be used to recover the secret. Gathering strictly less than k shares reveals no information about the secret.

N_A	nonce chosen by Alice
N_B	nonce chosen by Bob
ℓ_A	size of N_A in bits
ℓ_B	size of N_B in bits
G	a finite group
$\mathcal{R}$	$n \times m$ matrix over G
c_i	i-th challenge of Bob
$r_{i,j}$	an element of $\mathcal{R}$ (i-th row and j-th column) and a given share of Λ
m	number of rounds in TDB and TTDB
q	number of sub-rounds in TTDB and $m|q$
n	total number of shares
k	number of shares recovering the secret $k > 1$
$\mathcal{E}$	encryption algorithm
Λ	(n, k) threshold scheme over G
Λ'	(n, k) threshold scheme over G^q
f	pseudo-random function
$P_\mathcal{M}$	success probability of mafia fraud
$P_\mathcal{T}$	success probability of terrorist fraud
$P_\mathcal{B}$	success probability of birthday impersonation
$P_\mathcal{X}$	success probability of impersonation knowing X elements of each column of $\mathcal{R}$
BD-ADV	blind adversary
RES-ADV	adversary observing protocol result
RD-ADV	adversary observing round results

Table 1: Notations and parameters for TDB.

3.1 The TDB scheme

TDB is similar to the protocol of Hancke and Khun [17]. It is based on a decision problem, *i.e.*, Bob's challenges are used to select the answers of Alice amongst n possible shares. In [17], $n = 2$ and the shares of Alice are created using a pseudo-random function. In TDB, the computation of Alice's answers is done differently.

PREREQUISITE.
Alice and Bob share a secret s viewed as a vector $(s_1, \ldots, s_m)$ of m coordinates over a group G. They can both compute an (n, k) threshold scheme Λ and a pseudo-random function f. The protocol is composed of three phases (Figure 1): initialization, interactive, and result.

INITIALIZATION PHASE.
Alice and Bob exchange nonces N_A and N_B of respective size ℓ_A and ℓ_B generated using a random number generator. Then, Alice and Bob compute an $n \times m$ matrix $\mathcal{R}$. The details on the computation of this matrix are given later. There are no time constraints required for this protocol phase.

INTERACTIVE PHASE.
Bob asks Alice at round i to send the element $r_{c_i,i}$ of $\mathcal{R}$ (c_i-th row and i-th column). Bob measures the round trip times δt_i of each exchange. The accuracy and implementation details depend on the underlying technology and are out of scope in this paper.

RESULT PHASE.
Bob declares that the protocol succeeds if the received answers $r'_{c_i,i}$ match the expected values $r_{c_i,i}$ and if all round trip time $\delta t_i < \Delta$ where Δ is a given bound used to estimate if Alice is within the neighborhood of Bob. For now, we consider only noiseless communication. This result phase is the one targeted by the adversaries RES-ADV and RD-ADV.

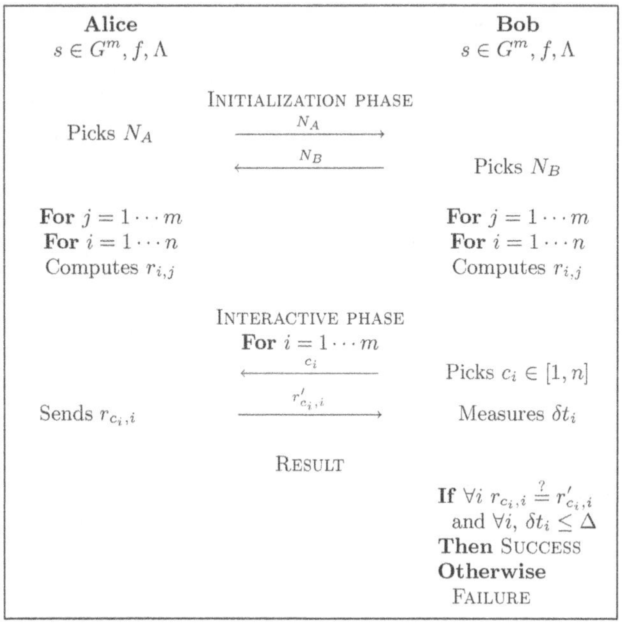

Figure 1: TDB protocol.

MATRIX COMPUTATION.

This is the core of TDB. Let us assume that $\mathcal{R}$ is generated randomly. It can be concluded that $I(s; \mathcal{R}) = 0$ where I denotes the mutual information, *i.e.*, the amount by which the uncertainty (entropy) of s is reduced by learning $\mathcal{R}$: $I(s; \mathcal{R}) = H(s) - H(s|\mathcal{R})$ in which $\mathcal{R}$ and s are assimilated to random variables on their respective domains and H is the Shannon's entropy. Alice can share $\mathcal{R}$ with Eve without revealing s. In order to defeat terrorist fraud, $\mathcal{R}$ must be computed such that Alice cannot reveal $\mathcal{R}$ to Eve without also leaking s, *i.e.*, $I(s; \mathcal{R}) > 0$.

The computation of $\mathcal{R}$ must satisfy two important criteria. First, the knowledge of any combination of k elements of a given column reveals a coordinate of the key. Second, Alice and Bob need to compute the same $n \times m$ matrix $\mathcal{R}$ over G. The first criterion is used to thwart the terrorist fraud and the latter is required for the RESULT phase. The matrix $\mathcal{R}$ is defined by:

$$\mathcal{R} = \begin{pmatrix} r_{1,1} & \cdots & r_{1,m} \\ \vdots & \ddots & \vdots \\ r_{n,1} & \cdots & r_{n,m} \end{pmatrix}$$

where each column $(r_{1,i}, r_{2,i}, \cdots, r_{n,i})^T$ of $\mathcal{R}$ is obtained using the (n, k) threshold scheme Λ applied on s_i. This construction is compliant with our first criterion. Indeed, we have for each column $i \in [1, m]$:

$$I(s_i; \varphi) = 0, \qquad \forall \varphi \in \Phi_{k-1}(r_{1,i}, \cdots, r_{n,i})$$
$$I(s_i; \varphi) = \lceil \log_2 |G| \rceil, \qquad \forall \varphi \in \Phi_k(r_{1,i}, \cdots, r_{n,i})$$

with $\Phi_k(r_{1,i}, \cdots, r_{n,i})$ being the set of the combinations for k elements belonging to the i-th column. The previous equations are a strict interpretation of our criterion and of threshold cryptography. By using Λ for the computation of $\mathcal{R}$, Alice should not reveal to Eve more than $k-1$ elements of each column of $\mathcal{R}$. In an (n, k) threshold scheme Λ, random values are often needed and it can be problematic if Alice and Bob are not synchronized, *i.e.*, producing different random numbers in different shares. For this reason, they use a pseudo-random generator initialized with s, N_A, and N_B. A concrete study case is given with Example 1.

The computational cost of $\mathcal{R}$ depends on n, k, and $|G|$. For instance, schemes with $n = k$ are easy to implement (see Example 1). For $n \neq k$ and $G = \mathbb{F}_{2^i}$, construction using MDS codes can be obtained at the cost of multiplication by a constant in $\mathbb{F}_{2^i}$. This can be implemented very efficiently [28] using linear feedback shift registers (LFSRs).

EXAMPLE 1 *Consider the case of $n = k = 3$ and $G = \mathbb{F}_2$. Then, computing $3 \times m$ binary matrix $\mathcal{R}$ requires generating a random value of $2m$ bits. This value can be obtained using the pseudo-random function f by computing $f(s, N_A, N_B)$. These $2m$ bits represent the rows of the matrix $(r_{1,1}, \cdots, r_{1,m})$ and $(r_{2,1}, \cdots, r_{2,m})$. The last row is the sum modulo two of all other rows plus the corresponding secret bit of s. Matrix $\mathcal{R}$ becomes:*

$$\mathcal{R} = \begin{pmatrix} r_{1,1} & \cdots & r_{1,m} \\ r_{2,1} & \cdots & r_{2,m} \\ s_1 \oplus r_{1,1} \oplus r_{2,1} & \cdots & s_m \oplus r_{1,m} \oplus r_{2,m} \end{pmatrix}.$$

The computation of $\mathcal{R}$ for any (n, m) easily follows.

REMARK 3 *The critical parameters for implementation on a radio device are n and $|G|$. Bob needs to send $\lceil \log_2 n \rceil$ bits per challenge. Alice replies with $\lceil \log_2 |G| \rceil$ bits. As the protocol does not target any given technology, we do not discuss on these values. The reader may consult [15, 16, 23, 29] for more details on this topic.*

3.2 The thrifty TDB scheme

The TDB and TTDB differ on three points: (1) the matrix computation, (2) the size of Alice's answers, and (3) additional conditions on the challenges sent by Bob.

We call this scheme thrifty because it reduces the number of systems of shares computed. First, TTDB works on vectors of q coordinates in G. An (n, k) threshold scheme Λ' compliant with this condition is used. The scheme Λ' is applied $\frac{m}{q}$ times with q a divisor of m. A column of $\mathcal{R}$ is used once in TDB, whereas in TTDB, it is used q times. Consequently, there are only $\frac{m}{q}$ distinct columns in $\mathcal{R}$. A column $(r_{1,i}, r_{2,i}, \cdots, r_{n,i})^T$ of $\mathcal{R}$ is obtained using the (n, k) threshold scheme Λ' applied on $(s_{qi-q+1}, \cdots, s_{qi})$. Each distinct column is repeated q times in the matrix. The overall number of challenges/responses is kept constant m. The resulting $n \times m$ matrix $\mathcal{R}$ over G^q is defined by:

$$\mathcal{R} = \begin{pmatrix} \overbrace{r_{1,1} \cdots r_{1,1}}^{q \text{ times}} & \cdots & \overbrace{r_{1,m/q} \cdots r_{1,m/q}}^{q \text{ times}} \\ \vdots & \ddots & \vdots \\ r_{n,1} \cdots r_{n,1} & \cdots & r_{n,m/q} \cdots r_{n,m/q} \end{pmatrix}.$$

The last difference between TDB and TTDB is how Bob generates challenges. When working on a giving distinct column of $\mathcal{R}$, the challenges c_i are not allowed to be repeated. We now define a round for TTDB as the series of q challenge/response (sub-rounds) with the same column.

As the following results will show, TTDB is a generalization of TDB for the terrorist fraud.

4. BLIND ADVERSARY

In Section 2, we saw that mafia fraud and terrorist fraud cannot be dissociated. We now show the results of our protocols against mafia fraud.

4.1 The analysis of TDB

This section describes how n and k should be chosen. The parameter n is critical regarding mafia fraud while k impacts the probability of a successful terrorist fraud. We also provide recommendations on the size of the nonces exchanged by Alice and Bob.

An important intermediate result in our analysis is the probability of a successful impersonation attack considering that Eve knows $X > 0$ elements of each column of $\mathcal{R}$. This probability, denoted P_X, is equal to:

$$P_X = \left(\frac{X}{n} + \frac{n - X}{n|G|} \right)^m$$

With this result, we derive all the probabilities needed to evaluate the security of TDB.

MAFIA FRAUD.

The probability $P_\mathcal{M}$ of mafia fraud is:

$$P_\mathcal{M} = \max\left(\left(\frac{1}{|G|}\right)^m, \left(\frac{1}{n} + \frac{n-1}{n|G|}\right)^m\right). \quad (2)$$

Note that $\left(\frac{1}{|G|}\right)^m$ corresponds to an adversary who attempts to answer on its own. Any value is possible and is referred to in the literature as the *no-ask strategy*. The right term is the probability of success of the *pre-ask strategy*. Within this strategy, the normal initialization phase is followed by Eve executing the interactive phase with Alice using her own challenges. Eve obtains m elements of $\mathcal{R}$ from Alice (one per column). Afterwards, Eve executes the interactive phase with Bob. The success probability for the pre-ask strategy is exactly $P_{X=1}$.

Equation 2 does not take into account the capability of Eve to observe different executions of the protocol. She can exploit the *birthday paradox* [38] and the *generalized birthday paradox*[1]. When both nonces are repeated, so does the matrix $\mathcal{R}$. An X-collision is the observation by Eve of X executions of the protocol between Alice and Bob with the same values N_A and N_B. Eve needs to observe:

$$C(X) \geq (X!)^{\frac{1}{X}} \times \left(2^{\ell_A + \ell_B}\right)^{\frac{X-1}{X}}, \quad (3)$$

to obtain an X-collision on both N_A and N_B with a probability greater than $\frac{1}{2}$ for a large value of $2^{\ell_A + \ell_B}$. This result is a direct application of the work of Suzuki, Tonien, Kurosawa, and Toyota in [35].

When the X-th collision occurs, the success probability $P_\mathcal{B}$ for this birthday impersonation is: $P_\mathcal{B} = P_X$.

The previous computation of $P_\mathcal{B}$ assumes that Eve has obtained X different shares for each round only from observing the protocol execution. The birthday paradox needs to be also applied on Bob's challenges. Eve will need more than an X-collision to obtain the success probability equal to P_X. Fortunately for Eve, she can circumvent this problem by using a pre-ask strategy. When a collision occurs, she executes the interactive phase with Alice using challenges not previously recorded. Then, she executes the interactive phase with Bob. To thwart such attacks, the nonce size must be chosen such that observing $C(X)$ is not feasible.

At this point, readers may be wondering about the case when $X = k$. Indeed, Eve can recover each coordinates s_i of the secret s. However, it requires $C(k)$ executions of the protocol (Equation 3). A more effective attack is possible as shown in the next paragraph.

KEY RECOVERY.

With the lesson learned by birthday impersonation, Eve can devise a key recovery attack more efficient than the one suggested previously. Instead of observing and tampering with messages between Alice and Bob during protocol execution, she directly executes the protocol with Alice. This attack is possible since the authentication is unilateral. In this way, Eve keeps the value of the nonce N_B constant and

---

[1]The term generalized birthday paradox is used abusively to describe very different problems. We refer here to multicollisions as used in the cryptography-related literature [20]

observes a k-collision with probability greater than $\frac{1}{2}$ for:

$$C'(k) \geq (k!)^{\frac{1}{k}} \times \left(2^{\ell_A}\right)^{\frac{k-1}{k}} \quad (4)$$

executions of the protocol. If ℓ_A is not chosen carefully, an attack against the secret s can be more efficient than an exhaustive search. To guarantee the security level of the key s, we require:

$$C'(k) \geq 2^m,$$
$$\ell_A \geq \frac{km}{k-1} - \frac{k \log_2 (k!)^{\frac{1}{k}}}{k-1},$$
$$\ell_A \geq \frac{km}{k-1},$$

since $(k!)^{\frac{1}{k}} > 1$. For $k = 2$, we need to have $\ell_A = 2m$. Choosing $k > 2$ allows the designer to reduce the size of the nonces generated and exchanged by Alice.

We claim that this attack is the only key-recovery attack available to Eve when she is a BD-ADV. She is unable to recover k elements of a column of $\mathcal{R}$ even if she observes or tampers with the protocol. This claim is more explicit when we deal with RES-ADV and RD-ADV in Section 5.

TERRORIST FRAUD.

How many elements of a column of $\mathcal{R}$ can be safely given to Eve? In the context of BD-ADV, this value is equal to $k-1$. The reasoning behind this choice is as follows: When Bob sends a challenge c_i for which Eve knows the answer $r_{c_i,i}$, there is no risk of information leakage on s. Otherwise, Eve tries to guess the answer. If her guess is correct, she obtains enough shares to recover a coordinate of the key. However, she is unable to detect a correct guess since we are dealing with a BD-ADV. Therefore, the success probability $P_T^{\text{BD-ADV}}$ of terrorist fraud is:

$$P_T^{\text{BD-ADV}} = P_{X=k-1} = \left(\frac{k-1}{n} + \frac{n-k+1}{n|G|}\right)^m. \quad (5)$$

EXAMPLE 2 *Let consider* TDB *implemented with an* $(2,2)$ *threshold scheme and* $G = \mathbb{F}_2$ *(similar to the protocol of Hancke and Khun [17]). In this case, the success probability against the mafia and terrorist frauds are respectively* $P_\mathcal{M} = \left(\frac{3}{4}\right)^m$ *and* $P_T^{\text{BD-ADV}} = \left(\frac{3}{4}\right)^m$. *It is secure against terrorist fraud:* $P_\mathcal{M} = P_T^{\text{BD-ADV}}$ *and* $P_\mathcal{M} < 1$. *Indeed,* TDB *implemented with* $(n,2)$ *threshold scheme is secure against terrorist fraud for any* $n \geq 2$ *if Eve is* BD-ADV.

Working with $n = k = 2$ *means that the birthday impersonation and the key recovery attack employ directly the birthday paradox:*

$$C(2) \approx 2^{\frac{\ell_A + \ell_B}{2}}$$
$$C'(2) \approx 2^{\frac{\ell_A}{2}}.$$

When a collision is observed, $P_\mathcal{B} = 1$. *Alice needs to choose a nonce* N_A *of length* $\ell_A = 2m$ *to guarantee the security level of her key* s.

4.2 The analysis of TTDB

The security analysis of TTDB is essentially the same as the one for TDB. The main difference is the computation of P_X.

In order to compute the success probability of mafia and terrorist frauds, we first analyze the success probability of an impersonation given that Eve knows X shares in each round, with $X > 0$.

Let consider a given round r_w ($1 \leq w \leq \frac{m}{q}$). The analysis becomes tricky because the sub-rounds of r_w are not independent. Given a bit string B of length q, we define the events $\mathcal{A}_B$ that Eve succeeds in round r_w and Bob asks her known shares when the bits of B are equal to 1. By varying B in $\mathbb{F}_2^q$, we cover all the possible sequences of challenges. As the $\mathcal{A}_B$s are pairwise disjoint, we deduce the success probability of Eve impersonating Alice regarding Bob in the round r_w:

$$\Pr\left(\text{succ } r_w\right) = \sum_{B \in \mathbb{F}_2^q} \Pr\left(\mathcal{A}_B\right). \tag{6}$$

Now, we define the function $f_{X,B}(i) : \{0, \ldots, q-1\} \mapsto [0, 1]$, by:

$$\frac{1}{n-i} \cdot \begin{cases} X - \sum_{j=0}^{j=i} B_j + 1 & \text{if } B_i = 1, \\ \left((n-i) - \left(X - \sum_{j=0}^{j=i} B_j\right)\right) \cdot \frac{1}{|G|^q} & \text{otherwise}, \end{cases}$$

where B_j is the jth bit of B. $f_{X,B}(i)$ represents the success probability of Eve in the $(i+1)$th sub-round. Indeed, two cases occur (a) Bob asks for a known share, this happens with probability $\frac{X - \sum_{j=0}^{j=i} B_j + 1}{n-i}$ and Eve wins with probability 1. Or (b) he does not and Eve has to guess the answer, so she succeeds with probability $\frac{1}{|G|^q}$. By definition of $f_{X,B}$:

$$\Pr\left(\mathcal{A}_B\right) = \prod_{i=0}^{i=q-1} f_{X,B}(i). \tag{7}$$

Hence, Equations 6, 7, yield to:

$$\Pr\left(\text{succ } r_w\right) = \sum_{B \in \mathbb{F}_2^q} \left(\prod_{i=0}^{i=q-1} f_{X,B}(i)\right).$$

Finally, by noticing that the rounds are independent, we find the probability of a successful impersonation given that Eve knows X shares in each round, P_X, as:

$$P_X = \left(\sum_{B \in \mathbb{F}_2^q} \left(\prod_{i=0}^{i=q-1} f_{X,B}(i)\right)\right)^{\frac{m}{q}} \tag{8}$$

Mafia fraud.

The success probability for mafia fraud is the maximum between the no-ask and pre-ask strategy:

$$P_{\mathcal{M}} = \max\left(\left(\frac{1}{|G|^q}\right)^m, P_{X=q}\right),$$

We compute the success probability of a birthday impersonation given that Eve has observed a x-collision as:

$$P_{\mathcal{B}} = P_{X=qx}.$$

Indeed, Eve learns q elements of column of $\mathcal{R}$ at each round and this for every collision she observed. $C(X)$ remains the same (Equation 3).

Key recovery.

Eve uses the same key recovery as in TDB. She executes the protocol with Alice with a fixed N_B. However, Eve collects more information during each collision with TTDB than with TDB. Indeed, a collision exposes q shares with TTDB for only one with TDB. Thus, we need:

$$C'\left(\left\lceil \frac{k}{q} \right\rceil\right) \geq 2^m$$

which implies from Equation 4:

$$\ell_A \geq m \cdot \left(1 + \frac{k}{q}\right),$$

considering $\lceil \frac{k}{q} \rceil \leq \frac{k}{q} + 1$ and Equation 4.

Terrorist fraud.

For each distinct column of $\mathcal{R}$, Alice can provide $k-1$ elements to Eve without revealing the key. We have:

$$P_T^{\text{BD-ADV}} = P_{X=k-1}. \tag{9}$$

Example 3 *Let consider* TTDB *implemented with an $(3, 3)$ threshold scheme, $q = 2$ and $|G| = 4$. The size of Alice's nonce is $\ell_A \approx 2m$. Using the previous equations, we have the following computations for $P_{X=2}$:*

$$\begin{aligned} P_{X=2} &= \left(\frac{2}{3} \cdot \frac{1}{2} + \frac{2}{3} \cdot \frac{1}{2} \cdot \frac{1}{16} + \frac{1}{3} \cdot \frac{1}{16} \cdot 1 + \frac{1}{3} \cdot \frac{1}{16} \cdot 0 \cdot \frac{1}{16}\right)^{\frac{m}{2}} \\ &= \left(\frac{3}{8}\right)^{\frac{m}{2}} = \left(\frac{\sqrt{3}}{2\sqrt{2}}\right)^m. \end{aligned}$$

Thus, the success probability against mafia and terrorist frauds are respectively $P_{\mathcal{M}} = \left(\frac{\sqrt{3}}{2\sqrt{2}}\right)^m$ and $P_T^{\text{BD-ADV}} = \left(\frac{\sqrt{3}}{2\sqrt{2}}\right)^m$. Hence, this scheme is secure against terrorist fraud: $P_{\mathcal{M}} = P_T^{\text{BD-ADV}}$ and $P_{\mathcal{M}} < 1$. This property is verified for TTDB if $q = k-1$.

5. STRONGER ADVERSARIES

Apart from the birthday results, the analysis found in Section 4 is the one used by the existing literature, and is limited to BD-ADV. Our analysis goes a step further with RES-ADV and RD-ADV and we see drastically different results. This section is dedicated to key recovery attacks pertaining the terrorist fraud.

5.1 The analysis of TDB

In Section 4, we concluded that TDB with $(n, 2)$ threshold cryptography is enough to defeat terrorist fraud. We now show under the same assumptions that Eve can recover the secret s using a *post-ask strategy* in RES-ADV and RD-ADV.

Post-ask strategy.

This strategy was originally designed to carry out mafia fraud against Brands and Chaum's protocol [8]. This protocol differs from Hancke and Khun [17] by requiring that Alice compute a signature over all received challenges c_i and all answers $r_{c_i, i}$ at the end of the protocol. She sends this signature to Bob for verification in addition to the initialization and interactive phases. The idea of the post-ask strategy is to force Alice to generate the final signature. When

Eve executes the interactive phase with Bob, she must also execute the interactive phase with Alice and forward the legitimate challenges. At the end, Alice transmits the correct signature and Eve relays it to Bob. Eve has "only" to succeed in the interactive phase with Bob. She does not solve a cryptographic problem.

The use of this strategy may look dubious on TDB for Eve at a first sight: TDB and TTDB are not using any final signature. However, a slight modification of this attack results in learning two elements of each column of $\mathcal{R}$ for each protocol round.

First consider the case of RD-ADV and the attack described in Figure 2. Eve executes the interactive phase with Bob. The challenge c_i is answered by $\hat{r}_{c_i,i}$. She observes the result of each round. If a round succeeds, then $\hat{r}_{c_i,i} = r_{c_i,i}$. She is now half way to recovering the secret key. Now, Eve sends her own challenges $\hat{c}_i$ to Alice such that they all differ from the legitimate ones, i.e., $\forall i$, $c_i \neq \hat{c}_i$. By doing so, Eve is guaranteed to obtain legitimate elements from $\mathcal{R}$ which are not expected by Bob. If a given round i succeeds, Eve has two distinct elements, $r_{\hat{c}_i,i}$ and $r_{c_i,i}$, of the same column of $\mathcal{R}$. With two shares, she can recover the corresponding coordinate s_i. On average $\frac{|G|}{2}$ post-ask attacks are needed to recover the whole secret s.

Now consider the case of RES-ADV. Eve allows the interactive phase to be carried out correctly except for a single round i. In this round, Eve modifies the challenge c_i sent by Bob. Alice receives $\hat{c}_i \neq c_i$. Then, Eve records the answer of Alice $r_{\hat{c}_i,i}$ and sends a random answer $\hat{r}_{c_i,i}$ to Bob. If the protocol succeeds, Eve knows that $\hat{r}_{c_i,i} = r_{c_i,i}$. Otherwise, she knows two elements of the same column $r_{c_i,i}$ and $r_{\hat{c}_i,i}$. She can recover the corresponding coordinate s_i of the secret. Eve needs on average $\frac{|G|}{2}$ executions of this attack to recover s_i. Repeating this process m times, once per coordinate, she recovers s using a typical divide-and-conquer strategy.

The main difference between RD-ADV and RES-ADV is that RD-ADV can work on all rounds in parallel. Eve is limited to a single round per attack with RES-ADV.

EXAMPLE 4 *Recall Example 2, i.e., $n = k = 2$ and $G = \mathbb{F}_2$. The attack described in Figure 2 can be obviously applied. However, there is a much simpler strategy for Eve to recover two shares at each round. It exploits the fact that $|G| = 2$. The post-ask attack given in Figure 2 can be replaced by a fault attack: Eve changes one or all the challenges of Bob.*

- *In RES-ADV, Eve changes only one challenge c_i. She knows that $r_{0,i} = r_{1,i}$ if the protocol succeeds. Otherwise, she concludes that $r_{0,i} \neq r_{1,i}$ and she observes either $r_{0,i}$ or $r_{1,i}$. After m executions of the protocol with one fault at a different round, she recovers the whole secret s. This strategy was first unveiled by Kim et al. in [22] against the protocol of Tu and Piramuthu [37].*

- *In RD-ADV, Eve can flip all the challenge bits and recover the secret s with only one execution of the protocol.*

For $|G| > 2$, this fault attack only reveals equality between the two shares. If all shares are different, this fault attack does not help Eve. This is most likely if $n \ll |G|$ (this is yet another application of the birthday paradox). The post-ask strategy directly attempts to recover two shares and is not affected by this problem.

We can conclude that TDB cannot be used with $(n, 2)$ threshold scheme if Alice has to deal with RES-ADV or RD-ADV. TDB is weak for $k = 2$ because Eve can recover two shares at each round. The parameter k must be chosen as $k = \alpha + 1$ where α is the maximum number of shares that can be recovered by Eve in a given round. For TDB, we have shown with the previous attack that $\alpha = 2$. So, $k \geq 3$ is a safe choice for TDB. If we refer to the result given for terrorist fraud in Section 4 (Equation 5), $k \geq 3$ implies that:

$$P_{\mathcal{M}} < P_T^{\text{BD-ADV}}.$$

So, it seems that our solution is not secure against terrorist fraud. However, the analysis of the terrorist fraud has to be re-computed taking into account the new capabilities of Eve (RES-ADV and RD-ADV).

TERRORIST FRAUD.

For now, $k \geq 3$ is only considered. In BD-ADV, it was assumed that Alice can provide $k - 1$ shares for each round of the protocol without revealing the secret s. Let us assume that Alice provided $k-1$ elements of each column of $\mathcal{R}$. Each time, Alice has not provided the legitimate answer $r_{c_i,i}$ to Eve, Eve sends $\hat{r}_{c_i,i}$. If the round succeeds $\hat{r}_{c_i,i} = r_{c_i,i}$, she recover s_i. Otherwise, she eliminates a possible value for s_i. On average, $\frac{|G|}{2}$ attempts are needed on a round for which Eve does not know the answer. Moreover, Eve with RD-ADV capabilities can explore on average $\frac{m}{2}$ rounds in parallel.

In the case of RES-ADV, Eve obtains less information. If the terrorist fraud is successful, she obtains on average $\frac{m}{2}$ coordinates of the key. Otherwise, Eve has chosen i coordinates for the secret s (on average $\frac{m}{2}$). These coordinates are incorrect since the protocol fails. The $|G|^{m-i}$ secrets with these coordinates can be eliminated by Eve. Several executions of terrorist fraud result in an exploration of the key space faster than exhaustive search. The same reasoning holds for mafia fraud.

Therefore, it is wiser for Alice in the terrorist fraud to expose to Eve only $k - 2$ shares at each round. When Eve succeeds in terrorist fraud, she obtains for some columns of $\mathcal{R}$ $k - 1$ elements. This is not enough to recover the corresponding coordinates of the key s_i. The probability of successful terrorist fraud becomes:

$$P_T^{\text{RES-ADV}} = P_T^{\text{RD-ADV}} = \left(\frac{k-2}{n} + \frac{n-k+2}{n|G|} \right)^m. \quad (10)$$

REMARK 4 *In the context of RES-ADV and RD-ADV, TDB used with $(n, 3)$ threshold schemes is secure against the terrorist fraud since we have for $k = 3$ and $|G| \geq 2$:*

$$\forall n \geq 3, \ P_T^{\text{RES-ADV}} = P_T^{\text{RD-ADV}} = P_{\mathcal{M}}.$$

5.2 The TTDB analysis

Fundamentally, the attacks against TTDB are identical to the ones used against TDB in RES-ADV and RD-ADV. The only modification is the overall number of shares recovered by Eve. For TDB, the post-ask helps to recover at most $\alpha = 2$ shares and explains why $(n, 3)$ schemes are safe. For TTDB, Eve can recover at most $\alpha = 2q$ shares with the same method. Therefore, $(n, 2q+1)$ threshold schemes ensure that TTDB never reveals enough information to the adversary.

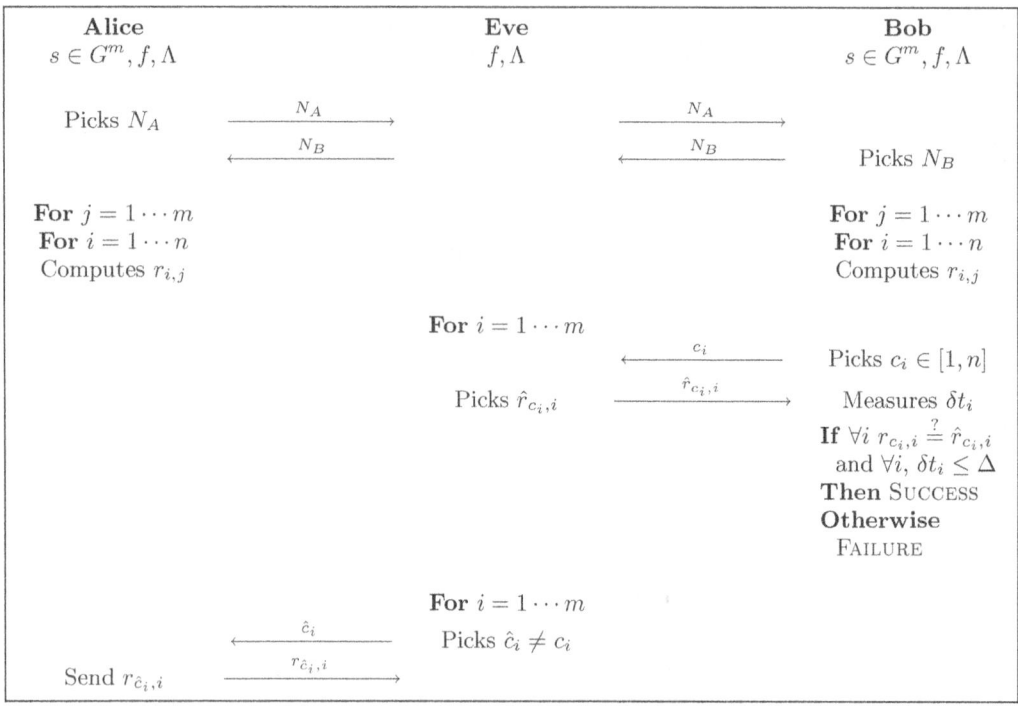

Alice	Eve	Bob
$s \in G^m, f, \Lambda$	f, Λ	$s \in G^m, f, \Lambda$

Picks N_A $\xrightarrow{\quad N_A \quad}$ $\xrightarrow{\quad N_A \quad}$

$\xleftarrow{\quad N_B \quad}$ $\xleftarrow{\quad N_B \quad}$ Picks N_B

For $j = 1 \cdots m$ — **For** $j = 1 \cdots m$
For $i = 1 \cdots n$ — **For** $i = 1 \cdots n$
Computes $r_{i,j}$ — Computes $r_{i,j}$

For $i = 1 \cdots m$

$\xleftarrow{\quad c_i \quad}$ Picks $c_i \in [1, n]$

Picks $\hat{r}_{c_i,i}$ $\xrightarrow{\quad \hat{r}_{c_i,i} \quad}$ Measures δt_i

If $\forall i \; r_{c_i,i} \stackrel{?}{=} \hat{r}_{c_i,i}$
and $\forall i, \delta t_i \leq \Delta$
Then SUCCESS
Otherwise
FAILURE

For $i = 1 \cdots m$
$\xleftarrow{\quad \hat{c}_i \quad}$ Picks $\hat{c}_i \neq c_i$

Send $r_{\hat{c}_i,i}$ $\xrightarrow{\quad r_{\hat{c}_i,i} \quad}$

Figure 2: Post-ask attack for RD-ADV against TDB.

Consequently, Alice can only reveal q shares to Eve. The probability of terrorist fraud is:

$$\forall n \geq 3 \text{ and } q \geq 1, \; P_T^{\text{RES-ADV}} = P_T^{\text{RD-ADV}} = P_{\mathcal{M}}.$$

6. RELATED WORKS

Although existing work is primarily based on (2,2) threshold schemes, individual constructions use matrix computation based on encryption, or, introduce a challenge verification step. We consider both approaches by studying, respectively, the protocols of Reid et al. [30], and Kim et al. [22].

6.1 Matrix computation based on encryption

This class of protocols is derived from the first solution to terrorist fraud by Bussard and Bagga [11]. This solution based on asymmetric encryption was adapted by Reid et al. [30] to symmetric encryption. The protocol is described in Figure 3.

Let us summarize the main differences between the protocol of Reid et al. [30] and TDB with respect to our notations. The protocol of Reid et al. uses an $2 \times m$ matrix $\mathcal{R}$ over $G = \mathbb{F}_2$. Let denote r_1 and r_2 the rows of $\mathcal{R}$. The first row r_1 is obtained using the pseudo random function f: $r_1 = f(s, A, B, N_A, N_B)$. The second row is obtained by encrypting s with r_1: $r_2 = \mathcal{E}_{r_1}(s)$. For the choice of $\mathcal{E}$, Reid et al. gave, in the early version of their paper [30], the following comment (with adapted notation for consistency):

$\mathcal{E}$ is a semantically secure encryption function, i.e. an adversary does not learn any (computational) information about the plaintext. In practice, because the strings to be encrypted are short and the key varies for each run of the protocol, we can use a one-time pad, i.e $\mathcal{E}_{r_1}(s) = s \oplus r_1$.

If $\mathcal{E}$ is the one-time pad, then we are exactly in the setup of Example 2. The protocol of Reid et al. is an instance of

TDB with a (2,2) threshold scheme and $G = \mathbb{F}_2$. Indeed, the additive cipher is the basic tool used to design (n, n) threshold scheme (see Appendix A). Section 5 has shown that such a scheme is not secure against the post-ask strategy for RES-ADV and RD-ADV.

If $\mathcal{E}$ is a block cipher or an asymmetric encryption scheme, the attack remains the same for RD-ADV. However, the case of RES-ADV is more difficult. Eve recovers $\frac{m}{2}$ bits of the key r_1 used to encrypt s and $\frac{m}{2} + 1$ of the ciphertext r_2. However, this information alone cannot be used to recover the secret s when $\mathcal{E}$ is a pseudo-random permutation. Otherwise, the information recovered may depend on the cipher characteristics. The additional cost of using a block cipher or an asymmetric encryption scheme must also be taken into account.

6.2 Challenge verification and (2,2) threshold

Amongst all the solutions to terrorist fraud, the Swiss-Knife RFID Distance Bounding Protocol [22] is particularly interesting. It uses an (2,2) threshold scheme that is combined with a challenge verification step. An extended analysis of this protocol is given below. The protocol is depicted in Figure 4.

PREREQUISITE.

Alice has an identifier A and a secret key $s \in \mathbb{F}_2^m$. Bob knows a database $\mathbb{DB}$ which consists of pair of the form (key,identifier). The pair (s, A) is included in Bob's database. Alice and Bob also share a constant Y. They can both compute a pseudo-random function f and a (2,2) threshold scheme.

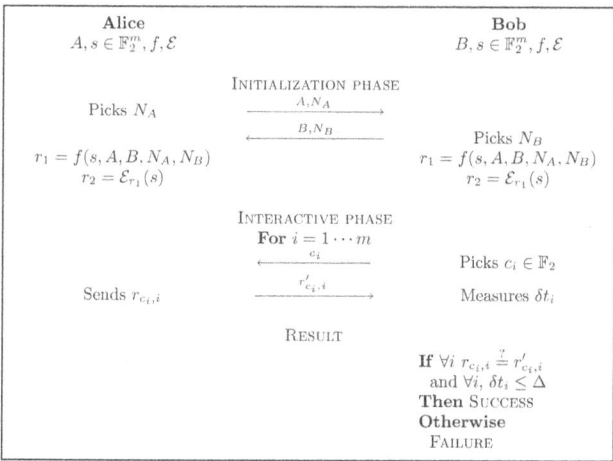

Figure 3: Reid *et al.*'s protocol. The use of the identifier A and B is made to solve a complexity issue at Bob's side [2]. They are omitted in TDB and TTDB for the sake of simplicity.

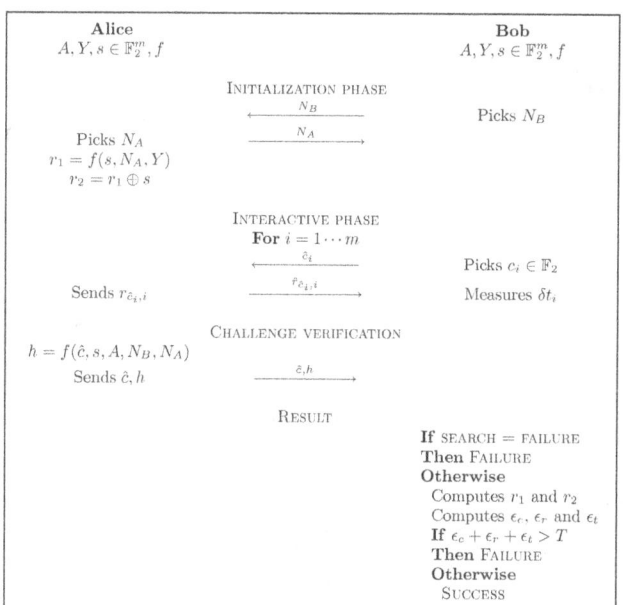

Figure 4: Kim *et al.*'s protocol.

INITIALIZATION PHASE.

Bob and Alice pick respectively the nonces N_B and N_A. Both nonces are exchanged. Then, Alice computes the $2 \times m$ matrix $\mathcal{R}$ over $\mathbb{F}_2$. The first row of the matrix is $r_1 = f(s, Y, N_A)$. The second row r_2 is given by $r_2 = r_1 \oplus s$.

INTERACTIVE PHASE.

At each of the m rounds of this phase, Bob picks randomly a challenge $c_i \in \mathbb{F}_2$. Alice received the challenge $\hat{c}_i$ and replies with $r_{\hat{c}_i, i}$. Bob receives $\hat{r}_{\hat{c}_i, i}$ and measures the timing of the round δt_i.

CHALLENGE VERIFICATION.

Alice computes a signature of the received challenge $\hat{c}_i$:

$$h = f(\hat{c}_1, \cdots, \hat{c}_m, A, N_A, N_B).$$

Then, Alice sends to Bob the vector $\hat{c} = (\hat{c}_1, \hat{c}_2, \cdots, \hat{c}_m)$ and h. A similar phase is also found in the protocol of Bussard and Bagga [11].

RESULT.

Bob first needs to recover the identity of the prover. He performs an exhaustive search on his database $\mathbb{DB}$ (SEARCH function) to match the value h using $\hat{c}$, Y, N_A and N_B. If this search is unsuccessful, the protocol fails. Otherwise, Bob recovers the pair (s, A). He computes the matrix $\mathcal{R}$ as done previously by Alice, along with the following quantities:

- ϵ_c the number of positions for which $c_i \neq \hat{c}_i$,

- ϵ_r the number of positions for which $c_i = \hat{c}_i$ but $r_{c_i, i} \neq \hat{r}_{c_i, i}$,

- ϵ_t the number of positions for which $c_i = \hat{c}_i$, $r_{c_i, i} = \hat{r}_{c_i, i}$ but $\delta t_i > \Delta$.

If $\epsilon_c + \epsilon_r + \epsilon_t \geq T$ the authentication fails. Otherwise, it succeeds.

REMARK 5 *Kim et al. propose a variant of this protocol in which the number of rounds is smaller than the key size m.*

At the beginning of each instance of the protocol, Bob picks a random mask of m bits and Hamming weight w. This mask is used to select w bits of the key s. The interactive phase consists of w rounds. This does not affect our analysis.

POST-ASK STRATEGY.

Assume that $T = 0$, *i.e.*, no error is tolerated. This scheme defeats the post-ask attack described in Section 5 for RES-ADV but not for RD-ADV. For RES-ADV, the attack is detected by the ϵ_c variable and the protocol can never succeed. Eve can attempt to bypass this problem by forging a valid signature for the legitimate challenges c_i. We assume that this cryptographic task cannot be afforded by Eve.

If $T > 1$, Eve can manipulate T challenges. However, the values sent by Eve are not taken into account when determining if the protocol succeeds or not. When $c_i \neq \hat{c}_i$, the corresponding answer is discarded.

TERRORIST FRAUD.

This protocol uses a $(2, 2)$ threshold scheme and, as pointed out in section 4, does not leak any information to a BD-ADV. We focus our discussion on RES-ADV and RD-ADV.

In order to mount a terrorist fraud, Eve first relays the initialization phase. Then she asks Alice for a row of the matrix $\mathcal{R}$, without loss of generality we assume that it is the first row. After the interaction phase with Bob, she transmits to Alice the challenges she received. Alice computes the signature, and sends it to Eve who ends the protocol with Bob by transmitting him this signature.

A RES-ADV Eve, capable of detecting protocol success, gains information about the secret. Indeed, if the protocol succeeds, she knows the answers given to Bob were all correct. Thus, for the answers coming from the second row of $\mathcal{R}$, Eve learns the corresponding secret bits. We conclude that Alice should never help Eve.

Finally, in the case of the RD-ADV, Eve knows whether the round succeeds or not. Hence, when Bob asks her for a second row element, she is able to determine the expected answer, and so she retrieves the corresponding secret bits. The conclusion is Alice must absolutely not provide any help to Eve.

7. CONCLUSION

We demonstrated in this paper that using threshold cryptography thwarts terrorist fraud. Previously proposed distance bounding protocols using a $(2, 2)$ threshold scheme do not resist to terrorist fraud with powerful adversaries. Our results show that, at least, a $(3, 3)$ threshold scheme should be used. We illustrated our results on the protocol of Hancke and Kuhn, yielding two variants: the threshold distance bounding (TDB) protocol and the thrifty threshold distance bounding (TTDB) protocol. We refined the adversary model, introducing three classes of adversaries: BD-ADV, RES-ADV, and RD-ADV. We provided an accurate analysis of our protocols, including the adversary's success probabilities. Finally, we applied our adversarial model to previous works, and highlighted their weaknesses.

Acknowledgement

The authors want to thank the reviewers for their comments and particularly John Solis for his help to clarify this work.

This work is partially funded by the Walloon Region Marshall plan through the SPW DG06 Project TRASILUX. Benjamin Martin was supported by a grant from Fonds pour la formation à la Recherche dans l'Industrie et dans l'Agriculture (FRIA), rue d'Egmont 5, 1000 Brussels, Belgium.

8. REFERENCES

[1] G. Avoine, M. A. Bingöl, S. Kardaş, C. Lauradoux, and B. Martin. A Framework for Analyzing RFID Distance Bounding Protocols. *Journal of Computer Security – Special Issue on RFID System Security*, 2010.

[2] G. Avoine, E. Dysli, and P. Oechslin. Reducing Time Complexity in RFID Systems. In *Selected Areas in Cryptography – SAC 2005*, volume 3897 of *Lecture Notes in Computer Science*, pages 291–306, Kingston, Canada, August 2005. Springer-Verlag.

[3] G. Avoine, C. Floerkemeier, and B. Martin. RFID Distance Bounding Multistate Enhancement. In *International Conference on Cryptology in India - Indocrypt 2009*, volume 5922 of *Lecture Notes in Computer Science*, pages 290–307. Springer-Verlag, 2009.

[4] S. Bengio, G. Brassard, Y. Desmedt, C. Goutier, and J.-J. Quisquater. Secure implementation of identification systems. *Journal of Cryptology*, 4(3):175–183, 1991.

[5] T. Beth and Y. Desmedt. Identification Tokens - or: Solving the Chess Grandmaster Problem. In *Advances in Cryptology - CRYPTO '90*, volume 537 of *Lecture Notes in Computer Science*, pages 169–177, Santa Barbara, CA, USA, August 1990. Springer-Verlag.

[6] G. R. Blakley. Safeguarding cryptographic keys. In *AFIPS 1979 National Computer Conference*, volume 48, pages 313–317, Arlington, NY, USA, 1979–317.

[7] M. Blaze. Looking on the Bright Side of Black-Box Cryptography (Transcript of Discussion). In *Security Protocols Workshop*, volume 2133 of *Lecture Notes in Computer Science*, pages 54–61, Cambridge, UK, April 2000. Springer-Verlag.

[8] S. Brands and D. Chaum. Distance-Bounding Protocols. In *Advances in Cryptology - EUROCRYPT'93*, volume 765 of *Lecture Notes in Computer Science*, pages 344–359, Lofthus, Norway, May 1993. Springer-Verlag.

[9] E. F. Brickell and D. M.Davenport. On the classification of ideal secret sharing schemes. *Journal of Cryptology*, 4:123–134, 1991.

[10] L. Bussard. *Trust Establishement Protocols for Communications Devices*. PhD thesis, Eurecom-ENST, 2004.

[11] L. Bussard and W. Bagga. Distance-bounding proof of knowledge to avoid real-time attacks. In *Security and Privacy in the Age of Ubiquitous Computing*, volume 181 of *IFIP International Federation for Information Processing*, pages 223–238. Springer-Verlag, 2005.

[12] L. Csirmaz. The Size of a Share Must Be Large. In *Advances in Cryptology - EUROCRYPT '94*, volume 950 of *Lecture Notes in Computer Science*, pages 13–22, Perugia, Italy, 1994. Springer-Verlag.

[13] Y. Desmedt, C. Goutier, and S. Bengio. Special Uses and Abuses of the Fiat-Shamir Passport Protocol. In *Advances in Cryptology - CRYPTO'87*, volume 293 of *Lecture Notes in Computer Science*, pages 21–39, Santa Barbara, CA, USA, August 1988. Springer-Verlag.

[14] S. Drimer and S. J. Murdoch. Keep your enemies close: distance bounding against smartcard relay attacks. In *16th USENIX Security Symposium on USENIX Security Symposium*, pages 1–16, Santa Clara, CA, USA, June 2007. USENIX Association.

[15] M. Flury, M. Poturalski, P. Papadimitratos, J.-P. Hubaux, and J.-Y. L. Boudec. Effectiveness of distance-decreasing attacks against impulse radio ranging. In *ACM Conference on Wireless Network Security - WISEC 2010*, pages 117–128, Hoboken, NJ, USA, 2010. ACM.

[16] G. P. Hancke. Design of a Secure Distance-Bounding Channel for RFID. *Journal of Network and Computer Applications*, May 2010.

[17] G. P. Hancke and M. Kuhn. An RFID Distance Bounding Protocol. In *Conference on Security and Privacy for Emerging Areas in Communication Networks – SecureComm 2005*, pages 67–73, Athens, Greece, September 2005. IEEE Computer Society.

[18] G. P. Hancke and M. G. Kuhn. Attacks on time-of-flight distance bounding channels. In *ACM Conference on Wireless Network Security - WISEC 2008*, pages 194–202, Alexandria, VA, USA, March 2008. ACM.

[19] International Organization for Standardization. ISO/IEC 9798 – Information technology – Security techniques – Entity authentication, 1997 - 2008.

[20] A. Joux. Multicollisions in Iterated Hash Functions. Application to Cascaded Constructions. In *Advances in Cryptology - CRYPTO 2004*, volume 3152 of *Lecture Notes in Computer Science*, pages 306–316,

Santa Barbara, CA, USA, August 2004. Springer-Verlag.

[21] C. H. Kim and G. Avoine. RFID distance bounding protocol with mixed challenges to prevent relay attacks. In *International Conference on Cryptology and Network Security - CANS*, volume 5888 of *Lecture Notes in Computer Science*, pages 119–133, Kanazawa, Ishikawa, Japan, December 2009. Springer-Verlag.

[22] C. H. Kim, G. Avoine, F. Koeune, F.-X. Standaert, and O. Pereira. The Swiss-Knife RFID Distance Bounding Protocol. In *International Conference on Information Security and Cryptology – ICISC'08*, volume 5461 of *Lecture Notes in Computer Science*, pages 98–115, Seoul, Korea, December 2008. Springer-Verlag.

[23] M. Kuhn, H. Luecken, and N. O. Tippenhauer. UWB Impulse Radio Based Distance Bounding. In *Workshop on Positioning, Navigation and Communication 2010 - WPNC'10*, Dresden, Germany, March 2010.

[24] J. L. Massey. Minimal Codewords and Secret Sharing. In *Proceedings of the 6th Joint Swedish-Russian International Workshop on Information Theory*, pages 276–279, 1993.

[25] R. J. McEliece and D. V. Sarwate. On sharing secrets and Reed-Solomon codes. *Communication of the ACM*, 24(9):583–584, 1981.

[26] A. Mitrokotsa, C. Dimitrakakis, P. Peris-Lopez, and J. C. Hernandez-Castro. Reid et al.'s Distance Bounding Protocol and Mafia Fraud Attacks over Noisy Channels. *IEEE Communications Letters*, 14(2):121–123, July 2010.

[27] J. Munilla and A. Peinado. Distance bounding protocols for RFID enhanced by using void-challenges and analysis in noisy channels. *Wireless Communications and Mobile Computing*, 8(9):1227–1232, 2008.

[28] C. Paar. *Efficient VLSI Architectures for Bit Parallel Computation in Galois Fields*. PhD thesis, Universität GH Essen, 1994.

[29] K. B. Rasmussen and S. Čapkun. Realization of RF Distance Bounding. In *USENIX Security Symposium*, Washington, DC, USA, August 2010.

[30] J. Reid, J. M. G. Nieto, T. Tang, and B. Senadji. Detecting relay attacks with timing-based protocols. In *ACM symposium on Information, computer and communications security - ASIACCS '07*, pages 204–213. ACM, 2007. Early version available at citeseerx.ist.psu.edu/viewdoc/summary?doi=10.1.1.70.5584.

[31] A. Saxena, B. Wyseur, and B. Preneel. Towards Security Notions for White-Box Cryptography. In *Information Security Conference- ISC 2009*, volume 5735 of *Lecture Notes in Computer Science*, pages 49–58, Pisa, Italy, September 2009. Springer-Verlag.

[32] A. Shamir. How to share a secret. *Communication of the ACM*, 22(11):612–613, 1979.

[33] G. J. Simmons. *Contemporary Cryptology: The Science of Information Integrity*. IEEE Press, 1991.

[34] D. Singelée and B. Preneel. Distance Bounding in Noisy Environments. In *European Workshop on Security in Ad-hoc and Sensor Networks - ESAS'07*, volume 4572 of *Lecture Notes in Computer Science*, pages 101–115, Cambridge, UK, July 2007. Springer-Verlag.

[35] K. Suzuki, D. Tonien, K. Kurosawa, and K. Toyota. Birthday Paradox for Multi-collisions. In *Information Security and Cryptology - ICISC 2006*, volume 4296 of *Lecture Notes in Computer Science*, pages 29–40, Busan, Korea, November 2006. Springer-Verlag.

[36] R. Trujillo Rasua, B. Martin, and G. Avoine. The Poulidor Distance-Bounding Protocol. In S. O. Yalcin, editor, *Workshop on RFID Security – RFIDSec'10*, volume 6370 of *Lecture Notes in Computer Science*, pages 239–257, Istanbul, Turkey, June 2010. Springer-Verlag.

[37] Y.-J. Tu and S. Piramuthu. RFID Distance Bounding Protocols. In *First International EURASIP Workshop on RFID Technology*, Vienna, Austria, September 2007.

[38] D. Wagner. A Generalized Birthday Problem. In *Advances in Cryptology - CRYPTO 2002*, volume 2442 of *Lecture Notes in Computer Science*, pages 288–303, Santa Barbara, CA, USA, August 2002. Springer-Verlag.

APPENDIX

A. SECRET SHARING

A secret-sharing scheme Λ allows a user to share a secret s amongst n participants according to an access control list Γ. Γ determines the subset of participants that are allowed to recover s. The parameter k of a secret-sharing scheme is the size of the smallest subset of participants that can recover the secret. The first solution for achieving secret-sharing was the threshold cryptography [6, 32]. In an (n, k) threshold scheme, any subset of k participants can recover s. Threshold schemes were first implemented by Shamir [32] using interpolation problem. It was subsequently re-interpreted by Sarwate and McEliece [25] in terms of Reed-Solomon codes. Several important results for secret-sharing coming from coding theory have followed [24]. To conclude this overview of secret-sharing, the classical construction of (n, n) threshold schemes is given. This textbook example is particularly useful since the existing works used $(2, 2)$ schemes and $(3, 3)$ schemes.

EXAMPLE 5 *Consider an additive group $(G, +)$ and a secret $s \in G$. To construct an (n, n) threshold scheme, the owner of s chooses randomly $n - 1$ shares $s_i \in G$, $i \in [1, n - 1]$. The last share s_n is defined by $s_n = s - \sum_{i=1}^{n-1} s_i$. Knowing all shares, one can compute $s = \sum_{i=1}^{n} s_i$. Knowing strictly less than n shares does not provide information about s.*

The size of shares in a secret sharing scheme is also an important problem. More details on this problem can be found in [9, 12, 33].

Short Paper: A Practical View of "Mixing" Identities in Vehicular Networks

Bisheng Liu
School of Computer Science
Fudan University
220 Handan Road, Shanghai, China 200433

bsliu@fudan.edu

Jerry T. Chiang, Jason J. Haas, Yih-Chun Hu
Department of Electrical and Computer Engineering
University of Illinois at Urbana-Champaign
1406 W. Green Street, Urbana, IL 61801-2918

{chiang2, jjhaas2, yihchun} @illinois.edu

ABSTRACT

In a Vehicular Ad hoc NETwork (VANET), vehicles broadcast safety messages disclosing their trajectory information in order to warn drivers of impending accidents. Precise location information needed for these safety applications, combined with the need to exclude attackers through the use of authentication, creates a significant privacy risk. One method proposed to improve privacy is the use of many pseudonyms, and changing pseudonyms while in a *mix zone* where all other vehicles also change pseudonyms. Previous work has evaluated the effectiveness of mix zones using traces generated based on traffic theory. In this paper, we analyze the privacy obtainable from using mix zones in VANETs based on actual recordings of vehicle movements. We choose *rank* instead of *entropy* as our privacy metric because, as we will show, entropy is difficult to measure in our scenarios.

Categories and Subject Descriptors

C.2.0 [**Computer-Communication Networks**]: General—Security and protection, (e.g., firewalls)

General Terms

Security, Performance

Keywords

Vehicular ad hoc networks, privacy, mix zones

1. INTRODUCTION

Researchers have proposed using Vehicular Ad hoc NETworks (VANETs) to disseminate safety messages to support vehicular safety applications, which they hope will improve drivers' safety. For example, the US Department of Transportation (US-DOT) has identified eight such applications [1]. Most of these safety applications require that each vehicle periodically broadcast its current location among other information (e.g., speed, timestamp, etc.) to its one-hop neighbors. Depending on the safety application, each vehicle may be required to broadcast safety messages at a rate of up to 10 Hz. While these applications could improve vehicular safety, an attacker can also try to track a single vehicle by eavesdropping on the unsuspecting vehicle's safety messages.

In order to preserve *anonymity* and ensure *untraceability*, each

vehicle could use randomly-changing and unlinkable pseudonyms to communicate with each other. Pseudonyms are sufficient for initiating communication since most safety applications are more concerned about vehicle trajectory than vehicle identity. However, using the temporal and spatial relationship between the current and previous locations of each vehicle, an attacker capable of monitoring all communications in the network could make pseudonym changes ineffective. To reduce an attacker's ability to correlate multiple pseudonyms from a single vehicle, the vehicle can choose to change its pseudonyms only in regions where the attacker is unable to monitor the communications, known as *mix zones* [2]. Several researchers [3][4] have suggested that mix zones in VANETs be created at predetermined locations where the density of vehicles is high and the speed and direction of vehicles change often, such as at intersections.

The obtainable privacy from a given mix zone depends not only on the sampled traffic traces crossing the mix zone, but also on the power of the tracking algorithm chosen by the attacker. Prior work [3][5] has often relied on simulating VANET environments to evaluate the effectiveness of mix zones, using traffic data generated by simulators based on traffic theory. To the best of our knowledge, we are the first to apply a realistic traffic model as a part of the analysis of the achieved privacy from a mix zone based on *real vehicle mobility data*. For a mix zone created at a busy intersection, we extend previously proposed tracking algorithms by taking traffic signals and lane changes into consideration; for mix zones created on a high-density straight road, we choose a heuristic tracking algorithm that correlates vehicles based on the sequence of vehicles entering and exiting the road section. Because an attacker that lacks a more sophisticated traffic model can always use our proposed tracking algorithm, our evaluations represent an *upper bound* on the amount of privacy that the mix zone under evaluation can provide. Moreover, prior research has used *entropy* [3] to measure the privacy obtainable from a mix zone based on a particular tracking algorithm. However, prior work calculates entropy using probabilities determined by a tracking algorithm, and may not be a very useful metric in evaluating privacy, as we will discuss in Section 3. Our research addresses the following questions. *How much privacy can we obtain from a mix zone in reality? How do we measure the obtained privacy?*

The remainder of this paper is organized as follows. In Section 2 we present related work, our assumptions, and our attacker model. In Section 3, we discuss our choice of privacy metrics. In Section 4, we present the tracking algorithm we use for mix zones created at road intersections and analyze the obtainable privacy. We then present the tracking algorithm we use for mix zones along straight roads and analyze the effectiveness of these mix zones in Section 5. Finally we conclude our work in Section 6.

2. BACKGROUND

2.1 Related Work

The privacy implications of VANETs are a major concern [6][7]. Researchers have proposed that vehicles should change pseudonyms while communicating in order to mitigate the threat of being tracked by an attacker [6][8][9]. However, an attacker might still be able to determine that two pseudonyms correspond to a single vehicle by using the information included in safety messages, such as the location and the speed of the vehicle, thereby compromising the driver's privacy.

Many authors have suggested using *silent periods* [10] to preserve anonymity; that is, when vehicles need to update their pseudonyms, they turn off their transceivers for a period of time. Sampigethaya et al. [11][12] proposed that vehicles in geographic proximity can form a group and elect a group leader so that the group leader can communicate on behalf of the whole group. Other group members could then safely extend their silent periods. The same researchers also developed a user-centric approach, *Swing & Swap* [13], to increase location privacy by loosely synchronizing pseudonym updates between vehicles. As we mentioned in Section 1, since many safety applications require each vehicle to periodically broadcast safety messages approximately every 100 milliseconds, the maximum silent period is bounded by the required broadcast interval.

Beresford et al. [2][14] proposed using *mix zones* for privacy preservation. Mix zones are locations where an attacker is unable to directly link vehicular communications to vehicle identities, and hence, the vehicle identities could be mixed in such areas. If many vehicles simultaneously update pseudonyms in a mix zone, an attacker is less likely to be able to associate each updated pseudonym to its previous pseudonym. Freudiger et al. [3] proposed that mix zones could be created at road intersections and used simulations to determine the effectiveness of their mix zones. Their approach is only effective against external attackers that have no legitimate credentials, because an attacker with legitimate credentials can understand all transmissions within the mix zone, thus able to track a vehicle from mix zone entry to exit. Other approaches have considered connecting several mix zones together to form a mix network that can accumulate the achieved privacy [4]. An attacker monitoring multiple mix zones could, however, thwart the privacy goals of the mix network. The work most similar to ours is that of Buttyan et al. [5], who examine the relationship between the strength of the attacker and the achieved privacy, using artificial traces. Their analysis suggests that an attacker monitoring 50% of the intersections in the road network could successfully track approximately 60% of the vehicles. Our research differs from these approaches because we evaluate the upper bound on the amount of privacy provided by a single mix zone, using actual vehicle mobility data.

2.2 Assumptions

We assume that each VANET will use a suitable public key infrastructure where a possibly-offline but trusted certificate authority (CA) manages the identities, cryptographic keys, and certificates of all vehicles in the network. We assume that every legitimate vehicle has a unique identity, several pairs of private and public keys, and certificates corresponding to each public key.

We assume each vehicle in a VANET is equipped with a GPS receiver and can obtain the vehicle's location and the current time. Each vehicle periodically broadcasts a safety message every 100 milliseconds [15]. A safety message includes the location of the transmitting vehicle, the time of transmission, and possibly other data. Each vehicle must sign every message it sends, and distribute the corresponding certificate so that neighbors can verify the signature of each received packet [16]. We assume that each vehicle periodically changes the certificate with which it signs messages, using each certificate for a short duration and never reusing a certificate. The duration of use is beyond the scope of this paper.

We assume the location of each mix zone in a VANET is published by the trusted CA, and that both legitimate vehicles and attackers know the exact locations of the mix zones. The selection of mix zone locations is beyond the scope of this paper. We further assume that each vehicle must change its pseudonym when the vehicle passes through any mix zone. This assumption provides maximal privacy. Our analysis techniques are applicable even when some vehicles do not change pseudonyms in a mix zone.

2.3 Adversary Model

In this paper, we assume an attacker can monitor communications immediately adjacent to a mix zone, and as such can hear messages from entering and exiting nodes. Moreover, we assume that an attacker cannot receive safety messages from vehicles in a mix zone. Against a weak adversary, this requirement may be fulfilled using symmetric encryption [3]. Meeting this assumption against a more powerful adversary requires the use of a *silent period*, so that vehicles inside the mix zone do not transmit any safety messages at all, which may negatively impact vehicular safety within the mix zone.

We assume that an attacker can, from a safety message, identify the sending vehicle's exact lane number. This assumption is reasonable since the typical lane width in the United States is more than 3 m [17] and many off-the-shelf GPS receivers could provide accuracy within 1.5 m with 95% confidence [18].

3. PRIVACY METRICS

In this section, we discuss possible metrics for measuring the privacy obtained from mix zones for a given tracking algorithm. In particular, we analyze three proposed privacy metrics: entropy, success probability, and rank.

3.1 Entropy

Beresford et al. first used entropy to measure the user privacy provided by mix zones in location-aware services [2]. Similarly, researchers [3][4][5] have adopted entropy to measure the level of privacy provided by mix zones in VANETs. For each vehicle v exiting the mix zone, the attacker calculates the probability that v corresponds to an entering vehicle i. We denote this probability as $p_{i,v}$. The mix zone is then claimed to provide a level of privacy to vehicle v defined by the entropy of $p_{i,v}$,

$$H(v) = -\sum_{i=1}^{N} p_{i,v} \log_2(p_{i,v}) \qquad (1)$$

However, the correctness of the entropy value depends on the correctness of the computed probability $p_{i,v}$. Because each value of $p_{i,v}$ is computed by the tracking algorithm, and because the tracking algorithm might not correctly estimate this probability, the actual entropy obtained by a mix zone may be greater than or less than the calculated entropy.

We use the following example to illustrate our argument, as shown in Fig. 1. Let us assume vehicle X enters the mix zone from the west and vehicle Y enters the mix zone from the north simultaneously. Before vehicle X exits from the east exit, X changes its pseudonym to Y'. Similarly, vehicle Y changes its pseudonym to X' before exiting from the south exit. Let there be an attacker who tries to track each vehicle by correlating their pseudonyms before and after each vehicle crosses the mix zone.

We consider two possible attackers. Attacker A relies on the spatial relation between the locations where a vehicle enters and exits the mix zone to link pseudonyms. For example, the tracking algorithm of attacker A states that vehicles coming from the west have an equal probability of exiting from the north, south, and east sides of the mix zone. Similarly, vehicles coming from the north have an equal probability of exiting from the south, west, and east sides of the mix zone. From attacker A's perspective, the probability that vehicle Y' and vehicle X are the same vehicle is 50%, the probability that vehicle Y' and vehicle Y are the same vehicle is 50% as well, and hence the entropy of vehicle Y' is 1 bit.

Attacker B, on the other hand, pairs the pseudonyms using a deterministic permutation. That is, attacker B believes that pseudonym X and X' should always belong to the same vehicle and pseudonym Y and Y' should always belong to the same vehicle. The tracking algorithm of attacker B may be incorrect in reality and be weaker than the tracking algorithm of attacker A. Nevertheless, the computed entropy of vehicle Y' is 0 since the tracking algorithm of B is deterministic. As a result, it seems that vehicle Y' has less privacy in the presence of attacker B compared to attacker A.

If we fix a single tracking algorithm and measure its entropy across several mix zones, the result tells us how confident the tracking algorithm is in different situations. However, as we have shown through our example, if multiple tracking algorithms are used, the resulting entropy values may provide very little insight for further analysis.

3.2 Success Probability and Rank

Another natural metric to measure the amount of privacy is the success probability of the attacker [5]. For each vehicle v exiting the mix zone, the attacker determines the corresponding entering vehicle i. The attacker can make this decision by calculating the probability of the mapping of an entering vehicle u_i to the exiting vehicle v, denoted as $p_{i,v}$, and pick the most likely mapping. The decision is then compared against ground truth. If the chosen vehicle u_i is indeed the same vehicle using pseudonym v, then the attacker is successful. The higher the success probability is, the less privacy the mix zone offers.

A more fine-grained metric than the success probability is the rank of the actual vehicle [19]. For each exiting vehicle v, the tracking algorithm sorts the entering vehicles based on $p_{i,v}$. We can then compare the ground truth with the rank chosen by the tracking algorithm. For example, if the algorithm chose the actual entering vehicle as the second most likely, the algorithm would have a rank of 2 in that case. An algorithm that consistently has low rank is one that is effective at tracking vehicles through the mix zone. We can show how often a tracking algorithm is effective by computing the probability that the rank is less than some value. This metric is a generalized form of success probability: The algorithm is successful if the rank equals to 1.

Since we use two different tracking algorithms for two different mix zone configurations, we will use the rank of the actual vehicle to measure the privacy provided by mix zones.

4. MIX ZONES AT INTERSECTIONS

Researchers have proposed using mix zones at certain intersections. Because vehicles often simultaneously change their directions and speeds at intersections, intersections form a promising mix context [20] in which a vehicle can update its pseudonym in a way that leaks minimal information linking its two pseudonyms. In order to evaluate the privacy provided by mix zones, we first choose a

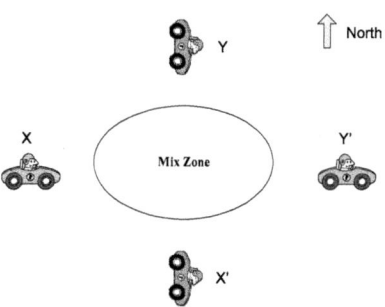

Figure 1. Vehicles X, Y enter the mix zone and change their pseudonyms to Y' and X' respectively after exiting.

tracking algorithm for an attacker and then measure the *upper bound* on the amount of privacy provided by the mix zone against that attacker.

4.1 Tracking at Intersections

We evaluate our algorithm using traditional machine-learning test protocols. We divide up our dataset into two phases: a training phase and a testing phase. During the training phase, an attacker (perfectly) observes incoming and outgoing traffic for a limited period of time to infer patterns with which entering vehicles correspond to exiting vehicles. During the testing phase, the attacker listens to each vehicle's location broadcasts as it enters and exits the mix zone. Then the attacker estimates the probability that a particular exiting vehicle corresponds to each of the candidate entering vehicles, using information learned during the training phase. Most proposed tracking algorithms [2][3][4][5] use two categories of information to correlate vehicles.

- Spatial correlation: The attacker observes a vehicle's location at entry and exit. Specifically, the attacker determines the probability that a node enters at location s and exits at location e.

- Temporal correlation: The attacker observes a vehicle's time of entry and exit; the elapsed time t follows a particular probability distribution.

We derive a more realistic traffic model by also considering lane changes and traffic lights, based upon our observations over real vehicle mobility data. As mentioned in Section 2.2, we assume that an attacker is able to identify the exact lane of traffic from which each vehicle enters and exits the mix zone. The attacker can then refine its spatial correlation technique by using lane information to help correlate entry-exit pairs. The lane-change information could provide significant advantages for the attacker. For example, based on our observations, *vehicles tend to remain in the same lane after crossing an intersection* (as long as the number of lanes remains the same before and after the intersection), and *vehicles turning right tend to stay in those lanes closer to the right edge of the road when exiting the intersection*.

Moreover, we refine the temporal correlation pattern by considering the status of traffic lights. In particular, we estimate the time that a vehicle takes to cross the intersection given the known traffic light status when the vehicle arrives at the intersection. If the light is red (we consider a yellow light to be the end of the green light cycle) when an entering vehicle wishes to cross the intersection, the vehicle has to wait a certain amount of time until the light turns green. *That vehicle would take longer to cross the intersection compared to vehicles that arrive at the intersection when the light is green.*

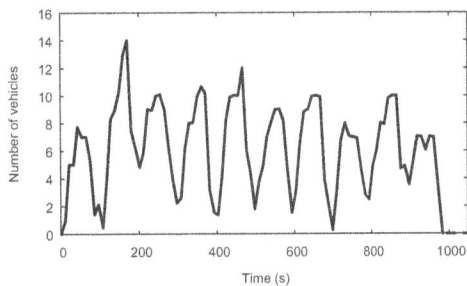

Figure 2. The number of vehicles near the southern entry of the intersection as a function of the time.

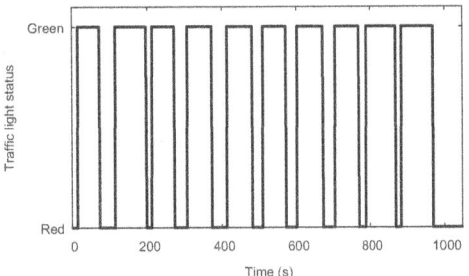

Figure 3. The estimated light status as a function of the time.

Our study assumes that the attacker knows, or can infer, the traffic light status. When lights are timed, an attacker can record their timing on one day and use it to estimate the status of the traffic light on another day. When lights respond in real-time to traffic conditions, the attacker can estimate the status of the light by monitoring the density and average speed at the entries and exits of the intersection. Though other intersections may use different traffic control devices such as stop signs, such intersections typically have much less traffic, making them less suitable as mix zones.

In the training phase of our tracking algorithm, we learn the probability distribution of all possible pairings of a vehicle entering the intersection in lane i at entry s and exiting in lane j at exit e, denoted as $p_{si,ej}$. Next, for each vehicle arriving at the intersection, we record the traffic light status and the amount of time that the vehicle took to cross the intersection. We model the crossing time using a normal distribution, with different parameters that depend on the trajectory of the vehicle and the light status. For a vehicle arriving at the intersection at entry s when the light status is l and exiting at exit e, the probability distribution of the crossing time $q_{s,e,l}(t)$ can be denoted as

$$q_{s,e,l}(t) \sim N_l(\mu_{s,e}, \sigma_{s,e}) \qquad (2)$$

where $l \in \{Green, Red\}$.

In the testing phase of our algorithm, we represent each exit event as a 4-tuple, (v, j, e, t_e) where v is the pseudonym of the exiting vehicle, j is the lane number, e is the exit at which v exits the mix zone, and t_e is the time of v exiting the mix zone. We represent each entering event as a 5-tuple (f, i, s, t_s, l) where f denotes the pseudonym of the entering vehicle, i is the lane number, s is the entrance at which v enters the mix zone, t_s is the time v enters the mix zone, and l is the light status at time t_s. For each entering and exiting event, we compute the probability that pseudonym v and f belong to the same vehicle as

$$P_{f,v} = p_{si,ej} q_{s,e,l}(t_e - t_s) \qquad (3)$$

Then, for each exiting vehicle v, we sort and rank all possible entering vehicles according to their computed probabilities.

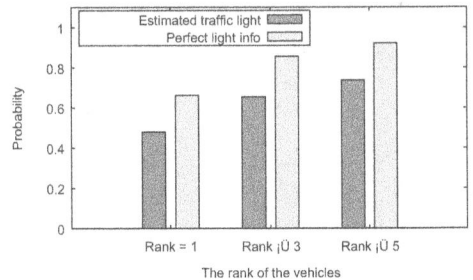

Figure 4. The obtainable privacy provided by the mix zone created at the sample intersection of Lankershim.

4.2 Case Study on Lankershim Data

In this subsection, we evaluate the level of privacy provided by a mix zone located at an intersection. We use real vehicle mobility data from the Lankershim datasets obtained from the Federal Highway Administration's (FHWA) Next Generation Simulation (NGSIM) project [21]. In the NGSIM data, both Lankershim Boulevard and Peachtree Street are multi-lane arterial roads that consist of several intersections. We choose to use the Lankershim data over the Peachtree data, because the Peachtree data has very little cross traffic in the east-west direction and all of the Peachtree intersections are either controlled by timer based traffic lights or have no traffic lights at all.

In the Lankershim data, we choose the intersection of Universal Hollywood Drive and Lankershim Boulevard because this intersection has the densest traffic. The traffic at this intersection is coordinated by adaptive traffic lights, which dynamically changes status based on the traffic condition around the intersection. The Lankershim data includes two sets of data, each lasting about 15 minutes. Across both data sets, 2,230 vehicles cross this intersection. We use the data starting from 8:30 am as the training dataset and the trace starting from 8:45 am as the testing dataset. We define a circular mix zone centered at the middle of the intersection. The radius of the mix zone is 24 meters, which covers approximately the entire intersection.

During the training phase, we assume the attacker knows the precise traffic light status at any time, which we derived from the recorded Lankershim video data. In the testing phase, we *estimate* the traffic light status every second during the entire 15-minute period. In our evaluation, we only use the change in vehicle density to estimate the light status. We monitor the number of vehicles near the southern entry of the intersection every second, as depicted in Fig. 2. We derive the status of the traffic light controlling the northbound traffic at every second, as depicted in Fig. 3 (details are omitted here due to space constraints). For comparison, we let the attacker know the exact light status at any second and run the same experiment again.

We plot the fraction of cases where the actual vehicle's rank was 1, at most 3, and at most 5. Fig. 4 shows our results. The attacker is able to correctly identify the entering vehicle for about 48.0% of the exiting vehicles. We also find that the probability of success could be significantly improved if the attacker can learn the exact times at which the traffic light changes. Simulations in previous work suggest if there are on average 7 vehicles crossing the intersection under high traffic congestion scenario, then less than 30% of the vehicles could be tracked [4]. However, our evaluation based on actual vehicle mobility data shows that a mix zone at a busy intersection only offers limited privacy. Vehicles crossing the mix zone would obtain even less privacy if the attacker could get accurate traffic light status along both directions of the intersection, or if the attacker uses more sophisticated tracking algorithms.

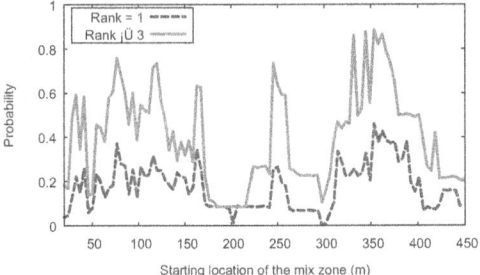

Figure 5. The obtainable privacy as a function of the starting location of the mix zone (l = 50 m, lane 5).

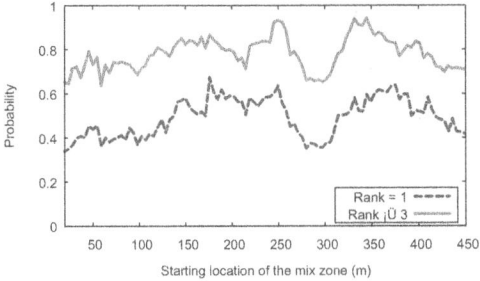

Figure 6. The obtainable privacy as a function of the starting location of the mix zone when 5% of the entering vehicles have already been tracked (l = 50 m, lane 5).

5. MIX ZONES ON STRAIGHT ROADS

Unlike at intersections, vehicles on straight roads rarely change directions. However, if the vehicle density on the roadway is relatively high, drivers might change lanes and speed, making these locations possible candidates for mix zones. In this section, we evaluate the effectiveness of mix zones created on a high density straight highway using the I-80 data from NGSIM.

5.1 Tracking on Straight Roads

In order to evaluate the effectiveness of mix zones on straight roads, we choose a tracking algorithm that correlates vehicles based on the sequence of vehicles entering and exiting the road section, similar to the idea proposed in [22].

Because straight-road tracking depends on typical driver behavior, errors can accumulate without the periodic injection of ground truth. An attacker can take advantage of easily tracked vehicles in order to obtain this ground truth. Some public vehicles, such as police cars, might be tracked easily if they send out distinct messages. Other VANET applications may also disclose information sufficient for such tracking. Other RF devices in a car, such as electronic toll collection or an RF tire pressure monitor, could also be used for tracking. These easily tracked vehicles can help an attacker reduce accumulations of error, as we show in our evaluations.

Our tracking algorithm is as follows. For each lane k on a straight road, we maintain a counter CI_k and assign a unique sequence number for every vehicle entering lane k. The counter CI_k starts from zero and is incremented by one when a vehicle enters the mix zone in lane k. Similarly, we maintain another counter CO_k and assign a unique sequence number for every vehicle exiting the mix zone in lane k. The counter CO_k starts from zero and is incremented by one when a vehicle exits the mix zone in lane k. The attacker could initiate tracking when there are no vehicles on the road, e.g., at some time during the night. The attacker then tries to track a vehicle by pairing the exit sequence number with the same entry sequence number; that is, the n-th vehicle entering the mix zone in lane k is paired with the n-th vehicle exiting the mix zone in lane k. One

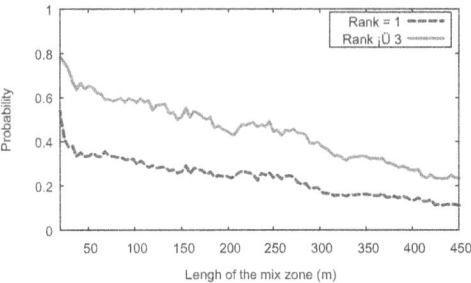

Figure 7. The obtained privacy as a function of the length of the mix zone (lane 5).

disadvantage of this approach is that if vehicle v enters the mix zone in lane k and later changes to lane q, all the vehicles following v in lane k will have their exit sequence number offset by 1. These errors could accumulate if additional vehicles in lane k change lanes. However, as previously mentioned, some vehicles could be tracked using other approaches; these vehicles could be used to remove the accumulated errors. Whenever a trackable vehicle enters and exits the mix zone in lane k, we reset the entry counter CI_k to zero when the vehicle enters the mix zone and reset the exit counter CO_k to zero when the vehicle exits the mix zone.

5.2 Case Study on I-80 Data

In this subsection, we study the privacy obtainable from mix zones built on a high-density straight road. We assume that the attacker uses the tracking algorithm described above; thus our evaluation results serve as an upper bound of obtainable privacy. In the NGSIM data, both I-80 and US-101 are major multi-lane freeways. We choose the I-80 data over the US-101 data because the I-80 data has denser traffic.

The I-80 data represents a stretch of roadway approximately 503 meters in length, including an on-ramp at Powell Street. There are six through lanes on I-80, excluding the on-ramp. Lane numbering starts from the left-most lane, which we number lane 1. Lane 6 is the closest to the on-ramp. In the I-80 data, we choose to study the 5:00 pm – 5:15 pm dataset because it contains the densest traffic among all three of the datasets, consisting of 1836 vehicles. The average density of the trace is 52.1 vehicles per km per lane. We exclude the traffic coming from the on-ramp (205 vehicles) from our evaluation.

We define a rectangular area on I-80 as the mix zone; the rectangular area is l meters in length, consisting of all six straight lanes. Both the starting location of the mix zone on I-80 and the value of l vary. We choose to evaluate the privacy of the vehicles entering the mix zone in lane 5, because of all six lanes, lane changes take place most frequently in lane 5. Fig. 5 shows the privacy obtained from mix zones built on I-80, where l = 50 m. We build the first mix zone starting from the southern edge of the I-80 data set and increment the starting location of the mix zone by 3 meters (approximately the length of one vehicle) for every run. The results suggest that the privacy obtained from the mix zone is highly dependent on the location of the mix zone.

We then investigate the impact of easily tracked vehicles on the privacy of other nodes around them. We uniformly at random choose 5% of the vehicles entering the mix zone in lane 5 and assume they can be easily tracked. We performed 100 runs for each mix zone and averaged the results. Comparing Fig. 6 to Fig. 5 shows that the attacker is much more successful if some vehicles can be easily tracked. Over 60% of all vehicles exiting the mix zone in lane 5 are one of the three highest ranked entering vehicles. For comparison, we also carry out the same evaluation in lane 1 and lane 2 (detailed results omitted due to space constraints). Vehicles in these lanes could not obtain as much privacy as those in lane 5, because lane 1 and lane 2 are farther away from the on-ramp than lane 5 and hence vehicles in lane 1 and 2 are less affected by the traffic coming from the on-ramp. In other words, true straight-line roads offer little privacy.

Finally we evaluate the impact the size of the mix zone has on the obtainable privacy. We fix the starting position of the mix zone near the southern edge of the I-80 dataset and gradually increase the length of the mix zone from 20 m to 500 m. As we expected, Figure 7 suggests that larger mix zones provide better privacy.

6. CONCLUSION

We took realistic traffic models into consideration and evaluated the effectiveness of mix zones at intersections and on straight roads using actual mobility traces. Contrary to implications of prior work, our results suggest that a single mix zone provides limited privacy because of the inherent lack of randomness in vehicle mobility. However, a vehicle might obtain more privacy by consecutively traversing several mix zones. Evaluating the effectiveness of a network of mix zones is beyond the scope of this paper and we leave this to future work. We believe that deciding whether or not the privacy provided by a single mix zone is sufficient should also be a policy question, which depends on the opinion of VANET policy-makers.

7. References

1. **The CAMP Vehicle Safety Communications Consortium.** *Vehicle Safety Communications Project Final Report: Identify Intelligent Vehicle Safety Applications Enabled by DSRC.* s.l. : U.S. Department of Transportation, National Highway Traffic Safety Administration, 2005. DOT HS 809 859.

2. *Mix-zones: User privacy in location-aware services.* **Beresford, A. R. and Stajano, F.** s.l. : IEEE, 2004. Proceedings of the First IEEE International Workshop on Pervasive Computing and Com-munication Security (PerSec).

3. *Mix-Zones for Location Privacy in Vehicular Networks.* **Freudiger, J., et al.** 2007. Proceedings of WiN-ITS.

4. *On the Optimal Placement of Mix Zones.* **Freudiger, J., Shokri, R. and Hubaux, J.-P.** 2009. Proceedings of the 9th Privacy Enhancing Technologies Symposium (PETS).

5. *On the effectiveness of changing pseudonyms to provide location privacy in VANETs.* **Buttyan, L., Holczer, T. and Vajda, I.** 2007. Proceedings of the 4th European Workshop on Security and Privacy in Ad Hoc and Sensor Networks (ESAS).

6. *Privacy issues in vehicular ad hoc networks.* **Dötzer, F.** 2005. Proceedings of the Workshop on Privacy Enhancing Technologies (PET).

7. **Hubaux, J.-P., Capkun, S. and Luo, J.** The Security and Privacy of Smart Vehicles. *IEEE Security & Privacy Magazine.* 2004, Vol. 2, 3.

8. *The Security of Vehicular Ad Hoc Networks.* **Raya, M. and Hubaux, J.-P.** 2005. Proceedings of the Third ACM Workshop on the Security of Ad Hoc and Sensor Networks (SASN).

9. *Architecture for Secure and Private Vehicular Communications.* **Papadimitratos, P., et al.** 2007. Proceedings of the International Conference on ITS Telecommunications (ITST).

10. *Enhancing wireless location privacy using silent period.* **Huang, L., et al.** 2005. Proceedings of the IEEE Wireless Communications and Networking Conference (WCNC).

11. *Caravan: Providing location privacy for VANET.* **Sampigethaya, K., et al.** 2005. Proceedings of the 3rd Annual Conference on Embedded Security in Cars (ESCAR).

12. *Amoeba: Robust location privacy scheme for VANET.* **Sampigethaya, K., et al.** 8, 2007, IEEE Journal on Selected Areas in Communications, Vol. 25, pp. 1569--1589.

13. *Swing and Swap: User-centric approaches towards maximizing location privacy.* **Li, M., et al.** 2006. Proceedings of the 5th ACM workshop on Privacy in electronic society (WPES).

14. *Location privacy in pervasive computing.* **Beresford, A. R. and Stajano, F.** 1, 2003, IEEE Pervasive Computing, Vol. 3, pp. 46-55.

15. **IEEE.** *5.9 GHz DSRC: Dedicated Short-Range Communications.* http://grouper.ieee.org/groups/scc32/dsrc/.

16. *IEEE 1609.2-Standard for Wireless Access in Vehicular Environments (WAVE) - Security Services for Applications and Management Messages.*

17. **Stein, William J. and Neuman, Timothy R.** *Mitigation Strategies for Design Exceptions.* http://safety.fhwa.dot.gov/geometric/pubs/mitigationstrategies/fhwa_sa_07011.pdf.

18. *Wide-Area Augmentation System Performance Analysis Report, Reporting Period: January 1 to March 31.* 2009. http://www.nstb.tc.faa.gov/.

19. *Location Privacy in Wireless Networks.* **Hu, Y.-C. and Wang, H. J.** 2005. Proceedings of the ACM SIGCOMM Asia Workshop.

20. *Privacy in VANETs using changing pseudonyms - ideal and real.* **Gerlach, M. and Gäuttler, F.** 2007. Proceedings of the 65th Vehicular Technology Conference (VTC).

21. NGSIM. Next Generation Simulation. [Online] http://www.ngsim.fhwa.dot.gov/.

22. *A Method for Deter-mining Real-Time Travel Times on Motorways.* **Westerman, M. and Immers, L.** 1992. Proceedings of the 25th International Symposium on Automotive Technology and Automation (ISATA). pp. 221--228.

Efficient and Secure Threshold-based Event Validation for VANETs*

Hsu-Chun Hsiao[†]   Ahren Studer[†]   Rituik Dubey[§]   Elaine Shi[°]   Adrian Perrig[†]

[†] CyLab/CMU   [§] Cisco   [°] PARC/UC Berkeley
{hchsiao, astuder, perrig}@cmu.edu   ritdubey@cisco.com   elaines@eecs.berkeley.edu

ABSTRACT

Determining whether the number of vehicles reporting an event is above a threshold is an important mechanism for VANETs, because many applications rely on a threshold number of notifications to reach agreement among vehicles, to determine the validity of an event, or to prevent the abuse of emergency alarms. We present the first efficient and secure threshold-based event validation protocol for VANETs. Quite counter-intuitively, we find that the z-smallest approach [3] offers the best tradeoff between security and efficiency since other approaches perform better for probabilistic counting. Analysis and simulation shows that our protocol provides > 99% accuracy despite the presence of attackers, collection and distribution of alerts in less than 1 second, and negligible impact on network performance.

Categories and Subject Descriptors

C.2.0 [**General**]: Security and protection; C.2.1 [**Network Architecture and Design**]: Wireless communication

General Terms

Algorithms, Design, Security

Keywords

VANETs, threshold-based event validation, multi-hop communication

*This research was supported by CyLab at Carnegie Mellon under grants DAAD19-02-1-0389 and W911NF-09-1-0273, and by MURI W 911 NF 0710287 from the Army Research Office, and by support from General Motors through the GM-CMU Collaborative Research Laboratory. The views and conclusions contained here are those of the authors and should not be interpreted as necessarily representing the official policies or endorsements, either express or implied, of ARO, CMU, GM, or the U.S. Government or any of its agencies.

1. INTRODUCTION

In Vehicular Ad-hoc NETworks (VANETs), vehicles' On-Board Units (OBUs) broadcast information, such as location, time, speed, and congestion level over the wireless channel for a variety of safety and convenience applications [2]. For example, the Emergency Electronic Brake Light (EEBL) application enables a vehicle performing emergency braking to broadcast a warning message to any following vehicles. Similarly, the Road Hazard Condition Notification (RHCN) application enables a vehicle to detect ice or obstacles on the road and alert the vehicles approaching the hazard zone. Such notification-based VANET applications can be classified into two types, single-hop-relevant and multi-hop-relevant, based on the number of alerts that are generated and the distance these alerts need to be propagated. In single-hop-relevant applications (such as emergency braking or lane change alerts), only one or a few vehicles — those vehicles involved in the event — will send out a notification to nearby vehicles. Such traffic information is irrelevant to vehicles multiple network hops away. In multi-hop-relevant applications (such as road hazard and congestion notification systems) a large number of vehicles are involved and report the event to vehicles that are potentially multiple network hops away, so recipients can respond appropriately. For example, congested road notifications may be transmitted several kilometers so drivers can find another route (e.g., take an exit to avoid a congested part of a highway).

Despite the great potential of VANET applications, security has long been a concern [10, 18, 24, 25, 28, 31], and thus it is imperative to provide functionality to validate an event reported by vehicles in both types of applications. Although the IEEE 1609.2 [14] standard is proposed to secure VANETs using digital signatures and certificates to prevent attacks (e.g., impersonation), the standard fails to address event falsification. For example, a selfish driver can still generate a false alert about congestion on a road segment, but other drivers will believe the alert since it is digitally signed using valid cryptographic credentials. As a result, these drivers will avoid this road, providing the selfish driver with an improved driving experience.

Counting the number of vehicles that report an event allows a recipient to evaluate the validity of a VANET event [13, 16, 29]. For example, a traffic jam reported by 2 vehicles is likely to be fake (or just started), but alerts from 50 vehicles is a strong indicator of road congestion. Particularly, we focus on **threshold-based event validation** where an event is considered valid if the number of reports exceeds a certain threshold. In contrast to counting alerts for single-hop-relevant applications, which can be done without collecting alerts from vehicles several hops away, correctly counting the number of reporting vehicles in **multi-hop-relevant (MH-relevant) applications** is challenging; it is crucial that the counting mechanism satisfies efficiency and security *at the same time*. Rebroadcasting all signed messages with certificates associated with an event is secure, yet causes network contention [23]. Messages without the signatures and certificates may elevate efficiency, but a vehicle could claim that an arbitrary number of vehicles have observed an event. Cooperative rebroadcasts have been proposed to reduce network contention [35], but it is still inefficient when combined with signatures and certificates. Hence, the major challenge is to securely and accurately estimate the number of vehicles that report an alert without requiring all of the associated data.

Prior work has proposed schemes for probabilistic counting to estimate the total number of items (e.g., unique elements in a database) based on a single pass over the data while requiring significantly less space [1, 3, 9]. In this paper, we leverage such counting schemes to perform *probabilistic threshold-based event validation* where a vehicle that receives a small subset of alerts can distinguish between a small number of potentially malicious alerts and a large number of alerts for a legitimate event. To reduce space requirements, probabilistic counting assumes that items follow a distribution. Based on this distribution, the reception of different items has (with high probability) different implications about the total number of items in existence. For example, item A may be so rare that receiving A implies there are 100 items. Probabilistic counting yields an estimate of the number of alerts, whereas threshold-based event validation only needs to indicate if the number of alerts is above a fixed threshold. By focusing on estimating a binary condition, i.e., whether the count is over or under a fixed threshold, rather than on the numerical value of the count itself, probabilistic threshold-based validation can sacrifice accuracy of the underlying counting schemes in order to further improve efficiency.

Current schemes for probabilistic counting assume the absence of malicious parties. Unfortunately, a malicious party can generate different variants of a single alert (e.g., by making small changes to the time, location, or randomness in the signature) until it acquires a rare enough alert instance that the scheme indicates the threshold was passed — a *decision changing attack*. To prevent such attacks, the scheme must limit the number of alerts one sender can generate for an event. We propose an event description format that uses coarse-grained event, time, and location descriptions to achieve this goal. We perform threshold-based validation on the event description and source of an alert while keeping the associated signature and certificate to verify the source that generated the alert. This combination of signatures and threshold-based validation based on messages of our format provides an efficient means to prevent malicious parties from abusing VANET applications.

Contributions. The main contributions of this work are:
1) We prove that threshold-based validation requires much less accuracy in counting than probabilistic counting does.
2) We propose a secure and efficient probabilistic threshold-based event validation protocol with an event description format to prevent decision changing attacks.
3) We design a message exchange protocol enabling timely collection and distribution of multi-hop alerts.
4) The evaluation shows that vehicles can accurately validate an event by storing and forwarding only 15 alerts while incurring limited packet loss due to bandwidth consumption associated with VANET applications.

2. BACKGROUND ON PROBABILISTIC COUNTING

In this paper, we propose a protocol for efficient and secure threshold-based event validation, building on probabilistic counting schemes. In this section, we provide an overview of probabilistic counting, one example of a specific probabilistic counting scheme, and a discussion of probabilistic counting schemes' trade-offs and limitations.

Probabilistic counting selects several representative elements, or a *synopsis* [22], as an estimator for the total number of distinct elements [1, 3, 9]. The synopsis summarizes the entire element set and thus permits estimation of the total size. Probabilistic counting provides a trade-off between synopsis size and accuracy: the more elements in the synopsis, the more accurate the count. The extreme trade-off points are to either keep all elements (achieving perfect accuracy) or to store only minimal statistical information. For example, storing only the lexicographically smallest element enables estimation of the total number of elements, because assuming uniformly distributed elements, the unbiased estimator for the total number is $(e_1 - e_0)/(e - e_0)$, where e represents the value of the smallest observed element, and e_0 and e_1 the minimal and maximal value, respectively.

Generally a probabilistic counting scheme provides three functions on synopses: *Generation*, *Fusion*, and *Evaluation* [22]. A *Generation* function selects the representative items from the input set I to use as a synopsis $\mathbb{S}$. In this paper, we consider a class of probabilistic counting schemes whose *Fusion* function prevents double counting and *Evaluation* function provides an error guarantee on its approximation $\tilde{n}$, such that we have high confidence $(1 - \delta)$ on a probabilistic statement that $\tilde{n}$ deviates from the real count n by only a small amount. Formally, each scheme provides the following functions:

Generation: **SG(.)** $\mathbb{S} = SG(I)$, where $\mathbb{S} \subseteq I$.

Fusion: **SF(.,.)** $SF(\mathbb{S}_1, \mathbb{S}_2) = SG(I_1 \cup I_2)$ when $\mathbb{S}_1 = SG(I_1)$ and $\mathbb{S}_2 = SG(I_2)$.

Evaluation: **SE(.)** $\tilde{n} = SE(\mathbb{S})$.

$$Pr[B_L(n) \leq \tilde{n} \leq B_U(n)] > 1 - \delta, \qquad (1)$$

where δ is in $[0, 1]$, and $B_L(\cdot)$ and $B_U(\cdot)$ are monotonically increasing functions that indicate the lower bound and the upper bound of $\tilde{n}$, respectively. This probability is taken

Table 1: Error bounded probabilistic counting schemes. $\epsilon < 1$ for z-smallest and FM sketch. $w > 4$ for AMS. The right most column shows the approximate size of a synopsis when $n = 10000$, $\epsilon = 0.1$, $\delta = 0.05$, $w = 5$.

scheme	$B_L(n)$	$B_U(n)$	synopsis size	
KeepAll	n	n	n	10000
z-smallest	$n(1-\epsilon)$	$n(1+\epsilon)$	$O(\frac{\ln(1/\delta)}{\epsilon^2})$	128
AMS	n/w	wn	$\frac{\ln(1/\delta)}{2(1/2-2/w)^2}$	150
FM sketch	$n(1-\epsilon)$	$n(1+\epsilon)$	$O(\frac{\ln 1/\delta \ln n}{\epsilon^2})$	1700

over the space of random items, not over the entire distribution of n, i.e., n is taken as given.

In this paper, we consider four error-bounded probabilistic counting schemes (KeepAll, AMS [1], FM sketch [9], and z-smallest [3]) which satisfy such requirements as examples for theoretical analysis and simulation. KeepAll is the approach where every unique item is part of the synopsis. Due to space limitations, we only provide a summary of z-smallest below, and refer readers to the original publications for more details [1,3,9]. After the example and a discussion of the accuracy and efficiency trade-off for probabilistic counting schemes, we discuss how maliciously crafted inputs can cause probabilistic counting schemes to produce unrealistically large estimates.

Probabilistic Counting Example. Bar-Yossef et al. [3] proposed using the zth-smallest hash value (v_z) as an estimator of the number of distinct elements (n). The intuition is that if the hashes of the elements are uniformly distributed in $[0, 1]$, the expected number of hashes falling into $[0, v_z]$ is $v_z n$. Hence, the estimator is $\tilde{n} = z/v_z$. For example, if the resulted hash set is $\{0.05, 0.1, 0.15, 0.2, \ldots\}$, with elements perfectly uniformly distributed in $[0, 1]$, the total number of elements can be estimated by the 2nd-smallest value (v_2): $\tilde{n} = 2/v_2 = 2/0.1 \approx 20$.

Accuracy and Efficiency Trade-off. Probabilistic counting schemes provide a trade-off between efficiency and accuracy. For example, KeepAll sacrifices efficiency to provide perfect accuracy. Other probabilistic counting schemes selectively store a subset of the data to shrink the synopsis while maintaining an accurate estimate. As the error bound ($B_U(n) - B_L(n)$) and the probability of an inaccurate estimate (δ) decrease, probabilistic counting schemes must increase the synopsis size. Table 1 provides a summary of these parameters for the four schemes we consider.

Vulnerability to Maliciously Crafted Inputs.
Probabilistic counting schemes were originally designed to operate in environments without malicious behavior. However, when an attacker controls the inputs to the *Generation* function, the attacker can craft inputs to bias the output of the estimator. Such manipulation of inputs is known as an *inflation attack*. Secure threshold-based event validation is unable to prevent minor inflation. However, our goal is to prevent decision changing attacks, where the threshold comparison output changes.

3. PROBLEM DEFINITION

To obtain high certainty for a MH-relevant event, vehicles rely on a threshold number of vehicles to report that event before alerting the driver. The core challenge in threshold-based event validation for VANETs is to create an efficient mechanism to combine and distribute event alerts with a low error rate in the presence of malicious entities.

3.1 Application Model

Fig. 1 provides an example of threshold-based validation for a congestion notification application. *Witnesses* (vehicles that observe the event directly and report the event) work collaboratively to collect alerts. If the number of witnesses (n) exceeds a threshold (τ), the witnesses generate a compact *event proof* proving that $n \geq \tau$, and distribute the event proof to vehicles multiple hops away. A vehicle that did not observe the event itself can verify the event proof to ensure that $n \geq \tau$. In our example, timely multi-hop distribution allows vehicles to avoid the congestion by taking another route. Next we provide more details about the Collection and Distribution phases of the applications.

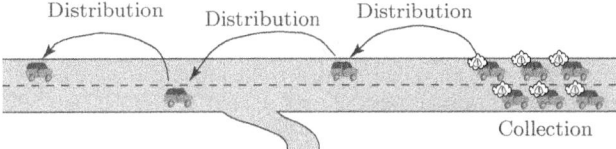

Figure 1: Example of road congestion. vehicles in the traffic jam collect alerts and distribute an event proof to warn vehicles behind.

Collection phase: Once a vehicle observes an event, that vehicle begins broadcasting alerts about the event and starts to collect other vehicles' alerts pertaining to the event. Specifically, a witness vehicle broadcasts a triple $\langle \mathcal{E}, \sigma, cert \rangle$, where $\mathcal{E}$ is an event description, σ is a signature on $\mathcal{E}$, and *cert* is a public-key certificate. To reduce communication overhead in the Collection phase, a witness only keeps a *synopsis*, a subset of alerts providing a rough estimate of number of alerts ($\tilde{n}$). The witness vehicles exchange synopses with each other using the *Message Exchange Protocol*. The Collection phase is finished when the *threshold-based validation algorithm* determines that the vehicle has collected sufficient alerts to generate an event proof (a synopsis showing $\tilde{n} \geq \tau$), or when the event expires. If $\tilde{n} \geq \tau$, the witnesses transit to the Distribution phase to spread the synopsis.

Distribution phase: After receiving an event proof that indicates $n \geq \tau$, vehicles rebroadcast the event proof to alert vehicles further away. Similar to in the Collection phase, in the Distribution phase, the rebroadcast frequency and message payload is determined by the *message exchange protocol*. By verifying an event proof, a vehicle away from the event scene can be assured that the total number of alerts exceeds a certain threshold value ($n \geq \tau$) without hearing all of the n alerts.

Figure 2 outlines the phase transitions in threshold-based applications. During the Standby phase, there is no active MH-relevant event. In the occurrence of multiple concurrent events, the applications maintain per-event phase and synopsis, but broadcast their synopses in the same beacon. We detail the Threshold-based Validation Algorithm in Section 4 and the Message Exchange Protocol in Section 5.

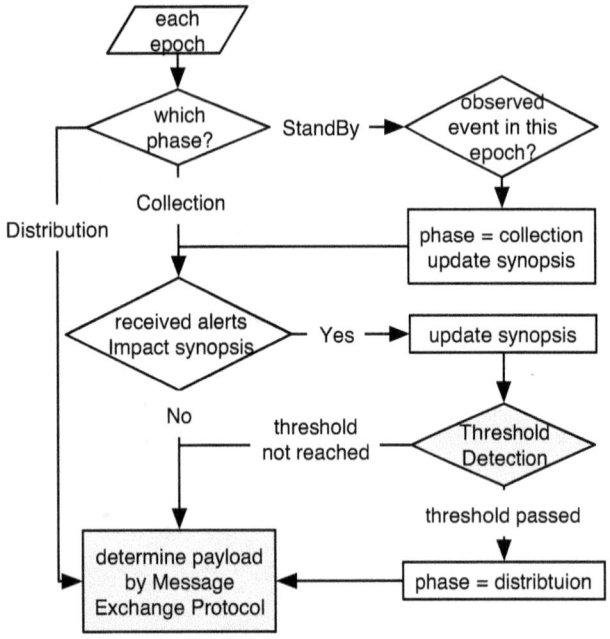

Figure 2: The phase transitions and operations in threshold-based applications.

In this work, we consider RSU-free collection and distribution. Roadside Units (RSUs) are immobile base stations that often play the role of a resource-abundant and trusted authority in many VANET proposals [2, 24, 34, 37]. In practice, however, it is difficult and costly to deploy RSUs along all roads and ensure their integrity. Our design allows vehicles to collect and distribute messages collaboratively, and thus no RSU is involved.

3.2 Problem Formulation

Successful operation of MH-relevant applications requires a threshold-based validation algorithm D, which outputs 1 when at least a threshold number of vehicles (τ) report an event and 0 otherwise. In the presence of adversaries, a threshold-based validation scheme may produce the wrong output. The error rate of D is expressed through false positive rate δ_1 and false negative rate δ_0. We define a *positive* as when the threshold-based validation algorithm outputs 1, and a *negative* when it outputs 0. Consequently, in a *false positive* (FP) D outputs 1 when less than τ vehicles report an event. In a *false negative* (FN), D outputs 0 when more than τ vehicles report an event. A *spurious* alert reports an event that did not occur. A *legitimate* alert reports an event that occurred. If receivers can verify the signature in an alert using the included public key and certificate, the alert is *valid*. Spurious and legitimate alerts can be valid.

More formally, in a setting with n_0 spurious alerts that try to report a fake event $\mathcal{E}$:

$$Pr[D(\mathcal{E}) = 1 | n_0 < \tau] \leq \delta_1 \qquad (2)$$

If n_1 legitimate alerts report a real event $\mathcal{E}$:

$$Pr[D(\mathcal{E}) = 0 | n_1 \geq \tau] \leq \delta_0 \qquad (3)$$

3.3 Evaluation Metrics

We evaluate the performance of a threshold-based event validation protocol based on the following metrics.

Overhead: The bandwidth associated with transmission of a synopsis provides a way to evaluate the efficiency of a threshold-based validation protocol. Because communication is limited, an efficient threshold-based validation protocol should consume a sub-linear amount of bandwidth with respect to the number of total alerts.

FP and FN rate: A secure threshold-based validation protocol should provide low FP and FN rates.

Delay: The time from vehicles' first alert until the reception of the event proof represents the delay, assuming that τ or more vehicles report the event.

3.4 Assumptions

PKI. We assume that a Public Key Infrastructure (PKI) exists, where each vehicle possesses one (and only one) valid public key and private key pair at a time.[1] For example, auto manufactures can act as certificate authorities to generate and sign key pairs. Each key pair will then be stored in an OBU, with tamper-resistant protection to protect the private key from compromise.

Bimodal distribution of number of alerts. We assume the number of alerts associated with events follows a bimodal distribution such that the number of spurious alerts during a fake event (n_0) is significantly smaller than the number of legitimate alerts (n_1) during a real event. That is, we assume that the majority of vehicles that participate in alert collection and distribution are honest. A honest participant complies with all VANET protocols and reports correct information. A temporary, localized dishonest majority may exist [21] (e.g., 7 out of 10 vehicles in one block are dishonest). However, such a small-scale dishonest majority has a limited impact on MH-relevant applications because the number of malicious entities is too small to successfully cause a decision changing attack. This disparity between n_0 and n_1 ensures that with high probability a large number of alerts represents a legitimate event while a small number of alerts, in the steady state, indicates a fake event. The actual values of n_0 and n_1 may vary based on the current circumstance (such as road capacity, speed, and number of spurious alerts that we want to tolerate). For instance, for a congestion notification application, we may have $n_1 = 100$ on a highway, but $n_1 = 50$ on a narrow local street. However, the mechanism to determine proper values is outside the scope of this paper. We assume the system knows a priori what values are appropriate for a given scenario.

Time and location information. Time and location information is required in each event description $\mathcal{E}$. The information can be provided by the Global Positioning Sys-

---

[1]VANETs can leverage multiple keys per vehicle to provide privacy [28, 33]. However, only one key pair is valid at any given time to prevent Sybil attacks [8] where one vehicle poses as many vehicles.

tem (GPS), which is available in many vehicles nowadays and necessary for VANET safety applications. We do not require secure positioning, and thus we tolerate vehicles lying about their location. So long as the majority are honest, a threshold-based application can limit the influence of fake reports.

Event detection. We assume a mechanism for event detection, either through human input or automatic detection through vehicle kinematics. A human observer may trigger an alert by pressing a button and selecting an event type. Automatic detection may rely on sensors (e.g., wheel slip to detect ice) or vehicle kinematics (e.g., vehicle standing on highway indicates congestion or danger) to detect an event and automatically send out an alert. After witness vehicles use the aforementioned mechanism(s) to detect the event, the vehicles can broadcast an alert reporting the event. However, our secure event validation protocol does not require such event detection mechanisms to be secure.

3.5 Attacker Model

In general, the attacker's goal is to bias other vehicles' views, i.e., cause a threshold-based validation algorithm to return an incorrect result. In particular, we consider *decision changing attacks*, where an attacker can make vehicles believe an inflated number of alerts such that a detection algorithm outputs "threshold detected" while in fact $n < \tau$ (a large FP rate of $P[D = 1|n < \tau] > \delta_1$).

We assume jamming and denial-of-service attacks can be mitigated by techniques such as spread spectrum [6], channel switching [28] or adaptive authentication [30]; providing reliable wireless communication is outside the scope of this paper. We do not consider deflation attacks, where an attacker covers up the occurrence of an event by dropping alerts or jamming the wireless channels because the attacker has difficulty to persistently (compared to the protocol execution time) isolate one group of vehicles from the other.

We assume the attacker targets an event or a set of similar events, all of them satisfy a specific intention. For example, the attacker intends to reduce her commute time when she goes to work in the early morning. Hence, any fake congestion event that falls in such a time frame (early morning) and space window (home to office) can serve the purpose of reducing commute time by misleading other drivers to take different paths. We do not consider an aimless attacker who just wants to cause trouble somewhere, e.g., any location within the US, because in most cases it is impractical for the attacker to ship and deploy a wireless device broadcasting fake alerts at that location, which may be far away. Note that attackers cannot distribute fake alerts over the Internet and rebroadcast by WiFi devices because WiFi operates in the 2.4GHz radio band while VANETs in 5.9GHz. Attackers could collude over the Internet by posting their fake alerts on a message board, from which others can download a message that successfully launches an attack. However, law enforcement can find such illegal sites and try to shut them down. Moreover, malicious vehicles would be easy to detect, because two messages would appear in a short timescale during which it would have been impossible to get from one location to the other.

4. EFFICIENT AND SECURE THRESHOLD-BASED VALIDATION

Multiple-hop-relevant VANET applications require a threshold number of alerts to validate an event. Witnesses to the event collect a subset of alerts, a synopsis, and distribute the subset to vehicles further away. The synopsis allows other vehicles to determine if the total number of alerts surpasses the threshold. Our goal is a small synopsis which provides an accurate threshold-based validation, because collecting and relaying every alert, digital signature, and certificate would cause severe link-layer contention. Moreover, such a synopsis should be secure against malicious manipulation that impacts the applications, i.e., a decision changing attack. This section describes how our proposed protocol achieves each of those goals.

Reducing the size of a synopsis. In this section, we formally *prove that threshold-based validation based on error bounded probabilistic counting can be efficient in MH-relevant applications*, where the expected number of legitimate alerts is much larger than the number of spurious alerts (Section 4.1). In contrast to a probabilistic counting scheme which requires a large synopsis for an accurate estimation of the number of alerts, a threshold-based validation scheme requires much less overhead to accurately detect a threshold number of alerts. We introduce a notion of *noise zone* to characterize the bimodal distribution of number of alerts in a MH-relevant application. The noise zone represents the value range from the *anticipated number of colluding attackers* to the *minimum number of legitimate witnesses*. When the actual count fails outside the noise zone, our threshold-based validation algorithm will return an accurate decision with high probability.

Securing synopses against manipulation. Every vehicle adds a digital signature (σ) and certificate (*cert*) to its alert to secure the threshold-based validation result. Certificates and signatures prevent an attacker from posing as a large number of vehicles reporting a fake event. An attacker, however, could subvert the decision of threshold-based validation by a single special message that represents a high count in a probabilistic threshold-based validation scheme. The attacker can obtain the special message by brute force search in a number of distinctly constructed alerts with equivalent meaning. To thwart such a decision changing attack, we propose a message description format that *specifies every event by a pre-defined structure and granularity* (Section 4.2). Such a format prevents the attacker from generating a large number of alerts by making small changes to the message (e.g., changing the longitude by a few meters).

4.1 Efficient threshold-based validation

We observe that a MH-relevant VANET application can be characterized by a *noise zone*, which is a value interval $[a, b)$ satisfying the following condition:

$$Pr[n \in [0, a] \cup [b, \infty)] > 1 - \eta, \qquad (4)$$

where η is close to zero. In other words, the number of alerts in a steady state (e.g., the state where no new alerts are observed for a certain amount of time) falls outside the noise zone with high probability. We give a formal definition:

DEFINITION 1. *A threshold-based validation algorithm D is (τ, a, b, δ)-guaranteed if for a threshold τ and a noise zone $[a, b]$, D can output a decision with false positive and false negative rates less than δ when $n \notin [a, b]$.*

Combining Definition 1 and (4) directly gives us Theorem 1, a probabilistic bound on a threshold-based validation algorithm over all inputs n.

THEOREM 1. *A (τ, a, b, δ)-guaranteed threshold-based validation scheme can output a correct decision with probability at least $(1 - \delta)(1 - \eta)$.*

Theorem 2 shows the relation between a noise zone $[a, b]$ and a threshold τ. We show that a threshold-based validation scheme guarantees an accurate decision when the number of alerts (n) is outside its noise zone; otherwise, the decision is interfered by "noise". Precisely, it can distinguish between a fake event and a real event with high probability, when at most a spurious alerts report a fake event or at least b legitimate alerts report a real event.

THEOREM 2. *Let ρ be a (B_L, B_U, δ) probabilistic counting scheme (i.e., satisfying (1), $Pr[B_L(n) \leq \tilde{n} \leq B_U(n)] > 1 - \delta$). a, b, and τ are values that satisfy the equation*

$$B_U(a) < \tau \leq B_L(b). \qquad (5)$$

Let $\mathcal{D}$ be the probabilistic threshold-based validation algorithm that runs ρ to receive an estimate $\tilde{n}$ of n, and outputs 0 when $\tilde{n} < \tau$ and 1 when $\tilde{n} \geq \tau$. Then $\mathcal{D}$ is a (τ, a, b, δ)-guaranteed probabilistic threshold-based validation algorithm.

Proof of Theorem 2: When $n \geq b$,

$$Pr[\tilde{n} \geq \tau] \geq Pr[\tilde{n} \geq B_L(n) \geq \tau]$$
$$= Pr[\tilde{n} \geq B_L(n) \text{ and } B_L(n) \geq \tau]$$
$$= Pr[\tilde{n} \geq B_L(n) | B_L(n) \geq \tau] Pr[B_L(n) \geq \tau]$$
$$> (1 - \delta) Pr[B_L(n) \geq \tau]$$
$$\geq (1 - \delta) Pr[B_L(b) \geq \tau]$$

$$\Rightarrow Pr[\tilde{n} < \tau] < \delta.$$

We replace $Pr[\tilde{n} \geq B_L(n)]$ by $1 - \delta$ based on (1), which holds unconditionally of n. Finally, we replace n with b because $B_L(\cdot)$ is a non-decreasing function.

Similarly, when $n \leq a$, $Pr[\tilde{n} \geq \tau] < \delta$. ∎

Theorem 2 shows that to achieve (τ, a, b, δ) guarantee, threshold-based validation algorithm should satisfy both (1) and (5), and output 1 when $\tilde{n} \geq \tau$ and output 0 when $\tilde{n} < \tau$.

4.1.1 Discussion

According to (5) and the $B_L(n)$ and $B_U(n)$ in Table 1 we can express the noise zone in terms of the threshold τ. For example, the D_z scheme has to satisfy

$$B_L(b) = b(1 - \epsilon) < \tau \leq B_U(a) = a(1 + \epsilon)$$

and thus $[a, b) = [\frac{\tau}{1+\epsilon}, \frac{\tau}{1-\epsilon})$, where ϵ is an adjustment parameter whose increment reduces the synopsis size but extends the noise zone. Note that probabilistic counting requires ϵ to be close to zero (e.g., 0.05) to have an accurate

Table 2: Comparison of four instantiations threshold-based validation.

scheme	$|\mathbb{S}|$	$[a, b)$
D_{KA}	$O(\tau)$	N/A
D_z	$O(\frac{\ln(1/\delta)}{\epsilon^2})$	$[\frac{\tau}{1+\epsilon}, \frac{\tau}{1-\epsilon})$
D_{AMS}	$O(\frac{\ln(1/\delta)}{2(1/2-2/w)^2})$	$[\tau/w, \tau w)$
D_{FM}	$O(\frac{\ln 1/\delta \ln \tau}{\epsilon^2})$	$[\frac{\tau}{1+\epsilon}, \frac{\tau}{1-\epsilon})$

count, whereas in threshold-based validation ϵ can be much higher (e.g., 0.5) thus greatly reducing the communication overhead caused by synopsis exchange.

Table 2 summarizes four (τ, a, b, δ)-guaranteed threshold-based validation algorithms, D_z, D_{FM}, and D_{AMS}, based on z-smallest, FM, and AMS sketch, respectively. D_{KA} represents a naive threshold-based validation scheme which keeps all alerts until τ alerts are stored.

Given a noise zone $[a, b]$ and a required false positive (negative) rate δ, an application can determine proper values of τ and ϵ and thus $|\mathbb{S}|$ based on Table 2. For example, when $[a, b) = [40, 90)$, we can set $\tau = 56$ and $\epsilon \leq 5/13$ for D_z.

In D_z, D_{FM}, and D_{AMS}, a wider $[a, b)$ implies a larger ϵ (or smaller w, the adjustment parameter for D_{AMS}) thus reducing the synopsis size. In Section 6, we analyze and simulate the schemes to determine the impact of synopsis size on false positives, false negatives and network performance. We find that D_z causes the lowest overhead among all schemes given the same error rates.

4.2 Event Description Format

To prevent a decision changing attack, we require that the valid message space is bounded. In other words, a valid event description $\mathcal{E}$ needs to conform to a prescribed format:

```
[emergency type] [time epoch] [location]
```

Both the time epoch and location are *coarse-grained*. For example, time epochs have the granularity of 10 minutes, and location is approximated to the nearest intersection or the previous highway exit. The approach limits the attacker to a single description for a given event, thereby preventing a decision changing attack.

Given every witness will generate the same $\mathcal{E}$, we hash the event descriptor along with the signer's public key as the input to a probabilistic counting scheme. Hence, each public key acts as an unique identifier of an alert, and allows our scheme to detect a threshold number of vehicles by estimating the number of distinct alerts. In VANETs, authorities assign key pairs to vehicles [28]. This prevents an attacker from selecting a specific public key as part of a decision changing attack; vehicles are limited to the public keys assigned to them. The advantage of hashing the above rather than signatures is that signatures are often randomized, and one can produce many signatures for the same message by supplying different random bits which would enable an attack. One way to address this is to use a deterministic signature scheme. However, if we hash the signer's public key along with the message, our design becomes independent of the underlying signature schemes.

Without our description format, the message field has high entropy and thus there are numerous equivalent messages indicating the same event. The attacker can thus find special messages to significantly inflate the estimation of the number of alerts with almost no delay. However, our description format slows down such an attack because it limits the entropy in the message field.

4.2.1 Discussion

In addition to our coarse-grained event format, the limitations on time and location help prevent decision changing attacks. Equation (6) models the relation between these limitations. A threshold-based validation scheme satisfying (6) is secure against decision changing attacks because an attacker can only launch such attacks with low probability.

Time limit. In VANETs, vehicles change public keys periodically (e.g., every 5 minutes) to prevent long-term location tracing. When vehicles are unable to connect to keying authorities on a frequent basis, the vehicles are allowed to preload multiple key pairs [28]. Let T_{PK} be the average time length between a public key is known by its owner and the key is being used. For example, $T_{PK} = 6$ months when vehicles download a year worth key pairs for the next year during annual inspection. To launch an effective decision changing attack, the attacker has to find a special description that causes significant inflation within T_{PK}.

Location limit. In most cases, an honest vehicle is unlikely to report events far away from each other in a short timescale, in contrast to an aimless attacker who would look for forgeable events regardless of location. Though such aimless attacks can be detected by law enforcement as explained in the previous section, law enforcement can further deter aimless attacks by running a posterior analysis on collected event proofs to detect such location inconsistency or proofs that indicate a single vehicle was in two places at once.

Coarse-grained event description. We denote N_E as the number of events available per time. For example, consider a time granularity of ten minutes and a location granularity of one square kilometer, and an attacker who wants to falsely report a congestion event occurs between her home at location (x, y) and office at $(x + 100km, y + 100km)$ between 7 am to 9 am, $N_E = 1.2 * 10^5$ per day.

Hence, our scheme is secure against a decision changing attack if the average time in finding a special description that triggers a decision changing attack, T_{attack}, is larger than the available time of public keys. The security condition holds when:

$$T_{attack} = 1/(P_{DC} * N_E) > T_{PK} \qquad (6)$$

where P_{DC} is the probability of a decision changing attack against one event. We derive formulas for P_{DC} in Section 6.1. P_{DC} is determined by the number of colluding attackers, and T_{PK} by the public key management mechanism in VANETs. An application can select a good trade-off value of N_E to satisfy this condition. For example, $T_{attack} = 8.3 * 10^2$ (days) $> T_{PK}$ when $N_E = 1.2 * 10^5$ (events per day), $P_{DC} = 10^{-8}$ per event (based on the analysis in Section 6), and $T_{PK} = 365$ days.

5. MESSAGE EXCHANGE PROTOCOL

Even with a smaller synopsis, unorganized collection and rebroadcasting of messages in the ad hoc network can cause severe channel contention [23]. In this section, we describe a message exchange protocol (MEP) to efficiently collect and distribute synopses in threshold-based validation scheme.

5.1 Protocol Overview

According to the IEEE 1609.2 specification [14], each vehicle sends a beacon every 100 ms. The beacon is a signed message that authenticates the sender's information (location, speed, etc.). Therefore, a vehicle can piggyback its current synopsis in a beacon. A synopsis of an event $\mathcal{E}$ is a set of representative alerts $\{A_1, A_2, \cdots, A_{|\mathbb{S}|}\}$ reporting that event, where $A_i = \langle \mathcal{E}, \sigma_i, cert_i \rangle$. Note that σ_i is a signature on $\mathcal{E}$ so we can represent a synopsis in a compressed form, i.e., $\{\mathcal{E}, \{\sigma_1, cert_1\}, \cdots, \{\sigma_{|\mathbb{S}|}, cert_{|\mathbb{S}|}\}\}$, without losing information by discarding other data in witnesses' beacons.

Our scheme relies on broadcast communication to deliver an event proof to vehicles multiple hops away. However, multihop broadcast may cause a broadcast storm [23] — severe link-layer contention and collision due to an excessive number of replicated messages. Various techniques have been proposed to alleviate the broadcast storm problem in general [17, 23, 32, 35]. Built upon existing broadcast storm solutions, we describe a customized message exchange protocol that can further reduce the bandwidth overhead by suppressing redundant broadcasts of synopses. For example, a vehicle only broadcasts its synopsis if the vehicle hears a different set of alerts from vehicles within its communication range.

5.1.1 Synopsis Advertisement

During synopsis advertisement, a vehicle advertises a digest of its current synopses. Hence, receivers can determine if they have the same information as the sender.

At any point in time, a total of K emergency events are active. This means that each vehicle maintains a total of K synopses/sets. We denote the K sets as $\mathbb{S}(\mathcal{E}_1)$, ..., $\mathbb{S}(\mathcal{E}_K)$. Each vehicle attaches a digest to its beacon:

$$\text{digest} = h(\mathcal{E}_1, \ldots, \mathcal{E}_K, \mathbb{S}(\mathcal{E}_1), \ldots, \mathbb{S}(\mathcal{E}_K))$$

where h is a hash function. Each alert in $\mathbb{S}$ is ordered based on the public keys.

A vehicle overhears the beacon of nearby vehicles, and checks if the digest matches its own. If the hashes differ, the vehicle verifies the signature on the digest, and if the signature is valid, it adds the other vehicle's public key to a list $\mathcal{N}$ that it maintains. The list $\mathcal{N}$ stores nearby vehicles whose views are different.

5.1.2 Synopsis Update

Whenever the list $\mathcal{N}$ becomes non-empty, a vehicle waits r beacons, where r is uniformly drawn from an interval (e.g., $[0, 10]$), before broadcasting its K sets. If vehicle V hears from V_s a new synopsis set that results in an updated digest, V's next beacon will act as an implicit acknowledgment, such that vehicles that hear this beacon with a now matching digest will delete V from their $\mathcal{N}$ list, and cancel any pending broadcast dedicated for V.

An attacker who keeps advertising different random strings as digests may trigger contention because none of her neighbors have the same digest and thus will broadcast their synopsis sets. To prevent such an abuse, we require every vehicle to maintain a blacklist of vehicles that have been added to $\mathcal{N}$ frequently. Advertisements from blacklisted vehicles will be dropped. Also law enforcement can track down the attacker by the blacklists.

Optimization. In the message exchange protocol, a vehicle suppresses its synopsis update when every received digest is the same as the vehicle's digest. A vehicle broadcasts its synopsis set when receiving a different digest, because seeing a different digest indicates that the vehicle may know alerts unknown to others. Nevertheless, the synopsis set may also include alerts that are already known to others. To avoid transmitting such redundant alerts and thus further optimize the message exchange protocol, we instead use a Bloom filter [4] as the digest. A Bloom filter allows constant time membership queries. Hence, the vehicle can reduce bandwidth usage by identifying absent alerts in the sender's synopsis set, and only broadcast those alerts. Specifically, a Bloom filter requires $1.44 \log_2(1/(1-0.999)) \approx 1.75$ bytes per alert to identify 99.9% of the absent alerts [4], rather than redundantly rebroadcasting all 181 bytes associated with each alert (64-byte Elliptic Curve DSA signature along with a 117-byte certificate [14]).

5.2 Discussion

Effective interval. To avoid an explosion of the number of events, a vehicle only stores alerts for recent events occurred in a nearby area. Specifically, a vehicle keeps track of an event occurring in L at T if

$$|L_{cur} - L| \leq \Delta L \text{ and } T_{cur} - T \leq \Delta T,$$

where L_{cur} is the current location of the vehicle and T_{cur} the current time, and ΔL and ΔT represent the acceptable location and time differences, respectively.

Collection delay. Our scheme provides accurate decision when the total number of alerts n is outside a certain noise zone $[a, b)$. However, alerts do not arrive in bursts. When first collecting alerts for an event, it is possible that only a few vehicles have observed the event, even if the event is occurring. To avoid such a false negative due to early evaluation, an witness vehicle keeps evaluating an event until the time $\mathcal{E}$ expires. Hence the vehicles can guarantee low false negatives while minimizing the collection delay (the time from the first alert reporting the event till the generation of an event proof) to enable timely reception of an event proof at the distant vehicles.

6. EVALUATION

Section 4 provides a summary of the asymptotic behavior of our scheme based on probabilistic counting, which was designed to work with large datasets (several thousands). In this section, we examine the behavior with hundreds of vehicles based on mathematical analysis and simulation. Our evaluation confirms that our scheme, with a reasonable error rate, can largely reduce the overhead compared to the baseline scheme, D_{KA}, which keeps all distinct alerts received by the vehicle.

6.1 Analysis of Threshold-based Validation Algorithms

We analyze three probabilistic threshold-based validation algorithms, D_z, D_{FM}, D_{AMS}, built on z-smallest, FM sketch, AMS probabilistic counting, respectively, and compare them to the D_{KA} scheme. To facilitate our analysis, we derive the probability that the estimate of number of vehicles ($\tilde{n}$) is larger than a given threshold value (τ). We denote the probability as $P_{\tilde{n} \geq \tau}$.

D_{KA}: $P_{\tilde{n} \geq \tau} = 0$ if $n < \tau$. Otherwise $P_{\tilde{n} \geq \tau} = 1$. The synopsis size is $|\mathbb{S}| = \tau$. D_{KA} keeps a threshold number of alerts to achieve perfect accuracy.

The probabilistic counting schemes run C copies of an algorithm, and take median in D_z and D_{AMS}, but mean in D_{FM} to increase the accuracy. Though FM sketch is proven to be asymptotic to a normal distribution when n is large, to our knowledge, there is no such asymptotic bound for AMS or z-smallest. On the other hand, using median in D_{FM} outputs a similar result as in D_{AMS}, where the estimate is limited to certain values, e.g., the power of 2.

D_z: First we consider one copy of the z-smallest algorithm storing z elements. The probability the estimate of n is larger than the threshold (τ) is: $p = 1 - \sum_{i=0}^{z-1} \binom{n}{i}(z/\tau)^i(1-z/\tau)^{n-i}$. When C copies of the probabilistic counting algorithms are used, the probability that the median of these C estimates exceeds the threshold is:

$$P_{\tilde{n} \geq \tau} = \sum_{j=\lceil C/2 \rceil}^{C} \binom{C}{j} p^j (1-p)^{C-j} \quad (7)$$

The size of a synopsis is $|\mathbb{S}| = Cz$.

D_{FM}: $p_{0,i} = (1 - 1/2^i)^\tau$. $p_i = p_{0,i} \prod_{j=1}^{i-1}(1 - p_{0,i})$. $u = C \log_2(0.77351\tau)$. x_i are integers $\forall i$. $|\mathbb{S}| \leq u$.

$$P_{\tilde{n} \geq \tau} = 1 - \sum_{(\sum_{i=1}^{C} x_i) < u} \left(\prod_{i=1}^{C} p_{x_i} \right) \quad (8)$$

D_{AMS}: $p = 1 - (1 - 1/\tau_1)^n$, where $\tau_1 = 2^{\lceil \log_2 \tau \rceil}$. $P_{\tilde{n} \geq \tau}$ can be derived from (7) as well. $|\mathbb{S}| = C$.

6.1.1 Configuring Parameters

We study the relations among τ (threshold value), n_0 (number of alerts reporting a fake event), n_1 (number of alerts reporting a real event), ER (error rate) and $\mathbb{S}$ (communication overhead in terms of synopsis size). We define ER as the summation of the false positive and false negative rates. Our default setting is $n_1 = 100$, $n_0 = 0.2n_1$, $|\mathbb{S}| \approx 15$. We set $[a, b) = [2n_0, 0.5n_1)$ to ensure n falls into the noise zone with low probability. Based on Table 2, we set the threshold value as $\tau = \lceil a(1 + \frac{b-a}{b+a}) \rceil = 45$ for D_z and D_{FM}, and $\tau = \lceil \sqrt{ab} \rceil = 45$ for D_{AMS}. Note that threshold-based validation schemes are compromised when the number of malicious vehicles surpasses the threshold (i.e., $n_0 = \tau$); in other word, our default setting is highly adversarial ($n_0/\tau = 0.44$).

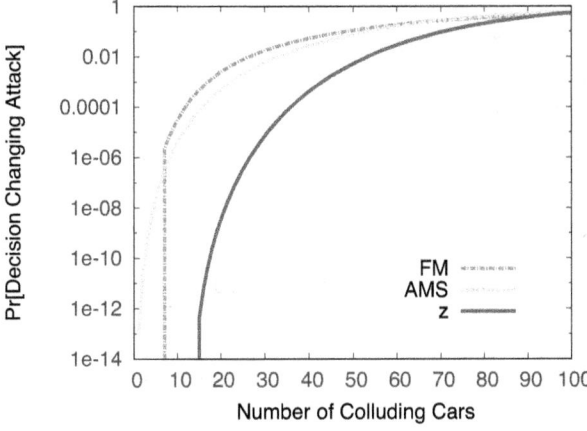

Figure 3: $\tau = 100.$ $|\mathbb{S}| \approx 15.$

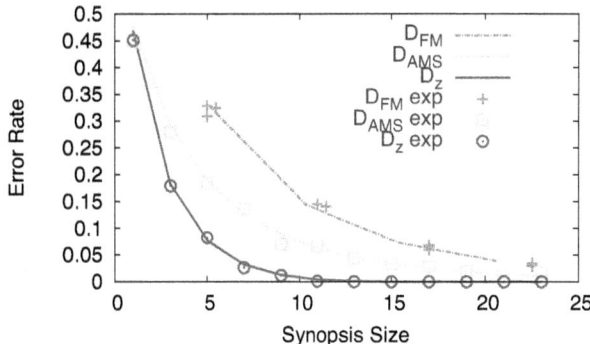

Figure 4: $n_1 = 100$, $n_0 = 20$.

6.1.2 Probability of decision changing attacks

A larger number of colluding attackers (n_0) is more likely to successfully claim a fake event. In an extreme situation where no malicious parties are present, the false positive rate is zero. In the presence of τ colluding attackers, the false positive rate is close to 0.5 because probabilistic threshold-based validation schemes have difficulty in distinguishing τ colluding attackers from τ honest participants.

Fig. 3 shows the probability of a decision changing attack (P_{DC}) vs. the number of colluding attackers when threshold value is 100 and the synopsis size is around 15 for a fair comparison among the different schemes. With such a constraint on the synopsis size, D_{KA} outputs "threshold detected" when the number of kept alerts passes the threshold or the size of the synopsis.

$P_{DC} = P_{\tilde{n} \geq \tau}$ when $n < \tau$. In contrast to D_{KA}, whose P_{DC} raises to 1 sharply as soon as $n \geq |\mathbb{S}|$, P_{DC} for other schemes gracefully increases as the number of colluding attackers increases. D_{KA} only works when the threshold number is small, for example 15. However, because the number of colluding attackers may be slightly larger, we require schemes for probabilistic threshold-based validation.

Given the same synopsis size, D_z is more secure (less chance of a decision changing attack) than the other schemes for any number of colluding vehicles. In the remainder of this analysis section, we focus on the three probabilistic threshold-based validation algorithms because this result shows that probabilistic counting largely reduces the synopsis size at the cost of slightly degraded accuracy.

6.1.3 Error Rate vs. Synopsis Size

Fig. 4 shows the error rate vs. communication overhead, expressed by the synopsis size. The error rate can be computed by $ER = P_{\tilde{n}_0 \geq \tau} + (1 - P_{\tilde{n}_1 \geq \tau})$. For each threshold-based validation, we simulate the decision process and records the error rate and synopsis size for a given threshold and number of vehicles. In the experiment, we obtain $P_{\tilde{n}_0 \geq \tau}$ and $P_{\tilde{n}_1 \geq \tau}$ by the percentage of false positives and true positives out of 1000 runs. The experimental result validates the correctness of our analytical result. We represent the analytical and experimental results by lines and points, respectively.

The graph confirms that we can improve the confidence on the output at the cost of communication overhead. The improvement is non-linear; storing more than 10–15 signatures has little advantage. For the same overhead, D_z has lowest (best) error rate while D_{FM} has the highest (worst).

6.1.4 Error Rate vs. Number of alerts

Fig. 5 shows the error rate vs. the number alerts reporting an event. We focus on the D_z scheme because it provided the best tradeoff in the previous two analyses. Fig. 5(a) shows that the error rate rate is lower when the number of alerts (n) falls outside the noise zone. Fig. 5(b) shows that given the same synopsis size ($|\mathbb{S}|$) and error rate (δ), increasing the threshold τ also increases the size of the noise zone.

In summary, the analysis shows that the D_z threshold-based validation algorithm provides the lowest error rates and requires the smallest synopsis size. These results make D_z most suitable for MH-relevant VANET applications.

6.2 Simulation

We use the NS-2 simulator to measure the impact of our threshold-based validation algorithms and message exchange protocol (MEP) on network performance and the delay associated with distributing an event proof. We summarize our NS-2 simulation settings and implementation, and present the results with respect to the packet reception rate and the delay for event proof collection and distribution. The results show that the MEP protocol, which rebroadcasts synopses intelligently, can distribute a proof of congestion to vehicles 4.5 kilometers away from the congestion area in less than 1 second with little impact on network performance.

6.2.1 Simulation Environment

The vehicles are represented as mobile nodes in the simulation. Every 0.1 seconds an vehicle sends out a beacon that contains the safety information and any MH-relevant application data. We use IEEE 802.11p with parameters to reflect VANET wireless conditions [15]. Without any MH-relevant application data, each beacon is 368 bytes [14]. When broadcasting a synopsis, each certificate is 117 bytes, each signature is 64 bytes, and each $\mathcal{E}$ is 136 bits (8 bit event type, 64 bit time, 32 bit longitude, and 32 bit latitude).

We simulate a straight road with traffic in two directions. One direction has three distinct regions. The first region

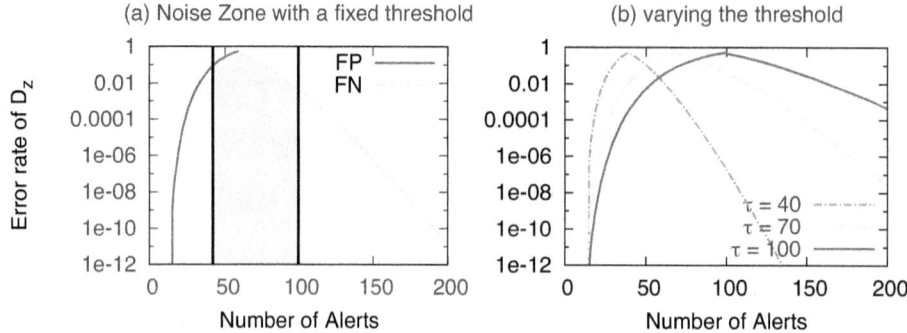

Figure 5: (a) Given $\tau = 60$ and $|\mathbb{S}| = 15$. When $\epsilon = 0.4$, the noise zone is $[a, b) = [42, 100)$ (indicated by the grey area) and $\delta = 0.076$. If we increase the ϵ value to 0.6, the noise zone becomes $[37, 150)$ and $\delta = 0.024$. Hence increasing the noise zone decreases the error rate when n is outside of the noise zone. (b) Given $\epsilon = 0.4$, $|\mathbb{S}| = 15$ and $\delta \approx 0.1$. Increasing τ from 40, 70 to 100 expands the noise zone from $[28, 67)$, $[50, 117)$, to $[72, 166)$.

(R_1) is 7.5 kilometers long and has 300 vehicles at a density of 1 vehicle per 25 meters. This is followed by a region (R_2) 3 kilometers long with 300 vehicles at a density of 1 vehicle per 10 meters. The last region (R_3) is 1.5 kilometers long and has 60 vehicles with a density of 1 vehicle per 25 meters. Travelling in the opposite direction of the three regions are vehicles with a density of 1 vehicle per 25 meters. R_2 represents a congested region while the other regions are non-congested. Vehicles in R_3 do not witness the congestion, but can utilize an event proof from vehicles in R_2 to notify the driver and avoid the congestion ahead. R_1 and oncoming traffic are included to simulate the wireless communication from nearby vehicles.

6.2.2 Simulation Details

At a fixed time, the first 100 vehicles in R_2 start sending out a congestion alert corresponding to a single event. The vehicles hearing the alerts will retain a synopsis to generate an event proof that at least 50 vehicles are reporting the event ($\tau = 50$). For D_z, the synopsis size is 15 alerts. In simulations without MEP, a vehicle rebroadcasts its current synopsis in every beacon.

To implement our message exchange protocol described in Section 5, each vehicle sends a beacon every 100ms and can be in one of the four states which dictate what MH-relevant application data is included in the next message: 1) include a synopsis advertisement, 2) include the synopsis, 3) wait some number of epochs (randomly selected from 1 to 10) before including the synopsis (only include the advertisement) 4) include no MH-relevant application data (the vehicle lacks knowledge of the event). The reception of a message from another vehicle triggers the transition from one state to another. The content of the received message and the current state determines the next state.

6.2.3 Results

Figure 6(a) presents the normalized packet reception rate per vehicle vs. the distance from the beginning of the congestion. We define normalized packet reception rate to be the number of successfully received packets with the MH-relevant application enabled divided by the number of suc-

cessfully received packets with MH-relevant applications disabled. This quantifies our protocol's impact on the network performance. The reception rates are lower in the congested area (0 to 3000 meters) and increase for vehicles away from the congestion. Without our MEP protocol, both D_{KA} and D_z lose on average 40% of packets. With MEP, D_z has a normalized packet reception rate close to 1 and greater reception in congested areas compared to D_{KA}. These results show smaller synopsis size and intelligent rebroadcast is needed to limit network degradation.

Figure 6(b) presents the collection and distribution delays vs. the distance from the beginning of the congestion. Despite the random backoff, MEP allows dissemination of an event proof within 1 second of the witnesses' original broadcasts. D_{KA} has a longer delay than D_z for both cases with and without MEP because D_{KA} experiences higher packet loss, which retards alert collection and distribution. Because beacons are not sent in synchrony, a message can spread more than one hop in less than 0.1 seconds, as shown in the distribution area of all four cases.

7. RELATED WORK

We are not aware of prior work on either threshold-based event validation or secure threshold detection. We thus discuss work in related topics: VANET event validation, secure aggregation, and probabilistic counting (detailed discussion on probabilistic counting is provided in Section 2).

VANET event validation.   The number of alerts from nearby vehicles is a strong indicator of the validity of an event [13, 16, 29]. However, prior work either focuses on one-hop-relevant applications where only one-hop alerts are counted or assumes all alerts are available for analysis regardless how the alert distribution works. Dietzel et al. adopts the notion of data-centric trust [29] for event validation [7]. However, their scheme results in high dissemination delay. In contrast, our protocol enables a bandwidth-efficient solution to promptly distribute alerts and provides the event validity indicator for multi-hop-relevant applications.

Secure count aggregation.   Work to secure the count aggregation problem uses cryptographic solutions [5, 11, 26,

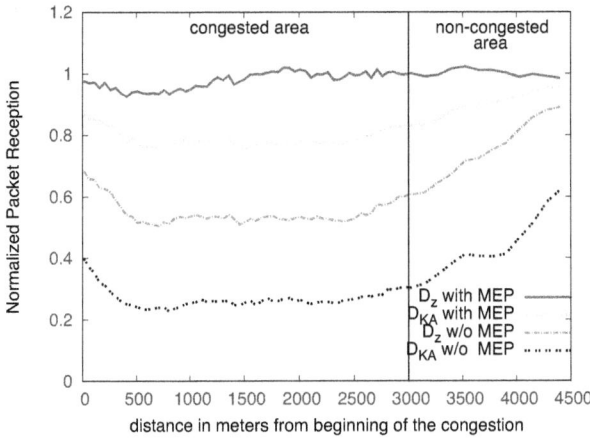 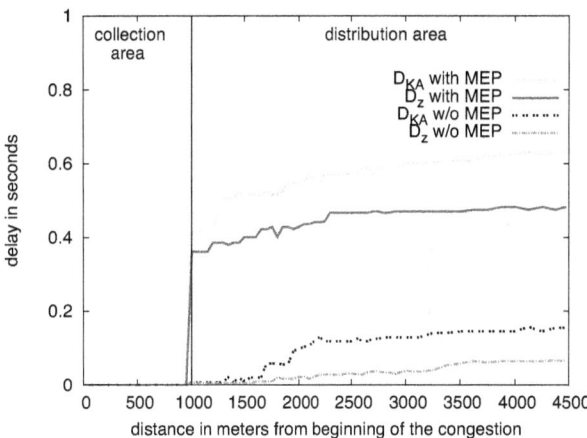

Figure 6: (a) Normalized packet reception rate at different distances. (b) Collection and distribution delays at different distances.

36] to defend against attacks, but their assumption of known network topology conflicts with vehicle mobility. Probabilistic counting has been proposed for efficient data dissemination in VANETs [20]. However, to secure probabilistic counting, most schemes need to store hundreds of signatures [12,19]; such overhead is impractical for VANET.

Aggregate signatures. Aggregate signatures have been widely studied for reducing the signature size for multiple signers but still require broadcasting one certificate per signer for verification. In VANETs, Raya et al. propose a sequential aggregation scheme to reduce the communication overhead for signature broadcast [27]. However, this scheme does not scale to hundreds of signatures because sequential aggregation is sensitive to topology change and duplication.

8. CONCLUSION

So far, security approaches for VANETs have mostly only focused on basic primitives and mechanisms, e.g., by simply adding a digital signature to messages. Unfortunately, digital signatures alone are woefully inadequate because most applications need specialized security properties. In this paper, we propose a secure and efficient threshold-based event validation protocol for MH-relevant applications. We convert probabilistic counting to threshold-based validation, and show that threshold-based validation schemes yield significant savings compared to just counting accurately and comparing to the threshold, because threshold-based validation schemes can output an accurate decision based on an inaccurate estimate. Since VANETs are expected to be deployed within five years, we hope that the research community will embrace these important research challenges to ensure that we have secure and reliable VANET applications ready upon deployment.

Acknowledgements

We gratefully thank Fan Bai, Bhargav Bellur, and Aravind Iyer for their insightful suggestions, as well as the anonymous reviewers for their valuable comments.

9. REFERENCES

[1] ALON, N., MATIAS, Y., AND SZEGEDY, M. The space complexity of approximating the frequency moments. *Journal of Computer and System Sciences 58*, 1 (1999), 137–147.

[2] BAI, F., KRISHNAN, H., SADEKAR, V., HOLLAND, G., AND ELBATT, T. Towards characterizing and classifying communication-based automotive applications from a wireless networking perspective. In *Proceedings of IEEE AutoNet* (2006).

[3] BAR-YOSSEF, Z., JAYRAM, T. S., KUMAR, R., SIVAKUMAR, D., AND TREVISAN, L. Counting distinct elements in a data stream. In *Proceedings of RANDOM* (2002).

[4] BLOOM, B. H. Space/time trade-offs in hash coding with allowable errors. *Communications of the ACM 13*, 7 (1970), 422–426.

[5] CHAN, H., PERRIG, A., AND SONG, D. X. Secure hierarchical in-network aggregation in sensor networks. In *Proceedings of ACM CCS* (2006).

[6] CHIANG, J. T., AND HU, Y.-C. dynamic jamming mitigation for wireless broadcast networks. In *Proceedings of IEEE INFOCOM* (2008).

[7] DIETZEL, S., SCHOCH, E., KÖNINGS, B., WEBER, M., AND KARGL, F. Resilient secure aggregation for vehicular networks. *IEEE Network: The Magazine of Global Internetworking 24* (2010), 26–31.

[8] DOUCEUR, J. R. The sybil attack. In *Proceedings of International Workshop on Peer-to-Peer Systems* (2002).

[9] FLAJOLET, P., AND MARTIN, G. N. Probabilistic counting algorithms for data base applications. *Journal of Computer and System Sciences 31*, 2 (1985), 182–209.

[10] FRANCILLON, A., DANEV, B., AND CAPKUN, S. Relay attacks on passive keyless entry and start systems in modern cars. In *Proceedings of NDSS* (2011).

[11] FRIKKEN, K. B., AND JOSEPH A. DOUGHERTY, I. An efficient integrity-preserving scheme for hierarchical

sensor aggregation. In *Proceedings of ACM WiSec* (2008).

[12] GAROFALAKIS, M. N., HELLERSTEIN, J. M., AND MANIATIS, P. Proof sketches: Verifiable in-network aggregation. In *Proceedings of IEEE ICDE* (2007).

[13] GOLLE, P., GREENE, D., AND STADDON, J. Detecting and correcting malicious data in vanets. In *Proceedings of ACM VANET* (2004).

[14] IEEE. 1609.2: Trial-use standard for wireless access in vehicular environments-security services for applications and management messages. IEEE Standards, 2006.

[15] JIANG, D., CHEN, Q., AND DELGROSSI, L. Optimal data rate selection for vehicle safety communications. In *Proceedings of ACM VANET* (2008).

[16] KIM, T. H.-J., STUDER, A., ZHANG, X., DUBEY, R., PERRIG, A., BAI, F., BELLUR, B., AND IYER, A. Vanet alert endorsement using multi-source filters. In *Proceedings of ACM VANET* (2010).

[17] KORKMAZ, G., EKICI, E., ÖZGÜNER, F., AND ÖZGÜNER, U. Urban multi-hop broadcast protocol for inter-vehicle communication systems. In *Proceedings of ACM VANET* (2004).

[18] KOSCHER, K., CZESKIS, A., ROESNER, F., PATEL, S., KOHNO, T., CHECKOWAY, S., MCCOY, D., KANTOR, B., ANDERSON, D., SHACHAM, H., AND SAVAGE, S. Experimental security analysis of a modern automobile. In *Proceedings of IEEE Symposium on Security and Privacy* (2010).

[19] KUHN, M. G. Probabilistic counting of large digital signature collections. In *Proceedings of USENIX Security Symposium* (2000).

[20] LOCHERT, C., SCHEUERMANN, B., AND MAUVE, M. Probabilistic aggregation for data dissemination in vanets. In *Proceedings of ACM VANET* (2007).

[21] MOORE, T., CLULOW, J., PAPADIMITRATOS, P., ANDERSON, R., AND PIERRE HUBAUX, J. Fast exclusion of errant devices from vehicular networks. In *Proceedings of IEEE SECON* (2008).

[22] NATH, S., GIBBONS, P. B., SESHAN, S., AND ANDERSON, Z. R. Synopsis diffusion for robust aggregation in sensor networks. *ACM Transactions on Sensor Networks 4*, 2 (2008).

[23] NI, S.-Y., TSENG, Y.-C., CHEN, Y.-S., AND SHEU, J.-P. The broadcast storm problem in a mobile ad hoc network. In *Proceedings of ACM MobiCom* (1999).

[24] PAPADIMITRATOS, P., GLIGOR, V., AND HUBAUX, J.-P. Securing Vehicular Communications - Assumptions, Requirements, and Principles. In *Proceedings of Workshop on Embedded Security in Cars* (2006).

[25] PARNO, B., AND PERRIG, A. Challenges in securing vehicular networks. In *Proceedings of ACM HotNets* (2005).

[26] PRZYDATEK, B., SONG, D. X., AND PERRIG, A. SIA: secure information aggregation in sensor networks. In *Proceedings of ACM SenSys* (2003).

[27] RAYA, M., AZIZ, A., AND HUBAUX, J.-P. Efficient secure aggregation in vanets. In *Proceedings of ACM VANET* (2006).

[28] RAYA, M., AND HUBAUX, J.-P. Securing vehicular ad hoc networks. *Journal of Computer Security 15* (2007), 39–68.

[29] RAYA, M., PAPADIMITRATOS, P., GLIGOR, V. D., AND PIERRE HUBAUX, J. On data centric trust establishment in ephemeral ad hoc networks. In *Proceedings of IEEE INFOCOM* (2008).

[30] RISTANOVIC, N., PAPADIMITRATOS, P., THEODORAKOPOULOS, G., HUBAUX, J.-P., AND LEBOUDEC, J.-Y. Adaptive message authentication for vehicular networks. In *Proceedings of ACM VANET* (2009).

[31] ROUF, I., MILLER, R., MUSTAFA, H., TAYLOR, T., OH, S., XU, W., GRUTESER, M., TRAPPE, W., AND SESKAR, I. Security and privacy vulnerabilities of in-car wireless networks: A tire pressure monitoring system case study. In *Proceedings of USENIX Security Symposium* (2010).

[32] STOJMENOVIC, I., SEDDIGH, M., AND ZUNIC, J. Dominating sets and neighbor elimination-based broadcasting algorithms in wireless networks. *IEEE Transactions on Parallel and Distributed Systems 13*, 1 (2002), 14–25.

[33] STUDER, A., SHI, E., BAI, F., AND PERRIG, A. TACKing together efficient authentication, revocation, and privacy in vanets. In *Proceedings of IEEE SECON* (2009).

[34] WISITPONGPHAN, N., BAI, F., MUDALIGE, P., AND TONGUZ, O. On the routing problem in disconnected vehicular ad-hoc networks. In *Proceedings of IEEE INFOCOM* (2007).

[35] WISITPONGPHAN, N., TONGUZ, O. K., PARIKH, J. S., MUDALIGE, P., BAI, F., AND SADEKAR, V. Broadcast storm mitigation techniques in vehicular ad hoc networks. *Wireless Communications, IEEE 14*, 6 (2007), 84–94.

[36] YANG, Y., WANG, X., ZHU, S., AND CAO, G. SDAP: a secure hop-by-hop data aggregation protocol for sensor networks. In *Proceedings of ACM MobiHoc* (2006).

[37] ZHANG, C., LU, R., LIN, X., HO, P.-H., AND SHEN, X. An efficient identity-based batch verification scheme for vehicular sensor networks. In *Proceedings of IEEE INFOCOM* (2008).

Author Index